# *Edmund's*

# USED CAR PRICES

D1555710

**"THE ORIGINAL CONSUMER PRICE AUTHORITY"**

Publisher: Peter Steinlauf

# USED CAR PRICES

## TABLE OF CONTENTS

**JUNE 1993**                    **VOL U2702**

Published by:
Edmund Publications Corp.
300 N Sepulveda   Suite 2050
Los Angeles, CA 90245
310-640-7840

SBN: 87759-419-8
ISSN: 0424-5059
Library of Congress Catalog
Card No: 71-80099

Creative
/Design Director:
Julie Finger

Production Coordinator:
Margalit Ward

Contributing Editor:
Patrick Barry

Copy Editor:
William Badnow

Production:
Rachel Abrash
Terrance Laurent

*Cover: Mitsubishi 3000 GT4*

REGIONAL PRICE DIFFERENCES: The pricing information contained in
Edmund Used Car Prices represents an average value for that vehicle
regardless of location. Bear in mind that there are minor regional
differences in values for some vehicles due to climate, local culture,
and current trends. Trucks are singled out by Edmund as deserving
special mention. Price data suggests that for areas approximately west
of the Mississippi, 5% should be added to the values in this guide.

*1985 Buick Skyhawk Custom Coupe*

*Lexus ES250*

NOTE: All information and prices published herein are gathered from sources which, in the editor's opinion, are considered reliable, but under no circumstances is the reader to assume that this information is official or final. All prices are represented as approximations only, and are rounded to the highest whole dollar amount over 50 cents. Unless otherwise noted, all prices are effective as of 10/1/92 but are subject to change without notice. The publisher does not assume responsibility for errors of omission or interpretation. ■ The computerized consumer pricing services advertised herein are not operated by nor are they the responsibility of the publisher. The publisher assumes no responsibility for claims made by advertisers regarding their products or services.

## USING EDMUND'S GUIDE TO USED CAR PRICES

As the industry pioneer in automotive price guides, Edmund's has gathered all the data you need to make an intelligent, informed pricing decision. Buying or selling...new or used . . . foreign or domestic...you will be able to determine the fair market value for virtually any car, van, truck or utility vehicle on the market, thanks to Edmund's.

**1** Select model and year of vehicle from Used Car Guide.

**2** Review Original List Price — the suggested base retail price of the vehicle when it was new, without optional accessories.

**3** Review Current Wholesale price — the approximate average price a seller may expect to receive from a dealer for a "clean" car in fine mechanical condition. For cars needing repair or reconditioning, the cost of the work should be deducted.

**4** Review Average Retail price – the current avg. price the buyer might expect to pay.

**5** Add Optional Equipment — Add the value of any optional equipment. Turn to Optional Equipment Locator on page 6 and 7. Match column listing (A-F) of the desired vehicle with Optional Equipment schedules listed on Pages 8-10. Add the value of the equipment to the Wholesale or Retail Price of selected vehicle.

**6** Review the Excessive Mileage Chart — Deduct amount listed on the table located on the next page.

The resulting value represents the fair market price you can expect for your selected vehicle. Compare value of several cars by filling out the Used Car Buying Worksheets on pages 202-203.

### THE REST IS UP TO YOU!

With an informed assesment of the vehicle's value, you will be able to negotiate with the pros. Whether buying, selling, or even swapping. Edmund's is your guide for making the best deal at the best possible price.

## UNDERSTANDING THE LANGUAGE OF AUTO BUYING

***Original List Price*** This term applies to the original suggested retail price. **American Car Valuations:** include automatic transmission, stereo, power steering and air conditioning. **Foreign Car Valuations (1985-1988):** include standard transmission and stereo. **Foreign Car Valuations (1989-1992):** include standard transmission, stereo, air conditioning and power steering. Original List Prices do not include state and local taxes or original transportation charges.

***Average Retail*** The current average price the buyer may expect to pay.

***Current Wholesale*** This term applies to the approximate average current sum a seller may expect to receive from a dealer for a "clean" car in fine mechanical condition. For cars needing repairs or reconditioning, the cost of said work should be deducted.

***Condition*** Within the industry, the generally accepted classification of used cars is as follows: "Extra Clean or Cream Puff"—this refers to a car in exceptionally fine condition that warrants a premium price. "Clean"—this is the classification for the valuations in Edmund's Used Car Prices; as mentioned, it is a car in fine mechanical and physical condition. "Average"— is a car that shows obvious wear and tear, but is still passable. "Rough"—is a below average car, still usable, but with body wear and needing mechanical repair.

*1985 Chevrolet Astro*

| VIN LETTER | | | | | | | | | |
|---|---|---|---|---|---|---|---|---|---|
| ▼ | YEAR | ▼ | YEAR | ▼ | YEAR | ▼ | YEAR | ▼ | YEAR |
| **B** | 1981 | **E** | 1984 | **H** | 1987 | **L** | 1990 | **P** | 1993 |
| **C** | 1982 | **F** | 1985 | **J** | 1988 | **M** | 1991 | | — |
| **D** | 1983 | **G** | 1986 | **K** | 1989 | **N** | 1992 | | — |

**How to Determine Model Year** To be sure you are paying the correct price for the car you want to buy you must be sure that the model year is correct. Fortunately, checking out the model year is not difficult. Just find the VIN (Vehicle Identification Number) usually located on the dash near the front window. The letter in the tenth position in the VIN identifies the model year. The chart below shows the letter and the corresponding years.

For example, here is a VIN for a 1987 Chevrolet Cavalier:

1G1JE1119**H**J162212

*The tenth position is "H" — this confirms that the car is a 1987 model.*

**Excessive Mileage** The table below represents generally accepted deductions for clean cars in good mechanical condition with excessive mileage. It is most important to keep in mind that the *condition* of the car is more important than the mileage. Late model cars with excessive mileage should be given special consideration. At the same time, older cars with low mileage have an additional worth. At no point is the deduction to be over 50% of the wholesale valuation. Using the table, deduct the lower figure for sub-compacts, compacts and intermediate cars. Deduct the higher figure for standard and luxury cars.

**Excessive Mileage Deduction Table**

| | 1991 | 1990 | 1989 | 1988 | 1987 | 1986 | 1985 |
|---|---|---|---|---|---|---|---|
| TO 15,000 Miles | $ — - $ — | $ — - $ — | $ — - $ — | $ — - $ — | $ — - $ — | $ — - $ — | $ — - $ — |
| 15,000 to 20,000 | 300 - 400 | — - — | — - — | — - — | — - — | — - — | — - — |
| 20,000 to 25,000 | 450 - 600 | — - — | — - — | — - — | — - — | — - — | — - — |
| 25,000 to 30,000 | 575 - 750 | 275 - 325 | — - — | — - — | — - — | — - — | — - — |
| 30,000 to 35,000 | 725 - 950 | 375 - 500 | — - — | — - — | — - — | — - — | — - — |
| 35,000 to 40,000 | 900 - 1150 | 550 - 700 | 200 - 275 | — - — | — - — | — - — | — - — |
| 40,000 to 45,000 | 1050 - 1300 | 725 - 900 | 350 - 500 | — - — | — - — | — - — | — - — |
| 45,000 to 50,000 | 1200 - 1500 | 850 - 1100 | 525 - 650 | 200 - 250 | — - — | — - — | — - — |
| 50,000 to 55,000 | 1350 - 1700 | 1025 - 1300 | 675 - 850 | 350 - 425 | — - — | — - — | — - — |
| 55,000 to 60,000 | 1525 - 1900 | 1175 - 1500 | 850 - 1050 | 500 - 650 | 175 - 200 | — - — | — - — |
| 60,000 to 65,000 | 1800 - 2100 | 1325 - 1700 | 1000 - 1250 | 650 - 825 | 300 - 400 | — - — | — - — |
| 65,000 to 70,000 | 1825 - 2300 | 1500 - 1900 | 1150 - 1450 | 800 - 1025 | 450 - 600 | 125 - 150 | 100 - 125 |
| GENERALLY ACCEPTED MILEAGE | 10,000 to 15,000 | 15,000 to 30,000 | 30,000 to 40,000 | 40,000 to 45,000 | 45,000 to 50,000 | 50,000 to 55,000 | 55,000 to 60,000 |

**DOMESTIC OPTIONAL EQUIPMENT LOCATOR**

Use this table to determine which schedule applies to your vehicle. Then use the Optional Equipment Schedules on the following pages to determine values for factory installed accessories. Each model indicates the equipment schedule you should use.

| MAKE | A | B | E | F |
|------|---|---|---|---|
| AMERICAN MOTORS | ALLIANCE<br>EAGLE<br>ENCORE<br>GTA | | | |
| BUICK | SKYHAWK<br>SKYLARK | CENTURY<br>ELECTRA<br>ESTATE WAGON<br>LESABRE<br>PARK AVENUE<br>REATTA<br>REGAL<br>RIVIERA | | |
| CADILLAC | | ALL MODELS | | |
| CHEVROLET | BERETTA<br>CAVALIER<br>CHEVETTE<br>CITATION<br>CORSICA<br>NOVA<br>SPECTRUM<br>SPRINT | CAMARO<br>CAPRICE<br>CELEBRITY<br>CORVETTE<br>LUMINA<br>MONTE CARLO | BLAZER<br>EL CAMINO<br>LUMINA APV<br>SAFARI<br>STD-SIZE PICKUPS<br>STD SIZE VANS<br>SUBURBAN | S-10 PICKUPS |
| CHRYSLER | | ALL CARS | TOWN & COUNTRY VAN | |
| DODGE | ARIES<br>CHARGER<br>OMNI<br>SHADOW | 600<br>DAYTONA<br>DYNASTY<br>DIPLOMAT<br>LANCER<br>MONACO<br>SPIRIT<br>STEALTH | CARAVAN<br>DAKOTA<br>RAIDER<br>STD-SIZE PICKUP<br>STD-SIZE VAN | RAM 50 |
| EAGLE | SUMMIT | MEDALLION<br>PREMIER<br>TALON | | |
| FORD | ESCORT<br>EXP<br>FESTIVA<br>TEMPO | CROWN VICTORIA<br>LTD<br>MUSTANG<br>PROBE<br>TAURUS<br>THUNDERBIRD | AEROSTAR<br>BRONCO<br>BRONCO II<br>EXPLORER<br>STD-SIZE PICKUP<br>STD-SIZE VAN | RANGER |
| GMC | | | CABALLERO<br>JIMMY<br>SAFARI<br>STD-SIZE PICKUP<br>STD-SIZE VAN<br>SUBURBAN | SONOMA |
| JEEP | | | CHEROKEE<br>COMANCHE<br>GRAND WAGONEER<br>J-10<br>J-20<br>WRANGLER | CJ |
| LINCOLN | | ALL MODELS | | |
| MERCURY | CAPRI (FWD)<br>LYNX<br>TOPAZ<br>TRACER | CAPRI (RWD)<br>COUGAR<br>GRAN MARQUIS<br>MARQUIS<br>MERKUR<br>SABLE | | |
| OLDSMOBILE | CUTLASS CALAIS<br>FIRENZA | CUSTOM CRUISER<br>CUTLASS CIERA<br>CUTLASS SUPREME<br>EIGHTY-EIGHT<br>NINETY-EIGHT<br>TORONADO | BRAVADA<br>SILHOUETTE | |
| PLYMOUTH | HORIZON<br>RELIANT<br>SUNDANCE<br>TURISMO | ACCLAIM<br>CARAVELLE<br>GRAN FURY<br>LASER | VOYAGER | |
| PONTIAC | 1000<br>FIERO<br>GRAND AM<br>LEMANS<br>SUNBIRD | 6000<br>BONNEVILLE<br>FIREBIRD<br>GRAND PRIX<br>PARISIENNE<br>SAFARI | TRANS SPORT | |
| SATURN | ALL MODELS | | | |

**FOREIGN** OPTIONAL EQUIPMENT LOCATOR

Use this table to determine which schedule applies to your vehicle. Then use the Optional Equipment Schedules on the following pages to determine values for factory installed accessories. Each model indicates the equipment schedule you should use.

| MAKE | C | D | E | F | No Schedule |
|------|---|---|---|---|-------------|
| ACURA | INTEGRA | LEGEND | | | |
| ALPHA ROMEO | SPIDER | 164<br>MILANO | | | |
| AUDI | | ALL MODELS | | | |
| BMW | | 318<br>325 | | | 525<br>535<br>635<br>735<br>750 |
| COLT | ALL MODELS | | | | |
| CONQUEST | | ALL MODELS | | | |
| DAIHATSU | CHARADE | ROCKY | | | |
| GEO | METRO<br>PRIZM<br>SPECTRUM<br>STORM | TRACKER | | | |
| HONDA | CIVIC<br>CRX | ACCORD<br>PRELUDE | | | |
| HYUNDAI | EXCEL<br>SCOUPE | SONATA | | | |
| ISUZU | I-MARK<br>STYLUS | IMPULSE | TROOPER | AMIGO<br>PICKUPS<br>RODEO | |
| JAGUAR | | XJBASE | | | SOVEREIGN<br>VANDEN PLAS |
| LEXUS | | ALL MODELS | | | |
| MAZDA | 323<br>GLC<br>MIATA<br>PROTEGE | 626<br>929<br>MX-6<br>RX-7 | | PICKUPS | |
| MERCEDES | | 190<br>300<br>350<br>380<br>420 | | | 560 |
| MITSUBISHI | MIRAGE<br>PRECIS<br>TREDIA | 300 GT<br>CORDIA<br>ECLIPSE<br>GALANT<br>SIGMA<br>STARION | MONTERO<br>VAN | TRUCKS | |
| INFINITI | | G-20<br>M30 | | | Q45 |
| NISSAN | 200 SX<br>NX<br>PULSAR<br>SENTRA | 240 SX<br>300 SX<br>MAXIMA<br>STANZA | AXXESS<br>PATHFINDER | PICKUPS<br>VANS | |
| PEUGEOT | | ALL MODELS | | | |
| PORSCHE | | 924S | | | 911<br>944 |
| RANGE ROVER | | | ALL MODELS | | |
| RENAULT | FUEGO | SPORTWAGON | | | |
| SAAB | | ALL MODELS | | | |
| STERLING | | ALL MODELS | | | |
| SUBARU | BRAT<br>DL<br>GL<br>JUSTY<br>LOYALE<br>RX<br>STANDARD<br>XT-6 | LEGACY | | | |
| SUZUKI | SWIFT | SAMURAI<br>SIDEKICK | | | |
| TOYOTA | COROLLA<br>MR2<br>TERCEL | CAMRY<br>CELICA<br>CRESSIDA<br>SUPRA | LAND CRUISER<br>PREVIA<br>VAN | TRUCKS | |
| VISTA | ALL MODELS | | | | |
| VW | FOX<br>GOLF<br>JETTA | CORRADO<br>PASSAT<br>QUANTUM | | VANAGON | |
| VOLVO | | ALL MODELS | | | |
| YUGO | ALL MODELS | | | | |

## OPTIONAL EQUIPMENT — SCHEDULE A

| Add for | 1992 | 1991 | 1990 | 1989 | 1988 | 1987 | 1986 | 1985 |
|---|---|---|---|---|---|---|---|---|
| | whlse/rtl | whlse/rtl | whlse/rtl | whlse/rtl | whlse/rtl | whlse/rtl | whlse/rtl | whlse/rtl |
| Power Windows | 175/200 | 150/175 | 125/150 | 100/125 | 75/100 | 50/75 | 50/50 | 50/50 |
| Power Seat | 150/175 | 125/150 | 100/125 | 50/75 | 50/75 | 25/25 | 25/25 | 25/25 |
| Power Door Locks | 125/150 | 100/125 | 100/125 | 50/75 | 50/75 | 50/50 | 25/25 | 25/25 |
| Tilt Steering Wheel | 150/175 | 125/150 | 100/125 | 50/75 | 50/75 | 50/75 | 50/50 | 25/25 |
| Cruise Control | 150/175 | 125/150 | 125/150 | 75/100 | 50/75 | 50/75 | 50/50 | 25/25 |
| Manual Sunroof | 175/225 | 150/200 | 150/175 | 125/150 | 100/125 | 75/100 | 50/75 | 50/75 |
| Power Sunroof | 400/450 | 375/425 | 350/400 | 300/350 | 250/300 | 200/250 | 175/200 | 150/175 |

| Deduct if no | 1992 | 1991 | 1990 | 1989 | 1988 | 1987 | 1986 | 1985 |
|---|---|---|---|---|---|---|---|---|
| | whlse/rtl | whlse/rtl | whlse/rtl | whlse/rtl | whlse/rtl | whlse/rtl | whlse/rtl | whlse/rtl |
| Automatic Transmission | 500/550 | 475/525 | 450/500 | 450/500 | 350/400 | 325/375 | 250/300 | 225/275 |
| Air Conditioning | 550/600 | 525/575 | 500/550 | 450/500 | 375/425 | 325/375 | 275/325 | 200/250 |
| Power Steering | 150/175 | 125/150 | 125/150 | 100/125 | 100/125 | 75/100 | 75/100 | 50/75 |
| AM/FM Stereo | 125/175 | 100/150 | 75/100 | 75/100 | 75/100 | 50/75 | 50/75 | 50/75 |

IMPORTANT: The value adjustments in these tables apply only to vehicles that did not have this equipment as standard, or that do not have specific values for this equipment assigned to them in the main text.

## OPTIONAL EQUIPMENT — SCHEDULE B

| Add for | 1992 | 1991 | 1990 | 1989 | 1988 | 1987 | 1986 | 1985 |
|---|---|---|---|---|---|---|---|---|
| | whlse/rtl | whlse/rtl | whlse/rtl | whlse/rtl | whlse/rtl | whlse/rtl | whlse/rtl | whlse/rtl |
| Power Windows | 200/225 | 175/200 | 150/175 | 125/150 | 100/125 | 75/100 | 75/100 | 50/50 |
| Power Seat | 175/200 | 150/175 | 100/125 | 75/100 | 75/100 | 50/75 | 50/50 | 25/25 |
| Power Door Locks | 175/200 | 150/175 | 125/150 | 100/125 | 75/100 | 50/75 | 50/50 | 50/50 |
| Tilt Steering Wheel | 175/200 | 150/175 | 125/150 | 100/125 | 75/100 | 50/75 | 50/75 | 50/50 |
| Cruise Control | 175/200 | 150/175 | 150/175 | 125/150 | 100/125 | 75/100 | 50/75 | 50/50 |
| Manual Sunroof | 175/225 | 150/200 | 150/175 | 125/150 | 100/125 | 75/100 | 50/75 | 50/75 |
| Power Sunroof | 575/650 | 550/625 | 375/450 | 350/425 | 325/400 | 250/300 | 200/250 | 175/200 |

| Deduct if no | 1992 | 1991 | 1990 | 1989 | 1988 | 1987 | 1986 | 1985 |
|---|---|---|---|---|---|---|---|---|
| | whlse/rtl | whlse/rtl | whlse/rtl | whlse/rtl | whlse/rtl | whlse/rtl | whlse/rtl | whlse/rtl |
| Automatic Transmission | 600/700 | 575/675 | 500/575 | 475/550 | 450/500 | 425/475 | 375/425 | 300/325 |
| Air Conditioning | 675/750 | 650/725 | 575/650 | 500/575 | 450/500 | 400/450 | 375/425 | 275/300 |
| Power Steering | 250/275 | 225/250 | 225/250 | 200/225 | 175/200 | 175/200 | 125/150 | 100/125 |
| AM/FM Stereo | 125/175 | 100/150 | 100/150 | 75/100 | 75/100 | 50/75 | 50/75 | 50/75 |

IMPORTANT: The value adjustments in these tables apply only to vehicles that did not have this equipment as standard, or that do not have specific values for this equipment assigned to them in the main text.

## OPTIONAL EQUIPMENT — SCHEDULE C

| Add for | 1992 | 1991 | 1990 | 1989 | 1988 | 1987 | 1986 | 1985 |
|---|---|---|---|---|---|---|---|---|
| | whlse/rtl | whlse/rtl | whlse/rtl | whlse/rtl | whlse/rtl | whlse/rtl | whlse/rtl | whlse/rtl |
| Automatic Transmission | 475/525 | 450/500 | 450/500 | 425/475 | 325/375 | 325/375 | 225/275 | 200/225 |
| Air Conditioning | —/— | —/— | —/— | —/— | 375/425 | 350/400 | 275/325 | 200/250 |
| Power Steering | —/— | —/— | —/— | —/— | 75/100 | 75/100 | 50/75 | 50/75 |
| Power Windows | 175/200 | 150/175 | 125/150 | 100/125 | 75/100 | 50/75 | 50/50 | 50/50 |
| Power Seat | 150/175 | 125/150 | 100/125 | 50/75 | 50/75 | 25/25 | 25/25 | 25/25 |
| Power Door Locks | 125/150 | 100/125 | 100/125 | 50/75 | 50/75 | 50/50 | 25/25 | 25/25 |
| Tilt Steering Wheel | 150/175 | 125/150 | 100/125 | 50/75 | 50/75 | 50/75 | 50/50 | 25/25 |
| Cruise Control | 150/175 | 125/150 | 125/150 | 75/100 | 50/75 | 50/75 | 50/50 | 25/25 |
| Manual Sunroof | 175/225 | 150/200 | 150/175 | 125/150 | 100/125 | 75/100 | 50/75 | 50/75 |
| Power Sunroof | 400/450 | 375/425 | 350/400 | 300/350 | 250/300 | 200/250 | 175/200 | 150/175 |

| Deduct if no | 1992 | 1991 | 1990 | 1989 | 1988 | 1987 | 1986 | 1985 |
|---|---|---|---|---|---|---|---|---|
| | whlse/rtl | whlse/rtl | whlse/rtl | whlse/rtl | whlse/rtl | whlse/rtl | whlse/rtl | whlse/rtl |
| Air Conditioning | 550/600 | 525/575 | 500/550 | 475/500 | —/— | —/— | —/— | —/— |
| Power Steering | 150/175 | 125/150 | 125/150 | 100/125 | —/— | —/— | —/— | —/— |
| AM/FM Stereo | 125/175 | 100/150 | 75/100 | 75/100 | 75/100 | 50/75 | 50/75 | 50/75 |

IMPORTANT: The value adjustments in these tables apply only to vehicles that did not have this equipment as standard, or that do not have specific values for this equipment assigned to them in the main text.

## OPTIONAL EQUIPMENT — SCHEDULE D

| Add for | 1992 | 1991 | 1990 | 1989 | 1988 | 1987 | 1986 | 1985 |
|---|---|---|---|---|---|---|---|---|
| | whlse/rtl | whlse/rtl | whlse/rtl | whlse/rtl | whlse/rtl | whlse/rtl | whlse/rtl | whlse/rtl |
| Automatic Transmission | 600/675 | 575/650 | 500/575 | 450/525 | 450/500 | 400/450 | 375/425 | 275/300 |
| Air Conditioning | —/— | —/— | —/— | —/— | 450/500 | 400/450 | 350/400 | 250/275 |
| Power Steering | —/— | —/— | —/— | —/— | 150/175 | 125/150 | 100/125 | 50/75 |
| Power Windows | 200/225 | 175/200 | 150/175 | 125/150 | 100/125 | 75/100 | 75/100 | 50/50 |
| Power Seat | 175/200 | 150/175 | 100/125 | 75/100 | 75/100 | 50/75 | 50/50 | 25/25 |
| Power Door Locks | 175/200 | 150/175 | 125/150 | 100/125 | 75/100 | 50/75 | 50/50 | 50/50 |
| Tilt Steering Wheel | 175/200 | 150/175 | 125/150 | 100/125 | 75/100 | 50/75 | 50/75 | 50/50 |
| Cruise Control | 175/200 | 150/175 | 150/175 | 125/150 | 100/125 | 75/100 | 50/75 | 50/50 |
| Manual Sunroof | 175/200 | 150/175 | 150/175 | 125/150 | 100/125 | 75/100 | 50/75 | 50/75 |
| Power Sunroof | 600/675 | 575/650 | 400/475 | 350/425 | 325/400 | 250/300 | 200/250 | 175/200 |

| Deduct if no | 1992 | 1991 | 1990 | 1989 | 1988 | 1987 | 1986 | 1985 |
|---|---|---|---|---|---|---|---|---|
| | whlse/rtl | whlse/rtl | whlse/rtl | whlse/rtl | whlse/rtl | whlse/rtl | whlse/rtl | whlse/rtl |
| Air Conditioning | 675/750 | 650/725 | 575/650 | 500/575 | —/— | —/— | —/— | —/— |
| Power Steering | 250/275 | 225/250 | 225/250 | 200/225 | —/— | —/— | —/— | —/— |
| AM/FM Stereo | 125/175 | 100/150 | 100/150 | 100/125 | 100/125 | 75/100 | 50/75 | 50/75 |

IMPORTANT: The value adjustments in these tables apply only to vehicles that did not have this equipment as standard, or that do not have specific values for this equipment assigned to them in the main text. However, it is likely that luxury models are fully equipped with the above optional equipment.

| Add for | 1992 | 1991 | 1990 | 1989 | 1988 | 1987 | 1986 | 1985 |
|---|---|---|---|---|---|---|---|---|
| | whlse/rtl | whlse/rtl | whlse/rtl | whlse/rtl | whlse/rtl | whlse/rtl | whlse/rtl | whlse/rtl |
| Auto Transmission | 500/575 | 475/550 | 450/525 | 425/475 | 400/450 | 350/400 | 300/350 | 250/300 |
| Air Conditioning | —/— | —/— | —/— | —/— | 450/500 | 400/450 | 325/375 | 275/325 |
| Power Steering | —/— | —/— | —/— | —/— | 175/200 | 175/200 | 150/175 | 100/125 |
| Power Windows | 200/225 | 175/200 | 150/175 | 125/150 | 125/150 | 100/125 | 75/100 | 50/75 |
| Power Seat | 175/200 | 150/175 | 100/125 | 100/125 | 75/100 | 50/75 | 50/50 | 25/25 |
| Power Door Locks | 125/150 | 100/125 | 75/100 | 75/100 | 75/100 | 50/75 | 50/75 | 25/25 |
| Tilt Steering Wheel | 150/175 | 125/150 | 125/150 | 100/125 | 75/100 | 50/75 | 50/50 | 50/50 |
| Cruise Control | 175/200 | 150/175 | 125/150 | 100/125 | 75/100 | 50/75 | 50/75 | 50/50 |
| 4-Wheel Drive | 1525/1725 | 1500/1700 | 1400/1600 | 1250/1400 | 1150/1300 | 1000/1100 | 900/1050 | 800/925 |
| Sliding Rear Window | 100/125 | 75/100 | 75/100 | 50/75 | 50/75 | 50/50 | 50/50 | 25/25 |
| Manual Sunroof | 200/225 | 175/200 | 150/175 | 125/150 | 100/125 | 75/100 | 50/75 | 50/75 |
| Power Sunroof | 500/575 | 475/550 | 375/450 | 325/375 | 300/350 | 250/300 | 200/250 | 150/200 |

| Deduct if no | 1992 | 1991 | 1990 | 1989 | 1988 | 1987 | 1986 | 1985 |
|---|---|---|---|---|---|---|---|---|
| | whlse/rtl | whlse/rtl | whlse/rtl | whlse/rtl | whlse/rtl | whlse/rtl | whlse/rtl | whlse/rtl |
| Air Conditioning | 575/650 | 550/625 | 525/600 | 525/600 | —/— | —/— | —/— | —/— |
| Power Steering | 300/325 | 275/300 | 275/300 | 250/275 | —/— | —/— | —/— | —/— |
| AM/FM Stereo | 125/175 | 100/150 | 100/150 | 75/100 | 75/100 | 50/75 | 50/75 | 50/75 |

IMPORTANT: The value adjustments in these tables apply only to vehicles that did not have this equipment as standard, or that do not have specific values for this equipment assigned to them in the main text.

| Add for | 1992 | 1991 | 1990 | 1989 | 1988 | 1987 | 1986 | 1985 |
|---|---|---|---|---|---|---|---|---|
| | whlse/rtl | whlse/rtl | whlse/rtl | whlse/rtl | whlse/rtl | whlse/rtl | whlse/rtl | whlse/rtl |
| Auto Transmission | 425/500 | 400/475 | 350/425 | 325/375 | 325/375 | 300/350 | 250/300 | 200/250 |
| Air Conditioning | —/— | —/— | —/— | —/— | 375/425 | 300/350 | 250/300 | 200/225 |
| Power Steering | —/— | —/— | —/— | —/— | 125/150 | 125/150 | 100/125 | 75/100 |
| Power Windows | 175/200 | 150/175 | 125/150 | 100/125 | 75/100 | 50/75 | 25/50 | 25/25 |
| Power Seat | 125/150 | 100/125 | 75/100 | 75/100 | 50/75 | 25/25 | 25/25 | —/— |
| Power Door Locks | 100/125 | 75/100 | 75/100 | 50/75 | 50/75 | 25/25 | 25/25 | 25/25 |
| Tilt Steering Wheel | 125/150 | 100/125 | 100/125 | 75/100 | 75/100 | 50/75 | 50/50 | 25/25 |
| Cruise Control | 150/175 | 125/150 | 100/100 | 75/100 | 50/75 | 50/75 | 50/50 | 25/25 |
| 4-Wheel Drive | 1425/1625 | 1400/1600 | 1300/1500 | 1150/1300 | 1100/1300 | 900/1050 | 800/900 | 750/850 |
| Sliding Rear Window | 100/125 | 75/100 | 75/100 | 50/75 | 50/75 | 50/50 | 50/50 | 25/25 |
| Manual Sunroof | 175/225 | 150/200 | 150/175 | 125/150 | 100/125 | 75/100 | 50/75 | 50/75 |
| Power Sunroof | 475/550 | 450/525 | 350/400 | 300/350 | 275/325 | 225/275 | 175/200 | 150/175 |

| Deduct if no | 1992 | 1991 | 1990 | 1989 | 1988 | 1987 | 1986 | 1985 |
|---|---|---|---|---|---|---|---|---|
| | whlse/rtl | whlse/rtl | whlse/rtl | whlse/rtl | whlse/rtl | whlse/rtl | whlse/rtl | whlse/rtl |
| Air Conditioning | 525/600 | 500/575 | 500/575 | 425/475 | —/— | —/— | —/— | —/— |
| Power Steering | 200/225 | 175/200 | 175/200 | 150/175 | —/— | —/— | —/— | —/— |
| AM/FM Stereo | 125/175 | 100/150 | 100/150 | 75/100 | 75/100 | 50/75 | 50/75 | 50/75 |

IMPORTANT: The value adjustments in these tables apply only to vehicles that did not have this equipment as standard, or that do not have specific values for this equipment assigned to them in the main text.

*1984 American Motors Eagle Sedan*

| Year/Model/ Body/Type | Original List | Current Whlse | Average Retail |
|---|---|---|---|
| **AMERICAN MOTORS** | | | |
| **1987** | | | |
| **ALLIANCE 4** | | | |
| 2 Dr Base Sdn | **7917** | 575 | 1075 |
| 4 Dr Base Sdn | **8117** | 675 | 1275 |
| 3 Dr Hbk | **7917** | 625 | 1175 |
| 2 Dr DL Sdn | **8944** | 900 | 1625 |
| 4 Dr DL Sdn | **9219** | 1000 | 1725 |
| 2 Dr DL Conv | **13418** | 2375 | 3250 |
| 3 Dr DL Hbk | **8994** | 950 | 1675 |
| 5 Dr DL Hbk | **9269** | 1050 | 1775 |
| 2 Dr L Sdn | **8443** | 750 | 1475 |
| 4 Dr L Sdn | **8718** | 850 | 1550 |
| 2 Dr L Conv | **12418** | 2200 | 3050 |
| 3 Dr L Hbk | **8397** | 800 | 1500 |
| 5 Dr L Hbk | **8672** | 875 | 1600 |
| 3 Dr GS Hbk | **9818** | 1275 | 2000 |
| **GTA 4** | | | |
| 2 Dr Sdn | **9704** | 1275 | 2000 |
| 2 Dr Conv | **13604** | 2675 | 3575 |
| **EAGLE 6** | | | |
| 4 Dr Sdn | **12927** | 2275 | 3150 |
| 4 Dr Wgn | **13743** | 2550 | 3425 |
| **EAGLE LIMITED 6** | | | |
| 4 Dr Wgn | **14475** | 3050 | 3950 |
| *ADD FOR:* | | | |
| Eagle Sport Pkg (Eagle) | **456** | 90 | 100 |

NOTE: Power brakes standard on all models.

| Year/Model/ Body/Type | Original List | Current Whlse | Average Retail |
|---|---|---|---|
| **1986** | | | |
| **ALLIANCE 4** | | | |
| 2 Dr Base Sdn | **7473** | 375 | 675 |
| 4 Dr Base Sdn | **7673** | 475 | 875 |
| 2 Dr DL Sdn | **8391** | 675 | 1275 |
| 4 Dr DL Sdn | **8414** | 775 | 1500 |
| 2 Dr DL Conv | **12966** | 1850 | 2700 |
| 2 Dr L Sdn | **7891** | 525 | 975 |
| 4 Dr L Sdn | **8141** | 625 | 1175 |
| 2 Dr L Conv | **12611** | 1725 | 2575 |
| **EAGLE 6** | | | |
| 4 Dr Sdn | **12196** | 1675 | 2525 |
| 4 Dr Wgn | **12966** | 1875 | 2725 |
| **EAGLE LIMITED 6** | | | |
| 4 Dr Wgn | **13656** | 2275 | 3150 |
| **ENCORE 4** | | | |
| 3 Dr S Lftbk | **7931** | 525 | 975 |
| 5 Dr S Lftbk | **8181** | 625 | 1175 |
| 3 Dr LS Lftbk | **8591** | 675 | 1275 |
| 5 Dr LS Lftbk | **8841** | 775 | 1500 |
| 3 Dr GS Lftbk | **9089** | 950 | 1675 |
| 3 Dr Electronic Lftbk | **8619** | 675 | 1275 |
| *ADD FOR:* | | | |
| Eagle Sport Pkg (Eagle) | **431** | 60 | 70 |

NOTE: Vinyl top standard on Eagle Sedan. Power brakes standard on all models.

| Year/Model/<br>Body/Type | Original<br>List | Current<br>Whlse | Average<br>Retail |
|---|---|---|---|
| **1985** | | | |
| **ALLIANCE 4** | | | |
| 2 Dr Base Sdn | **7200** | 300 | 575 |
| 2 Dr DL Sdn | **8114** | 525 | 975 |
| 4 Dr DL Sdn | **8364** | 625 | 1175 |
| 2 Dr DL Conv | **12316** | 1550 | 2400 |
| 2 Dr L Sdn | **7514** | 425 | 775 |
| 4 Dr L Sdn | **7764** | 525 | 975 |
| 2 Dr L Conv | **11637** | 1450 | 2225 |
| 4 Dr Limited Sdn | **8764** | 850 | 1550 |
| **EAGLE 6** | | | |
| 4 Dr Sdn | **11698** | 950 | 1675 |
| 4 Dr Wgn | **12459** | 1175 | 1900 |
| **EAGLE LIMITED 6** | | | |
| 4 Dr Wgn | **13135** | 1500 | 2350 |
| **ENCORE 4** | | | |
| 3 Dr Base Lftbk (4 spd) | **5986** | 300 | 575 |
| 3 Dr S Lftbk | **7702** | 450 | 825 |
| 5 Dr S Lftbk | **7952** | 550 | 1025 |
| 3 Dr LS Lftbk | **8402** | 550 | 1025 |
| 5 Dr LS Lftbk | **8652** | 650 | 1225 |
| 3 Dr GS Lftbk | **8902** | 800 | 1500 |

NOTE: 5 speed transmission standard on Encore LS and GS. Power brakes standard on all models.

| Year/Model/<br>Body/Type | Original<br>List | Current<br>Whlse | Average<br>Retail |
|---|---|---|---|
| **1984** | | | |
| **ALLIANCE 4** | | | |
| 2 Dr Base Sdn | **7346** | 110 | 300 |
| 2 Dr L Sdn | **7734** | 110 | 300 |
| 4 Dr L Sdn | **7984** | 125 | 325 |
| 2 Dr DL Sdn | **8334** | 110 | 300 |
| 4 Dr DL Sdn | **8634** | 200 | 400 |
| 4 Dr Limited Sdn | **9296** | 300 | 575 |
| 2 Dr Diamond Edit.<br>Sdn | **8984** | 250 | 525 |
| 4 Dr Diamond Edit.<br>Sdn | **9284** | 275 | 550 |
| **EAGLE 4\*** | | | |
| 4 Dr Sdn | **10331** | 625 | 1175 |
| 4 Dr Wgn | **11061** | 800 | 1500 |
| **EAGLE LIMITED 4\*** | | | |
| 4 Dr Wgn | **11531** | 1100 | 1825 |

*For 6 cyl models add $200 whsle/$200 retail.

| Year/Model/<br>Body/Type | Original<br>List | Current<br>Whlse | Average<br>Retail |
|---|---|---|---|
| **ENCORE 4** | | | |
| 3 Dr Base Sdn | **7142** | 110 | 300 |
| 3 Dr S Lftbk | **7668** | 110 | 300 |
| 5 Dr S Lftbk | **7618** | 110 | 300 |
| 3 Dr LS Lftbk | **8298** | 110 | 300 |

| Year/Model/<br>Body/Type | Original<br>List | Current<br>Whlse | Average<br>Retail |
|---|---|---|---|
| 5 Dr LS Lftbk | **8498** | 175 | 375 |
| 3 Dr GS Lftbk | **8850** | 200 | 400 |
| 3 Dr Diamond Edit.<br>Lftbk | **8873** | 275 | 550 |
| 5 Dr Diamond Edit.<br>Lftbk | **9073** | 350 | 625 |

| **1983 — ALL BODY STYLES** | | | |
|---|---|---|---|
| ALLIANCE 4 | — | 150 | 350 |
| BASE CONCORD | — | 200 | 400 |
| CONCORD DL | — | 300 | 575 |
| CONCORD LIMITED | — | 450 | 825 |
| EAGLE | — | 525 | 975 |
| EAGLE LIMITED | — | 825 | 1525 |
| EAGLE SX/4 | — | 300 | 575 |
| EAGLE SX/4 DL | — | 400 | 725 |
| SPIRIT DL | — | 175 | 375 |
| SPIRIT GT | — | 225 | 475 |

## BUICK

| **1992** | | | |
|---|---|---|---|
| **CENTURY CUSTOM 4\*** | | | |
| 4 Dr Sdn | **14755** | 9575 | 11025 |
| 2 Dr Cpe | **14550** | 9475 | 10925 |
| 4 Dr Wgn | **15660** | 9975 | 11500 |
| **CENTURY LIMITED 4\*** | | | |
| 4 Dr Sdn | **15695** | 10225 | 11800 |
| 4 Dr Wgn | **16395** | 10675 | 12325 |
| **CENTURY SPECIAL 4\*** | | | |
| 4 Dr Sdn | **13795** | 9175 | 10575 |

*For 6 cyl models add $500 whsle/$500 retail.

| *ADD FOR:* | | | |
|---|---|---|---|
| Leather Seat Trim | **500** | 250 | 280 |
| Aluminum Wheels | **295** | 180 | 200 |
| **LE SABRE CUSTOM 6** | | | |
| 4 Dr Sdn | **18695** | 13425 | 15750 |
| **LE SABRE LIMITED 6** | | | |
| 4 Dr Sdn | **20775** | 14625 | 17175 |
| *ADD FOR:* | | | |
| Leather Seat Trim | **500** | 250 | 280 |
| Aluminum Wheels | **325** | 180 | 200 |
| **PARK AVENUE 6** | | | |
| 4 Dr Base Sdn | **25285** | 17250 | 19900 |
| 4 Dr Ultra Sdn | **28780** | 20225 | 23275 |
| *ADD FOR:* | | | |
| Leather Seat Trim | | | |

| Year/Model/ Body/Type | Original List | Current Whlse | Average Retail |
|---|---|---|---|
| (Base Sdn) | **500** | 250 | 280 |
| **REGAL CUSTOM 6** | | | |
| 4 Dr Sdn | **16865** | 10850 | 12525 |
| 2 Dr Cpe | **16610** | 10850 | 12525 |
| **REGAL GRAN SPORT 6** | | | |
| 4 Dr Sdn | **19300** | 12350 | 14400 |
| 2 Dr Cpe | **18600** | 12350 | 14400 |
| **REGAL LIMITED 6** | | | |
| 4 Dr Sdn | **18110** | 11725 | 13550 |
| 2 Dr Cpe | **17790** | 11725 | 13550 |
| ADD FOR: | | | |
| 3.8 Liter 6 Cyl Eng | | | |
| (Custom, Limited) | **395** | 180 | 200 |
| Anti-Lock Brakes (Custom) | **450** | 300 | 330 |
| Leather Seat Trim | **500** | 250 | 280 |
| Aluminum Wheels | | | |
| (Custom, Limited) | **295** | 180 | 200 |
| Wire Whls (Custom, Ltd) | **240** | 160 | 180 |
| **RIVIERA 6** | | | |
| 2 Dr Cpe | **25415** | 17850 | 20500 |
| ADD FOR: | | | |
| Vinyl Roof | **695** | 200 | 230 |
| Leather Seat Trim | **600** | 250 | 280 |
| **ROADMASTER 8** | | | |
| 4 Dr Base Sdn | **21865** | 15425 | 18075 |
| 4 Dr Limited Sdn | **24195** | 17075 | 19725 |
| 4 Dr Estate Wgn | **23040** | 18125 | 20850 |
| ADD FOR: | | | |
| Vinyl Roof | **695** | 200 | 230 |
| Leather Seat Trim | **700** | 250 | 280 |
| Wire Wheel Covers | | | |
| (Base, Limited) | **240** | 160 | 180 |
| Aluminum Wheels | | | |
| (Base, Limited) | **325** | 180 | 200 |
| **SKYLARK 4\*** | | | |
| 4 Dr Sdn | **14705** | 9250 | 10650 |
| 2 Dr Cpe | **14705** | 9250 | 10650 |
| *For 6 cyl models add $450 whsle/$450 retail. | | | |
| **SKYLARK GRAN SPORT 6** | | | |
| 4 Dr Sdn | **16700** | 10800 | 12475 |
| 2 Dr Cpe | **16700** | 10800 | 12475 |
| ADD FOR: | | | |
| Automatic Leveling System | | | |
| (Base) | **380** | 250 | 280 |

NOTE: Power windows standard on LeSabre, Park Avenue, Riviera and Roadmaster. Power door locks standard on Century, Park Avenue, Regal, Riviera, Roadmaster and Skylark. Power seat standard on

Century, Park Avenue Ultra and Roadmaster Limited. Tilt steering wheel standard on Park Avenue, Regal, Riviera and Roadmaster. Cruise control standard on Park Avenue, Riviera and Roadmaster Base.

## 1991

| Year/Model/ Body/Type | Original List | Current Whlse | Average Retail |
|---|---|---|---|
| **CENTURY CUSTOM 4\*** | | | |
| 4 Dr Sdn | **13685** | 7625 | 8850 |
| 2 Dr Cpe | **13785** | 6550 | 7625 |
| 4 Dr Wgn | **15310** | 8025 | 9275 |
| **CENTURY LIMITED 4\*** | | | |
| 4 Dr Sdn | **14795** | 8250 | 9525 |
| 4 Dr Wgn | **16230** | 8450 | 9750 |
| **CENTURY SPECIAL 4\*** | | | |
| 4 Dr Sdn | **13240** | 7275 | 8450 |
| *For 6 cyl models add $425 whsle/$425 retail. | | | |
| **LE SABRE 6** | | | |
| 2 Dr Cpe | **17180** | 10200 | 11775 |
| **LE SABRE CUSTOM 6** | | | |
| 4 Dr Sdn | **17180** | 10350 | 11950 |
| **LE SABRE LIMITED 6** | | | |
| 4 Dr Sdn | **18430** | 11425 | 13200 |
| 2 Dr Cpe | **18330** | 11250 | 13000 |
| **PARK AVENUE 6** | | | |
| 4 Dr Sdn | **24385** | 14400 | 16900 |
| 4 Dr Ultra Sdn | **27420** | 17000 | 19650 |
| **REATTA 6** | | | |
| 2 Dr Cpe | **29300** | 16200 | 18850 |
| 2 Dr Conv | **35965** | — | — |
| **REGAL CUSTOM 6** | | | |
| 4 Dr Sdn | **15910** | 8900 | 10275 |
| 2 Dr Cpe | **15690** | 8900 | 10275 |
| **REGAL LIMITED 6** | | | |
| 4 Dr Sdn | **16735** | 9475 | 10925 |
| 2 Dr Cpe | **16455** | 9475 | 10925 |
| **RIVIERA 6** | | | |
| 2 Dr Cpe | **24560** | 14775 | 17350 |
| **ROADMASTER 8** | | | |
| 4 Dr Base Sdn | **20890** | 13800 | 16175 |
| 4 Dr Limited Sdn | **23245** | 15250 | 17900 |
| 4 Dr Estate Wgn | **21445** | 15250 | 17900 |
| **SKYLARK 4\*** | | | |
| 2 Dr Cpe | **11570** | 6575 | 7650 |

| Year/Model/Body/Type | Original List | Current Whlse | Average Retail |
|---|---|---|---|
| 4 Dr Sdn | **11470** | 6575 | 7650 |
| **SKYLARK CUSTOM 4*** | | | |
| 4 Dr Sdn | **12765** | 7075 | 8225 |
| **2 Dr Cpe** | 12765 | 7075 | |
| **SKYLARK GRAN SPORT 4*** | | | |
| 2 Dr Cpe | **14410** | 7550 | 8775 |
| **SKYLARK LUXURY EDITION 4*** | | | |
| 4 Dr Sdn | **14610** | 7750 | 9000 |

*For 6 cyl or quad 4 eng models add $400 whsle/$400 rtl.

*ADD FOR:*

| | Original List | Current Whlse | Average Retail |
|---|---|---|---|
| Anti-lock Brakes (Le Sabre, Regal, Skylark Gran Sport) | **925** | 390 | 430 |
| Vinyl Landau Roof (Roadmaster) | **695** | 230 | 250 |
| Leather Seats (Le Sabre Ltd, Park Ave. Base,Regal) | **500** | 220 | 240 |
| (Reatta) | **680** | 260 | 280 |
| (Roadmaster Sdn) | **760** | 260 | 280 |
| (Roadmaster Estate Wgn) | **540** | 220 | 240 |
| CD Player (Reatta) | **396** | 130 | 140 |
| (Regal) | **414** | 130 | 140 |

NOTE: Power windows, power door locks and power seat standard on Park Avenue, Reatta, Riviera and Roadmaster. Anti-lock brakes and driver side air bag standard on Park Avenue, Reatta and Roadmaster. Power brakes standard on all models.

## 1990

| | Original List | Current Whlse | Average Retail |
|---|---|---|---|
| **CENTURY CUSTOM 4*** | | | |
| 4 Dr Sdn | **13150** | 5325 | 6250 |
| 2 Dr Cpe | **13250** | 5225 | 6150 |
| 4 Dr Wgn | **14570** | 5725 | 6650 |
| **CENTURY LIMITED 4*** | | | |
| 4 Dr Sdn | **14075** | 5875 | 6800 |
| 4 Dr Wgn | **15455** | 6250 | 7275 |

*For 6 cyl models add $400 whsle/$400 retail.

| | Original List | Current Whlse | Average Retail |
|---|---|---|---|
| **ELECTRA LIMITED 6** | | | |
| 4 Dr Sdn | **20225** | 9325 | 10750 |
| **ELECTRA PARK AVENUE 6** | | | |
| 4 Dr Sdn | **21750** | 10175 | 11750 |
| **ELECTRA PARK AVENUE ULTRA 6** | | | |
| 4 Dr Sdn | **27825** | 12600 | 14925 |
| **ELECTRA T TYPE 6** | | | |
| 4 Dr Sdn | **23025** | 9800 | 11300 |

| Year/Model/Body/Type | Original List | Current Whlse | Average Retail |
|---|---|---|---|
| **ESTATE WAGON 8** | | | |
| 4 Dr Wgn | **17940** | 9250 | 10650 |
| **LE SABRE 6** | | | |
| 2 Dr Cpe | **16145** | 7450 | 8650 |
| **LE SABRE CUSTOM 6** | | | |
| 4 Dr Sdn | **16050** | 7600 | 8825 |
| **LE SABRE LIMITED 6** | | | |
| 2 Dr Cpe | **17300** | 8400 | 9700 |
| 4 Dr Sdn | **17400** | 8550 | 9875 |
| **REATTA 6** | | | |
| 2 Dr Cpe | **28335** | 12650 | 14975 |
| 2 Dr Conv | **34995** | 16550 | 19200 |
| **REGAL CUSTOM 6** | | | |
| 2 Dr Cpe | **15200** | 7400 | 8600 |
| **REGAL LIMITED 6** | | | |
| 2 Dr Cpe | **15860** | 7900 | 9175 |
| **RIVIERA 6** | | | |
| 2 Dr Cpe | **23040** | 11025 | 12725 |
| **SKYLARK 4** | | | |
| 2 Dr Cpe | **11285** | 5050 | 5975 |
| 4 Dr Sdn | **11185** | 5050 | 5975 |
| **SKYLARK CUSTOM 4*** | | | |
| 2 Dr Cpe | **12180** | 5500 | 6425 |
| 4 Dr Sdn | 12180 | 5500 | 6425 |
| **SKYLARK GRAN SPORT 4*** | | | |
| 2 Dr Cpe | **13655** | 5950 | 6875 |
| **SKYLARK LUXURY EDITION 4*** | | | |
| 4 Dr Sdn | **13865** | 6125 | 7125 |

*For 6 cyl or quad 4 eng models add $350 whsle/$350 rtl.

*ADD FOR:*

| | Original List | Current Whlse | Average Retail |
|---|---|---|---|
| Anti-lock Brakes (Electra Limited & Park Ave., Le Sabre, Regal, Riviera) | **925** | 360 | 400 |
| 3.8 Liter V6 Eng (Regal) | **395** | 170 | 190 |
| Leather Bucket Seats (Reatta) | **680** | 240 | 260 |
| 4-Seater Pkg (Regal) | **409** | 170 | 190 |
| Delco/Bose Music System (Riviera) | **1399** | 350 | 380 |

NOTE: Power windows standard on Electra Series, Reatta and Riviera. Power door locks standard on Electra Park Avenue, Electra Ultra, Reatta and Riviera. Power driver's seat standard on Electra Series, Reatta and Riviera. Full vinyl roof standard on Skylark Luxury Edition. Power brakes standard on all models.

| Year/Model/ Body/Type | Original List | Current Whlse | Average Retail |
|---|---|---|---|
| **1989** | | | |
| **CENTURY CUSTOM 4\*** | | | |
| 4 Dr Sdn | **13554** | 3975 | 4875 |
| 2 Dr Cpe | **13324** | 3875 | 4775 |
| 4 Dr Wgn | **14396** | 4275 | 5200 |
| **CENTURY ESTATE WAGON 4\*** | | | |
| 4 Dr Wgn | **15196** | 4650 | 5575 |
| **CENTURY LIMITED 4\*** | | | |
| 4 Dr Sdn | **14481** | 4500 | 5425 |
| *For 6 cyl models add $375 whsle/$375 retail.* | | | |
| **ELECTRA LIMITED 6** | | | |
| 4 Dr Sdn | **18525** | 7125 | 8275 |
| **ELECTRA ESTATE WAGON 8** | | | |
| 4 Dr Wgn | **19860** | 8125 | 9375 |
| **ELECTRA PARK AVENUE 6** | | | |
| 4 Dr Sdn | **20460** | 7800 | 8925 |
| **ELECTRA PARK AVENUE ULTRA 6** | | | |
| 4 Dr Sdn | **26218** | 9925 | 11425 |
| **ELECTRA T TYPE 6** | | | |
| 4 Dr Sdn | **21325** | 7450 | 8650 |
| **LE SABRE 6** | | | |
| 2 Dr Cpe | **15425** | 5975 | 6900 |
| **LE SABRE CUSTOM 6** | | | |
| 4 Dr Sdn | **15330** | 6125 | 7125 |
| **LE SABRE ESTATE WAGON 8** | | | |
| 4 Dr Wgn | **16770** | 6550 | 7625 |
| **LE SABRE LIMITED 6** | | | |
| 2 Dr Cpe | **16630** | 6750 | 7850 |
| 4 Dr Sdn | **16730** | 6925 | 8050 |
| **REATTA 6** | | | |
| 2 Dr Cpe | **26700** | 9675 | 11150 |
| **REGAL CUSTOM 6** | | | |
| 2 Dr Cpe | **14614** | 5650 | 6575 |
| **REGAL LIMITED 6** | | | |
| 2 Dr Cpe | **15139** | 6050 | 6950 |
| **RIVIERA 6** | | | |
| 2 Dr Cpe | **22540** | 8000 | 9300 |
| **SKYHAWK 4** | | | |
| 2 Dr Cpe | **10420** | 4175 | 5100 |

| Year/Model/ Body/Type | Original List | Current Whlse | Average Retail |
|---|---|---|---|
| 4 Dr Sdn | **10420** | 4275 | 5200 |
| 4 Dr Wgn | **11365** | 4475 | 5400 |
| **SKYLARK CUSTOM 4\*** | | | |
| 2 Dr Cpe | **11691** | 4475 | 5400 |
| 4 Dr Sdn | **11691** | 4475 | 5400 |
| **SKYLARK LIMITED 4\*** | | | |
| 2 Dr Cpe | **12921** | 4800 | 5725 |
| 4 Dr Sdn | **12921** | 4800 | 5725 |
| *For 6 cyl models add $325 whsle/$325 retail. For quad 4 eng add $275 whsle/$275 retail.* | | | |
| *ADD FOR:* | | | |
| S/E Pkg (Skyhawk Cpe) | **1095** | 350 | 380 |
| (Skylark Custom) | **1134** | 390 | 430 |
| 4-Seater Pkg (Regal) | **409** | 160 | 170 |
| Gran Spt Pkg (Regal Custom) | **1212** | 440 | 480 |
| T-Type Pkg (Le Sabre) | **1005** | 350 | 380 |
| 16-way Adj. Driver's Seat (Riviera) | **1230** | 220 | 240 |
| (Reatta) | **895** | 170 | 190 |
| Anti-Lock Brakes (Regal, Le Sabre, Electra Ltd, Electra Park Ave., Riviera) | **925** | 300 | 330 |
| Leather Seats (Regal Ltd, Le Sabre) | **450** | 160 | 170 |

NOTE: Power brakes standard on all models. Power windows standard on Electra Series, Riviera and Reatta. Power locks standard on Electra Park Ave., Riviera and Reatta. Power seat standard on Electra Park Ave., Ultra Riviera and Reatta. Vinyl roof standard on Le Sabre Coupe and Electra Park Avenue Ultra. Anti-Lock brakes standard on Electra T Type, Electra Park Avenue and Reatta.

| Year/Model/ Body/Type | Original List | Current Whlse | Average Retail |
|---|---|---|---|
| **1988** | | | |
| **CENTURY CUSTOM 4\*** | | | |
| 4 Dr Sdn | **12679** | 2950 | 3850 |
| 2 Dr Cpe | **12529** | 2850 | 3750 |
| 4 Dr Wgn | **13346** | 3175 | 4075 |
| **CENTURY ESTATE WAGON 4\*** | | | |
| 4 Dr Wgn | **14553** | 3625 | 4525 |
| **CENTURY LIMITED 4\*** | | | |
| 4 Dr Sdn | **13729** | 3375 | 4275 |
| 2 Dr Cpe | **13526** | 3275 | 4175 |
| *For 6 cyl models add $350 whsle/$350 retail.* | | | |
| **ELECTRA LIMITED 6** | | | |
| 4 Dr Sdn | **17479** | 5175 | 6100 |
| **ELECTRA ESTATE WAGON 8** | | | |
| 4 Dr Wgn | **18954** | 6500 | 7575 |

*Refer to optional equipment schedules*

| Year/Model/ Body/Type | Original List | Current Whlse | Average Retail |
|---|---|---|---|
| **ELECTRA PARK AVENUE 6** | | | |
| 4 Dr Sdn | **19464** | 5850 | 6775 |
| **ELECTRA T TYPE 6** | | | |
| 4 Dr Sdn | **20229** | 5550 | 6475 |
| **LE SABRE 6** | | | |
| 2 Dr Cpe | **14560** | 4200 | 5125 |
| **LE SABRE CUSTOM 6** | | | |
| 4 Dr Sdn | **14405** | 4350 | 5275 |
| **LE SABRE LIMITED 6** | | | |
| 4 Dr Sdn | **15475** | 5000 | 5925 |
| 2 Dr Cpe | **16350** | 4850 | 5775 |
| **LE SABRE ESTATE WAGON 8** | | | |
| 4 Dr Wgn | **16040** | 5025 | 5950 |
| **REATTA 6** | | | |
| 2 Dr Cpe | **25000** | 8450 | 9750 |
| **REGAL CUSTOM 6** | | | |
| 2 Dr Cpe | **13452** | 4325 | 5250 |
| **REGAL LIMITED 6** | | | |
| 2 Dr Cpe | **14015** | 4625 | 5550 |
| **RIVIERA 6** | | | |
| 2 Dr Cpe | **21615** | 5875 | 6800 |
| **SKYHAWK 4** | | | |
| 4 Dr Sdn | **9974** | 3100 | 4000 |
| 2 Dr Cpe | **9974** | 3000 | 3900 |
| 4 Dr Wgn | **10887** | 3250 | 4150 |
| **SKYLARK CUSTOM 4\*** | | | |
| 4 Dr Sdn | **11074** | 3350 | 4250 |
| 2 Dr Cpe | **11359** | 3350 | 4250 |
| **SKYLARK LIMITED 4\*** | | | |
| 4 Dr Sdn | **12396** | 3650 | 4550 |
| 2 Dr Cpe | **12466** | 3650 | 4550 |

*For quad 4 or 6 cyl models add $275 whsle/$275 retail.

| ADD FOR: | | | |
|---|---|---|---|
| T-Type Pkg (Le Sabre | | | |
| Custom Cpe) | **1958** | 600 | 670 |
| (Riviera) | **1844** | 560 | 630 |
| Turbo Pkg (Skyhawk Ltd) | **1547** | 440 | 480 |
| Anti-Lock Brakes | | | |
| (Electra Ltd Park Ave., | | | |
| Le Sabre, Riviera) | **925** | 240 | 260 |
| Cellular Phone (Riviera) | **2850** | 170 | 190 |
| 231 CID V6 Eng (Century) | **745** | 170 | 190 |

NOTE: Power brakes standard on all models. Power windows standard on Electra Series, Riviera and Reatta.

Power door locks standard on Electra Park Avenue, Electra Estate Wagon, Riviera and Reatta. Power seat standard on Electra Series, Riviera and Reatta.

## 1987

| Year/Model/ Body/Type | Original List | Current Whlse | Average Retail |
|---|---|---|---|
| **CENTURY CUSTOM 4\*** | | | |
| 4 Dr Sdn | **11764** | 2225 | 3075 |
| 2 Dr Cpe | **11619** | 2150 | 3000 |
| 4 Dr Wgn | **12253** | 2425 | 3300 |
| **CENTURY ESTATE WAGON 4\*** | | | |
| 4 Dr Wgn | **12773** | 2850 | 3750 |
| **CENTURY LIMITED 4\*** | | | |
| 4 Dr Sdn | **12368** | 2625 | 3525 |
| 2 Dr Cpe | **12172** | 2525 | 3400 |

*For 6 cyl models add $300 whsle/$300 retail.

| | | | |
|---|---|---|---|
| **ELECTRA LIMITED 6** | | | |
| 4 Dr Sdn | **16902** | 3700 | 4600 |
| **ELECTRA ESTATE WAGON 8** | | | |
| 4 Dr Wgn | **17697** | 4800 | 5725 |
| **ELECTRA PARK AVENUE 6** | | | |
| 4 Dr Sdn | **18769** | 4250 | 5175 |
| 2 Dr Cpe | **18577** | 4100 | 5025 |
| **ELECTRA T TYPE 6** | | | |
| 4 Dr Sdn | **18224** | 4000 | 4900 |
| **LE SABRE 6** | | | |
| 4 Dr Sdn | **13438** | 3100 | 4000 |
| **LE SABRE CUSTOM 6** | | | |
| 4 Dr Sdn | **13616** | 3350 | 4250 |
| 2 Dr Cpe | **13616** | 3225 | 4125 |
| **LE SABRE LIMITED 6** | | | |
| 4 Dr Sdn | **14918** | 3925 | 4825 |
| 2 Dr Cpe | **14918** | 3775 | 4675 |
| **LE SABRE ESTATE WAGON 8** | | | |
| 4 Dr Wgn | **14724** | 3825 | 4725 |
| **REGAL 6\*** | | | |
| 2 Dr Cpe | **12337** | 2975 | 3875 |
| **REGAL LIMITED 6\*** | | | |
| 2 Dr Cpe | **13078** | 3275 | 4175 |

*For 8 cyl models add $350 whsle/$350 retail.

| | | | |
|---|---|---|---|
| **RIVIERA 6** | | | |
| 2 Dr Cpe | **20337** | 4075 | 5000 |

| Year/Model/ Body/Type | Original List | Current Whsle | Average Retail |
|---|---|---|---|
| **SKYHAWK CUSTOM 4** | | | |
| 4 Dr Sdn | **9949** | 2075 | 2925 |
| 2 Dr Cpe | **9912** | 1975 | 2825 |
| 4 Dr Wgn | **10639** | 2175 | 3025 |
| **SKYHAWK LIMITED 4** | | | |
| 4 Dr Sdn | **10893** | 2400 | 3275 |
| 2 Dr Cpe | **10835** | 2300 | 3175 |
| 4 Dr Wgn | **11231** | 2525 | 3400 |
| **SKYHAWK SPORT 4** | | | |
| 2 Dr Hbk | **10355** | 2075 | 2925 |
| **SKYLARK CUSTOM 4*** | | | |
| 4 Dr Sdn | **11080** | 2275 | 3150 |
| **SKYLARK LIMITED 4*** | | | |
| 4 Dr Sdn | **12168** | 2500 | 3375 |
| **SOMERSET CUSTOM 4*** | | | |
| 2 Dr Cpe | **11122** | 2275 | 3150 |
| **SOMERSET LIMITED 4*** | | | |
| 2 Dr Cpe | **12168** | 2500 | 3375 |
| *For 6 cyl models add $300 whsle/$300 retail. | | | |

ADD FOR:
| | | | |
|---|---|---|---|
| Grand National Package (Regal) | **3574** | 860 | 960 |
| T-Type Pkg (Le Sabre Custom Cpe) | **1975** | 440 | 480 |
| (Riviera) | **1844** | 390 | 430 |
| T Pkg (Skyhawk, Skylark, Somerset) | **592** | 150 | 160 |
| (Le Sabre, Electra, Regal) | **508** | 120 | 130 |
| (Riviera) | **581** | 140 | 150 |
| (Electra Park Ave) | **407** | 130 | 140 |
| Turbo Pkg (Skyhawk) | **1607** | 300 | 330 |
| (Regal) | **1422** | 350 | 380 |
| 231 CID V6 Eng (Century) | **745** | 130 | 140 |
| 307 CID V8 Eng (Regal) | **590** | 160 | 170 |
| Hatch Roof (Regal) | **895** | 220 | 240 |

NOTE: Power brakes standard on all models. Power windows standard on Riviera and Electra Series. Power locks standard on Riviera and Electra Park Avenue.

## 1986

| | Original List | Current Whsle | Average Retail |
|---|---|---|---|
| **CENTURY CUSTOM 4*** | | | |
| 4 Dr Sdn | **11259** | 1500 | 2350 |
| 2 Dr Cpe | **11078** | 1400 | 2150 |
| 4 Dr Wgn | **11689** | 1700 | 2550 |
| **CENTURY ESTATE WAGON 4*** | | | |
| 4 Dr Wgn | **12162** | 2000 | 2850 |

| Year/Model/ Body/Type | Original List | Current Whsle | Average Retail |
|---|---|---|---|
| **CENTURY LIMITED 4*** | | | |
| 4 Dr Sdn | **11772** | 1800 | 2650 |
| 2 Dr Cpe | **11582** | 1725 | 2575 |
| **CENTURY T TYPE 6** | | | |
| 4 Dr Sdn | **13304** | 2175 | 3025 |
| *For 6 cyl models add $300 whsle/$300 retail. | | | |
| **ELECTRA 6** | | | |
| 4 Dr Sdn | **16071** | 2950 | 3850 |
| 2 Dr Cpe | **15873** | 2800 | 3700 |
| **ELECTRA ESTATE WAGON 8** | | | |
| 4 Dr Wgn | **16911** | 3200 | 4100 |
| **ELECTRA PARK AVENUE 6** | | | |
| 4 Dr Sdn | **17875** | 3400 | 4300 |
| 2 Dr Cpe | **17690** | 3250 | 4150 |
| **ELECTRA T TYPE 6** | | | |
| 4 Dr Sdn | **17348** | 3225 | 4125 |
| **LE SABRE CUSTOM 6** | | | |
| 4 Dr Sdn | **12699** | 2625 | 3525 |
| 2 Dr Cpe | **12699** | 2475 | 3350 |
| **LE SABRE LIMITED 6** | | | |
| 4 Dr Sdn | **13838** | 3100 | 4000 |
| 2 Dr Cpe | **13838** | 2950 | 3850 |
| **LE SABRE ESTATE WAGON 8** | | | |
| 4 Dr Wgn | **14044** | 2400 | 3275 |
| **REGAL 6*** | | | |
| 2 Dr Cpe | **11770** | 2150 | 3000 |
| **REGAL LIMITED 6*** | | | |
| 2 Dr Cpe | **12485** | 2425 | 3300 |
| **REGAL T TYPE 6** | | | |
| 2 Dr Cpe | **14153** | 3750 | 4650 |
| *For 8 cyl models add $325 whsle/$325 retail. | | | |
| **RIVIERA 6** | | | |
| 2 Dr Cpe | **20267** | 3275 | 4175 |
| **RIVIERA T TYPE 6** | | | |
| 2 Dr Cpe | **22052** | 3650 | 4550 |
| **SKYHAWK CUSTOM 4** | | | |
| 4 Dr Sdn | **9682** | 1625 | 2475 |
| 2 Dr Cpe | **9444** | 1525 | 2375 |
| 4 Dr Wgn | **10044** | 1700 | 2550 |
| **SKYHAWK LIMITED 4** | | | |
| 4 Dr Sdn | **10220** | 1875 | 2725 |

| Year/Model/Body/Type | Original List | Current Whlse | Average Retail |
| --- | --- | --- | --- |
| 2 Dr Cpe | 10024 | 1775 | 2625 |
| 4 Dr Wgn | 10541 | 1975 | 2825 |
| **SKYHAWK T TYPE 4** | | | |
| 2 Dr Cpe | 10528 | 2100 | 2950 |
| 2 Dr Hbk | 10983 | 2175 | 3025 |
| **SKYLARK CUSTOM 4*** | | | |
| 4 Dr Sdn | 10997 | 1600 | 2450 |
| **SKYLARK LIMITED 4*** | | | |
| 4 Dr Sdn | 11681 | 1775 | 2625 |
| **SOMERSET CUSTOM 4*** | | | |
| 2 Dr Cpe | 10797 | 1600 | 2450 |
| **SOMERSET LIMITED 4*** | | | |
| 2 Dr Cpe | 11482 | 1775 | 2625 |
| **SOMERSET T TYPE 6** | | | |
| 2 Dr Cpe | 11241 | 2275 | 3150 |

*For 6 cyl models add $275 whsle/$275 retail.

*ADD FOR:*

| | Original List | Current Whlse | Average Retail |
| --- | --- | --- | --- |
| 110 CID Turbo Eng (Skyhawk T Type) | 800 | 130 | 140 |
| 173 CID V6 Eng (Century except T Type) | 485 | 70 | 80 |
| 181 CID V6 Eng (Skylark, Somerset except T Type) | 660 | 100 | 110 |
| 231 CID V6 Eng (Century except T Type) | 745 | 90 | 100 |
| 307 CID V8 Eng (Regal except T Type) | 590 | 90 | 100 |
| Hatch Roof (Regal) | 895 | 140 | 150 |

NOTE: Power windows and power seat standard on Electra and Riviera.

## 1985

| Year/Model/Body/Type | Original List | Current Whlse | Average Retail |
| --- | --- | --- | --- |
| **CENTURY CUSTOM 4*** | | | |
| 4 Dr Sdn | 10485 | 1325 | 2050 |
| 2 Dr Cpe | 10315 | 1250 | 1975 |
| 4 Dr Wgn | 10890 | 1475 | 2300 |
| **CENTURY LIMITED 4*** | | | |
| 4 Dr Sdn | 10965 | 1575 | 2425 |
| 2 Dr Cpe | 10790 | 1475 | 2300 |
| 4 Dr Wgn | 11335 | 1725 | 2575 |
| **CENTURY T TYPE 6** | | | |
| 4 Dr Sdn | 12395 | 1675 | 2525 |
| 2 Dr Cpe | 12225 | 1675 | 2525 |

*For 6 cyl models add $300 whsle/$300 retail.

| Year/Model/Body/Type | Original List | Current Whlse | Average Retail |
| --- | --- | --- | --- |
| **ELECTRA 6** | | | |
| 4 Dr Sdn | 14883 | 2175 | 3025 |
| 2 Dr Cpe | 14697 | 2025 | 2875 |
| **ELECTRA ESTATE WAGON 8** | | | |
| 4 Dr Wgn | 15629 | 2375 | 3250 |
| **ELECTRA PARK AVENUE 6** | | | |
| 4 Dr Sdn | 16566 | 2550 | 3425 |
| 2 Dr Cpe | 16398 | 2400 | 3275 |
| **ELECTRA T TYPE 6** | | | |
| 4 Dr Sdn | 15879 | 2375 | 3250 |
| 2 Dr Cpe | 15694 | 2250 | 3100 |
| **LE SABRE CUSTOM 6*** | | | |
| 4 Dr Sdn | 11565 | 1775 | 2625 |
| 2 Dr Cpe | 11412 | 1675 | 2525 |
| **LE SABRE ESTATE WAGON 8** | | | |
| 4 Dr Wgn | 12958 | 1800 | 2650 |
| **LE SABRE LTD COLLECTORS EDIT 6*** | | | |
| 4 Dr Sdn | 12904 | 2150 | 3000 |
| 2 Dr Cpe | 12736 | 2000 | 2850 |

*For 8 cyl models add $400 whsle/$400 retail.

| Year/Model/Body/Type | Original List | Current Whlse | Average Retail |
| --- | --- | --- | --- |
| **REGAL 6** | | | |
| 2 Dr Cpe | 10879 | 1500 | 2350 |
| **REGAL LIMITED 6** | | | |
| 2 Dr Cpe | 11543 | 1750 | 2600 |
| **REGAL T TYPE 6** | | | |
| 2 Dr Cpe | 12890 | 2825 | 3725 |
| **RIVIERA 8** | | | |
| 2 Dr Cpe | 17044 | 2400 | 3275 |
| **RIVIERA CONVERTIBLE 8** | | | |
| 2 Dr Conv | 27335 | 5275 | 6200 |
| **RIVIERA T TYPE 6** | | | |
| 2 Dr Cpe | 17995 | 1950 | 2800 |
| **SKYHAWK CUSTOM 4** | | | |
| 4 Dr Sdn | 9019 | 1175 | 1900 |
| 2 Dr Cpe | 8798 | 1075 | 1800 |
| 4 Dr Wgn | 9362 | 1250 | 1975 |
| **SKYHAWK LIMITED 4** | | | |
| 4 Dr Sdn | 9529 | 1375 | 2125 |
| 2 Dr Cpe | 9325 | 1300 | 2025 |
| 4 Dr Wgn | 9832 | 1450 | 2225 |
| **SKYHAWK T TYPE 4** | | | |
| 2 Dr Cpe | 9851 | 1525 | 2375 |

| Year/Model/ Body/Type | Original List | Current Whlse | Average Retail |
|---|---|---|---|
| **SKYLARK CUSTOM 4*** | | | |
| 4 Dr Sdn | **9061** | 925 | 1650 |
| **SKYLARK LIMITED 4*** | | | |
| 4 Dr Sdn | **9649** | 1125 | 1850 |
| **SOMERSET REGAL 4*** | | | |
| 2 Dr Cpe | **10104** | 1350 | 2100 |
| **SOMERSET REGAL LIMITED 4*** | | | |
| 2 Dr Cpe | **10725** | 1550 | 2400 |
| *For 6 cyl models add $200 whsle/$200 retail. | | | |
| *ADD FOR:* | | | |
| 110 CID Turbo Eng (Skyhawk T Type) | **800** | 90 | 100 |
| 173 CID MFI V6 Eng (Skylark) | **510** | 60 | 60 |
| 181 CID MFI V6 Eng (Somerset Regal) | **560** | 60 | 70 |
| 231 CID MFI V6 Eng (Century Custom & Ltd) | **595** | 60 | 70 |
| 231 CID V6 Turbo Eng (Riviera) | **735** | 70 | 80 |

NOTE: Power windows standard on Electra and Riviera. Power door locks standard on Electra. Power brakes standard on all models. Power seat standard on Electra, Le Sabre Ltd Collector's Edit and Riviera.

## 1984

| Year/Model/ Body/Type | Original List | Current Whlse | Average Retail |
|---|---|---|---|
| **CENTURY CUSTOM 4*** | | | |
| 4 Dr Sdn | **10004** | 1050 | 1775 |
| 2 Dr Cpe | **9840** | 950 | 1675 |
| 4 Dr Wgn | **10390** | 1175 | 1900 |
| **CENTURY LIMITED 4*** | | | |
| 4 Dr Sdn | **10459** | 1225 | 1950 |
| 2 Dr Cpe | **10292** | 1150 | 1875 |
| 4 Dr Wgn | **10817** | 1325 | 2050 |
| *For 6 cyl models add $200 whsle/$200 retail. | | | |
| **CENTURY T TYPE 6** | | | |
| 4 Dr Sdn | **11404** | 1275 | 2000 |
| 2 Dr Cpe | **11240** | 1275 | 2000 |
| **ELECTRA LIMITED 6*** | | | |
| 4 Dr Sdn | **13530** | 1775 | 2625 |
| 2 Dr Cpe | **13353** | 1675 | 2525 |
| **ELECTRA PARK AVENUE 6*** | | | |
| 4 Dr Sdn | **15044** | 2150 | 3000 |
| 2 Dr Cpe | **14888** | 2025 | 2875 |
| *For 8 cyl models add $300 whsle/$300 retail. | | | |

| Year/Model/ Body/Type | Original List | Current Whlse | Average Retail |
|---|---|---|---|
| **ESTATE WAGON 8** | | | |
| 4 Dr Wgn | **14681** | 1725 | 2575 |
| **LE SABRE CUSTOM 6*** | | | |
| 4 Dr Sdn | **10971** | 1300 | 2025 |
| 2 Dr Cpe | **10826** | 1175 | 1900 |
| **LE SABRE LIMITED 6*** | | | |
| 4 Dr Sdn | **11782** | 1500 | 2350 |
| 2 Dr Cpe | **11622** | 1375 | 2125 |
| *For 8 cyl models add $300 whsle/$300 retail. | | | |
| **REGAL 6** | | | |
| 4 Dr Sdn | **10513** | 1075 | 1800 |
| 2 Dr Cpe | **10329** | 1250 | 1975 |
| **REGAL LIMITED 6** | | | |
| 4 Dr Sdn | **11105** | 1300 | 2025 |
| 2 Dr Cpe | **10967** | 1450 | 2225 |
| **REGAL T TYPE 6** | | | |
| 2 Dr Cpe | **12230** | 2150 | 3000 |
| **RIVIERA 6*** | | | |
| 2 Dr Cpe | **15967** | 2000 | 2850 |
| **RIVIERA CONVERTIBLE 6*** | | | |
| 2 Dr Conv | **25832** | 4900 | 5825 |
| *For 8 cyl models add $300 whsle/$300 retail. | | | |
| **RIVIERA T TYPE 6** | | | |
| 2 Dr Cpe | **17050** | 1700 | 2550 |
| **SKYHAWK CUSTOM 4** | | | |
| 4 Dr Sdn | **8574** | 800 | 1500 |
| 2 Dr Cpe | **8362** | 725 | 1375 |
| 4 Dr Wgn | **8906** | 850 | 1550 |
| **SKYHAWK LIMITED 4** | | | |
| 4 Dr Sdn | **9066** | 925 | 1650 |
| 2 Dr Cpe | **8870** | 875 | 1600 |
| 4 Dr Wgn | **9356** | 975 | 1700 |
| **SKYHAWK T TYPE 4** | | | |
| 2 Dr Cpe | **9306** | 1000 | 1725 |
| **SKYLARK CUSTOM 4*** | | | |
| 4 Dr Sdn | **8862** | 600 | 1125 |
| 2 Dr Cpe | **8700** | 550 | 1025 |
| **SKYLARK LIMITED 4*** | | | |
| 4 Dr Sdn | **9438** | 775 | 1500 |
| 2 Dr Cpe | **9274** | 725 | 1375 |
| *For 6 cyl models add $150 whsle/$150 retail. | | | |

| Year/Model/ Body/Type | Original List | Current Whlse | Average Retail |
|---|---|---|---|
| **SKYLARK T TYPE 6** | | | |
| 2 Dr Cpe | **10712** | 900 | 1625 |
| **1983 — ALL BODY STYLES** | | | |
| CENTURY CUSTOM | — | 900 | 1600 |
| CENTURY LIMITED | — | 975 | 1700 |
| CENTURY T TYPE | — | 1050 | 1775 |
| ELECTRA LIMITED | — | 1250 | 1975 |
| ELECTRA PARK AVENUE | — | 1500 | 2350 |
| ESTATE WAGON | — | 1300 | 2025 |
| LE SABRE CUSTOM | — | 975 | 1700 |
| LE SABRE ESTATE WAGON | — | 1125 | 1850 |
| LE SABRE LIMITED | — | 1175 | 1900 |
| REGAL | — | 900 | 1625 |
| REGAL ESTATE WAGON | — | 900 | 1625 |
| REGAL LIMITED | — | 1175 | 1900 |
| REGAL T TYPE | — | 950 | 1675 |
| RIVIERA | — | 1625 | 2475 |
| RIVIERA CONV | — | 4425 | 5350 |
| SKYHAWK CUSTOM | — | 550 | 1025 |
| SKYHAWK LIMITED | — | 650 | 1225 |
| SKYHAWK T TYPE | — | 650 | 1225 |
| SKYLARK CUSTOM | — | 400 | 725 |
| SKYLARK LIMITED | — | 500 | 925 |
| SKYLARK T TYPE | — | 600 | 1125 |

## CADILLAC

### 1992

**ALLANTE 8**

| | Original List | Current Whlse | Average Retail |
|---|---|---|---|
| Cpe/Conv | **62790** | — | — |
| Conv | **57170** | — | — |
| *ADD FOR:* | | | |
| Digital Instrument Cluster (Conv) | **495** | 300 | 330 |
| Pearl White Paint | **700** | 230 | 250 |
| **BROUGHAM 8** | | | |
| Sdn | **31740** | 20225 | 23275 |
| *ADD FOR:* | | | |
| 5.7 Liter 8 Cyl Eng | **250** | 180 | 200 |
| D'Elegance, Cloth | **1875** | 1230 | 1360 |
| D'Elegance, Leather | **2445** | 1570 | 1750 |
| Leather Seat Trim | **570** | 340 | 380 |
| Wire Wheels | **1000** | 550 | 610 |
| **DE VILLE 8** | | | |
| Cpe | **31740** | 19200 | 22250 |
| Sdn | **31740** | 19400 | 22450 |
| Touring Sdn | **35190** | 21550 | 24850 |
| *ADD FOR:* | | | |
| Cabriolet Roof | **1095** | 360 | 400 |

| Year/Model/ Body/Type | Original List | Current Whlse | Average Retail |
|---|---|---|---|
| Phaeton Roof | **1095** | 360 | 400 |
| Full Vinyl Roof | **925** | 340 | 380 |
| Leather Seat Trim (Base) | **570** | 340 | 380 |
| **ELDORADO 8** | | | |
| Cpe | **32470** | 24950 | 28275 |
| *ADD FOR:* | | | |
| Sports & Stripes Pkg | **1900** | — | — |
| Touring Pkg | **4000** | — | — |
| Leather Seat Trim | **650** | 375 | 450 |
| **FLEETWOOD 8** | | | |
| Cpe | **36360** | 21650 | 24950 |
| Sdn | **36360** | 21850 | 25150 |
| Sixty Special Sdn | **39860** | — | — |
| *ADD FOR:* | | | |
| Leather Seat Trim | **570** | 340 | 380 |
| **SEVILLE 8** | | | |
| Sdn | **34975** | 26650 | 29975 |
| Touring Sdn | **37975** | 29450 | 32800 |
| *ADD FOR:* | | | |
| Leather Seat Trim | **650** | 375 | 450 |

NOTE: Power windows, power door locks, power seat, cruise control and tilt steering wheel standard on all models.

### 1991

**ALLANTE 8**

| | Original List | Current Whlse | Average Retail |
|---|---|---|---|
| Cpe/Conv | **62810** | 28425 | 31775 |
| Conv | **57260** | 30900 | 34350 |
| **BROUGHAM 8** | | | |
| Sdn | **30455** | 16550 | 19200 |
| **DE VILLE 8** | | | |
| Cpe | **30455** | 16200 | 18850 |
| Sdn | **30455** | 16400 | 19050 |
| **ELDORADO 8** | | | |
| Cpe | **31495** | 18450 | 21500 |
| **FLEETWOOD 8** | | | |
| Cpe | **35195** | 18350 | 21300 |
| Sdn | **35195** | 18550 | 21600 |
| Sixty Special Sdn | **38695** | 19550 | 22600 |
| **SEVILLE 8** | | | |
| Sdn | **34195** | 17550 | 20200 |
| Touring Sdn | **37395** | 20000 | 23050 |
| **TOURING SEDAN 8** | | | |
| Sdn | **33455** | 18300 | 21200 |

| Year/Model/ Body/Type | Original List | Current Whlse | Average Retail |
|---|---|---|---|
| *ADD FOR:* | | | |
| D'Elegance, Cloth (Brougham) | **1875** | 860 | 960 |
| D'Elegance, Leather (Brougham) | **2445** | 1080 | 1200 |
| Touring Coupe Pkg (Eldorado) | **2050** | 1040 | 1150 |
| Spring Edit Pkg (Coupe De Ville) | **1481** | 690 | 770 |
| Leather Seats (Brougham, De Ville, Fleetwood ex. | | | |
| 60 Special) | **570** | 280 | 310 |
| (Eldorado) | **555** | 280 | 310 |
| (Seville Base) | **460** | 260 | 280 |
| Formal Cabriolet Roof (Coupe De Ville) | **925** | 300 | 330 |
| Full Cabriolet Roof (Coupe De Ville, Eldorado) | **1095** | 310 | 340 |
| Full Padded Vinyl Roof (Sedan De Ville) | **925** | 300 | 330 |
| (Eldorado) | **1095** | 310 | 340 |
| Phaeton Roof (Sedan De Ville) | **1095** | 310 | 340 |
| (Seville Base) | **1195** | 380 | 420 |

NOTE: Power windows, power door locks, power seat, and power anti-lock brakes standard on all models. Vinyl roof standard on Brougham and Fleetwood. Air bag standard on Allante, De Ville, Eldorado, Fleetwood and Seville.

## 1990

### ALLANTE 8

| | | | |
|---|---|---|---|
| Cpe/Conv | **58638** | 24375 | 27675 |
| Conv | **53050** | 26400 | 29725 |

### BROUGHAM 8

| | | | |
|---|---|---|---|
| Sdn (307 CID V8) | **27400** | 12900 | 15225 |
| Sdn (350 CID V8) | **28250** | 13125 | 15450 |

### DE VILLE 8

| | | | |
|---|---|---|---|
| Cpe | **26960** | 13050 | 15375 |
| Sdn | **27540** | 13250 | 15575 |

### ELDORADO 8

| | | | |
|---|---|---|---|
| Cpe | **28855** | 14250 | 16725 |

### FLEETWOOD 8

| | | | |
|---|---|---|---|
| Cpe | **32400** | 14450 | 16975 |
| Sdn | **32980** | 14625 | 17175 |
| Sixty Special Sdn | **36980** | 16000 | 18650 |

### SEVILLE 8

| | | | |
|---|---|---|---|
| Sdn | **31830** | 14200 | 16675 |
| Touring Sdn | **36320** | 16175 | 18825 |

| Year/Model/ Body/Type | Original List | Current Whlse | Average Retail |
|---|---|---|---|
| *ADD FOR:* | | | |
| Anti-Lock Brakes (De Ville, Eldorado, Seville Base) | **925** | 390 | 430 |
| Cellular Phone (Allante) | **1195** | 160 | 180 |
| D'Elegance, Cloth (Brougham) | **2171** | 740 | 820 |
| D'Elegance, Leather (Brougham) | **2731** | 820 | 910 |
| Formal Cabriolet Roof (Coupe De Ville) | **825** | 200 | 220 |
| Full Cabriolet Roof (Coupe De Ville, Eldorado) | **1095** | 260 | 290 |
| Full Padded Vinyl Roof (Eldorado) | **1095** | 260 | 290 |

NOTE: Power windows, power door locks, power seat and power brakes standard on all models. Air bag standard on all models except Brougham. Anti-lock brakes standard on Allante, Brougham, Fleetwood Series and Seville Touring Sedan. Full vinyl roof standard on Brougham and Fleetwood Series. Formal cabriolet roof standard on Fleetwood Coupe.

## 1989

### ALLANTE 8

| | | | |
|---|---|---|---|
| Cpe/Conv | **57183** | 18950 | 21950 |

### BROUGHAM 8

| | | | |
|---|---|---|---|
| Sdn | **25699** | 8325 | 9500 |

### DE VILLE 8

| | | | |
|---|---|---|---|
| Cpe | **25285** | 10450 | 12100 |
| Sdn | **25760** | 10700 | 12400 |

### ELDORADO 8

| | | | |
|---|---|---|---|
| Cpe | **26915** | 11450 | 13125 |

### FLEETWOOD 8

| | | | |
|---|---|---|---|
| Cpe | **30365** | 11250 | 13000 |
| Sdn | **30840** | 11450 | 13225 |
| Sixty Special Sdn | **34840** | 12450 | 14600 |

### SEVILLE 8

| | | | |
|---|---|---|---|
| Sdn | **29935** | 11100 | 12825 |
| *ADD FOR:* | | | |
| Biarritz, Cloth (Eldorado) | **2875** | 670 | 750 |
| Biarritz, Leather (Eldorado) | **3325** | 820 | 910 |
| Full Vinyl Roof (Eldorado) | **1095** | 230 | 250 |
| D'Elegance, Cloth (Brougham) | **2286** | 690 | 770 |
| D'Elegance, Leather | | | |

| Year/Model/Body/Type | Original List | Current Whlse | Average Retail |
|---|---|---|---|
| (Brougham) | **2846** | 820 | 910 |
| STS Pkg (Seville) | **5754** | 2080 | 2300 |
| Anti-Lock Brakes | | | |
| (De Ville, Eldorado,Seville) | **925** | 300 | 330 |

NOTE: Power windows, power door locks, and power brakes standard on all models.

## 1988

### ALLANTE 8

| | Original List | Current Whlse | Average Retail |
|---|---|---|---|
| Cpe/Conv | **56533** | 16450 | 19100 |

### BROUGHAM 8

| | | | |
|---|---|---|---|
| Sdn | **23486** | 7325 | 8500 |

### CIMARRON 6

| | | | |
|---|---|---|---|
| Sdn | **16486** | 4100 | 5025 |

### DE VILLE 8

| | | | |
|---|---|---|---|
| Cpe | **23049** | 7500 | 8700 |
| Sdn | **23404** | 7700 | 8950 |

### ELDORADO 8

| | | | |
|---|---|---|---|
| Cpe | **24891** | 8250 | 9525 |

### FLEETWOOD 8

| | | | |
|---|---|---|---|
| d'Elegance | **28025** | 8525 | 9850 |
| Sixty Special | **34750** | 9225 | 10625 |

### SEVILLE 8

| | | | |
|---|---|---|---|
| Sdn | **27627** | 8150 | 9425 |

ADD FOR:

| | | | |
|---|---|---|---|
| Biarritz, Cloth (Eldorado) | **2845** | 510 | 570 |
| Biarritz, Leather (Eldorado) | **3255** | 560 | 630 |
| D'Elegance, Cloth (Brougham) | **2335** | 450 | 500 |
| D'Elegance, Leather (Brougham) | **2895** | 520 | 580 |
| Elegante, Cloth (Seville) | **3345** | 570 | 640 |
| Elegante, Leather (Seville) | **3755** | 620 | 690 |
| Touring Car Opt. (De Ville) | **2880** | 780 | 870 |
| Anti-Lock Brakes (De Ville, Eldorado, Seville, Fleetwood d'Elegance | **925** | 260 | 280 |
| Full Vinyl Roof (Eldorado) | **995** | 270 | 150 |
| Formal Cabriolet Roof (De Ville Cpe) | **713** | 170 | 190 |
| Phaeton Roof (Seville) | **1095** | 300 | 330 |
| Premier Formal Vinyl | | | |

| Year/Model/Body/Type | Original List | Current Whlse | Average Retail |
|---|---|---|---|
| Roof (Brougham) | **1095** | 300 | 330 |

NOTE: Power windows, power door locks, and power brakes standard on all models. Sunroof standard on Allante.

## 1987

### ALLANTE 8

| | | | |
|---|---|---|---|
| Cpe/Conv | **54700** | 13550 | 15925 |

### CIMARRON 4*

| | | | |
|---|---|---|---|
| Sdn | **15032** | 2800 | 3700 |

*For 6 cyl models add $425 whlse/$425 retail.

### DE VILLE 8

| | | | |
|---|---|---|---|
| Cpe | **21316** | 5125 | 6050 |
| Sdn | **21659** | 5325 | 6250 |

### ELDORADO 8

| | | | |
|---|---|---|---|
| Cpe | **23740** | 6000 | 6925 |

### FLEETWOOD 8

| | | | |
|---|---|---|---|
| Limousine | **36510** | 6500 | 7575 |
| Formal Limousine | **38580** | 8000 | 9300 |
| Brougham | **22637** | 4925 | 5850 |
| d'Elegance | **26104** | 5925 | 6850 |
| Sixty Special | **34850** | 6625 | 7700 |

### SEVILLE 8

| | | | |
|---|---|---|---|
| Sdn | **26326** | 6000 | 6925 |

ADD FOR:

| | | | |
|---|---|---|---|
| Biarritz, Cloth (Eldorado) | **3095** | 390 | 430 |
| Biarritz, Leather (Eldorado) | **3505** | 440 | 480 |
| D'Elegance, Cloth (Brougham) | **1950** | 310 | 340 |
| D'Elegance, Leather (Brougham) | **2510** | 360 | 390 |
| Elegante, Cloth (Seville) | **3595** | 520 | 580 |
| Elegante, Leather (Seville) | **4005** | 600 | 670 |
| Touring Car Opt (De Ville) | **2880** | 650 | 720 |
| Formal Cabriolet Roof (De Ville) | **713** | 130 | 140 |

NOTE: Power windows, power brakes, and power seat standard on all models.

## 1986

### CIMARRON 4*

| | | | |
|---|---|---|---|
| Sdn | **13974** | 1925 | 2775 |

*For 6 cyl models add $400 whlse/$400 retail.

*1991 Cadillac Allanté*

| Year/Model/<br>Body/Type | Original<br>List | Current<br>Whlse | Average<br>Retail |
|---|---|---|---|
| **DE VILLE 8** | | | |
| Cpe (FWD) | **20254** | 3625 | 4525 |
| Sdn (FWD) | **20585** | 3825 | 4725 |
| **ELDORADO 8** | | | |
| Cpe | **25032** | 4775 | 5700 |
| **FLEETWOOD 8** | | | |
| Limousine | **34934** | 4350 | 5275 |
| Formal Limousine | **36934** | 5575 | 6500 |
| Brougham Sdn | **21633** | 4250 | 5175 |
| **SEVILLE 8** | | | |
| Sdn | **27618** | 4800 | 5725 |
| *ADD FOR:* | | | |
| Biarritz, Cloth<br>(Eldorado) | **3095** | 260 | 280 |
| Biarritz, Leather<br>(Eldorado) | **3505** | 300 | 330 |
| D'Oro (Cimarron) | **975** | 120 | 130 |
| Elegante, Cloth<br>(Seville) | **3595** | 300 | 330 |
| Elegante, Leather<br>(Seville) | **4005** | 350 | 380 |
| Fleetwood Cloth Opt<br>(De Ville) | **3150** | 280 | 310 |
| Fleetwood Leather Opt<br>(De Ville) | **3700** | 330 | 360 |
| Touring Car Opt<br>(De Ville) | **2880** | 350 | 380 |
| Formal Cabriolet Roof<br>(De Ville) | **713** | 110 | 120 |

NOTE: Power windows and power brakes standard on all models. Power seat standard on Formal Limousine and

| Year/Model/<br>Body/Type | Original<br>List | Current<br>Whlse | Average<br>Retail |
|---|---|---|---|
| Fleetwood Brougham Sedan. Vinyl top standard on Limousines and Fleetwood Brougham Sedan. | | | |

## 1985

| | Original<br>List | Current<br>Whlse | Average<br>Retail |
|---|---|---|---|
| **DE VILLE 8** | | | |
| Cpe (FWD) | **18355** | 2950 | 3850 |
| Sdn (FWD) | **18947** | 3125 | 4025 |
| **FLEETWOOD 8** | | | |
| Cpe (FWD) | **21495** | 3250 | 4150 |
| Sdn (FWD) | **21466** | 3450 | 4350 |
| Limousine (FWD) | **32640** | 3450 | 4350 |
| Brougham Cpe (RWD) | **21219** | 2850 | 3750 |
| Brougham Sdn (RWD) | **21835** | 3050 | 3950 |
| Eldorado Cpe | **21355** | 3275 | 4175 |
| Eldorado Biarritz Conv. | **32105** | 7775 | 9025 |
| Seville Sdn | **23729** | 3500 | 4400 |
| Cimarron Sdn (4 cyl) | **13312** | 1600 | 2450 |
| *ADD FOR:* | | | |
| Brougham d'Elegance,<br>Cloth | **1295** | 130 | 140 |
| Brougham d'Elegance,<br>Leather | **1845** | 170 | 190 |
| Fleetwood d'Elegance,<br>Leather | **1845** | 170 | 190 |
| Formal Cabriolet<br>(De Ville Cpe, Fleet-<br>wood Sdn) | **698** | 70 | 80 |
| Full Cabriolet (Eldorado<br>Cpe, Seville) | **995** | 100 | 110 |
| D'Oro (Cimarron) | **975** | 100 | 110 |

NOTE: Power brakes standard on all models. Power windows, power door locks and power seat standard on all models except Cimarron.

*Refer to optional equipment schedules*

| Year/Model/Body/Type | Original List | Current Whlse | Average Retail |
|---|---|---|---|
| **1984** | | | |
| **CIMARRON 4** | | | |
| Sdn | **12605** | 1250 | 1975 |
| **DE VILLE 8** | | | |
| Cpe (RWD) | **17128** | 2050 | 2900 |
| Sdn (RWD) | **17613** | 2175 | 3025 |
| Cpe (FWD) | **17472** | — | — |
| Sdn (FWD) | **17957** | — | — |
| **FLEETWOOD 8** | | | |
| Eldorado Cpe | **20330** | 2900 | 3800 |
| Eldorado Biarritz Conv. | **31274** | 6625 | 7700 |
| Brougham Cpe | **19930** | 2400 | 3275 |
| Brougham Sdn | **20439** | 2525 | 3400 |
| Limousine | **30439** | 3175 | 4075 |
| Formal Limousine | **31497** | 3700 | 4600 |
| Seville Sdn | **22456** | 2825 | 3725 |

NOTE: Power windows (except Cimarron), tinted glass, and power disc brakes standard on all models. Cabriolet roof standard on Brougham Coupe. Full vinyl roof standard on Brougham Sedan, Limousine and Formal Limousine.

| **1983** — ALL BODY STYLES | | | |
|---|---|---|---|
| CIMARRON | — | 950 | 1675 |
| DE VILLE | — | 1775 | 2625 |
| FLEETWOOD ELDORADO | — | 2200 | 3050 |
| FLEETWOOD BROUGHAM | — | 2125 | 2975 |
| FLEETWOOD LIMOUSINE | — | 2975 | 3875 |
| FLEETWOOD FORMAL LIMOUSINE | — | 3300 | 4200 |
| SEVILLE | — | 2575 | 3450 |

## CHEVROLET

| **1992** | | | |
|---|---|---|---|
| **BERETTA 4\*** | | | |
| 2 Dr Base Cpe | **12359** | 8050 | 9300 |

*For 6 cyl models add $450 whsle/$450 retail.

| **BERETTA GTZ 4** | | | |
|---|---|---|---|
| 2 Dr Cpe | **16755** | 10525 | 12150 |
| **BERETTA GT 4\*** | | | |
| 2 Dr Cpe | **13935** | 9550 | 11000 |

*For 6 cyl models add $450 whsle/$450 retail.

| **DEDUCT FOR:** | | | |
|---|---|---|---|
| 6 Cyl Eng (GTZ) | — | 200 | 200 |

| Year/Model/Body/Type | Original List | Current Whlse | Average Retail |
|---|---|---|---|
| **CAMARO 6\*** | | | |
| 2 Dr RS Cpe | **13435** | 10100 | 11650 |
| 2 Dr RS Conv | **19415** | 10575 | 12200 |

*For 8 cyl models add $500 whsle/$500 retail.

| **CAMARO 8** | | | |
|---|---|---|---|
| 2 Dr Z28 Cpe | **17415** | 13800 | 16175 |
| 2 Dr Z28 Conv | **22860** | — | — |
| *ADD FOR:* | | | |
| 5.7 Liter 8 Cyl Eng (Z28 Cpe) | **300** | 200 | 220 |
| Custom Cloth Seats | **327** | 210 | 230 |
| Leather Seats | **850** | 530 | 590 |
| Aluminum Wheels (RS) | **225** | 150 | 160 |
| Removable Roof Panels | **895** | 580 | 650 |

| **CAPRICE 8** | | | |
|---|---|---|---|
| 4 Dr Sdn | **17300** | 10800 | 12475 |
| 4 Dr Wgn | **18700** | 13825 | 16200 |

| **CAPRICE CLASSIC 8** | | | |
|---|---|---|---|
| 4 Dr Sdn | **19300** | 12575 | 14850 |
| *ADD FOR:* | | | |
| 5.7 Liter Eng | **250** | 160 | 180 |
| Leather Seat Trim | **645** | 390 | 430 |
| Wire Whl Covers (Base) | **215** | — | — |

| **CAVALIER 4\*** | | | |
|---|---|---|---|
| 2 Dr VL Cpe | **10471** | 6400 | 7450 |
| 4 Dr VL Sdn | **10571** | 6500 | 7575 |
| 4 Dr VL Wgn | **11176** | 6850 | 7975 |
| 2 Dr RS Cpe | **11239** | 7125 | 8275 |
| 2 Dr RS Conv | **17175** | 10775 | 12425 |
| 4 Dr RS Sdn | **11439** | 7200 | 8350 |
| 4 Dr RS Wgn | **11944** | 7550 | 8775 |

*For 6 cyl models add $425 whsle/$425 retail.

| **CAVALIER 6** | | | |
|---|---|---|---|
| 2 Dr Z24 Sport Cpe | **14235** | 10200 | 11775 |
| 2 Dr Z24 Conv | **19545** | 13825 | 16200 |

| **CORSICA LT 4\*** | | | |
|---|---|---|---|
| 4 Dr Ntchbk Sdn | **12359** | 7550 | 8775 |

*For 6 cyl models add $450 whsle/$450 retail.

| *ADD FOR:* | | | |
|---|---|---|---|
| Sport Handling Pkg | **395** | 260 | 280 |

| **CORVETTE 8** | | | |
|---|---|---|---|
| Hbk Cpe | **33635** | 24950 | 28275 |
| Conv | **40145** | — | — |
| *ADD FOR:* | | | |
| ZR1 Spec Perf Pkg | **31378** | — | — |
| Handling Pkg | **2045** | 1340 | 1480 |
| Removable Hardtop | | | |

| Year/Model/ Body/Type | Original List | Current Whlse | Average Retail |
|---|---|---|---|
| Roof | **1995** | 1310 | 1450 |
| Removable Roof Panels | **650** | 430 | 480 |
| Dual Removable Rf Panels | **950** | 620 | 690 |
| Leather Seat Trim | **475** | 310 | 340 |
| Spt Leather Seat Trim | **1100** | 720 | 800 |
| Selective Ride & Handling Suspension | **1695** | 1110 | 1230 |

**LUMINA 4***

| | | | |
|---|---|---|---|
| 2 Dr Cpe | **14030** | 9125 | 10500 |
| 4 Dr Sdn | **14230** | 9125 | 10500 |

*For 6 cyl models add $500 whsle/$500 retail.

**LUMINA 6**

| | | | |
|---|---|---|---|
| 2 Dr Euro Cpe | **15600** | 11125 | 12850 |
| 4 Dr Euro Sdn | **15800** | 11125 | 12850 |
| 2 Dr Z34 Cpe | **18600** | 13375 | 15700 |

*ADD FOR:*

| | | | |
|---|---|---|---|
| Euro 3.4 Pkg (Euro Sdn) | **1885** | 1570 | 1750 |
| Anti-Lock Brakes (Base) | **450** | 290 | 320 |
| Custom Cloth Bench Seats | **234** | — | — |
| Custom Cloth Bucket Seats | **284** | 180 | 200 |

NOTE: Power windows standard on Cavalier Convertible & Z24 and Corvette. Power door locks standard on Caprice Classic and Corvette. Tilt steering wheel standard on Camaro, Caprice, Corvette and Lumina Z34. Cruise control standard on Corvette and Lumina Z34.

## 1991

**BERETTA 4***

| | | | |
|---|---|---|---|
| 2 Dr Base Cpe | **11725** | 7025 | 8150 |
| 2 Dr GTZ Cpe | **15005** | 9150 | 10550 |

*For Base Cpe with 6 cyl eng add $375 whsle/$375 retail.

**BERETTA GT**

| | | | |
|---|---|---|---|
| 2 Dr GT Cpe | **13705** | 8700 | 10050 |

**CAMARO RS 6***

| | | | |
|---|---|---|---|
| 2 Dr Cpe | **13010** | 7675 | 8900 |
| 2 Dr Conv | **18790** | 12175 | 14050 |

*For 8 cyl models add $450 whsle/$450 retail.

**CAMARO Z28 8**

| | | | |
|---|---|---|---|
| 2 Dr Cpe | **16805** | 11000 | 12700 |
| 2 Dr Conv | **22175** | 15525 | 18175 |

**CAPRICE 8**

| | | | |
|---|---|---|---|
| 4 Dr Sdn | **16515** | 8400 | 9700 |
| 4 Dr Wgn | **17872** | 11150 | 12875 |

**CAPRICE CLASSIC 8**

| | | | |
|---|---|---|---|
| 4 Dr Sdn | **18470** | 9925 | 11425 |

| Year/Model/ Body/Type | Original List | Current Whlse | Average Retail |
|---|---|---|---|
| **CAVALIER 4*** | | | |
| 2 Dr VL Cpe | **9567** | 5375 | 6300 |
| 4 Dr VL Sdn | **9842** | 5500 | 6425 |
| 4 Dr VL Wgn | **10302** | 5800 | 6725 |
| 2 Dr RS Cpe | **10305** | 6050 | 6950 |
| 4 Dr RS Sdn | **10505** | 6150 | 7150 |
| 4 Dr RS Wgn | **11015** | 6450 | 7500 |

*For 6 cyl models add $375 whsle/$375 retail.

**CAVALIER 6**

| | | | |
|---|---|---|---|
| 2 Dr RS Conv | **16454** | 9750 | 11225 |
| 4 Dr Z24 Sport Cpe | **13290** | 8900 | 10275 |

**CORSICA LT 4***

| | | | |
|---|---|---|---|
| 4 Dr Ntchbk Sdn | **11430** | 6525 | 7600 |
| 5 Dr Hbk Sdn | **12105** | 6700 | 7800 |

*For 6 cyl models add $375 whsle/$375 retail.

**CORVETTE 8**

| | | | |
|---|---|---|---|
| Cpe | **32455** | 20875 | 23925 |
| Conv | **38770** | 25600 | 28925 |

**LUMINA 4***

| | | | |
|---|---|---|---|
| 2 Dr Base Cpe | **13500** | 6950 | 8100 |
| 4 Dr Base Sdn | **13700** | 6950 | 8100 |

*For 6 cyl models add $475 whsle/$475 retail.

**LUMINA 6**

| | | | |
|---|---|---|---|
| 2 Dr Euro Cpe | **14795** | 8750 | 10100 |
| 4 Dr Euro Sdn | **14995** | 8750 | 10100 |
| 2 Dr Z34 Cpe (NA w/Auto Trans) | **17275** | 10750 | 12400 |

*ADD FOR:*

| | | | |
|---|---|---|---|
| Special Perf Pkg (ZR-1) (Corvette) | **31683** | 16000 | 17760 |
| Leather Seats Camaro) (Caprice Classic) | **850** | 360 | 400 |
| | **645** | 290 | 320 |
| (Corvette) | **1100** | 440 | 480 |
| Removable Roof Panels (Camaro Cpe) | **895** | 370 | 410 |
| (Corvette Cpe) | **650** | 300 | 330 |
| Dual Removable Roof Panels (Corvette Cpe) | **950** | 410 | 460 |

NOTE: Power brakes standard on all models. Power door locks and power windows standard on Caprice Classic, Corvette and Cavalier RS Convertible & Z24. Anti-lock brakes standard on Caprice and Corvette. Air bag standard on Beretta, Camaro, Caprice and Corvette.

## 1990

**BERETTA 4***

| | | | |
|---|---|---|---|
| 2 Dr Cpe | **11640** | 5050 | 5975 |

*For 6 cyl models add $350 whsle/$350 retail.

---

| Year/Model/Body/Type | Original List | Current Whlse | Average Retail |
|---|---|---|---|
| **BERETTA GTZ 4** | | | |
| 2 Dr Cpe (NA w/auto trans) | **13750** | 6750 | 7850 |
| **BERETTA GT 6** | | | |
| 2 Dr Cpe | **13040** | 6500 | 7575 |
| **CAMARO 6*** | | | |
| 2 Dr RS Cpe | **12315** | 5650 | 6575 |
| *For 8 cyl models add $400 whlse/$400 retail. | | | |
| **CAMARO 8** | | | |
| 2 Dr RS Conv | **18200** | 10125 | 11675 |
| 2 Dr IROC-Z Cpe | **15875** | 8675 | 10025 |
| 2 Dr IROC-Z Conv | **21515** | 12750 | 15075 |
| **CAPRICE 8** | | | |
| 4 Dr Sdn | **14525** | 5500 | 6425 |
| **CAPRICE CLASSIC 8** | | | |
| 4 Dr Sdn | **15125** | 6750 | 7850 |
| 4 Dr Wgn | **15725** | 7125 | 8275 |
| **CAPRICE CLASSIC BROUGHAM 8** | | | |
| 4 Dr Sdn | **16325** | 7500 | 8700 |
| 4 Dr LS Sdn | **17525** | 8275 | 9550 |
| **CAVALIER 4*** | | | |
| 2 Dr VL Cpe | **9369** | 3650 | 4550 |
| 4 Dr VL Sdn | **8962** | 3750 | 4650 |
| 4 Dr VL Wgn | **9350** | 4000 | 4900 |
| 2 Dr Cpe | **9805** | 4250 | 5175 |
| 4 Dr Sdn | **10005** | 4350 | 5275 |
| 4 Dr Wgn | **10380** | 4600 | 5525 |
| *For 6 cyl models add $300 whlse/$300 retail. | | | |
| **CAVALIER 6** | | | |
| 2 Dr Z24 Cpe | **12690** | 6775 | 7875 |
| **CELEBRITY 4*** | | | |
| 4 Dr 2 Seat Wgn | **13200** | 5825 | 6750 |
| 4 Dr 3 Seat Wgn | **13450** | 6100 | 7000 |
| *For 6 cyl models add $400 whlse/$400 retail. | | | |
| **CORSICA 4*** | | | |
| 4 Dr LT Ntchbk Sdn | **10815** | 4600 | 5525 |
| 4 Dr LT Hbk Sdn | **11215** | 4775 | 5700 |
| *For 6 cyl models add $350 whlse/$350 retail. | | | |
| **CORSICA 6** | | | |
| 4 Dr LTZ Ntchbk Sdn | **13335** | 6350 | 7400 |
| **CORVETTE 8** | | | |
| Hbk Cpe | **31979** | 17800 | 20450 |
| Conv | **37264** | 22100 | 25400 |

| Year/Model/Body/Type | Original List | Current Whlse | Average Retail |
|---|---|---|---|
| **LUMINA 4*** | | | |
| 2 Dr Cpe | **12945** | 4775 | 5700 |
| 4 Dr Sdn | **13145** | 4775 | 5700 |
| *For 6 cyl models add $475 whlse/$475 retail. | | | |
| **LUMINA EURO 6** | | | |
| 2 Dr Euro Cpe | **14040** | 6275 | 7300 |
| 4 Dr Euro Sdn | **14240** | 6275 | 7300 |
| *ADD FOR:* | | | |
| 5.7 Liter Eng | **300** | 140 | 150 |
| Estate Equipment (Caprice Classic Wgn) | **307** | 140 | 150 |
| Eurosport Pkg (Celebrity) | **2011** | 820 | 910 |
| Performance Handling Pkg (Corvette Hbk) | **460** | 210 | 230 |
| Selective Ride Handling Pkg (Corvette Hbk) | **1695** | 690 | 770 |
| Leather Bucket Seats (Camaro) | **800** | 300 | 330 |
| (Corvette) | **425** | 190 | 210 |
| Leather Sport Bucket Seats (Corvette Hbk) | **1050** | 350 | 380 |
| Removable Roof Panels (Camaro Cpe) | **866** | 350 | 380 |
| (Corvette Hbk) | **615** | 260 | 280 |
| Dual Removable Roof Panels (Corvette Hbk) | **915** | 390 | 430 |

NOTE: Power windows and power door locks standard on Beretta Convertible and Corvette. Power brakes standard on all models.

## 1989

| Year/Model/Body/Type | Original List | Current Whlse | Average Retail |
|---|---|---|---|
| **BERETTA 4*** | | | |
| 2 Dr Cpe | **11860** | 4150 | 5075 |
| *For 6 cyl models add $300 whlse/$300 retail. | | | |
| **BERETTA GT 6** | | | |
| 2 Dr Cpe | **13200** | 5350 | 6275 |
| **CAMARO 6*** | | | |
| 2 Dr RS Cpe | **12805** | 4675 | 5600 |
| *For 8 cyl models add $350 whlse/$350 retail. | | | |
| **CAMARO 8** | | | |
| 2 Dr RS Conv | **18305** | 8900 | 10275 |
| 2 Dr IROC Spt Cpe | **15455** | 7400 | 8600 |
| 2 Dr IROC Conv | **20255** | 11225 | 12975 |
| **CAPRICE 8** | | | |
| 4 Dr Sdn | **13865** | 4675 | 5600 |
| **CAPRICE CLASSIC 8** | | | |
| 4 Dr Sdn | **14445** | 5825 | 6750 |

| Year/Model/Body/Type | Original List | Current Whlse | Average Retail |
|---|---|---|---|
| 4 Dr Wgn | **15025** | 6125 | 7125 |
| **CAPRICE CLASSIC BROUGHAM 8** | | | |
| 4 Dr Sdn | **15615** | 6500 | 7575 |
| 4 Dr LS Sdn | **16835** | 7150 | 8300 |
| **CAVALIER 4\*** | | | |
| 2 Dr VL Cpe | **8919** | 2775 | 3675 |
| 2 Dr Cpe | **9530** | 3275 | 4175 |
| 4 Dr Sdn | **9730** | 3375 | 4275 |
| 4 Dr Wgn | **10110** | 3575 | 4475 |
| *For 6 cyl models add $300 whsle/$300 retail. | | | |
| **CAVALIER 6** | | | |
| 2 Dr Z24 Sport Cpe | **12435** | 5575 | 6500 |
| 2 Dr Z24 Conv | **17725** | 8100 | 9350 |
| **CELEBRITY 4\*** | | | |
| 4 Dr Sdn | **12290** | 3700 | 4600 |
| 4 Dr 2 Seat Wgn | **12720** | 4000 | 4900 |
| 4 Dr 3 Seat Wgn | **12970** | 4225 | 5150 |
| *For 6 cyl models add $350 whsle/$350 retail. | | | |
| **CORSICA 4\*** | | | |
| 4 Dr Ntchbk Sdn | **11270** | 3650 | 4550 |
| 5 Dr Hbk Sdn | **11660** | 3850 | 4750 |
| *For 6 cyl models add $300 whsle/$300 retail. | | | |
| **CORSICA 6** | | | |
| 4 Dr LTZ Ntchbk Sdn | **13340** | 5125 | 6050 |
| **CORVETTE 8** | | | |
| Hbk Cpe | **31545** | 15100 | 17750 |
| Conv | **36785** | 18925 | 21975 |
| *ADD FOR:* | | | |
| Eurosport Pkg (Celebrity) | **230** | 90 | 100 |
| Estate Equip (Caprice Wgn) | **307** | 120 | 130 |
| Removable Roof Panels (Camaro Cpe) | **866** | 300 | 330 |
| (Corvette) | **615** | 220 | 240 |
| Dual Removable Roof Panels (Corvette) | **915** | 300 | 330 |
| Removable Hardtop (Corvette Conv) | **1995** | 650 | 720 |
| Leather Sport Bucket Seats (Corvette Cpe) | **1050** | 330 | 360 |
| Selective Ride & Handling Suspension (Corvette Cpe) | **1695** | 520 | 580 |

NOTE: Power brakes standard on all models. Power windows and power door locks standard on Cavalier Z24 Convertible and Corvette.

| Year/Model/Body/Type | Original List | Current Whlse | Average Retail |
|---|---|---|---|
| **1988** | | | |
| **BERETTA 4\*** | | | |
| 2 Dr Cpe | **11375** | 3225 | 4125 |
| *For 6 cyl models add $300 whsle/$300 retail. | | | |
| **CAMARO 6\*** | | | |
| Sport Cpe | **12260** | 3700 | 4600 |
| *For 8 cyl models add $325 whsle/$325 retail. | | | |
| **CAMARO 8** | | | |
| Sport Cpe Conv | **17520** | 7525 | 8725 |
| IROC-Z Sport Cpe | **14755** | 6200 | 7225 |
| IROC-Z Sport Cpe Conv | **19280** | 9700 | 11175 |
| **CAPRICE 6\*** | | | |
| 4 Dr Sdn | **12805** | 2825 | 3725 |
| **CAPRICE CLASSIC 6\*** | | | |
| 4 Dr Sdn | **12575** | 4075 | 5000 |
| **CAPRICE CLASSIC BROUGHAM 6\*** | | | |
| 4 Dr Sdn | **13645** | 4625 | 5550 |
| 4 Dr LS Sdn | **14820** | 5200 | 6125 |
| *For 8 cyl models add $475 whsle/$475 retail. | | | |
| **CAPRICE CLASSIC 8** | | | |
| 4 Dr Wgn | **14340** | 4750 | 5675 |
| **CAVALIER 4\*** | | | |
| 2 Dr VL Cpe | **8310** | 1850 | 2700 |
| 2 Dr Cpe | **9435** | 2300 | 3175 |
| 4 Dr Sdn | **9510** | 2400 | 3275 |
| 4 Dr Wgn | **9805** | 2575 | 3450 |
| 2 Dr RS Cpe | **10265** | 2825 | 3725 |
| 4 Dr RS Sdn | **10475** | 2925 | 3825 |
| *For 6 cyl models add $250 whsle/$250 retail. | | | |
| **CAVALIER 6** | | | |
| 2 Dr Z24 Sport Cpe | **11815** | 4325 | 5250 |
| 2 Dr Z24 Conv | **17080** | 6625 | 7700 |
| **CELEBRITY 4\*** | | | |
| 2 Dr Cpe | **11360** | 2575 | 3450 |
| 4 Dr Sdn | **11800** | 2675 | 3575 |
| 4 Dr 2 Seat Wgn | **12125** | 2925 | 3825 |
| 4 Dr 3 Seat Wgn | **12365** | 3100 | 4000 |
| *For 6 cyl models add $325 whsle/$325 retail. | | | |
| **CORSICA 4\*** | | | |
| 4 Dr Sdn | **10795** | 2750 | 3650 |
| *For 6 cyl models add $300 whsle/$300 retail. | | | |
| **CORVETTE 8** | | | |
| Hbk Cpe | **29480** | 12925 | 15250 |

| Year/Model/Body/Type | Original List | Current Whlse | Average Retail |
|---|---|---|---|
| Conv | **34820** | 16300 | 18950 |

## MONTE CARLO 6*

| | | | |
|---|---|---|---|
| 2 Dr LS Cpe | **13105** | 4000 | 4900 |

*For 8 cyl models add $375 whsle/$375 retail.

## MONTE CARLO 8

| | | | |
|---|---|---|---|
| 2 Dr SS Sport Cpe | **15095** | 6450 | 7500 |

## NOVA 4

| | | | |
|---|---|---|---|
| 4 Dr Ntchbk Sdn | **10310** | 2425 | 3300 |
| 4 Dr Twin Cam Ntchbk Sdn | **12860** | 3125 | 4025 |
| 5 Dr Hbk Sdn | **10565** | 2525 | 3400 |

## SPECTRUM

| | | | |
|---|---|---|---|
| 4 Dr Ntchbk Sdn | **9587** | 1650 | 2500 |
| 4 Dr Turbo Ntchbk Sdn (NA w/auto trans, pwr steering or radio) | **8900** | 2225 | 3075 |
| 2 Dr Hbk Cpe | **9800** | 1550 | 2400 |
| 2 Dr Express Hbk Cpe (NA w/auto trans, pwr strng or radio) | **7155** | 925 | 1650 |

## SPRINT 3

| | | | |
|---|---|---|---|
| 2 Dr Metro Hbk Cpe (NA w/pwr strng) | **6996** | 1025 | 1750 |
| 2 Dr Hbk Cpe (NA w/pwr strng) | **7881** | 1300 | 2025 |
| 2 Dr Turbo Hbk Cpe (NA w/auto trans or pwr strng) | **9017** | 1725 | 2575 |
| 4 Dr Hbk Sdn (NA w/pwr strng) | **8086** | 1375 | 2125 |

*ADD FOR:*

| | | | |
|---|---|---|---|
| Sport Handling Pkg (Corvette) | **970** | 260 | 280 |
| Perf Handling Pkg (Corvette) | **1295** | 330 | 360 |
| Dual Removable Roof Panels (Corvette) | **915** | 260 | 280 |
| Removable Roof Panels (Camaro Cpe) | **866** | 240 | 260 |
| (Corvette) | **615** | 170 | 190 |
| (Monte Carlo) | **895** | 240 | 260 |
| 5.0 Liter V8 TPI Eng (Camaro IROC-Z) | **745** | 220 | 240 |
| 5.7 Liter V8 TPI Eng (Camaro IROC-Z Cpe) | **1045** | 330 | 360 |

NOTE: Power brakes standard on all models. Power windows and power door locks standard on Cavalier Z24 Convertible and Corvette.

| Year/Model/Body/Type | Original List | Current Whlse | Average Retail |
|---|---|---|---|
| **1987** | | | |

## CAMARO 6*

| | | | |
|---|---|---|---|
| Sport Cpe | **11260** | 2775 | 3675 |
| Conv | **15689** | 4850 | 5775 |

*For 8 cyl models add $300 whsle/$300 retail.

## CAMARO 8

| | | | |
|---|---|---|---|
| Z28 Sport Cpe | **14084** | 4550 | 5475 |
| Z28 Conv | **18483** | 7625 | 8850 |

## CAPRICE 6*

| | | | |
|---|---|---|---|
| 4 Dr Sdn | **11770** | 2125 | 2975 |

## CAPRICE CLASSIC 6*

| | | | |
|---|---|---|---|
| 2 Dr Sport Cpe | **12167** | 3075 | 3975 |
| 4 Dr LS Sdn | **12335** | 3200 | 4100 |

## CAPRICE CLASSIC BROUGHAM 6*

| | | | |
|---|---|---|---|
| 4 Dr Sdn | **13324** | 3600 | 4500 |
| 4 Dr LS Sdn | **14580** | 3975 | 4875 |

*For 8 cyl models add $450 whsle/$450 retail.

## CAPRICE 8

| | | | |
|---|---|---|---|
| 4 Dr Wgn | **12770** | 2650 | 3550 |

## CAPRICE CLASSIC 8

| | | | |
|---|---|---|---|
| 4 Dr Wgn | **13361** | 3750 | 4650 |

## CAVALIER 4*

| | | | |
|---|---|---|---|
| 2 Dr Cpe | **8737** | 1825 | 2675 |
| 4 Dr Sdn | **8961** | 1925 | 2775 |
| 4 Dr Wgn | **9127** | 2050 | 2900 |
| 2 Dr CS Hbk Cpe | **9368** | 2050 | 2900 |
| 4 Dr CS Sdn | **9343** | 2050 | 2900 |
| 4 Dr CS Wgn | **9530** | 2175 | 3025 |
| 2 Dr RS Conv | **14611** | 4500 | 5425 |
| 2 Dr RS Cpe | **9483** | 2175 | 3025 |
| 2 Dr RS Hbk Cpe | **9685** | 2275 | 3150 |
| 4 Dr RS Sdn | **9664** | 2275 | 3150 |
| 4 Dr RS Wgn | **9842** | 2375 | 3250 |

*For 6 cyl models add $200 whsle/$200 retail.

## CAVALIER 6

| | | | |
|---|---|---|---|
| 2 Dr Z24 Sport Cpe | **11078** | 3450 | 4350 |
| 2 Dr Z24 Hbk | **11280** | 3550 | 4450 |

## CELEBRITY 4*

| | | | |
|---|---|---|---|
| 2 Dr Cpe | **10770** | 1725 | 2575 |
| 4 Dr Sdn | **11040** | 1800 | 2650 |
| 4 Dr 2 Seat Wgn | **11200** | 2025 | 2875 |
| 4 Dr 3 Seat Wgn | **11447** | 2050 | 2900 |

*For 6 cyl models add $300 whsle/$300 retail.

## CHEVETTE 4

| | | | |
|---|---|---|---|
| 2 Dr CS Hbk Cpe | **6345** | 875 | 1600 |

| Year/Model/Body/Type | Original List | Current Whlse | Average Retail |
|---|---|---|---|
| 4 Dr CS Hbk Sdn | **6845** | 950 | 1675 |
| **CORVETTE 8** | | | |
| Hbk Cpe | **27999** | 10675 | 12325 |
| Conv | **33172** | 13850 | 16225 |
| **MONTE CARLO 6*** | | | |
| 2 Dr LS Cpe | **12081** | 2750 | 3650 |
| *For 8 cyl models add $350 whsle/$350 retail. | | | |
| **MONTE CARLO 8** | | | |
| 2 Dr SS Sport Cpe | **14238** | 4800 | 5725 |
| 2 Dr SS Aero Cpe | **15613** | 6900 | 8025 |
| **NOVA 4** | | | |
| 4 Dr Ntchbk Sdn | **9200** | 1875 | 2725 |
| 5 Dr Hbk Sdn | **9630** | 1975 | 2825 |
| **SPECTRUM 4** | | | |
| 4 Dr Ntchbk Sdn | **9200** | 1350 | 2100 |
| 2 Dr Hbk Cpe | **8903** | 1275 | 2000 |
| **SPRINT 3** | | | |
| 2 Dr Hbk Cpe | **7486** | 950 | 1675 |
| 2 Dr ER Hbk Cpe | **7601** | 1000 | 1725 |
| 2 Dr Turbo Hbk Cpe | **9181** | 1325 | 2050 |
| 4 Dr Hbk Sdn | **7686** | 1050 | 1775 |
| *ADD FOR:* | | | |
| LT Opt Pkg 1 (Camaro Base Sport Cpe) | **1522** | 350 | 380 |
| LT Opt Pkg 2 (Camaro Base Sport Cpe) | **1938** | 440 | 480 |
| LT Opt Pkg 3 (Camaro Base Sport Cpe) | **2387** | 540 | 600 |
| LT Opt Pkg 4 (Camaro Base Sport Cpe) | **2858** | 650 | 720 |
| Nova CL Opt Pkg 1 | **2405** | 520 | 580 |
| Nova CL Opt Pkg 2 | **2625** | 560 | 630 |
| Nova CL Opt Pkg 3 | **3200** | 650 | 720 |
| 5.7 Liter TPI V8 Eng (Camaro) | **1045** | 260 | 280 |
| Removable Glass Roof Panels (Camaro, Monte Carlo) | **895** | 220 | 240 |
| (Corvette) | **615** | 150 | 160 |
| Dual Removable Glass Roof Panels (Corvette) | **915** | 220 | 240 |

NOTE: Power windows standard on Cavalier Convertible and Corvette. Power brakes standard on all models except Chevette.

## 1986

| | | | |
|---|---|---|---|
| **CAMARO 4** | | | |
| Sport Cpe | **10414** | 2050 | 2900 |

| Year/Model/Body/Type | Original List | Current Whlse | Average Retail |
|---|---|---|---|
| **CAMARO 6*** | | | |
| Berlinetta Cpe | **12963** | 2975 | 3875 |
| *For 8 cyl models add $300 whsle/$300 retail. | | | |
| **CAMARO 8** | | | |
| Z28 Sport Cpe | **12963** | 3875 | 4775 |
| **CAPRICE 6*** | | | |
| 4 Dr Sdn | **11264** | 1700 | 2550 |
| **CAPRICE CLASSIC 6*** | | | |
| 2 Dr Sport Cpe | **11665** | 2500 | 3375 |
| 4 Dr Sdn | **11829** | 2650 | 3550 |
| 4 Dr Brougham Sdn | **12478** | 3075 | 3975 |
| 4 Dr Wgn (8 cyl) | **12562** | 3150 | 4050 |
| *For 8 cyl models add $400 whsle/$400 retail. | | | |
| **CAVALIER 4*** | | | |
| 2 Dr Cpe | **8258** | 1275 | 2000 |
| 4 Dr Sdn | **8443** | 1350 | 2100 |
| 4 Dr Wgn | **8606** | 1450 | 2225 |
| 2 Dr CS Hbk Cpe | **8940** | 1450 | 2225 |
| 4 Dr CS Sdn | **8916** | 1450 | 2225 |
| 4 Dr CS Wgn | **9097** | 1550 | 2400 |
| 2 Dr RS Conv | **13996** | 3375 | 4275 |
| 2 Dr RS Cpe | **8988** | 1550 | 2400 |
| 2 Dr RS Hbk Cpe | **9183** | 1650 | 2500 |
| 4 Dr RS Sdn | **9163** | 1650 | 2500 |
| 4 Dr RS Wgn | **9335** | 1725 | 2575 |
| *For 6 cyl models add $200 whsle/$200 retail. | | | |
| **CAVALIER 6** | | | |
| 2 Dr Z24 Sport Cpe | **10256** | 2550 | 3425 |
| 2 Z24 Hbk Sport Cpe | **10451** | 2650 | 3550 |
| **CELEBRITY 4*** | | | |
| 2 Dr Cpe | **10243** | 1250 | 1975 |
| 4 Dr Sdn | **10444** | 1325 | 2050 |
| 4 Dr 2 Seat Wgn | **10598** | 1500 | 2350 |
| 4 Dr 3 Seat Wgn | **10836** | 1525 | 2375 |
| *For 6 cyl models add $300 whsle/$300 retail. | | | |
| **CHEVETTE 4** | | | |
| CS Hbk Cpe | **7125** | 800 | 1500 |
| CS Hbk Sdn | **7309** | 875 | 1600 |
| CS Diesel Hbk Cpe | **6507** | 350 | 625 |
| CS Diesel Hbk Sdn | **6712** | 500 | 925 |
| (Diesel models not available w/automatic transmission) | | | |
| **CORVETTE 8** | | | |
| Hbk Cpe | **27405** | 9000 | 10400 |
| Conv | **32480** | 11850 | 13675 |
| **MONTE CARLO 6*** | | | |
| 2 Dr Sport Cpe | **10344** | 2000 | 2850 |

*Refer to optional equipment schedules*

| Year/Model/Body/Type | Original List | Current Whlse | Average Retail |
|---|---|---|---|
| 2 Dr LS Cpe | **13640** | 2050 | 2900 |

*For 8 cyl models add $325 whsle/$325 retail.

### MONTE CARLO 8

| | | | |
|---|---|---|---|
| 2 Dr SS Sport Cpe | **13640** | 3900 | 4800 |

### NOVA 4

| | | | |
|---|---|---|---|
| 4 Dr Ntchbk Sdn | **9176** | 1425 | 2175 |
| 4 Dr Hbk Sdn | **9417** | 1525 | 2375 |

### SPECTRUM 4

| | | | |
|---|---|---|---|
| 4 Dr Ntchbk Sdn | **8728** | 1150 | 1875 |
| 2 Dr Ntchbk Cpe | **8444** | 1050 | 1775 |

### SPRINT 3

| | | | |
|---|---|---|---|
| 2 Dr Hbk Cpe | **6891** | 750 | 1475 |
| 2 Dr ER Hbk Cpe | **6996** | 775 | 1500 |
| 4 Dr Plus Hbk Sdn | **7101** | 850 | 1550 |
| (Power steering not available) | | | |

*ADD FOR:*

| | | | |
|---|---|---|---|
| Performance Handling Pkg (Corvette) | **470** | 70 | 80 |
| Nova CL Pkg 1 | **1780** | 260 | 280 |
| Nova CL Pkg 2 | **2190** | 330 | 360 |
| Nova CL Pkg 3 | **2590** | 360 | 400 |
| Nova CL Pkg 4 | **2700** | 390 | 430 |
| I.R.O.C. Sport Equip Pkg (Camaro) | **669** | 100 | 110 |
| 2.8 Liter MFI V6 Eng (Celebrity) | **610** | 90 | 100 |
| (Cavalier except Z24) | **660** | 90 | 100 |
| 5.0 Liter TPI V8 Eng (Camaro) | **745** | 120 | 130 |
| 5.0 Liter HO V8 Eng (Camaro) | **745** | 120 | 130 |
| Removable Glass Roof Panels (Camaro, Monte Carlo) | **866** | 140 | 150 |
| (Corvette) | **615** | 90 | 100 |
| Dual Removable Glass Roof Panels (Corvette) | **915** | 150 | 160 |

NOTE: Power brakes standard on all models except Chevette. Power windows standard on Corvette.

## 1985

### CAMARO 4*

| | | | |
|---|---|---|---|
| Sport Cpe | **9705** | 1600 | 2450 |

*For models with 6 cyl eng add $350 whsle/$350 retail. For models with 5.0 liter T.P.I. V8 eng add $450 whsle/$450 retail. For models with 5.0 liter H.O. V8 eng add $600 whsle/$600 retail. For models with 5.0 liter V8 4 bbl. eng add $600 whsle/$600 retail.

### CAMARO 6*

| | | | |
|---|---|---|---|
| Berlinetta Cpe | **12456** | 2250 | 3100 |

*For models with 5.0 liter T.P.I. V8 eng add $300 whsle/$300 retail. For models with 5.0 liter H.O. V8 eng add $300 whsle/$300 retail. For models with 5.0 liter V8 4 bbl. eng add $300 whsle/$300 retail.

### CAMARO 8

| | | | |
|---|---|---|---|
| Z28 Sport Cpe | **12456** | 2975 | 3875 |

### CAPRICE CLASSIC 6*

| | | | |
|---|---|---|---|
| 2 Dr Sport Cpe | **10917** | 1800 | 2650 |
| 4 Dr Sdn | **11071** | 1950 | 2800 |

*For 8 cyl models add $350 whsle/$350 retail.

### CAPRICE CLASSIC WAGON 8

| | | | |
|---|---|---|---|
| 4 Dr 3 Seat Wgn | **11760** | 2025 | 2875 |

### CAVALIER 4*

| | | | |
|---|---|---|---|
| 4 Dr Sdn | **8003** | 925 | 1650 |
| 4 Dr Wgn | **8164** | 1000 | 1725 |
| 2 Dr Conv | **12997** | 2525 | 3400 |
| 2 Dr Cpe Type 10 | **8157** | 1025 | 1750 |
| 2 Dr Hbk Cpe Type 10 | **8342** | 1125 | 1850 |
| 4 Dr CS Sdn | **8323** | 1050 | 1775 |
| 4 Dr CS Wgn | **8492** | 1125 | 1850 |

*For 6 cyl models add $150 whsle/$150 retail.

### CELEBRITY 4*

| | | | |
|---|---|---|---|
| 2 Dr Cpe | **9464** | 975 | 1700 |
| 4 Dr Sdn | **9654** | 1075 | 1800 |
| 4 Dr 2 Seat Wgn | **9849** | 1250 | 1975 |
| 4 Dr 3 Seat Wgn | **10073** | 1325 | 2025 |

*For 6 cyl models add $250 whsle/$250 retail. For 6 cyl M.F.I. engs add $250 whsle/$250 retail.

### CHEVETTE 4

| | | | |
|---|---|---|---|
| CS Hbk Cpe | **6755** | 675 | 1275 |
| CS Hbk Sdn | **7075** | 775 | 1500 |
| CS Diesel Hbk Cpe | **7265** | 250 | 500 |
| CS Diesel Hbk Sdn | **7600** | 250 | 500 |

### CITATION 4*

| | | | |
|---|---|---|---|
| 2 Dr Hbk | **8494** | 625 | 1175 |
| 4 Dr Hbk | **8647** | 725 | 1375 |

*For 6 cyl models add $175 whsle/$175 retail. For V6 M.F.I. eng models add $175 whsle/$175 retail.

### CORVETTE 8

| | | | |
|---|---|---|---|
| Hbk Cpe | **24891** | 7700 | 8950 |

### IMPALA 6*

| | | | |
|---|---|---|---|
| 4 Dr Sdn | **10541** | 1000 | 1725 |

### MONTE CARLO 6*

| | | | |
|---|---|---|---|
| 2 Dr Sport Cpe | **10481** | 1550 | 2400 |

*For 8 cyl models add $300 whsle/$300 retail.

| Year/Model/ Body/Type | Original List | Current Whlse | Average Retail |
|---|---|---|---|
| **MONTE CARLO SS 8** | | | |
| 2 Dr SS Sport Cpe | **12358** | 3150 | 4050 |
| **NOVA 4** | | | |
| 4 Dr Ntchbk | **8410** | 1250 | 1975 |
| **SPECTRUM 4** | | | |
| 2 Dr Hbk Cpe | **7689** | 775 | 1500 |
| 4 Dr Ntchbk Sdn | **7969** | 875 | 1600 |
| **SPRINT 3** | | | |
| 2 Dr Hbk Cpe | **5941** | 625 | 1175 |
| *ADD FOR:* | | | |
| X-11 Sport Equipment Pkg (Citation II) | **1016** | 110 | 120 |
| I.R.O.C. Sport Equipment Pkg (Camaro) | **659** | 70 | 80 |
| Removable Glass Roof Panels (Camaro, Monte Carlo) | **850** | 90 | 100 |

NOTE: Power windows standard on Corvette. Power brakes standard on Camaro, Impala, Caprice Classic, Cavalier, Celebrity, Chevette Diesel, Corvette, Monte Carlo, Sprint and Spectrum.

## 1984

| | Original List | Current Whlse | Average Retail |
|---|---|---|---|
| **CAMARO 4*** | | | |
| Sport Cpe | **9352** | 1325 | 2050 |

*For models with 6 cyl eng add $200 whsle/$200 retail. For models with 5.0 liter C.F.I. V8 eng add $350 whsle/$350 retail. For models with 5.0 liter 4 bbl. V8 eng add $350 whsle/$350 retail.

| | Original List | Current Whlse | Average Retail |
|---|---|---|---|
| **CAMARO 6*** | | | |
| Berlinetta Cpe | **12022** | 1775 | 2625 |

*For models with 5.0 liter C.F.I. V8 eng add $200 whsle/$200 retail. For models with 5.0 liter 4 bbl. V8 eng add $200 whsle/$200 retail.

| | Original List | Current Whlse | Average Retail |
|---|---|---|---|
| **CAMARO 8** | | | |
| Z28 Sport Cpe | **11745** | 2400 | 3275 |
| **CAPRICE CLASSIC 6*** | | | |
| 2 Dr Sport Cpe | **10084** | 1025 | 1750 |
| 4 Dr Sdn | **10230** | 1150 | 1875 |

*For 8 cyl models add $300 whsle/$300 retail.

| | Original List | Current Whlse | Average Retail |
|---|---|---|---|
| **CAPRICE CLASSIC WAGON 8** | | | |
| 4 Dr Wgn | **11040** | 1175 | 1900 |
| **CAVALIER 4** | | | |
| 4 Dr Sdn | **7555** | 525 | 975 |
| 4 Dr Wgn | **7708** | 575 | 1075 |
| 2 Dr Conv | **12428** | 1875 | 2725 |

| Year/Model/ Body/Type | Original List | Current Whlse | Average Retail |
|---|---|---|---|
| 2 Dr Cpe Type 10 | **7698** | 600 | 1125 |
| 2 Dr Hbk Cpe Type 10 | **7875** | 675 | 1275 |
| 4 Dr CS Sdn | **7887** | 625 | 1175 |
| 4 Dr CS Wgn | **8042** | 675 | 1275 |
| **CELEBRITY 4*** | | | |
| 2 Dr Cpe | **8857** | 825 | 1525 |
| 4 Dr Sdn | **9036** | 900 | 1625 |
| 4 Dr 2 Seat Wgn | **9360** | 1000 | 1725 |
| 4 Dr 3 Seat Wgn | **9575** | 1025 | 1750 |

*For 6 cyl models add $200 whsle/$200 retail.

| | Original List | Current Whlse | Average Retail |
|---|---|---|---|
| **CHEVETTE 4** | | | |
| CS Hbk Cpe | **6711** | 200 | 400 |
| CS Hbk Sdn | **6858** | 300 | 575 |
| Hbk Cpe | **6301** | 110 | 300 |
| Hbk Sdn | **6555** | 150 | 350 |
| CS Diesel Hbk Cpe | **7221** | 55 | 225 |
| CS Diesel Hbk Sdn | **7383** | 55 | 225 |
| **CITATION 4*** | | | |
| 2 Dr Cpe | **7801** | 275 | 550 |
| 2 Dr Hbk Cpe | **8256** | 350 | 625 |
| 4 Dr Hbk Sdn | **8402** | 400 | 725 |

*For 6 cyl models add $150 whsle/$150 retail.

| | Original List | Current Whlse | Average Retail |
|---|---|---|---|
| **CORVETTE 8** | | | |
| Hbk Cpe | **23346** | 6950 | 8100 |
| **IMPALA 6*** | | | |
| 4 Dr Sdn | **9726** | 475 | 875 |
| **MONTE CARLO 6*** | | | |
| 2 Dr Sport Cpe | **9768** | 1275 | 2000 |

*For 8 cyl models add $200 whsle/$200 retail.

| | Original List | Current Whlse | Average Retail |
|---|---|---|---|
| **MONTE CARLO SS 8** | | | |
| 2 Dr SS Sport Cpe | **11530** | 2650 | 3550 |

NOTE: Power brakes standard on all models except Chevette gasoline models. Power windows standard on Corvette.

## 1983 — ALL BODY STYLES

| | | Current Whlse | Average Retail |
|---|---|---|---|
| CAMARO SPORT CPE | — | 1175 | 1900 |
| CAMARO BERLINETTA | — | 1500 | 2350 |
| CAMARO Z28 | — | 2100 | 2950 |
| CAPRICE CLASSIC | — | 900 | 1625 |
| CAPRICE WAGON | — | 900 | 1625 |
| CAVALIER | — | 500 | 925 |
| CELEBRITY | — | 675 | 1275 |
| CHEVETTE | — | 110 | 300 |
| CITATION | — | 225 | 475 |
| IMPALA | — | 275 | 550 |
| MALIBU | — | 625 | 1175 |
| MONTE CARLO | — | 1025 | 1750 |
| MONTE CARLO SS | — | 2150 | 3000 |

*Refer to optional equipment schedules*

| Year/Model/<br>Body/Type | Original<br>List | Current<br>Whlse | Average<br>Retail |
|---|---|---|---|
| **CHRYSLER** | | | |
| **1992** | | | |
| **IMPERIAL 6** | | | |
| 4 Dr Sdn | **28453** | 15500 | 18150 |
| *ADD FOR:* | | | |
| Elect Feature Group | **1011** | 590 | 660 |
| Elec Air Suspension | **650** | 330 | 360 |
| **LE BARON 4\*** | | | |
| 2 Dr Cpe | **13988** | 9425 | 10850 |
| 2 Dr Conv | **17565** | 12700 | 15025 |
| 4 Dr Sdn | **13998** | 10450 | 10450 |
| 4 Dr Landau Sdn | **15710** | 10150 | 11725 |
| *For 6 cyl models add $500 whlse/$500 retail.* | | | |
| **LE BARON 6** | | | |
| 2 Dr LX Cpe | **16094** | 10900 | 12575 |
| 2 Dr LX Conv | **20130** | 14250 | 16725 |
| 2 Dr GTC Cpe | **16844** | 11225 | 12975 |
| 2 Dr GTC Conv | **19665** | — | — |
| 4 Dr LX Sdn | **16079** | 10075 | 11625 |
| *ADD FOR:* | | | |
| 4 Cyl Turbo Eng | **694** | 460 | 500 |
| Anti-Lock Brakes | **899** | 460 | 500 |
| Leather Seat Trim | | | |
| (LX Cpe & GTC Cpe) | **1016** | 460 | 500 |
| (GTC Conv) | **1233** | 460 | 500 |
| (Landau Sdn) | **668** | 430 | 480 |
| Cast Alum Whls (Base) | **328** | 210 | 230 |
| (LX) | **532** | 260 | 290 |
| (GTC) | **188** | 130 | 140 |
| **NEW YORKER 6** | | | |
| 4 Dr Fifth Ave Sdn | **21874** | 13975 | 16350 |
| 4 Dr Salon Sdn | **18849** | 11275 | 13025 |
| *ADD FOR:* | | | |
| 3.8 Liter 6 Cyl Eng | | | |
| (Fifth Ave) | **262** | 170 | 190 |
| Anti-Lock Brakes | **899** | 460 | 500 |
| Vinyl Landau Roof (Salon) | **325** | 200 | 220 |
| Leather Seat Trim (Salon) | **590** | 390 | 430 |
| Wire Wheels | **240** | 160 | 170 |
| Cast Alum Whls (Fifth Ave) | **278** | 180 | 200 |
| **TOWN & COUNTRY 6** | | | |
| 2 Dr FWD Wgn | **24716** | 17750 | 20400 |
| 2 Dr AWD Wgn | **26611** | — | — |

NOTE: Power windows standard on Imperial, LeBaron Coupe & Convertible and New Yorker. Power door locks standard on Imperial and New Yorker Fifth Avenue. Power seat standard on Imperial, LeBaron LX Convertible and New Yorker Fifth Avenue. Tilt steering wheel and cruise control standard on Imperial, LeBaron Sedan and New Yorker Fifth Avenue.

| Year/Model/<br>Body/Type | Original<br>List | Current<br>Whlse | Average<br>Retail |
|---|---|---|---|
| **1991** | | | |
| **IMPERIAL 6** | | | |
| 4 Dr Sdn | **26978** | 13700 | 16075 |
| **LE BARON 4\*** | | | |
| 2 Dr Highline Cpe | **13816** | 6900 | 8025 |
| 2 Dr Highline Conv | **16797** | 10025 | 11575 |
| 2 Dr Prem LX Cpe (6 cyl) | **15520** | 8275 | 9550 |
| 2 Dr Prem LX Conv (6 cyl) | **19226** | 11425 | 13200 |
| 2 Dr GTC Cpe (6 cyl) | **15977** | 9375 | 10800 |
| 2 Dr GTC Conv (6 cyl) | **18533** | 12425 | 14550 |
| 4 Dr Sdn (6 cyl) | **16501** | 9175 | 10575 |
| *For 6 cyl or 4 cyl turbo eng models add $— whlse/$— retail.* | | | |
| **NEW YORKER 6** | | | |
| 4 Dr Fifth Avenue Sdn | **20875** | 12375 | 14125 |
| 4 Dr Salon Sdn | **17971** | 9975 | 11500 |
| **TC MASERATI 6** | | | |
| 2 Dr Conv (auto) | **37000** | — | — |
| **TOWN & COUNTRY 6** | | | |
| 4 Dr Wgn | **23956** | 15550 | 18200 |
| *ADD FOR:* | | | |
| Anti-lock Brakes | | | |
| (New Yorker) | **899** | 410 | 460 |
| Elec Features Pkg | | | |
| (Imperial, New Yorker | | | |
| Fifth Avenue) | **1689** | 720 | 800 |
| Mark Cross Pkg | | | |
| (Imperial) | **649** | 390 | 430 |
| (New Yorker Fifth Ave.) | **2089** | 850 | 940 |
| Leather Premium Seats | | | |
| (Le Baron Cpe) | **1006** | 330 | 360 |
| (Le Baron GTC Conv) | **1223** | 360 | 390 |
| Leather Sport Seats | | | |
| (Le Baron GTC Cpe) | **639** | 250 | 270 |
| Leather Ultrahyde Seats | | | |
| (Le Baron Sdn) | **668** | 260 | 280 |

NOTE: Power brakes standard on all models. Air bag standard on Imperial, Le Baron, New Yorker & TC by Maserati. Anti-lock brakes standard on Imperial, TC by Maserati and Town & Country. Power windows standard on Imperial, Le Baron, New Yorker, TC by Maserati and Town & Country. Power door locks standard on Imperial, Le Baron Permium LX, Le Baron GTC, Le Baron Sedan, New Yorker Fifth Avenue, TC by Maserati and Town & Country. Power seat standard on Imperial, New Yorker Fifth Ave., TC by Maserati and Town & Country. Vinyl roof standard on Imperial, Le Baron Sedan and New Yorker Fifth Ave.

| Year/Model/<br>Body/Type | Original<br>List | Current<br>Whlse | Average<br>Retail |
|---|---|---|---|
| **1990** | | | |
| **IMPERIAL 6** | | | |
| 4 Dr Sdn | **25495** | 11300 | 13050 |

| Year/Model/ Body/Type | Original List | Current Whlse | Average Retail |
|---|---|---|---|
| **LE BARON 4*** | | | |
| 2 Dr Highline Cpe | **13300** | 5925 | 6850 |
| 2 Dr Highline Conv | **15800** | 8775 | 10125 |
| 2 Dr Prem Cpe (6 cyl) | **16415** | 7200 | 8350 |
| 2 Dr Prem Conv (6 cyl) | **19595** | 10025 | 11575 |
| 2 Dr GT Cpe (6 cyl) | **16214** | 7425 | 8625 |
| 2 Dr GT Conv (6 cyl) | **18293** | 10325 | 11925 |
| 2 Dr GTC Cpe | **17811** | 7725 | 8975 |
| 2 Dr GTC Conv | **20052** | 10575 | 12200 |
| 4 Dr Sdn (6 cyl) | **15995** | 7450 | 8650 |

*For 6 cyl models add $400 whlse/$400 retail.

| | Original List | Current Whlse | Average Retail |
|---|---|---|---|
| **NEW YORKER 6** | | | |
| 4 Dr Fifth Avenue Sdn | **20860** | 9575 | 11025 |
| 4 Dr Landau Sdn | **19080** | 8675 | 10025 |
| 4 Dr Salon Sdn | **17147** | 7650 | 8875 |
| **TC MASERATI 4** | | | |
| 2 Dr Conv (5 spd) | **35000** | — | — |
| **TC MASERATI 6** | | | |
| 2 Dr Conv (auto) | **35000** | — | — |
| **TOWN & COUNTRY 6** | | | |
| 4 Dr Wgn | **23500** | 12025 | 13900 |

*ADD FOR:*

| | Original List | Current Whlse | Average Retail |
|---|---|---|---|
| Anti-Lock Brakes (New Yorker) | **926** | 350 | 380 |
| Electronics Feature Pkg (Imperial) | **1572** | 480 | 540 |
| (New Yorker ex. Salon) | **1216** | 400 | 440 |
| 2.5 Liter Turbo Eng (Le Baron Highline) | **680** | 290 | 320 |
| Mark Cross Pkg (New Yorker Fifth Avenue) | **2129** | 780 | 870 |
| (New Yorker Landau) | **2324** | 860 | 960 |

NOTE: Power brakes standard on all models. Anti-lock brakes standard on Imperial. Power seat standard on Imperial, Le Baron GTC Convertible, New Yorker Fifth Avenue and Maserati. Vinyl roof standard on New Yorker Landau. Power windows standard on Le Baron Series except Sedan, New Yorker Landau, New Yorker Fifth Avenue, Maserati and Town & Country. Power door locks standard on Imperial, Le Baron Premium Coupe, Le Baron GT Coupe, Le Baron GTC Coupe, Le Baron Premium Convertible, Le Baron GT Convertible, Le Baron GTC Convertible, New Yorker Fifth Avenue, Maserati and Town & Country.

## 1989

| **FIFTH AVENUE 8** | Original List | Current Whlse | Average Retail |
|---|---|---|---|
| 4 Dr Sdn | **18345** | 6150 | 7150 |
| **LE BARON 4** | | | |
| 2 Dr Highline Cpe | **12806** | 4200 | 5125 |

| Year/Model/ Body/Type | Original List | Current Whlse | Average Retail |
|---|---|---|---|
| 2 Dr Highline Conv | **15306** | 6525 | 7600 |
| 5 Dr Highline Spt Sdn | **12806** | 3900 | 4800 |
| 2 Dr Premium Cpe | **14695** | 4950 | 5875 |
| 2 Dr Premium Conv | **18195** | 7300 | 8475 |
| 5 Dr Premium Spt Sdn | **14031** | 4450 | 5375 |
| **LE BARON GT 4** | | | |
| 2 Dr Cpe | **15331** | 5375 | 6300 |
| 2 Dr Conv | **17731** | 7900 | 9175 |
| **LE BARON GTC 4** | | | |
| 2 Dr Cpe | **17435** | 6050 | 6950 |
| 2 Dr Conv | **19666** | 8450 | 9750 |
| **LE BARON GTS 4** | | | |
| 5 Dr Sport Sdn | **17095** | 5575 | 6500 |
| **NEW YORKER 6** | | | |
| 4 Dr Sdn | **17416** | 6125 | 7125 |
| **NEW YORKER LANDAU 6** | | | |
| 4 Dr Sdn | **19509** | 7075 | 8225 |
| **TC 4** | | | |
| 2 Dr Conv | **33000** | — | — |

*ADD FOR:*

| | Original List | Current Whlse | Average Retail |
|---|---|---|---|
| Power Leather Seats (Le Baron GTC) | **627** | 220 | 240 |
| Leather Seats (Le Baron Prem Cpe) | **627** | 190 | 210 |
| (Le Baron Prem Conv) | **1080** | 200 | 220 |
| (Le Baron GT Cpe) | **867** | 200 | 220 |
| (Le Baron GT Conv) | **1080** | 200 | 220 |
| (Le Baron Prem Sdn) | **625** | 170 | 190 |
| (Le Baron GTS Sdn) | **566** | 170 | 190 |
| Mark Cross Edit. (New Yorker Base) | **2069** | 690 | 770 |
| (New Yorker Landau) | **2467** | 780 | 870 |
| Anti-Lock Brakes (New Yorker) | **670** | 260 | 280 |
| 2.5 Liter Turbo Eng (Le Baron Highline Sdn) | **536** | 190 | 210 |
| (Le Baron Prem Sdn) | **678** | 190 | 210 |
| (Le Baron Highline & Premium Conv) | **678** | 220 | 240 |

NOTE: Power brakes standard on all models. Power windows standard on Le Baron GTC, Le Baron GTS Sport Sedan, New Yorker Series, Town & Country and Fifth Avenue. Power door locks standard on Le Baron Premium, Le Baron GTC, Le Baron Premium Sport Sedan, New Yorker Landau and Town & Country.

## 1988

| **FIFTH AVENUE 8** | Original List | Current Whlse | Average Retail |
|---|---|---|---|
| 4 Dr Sdn | **17243** | 4525 | 5450 |

| Year/Model/ Body/Type | Original List | Current Whlse | Average Retail |
|---|---|---|---|
| **LE BARON 4** | | | |
| 2 Dr Highline Cpe | **12306** | 3175 | 4075 |
| 2 Dr High Conv | **14806** | 5125 | 6050 |
| 2 Dr Premium Cpe | **13995** | 3800 | 4700 |
| 2 Dr Premium Conv | **17495** | 5800 | 6725 |
| 4 Dr Sdn | **12061** | 2800 | 3700 |
| **LE BARON GTS 4** | | | |
| 5 Dr High Sport Sdn | **12109** | 2925 | 3825 |
| 5 Dr Prem Sport Sdn | **13507** | 3375 | 4275 |
| **NEW YORKER 6** | | | |
| 4 Dr Sdn | **17416** | 5100 | 6025 |
| **NEW YORKER LANDAU 6** | | | |
| 4 Dr Sdn | **19509** | 5975 | 6900 |
| **NEW YORKER TURBO 4** | | | |
| 4 Dr Sdn | **17373** | 4525 | 5450 |
| **TOWN & COUNTRY 4** | | | |
| 4 Dr Wgn | **13664** | 3525 | 4425 |
| *ADD FOR:* | | | |
| Electronic Feature Pkg | | | |
| (Le Baron GTS Prem) | **272** | 90 | 100 |
| (Le Baron Prem Cpe & Conv) | **477** | 160 | 170 |
| Mark Cross Pkg (Le | | | |
| Baron Town & Country) | **1019** | 300 | 330 |
| (New Yorker Std) | **2374** | 600 | 670 |
| (New Yorker Landau) | **2066** | 560 | 630 |
| Turbo Coupe Pkg (Le | | | |
| Baron Highline Cpe) | **4000** | 860 | 960 |
| (Le Baron Highline Conv) | **3848** | 860 | 960 |
| 2.2 Liter Turbo Eng | | | |
| (Le Baron, Le Baron | | | |
| GTS Premium) | **678** | 170 | 190 |
| (Le Baron GTS Highline) | **399** | 170 | 190 |
| Leather Seating Pkg | | | |
| (Le Baron Highline | | | |
| Cpe, Le Baron | | | |
| Premium Cpe) | **627** | 150 | 160 |
| (Le Baron Prem Conv) | **1080** | 240 | 260 |
| (Le Baron GTS Prem) | **625** | 150 | 160 |

NOTE: Power brakes standard on all models. Power door locks standard on Le Baron GTS Premium, New Yorker Landau and New Yorker Turbo. Power seat standard on New Yorker Landau. Power windows standard on Fifth Avenue, Le Baron GTC Convertible, Le Baron Highline Convertible, Le Baron Premium, New Yorker Turbo and New Yorker Series.

## 1987

**FIFTH AVENUE 8**

| | | | |
|---|---|---|---|
| 4 Dr Sdn | **15966** | 3425 | 4325 |

| Year/Model/ Body/Type | Original List | Current Whlse | Average Retail |
|---|---|---|---|
| **LE BARON COUPE 4** | | | |
| 2 Dr Highline Cpe | **12606** | 2600 | 3475 |
| 2 Dr Premium Cpe | **13742** | 3125 | 4025 |
| **LE BARON 4** | | | |
| 4 Dr Sdn | **11489** | 1950 | 2800 |
| 2 Dr Conv | **14899** | 4500 | 5425 |
| **LE BARON GTS 4** | | | |
| 5 Dr High Sport Sdn | **11077** | 2100 | 2950 |
| 5 Dr Prem Sport Sdn | **12692** | 2475 | 3350 |
| **NEW YORKER 4** | | | |
| 4 Dr Sdn | **15321** | 2950 | 3850 |
| **TOWN & COUNTRY 4** | | | |
| 4 Dr Wgn | **13037** | 2650 | 3550 |
| *ADD FOR:* | | | |
| Electronic Feature Pkg | | | |
| (Le Baron GTS Prem) | **382** | 110 | 120 |
| (Le Baron Prem Cpe) | **687** | 130 | 140 |
| Leather Seating Pkg | | | |
| (Le Baron GTS Prem) | **625** | 160 | 170 |
| (Le Baron Prem Cpe) | **807** | 160 | 170 |
| Mark Cross Pkg | | | |
| (Le Baron Sdn, Town | | | |
| & Country) | **1018** | 170 | 190 |
| Turbo Coupe Pkg | | | |
| (Le Baron Cpe) | **1434** | 240 | 260 |
| Turbo Eng Pkg | | | |
| (Le Baron GTS) | **678** | 110 | 120 |
| 2.2 Liter Turbo Eng | | | |
| (Le Baron, New Yorker) | **678** | 90 | 100 |

NOTE: Power windows standard on Fifth Avenue and New Yorker. Power brakes standard on all models.

## 1986

**FIFTH AVENUE 8**

| | | | |
|---|---|---|---|
| 4 Dr Sdn | **14910** | 2525 | 3400 |

**LASER 4**

| | | | |
|---|---|---|---|
| 2 Dr Hbk | **10625** | 1450 | 2225 |

**LASER XE 4**

| | | | |
|---|---|---|---|
| 2 Dr Hbk | **12762** | 2000 | 2850 |

**LASER XT TURBO 4**

| | | | |
|---|---|---|---|
| 2 Dr Hbk | **13115** | 2150 | 3000 |

**LE BARON GTS 4**

| | | | |
|---|---|---|---|
| 5 Dr High Sport Sdn | **11015** | 1550 | 2400 |
| 5 Dr Prem Sport Sdn | **11941** | 1900 | 2750 |

**LE BARON 4**

| Year/Model/Body/Type | Original List | Current Whlse | Average Retail |
|---|---|---|---|
| 2 Dr Cpe | 10734 | 1475 | 2300 |
| 4 Dr Sdn | 10884 | 1575 | 2425 |
| 2 Dr Conv | 13452 | 2725 | 3625 |
| **LE BARON MARK CROSS CONV. 4** | | | |
| 2 Dr Conv | 16595 | 3250 | 4150 |
| 2 Dr Town & Country Conv | 17595 | 3900 | 4800 |
| **NEW YORKER 4** | | | |
| 4 Dr Sdn | 14309 | 2100 | 2950 |
| **TOWN & COUNTRY 4** | | | |
| 4 Dr Wgn | 12127 | 2200 | 3050 |
| *ADD FOR:* | | | |
| Electronic Feature Pkg (Le Baron GTS) | 382 | 60 | 70 |
| Mark Cross Pkg (Le Baron, Town & Country) | 1009 | 130 | 140 |
| 2.2 Liter Turbo Eng (Base Laser) | 990 | 160 | 170 |
| (Laser XE) | 730 | 160 | 170 |
| (Le Baron, New Yorker) | 628 | 90 | 100 |
| 2.5 Liter EFI Eng (Base Laser, Le Baron except Mark Cross Conv. and Town & Country Wgn) | 279 | 60 | 70 |
| T-Bar Roof (Laser) | 1316 | 170 | 190 |

NOTE: Vinyl top and power windows standard on Fifth Avenue and New Yorker. Power brakes standard on all models.

## 1985

| Year/Model/Body/Type | Original List | Current Whlse | Average Retail |
|---|---|---|---|
| **EXECUTIVE LIMOUSINE 4** | | | |
| 4 Dr Limousine | 26318 | — | — |
| **FIFTH AVENUE 8** | | | |
| 4 Dr Sdn | 14428 | 2025 | 2875 |
| **LASER 4** | | | |
| 2 Dr Hbk | 10030 | 975 | 1700 |
| **LASER XE 4** | | | |
| 2 Dr Hbk | 11952 | 1325 | 2050 |
| **LE BARON 4** | | | |
| 2 Dr Cpe | 10331 | 1200 | 1925 |
| 4 Dr Sdn | 10176 | 1275 | 2000 |
| 2 Dr Conv | 12809 | 2200 | 3050 |
| **LE BARON GTS 4** | | | |
| 5 Dr High Sport Sdn | 10465 | 1225 | 1950 |

| Year/Model/Body/Type | Original List | Current Whlse | Average Retail |
|---|---|---|---|
| 5 Dr Prem Sport Sdn | 11379 | 1450 | 2225 |
| **LE BARON MARK CROSS CONV. 4** | | | |
| 2 Dr Conv | 16951 | 2650 | 3550 |
| 2 Dr Town & Country Conv | 17951 | 3200 | 4100 |
| **NEW YORKER 4** | | | |
| 4 Dr Sdn | 13678 | 1650 | 2500 |
| **TOWN & COUNTRY 4** | | | |
| 4 Dr Wgn | 11252 | 1825 | 2675 |
| *ADD FOR:* | | | |
| Mark Cross Pkg (Le Baron Cpe) | 833 | 100 | 110 |
| (Le Baron Sdn, Town & Country Wgn) | 1009 | 110 | 120 |
| Turbo Sport Pkg (Le Baron GTS High) | 1098 | 120 | 130 |
| (Le Baron GTS Prem) | 1050 | 120 | 130 |
| 2.2 Liter Turbo Eng (Base Laser) | 964 | 100 | 110 |
| (Laser XE) | 872 | 100 | 110 |
| (Le Baron, New Yorker) | 610 | 90 | 100 |

NOTE: Power brakes standard on Executive Limousine, Fifth Avenue, Laser, Le Baron, Le Baron GTS and New Yorker. Vinyl top standard on Executive Limousine, Fifth Avenue, Le Baron Sedan, Le Baron Coupe and New Yorker. Power windows standard on Executive Limousine, Fifth Avenue and New Yorker. Power locks and power seat standard on Executive Limousine.

## 1984

| Year/Model/Body/Type | Original List | Current Whlse | Average Retail |
|---|---|---|---|
| **E CLASS 4** | | | |
| 4 Dr Sdn | 10294 | 700 | 1325 |
| **EXECUTIVE 4** | | | |
| 4 Dr Sdn | 18967 | — | — |
| 4 Dr Limousine | 21967 | — | — |
| **LASER 4** | | | |
| 2 Dr Hbk | 9814 | 600 | 1125 |
| **LASER XE 4** | | | |
| 2 Dr Hbk | 11712 | 900 | 1625 |
| **LE BARON 4** | | | |
| 2 Dr Cpe | 9951 | 875 | 1600 |
| 4 Dr Sdn | 9796 | 925 | 1650 |
| 2 Dr Conv | 12324 | 1725 | 2575 |
| **LE BARON MARK CROSS CONV. 4** | | | |
| 2 Dr Conv | 16224 | 1900 | 2750 |
| 2 Dr Town & Country Conv | 17724 | 2300 | 3175 |

| Year/Model/<br>Body/Type | Original<br>List | Current<br>Whlse | Average<br>Retail |
|---|---|---|---|
| **NEW YORKER 4** | | | |
| 4 Dr Sdn | **13179** | 1500 | 2350 |
| **NEW YORKER FIFTH AVE. 8** | | | |
| 4 Dr Sdn | **13978** | 1800 | 2650 |
| **TOWN & COUNTRY 4** | | | |
| 4 Dr Wgn | **10856** | 1325 | 2050 |

NOTE: Vinyl roof standard on New Yorker, Executive, Le Baron Coupe & Sedan, and New Yorker Fifth Avenue. Power windows standard on New Yorker, Executive and New Yorker Fifth Avenue.

### 1983 — ALL BODY STYLES

| | | | |
|---|---|---|---|
| CORDOBA | — | 725 | 1375 |
| E CLASS | — | 525 | 975 |
| IMPERIAL | — | 1575 | 2425 |
| LE BARON | — | 750 | 1475 |
| LE BARON CONV. | — | 1500 | 2350 |
| LE BARON MARK CROSS CONV. | — | 1700 | 2550 |
| NEW YORKER | — | 1200 | 1925 |
| NEW YORKER FIFTH AVE | — | 1500 | 2350 |
| TOWN & COUNTRY | — | 1050 | 1775 |

## DODGE

### 1992

**DAYTONA 4***

| | | | |
|---|---|---|---|
| 2 Dr Hbk | **11857** | 8900 | 10275 |
| 2 Dr ES Hbk | **12898** | 9650 | 11125 |
| 2 Dr IROC R/T Hbk | **19222** | — | — |

*For 6 cyl models add $475 whlse/$475 retail.

**DAYTONA 6**

| | | | |
|---|---|---|---|
| 2 Dr IROC Hbk<br>(NA w/auto trans) | **13636** | — | — |
| *ADD FOR:* | | | |
| V6 Perf Pkg (ES) | **319** | — | — |
| Anti-Lock Brakes<br>(ES, IROC) | **899** | — | — |
| Leather Enthusiast Seats | **1412** | — | — |
| Cloth Enthusiast Seats<br>(ES, IROC, IROC R/T) | **761** | — | — |
| Cast Alum Whls (Base) | **328** | — | — |

**DYNASTY 4***

| | | | |
|---|---|---|---|
| 4 Dr Sdn | **15108** | 9125 | 10500 |

*For 6 cyl models add $500 whlse/$500 retail.

**DYNASTY LE 6**

| | | | |
|---|---|---|---|
| 4 Dr Sdn | **16598** | 10300 | 11875 |

| Year/Model/<br>Body/Type | Original<br>List | Current<br>Whlse | Average<br>Retail |
|---|---|---|---|
| *ADD FOR:* | | | |
| Anti-Lock Brakes | **899** | 460 | 500 |
| Vinyl Landau Roof | **325** | 200 | 220 |
| Leather Seat Trim | **590** | 380 | 420 |
| Wire Wheel Covers | **240** | 160 | 170 |
| Cast Aluminum Wheels | **278** | 170 | 190 |
| **MONACO 6** | | | |
| 4 Dr LE Sdn | **15241** | — | — |
| 4 Dr ES Sdn | **17203** | — | — |
| *ADD FOR:* | | | |
| Anti-Lock Brakes | **799** | — | — |
| Leather Seat Trim | **891** | — | — |
| Cast Aluminum Wheels | **523** | — | — |
| **SHADOW 4** | | | |
| 2 Dr America Hbk | **9733** | 6375 | 7425 |
| 4 Dr America Sdn Hbk | **10133** | 6500 | 7575 |
| 2 Dr Highline Hbk | **10793** | 7225 | 8400 |
| 4 Dr Highline Sdn Hbk | **11193** | 7325 | 8500 |
| 2 Dr ES Hbk | **10762** | 8250 | 9525 |
| 4 Dr ES Sdn Hbk | **11162** | 8350 | 9650 |
| 2 Dr Highline Conv | **14836** | — | — |
| 2 Dr ES Conv | **15042** | — | — |
| *ADD FOR:* | | | |
| Cast Aluminum Wheels | **328** | 210 | 230 |
| 2.5 Liter 4 Cyl Eng<br>(America, Highline<br>Hbk & Sdn Hbk) | **286** | 200 | 220 |
| 2.5 Liter 4 Cyl Turbo Eng<br>(Highline Conv & ES) | **760** | 490 | 540 |
| 3.0 Liter 6 Cyl Eng<br>(ES) | **694** | 490 | 540 |
| (Conv) | **905** | 490 | 540 |
| **SPIRIT 4*** | | | |
| 4 Dr Sdn | **12858** | 7775 | 9025 |
| 4 Dr LE Sdn | **14361** | 8425 | 9725 |
| 4 Dr ES Sdn | **15829** | 9275 | 10675 |
| 4 Dr R/T Sdn<br>(NA w/auto trans) | **18674** | — | — |

*For 6 cyl models add $450 whlse/$450 retail.

| | | | |
|---|---|---|---|
| *ADD FOR:* | | | |
| 2.5 Liter 4 Cyl Turbo<br>Eng (LE) | **725** | 460 | 500 |
| Anti-Lock Brakes | **899** | 460 | 500 |
| Cast Aluminum Wheels | **328** | 210 | 230 |
| **STEALTH 6** | | | |
| 2 Dr Base Cpe | **18167** | 15125 | 17775 |
| 2 Dr ES Cpe | **20594** | 16225 | 18875 |
| 2 Dr R/T Cpe | **25747** | 19575 | 22625 |
| 2 Dr R/T Turbo Cpe | | | |

| Year/Model/Body/Type | Original List | Current Whlse | Average Retail |
|---|---|---|---|
| (NA w/auto trans) | **31185** | 22575 | 25875 |
| *ADD FOR:* | | | |
| Anti-Lock Brakes | **1395** | 590 | 660 |
| Leather Seat Trim | **843** | 460 | 500 |

### VIPER 10

| Year/Model/Body/Type | Original List | Current Whlse | Average Retail |
|---|---|---|---|
| 2 Dr Sport Cpe | | | |
| (NA w/auto trans) | **50000** | — | — |

NOTE: Power windows standard on Shadow Convertible, Stealth R/T & R/T Turbo. Power door locks and power seat standard on Stealth R/T & R/T Turbo. Tilt steering wheel standard on Spirit LE & ES, Stealth and Viper. Cruise control standard on Spirit LE, ES & R/T, Stealth R/T & R/T Turbo.

## 1991

### DAYTONA 4*

| Year/Model/Body/Type | Original List | Current Whlse | Average Retail |
|---|---|---|---|
| 2 Dr Hbk | **12080** | 6625 | 7700 |
| 2 Dr ES Hbk | **13325** | 7225 | 8400 |
| 2 Dr Shelby Turbo Hbk | **14596** | — | — |

*For 6 cyl models add $400 whsle/$400 retail.

### DAYTONA 6

| | Original List | Current Whlse | Average Retail |
|---|---|---|---|
| 2 Dr IROC Hbk | **14626** | — | — |

### DYNASTY 4*

| | Original List | Current Whlse | Average Retail |
|---|---|---|---|
| 4 Dr Sdn | **14518** | 7425 | 8625 |

*For 6 cyl models add $400 whsle/$400 retail.

### DYNASTY LE 6

| | Original List | Current Whlse | Average Retail |
|---|---|---|---|
| 4 Dr Sdn | **15958** | 8550 | 9875 |

### MONACO 6

| | Original List | Current Whlse | Average Retail |
|---|---|---|---|
| 4 Dr LE Sdn | **14624** | 5875 | 6800 |
| 4 Dr ES Sdn | **16492** | 6750 | 7850 |

### SHADOW 4

| | Original List | Current Whlse | Average Retail |
|---|---|---|---|
| 2 Dr America Hbk | **9321** | 4850 | 5775 |
| 4 Dr America Hbk | **9621** | 4925 | 5850 |
| 2 Dr Highline Hbk | **10286** | 5600 | 6525 |
| 4 Dr Highline Hbk | **10586** | 5725 | 6650 |
| 2 Dr ES Hbk | **11762** | 6500 | 7575 |
| 4 Dr ES Hbk | **12062** | 6600 | 7675 |
| 2 Dr Highline Conv | **14333** | 8625 | 9950 |
| 2 Dr ES Conv | **15406** | 9525 | 10975 |

### SPIRIT 4*

| | Original List | Current Whlse | Average Retail |
|---|---|---|---|
| 4 Dr Sdn | **11523** | 6550 | 7625 |
| 4 Dr LE Sdn | **13797** | 7125 | 8275 |
| 4 Dr ES Sdn | **15128** | 7875 | 9150 |
| 4 Dr R/T Sdn | | | |
| (NA w/auto trans) | **17871** | — | — |

*For 6 cyl models add $400 whsle/$400 retail.

### STEALTH 6

| Year/Model/Body/Type | Original List | Current Whlse | Average Retail |
|---|---|---|---|
| 2 Dr Base Cpe | **17952** | 13100 | 15425 |
| 2 Dr ES Cpe | **19715** | 14075 | 16525 |
| 2 Dr R/T Cpe | **24968** | 17100 | 19750 |
| 2 Dr R/T Turbo Cpe | | | |
| (NA w/auto trans) | **29267** | 19775 | 22825 |

*ADD FOR:*

| | Original List | Current Whlse | Average Retail |
|---|---|---|---|
| Anti-lock Brakes | | | |
| (Dynasty, Spirit) | **899** | 440 | 480 |
| (Monaco) | **799** | 390 | 430 |
| V6 Perf. Pkg (Daytona ES) | **1013** | 500 | 560 |
| Leather Seats (Stealth) | **843** | 350 | 380 |
| 50/50 Leather Seats | | | |
| (Dynasty LE) | **590** | 260 | 280 |
| Power 8-Way Leather Seat | | | |
| (Daytona ex. Base) | **1402** | 630 | 700 |
| Opt Pkg 2 (Stealth Base) | **836** | 410 | 460 |
| (Stealth ES) | **766** | 360 | 400 |
| (Stealth RT) | **424** | 170 | 190 |
| Opt Pkg 3 (Stealth Base) | **969** | 440 | 480 |
| (Stealth ES) | **1186** | 560 | 630 |
| Opt Pkg 4 (Stealth Base) | **1445** | 650 | 720 |
| (Stealth ES) | **2436** | 1060 | 1170 |
| Opt Pkg 5 (Stealth Base) | **2219** | 980 | 1090 |
| (Stealth ES) | **2860** | 1280 | 1420 |
| Opt Pkg 6 (Stealth Base) | **3119** | 1460 | 1620 |
| (Stealth ES) | **3221** | 1470 | 1640 |

NOTE: Power brakes standard on all models. Air bag standard on Base Daytona, Dynasty, Shadow, Spirit and Stealth. Anti-lock brakes and power door locks standard on Stealth R/T. Power windows standard on Stealth R/T and Shadow Highline Convertible and ES.

## 1990

### DAYTONA 4*

| | Original List | Current Whlse | Average Retail |
|---|---|---|---|
| 2 Dr Hbk | **11335** | 5275 | 6200 |
| 2 Dr ES Hbk | **12535** | 5850 | 6775 |
| 2 Dr ES Turbo Hbk | **13431** | 6650 | 7750 |
| 2 Dr Shelby Turbo | | | |
| Hbk (NA w/auto trans) | **15403** | 7225 | 8400 |

*For 6 cyl models add $400 whsle/$400 retail.

### DYNASTY 4*

| | Original List | Current Whlse | Average Retail |
|---|---|---|---|
| 4 Dr Sdn | **13800** | 5000 | 5925 |

*For 6 cyl models add $375 whsle/$375 retail.

### DYNASTY LE 6

| | Original List | Current Whlse | Average Retail |
|---|---|---|---|
| 4 Dr Sdn | **15200** | 6000 | 6925 |

### OMNI 4

| | Original List | Current Whlse | Average Retail |
|---|---|---|---|
| 5 Dr Hbk | **7998** | 2975 | 3875 |

### MONACO 6

| | Original List | Current Whlse | Average Retail |
|---|---|---|---|
| 4 Dr LE Sdn | **15855** | 5225 | 6150 |

| Year/Model/Body/Type | Original List | Current Whlse | Average Retail |
|---|---|---|---|
| 4 Dr ES Sdn | **17595** | 6025 | 6950 |
| **SHADOW 4** | | | |
| 3 Dr Lftbk Cpe | **10096** | 4200 | 5125 |
| 5 Dr Lftbk Sdn | **10296** | 4300 | 5225 |
| **SPIRIT 4*** | | | |
| 4 Dr Sdn | **11031** | 4600 | 5525 |
| 4 Dr LE Sdn | **13246** | 5050 | 5975 |
| 4 Dr ES Sdn | **14546** | 5800 | 6725 |
| *For 6 cyl models add $400 whsle/$400 retail. | | | |
| ADD FOR: | | | |
| Anti-Lock Brakes (Dynasty) | **926** | 390 | 430 |
| Competition Pkg (Shadow Cpe) | **2558** | 950 | 1050 |
| C/S Competition Pkg (Base Daytona) | **2702** | 1130 | 1250 |
| C/S Performance Disc Pkg (Base Daytona) | **1502** | 650 | 720 |
| Power 8-way Leather Seat (Daytona ex. Base) | **974** | 330 | 360 |
| 3.0 Liter V6 Eng (Base Daytona) | **680** | 300 | 330 |
| NOTE: Power brakes standard on all models. | | | |

## 1989

| **ARIES AMERICA 4** | | | |
|---|---|---|---|
| 2 Dr Sdn | **9298** | 2525 | 3400 |
| 4 Dr Sdn | **9298** | 2625 | 3525 |
| **DAYTONA 4** | | | |
| 2 Dr Hbk | **10606** | 3750 | 4650 |
| 2 Dr ES Hbk | **11706** | 4250 | 5175 |
| 2 Dr ES Turbo Hbk | **12531** | 4950 | 5875 |
| 2 Dr Shelby Turbo Hbk (NA w/auto trans) | **13295** | 5475 | 6400 |
| **DIPLOMAT 8** | | | |
| 4 Dr Salon Sdn | **12850** | 3250 | 4150 |
| 4 Dr SE Sdn | **14795** | 4050 | 4950 |
| **DYNASTY 4*** | | | |
| 4 Dr Sdn | **13070** | 4025 | 4925 |
| *For 6 cyl models add $400 whsle/$400 retail. | | | |
| **DYNASTY LE 6** | | | |
| 4 Dr Sdn | **14370** | 4875 | 5800 |
| **LANCER 4** | | | |
| 5 Dr Sport Sdn | **12506** | 3800 | 4700 |
| 5 Dr ES Turbo Sport Sdn | **14231** | 4350 | 5275 |

| Year/Model/Body/Type | Original List | Current Whlse | Average Retail |
|---|---|---|---|
| 5 Dr Shelby Spt Sdn | **17220** | 5525 | 6450 |
| **OMNI AMERICA 4** | | | |
| 5 Dr Hbk | **8298** | 2050 | 2900 |
| **SHADOW 4** | | | |
| 3 Dr Lftbk Cpe | **9706** | 3425 | 4325 |
| 5 Dr Lftbk Sdn | **9906** | 3525 | 4425 |
| **SPIRIT 4** | | | |
| 4 Dr Sdn | **10531** | 3725 | 4625 |
| 4 Dr LE Sdn | **12506** | 4200 | 5125 |
| 4 Dr ES Turbo Sdn | **13886** | 4750 | 5675 |
| ADD FOR: | | | |
| Competition Pkg (Shadow Cpe) | **1515** | 560 | 630 |
| ES Pkg (Shadow Cpe) | **1977** | 690 | 770 |
| (Shadow Sdn) | **2039** | 690 | 770 |
| C/S Competition Pkg (Base Daytona) | **2879** | 990 | 1100 |
| C/S Performance Pkg (Base Daytona) | **1443** | 520 | 580 |
| T-Bar Roof Pkg (Base Daytona, Daytona ES) | **1513** | 470 | 520 |
| (Daytona ES Turbo, Daytona Shelby) | **1298** | 470 | 520 |
| Turbo Eng Pkg (Shadow) | **923** | 350 | 380 |
| (Base Lancer) | **536** | 220 | 240 |
| NOTE: Power windows standard on Lancer Shelby. Power locks standard on Lancer ES and Lancer Shelby. | | | |

## 1988

| **600 4** | | | |
|---|---|---|---|
| 4 Dr Sdn | **11434** | 2575 | 3450 |
| 4 Dr SE Sdn | **12403** | 2950 | 3850 |
| **ARIES AMERICA 4** | | | |
| 2 Dr Sdn | **9064** | 2175 | 3025 |
| 4 Dr Sdn | **9064** | 2250 | 3100 |
| 4 Dr Wgn | **9458** | 2625 | 3525 |
| **DAYTONA 4** | | | |
| 2 Dr Base Hbk | **10299** | 2575 | 3450 |
| 2 Dr Pacifica Hbk | **15054** | 3875 | 4775 |
| 2 Dr Shelby Z Hbk | **14650** | 3800 | 4700 |
| **DIPLOMAT 8** | | | |
| 4 Dr Base | **12127** | 2800 | 3700 |
| 4 Dr Salon | **12237** | 2350 | 3225 |
| 4 Dr SE | **14221** | 3100 | 4000 |
| **DYNASTY 4*** | | | |
| 4 Dr Sdn | **12441** | 3250 | 4150 |

| Year/Model/Body/Type | Original List | Current Whlse | Average Retail |
|---|---|---|---|
| 4 Dr Premier Sdn | **13001** | 3500 | 4400 |
| *For 6 cyl models add $375 whsle/$375 retail. | | | |
| **LANCER 4** | | | |
| 5 Dr Sport Sdn | **11793** | 2825 | 3725 |
| 5 Dr ES Sport Sdn | **13251** | 3275 | 4175 |
| **OMNI AMERICA 4** | | | |
| 5 Dr Hbk | **7868** | 1550 | 2400 |
| **SHADOW 4** | | | |
| 2 Dr Lftbk Cpe | **9225** | 2325 | 3200 |
| 4 Dr Lftbk Sdn | **9475** | 2425 | 3300 |
| *ADD FOR:* | | | |
| Electronic Features Pkg (Lancer ES) | **571** | 160 | 170 |
| Lancer Shelby Pkg (Lancer ES) | **3830** | 1040 | 1150 |
| T-Bar Roof Pkg (Daytona) | **1468** | 360 | 400 |
| (Daytona Shelby Z) | **1258** | 360 | 400 |
| (Daytona Pacifica) | **955** | 360 | 400 |
| Turbo Eng Pkg (Shadow) | **780** | 260 | 280 |
| Turbo I Eng Pkg (Base Daytona) | **837** | 270 | 300 |
| Turbo Sport Discount Pkg (Lancer ES) | **1465** | 430 | 500 |
| 2.2 Liter 4 Cyl Turbo Eng (Base 600, Base Lancer) | **399** | 130 | 140 |
| (600 SE, Lancer ES) | **678** | 170 | 190 |
| (Dynasty) | **660** | 170 | 190 |

NOTE: Power brakes standard on all models. Power door locks standard on Lancer ES.

## 1987

**600 4**

| Year/Model/Body/Type | Original List | Current Whlse | Average Retail |
|---|---|---|---|
| 4 Dr Sdn | **10792** | 1625 | 2475 |
| 4 Dr SE Sdn | **11454** | 1875 | 2725 |
| *For 158 CID 4 cyl eng add $— whsle/$— retail. | | | |
| **ARIES 4*** | | | |
| 2 Dr Sdn | **9430** | 1150 | 1875 |
| 4 Dr Sdn | **9430** | 1250 | 1975 |
| 2 Dr LE Sdn | **9915** | 1350 | 2100 |
| 4 Dr LE Sdn | **9915** | 1450 | 2225 |
| 4 Dr LE Wgn | **10359** | 1775 | 2625 |
| *For 158 CID 4 cyl eng add $— whsle/$— retail. | | | |
| **CHARGER 4** | | | |
| 3 Dr Base Hbk | **9199** | 1425 | 2175 |
| 3 Dr Shelby Hbk (NA w/auto trans) | **10541** | 2100 | 2950 |

| Year/Model/Body/Type | Original List | Current Whlse | Average Retail |
|---|---|---|---|
| **DAYTONA 4** | | | |
| 2 Dr Base Hbk | **11110** | 2225 | 3075 |
| 2 Dr Pacifica Hbk | **14441** | 3125 | 4025 |
| 2 Dr Shelby Z Hbk (NA w/auto trans) | **12749** | 3125 | 4025 |
| **DIPLOMAT 8** | | | |
| 4 Dr Salon | **11435** | 1775 | 2625 |
| 2 Dr SE | **12515** | 2300 | 3175 |
| **LANCER 4*** | | | |
| 5 Dr Sport Sdn | **11163** | 2000 | 2850 |
| 5 Dr ES Sport Sdn | **12117** | 2375 | 3250 |
| *For 158 CID 4 cyl models add $— whsle/$— retail. | | | |
| **OMNI 4** | | | |
| 5 Dr America Hbk | **7799** | 1075 | 1800 |
| **SHADOW 4** | | | |
| 2 Dr Lftbk Cpe | **8722** | 1650 | 2500 |
| 4 Dr Lftbk Sdn | **8922** | 1725 | 2575 |
| *ADD FOR:* | | | |
| Electronic Features Pkg (Lancer ES) | **681** | 130 | 140 |
| Leather Seating Pkg (Daytona Shelby Z) | **939** | 190 | 210 |
| (Daytona Pacifica) | **488** | 130 | 140 |
| (Lancer ES) | **625** | 160 | 170 |
| Shadow ES Pkg | **1720** | 130 | 140 |
| T-Bar Roof Pkg (Daytona) | **1468** | 330 | 360 |
| (Daytona Shelby Z) | **1560** | 330 | 360 |
| (Daytona Pacifica) | **1165** | 330 | 360 |
| Turbo Eng Pkg (Shadow Sdn) | **806** | 170 | 190 |
| Turbo I Eng Pkg (Base Daytona) | **837** | 190 | 210 |
| 2.2 Liter Turbo Eng (600, Lancer) | **678** | 170 | 190 |

NOTE: Sunroof standard on Shelby Charger. Power brakes standard on all models.

## 1986

**600 4**

| Year/Model/Body/Type | Original List | Current Whlse | Average Retail |
|---|---|---|---|
| 2 Dr Cpe | **10034** | 1075 | 1800 |
| 2 Dr Conv | **12682** | 2300 | 3175 |
| 4 Dr Sdn | **10127** | 1175 | 1900 |
| **600 ES TURBO CONVERTIBLE 4** | | | |
| 2 Dr Conv (pwr strng NA) | **15613** | 2800 | 3700 |
| **600 SE 4** | | | |
| 4 Dr Sdn | **10785** | 1400 | 2150 |

| Year/Model/Body/Type | Original List | Current Whlse | Average Retail |
|---|---|---|---|
| **ARIES 4\*** | | | |
| 2 Dr | 8675 | 900 | 1625 |
| 4 Dr | 8792 | 1000 | 1725 |
| **ARIES LE 4\*** | | | |
| 2 Dr Sdn | 9578 | 1200 | 1925 |
| 4 Dr Sdn | 9698 | 1275 | 2000 |
| 4 Dr Wgn | 10197 | 1575 | 2425 |
| **ARIES SE 4\*** | | | |
| 2 Dr | 9130 | 1050 | 1775 |
| 4 Dr | 9250 | 1150 | 1875 |
| 4 Dr Wgn | 9677 | 1425 | 2175 |
| *For 158 CID 4 cyl models add $50 whsle/$50 retail.* | | | |
| **CHARGER 4\*** | | | |
| 2 Dr Hbk | 8297 | 1125 | 1850 |
| **CHARGER 2.2 4\*** | | | |
| 2 Dr Hbk | 9129 | 1500 | 2350 |
| **SHELBY CHARGER 4** | | | |
| 2 Dr Hbk | 10528 | 1700 | 2550 |
| **DAYTONA 4** | | | |
| 2 Dr Hbk | 10274 | 1450 | 2225 |
| **DAYTONA TURBO Z 4** | | | |
| 2 Dr Hbk | 12562 | 2300 | 3175 |
| **DIPLOMAT SALON 8** | | | |
| 4 Dr | 10898 | 1200 | 1925 |
| **DIPLOMAT SE 8** | | | |
| 4 Dr | 11978 | 1675 | 2525 |
| **LANCER 4** | | | |
| 5 Dr Sport Sdn | 10687 | 1500 | 2350 |
| **LANCER 'ES' 4** | | | |
| 5 Dr Sport Sdn | 11583 | 1850 | 2700 |
| **OMNI 4\*** | | | |
| 4 Dr Hbk | 7719 | 800 | 1500 |
| **OMNI GLH 4** | | | |
| 4 Dr Hbk (automatic transmission NA) | 8581 | 1500 | 2350 |
| **OMNI SE 4\*** | | | |
| 4 Dr Hbk | 7955 | 1075 | 1800 |
| *For 135 CID 4 cyl eng add $50 whsle/$50 retail.* | | | |
| *ADD FOR:* | | | |
| Electronics Features Pkg (Lancer) | 637 | 100 | 110 |

| Year/Model/Body/Type | Original List | Current Whlse | Average Retail |
|---|---|---|---|
| (Daytona Turbo) | 583 | 90 | 100 |
| (Base Daytona) | 272 | 50 | 50 |
| T-Bar Roof Pkg (Dodge, Daytona, Turbo Z) | 1351 | 220 | 240 |
| Turbo Sport Pkg (Lancer ES) | 1415 | 220 | 240 |
| 2.2 Liter Turbo Eng (600, Lancer) | 628 | 100 | 110 |
| (Base Daytona, Omni GLH) | 898 | 150 | 160 |
| NOTE: Power brakes standard on all models. | | | |

## 1985

| Year/Model/Body/Type | Original List | Current Whlse | Average Retail |
|---|---|---|---|
| **600 4\*** | | | |
| 2 Dr Cpe | 9931 | 900 | 1625 |
| 2 Dr Conv | 12028 | 1975 | 2825 |
| **600 ES TURBO CONVERTIBLE 4** | | | |
| 2 Dr Conv | 15171 | 2300 | 3175 |
| **600 SE 4\*** | | | |
| 4 Dr Sdn | 9838 | 975 | 1700 |
| **ARIES 4** | | | |
| 2 Dr | 8432 | 800 | 1500 |
| 4 Dr | 8547 | 875 | 1600 |
| **ARIES LE 4** | | | |
| 2 Dr | 9054 | 1025 | 1750 |
| 4 Dr | 9187 | 1125 | 1850 |
| 4 Dr Wgn | 9554 | 1325 | 2050 |
| **ARIES SE 4** | | | |
| 2 Dr | 8716 | 900 | 1625 |
| 4 Dr | 8834 | 975 | 1700 |
| 4 Dr Wgn | 9334 | 1225 | 1950 |
| **CHARGER 4\*** | | | |
| 2 Dr Hbk | 7885 | 975 | 1700 |
| **CHARGER 2.2 4\*** | | | |
| 2 Dr Hbk | 8816 | 1325 | 2050 |
| **SHELBY CHARGER 4** | | | |
| 2 Dr Hbk | 10077 | 1425 | 2175 |
| **DAYTONA 4** | | | |
| 2 Dr Hbk | 9681 | 925 | 1650 |
| **DAYTONA TURBO 4** | | | |
| 2 Dr Hbk | 11462 | 1275 | 2000 |
| **DAYTONA TURBO Z 4** | | | |
| 2 Dr Hbk | 12796 | 1700 | 2550 |

*1990 Dodge Daytona Shelby*

| Year/Model/Body/Type | Original List | Current Whlse | Average Retail |
|---|---|---|---|
| **DIPLOMAT SALON 8** | | | |
| 4 Dr | **10470** | 900 | 1625 |
| **DIPLOMAT SE 8** | | | |
| 4 Dr | **11513** | 1275 | 2000 |
| **LANCER 4** | | | |
| 5 Dr Sport Sdn | **10148** | 1225 | 1950 |
| **LANCER 'ES' 4** | | | |
| 5 Dr Sport Sdn | **11093** | 1450 | 2225 |
| **OMNI 4\*** | | | |
| 4 Dr Hbk | **7413** | 700 | 1325 |
| **OMNI GLH 4** | | | |
| 4 Dr Hbk | **9034** | 1225 | 1950 |
| **OMNI SE 4** | | | |
| 4 Dr Hbk | **7756** | 950 | 1675 |
| *ADD FOR:* | | | |
| Turbo Sport Pkg | | | |
| (Base Lancer) | **1098** | 120 | 130 |
| (Lancer ES) | **1397** | 160 | 170 |
| Turbo Eng (Lancer, 600) | **610** | 80 | 80 |
| (Base Daytona) | **964** | 110 | 120 |
| (Omni GLH) | **872** | 110 | 120 |

NOTE: Power brakes standard on all models. Vinyl top standard on 600 Coupe.

## 1984

| Year/Model/Body/Type | Original List | Current Whlse | Average Retail |
|---|---|---|---|
| **600** | | | |
| 2 Dr Cpe | **9544** | 600 | 1125 |

| Year/Model/Body/Type | Original List | Current Whlse | Average Retail |
|---|---|---|---|
| 2 Dr Conv | **11543** | 1525 | 2375 |
| 4 Dr Sdn | **9632** | 675 | 1275 |
| 4 Dr 'ES' Sdn | **10254** | 875 | 1600 |
| **ARIES** | | | |
| 2 Dr | **8337** | 400 | 725 |
| 4 Dr | **8449** | 475 | 875 |
| **ARIES CUSTOM** | | | |
| 4 Dr Wgn | **9123** | 650 | 1225 |
| **ARIES SPECIAL EDITION** | | | |
| 2 Dr | **8840** | 575 | 1075 |
| 4 Dr | **8976** | 650 | 1225 |
| 4 Dr Wgn | **9363** | 850 | 1550 |
| **CHARGER 4\*** | | | |
| 2 Dr Hbk | **7900** | 525 | 975 |
| **CHARGER 2.2** | | | |
| 2 Dr Hbk | **8581** | 750 | 1475 |
| **DAYTONA** | | | |
| 2 Dr Hbk | **9474** | 600 | 1125 |
| **DAYTONA TURBO** | | | |
| 2 Dr Hbk | **10954** | 900 | 1625 |
| **DIPLOMAT SALON** | | | |
| 4 Dr | **9961** | 750 | 1475 |
| **DIPLOMAT SE** | | | |
| 4 Dr | **10957** | 925 | 1650 |
| **OMNI** | | | |
| 4 Dr Hbk | **7236** | 250 | 500 |

| Year/Model/Body/Type | Original List | Current Whlse | Average Retail |
|---|---|---|---|
| **OMNI SE** | | | |
| 4 Dr Hbk | **7441** | 475 | 875 |
| **SHELBY CHARGER** | | | |
| Shelby Charger | **9834** | 900 | 1625 |
| NOTE: Power brakes standard on all models. | | | |

**1983 — ALL BODY STYLES**

| Year/Model/Body/Type | Original List | Current Whlse | Average Retail |
|---|---|---|---|
| 400 | — | 675 | 1275 |
| 400 CONV | — | 1350 | 2100 |
| 600 | — | 575 | 1075 |
| ARIES | — | 250 | 500 |
| ARIES CUSTOM | — | 425 | 775 |
| ARIES SPECIAL EDITION | — | 400 | 725 |
| CHARGER | — | 225 | 475 |
| CHARGER 2.2 | — | 400 | 725 |
| DIPLOMAT MEDALLION | — | 675 | 1275 |
| DIPLOMAT SALON | — | 550 | 1025 |
| MIRADA | — | 725 | 1375 |
| OMNI | — | 110 | 300 |
| OMNI CUSTOM | — | 150 | 350 |

## EAGLE

### 1992

| Year/Model/Body/Type | Original List | Current Whlse | Average Retail |
|---|---|---|---|
| **PREMIER 6** | | | |
| 4 Dr LX Sdn | **15716** | — | — |
| 4 Dr ES Sdn | **18057** | — | — |
| 4 Dr ES Limited Sdn | **20212** | — | — |
| *ADD FOR:* | | | |
| Anti-Lock Brakes (LX, ES) | **799** | — | — |
| Leather Seat Trim (ES) | **873** | — | — |
| Cast Aluminum Wheels | | | |
| (LX) | **523** | — | — |
| (ES) | **301** | — | — |
| **SUMMIT 4** | | | |
| 3 Dr Hbk | **9326** | — | — |
| 4 Dr Sdn | **10710** | — | — |
| 3 Dr ES Hbk | **9739** | — | — |
| 4 Dr ES Sdn | **11871** | — | — |
| 4 Dr DL Wgn | **13173** | — | — |
| 4 Dr LX Wgn | **13617** | — | — |
| 4 Dr AWD Wgn | **15571** | — | — |
| *ADD FOR:* | | | |
| 2.4 Liter 4 Cyl Eng (Wgns) | **181** | — | — |
| Anti-Lock Brakes (Wgn) | **913** | — | — |
| Cast Alum Whls (ES Sdn) | **275** | — | — |
| **TALON 4** | | | |
| 2 Dr Cpe | **15390** | 10875 | 12550 |

| Year/Model/Body/Type | Original List | Current Whlse | Average Retail |
|---|---|---|---|
| 2 Dr TSi Turbo Cpe | **17847** | — | — |
| 2 Dr 4WD TSi Turbo Cpe | **19854** | — | — |
| *ADD FOR:* | | | |
| Anti-Lock Brakes | **943** | — | — |
| Leather Seat Trim (TSi) | **435** | — | — |
| Cast Aluminum Wheels (TSi 2WD) | **284** | — | — |

NOTE: Power windows and power seat standard on Premier ES Limited. Power door locks and cruise control standard on Premier ES & ES Limited. Tilt steering wheel standard on Premier ES & ES Limited, Sundance ES Sdn, LX Wagon & AWD Wagon and Talon.

### 1991

| Year/Model/Body/Type | Original List | Current Whlse | Average Retail |
|---|---|---|---|
| **PREMIER 6** | | | |
| 4 Dr LX Sdn | **15051** | 6800 | 7950 |
| 4 Dr ES Sdn | **17238** | 7650 | 8775 |
| 4 Dr ES Limited Sdn | **19478** | 8850 | 9975 |
| **SUMMIT 4** | | | |
| 3 Dr Hbk | **7132** | 4875 | 5725 |
| 4 Dr Sdn | **10333** | 5800 | 6725 |
| 3 Dr ES Hbk | **9573** | 5475 | 6300 |
| 4 Dr ES Sdn | **11079** | 6075 | 6975 |
| **TALON 4** | | | |
| 2 Dr Cpe | **14489** | 9050 | 10425 |
| 2 Dr TSi Turbo Cpe | **17026** | 10275 | 11850 |
| 2 Dr 4WD T3i Turbo Cpe | **18930** | 12600 | 14925 |
| *ADD FOR:* | | | |
| Anti-lock Brakes | | | |
| (Premier LX & ES) | **799** | 390 | 430 |
| (Talon ex. TSi 4WD) | **925** | 430 | 500 |
| (Talon TSi 4WD) | **681** | 390 | 430 |
| Leather Seats (Talon) | **427** | 190 | 210 |

NOTE: Power brakes standard on all models. Power windows, power seat and anti-lock brakes standard on Eagle Premier ES Limited. Power door locks standard on Eagle Premier ES & ES Limited.

### 1990

| Year/Model/Body/Type | Original List | Current Whlse | Average Retail |
|---|---|---|---|
| **PREMIER 6** | | | |
| 4 Dr LX Sdn | **16210** | 5025 | 5950 |
| 4 Dr ES Sdn | **17845** | 5850 | 6775 |
| 4 Dr ES Limited Sdn | **20284** | 6950 | 8100 |
| **SUMMIT 4** | | | |
| 4 Dr Sdn | **10582** | 3450 | 4350 |
| 4 Dr DL Sdn | **11330** | 3750 | 4650 |
| 4 Dr LX Sdn | **12014** | 4250 | 5175 |
| 4 Dr ES Sdn | **13052** | 4625 | 5550 |

| Year/Model/Body/Type | Original List | Current Whlse | Average Retail |
|---|---|---|---|
| **TALON 4** | | | |
| 2 Dr Cpe | **14479** | 7450 | 8650 |
| 2 Dr TSI Turbo Cpe (NA w/auto trans) | **15555** | 8650 | 10000 |
| 2 Dr 4WD TSi Turbo Cpe (NA w/auto trans) | **17239** | 10475 | 12100 |
| *ADD FOR:* | | | |
| 1.6 Liter DOHC Pkg (Summit LX) | **1319** | 560 | 630 |
| 45/45 Leather/Vinyl Seats (Premier ES) | **566** | 240 | 260 |
| Leather Bucket Seats (Talon TSi) | **430** | 170 | 190 |

NOTE: Power windows and power door locks standard on Eagle ES Limited. Power brakes standard on all models.

### 1989

| | Original List | Current Whlse | Average Retail |
|---|---|---|---|
| **MEDALLION 4** | | | |
| 4 Dr DL Sdn | **11204** | 1900 | 2750 |
| 4 Dr DL Wgn | **12448** | 2275 | 3150 |
| 4 Dr LX Sdn | **11737** | 2100 | 2950 |
| 4 Dr LX Wgn | **13074** | 2450 | 3325 |
| **PREMIER LX 4*** | | | |
| 4 Dr Sdn | **14406** | 3200 | 4100 |

*For 6 cyl models add $375 whsle/$375 retail.

| | Original List | Current Whlse | Average Retail |
|---|---|---|---|
| **PREMIER ES 6** | | | |
| 4 Dr Sdn | **16689** | 4125 | 5050 |
| **PREMIER ES LIMITED 6** | | | |
| 4 Dr Sdn | **19181** | 5150 | 6075 |
| **SUMMIT 4** | | | |
| 4 Dr DL Sdn | **11281** | 2600 | 3475 |
| 4 Dr LX Sdn | **11617** | 3125 | 4025 |
| *ADD FOR:* | | | |
| Enthusiast Group (Premier LX) | **640** | 240 | 260 |
| Driving Group (Medallion LX) | **404** | 130 | 140 |

NOTE: Power brakes standard on all models.

### 1988

| | Original List | Current Whlse | Average Retail |
|---|---|---|---|
| **EAGLE 6** | | | |
| 4 Dr Wgn | **12995** | 3200 | 4100 |
| **MEDALLION 4** | | | |
| 4 Dr DL Sdn | **11200** | 1300 | 2025 |
| 4 Dr DL Wgn | **11928** | 1600 | 2450 |

| Year/Model/Body/Type | Original List | Current Whlse | Average Retail |
|---|---|---|---|
| 4 Dr LX Sdn | **11714** | 1450 | 2225 |
| **PREMIER LX 4** | | | |
| 4 Dr Sdn | **13304** | 2675 | 3575 |
| **PREMIER ES 6** | | | |
| 4 Dr Sdn | **14909** | 3125 | 4025 |
| *ADD FOR:* | | | |
| Driving Grp (Medallion LX, DL Wgn) | **417** | 110 | 120 |

NOTE: Power brakes standard on all models.

## FORD

### 1992

| | Original List | Current Whlse | Average Retail |
|---|---|---|---|
| **CROWN VICTORIA 8** | | | |
| 4 Dr Sdn | **19563** | 13250 | 15575 |
| 4 Dr LX Sdn | **20887** | 14150 | 16600 |
| 4 Dr Touring Sdn | **23832** | 15550 | 18200 |
| *ADD FOR:* | | | |
| Anti-Lock Brakes (Base, LX) | **695** | 450 | 500 |
| Leather Seat Trim (LX) | **555** | 260 | 290 |
| (Touring Sdn) | **339** | 260 | 290 |
| Spoke Wheel Covers | **311** | 200 | 220 |
| Cast Alum Whls (Base) | **440** | 290 | 320 |
| **ESCORT PONY 4** | | | |
| 2 Dr Hbk (NA w/pwr strng) | **9399** | 6100 | 7000 |
| **ESCORT GT 4** | | | |
| 2 Dr Hbk | **13362** | 8400 | 9700 |
| **ESCORT LX 4** | | | |
| 2 Dr Hbk | **10807** | 6625 | 7700 |
| 4 Dr Hbk | **11235** | 6925 | 8050 |
| 4 Dr Sdn | **11547** | 7075 | 8225 |
| 4 Dr Wgn | **11819** | 7550 | 8775 |
| **ESCORT LX-E 4** | | | |
| 4 Dr Sdn | **13424** | 8350 | 9650 |
| *ADD FOR:* | | | |
| Sport Appearance Grp (LX) | **757** | 470 | 520 |
| **FESTIVA 4** | | | |
| 2 Dr L Hbk (NA w/auto trans, or pwr strng) | **7253** | 5000 | 5925 |
| 2 Dr GL Hbk (NA w/pwr strng) | **9358** | 5750 | 6675 |

*Refer to optional equipment schedules*

| Year/Model/<br>Body/Type | Original<br>List | Current<br>Whlse | Average<br>Retail |
|---|---|---|---|
| **ADD FOR:** | | | |
| Sport Opt Pkg | **341** | 230 | 250 |
| **MUSTANG 4** | | | |
| 2 Dr LX Sdn | **11627** | 7750 | 9000 |
| 2 Dr LX Hbk | **11538** | 7900 | 9175 |
| 2 Dr LX Conv | **18311** | 11550 | 13350 |
| **MUSTANG 8** | | | |
| 2 Dr LX 5.0L Sdn | **14834** | 9350 | 10775 |
| 2 Dr LX 5.0L Hbk | **15619** | 9500 | 10950 |
| 2 Dr LX 5.0L Conv | **21056** | 13125 | 15450 |
| 2 Dr GT Hbk | **16655** | 11175 | 12900 |
| 2 Dr GT Conv | **21611** | 14800 | 17375 |
| **ADD FOR:** | | | |
| Leather Seat Trim | | | |
| (LX 5.0L, GT) | **523** | 260 | 290 |
| Cast Alum Wheels | **401** | — | — |
| **PROBE 4** | | | |
| 2 Dr GL Hbk | **13806** | 9025 | 10400 |
| 2 Dr GT Hbk | **16406** | 11425 | 13200 |
| **PROBE 6** | | | |
| 2 Dr LX Hbk | **14806** | 10025 | 11575 |
| **ADD FOR:** | | | |
| Anti-Lock Brakes | **924** | 450 | 500 |
| Leather Seat Trim | **523** | 260 | 290 |
| Elec Instrument | | | |
| Cluster (LX) | **463** | 300 | 330 |
| Cast Alum Whls (GL) | **313** | 200 | 220 |
| **TAURUS 6** | | | |
| 4 Dr L Sdn | **15821** | 10225 | 11800 |
| 4 Dr L Wgn | **16854** | 11050 | 12775 |
| 4 Dr GL Sdn | **16121** | 11025 | 12725 |
| 4 Dr GL Wgn | **17131** | 11850 | 13675 |
| 4 Dr LX Sdn | **17775** | 12450 | 14600 |
| 4 Dr LX Wgn | **19464** | 13275 | 15600 |
| 4 Dr SHO Sdn | | | |
| (NA w/auto trans) | **23839** | 15775 | 18425 |
| **ADD FOR:** | | | |
| 3.8 Liter 6 Cyl Eng | | | |
| (GL, LX Sdn) | **555** | 270 | 300 |
| Anti-Lock Brakes | | | |
| (L, GL, LX) | **595** | 450 | 500 |
| Leather Seat Trim | **515** | 260 | 290 |
| Cast Aluminum Wheels | **389** | 260 | 280 |
| **TEMPO 4\*** | | | |
| 2 Dr GL Sdn | **11367** | 7100 | 8250 |
| 4 Dr GL Sdn | **11517** | 7175 | 8325 |
| 4 Dr LX Sdn | **12495** | 7825 | 9075 |

*For 6 cyl models add $475 whsle/$475 retail.

| Year/Model/<br>Body/Type | Original<br>List | Current<br>Whlse | Average<br>Retail |
|---|---|---|---|
| **TEMPO 6** | | | |
| 2 Dr GLS Sdn | **13215** | 8000 | 9300 |
| 4 Dr GLS Sdn | **13363** | 8100 | 9350 |
| **THUNDERBIRD 6** | | | |
| 2 Dr Cpe | **16345** | 10225 | 11800 |
| 2 Dr LX Cpe | **18783** | 11275 | 13025 |
| 2 Dr Super Cpe | **22641** | 14625 | 17175 |
| **THUNDERBIRD 8** | | | |
| 2 Dr Sport Cpe | **18611** | 10725 | 12375 |
| **ADD FOR:** | | | |
| 8 Cyl (Standard & LX) | **1080** | 710 | 790 |
| Anti-Lock Brakes | | | |
| (Base Sport, LX) | **1085** | 450 | 500 |
| Leather Seat Trim | | | |
| (LX, Sport) | **515** | 260 | 290 |
| (Super Cpe) | **648** | 270 | 300 |

NOTE: Power windows standard on Crown Victoria, Mustang LX Convertible, LX 5.0L & GT, Taurus LX & SHO and Thunderbird. Power door locks standard on Mustang LX Convertible, LX 5.0L & GT and Taurus LX & SHO. Power seat standard on Crown Victoria LX & Touring Sedan, Taurus LX & SHO and Thunderbird LX. Tilt steering wheel standard on Crown Victoria, Taurus, Tempo LX, Thunderbird Sport & LX. Cruise control standard on Crown Victoria Touring Sedan and Taurus SHO.

## 1991

| Year/Model/<br>Body/Type | Original<br>List | Current<br>Whlse | Average<br>Retail |
|---|---|---|---|
| **ESCORT PONY 4** | | | |
| 2 Dr Hbk | | | |
| (NA w/pwr strng) | **8993** | 4525 | 5450 |
| **ESCORT GT 4** | | | |
| 2 Dr Hbk | **13000** | 6600 | 7675 |
| **ESCORT LX 4** | | | |
| 2 Dr Hbk | **10419** | 4975 | 5900 |
| 4 Dr Hbk | **10847** | 5275 | 6200 |
| 4 Dr Wgn | **11432** | 5875 | 6800 |
| **FESTIVA 4** | | | |
| 2 Dr L Hbk (NA w/auto | | | |
| trans or pwr strng) | **6893** | 3500 | 4400 |
| 2 Dr GL Hbk | **9111** | 4100 | 5025 |
| **LTD CROWN VICTORIA 8** | | | |
| 4 Dr Standard Sdn | **18227** | 9100 | 10475 |
| 4 Dr LX Sdn | **18863** | 9875 | 11375 |
| 4 Dr Standard Crown | | | |
| Victoria Wgn | **18083** | 9200 | 10600 |
| 4 Dr Standard Country | | | |
| Squire Wgn | **18335** | 9700 | 11175 |
| 4 Dr LX Wgn | **18833** | 9975 | 11500 |
| 4 Dr Country Squire | | | |
| LX Wgn | **19085** | 10425 | 12025 |

| Year/Model/ Body/Type | Original List | Current Whlse | Average Retail |
|---|---|---|---|
| **MUSTANG 4** | | | |
| 2 Dr LX Sdn | **11727** | 6650 | 7750 |
| 2 Dr LX Hbk | **12233** | 6825 | 7950 |
| 2 Dr LX Conv | **17692** | 10100 | 11650 |
| **MUSTANG 8** | | | |
| 2 Dr LX 5.0L Spt Sdn | **14740** | 8100 | 9350 |
| 2 Dr LX 5.0L Spt Hbk | **15525** | 8250 | 9525 |
| 2 Dr LX 5.0L Spt Conv | **20712** | 11525 | 13300 |
| 2 Dr GT Hbk | **16504** | 9700 | 11175 |
| 2 Dr GT Conv | **21334** | 12950 | 15275 |
| **PROBE 4** | | | |
| 2 Dr GL Hbk | **13412** | 7475 | 8675 |
| 2 Dr GT Hbk | **16748** | 9650 | 11125 |
| **PROBE 6** | | | |
| 2 Dr LX Hbk | **15013** | 8425 | 9725 |
| **TAURUS 4*** | | | |
| 4 Dr L Sdn | **14751** | 7150 | 8300 |
| 4 Dr GL Sdn | **14980** | 7875 | 9150 |
| *For 6 cyl models add $500 whlse/$500 retail. | | | |
| **TAURUS 6*** | | | |
| 4 Dr L Wgn | **15662** | 8400 | 9700 |
| 4 Dr GL Wgn | **15868** | 9125 | 10500 |
| 4 Dr LX Sdn | **17434** | 9775 | 11250 |
| 4 Dr LX Wgn | **19024** | 10450 | 12050 |
| 4 Dr SHO Sdn (NA w/auto trans) | **22132** | 12600 | 14925 |
| **TEMPO 4** | | | |
| 2 Dr L Sdn | **9730** | 5250 | 6175 |
| 4 Dr L Sdn | **9873** | 5350 | 6275 |
| 2 Dr GL Sdn | **10967** | 5875 | 6800 |
| 4 Dr GL Sdn | **11117** | 6000 | 6925 |
| 2 Dr GLS Sdn | **11785** | 6275 | 7300 |
| 4 Dr GLS Sdn | **11932** | 6400 | 7450 |
| 4 Dr LX Sdn | **12089** | 6575 | 7650 |
| 4 Dr All Whl Drv Sdn | **12253** | 7300 | 8475 |
| **THUNDERBIRD 6** | | | |
| 2 Dr Standard Cpe | **15385** | 8625 | 9950 |
| 2 Dr LX Cpe | **17801** | 9550 | 11000 |
| 2 Dr Super Cpe | **21661** | 12575 | 14850 |
| *ADD FOR:* | | | |
| Anti-Lock Brakes (Probe LX & GT) | **924** | 460 | 500 |
| (Taurus) | **985** | 500 | 560 |
| (Thunderbird ex. Super Cpe) | **1085** | 510 | 570 |

| Year/Model/ Body/Type | Original List | Current Whlse | Average Retail |
|---|---|---|---|
| Electronic Instrument Cluster (Probe LX) | **396** | 190 | 210 |
| Leather Bucket Seats (Taurus LX & SHO) | **489** | 250 | 270 |
| (Taurus GL) | **593** | 290 | 320 |
| Leather Seats (Thunderbird LX) | **489** | 250 | 270 |
| (Thunderbird Super Cpe) | **622** | 310 | 340 |
| 5.0L V8 EFI HO Eng (Thunderbird ex. Super Cpe) | **1080** | 510 | 570 |
| Half Brougham Roof (LTD Crown Victoria) | **726** | 300 | 330 |

NOTE: Power brakes standard on all models. Air bag standard on Crown Victoria, Mustang and Taurus. Anti-lock brakes standard on Thunderbird Super Coupe. Power windows standard on Crown Victoria, Mustang LX Standard Convertible, LX 5.0L Sport & GT, Taurus LX Sedan & LX Wagon, SHO and Thunderbird. Power seat standard on Taurus LX Sedan & LX Wagon, SHO and Thunderbird LX.

## 1990

| Year/Model/ Body/Type | Original List | Current Whlse | Average Retail |
|---|---|---|---|
| **ESCORT PONY 4** | | | |
| 2 Dr Hbk (NA w/pwr strng) | **7995** | 3375 | 4275 |
| **ESCORT GT 4** | | | |
| 2 Dr Hbk (NA w/auto trans) | **10588** | 5100 | 6025 |
| **ESCORT LX 4** | | | |
| 2 Dr Hbk | **9324** | 3825 | 4725 |
| 4 Dr Hbk | **9654** | 3925 | 4825 |
| 4 Dr Wgn | **10179** | 4150 | 5075 |
| **FESTIVA 4** | | | |
| 2 Dr L Hbk (NA w/auto trans or pwr strng) | **6564** | 2075 | 2925 |
| 2 Dr L Plus Hbk | **8710** | 2350 | 3225 |
| 2 Dr LX Hbk | **9244** | 2650 | 3550 |
| **LTD CROWN VICTORIA 8** | | | |
| 4 Dr Standard Sdn | **17257** | 7200 | 8350 |
| 4 Dr LX Sdn | **17894** | 7925 | 9200 |
| 4 Dr Standard Crown Victoria Wgn | **17668** | 7300 | 8475 |
| 4 Dr Country Squire Wgn | **17921** | 7750 | 9000 |
| 4 Dr LX Wgn | **18418** | 8025 | 9275 |
| 4 Dr Country Squire LX Wgn | **18671** | 8475 | 9800 |
| **MUSTANG 4** | | | |
| 2 Dr LX Sdn | **11051** | 4875 | 5800 |

| Year/Model/Body/Type | Original List | Current Whlse | Average Retail |
|---|---|---|---|
| 2 Dr LX Hbk | **11557** | 5025 | 5950 |
| 2 Dr LX Conv | **16636** | 8025 | 9275 |
| **MUSTANG 8** | | | |
| 2 Dr LX 5.0L Spt Sdn | **12842** | 6200 | 7225 |
| 2 Dr LX 5.0L Spt Hbk | **13685** | 6350 | 7400 |
| 2 Dr LX 5.0L Spt Conv | **18861** | 9325 | 10750 |
| 2 Dr GT Hbk | **14664** | 7725 | 8975 |
| 2 Dr GT Conv | **19483** | 10700 | 12350 |
| **PROBE 4** | | | |
| 2 Dr GL Hbk | **13139** | 5850 | 6775 |
| 2 Dr GT Hbk | **16275** | 7750 | 9000 |
| **PROBE 6** | | | |
| 2 Dr LX Hbk | **14557** | 6675 | 7775 |
| **TAURUS 4*** | | | |
| 4 Dr L Sdn | **13457** | 4900 | 5825 |
| 4 Dr GL Sdn | **13930** | 5575 | 6500 |
| *For 6 cyl models add $450 whlse/$450 retail. | | | |
| **TAURUS 6** | | | |
| 4 Dr L Wgn | **15089** | 6025 | 6950 |
| 4 Dr GL Wgn | **15539** | 6650 | 7750 |
| 4 Dr SHO Sdn (NA w/auto trans) | **21633** | 9850 | 11350 |
| 4 Dr LX Sdn | **16180** | 7150 | 8300 |
| 4 Dr LX Wgn | **17771** | 7800 | 9050 |
| **TEMPO 4** | | | |
| 2 Dr GL Sdn | **10863** | 4350 | 5275 |
| 4 Dr GL Sdn | **11013** | 4450 | 5375 |
| 2 Dr GLS Sdn | **11680** | 4700 | 5625 |
| 4 Dr GLS Sdn | **11828** | 4775 | 5700 |
| 4 Dr LX Sdn | **11985** | 4925 | 5850 |
| 4 Dr All Whl Drv Sdn | **12148** | 5675 | 6600 |
| **THUNDERBIRD 6** | | | |
| 2 Dr Standard Cpe | **14980** | 7225 | 8400 |
| 2 Dr LX Cpe | **17263** | 8075 | 9325 |
| 2 Dr Super Cpe | **20985** | 10625 | 12250 |
| *ADD FOR:* | | | |
| Air Bag Restraint System (Tempo GL) | **815** | 310 | 340 |
| (Tempo LX) | **690** | 220 | 240 |
| Anti-Lock Brakes (Probe) | **924** | 360 | 390 |
| (Taurus GL Sdn & LX Sdn) | **985** | 360 | 390 |
| (Thunderbird) | **1085** | 390 | 430 |
| Leather Upholstery (Thunderbird LX) | **489** | 170 | 190 |
| (Thunderbird Super Cpe) | **622** | 220 | 240 |
| Brougham Roof (LTD Crown Victoria) | **665** | 170 | 190 |

| Year/Model/Body/Type | Original List | Current Whlse | Average Retail |
|---|---|---|---|

NOTE: Power brakes standard on all models. Power seat standard on Taurus LX & SHO and Thunderbird LX. Power door locks standard on Mustang LX Standard Convertible, Mustang LX 5.0L Sport & GT, Taurus SHO and Thunderbird LX. Power windows standard on Mustang LX Standard Convertible & GT, LTD Crown Victoria Series, Taurus LX & SHO, Thunderbird Series.

## 1989

| | Original List | Current Whlse | Average Retail |
|---|---|---|---|
| **CROWN VICTORIA 8** | | | |
| 4 Dr S Sdn | **15434** | 4800 | 5725 |
| 4 Dr Sdn | **15851** | 5800 | 6725 |
| 4 Dr Wgn | **16209** | 5875 | 6800 |
| 4 Dr LX Sdn | **16727** | 6450 | 7500 |
| 4 Dr LX Wgn | **17238** | 6525 | 7600 |
| 4 Dr Country Squire Wgn | **16527** | 6275 | 7300 |
| 4 Dr Country Squire LX Wgn | **17556** | 6925 | 8050 |
| **ESCORT PONY 4** | | | |
| 2 Dr Hbk (NA w/pwr strng) | **7508** | 2225 | 3075 |
| **ESCORT GT 4** | | | |
| 2 Dr Hbk (NA w/auto trans) | **10003** | 3750 | 4650 |
| **ESCORT LX 4** | | | |
| 2 Dr Hbk | **8877** | 2600 | 3475 |
| 4 Dr Hbk | **9207** | 2700 | 3600 |
| 4 Dr Wgn | **9733** | 2900 | 3800 |
| **FESTIVA 4** | | | |
| 2 Dr L Hbk (NA w/auto trans or pwr strng) | **6124** | 1600 | 2450 |
| 2 Dr L Plus Hbk (NA w/pwr strng) | **7943** | 1825 | 2675 |
| 2 Dr LX Hbk (NA w/pwr strng) | **8567** | 2100 | 2950 |
| **MUSTANG 4** | | | |
| 2 Dr LX Sdn | **10745** | 3500 | 4400 |
| 2 Dr LX Hbk | **11251** | 3650 | 4550 |
| 2 Dr LX Conv | **15835** | 6425 | 7475 |
| **MUSTANG 8** | | | |
| 2 Dr LX Spt Sdn | **13105** | 4675 | 5600 |
| 2 Dr LX Spt Hbk | **13960** | 4800 | 5725 |
| 2 Dr LX Spt Conv | **18696** | 7575 | 8800 |
| 2 Dr GT Hbk | **14967** | 6150 | 7150 |
| 2 Dr GT Conv | **19207** | 8850 | 10225 |
| **PROBE 4** | | | |
| 2 Dr GL Hbk | **12246** | 4450 | 5375 |

# AMERICAN CARS

| Year/Model/Body/Type | Original List | Current Whlse | Average Retail |
|---|---|---|---|
| 2 Dr LX Hbk | **13072** | 4975 | 5900 |
| 2 Dr GT Hbk (NA w/auto trans) | **14865** | 6175 | 7200 |
| **TAURUS 4\*** | | | |
| 4 Dr L Sdn | **12566** | 3450 | 4350 |
| 4 Dr GL Sdn | **12990** | 4050 | 4950 |
| *For 6 cyl models add $400 whlse/$400 retail.* | | | |
| **TAURUS 6** | | | |
| 4 Dr L Wgn | **13931** | 4475 | 5400 |
| 4 Dr GL Wgn | **14332** | 5025 | 5950 |
| 4 Dr SHO Sdn | **19739** | 7575 | 8800 |
| 4 Dr LX Sdn | **15282** | 5425 | 6350 |
| 4 Dr LX Wgn | **16524** | 6050 | 6950 |
| **TEMPO 4** | | | |
| 2 Dr GL Sdn | **10360** | 3050 | 3950 |
| 4 Dr GL Sdn | **10510** | 3125 | 4025 |
| 2 Dr GLS Sdn | **11000** | 3325 | 4225 |
| 4 Dr GLS Sdn | **11151** | 3425 | 4325 |
| 4 Dr LX Sdn | **11459** | 3575 | 4475 |
| 4 Dr All Wheel Drive Sdn | **11648** | 4225 | 5150 |
| **THUNDERBIRD 6** | | | |
| 2 Dr Cpe | **14612** | 5875 | 6800 |
| 2 Dr LX Cpe | **16817** | 6625 | 7700 |
| 2 Dr Super Cpe | **19823** | 8500 | 9825 |
| *ADD FOR:* | | | |
| Sport App Group (Tempo GLS) | **1178** | 370 | 410 |
| Air Bag Restraint System (Tempo GL) | **815** | 290 | 320 |
| (Tempo LX) | **751** | 290 | 320 |
| 3.8 Liter 6 Cyl Eng (Taurus GL Wgn & LX Sdn) | **400** | 150 | 160 |
| (Taurus GL Sdn) | **1072** | 220 | 240 |
| Anti-Lock Brakes (Tbird Base & LX) | **1085** | 340 | 370 |

NOTE: Power brakes standard on all models. Power windows standard on Mustang Convertible and Thunderbird. Power door locks standard on Thunderbird LX.

## 1988½

**ESCORT PONY 4**

| Year/Model/Body/Type | Original List | Current Whlse | Average Retail |
|---|---|---|---|
| 2 Dr Hbk (NA w/power steering) | **7291** | 1700 | 2550 |
| **ESCORT LX 4** | | | |
| 2 Dr Hbk | **8540** | 1950 | 2800 |
| 4 Dr Hbk | **8870** | 2050 | 2900 |
| 4 Dr Wgn | **9396** | 2200 | 3050 |

| Year/Model/Body/Type | Original List | Current Whlse | Average Retail |
|---|---|---|---|
| **ESCORT EXP 4** | | | |
| 2 Dr Luxury Cpe | **9362** | 2100 | 2950 |
| **ESCORT GT 4** | | | |
| 2 Dr Hbk (NA w/auto trans) | **10196** | 3025 | 3925 |
| NOTE: Power brakes standard on all models. | | | |

## 1988

**ESCORT PONY 4**

| Year/Model/Body/Type | Original List | Current Whlse | Average Retail |
|---|---|---|---|
| 2 Dr Hbk | **7115** | 1625 | 2475 |
| **ESCORT GL 4** | | | |
| 2 Dr Hbk | **8362** | 1850 | 2700 |
| 4 Dr Hbk | **8692** | 1950 | 2800 |
| 4 Dr Wgn | **9205** | 2125 | 2975 |
| **ESCORT GT 4** | | | |
| 2 Dr Hbk (NA w/auto trans) | **9665** | 2875 | 3775 |
| **ESCORT EXP 4** | | | |
| 2 Dr Luxury Cpe | **9364** | 2000 | 2850 |
| **FESTIVA 4** | | | |
| 2 Dr L Hbk (NA w/auto trans or power steering) | **5652** | 1175 | 1900 |
| 2 Dr L Plus (NA w/auto trans or pwr strng) | **7002** | 1325 | 2050 |
| 2 Dr LX Hbk (NA w/auto trans or power steering) | **7489** | 1625 | 2475 |
| **LTD CROWN VICTORIA 8** | | | |
| 4 Dr S Sdn | **14675** | 3275 | 4175 |
| 4 Dr Std Sdn | **15241** | 4175 | 5100 |
| 4 Dr LX Sdn | **16157** | 4725 | 5650 |
| 4 Dr Crown Victoria Wgn | **15311** | 4200 | 5125 |
| 4 Dr Country Squire Wgn | **15744** | 4550 | 5475 |
| 4 Dr LX Crown Victoria Wgn | **16455** | 4750 | 5675 |
| 4 Dr LX Country Squire Wgn | **16773** | 5075 | 6000 |
| **MUSTANG 4** | | | |
| 2 Dr LX Sdn | **10138** | 2450 | 3325 |
| 2 Dr LX Hbk | **10644** | 2600 | 3475 |
| 2 Dr LX Conv | **15005** | 5100 | 6025 |
| 2 Dr GT Hbk (8 cyl) | **14048** | 4950 | 5875 |
| 2 Dr GT Conv (8 cyl) | **17193** | 7400 | 8600 |

| Year/Model/Body/Type | Original List | Current Whlse | Average Retail |
|---|---|---|---|
| **TAURUS 4*** | | | |
| 4 Dr L Sdn | **12351** | 2650 | 3550 |
| 4 Dr GL Sdn | **12958** | 3075 | 3975 |
| 4 Dr MT-5 Sdn (NA w/auto trans) | **13471** | 2600 | 3475 |
| *For 6 cyl models add $400 whsle/$400 retail. | | | |
| **TAURUS 6** | | | |
| 4 Dr L Wgn | **13655** | 3450 | 4350 |
| 4 Dr GL Wgn | **14138** | 3975 | 4875 |
| 4 Dr LX Sdn | **14966** | 4300 | 5225 |
| 4 Dr LX Wgn | **15698** | 4825 | 5750 |
| **TEMPO 4** | | | |
| 2 Dr GL Sdn | **9913** | 2325 | 3200 |
| 4 Dr GL Sdn | **10063** | 2425 | 3300 |
| 2 Dr GLS Sdn | **10504** | 2625 | 3525 |
| 4 Dr GLS Sdn | **10655** | 2725 | 3625 |
| 4 Dr LX Sdn | **10992** | 2825 | 3725 |
| 4 Dr All Whl Drive Sdn | **11186** | 3375 | 4275 |
| **THUNDERBIRD 6** | | | |
| 2 Dr Std | **13495** | 3975 | 4875 |
| 2 Dr LX | **15782** | 5050 | 5975 |
| 2 Dr Turbo Cpe (4 cyl) | **17661** | 4625 | 5550 |
| 2 Dr Sport (8 cyl) | **15927** | 4375 | 5300 |
| *ADD FOR:* | | | |
| Leather Seat Trim (Thunderbird) | **415** | 120 | 130 |
| Leather Articulated Sport Seats (Mustang LX Conv) | **780** | 230 | 250 |
| (Mustang GT Conv) | **415** | 120 | 130 |
| Electronic Instrument Cluster (Taurus L, GL & MT-5) | **351** | 110 | 120 |
| (Taurus LX) | **239** | 70 | 80 |
| Premium Lux Pkg (Thunderbird) | **832** | 250 | 270 |
| 5.0 Liter 8 Cyl EFI Eng (Thunderbird Base & LX) | **721** | 220 | 240 |
| 5.0 Liter HO 8 Cyl Eng (Mustang LX) | **2007** | 580 | 650 |

NOTE: Power brakes standard on all models. Power seat standard on Taurus LX. Power locks standard on Tempo LX, Taurus LX and Thunderbird LX. Power windows standard on Taurus LX, Thunderbird LX and Turbo Coupe, Crown Victoria LX and Country Squire LX.

# 1987

| Year/Model/Body/Type | Original List | Current Whlse | Average Retail |
|---|---|---|---|
| **ESCORT PONY 4** | | | |
| 2 Dr Hbk (NA w/auto trans or pwr strng) | **6625** | 1050 | 1775 |

| Year/Model/Body/Type | Original List | Current Whlse | Average Retail |
|---|---|---|---|
| **ESCORT GL 4** | | | |
| 2 Dr Hbk | **8362** | 1225 | 1950 |
| 4 Dr Hbk | **8576** | 1300 | 2025 |
| 4 Dr Wgn | **8857** | 1400 | 2150 |
| **ESCORT GT 4** | | | |
| 2 Dr Hbk (NA w/auto trans) | **9548** | 2075 | 2925 |
| **ESCORT EXP 4** | | | |
| 2 Dr Luxury Cpe | **9129** | 1425 | 2175 |
| 2 Dr Sport Cpe (NA w/auto trans) | **9653** | 1800 | 2650 |
| **LTD CROWN VICTORIA 8** | | | |
| 2 Dr Std Cpe | **14709** | 2550 | 3425 |
| 4 Dr Std Sdn | **14349** | 2700 | 3600 |
| 2 Dr LX Cpe | **15378** | 3050 | 3950 |
| 4 Dr LX Sdn | **15410** | 3175 | 4075 |
| 4 Dr Crown Victoria Wgn | **14315** | 2575 | 3450 |
| 4 Dr Country Squire Wgn | **14567** | 2875 | 3775 |
| 4 Dr LX Crown Victoria Wgn | **15489** | 3075 | 3975 |
| 4 Dr LX Country Squire Wgn | **15741** | 3325 | 4225 |
| **MUSTANG 4** | | | |
| 2 Dr LX Sdn | **9574** | 1975 | 2825 |
| 2 Dr LX Hbk | **9993** | 2125 | 2975 |
| 2 Dr LX Conv | **14355** | 4425 | 5350 |
| 2 Dr GT Hbk (8 cyl) | **13409** | 4225 | 5150 |
| 2 Dr GT Conv (8 cyl) | **17155** | 6275 | 7300 |
| **TAURUS 4** | | | |
| 4 Dr L Sdn | **11438** | 1775 | 2625 |
| 4 Dr GL Sdn | **12410** | 2225 | 3075 |
| 4 Dr MT5 Sdn (NA w/auto trans) | **12117** | 1775 | 2625 |
| 4 Dr MT5 Wgn (NA w/auto trans) | **12678** | 2250 | 3100 |
| **TAURUS 6** | | | |
| 4 Dr L Wgn | **12658** | 2525 | 3400 |
| 4 Dr GL Wgn | **13590** | 3000 | 3900 |
| 4 Dr LX Sdn | **14633** | 3150 | 4050 |
| 4 Dr LX Wgn | **15243** | 3625 | 4525 |
| **TEMPO 4** | | | |
| 2 Dr GL Sdn | **9415** | 1650 | 2500 |
| 4 Dr GL Sdn | **9565** | 1725 | 2575 |
| 2 Dr Sport GL Sdn | **10191** | 1800 | 2650 |
| 4 Dr Sport GL Sdn | **10341** | 1900 | 2750 |
| 2 Dr LX Sdn | **10576** | 1900 | 2750 |
| 4 Dr LX Sdn | **10775** | 2000 | 2850 |

| Year/Model/ Body/Type | Original List | Current Whlse | Average Retail |
|---|---|---|---|
| 2 Dr All Whl Drv Sdn | **10817** | 2400 | 3275 |
| 4 Dr All Whl Drv Sdn | **10967** | 2500 | 3375 |

**THUNDERBIRD 6**

| | Original List | Current Whlse | Average Retail |
|---|---|---|---|
| 2 Dr Std | **13028** | 2625 | 3525 |
| 2 Dr LX | **15357** | 3600 | 4500 |
| 2 Dr Turbo Cpe (4 cyl) | **16600** | 3125 | 4025 |
| 2 Dr Sport (8 cyl) | **15065** | 3625 | 4525 |

ADD FOR:

| | Original List | Current Whlse | Average Retail |
|---|---|---|---|
| Electronic Instrument Cluster (Taurus) | **351** | 80 | 90 |
| 3.0 Liter 6 Cyl Eng w/overdrive trans (Taurus Sdn) | **672** | 210 | 230 |
| 5.0 Liter 8 Cyl EFI Eng (T bird Std & LX) | **639** | 200 | 220 |
| 5.0 Liter HO 8 Cyl Eng (Mustang) | **1885** | 570 | 640 |

NOTE: Power brakes standard on all models. Power windows standard on Taurus LX, 2 Door Crown Victoria, Thunderbird LX and Turbo Coupe.

## 1986

**ESCORT PONY 4**

| | Original List | Current Whlse | Average Retail |
|---|---|---|---|
| 2 Dr Hbk (NA w/auto trans) | **6052** | 725 | 1375 |

**ESCORT L 4**

| | Original List | Current Whlse | Average Retail |
|---|---|---|---|
| 2 Dr Hbk | **7676** | 875 | 1600 |
| 4 Dr Hbk | **7890** | 950 | 1675 |
| 4 Dr Wgn | **8171** | 1050 | 1775 |

**ESCORT LX 4**

| | Original List | Current Whlse | Average Retail |
|---|---|---|---|
| 2 Dr Hbk | **8281** | 1125 | 1850 |
| 4 Dr Hbk | **8495** | 1225 | 1950 |
| 4 Dr Wgn | **8776** | 1300 | 2025 |

**ESCORT EXP 4**

| | Original List | Current Whlse | Average Retail |
|---|---|---|---|
| 2 Dr Luxury Cpe | **8415** | 1150 | 1875 |
| 2 Dr Sport Cpe | **9238** | 1475 | 2300 |

**ESCORT GT 4**

| | Original List | Current Whlse | Average Retail |
|---|---|---|---|
| 2 Dr Hbk | **9177** | 1625 | 2475 |

**LTD 6**

| | Original List | Current Whlse | Average Retail |
|---|---|---|---|
| 4 Dr Sdn | **10794** | 1250 | 1975 |
| 4 Dr Brougham Sdn | **11182** | 1575 | 2425 |
| 4 Dr Wgn | **10894** | 1425 | 2175 |

**LTD CROWN VICTORIA 8**

| | Original List | Current Whlse | Average Retail |
|---|---|---|---|
| 2 Dr Cpe | **13784** | 2000 | 2850 |
| 2 Dr LX Cpe | **14514** | 2375 | 3250 |
| 4 Dr Sdn | **13324** | 2150 | 3000 |
| 4 Dr LX Sdn | **14546** | 2525 | 3400 |

| Year/Model/ Body/Type | Original List | Current Whlse | Average Retail |
|---|---|---|---|
| 4 Dr S Sdn | **12950** | 1500 | 2350 |
| Country Squire Wagon | **13417** | 1950 | 2800 |
| Country Squire LX Wgn | **14579** | 2575 | 3450 |
| Crown Victoria Wgn | **13167** | 1325 | 2050 |
| Crown Victoria LX Wgn | **14329** | 2325 | 3200 |
| Crown Victoria S Wgn | **13230** | 1325 | 2050 |

**MUSTANG 4\***

| | Original List | Current Whlse | Average Retail |
|---|---|---|---|
| 2 Dr LX Sdn | **8461** | 1350 | 2100 |
| 3 Dr LX Hbk | **9016** | 1500 | 2350 |
| 2 Dr LX Conv (6 cyl) | **13641** | 3750 | 4650 |
| 3 Dr GT Hbk (8 cyl) | **12162** | 3300 | 4200 |
| 2 Dr GT Conv (8 cyl) | **15994** | 5050 | 5975 |
| 2 Dr SVO Hbk (auto trans NA on SVO) | **15272** | 4025 | 4925 |

*For 6 cyl models add $300 whsle/$300 retail.

**TAURUS 4**

| | Original List | Current Whlse | Average Retail |
|---|---|---|---|
| 4 Dr L Sdn | **10407** | 1425 | 2175 |
| 4 Dr L Wgn | **11586** | 1825 | 2675 |
| 4 Dr MT5 Sdn | **11038** | 1400 | 2150 |
| 4 Dr MT5 Wgn | **11503** | 1800 | 2650 |

**TAURUS 6**

| | Original List | Current Whlse | Average Retail |
|---|---|---|---|
| 4 Dr GL Sdn | **12145** | 2025 | 2875 |
| 4 Dr GL Wgn | **12613** | 2425 | 3300 |
| 4 Dr LX Sdn | **13412** | 2525 | 3400 |
| 4 Dr LX Wgn | **13921** | 2975 | 3875 |

**TEMPO GL 4**

| | Original List | Current Whlse | Average Retail |
|---|---|---|---|
| 2 Dr Sdn | **8772** | 1150 | 1875 |
| 4 Dr Sdn | **8922** | 1250 | 1975 |

**TEMPO LX 4**

| | Original List | Current Whlse | Average Retail |
|---|---|---|---|
| 2 Dr Sdn | **9769** | 1350 | 2100 |
| 4 Dr Sdn | **9968** | 1450 | 2225 |

**THUNDERBIRD 6\***

| | Original List | Current Whlse | Average Retail |
|---|---|---|---|
| 2 Dr | **11782** | 1825 | 2675 |
| 2 Dr Turbo (4 cyl) | **14905** | 2100 | 2950 |
| 2 Dr Elan | **13316** | 2625 | 3525 |

*For 8 cyl models add $325 whsle/$325 retail.

ADD FOR:

| | Original List | Current Whlse | Average Retail |
|---|---|---|---|
| Sport GL Pkg (Tempo GL) | **983** | 160 | 170 |
| "T" Roof (Mustang) | **1100** | 190 | 210 |
| Moonroof (Taurus, Thunderbird) | **701** | 100 | 120 |
| Interior Luxury Group (LTD Base Wgn) | **388** | 70 | 70 |
| 3.0 Liter 6 Cyl Eng w/overdrive trans (Taurus L Sdn) | **672** | 210 | 230 |
| 5.0 Liter 8 Cyl EFI Eng (Thunderbird) | **639** | 200 | 220 |

| Year/Model/Body/Type | Original List | Current Whlse | Average Retail |
|---|---|---|---|
| 5.0 Liter HO 8 Cyl Eng (Mustang LX Sdn & Hbk) | **1211** | 360 | 400 |
| *DEDUCT FOR:* | | | |
| 2.0 Liter 4 Cyl Diesel | | | |
| Eng (Escort) | **591** | 380 | 380 |
| (Tempo) | **509** | 380 | 380 |

NOTE: Power windows standard on Mustang SVO and Thunderbird Elan. Power brakes standard on all models.

## 1985½

### ESCORT 4

| | | | |
|---|---|---|---|
| 2 Dr Hbk | **6361** | 675 | 1275 |

### ESCORT GL 4

| | | | |
|---|---|---|---|
| 2 Dr Hbk | **7146** | 975 | 1700 |
| 4 Dr Hbk | **7360** | 1075 | 1800 |
| 4 Dr Wgn | **7641** | 1125 | 1850 |
| 2 Dr Diesel Hbk | **7710** | 350 | 625 |
| 4 Dr Diesel Hbk | **7924** | 400 | 725 |
| 4 Dr Diesel Wgn | **8205** | 500 | 925 |

### ESCORT L 4

| | | | |
|---|---|---|---|
| 2 Dr Hbk | **6632** | 775 | 1375 |
| 4 Dr Hbk | **6846** | 900 | 1625 |
| 4 Dr Wgn | **7127** | 950 | 1675 |
| 2 Dr Diesel Hbk | **7196** | 300 | 575 |
| 4 Dr Diesel Hbk | **7410** | 375 | 675 |
| 4 Dr Diesel Wgn | **7691** | 425 | 775 |

## 1985

### ESCORT 4

| | | | |
|---|---|---|---|
| 2 Dr Hbk | **6956** | 650 | 1225 |
| 4 Dr Hbk | **7163** | 750 | 1475 |

### ESCORT GL 4

| | | | |
|---|---|---|---|
| 2 Dr Hbk | **7670** | 950 | 1675 |
| 4 Dr Hbk | **7884** | 1050 | 1775 |
| 4 Dr Wgn | **8061** | 1100 | 1825 |
| 2 Dr Diesel Hbk | **8228** | 350 | 625 |
| 4 Dr Diesel Hbk | **8442** | 400 | 725 |
| 4 Dr Diesel Wgn | **8618** | 425 | 775 |

### ESCORT GT 4

| | | | |
|---|---|---|---|
| 2 Dr Hbk | **8806** | 1225 | 1950 |
| 2 Dr Turbo Hbk | **9686** | 1250 | 1975 |

### ESCORT L 4

| | | | |
|---|---|---|---|
| 2 Dr Hbk | **7212** | 825 | 1525 |
| 4 Dr Hbk | **7427** | 900 | 1625 |
| 4 Dr Wgn | **7641** | 925 | 1650 |
| 2 Dr Diesel Hbk | **7770** | 225 | 475 |
| 4 Dr Diesel Hbk | **7984** | 275 | 550 |
| 4 Dr Diesel Wgn | **8198** | 325 | 600 |

### ESCORT LX 4

| | | | |
|---|---|---|---|
| 4 Dr Hbk | **9136** | 1125 | 1850 |
| 4 Dr Wgn | **9227** | 1175 | 1900 |

### EXP 4

| | | | |
|---|---|---|---|
| 3 Dr Cpe | **7918** | 675 | 1275 |
| 3 Dr Luxury Cpe | **8806** | 925 | 1650 |
| 3 Dr Turbo Cpe | **11003** | 825 | 1525 |

### LTD 4*

| | | | |
|---|---|---|---|
| 4 Dr Sdn | **9828** | 850 | 1550 |
| 4 Dr Brougham Sdn | **10216** | 1100 | 1825 |

*For 6 cyl models add $300 wholesale add $300 retail.

### LTD 6

| | | | |
|---|---|---|---|
| 4 Dr Wgn | **10417** | 1125 | 1850 |

### LTD 8

| | | | |
|---|---|---|---|
| 4 Dr LX Sdn | **12457** | 1675 | 2525 |

### LTD CROWN VICTORIA 8

| | | | |
|---|---|---|---|
| 2 Dr Sdn | **12674** | 1575 | 2425 |
| 4 Dr Sdn | **12674** | 1700 | 2550 |
| Country Squire Wagon | **12862** | 1725 | 2575 |
| 4 Dr S Sdn | **12322** | 1200 | 1925 |
| 4 Dr Wgn | **12612** | 1525 | 2375 |
| 4 Dr S Wgn | **12675** | 950 | 1675 |

### MUSTANG 4*

| | | | |
|---|---|---|---|
| 2 Dr LX Sdn | **8221** | 1050 | 1775 |
| 3 Dr LX Sdn | **8741** | 1200 | 1925 |
| 2 Dr LX Conv (6 cyl) | **12999** | 3000 | 3900 |
| 3 Dr GT Sdn (8 cyl) | **11456** | 2600 | 3475 |
| 2 Dr GT Conv (8 cyl) | **15162** | 4150 | 5075 |
| 3 Dr SVO Sdn (NA w/auto trans) | **15568** | 3575 | 4475 |

*For 6 cyl models add $300 whsle/$300 retail.

### TEMPO GL 4

| | | | |
|---|---|---|---|
| 2 Dr | **8489** | 900 | 1625 |
| 4 Dr | **8489** | 1000 | 1725 |
| 2 Dr Diesel | **8968** | 575 | 1075 |
| 4 Dr Diesel | **8968** | 675 | 1275 |

### TEMPO GLX 4

| | | | |
|---|---|---|---|
| 2 Dr | **9359** | 1075 | 1800 |
| 4 Dr | **9408** | 1175 | 1900 |
| 2 Dr Diesel | **9838** | 725 | 1375 |
| 4 Dr Diesel | **9887** | 775 | 1500 |

### TEMPO L 4

| | | | |
|---|---|---|---|
| 2 Dr | **8381** | 750 | 1475 |
| 4 Dr | **8381** | 850 | 1550 |
| 2 Dr Diesel | **8860** | 225 | 475 |
| 4 Dr Diesel | **8860** | 275 | 550 |

*Refer to optional equipment schedules*

©1993 by Edmund Publications Corporation

| Year/Model/ Body/Type | Original List | Current Whlse | Average Retail |
|---|---|---|---|
| **THUNDERBIRD 6*** | | | |
| 2 Dr | **11205** | 1625 | 2475 |
| 2 Dr Turbo Cpe (4 cyl) | **14340** | 1775 | 2625 |
| 2 Dr Elan | **12886** | 2275 | 3150 |
| 2 Dr Fila | **15956** | 2550 | 3425 |

*For 8 cyl models add $275 whsle/$275 retail.

| *ADD FOR:* | | | |
|---|---|---|---|
| Sport GL Pkg (Tempo GL) | **677** | 70 | 80 |
| "T" Roof (Mustang) | **1100** | 160 | 180 |
| 302 V8 Eng (Mustang LX Sdn) | **1020** | 360 | 400 |

NOTE: Power brakes standard on all models except Base Escort. Vinyl top standard on LTD Crown Victoria Sedan. Power door locks standard on Tempo GLX.

## 1984

| | Original List | Current Whlse | Average Retail |
|---|---|---|---|
| **ESCORT 4** | | | |
| 2 Dr Hbk | **6956** | 350 | 675 |
| 4 Dr Hbk | **7163** | 400 | 725 |
| **ESCORT GL 4** | | | |
| 2 Dr Hbk | **7671** | 525 | 975 |
| 4 Dr Hbk | **7885** | 600 | 1125 |
| 4 Dr Wgn | **8062** | 675 | 1275 |
| 2 Dr Diesel Hbk | **8229** | 110 | 300 |
| 4 Dr Diesel Hbk | **8443** | 150 | 350 |
| 4 Dr Diesel Wgn | **8658** | 200 | 400 |
| **ESCORT GT 4** | | | |
| 2 Dr Hbk | **8806** | 750 | 1475 |
| 2 Dr Turbo Hbk | **9497** | 775 | 1500 |
| **ESCORT L 4** | | | |
| 2 Dr Hbk | **7212** | 400 | 725 |
| 4 Dr Hbk | **7427** | 475 | 875 |
| 4 Dr Wgn | **7641** | 550 | 1025 |
| 2 Dr Diesel Hbk | **7770** | 95 | 300 |
| 4 Dr Diesel Hbk | **7984** | 150 | 350 |
| 4 Dr Diesel Wgn | **8198** | 175 | 375 |
| **ESCORT LX 4** | | | |
| 4 Dr Wgn | **9152** | 700 | 1325 |
| 4 Dr Hbk | **9061** | 625 | 1175 |
| **EXP 4** | | | |
| 3 Dr Cpe | **7866** | 300 | 575 |
| 3 Dr Luxury Cpe | **8752** | 475 | 875 |
| 3 Dr Turbo Cpe | **11110** | 325 | 600 |
| **LTD 4*** | | | |
| 4 Dr Sdn | **9405** | 800 | 1500 |
| 4 Dr Brougham Sdn | **9793** | 950 | 1675 |
| 4 Dr Wgn (6 cyl) | **9902** | 900 | 1625 |

*For 6 cyl models add $200 whsle/$200 retail.

| Year/Model/ Body/Type | Original List | Current Whlse | Average Retail |
|---|---|---|---|
| **LTD CROWN VICTORIA 8** | | | |
| 2 Dr Sdn | **11686** | 1325 | 2050 |
| 4 Dr Sdn | **11686** | 1450 | 2225 |
| 4 Dr S Sdn | **10558** | 950 | 1675 |
| **LTD CROWN VICTORIA WAGONS 8** | | | |
| Country Squire | **11842** | 1450 | 2225 |
| 4 Dr Wgn | **11592** | 1225 | 1950 |
| 4 Dr S Wgn | **10867** | 725 | 1375 |
| **MUSTANG 4*** | | | |
| 2 Dr L Sdn | **8473** | 825 | 1525 |
| 3 Dr L Sdn | **8644** | 900 | 1625 |
| 2 Dr LX Sdn | **8665** | 925 | 1650 |
| 3 Dr LX Sdn | **8871** | 1050 | 1775 |
| 2 Dr LX Conv (6 cyl) | **12785** | 2375 | 3250 |
| 3 Dr GT Sdn | **10956** | 1925 | 2775 |
| 3 Dr GT Turbo Sdn | **11140** | 1325 | 2050 |
| 2 Dr GT Conv (8 cyl) | **14429** | 3250 | 4150 |
| 2 Dr GT Turbo Conv | **14623** | 2625 | 3525 |
| 3 Dr SVO Sdn | **16530** | 2700 | 3600 |

*For 6 cyl models add $200 whsle/$200 retail.

| **TEMPO GL 4** | | | |
|---|---|---|---|
| 2 Dr | **8556** | 475 | 875 |
| 4 Dr | **8556** | 575 | 1075 |
| 2 Dr Diesel | **9114** | 110 | 300 |
| 4 Dr Diesel | **9114** | 125 | 325 |
| **TEMPO GLX 4** | | | |
| 2 Dr | **9018** | 600 | 1125 |
| 4 Dr | **9018** | 675 | 1275 |
| 2 Dr Diesel | **9576** | 175 | 375 |
| 4 Dr Diesel | **9576** | 200 | 400 |
| **TEMPO L 4** | | | |
| 2 Dr | **8333** | 325 | 600 |
| 4 Dr | **8333** | 400 | 725 |
| 2 Dr Diesel | **8891** | 95 | 300 |
| 4 Dr Diesel | **8891** | 95 | 300 |
| **THUNDERBIRD 6*** | | | |
| 2 Dr | **10366** | 1450 | 2225 |
| 2 Dr Turbo Cpe | **13097** | 1400 | 2150 |
| 2 Dr Elan | **13394** | 2000 | 2850 |
| 2 Dr Fila | **14789** | 2175 | 3025 |

*For 8 cyl models add $200 whsle/$200 retail.

## 1983 — ALL BODY STYLES

| | | Current Whlse | Average Retail |
|---|---|---|---|
| ESCORT GL | — | 350 | 625 |
| ESCORT GLX | — | 400 | 725 |
| ESCORT GT | — | 500 | 925 |
| ESCORT L | — | 250 | 500 |
| EXP | — | 200 | 400 |
| FAIRMONT FUTURA | — | 300 | 575 |

©1993 by Edmund Publications Corporation

*Refer to optional equipment schedules*

| Year/Model/Body/Type | Original List | Current Whlse | Average Retail |
|---|---|---|---|
| LTD | — | 750 | 1475 |
| LTD CROWN VICTORIA | — | 1250 | 1975 |
| MUSTANG | — | 750 | 1475 |
| MUSTANG GT | — | 1700 | 2550 |
| MUSTANG GT CONV | — | 2800 | 3700 |
| MUSTANG GLX CONV | — | 2275 | 3150 |
| THUNDERBIRD | — | 1275 | 2000 |

## LINCOLN

### 1992

#### CONTINENTAL 6

| Year/Model/Body/Type | Original List | Current Whlse | Average Retail |
|---|---|---|---|
| 4 Dr Executive Sdn | 32263 | 18800 | 21850 |
| 4 Dr Sig Series Sdn | 34253 | 20650 | 23700 |
| ADD FOR: | | | |
| Styled Aluminum Wheels (Executive) | 556 | 320 | 350 |
| Cellular Telephone | 459 | 270 | 300 |

#### MARK VII 8

| | | | |
|---|---|---|---|
| 2 Dr Bill Blass Designer Series | 32156 | 21225 | 24525 |
| 2 Dr LSC Series | 32032 | 21300 | 24600 |
| ADD FOR: | | | |
| Special Edit Pkg (LSC) | 680 | 450 | 500 |
| Cellular Telephone | 459 | 300 | 330 |

#### TOWN CAR 8

| | | | |
|---|---|---|---|
| 4 Dr Executive Sdn | 31211 | 19275 | 22325 |
| 4 Dr Signature Series | 34252 | 21125 | 24350 |
| 4 Dr Cartier Designer Series | 36340 | 22275 | 25575 |
| ADD FOR: | | | |
| Jack Nicklaus Spec Edit (Signature) | 1279 | 840 | 930 |
| Vinyl Roof | 800 | 530 | 590 |
| Leather Seat Trim (Executive, Signature) | 570 | 270 | 300 |
| Cellular Telephone (Signature, Designer) | 459 | 270 | 300 |
| Alum Whls (Executive) | 556 | 320 | 350 |

NOTE: Power windows, power door locks, power seat, tilt steering wheel and cruise control standard on all models.

### 1991

#### CONTINENTAL 6

| | | | |
|---|---|---|---|
| 4 Dr Executive Sdn | 30335 | 15350 | 18000 |
| 4 Dr Signature Series | 32243 | 17000 | 19650 |

#### MARK VII 8

| | | | |
|---|---|---|---|
| 2 Dr LSC Series | 30362 | 18100 | 20800 |

| Year/Model/Body/Type | Original List | Current Whlse | Average Retail |
|---|---|---|---|
| 2 Dr Bill Blass Designer Series | 30485 | 18050 | 20700 |

#### TOWN CAR 8

| | | | |
|---|---|---|---|
| 4 Dr Executive Sdn | 29581 | 16075 | 18725 |
| 4 Dr Signature Series | 32540 | 17675 | 20325 |
| 4 Dr Cartier Designer Series | 34627 | 18750 | 21800 |
| ADD FOR: | | | |
| Special Edit Pkg (Mark VII LSC) | 680 | 330 | 360 |
| Comfort/Conv Pkg (Continental Executive) | 828 | 390 | 430 |

NOTE: Power anti-lock brakes, air bag, power windows, power door locks and power seat standard on all models.

### 1990

#### CONTINENTAL 6

| | | | |
|---|---|---|---|
| 4 Dr | 29422 | 11675 | 13475 |
| 4 Dr Signature Series | 31346 | 13025 | 15350 |

#### MARK VII 8

| | | | |
|---|---|---|---|
| 2 Dr LSC Series | 29468 | 13650 | 16025 |
| 2 Dr Bill Blass Designer Series | 29246 | 13600 | 15975 |

#### TOWN CAR 8

| | | | |
|---|---|---|---|
| 4 Dr | 27986 | 13050 | 15375 |
| 4 Dr Signature Series | 30721 | 14425 | 16925 |
| 4 Dr Cartier Series | 32809 | 15125 | 17775 |
| ADD FOR: | | | |
| Anti-Lock Brakes (Town Car) | 936 | 380 | 420 |
| Comfort/Conv Pkg (Continental Base) | 819 | 340 | 370 |
| (Town Car Base) | 694 | 280 | 310 |

NOTE: Power brakes, power windows, power door locks and power seat standard on all models. Anti-lock brakes standard on Continental Series and Mark VII Series.

### 1989

#### CONTINENTAL 6

| | | | |
|---|---|---|---|
| 4 Dr | 28032 | 8300 | 9575 |
| 4 Dr Signature Series | 29910 | 9500 | 10950 |

#### MARK VII 8

| | | | |
|---|---|---|---|
| 2 Dr LSC Series | 27569 | 10050 | 11600 |
| 2 Dr Bill Blass Designer Series | 27569 | 10025 | 11575 |

#### TOWN CAR 8

| | | | |
|---|---|---|---|
| 4 Dr | 25562 | 8925 | 10300 |
| 4 Dr Signature Series | 28562 | 10075 | 11625 |

| Year/Model/Body/Type | Original List | Current Whlse | Average Retail |
|---|---|---|---|
| 4 Dr Cartier Series | **29709** | 10750 | 12400 |
| *ADD FOR:* | | | |
| Comfort/Conv Pkg | | | |
| (Town Car Base) | **694** | 220 | 240 |
| (Continental Base) | **819** | 290 | 320 |
| Carriage Roof | | | |
| (Town Car Base) | **1069** | 220 | 240 |
| (Signature Town Car) | **710** | 180 | 200 |
| Electronic Instrument | | | |
| Panel (Town Car) | **822** | 220 | 240 |

NOTE: Power brakes, power windows, power door locks and power seat standard on all models.

## 1988

### CONTINENTAL 6

| | | | |
|---|---|---|---|
| 4 Dr | **26078** | 6550 | 7625 |
| 4 Dr Signature Series | **27944** | 7525 | 8725 |

### MARK VII 8

| | | | |
|---|---|---|---|
| 2 Dr LSC Series | **26380** | 7400 | 8600 |
| 2 Dr Bill Blass Designer Series | **26380** | 7375 | 8550 |

### TOWN CAR 8

| | | | |
|---|---|---|---|
| 4 Dr | **24373** | 6850 | 7975 |
| 4 Dr Signature Series | **27374** | 7825 | 9075 |
| 4 Dr Cartier Designer Series | **28520** | 8525 | 9850 |
| *ADD FOR:* | | | |
| Comfort/Conv Pkg | | | |
| (Continental Base) | **819** | 250 | 270 |
| Carriage Roof | | | |
| (Base Town Car) | **1069** | 160 | 170 |
| (Signature Town Car) | **710** | 160 | 170 |
| Preferred Equip Pkg | | | |
| (Town Car Base) | **2461** | 610 | 680 |
| Elec Instrument | | | |
| Panel (Town Car) | **822** | 180 | 200 |

NOTE: Power brakes, power windows, power door locks and power seat standard on all models.

## 1987

### CONTINENTAL 8

| | | | |
|---|---|---|---|
| 4 Dr | **25484** | 4550 | 5475 |
| 4 Dr Givenchy Designer Series | **27899** | 5425 | 6350 |

### MARK VII 8

| | | | |
|---|---|---|---|
| 2 Dr | **23246** | 4650 | 5575 |
| 2 Dr Bill Blass Designer Series | **25016** | 5500 | 6425 |
| 2 Dr LSC Series | **25016** | 5525 | 6450 |

| Year/Model/Body/Type | Original List | Current Whlse | Average Retail |
|---|---|---|---|
| **TOWN CAR 8** | | | |
| 4 Dr | **22837** | 5075 | 6000 |
| 4 Dr Signature Series | **25743** | 6025 | 6950 |
| 4 Dr Cartier Designer Series | **27026** | 6675 | 7775 |
| *ADD FOR:* | | | |
| Cambria Carriage Roof | | | |
| (Town Car Base & Signature) | **1069** | 120 | 130 |
| Bayville Carriage Roof | | | |
| (Town Car Signature) | **726** | 100 | 110 |
| Electronic Instrument | | | |
| Panel (Town Car) | **822** | 150 | 160 |

NOTE: Power windows, power seat, and power brakes standard on all models.

## 1986

### CONTINENTAL 8

| | | | |
|---|---|---|---|
| 4 Dr | **24556** | 3975 | 4875 |
| 4 Dr Givenchy Designer Series | **26960** | 4575 | 5500 |

### MARK VII 8

| | | | |
|---|---|---|---|
| 2 Dr | **22399** | 4450 | 5375 |
| 2 Dr Bill Blass Designer Series | **23980** | 5000 | 5925 |
| 2 Dr LSC Series | **23980** | 5125 | 6050 |

### TOWN CAR 8

| | | | |
|---|---|---|---|
| 4 Dr | **20764** | 4300 | 5225 |
| 4 Dr Signature Series | **23972** | 4925 | 5850 |
| 4 Dr Cartier Designer Series | **25235** | 5225 | 6150 |
| *ADD FOR:* | | | |
| Electronic Instrument | | | |
| Panel (Town Car) | **822** | 110 | 120 |

NOTE: Power windows, power seat, and power brakes standard on all models.

## 1985

### CONTINENTAL 8

| | | | |
|---|---|---|---|
| 4 Dr | **23066** | 3050 | 3950 |
| 4 Dr Turbo Diesel | **24321** | 2600 | 3475 |
| 4 Dr Valentino Designer Series | **26616** | 3600 | 4500 |
| 4 Dr Valentino Designer Series Turbo Diesel | **27388** | 3125 | 4025 |
| 4 Dr Givenchy Designer Series | **26321** | 3600 | 4500 |
| 4 Dr Givenchy Designer Series | | | |

| Year/Model/Body/Type | Original List | Current Whlse | Average Retail |
|---|---|---|---|
| Turbo Diesel | **27093** | 3125 | 4025 |
| **MARK VII 8** | | | |
| 2 Dr | **22399** | 3225 | 4125 |
| 2 Dr Turbo Diesel | **23633** | 2850 | 3750 |
| 2 Dr Bill Blass Designer Series | **26659** | 3700 | 4600 |
| 2 Dr Bill Blass Designer Turbo Diesel | **27431** | 3225 | 4125 |
| 2 Dr Versace Designer Series | **26578** | 3700 | 4600 |
| 2 Dr Versace Designer Series Turbo Diesel | **27349** | 3225 | 4125 |
| 2 Dr LSC Series | **24332** | 3900 | 4800 |
| 2 Dr LSC Series Turbo Diesel | **25104** | 2850 | 3750 |
| **TOWN CAR 8** | | | |
| 4 Dr | **19458** | 3225 | 4125 |
| 4 Dr Signature Series | **22573** | 3900 | 4800 |
| 4 Dr Cartier Designer Series | **24091** | 4025 | 4925 |
| *ADD FOR:* | | | |
| Carriage Roof (Town Car Signature) | **726** | 60 | 60 |
| (Town Car, Town Car Designer) | **1069** | 60 | 60 |

NOTE: Power windows, power disc brakes, and power seat standard on all models.

## 1984

### CONTINENTAL 8

| | Original List | Current Whlse | Average Retail |
|---|---|---|---|
| 4 Dr | **21757** | 2700 | 3600 |
| 4 Dr Turbo Dsl (6 cyl) | **22991** | 2400 | 3275 |
| 4 Dr Valentino Designer Series | **24205** | 2800 | 3700 |
| 4 Dr Valentino Designer Series Diesel (6 cyl) | **25440** | 2500 | 3375 |
| 4 Dr Givenchy Designer Series | **24230** | 2800 | 3700 |
| 4 Dr Givenchy Designer Series Turbo Diesel (6 cyl) | **25464** | 2500 | 3375 |

### MARK VII 8

| | Original List | Current Whlse | Average Retail |
|---|---|---|---|
| 2 Dr | **21695** | 2850 | 3750 |
| 2 Dr Turbo Diesel (6 cyl) | **22930** | 2525 | 3400 |
| 2 Dr Bill Blass Designer Series | **24795** | 3025 | 3925 |
| 2 Dr Bill Blass Designer Turbo Diesel (6 cyl) | **26030** | 2700 | 3600 |
| 2 Dr Versace | | | |

| Year/Model/Body/Type | Original List | Current Whlse | Average Retail |
|---|---|---|---|
| Designer Series | **24394** | 3025 | 3925 |
| 2 Dr Versace Designer Series Turbo Diesel (6 cyl) | **25628** | 2700 | 3600 |
| 2 Dr LSC Series | **23694** | 3025 | 3925 |
| 2 Dr LSC Series Turbo Diesel (6 cyl) | **24928** | 2725 | 3625 |
| **TOWN CAR 8** | | | |
| 4 Dr | **18059** | 3225 | 4125 |
| 4 Dr Signature Series | **20028** | 3325 | 4225 |
| 4 Dr Cartier Designer Series | **21694** | 3425 | 4325 |

NOTE: Power windows, power disc brakes, vinyl roof and power seat standard on all models.

## 1983 — ALL BODY STYLES

| | Original List | Current Whlse | Average Retail |
|---|---|---|---|
| CONTINENTAL | — | 2350 | 3225 |
| MARK VI | — | 1925 | 2775 |
| TOWN CAR | — | 1550 | 2400 |

## MERCURY

### 1992

#### CAPRI 4

| | Original List | Current Whlse | Average Retail |
|---|---|---|---|
| 2 Dr Conv | **16001** | — | — |
| 2 Dr XR2 Conv (NA w/auto trans) | **17250** | — | — |
| *ADD FOR:* | | | |
| Removable Hardtop Roof | **1383** | 910 | 1010 |
| Aluminum Wheels | **351** | 230 | 250 |

#### COUGAR 6*

| | Original List | Current Whlse | Average Retail |
|---|---|---|---|
| 2 Dr LS Cpe | **16460** | 10725 | 12375 |

*For 8 cyl models add $475 whsle/$475 retail.

#### COUGAR XR-7 8

| | Original List | Current Whlse | Average Retail |
|---|---|---|---|
| 2 Dr XR-7 Cpe | **22054** | 13975 | 16350 |
| *ADD FOR:* | | | |
| Anti-Lock Brakes (LS) | **695** | 645 | 1550 |
| Leather Seat Trim | **515** | 260 | 290 |
| Cast Alum Whls (LS) | **306** | 200 | 220 |

#### GRAND MARQUIS 8

| | Original List | Current Whlse | Average Retail |
|---|---|---|---|
| 4 Dr GS Sdn | **20216** | 14150 | 16600 |
| 4 Dr LS Sdn | **20644** | 15000 | 17600 |
| *ADD FOR:* | | | |
| Anti-Lock Brakes | **695** | 460 | 500 |
| Vinyl Roof | **1185** | — | — |
| Leather Seat Trim | **555** | 260 | 290 |
| Spoke Wheels | **311** | 200 | 220 |

| Year/Model/Body/Type | Original List | Current Whlse | Average Retail |
|---|---|---|---|
| Cast Aluminum Wheels | **440** | 290 | 320 |
| **SABLE 6** | | | |
| 4 Dr GS Sdn | **16418** | 11100 | 12825 |
| 4 Dr LS Sdn | **17368** | 12150 | 14025 |
| 4 Dr GS Wgn | **17396** | 11925 | 13775 |
| 4 Dr LS Wgn | **18395** | 12975 | 15300 |
| *ADD FOR:* | | | |
| 3.8 Liter 6 Cyl Eng | **555** | 360 | 400 |
| Anti-Lock Brakes | **595** | 450 | 500 |
| Leather Seat Trim | **515** | 260 | 290 |
| Aluminum Wheels | **270** | 170 | 190 |
| **TOPAZ 4\*** | | | |
| 2 Dr GS Sdn | **11892** | 7225 | 8400 |
| 4 Dr GS Sdn | **12058** | 7325 | 8500 |
| 4 Dr LS Sdn | **13437** | 8075 | 9325 |
| *For 6 cyl models add $475 whsle/$475 retail.* | | | |
| **TOPAZ 6** | | | |
| 2 Dr XR5 Sdn | **14015** | 8275 | 9550 |
| 2 Dr LTS Sdn | **14807** | — | — |
| *ADD FOR:* | | | |
| Cast Aluminum Wheels | **278** | 180 | 200 |
| **TRACER 4** | | | |
| 4 Dr Ntchbk | **11525** | 7025 | 8150 |
| 4 Dr LTS Ntchbk | **13514** | 8250 | 9525 |
| 4 Dr Wgn | **12285** | 7700 | 8950 |

NOTE: Power windows standard on Capri, Cougar, Grand Marquis, Sable LS, Topaz LS, XR5 & LTS. Power door locks standard on Topaz LS & LTS. Power seat standard on Topaz LTS. Tilt steering wheel standard on Grand Marquis, Sable, Topaz XR5 & LTS, Tracer LTS. Cruise control standard on Capri, Topaz LS & LTS, Tracer LTS.

## 1991

| CAPRI 4 | | | |
|---|---|---|---|
| 2 Dr Conv | **15239** | 8175 | 9450 |
| 2 Dr XR2 Conv (NA w/auto trans) | **16620** | 9300 | 10725 |

| COUGAR 6\* | | | |
|---|---|---|---|
| 2 Dr LS Cpe | **15696** | 9175 | 10575 |

*For 8 cyl models add $475 whsle/$475 retail.*

| COUGAR XR-7 8 | | | |
|---|---|---|---|
| 2 Dr XR-7 Cpe | **20972** | 12100 | 13975 |

| GRAND MARQUIS 8 | | | |
|---|---|---|---|
| 4 Dr GS Sdn | **18741** | 9875 | 11375 |
| 4 Dr LS Sdn | **19241** | 10625 | 12250 |
| Colony Park GS Wgn | **18918** | 10500 | 12125 |
| Colony Park LS Wgn | **19490** | 11300 | 13050 |

| Year/Model/Body/Type | Original List | Current Whlse | Average Retail |
|---|---|---|---|
| **SABLE 6\*** | | | |
| 4 Dr GS Sdn | **15372** | 8575 | 9900 |
| 4 Dr LS Sdn | **16215** | 9500 | 10950 |
| 4 Dr GS Wgn | **16317** | 9325 | 10750 |
| 4 Dr LS Wgn | **17185** | 10175 | 11750 |
| *For models w/231 CID 6 cyl eng add $300 whsle/$300 rtl.* | | | |
| **TOPAZ 4** | | | |
| 2 Dr GS Sdn | **11492** | 5975 | 6800 |
| 4 Dr GS Sdn | **11649** | 6050 | 6950 |
| 2 Dr XR5 Sdn | **12490** | 6550 | 7625 |
| 4 Dr LS Sdn | **13028** | 6700 | 7800 |
| 4 Dr LTS Sdn | **13235** | 7150 | 8300 |
| **TRACER 4** | | | |
| 4 Dr Standard Ntchbk | **11138** | 5425 | 6350 |
| 4 Dr LTS Ntchbk | **13153** | 6625 | 7700 |
| 4 Dr Wgn | **11924** | 6050 | 6950 |
| *ADD FOR:* | | | |
| All Wheel Drive Pkg | | | |
| (Topaz GS) | **1490** | 690 | 770 |
| (Topaz LTS) | **1380** | 690 | 770 |
| (Topaz LS) | **1478** | 690 | 770 |
| Anti-lock Brakes | | | |
| (Cougar LS, Sable) | **985** | 440 | 480 |
| Leather Seats | | | |
| (Cougar LS, Grand Marquis LS, Sable) | **489** | 220 | 240 |
| Formal Coach Vinyl Roof | | | |
| (Grand Marquis) | **726** | 250 | 270 |
| Carrige Roof | | | |
| (Grand Marquis) | **1537** | 390 | 430 |
| Removable Hardtop | | | |
| (Capri) | **1287** | 540 | 600 |

NOTE: Power brakes standard on all models. Anti-lock brakes standard on Cougar XR7. Air bag standard on Capri, Grand Marquis and Sable. Power door locks standard on Capri XR2 and Topaz LS & LTS. Power seat standard on Cougar XR7 and Sable LS. Power windows standard on Capri, Cougar, Grand Marquis, Sable LS and Topaz LS & LTS.

## 1990

| COUGAR 6 | | | |
|---|---|---|---|
| 2 Dr LS Cpe | **15816** | 7800 | 9050 |
| 2 Dr XR-7 Cpe | **20808** | 10150 | 11725 |

| GRAND MARQUIS 8 | | | |
|---|---|---|---|
| 4 Dr GS Sdn | **17784** | 7875 | 9150 |
| 4 Dr LS Sdn | **18284** | 8600 | 9925 |
| Colony Park GS Wgn | **18504** | 8475 | 9800 |
| Colony Park LS Wgn | **19076** | 9200 | 10600 |

| SABLE 6\* | | | |
|---|---|---|---|
| 4 Dr GS Sdn | **15065** | 6200 | 7225 |

| Year/Model/Body/Type | Original List | Current Whlse | Average Retail |
|---|---|---|---|
| 4 Dr LS Sdn | **16067** | 7000 | 8150 |
| 4 Dr GS Sdn | **16010** | 6850 | 7975 |
| 4 Dr LS Wgn | **17038** | 7625 | 8850 |

*For models w/231 CID 6 cyl eng add $300 whlse/$300 rtl.

### TOPAZ 4

| | | | |
|---|---|---|---|
| 2 Dr GS Sdn | **11363** | 4475 | 5400 |
| 4 Dr GS Sdn | **11520** | 4575 | 5500 |
| 2 Dr XR5 Sdn | **12362** | 4975 | 5900 |
| 4 Dr LS Sdn | **12899** | 5150 | 6075 |
| 4 Dr LTS Sdn | **13106** | 5550 | 6475 |

*ADD FOR:*
| | | | |
|---|---|---|---|
| All Wheel Drive Pkg | | | |
| (Topaz GS) | **1490** | 620 | 690 |
| (Topaz LTS) | **1380** | 620 | 690 |
| (Topaz LS) | **1478** | 620 | 690 |
| Anti-Lock Brakes | | | |
| (Cougar LS, Sable) | **985** | 390 | 430 |
| Formal Coach Vinyl | | | |
| Roof (Grand Marquis) | **665** | 220 | 240 |
| Leather Upholstery | | | |
| (Cougar, Grand | | | |
| Marquis, Sable) | **489** | 170 | 190 |

NOTE: Power brakes standard on all models. Power seat standard on Topaz LTS. Power door locks standard on Topaz LS & LTS. Power windows standard on Cougar Series, Grand Marquis Series, Sable LS Topaz LS & LTS. Anti-lock brakes standard on XR-7.

## 1989

### COUGAR 6

| | | | |
|---|---|---|---|
| 2 Dr LS Cpe | **15448** | 6275 | 7300 |
| 2 Dr XR-7 Cpe | **20165** | 8250 | 9525 |

### GRAND MARQUIS 8

| | | | |
|---|---|---|---|
| 4 Dr GS Sdn | **16701** | 6675 | 7775 |
| 4 Dr LS Sdn | **17213** | 7325 | 8500 |
| Colony Park GS Wgn | **17338** | 7200 | 8350 |
| Colony Park LS Wgn | **17922** | 7850 | 9125 |

### SABLE 6*

| | | | |
|---|---|---|---|
| 4 Dr GS Sdn | **14101** | 4800 | 5725 |
| 4 Dr LS Sdn | **15094** | 5500 | 6425 |
| 4 Dr GS Wgn | **14804** | 5375 | 6300 |
| 4 Dr LS Wgn | **15872** | 6125 | 7125 |

*For models w/231 CID 6 cyl eng add $250 whlse/$250 rtl.

### SCORPIO 6

| | | | |
|---|---|---|---|
| Scorpio | **25602** | 7550 | 8775 |

### TOPAZ 4

| | | | |
|---|---|---|---|
| 2 Dr GS Sdn | **10880** | 3250 | 4150 |
| 4 Dr GS Sdn | **11037** | 3325 | 4225 |
| 2 Dr XR5 Sdn | **11801** | 3725 | 4625 |
| 4 Dr LS Sdn | **12333** | 3900 | 4800 |

| Year/Model/Body/Type | Original List | Current Whlse | Average Retail |
|---|---|---|---|
| 4 Dr LTS Sdn | **12495** | 4225 | 5150 |

### TRACER 4

| | | | |
|---|---|---|---|
| 2 Dr Hbk | **9659** | 2425 | 3300 |
| 4 Dr Hbk | **10345** | 2575 | 3450 |
| 4 Dr Wgn | **10829** | 2875 | 3775 |

### XR4Ti 4

| | | | |
|---|---|---|---|
| XR4Ti | **20238** | 5350 | 6275 |

*ADD FOR:*
| | | | |
|---|---|---|---|
| Leather Trim (XR4Ti) | **969** | 270 | 300 |
| Touring Pkg (Scorpio) | **2635** | 580 | 650 |
| All Wheel Drive Pkg | | | |
| (Topaz GS & LS) | **1441** | 520 | 580 |
| (Topaz LTS) | **1332** | 520 | 580 |
| Anti-Lock Brakes | | | |
| (Cougar) | **985** | 270 | 300 |
| Formal Coach Vinyl | | | |
| Roof (Grand Marquis) | **665** | 160 | 170 |

NOTE: Power brakes standard on all models. Power windows standard on Topaz LS, Topaz LTS, Sable, Grand Marquis, Cougar, Scorpio and XR4Ti. Power door locks standard on Topaz LS and LTS, Scorpio and XR4Ti.

## 1988

### COUGAR 6*

| | | | |
|---|---|---|---|
| 2 Dr LS | **14026** | 4475 | 5400 |
| 2 Dr XR-7 (8 cyl) | **16157** | 5575 | 6500 |

*For 8 cyl models add $375 whlse/$375 retail.

### GRAND MARQUIS 8

| | | | |
|---|---|---|---|
| 4 Dr GS Sdn | **16079** | 4825 | 5750 |
| 4 Dr LS Sdn | **16591** | 5375 | 6300 |
| Colony Park GS Wgn | **16428** | 5225 | 6150 |
| Colony Park LS Wgn | **17012** | 5825 | 6750 |

### MERKUR SCORPIO 6

| | | | |
|---|---|---|---|
| Scorpio | **24598** | 4775 | 5700 |

### MERKUR XR4Ti 4

| | | | |
|---|---|---|---|
| XR4Ti | **19492** | 3900 | 4800 |

### SABLE 6

| | | | |
|---|---|---|---|
| 4 Dr GS Sdn | **13772** | 3600 | 4500 |
| 4 Dr LS Sdn | **14765** | 4225 | 5150 |
| 4 Dr GS Wgn | **14413** | 4150 | 5075 |
| 4 Dr LS Wgn | **15432** | 4750 | 5675 |

### TOPAZ 4

| | | | |
|---|---|---|---|
| 2 Dr GS Sdn | **10421** | 2450 | 3325 |
| 4 Dr GS Sdn | **10578** | 2550 | 3425 |
| 2 Dr XR5 Sdn | **11313** | 2950 | 3850 |
| 4 Dr LS Sdn | **11846** | 3050 | 3950 |
| 4 Dr LTS Sdn | **12023** | 3325 | 4225 |

| Year/Model/Body/Type | Original List | Current Whlse | Average Retail |
|---|---|---|---|
| **TRACER 4** | | | |
| 2 Dr Hbk | **9438** | 1825 | 2675 |
| 4 Dr Hbk | **9901** | 1975 | 2825 |
| 4 Dr Wgn | **10386** | 2175 | 3025 |
| *ADD FOR:* | | | |
| Formal Coach Vinyl Roof (Grand Marquis) | **665** | 160 | 170 |
| Leather Seat Trim (Merkur XR4Ti) | **890** | 250 | 270 |
| Touring Pkg (Merkur Scorpio) | **2465** | 400 | 440 |

NOTE: Power brakes standard on all models. Power seat standard on Topaz LTS. Power locks standard on Topaz LS and LTS. Power windows standard on Topaz LS and LTS, Sable LS and Grand Marquis Series.

## 1987

| Year/Model/Body/Type | Original List | Current Whlse | Average Retail |
|---|---|---|---|
| **COUGAR 6\*** | | | |
| 2 Dr LS | **13630** | 3050 | 3950 |
| 2 Dr XR-7 (8 cyl) | **15660** | 4025 | 4925 |
| *For 8 cyl models add $350 whsle/$350 retail.* | | | |
| **GRAND MARQUIS 8** | | | |
| 4 Dr GS Sdn | **15163** | 3225 | 4125 |
| 2 Dr LS Sdn | **15478** | 3550 | 4450 |
| 4 Dr LS Sdn | **15621** | 3700 | 4600 |
| Colony Park GS Wgn | **15500** | 3425 | 4325 |
| Colony Park LS Wgn | **16029** | 3925 | 4825 |
| **LYNX 4** | | | |
| 2 Dr L Hbk (NA w/auto trans) | **6755** | 900 | 1625 |
| 2 Dr GS Hbk | **8507** | 1175 | 1900 |
| 4 Dr GS Hbk | **8721** | 1275 | 2000 |
| 4 Dr GS Wgn | **9003** | 1325 | 2050 |
| 2 Dr XR3 Hbk (NA w/auto trans) | **9630** | 1675 | 2525 |
| **MERKUR XR4Ti 4** | | | |
| XR4Ti | **18259** | 2850 | 3750 |
| **SABLE 6** | | | |
| 4 Dr GS Sdn | **13128** | 2700 | 3600 |
| 4 Dr LS Sdn | **14544** | 3200 | 4100 |
| 4 Dr GS Wgn | **13692** | 3175 | 4075 |
| 4 Dr LS Wgn | **15089** | 3675 | 4575 |
| **TOPAZ 4** | | | |
| 2 Dr GS | **9919** | 1700 | 2550 |
| 4 Dr GS | **10069** | 1775 | 2625 |
| 2 Dr GS Sport | **10574** | 1850 | 2700 |
| 4 Dr GS Sport | **10724** | 1950 | 2800 |
| 4 Dr LS | **11548** | 2050 | 2900 |

| Year/Model/Body/Type | Original List | Current Whlse | Average Retail |
|---|---|---|---|
| *ADD FOR:* | | | |
| Electronic Instrument Cluster (Cougar) | **330** | 80 | 90 |
| Formal Coach Vinyl Roof (Grand Marquis) | **665** | 120 | 130 |

NOTE: Power windows standard on Grand Marquis Series, Sable LS and Topaz LS. Power brakes standard on all models.

## 1986

| Year/Model/Body/Type | Original List | Current Whlse | Average Retail |
|---|---|---|---|
| **CAPRI 4\*** | | | |
| 3 Dr GS | **9603** | 1350 | 2100 |
| 3 Dr 5.0 Liter (8 cyl) | **12421** | 3275 | 4175 |
| *For 6 cyl models add $275 whsle/$275 retail.* | | | |
| **COUGAR 6\*** | | | |
| 2 Dr GS | **12183** | 1975 | 2825 |
| 2 Dr LS | **13519** | 2500 | 3375 |
| 2 Dr XR-7 (4 cyl) | **15454** | 2225 | 3075 |
| *For 8 cyl models add $325 whsle/$325 retail.* | | | |
| **GRAND MARQUIS 8** | | | |
| 2 Dr Sdn | **14242** | 2550 | 3425 |
| 4 Dr Sdn | **14266** | 2700 | 3600 |
| 2 Dr LS Sdn | **14691** | 2975 | 2875 |
| 4 Dr LS Sdn | **14714** | 3125 | 4025 |
| Colony Park Wgn | **14486** | 2750 | 3650 |
| **LYNX 4** | | | |
| 2 Dr Hbk | **6221** | 725 | 1375 |
| 2 Dr L Hbk | **7821** | 900 | 1625 |
| 2 Dr GS Hbk | **8435** | 1175 | 1900 |
| 2 Dr XR3 Hbk | **8869** | 1675 | 2525 |
| 4 Dr L Hbk | **8035** | 1000 | 1725 |
| 4 Dr GS Hbk | **8649** | 1275 | 2000 |
| 4 Dr L Wgn | **8316** | 1100 | 1825 |
| 4 Dr GS Wgn | **8930** | 1325 | 2050 |
| **MARQUIS 4\*** | | | |
| 4 Dr Sdn | **10422** | 1025 | 1750 |
| 4 Dr Brougham Sdn | **10810** | 1350 | 2100 |
| Marquis Wgn (6 cyl) | **11016** | 1500 | 2350 |
| Marquis Brougham Wgn (6 cyl) | **11375** | 1650 | 2500 |
| *For 6 cyl models add $300 whsle/$300 retail.* | | | |
| **MERKUR XR4Ti 4** | | | |
| XR4Ti | **16788** | 2150 | 3000 |
| **SABLE 4\*** | | | |
| 4 Dr GS | **11462** | 2175 | 3050 |
| *For 6 cyl models add $300 whsle/$300 retail.* | | | |
| **SABLE 6** | | | |
| 4 Dr LS Sdn | **13397** | 2725 | 3625 |

| Year/Model/Body/Type | Original List | Current Whlse | Average Retail |
|---|---|---|---|
| 4 Dr GS Wgn | **12599** | 2700 | 3600 |
| 4 Dr LS Wgn | **13891** | 3150 | 4050 |

**TOPAZ 4**

| | | | |
|---|---|---|---|
| 2 Dr GS | **9276** | 1225 | 1950 |
| 4 Dr GS | **9426** | 1300 | 2025 |
| 2 Dr LS | **10415** | 1425 | 2175 |
| 4 Dr LS | **10685** | 1525 | 2375 |

*ADD FOR:*

| | | | |
|---|---|---|---|
| Grand Marquis LS Decor Option | **521** | 80 | 90 |
| "T" Roof (Capri) | **1100** | 170 | 190 |

NOTE: Power brakes standard on all models. Power windows standard on Capri, Cougar GS & LS, Merkur XR4Ti, Topaz LS and Sable LS.

## 1985

**CAPRI 4\***

| | | | |
|---|---|---|---|
| 3 Dr GS | **9363** | 1050 | 1775 |
| 3 Dr 5.0 Liter (8 cyl) | **11716** | 2575 | 3450 |

*For 6 cyl models add $250 whlse/$250 retail.

**COUGAR 6\***

| | | | |
|---|---|---|---|
| 2 Dr | **11606** | 1600 | 2450 |
| 2 Dr LS | **12821** | 2075 | 2925 |
| 2 Dr XR-7 (4 cyl) | **14574** | 1750 | 2600 |

*For 8 cyl models add $275 whlse/$275 retail.

**GRAND MARQUIS 8**

| | | | |
|---|---|---|---|
| 2 Dr Sdn | **13358** | 2075 | 2925 |
| 4 Dr Sdn | **13423** | 2200 | 3050 |
| 2 Dr LS Sdn | **13912** | 2375 | 3250 |
| 4 Dr LS Sdn | **13977** | 2525 | 3400 |
| Colony Park Wgn | **13635** | 2225 | 3075 |

**LYNX 4**

| | | | |
|---|---|---|---|
| 3 Dr Hbk | **6647** | 650 | 1225 |
| 3 Dr L Hbk | **7467** | 825 | 1525 |
| 3 Dr GS Hbk | **7928** | 950 | 1675 |
| 5 Dr L Hbk | **7681** | 900 | 1625 |
| 5 Dr GS Hbk | **8142** | 1050 | 1775 |
| 4 Dr L Wgn | **7805** | 925 | 1650 |
| 4 Dr GS Wgn | **8199** | 1100 | 1825 |
| 3 Dr L Diesel Hbk | **8025** | 325 | 600 |
| 3 Dr GS Diesel Hbk | **8343** | 500 | 925 |
| 5 Dr L Diesel Hbk | **8239** | 450 | 825 |
| 5 Dr GS Diesel Hbk | **8558** | 575 | 1075 |
| 4 Dr Diesel Wgn | **8363** | 600 | 1125 |
| 4 Dr GS Diesel Wgn | **8609** | 550 | 1025 |

**MARQUIS 4\***

| | | | |
|---|---|---|---|
| 4 Dr Sdn | **9950** | 1075 | 1800 |
| 4 Dr Brougham Sdn | **10338** | 1325 | 2050 |
| Marquis Wgn (6 cyl) | **10539** | 1250 | 1975 |

| Year/Model/Body/Type | Original List | Current Whlse | Average Retail |
|---|---|---|---|
| Marquis Wgn w/Brougham Decor Option (6 cyl) | **10899** | 1500 | 2350 |

*For 6 cyl models add $200 whlse/$200 retail.

**MERKUR XR4Ti 4**

| | | | |
|---|---|---|---|
| XR4Ti | **16788** | 1650 | 2500 |

**TOPAZ 4**

| | | | |
|---|---|---|---|
| 2 Dr GS | **8875** | 950 | 1675 |
| 4 Dr GS | **8875** | 1050 | 1775 |
| 2 Dr LS | **10039** | 1125 | 1850 |
| 4 Dr LS | **10088** | 1225 | 1950 |
| 2 Dr GS Diesel | **9354** | 450 | 825 |
| 4 Dr GS Diesel | **9354** | 500 | 925 |
| 2 Dr LS Diesel | **10518** | 725 | 1375 |
| 4 Dr LS Diesel | **10567** | 700 | 1325 |

*ADD FOR:*

| | | | |
|---|---|---|---|
| 5.0 Liter HO 4 bbl 8 Cyl Eng (Capri GS) | **1257** | 110 | 120 |
| Formal Coach Vinyl Roof (Grand Marquis) | **650** | 60 | 60 |
| "T" Roof (Capri) | **1100** | 170 | 190 |

NOTE: Power brakes standard on Capri, Cougar, Grand Marquis, Lynx L and GS, Marquis and Topaz. Vinyl top standard on Grand Marquis. Power windows standard on Capri, Cougar, Grand Marquis and Merkur XR4Ti.

## 1984

**CAPRI 4\***

| | | | |
|---|---|---|---|
| 3 Dr GS | **9133** | 825 | 1525 |
| 3 Dr RS (8 cyl) | **10810** | 1750 | 2600 |
| 3 Dr RS Turbo | **10994** | 1050 | 1775 |

*For 6 cyl models add $200 whlse/$200 retail.

**COUGAR 6\***

| | | | |
|---|---|---|---|
| 2 Dr | **10711** | 1325 | 2050 |
| 2 Dr LS | **11998** | 1675 | 2525 |
| 2 Dr XR-7 (4 cyl) | **14272** | 1300 | 2025 |

*For 8 cyl models add $200 whlse/$200 retail.

**GRAND MARQUIS 8**

| | | | |
|---|---|---|---|
| 2 Dr Sdn | **12308** | 1575 | 2425 |
| 4 Dr Sdn | **12372** | 1700 | 2550 |
| 2 Dr LS Sdn | **12863** | 1775 | 2625 |
| 4 Dr LS Sdn | **12927** | 1900 | 2750 |
| Colony Park Wgn | **12547** | 1700 | 2550 |

**LYNX 4**

| | | | |
|---|---|---|---|
| 3 Dr Hbk | **7086** | 300 | 575 |
| 3 Dr L Hbk | **7347** | 400 | 725 |
| 3 Dr GS Hbk | **7784** | 500 | 925 |
| 3 Dr RS Hbk | **8854** | 725 | 1375 |
| 5 Dr Hbk | **7293** | 375 | 675 |

*1985 Mercury Merkur XR4Ti*

| Year/Model/ Body/Type | Original List | Current Whlse | Average Retail |
|---|---|---|---|
| 5 Dr L Hbk | **7522** | 475 | 875 |
| 5 Dr GS Hbk | **7998** | 600 | 1125 |
| 5 Dr LTS Hbk | **9092** | 600 | 1125 |
| 4 Dr L Wgn | **7776** | 525 | 975 |
| 4 Dr GS Wgn | **8176** | 650 | 1225 |
| 3 Dr L Diesel Hbk | **7904** | 110 | 300 |
| 3 Dr GS Diesel Hbk | **8342** | 125 | 325 |
| 5 Dr L Diesel Hbk | **8118** | 110 | 300 |
| 5 Dr GS Diesel Hbk | **8557** | 250 | 500 |
| 4 Dr L Diesel Wgn | **8334** | 175 | 375 |
| 4 Dr GS Diesel Wgn | **8733** | 275 | 550 |

**MARQUIS 4***

| | | | |
|---|---|---|---|
| 4 Dr Sdn | **9461** | 700 | 1325 |
| 4 Dr Brougham Sdn | **9764** | 875 | 1600 |
| Marquis Wgn (6 cyl) | **9958** | 825 | 1525 |
| Marquis Wgn w/Brougham Decor Option (6 cyl) | **10232** | 950 | 1675 |

**TOPAZ 4**

| | | | |
|---|---|---|---|
| 2 Dr GS | **8874** | 500 | 925 |
| 4 Dr GS | **8874** | 600 | 1125 |
| 2 Dr LS | **9277** | 600 | 1125 |
| 4 Dr LS | **9277** | 700 | 1325 |
| 2 Dr GS Diesel | **9432** | 150 | 350 |
| 4 Dr GS Diesel | **9432** | 200 | 400 |
| 2 Dr LS Diesel | **9834** | 200 | 400 |
| 4 Dr LS Diesel | **9834** | 250 | 500 |

NOTE: Power brakes standard on Capri, Lynx Wagons, Marquis, Grand Marquis, Topaz and Cougar. Power windows standard on Grand Marquis and Cougar LS. .

**1983 — ALL BODY STYLES**

| | | | |
|---|---|---|---|
| CAPRI | — | 725 | 1375 |

| Year/Model/ Body/Type | Original List | Current Whlse | Average Retail |
|---|---|---|---|
| CAPRI RS | — | 1525 | 2375 |
| COUGAR | — | 1225 | 1950 |
| GRAND MARQUIS | — | 1100 | 1825 |
| LN7 | — | 200 | 400 |
| LYNX | — | 350 | 625 |
| MARQUIS | — | 700 | 1325 |
| ZEPHYR | — | 475 | 875 |

## OLDSMOBILE

### 1992

**ACHIEVA 4**

| | | | |
|---|---|---|---|
| 2 Dr S Cpe | **14100** | 9875 | 11375 |
| 4 Dr S Sdn | **14200** | 9875 | 11375 |
| 2 Dr SL Cpe | **15325** | 10725 | 12375 |
| 4 Dr SL Sdn | **15425** | 10725 | 12375 |

*ADD FOR:*

| | | | |
|---|---|---|---|
| 2.3 Liter 16V 4 Cyl Eng (S) | **410** | 270 | 300 |
| Styled Aluminum Wheels (S) | **391** | 260 | 280 |
| (SL) | **218** | 150 | 160 |

**CUSTOM CRUISER 8**

| | | | |
|---|---|---|---|
| 4 Dr Wgn | **20995** | 17000 | 19650 |

*ADD FOR:*

| | | | |
|---|---|---|---|
| 5.7 Liter 8 Cyl Eng | **250** | 160 | 180 |
| Leather Seat Trim | **515** | 260 | 290 |
| Cast Aluminum Wheels | **330** | 220 | 240 |

**CUTLASS CIERA 4***

| Year/Model/Body/Type | Original List | Current Whsle | Average Retail |
|---|---|---|---|
| 4 Dr S Sdn | **13585** | 9425 | 10850 |
| 4 Dr S Cruiser Wgn | **14690** | 9850 | 11350 |
| 4 Dr SL Sdn (6 cyl) | **16895** | 10575 | 12200 |
| 4 Dr SL Cruiser Wgn (6 cyl) | **17395** | 11225 | 12975 |

*For 6 cyl models add $500 whsle/$500 retail.

ADD FOR:

| | | | |
|---|---|---|---|
| Leather Seat Trim (SL) | **515** | 260 | 290 |
| Wire Wheel Discs | **240** | 160 | 170 |
| Styled Aluminum Wheels | **295** | 190 | 210 |

### CUTLASS SUPREME 6

| | | | |
|---|---|---|---|
| 2 Dr S Cpe | **15695** | 11275 | 13025 |
| 4 Dr S Sdn | **15795** | 11275 | 13025 |
| 2 Dr Conv | **21995** | — | — |
| 2 Dr International Cpe | **21795** | 13625 | 16000 |
| 4 Dr International Sdn | **21895** | 13625 | 16000 |

ADD FOR:

| | | | |
|---|---|---|---|
| 3.4 Liter 6 Cyl Eng (S Cpe) | **1285** | 660 | 660 |
| (S Sdn) | **1570** | 710 | 710 |
| Anti-Lock Brakes (S, Conv) | **450** | 370 | 410 |
| Leather Seat Trim (S, Conv) | **515** | 260 | 290 |
| (International) | **425** | 260 | 290 |
| Cast Aluminum Wheels | **285** | 180 | 200 |

### EIGHTY-EIGHT ROYALE 6

| | | | |
|---|---|---|---|
| 4 Dr Sdn | **18495** | 13425 | 15750 |
| 4 Dr LS Sdn | **21395** | 14625 | 17175 |

ADD FOR:

| | | | |
|---|---|---|---|
| LSS Pkg (LS) | **1995** | 1310 | 1450 |
| Anti-Lock Brakes (Base) | **450** | 370 | 410 |
| Electronic Instrument Cluster (LS) | **449** | 270 | 300 |
| Wire Wheel Discs | **240** | 160 | 170 |
| Styled Aluminum Wheels | **274** | 180 | 200 |

### NINETY-EIGHT REGENCY 6

| | | | |
|---|---|---|---|
| 4 Dr Sdn | **24595** | 16050 | 18700 |

### NINETY-EIGHT REGENCY ELITE 6

| | | | |
|---|---|---|---|
| 4 Dr Sdn | **26195** | 17450 | 20100 |

### NINETY-EIGHT TOURING 6

| | | | |
|---|---|---|---|
| 4 Dr Sdn | **28995** | 19725 | 22775 |

ADD FOR:

| | | | |
|---|---|---|---|
| 3.8 Liter Supercharged 6 Cyl Eng (Touring) | **1022** | 670 | 750 |
| Elec Instrument Cluster (Regency, Elite) | **449** | 290 | 320 |
| Leather Seat Trim (Regency, Elite) | **515** | 260 | 290 |

### TORONADO 6

| | Original List | Current Whsle | Average Retail |
|---|---|---|---|
| 2 Dr Cpe | **24695** | 15900 | 18550 |
| 2 Dr Trofeo Cpe | **27295** | 18075 | 20750 |

ADD FOR:

| | | | |
|---|---|---|---|
| Visual Info System | **1295** | 730 | 810 |
| Leather Seat Trim (Base) | **425** | 260 | 290 |
| Mobile Telephone | **995** | 270 | 300 |

NOTE: Power windows standard on Cutlass Supreme Convertible & Intl., Eighty-Eight Royale, Ninety-Eight and Toronado. Power door locks standard on Achieva, Cutlass Ciera, Cutlass Supreme Intl., Eight-Eight Royale LS, Ninety-Eight and Toronado. Power seat standard on Cutlass Ciera SL, Ninety-Eight Elite & Touring and Toronado. Tilt steering wheel standard on Cutlass Supreme Intl., Eighty-Eight Royale, Custom Cruiser, Ninety-Eight and Toronado. Cruise control standard on Cutlass Supreme International, Eighty-Eight Royale LS, Ninety-Eight and Toronado.

## 1991

### BRAVADA 6

| | | | |
|---|---|---|---|
| 4 Dr 4WD Wgn | **23795** | 15600 | 18250 |

### CUSTOM CRUISER 8

| | | | |
|---|---|---|---|
| 4 Dr Wgn | **20495** | 14200 | 16675 |

### CUTLASS CALAIS 4*

| | | | |
|---|---|---|---|
| 2 Dr Cpe | **11595** | 6325 | 7350 |
| 4 Dr Sdn | **11595** | 6325 | 7350 |
| 2 Dr S Cpe | **11795** | 6825 | 7950 |
| 4 Dr S Sdn | **12895** | 6825 | 7950 |
| 2 Dr SL Cpe | **15095** | 7575 | 8800 |
| 4 Dr SL Sdn | **15195** | 7575 | 8800 |
| 2 Dr International Cpe | **16295** | 8875 | 10250 |
| 4 Dr International Sdn | **16395** | 8875 | 10250 |

*For models w/quad 4 eng (std on SL) add $375 whsle/$375 retail.

### CUTLASS CIERA 4*

| | | | |
|---|---|---|---|
| 4 Dr Sdn | **13325** | 7100 | 8250 |
| 2 Dr S Cpe | **14225** | 7325 | 8500 |
| 4 Dr S Sdn | **13825** | 7425 | 8625 |
| 4 Dr S Cruiser Wgn | **14725** | 7825 | 9075 |
| 4 Dr SL Sdn (6 cyl) | **15895** | 8500 | 9825 |
| 4 Dr SL Cruiser Wgn (6 cyl) | **16595** | 9075 | 10450 |

*For 6 cyl models add $450 whsle/$450 retail.

### CUTLASS SUPREME 4*

| | | | |
|---|---|---|---|
| 2 Dr Cpe | **14995** | 8700 | 10050 |
| 4 Dr Sdn | **15095** | 8700 | 10050 |
| 2 Dr SL Cpe (6 cyl) | **16895** | 9650 | 11125 |
| 4 Dr SL Sdn (6 cyl) | **16995** | 9650 | 11125 |
| 2 Dr Intl Cpe (6 cyl) | **19695** | 10900 | 12575 |
| 4 Dr Intl Sdn (6 cyl) | **19795** | 10900 | 12575 |
| 2 Dr Conv Cpe (6 cyl) | **20995** | — | — |

*For 6 cyl models add $200 whsle/$200 retail.

| Year/Model/Body/Type | Original List | Current Whlse | Average Retail |
|---|---|---|---|
| **EIGHTY-EIGHT ROYALE 6** | | | |
| 2 Dr Cpe | **17095** | 9275 | 10675 |
| 4 Dr Sdn | **17195** | 9425 | 10850 |
| 2 Dr Brougham Cpe | **18695** | 10250 | 11825 |
| 4 Dr Brougham Sdn | **18795** | 10400 | 12000 |
| **NINETY-EIGHT REGENCY 6** | | | |
| 4 Dr Elite Sdn | **23695** | 14625 | 17175 |
| **NINETY-EIGHT TOURING SEDAN 6** | | | |
| 4 Dr Sdn | **28595** | 16575 | 19225 |
| **TORONADO 6** | | | |
| 2 Dr Cpe | **23795** | 12850 | 15175 |
| 2 Dr Trofeo Cpe | **26495** | 14750 | 17325 |
| *ADD FOR:* | | | |
| Anti-lock Brakes | | | |
| (Cutlass Supreme) | **925** | 390 | 430 |
| Leather Pkg (Bravada) | **545** | 240 | 260 |
| (Calais Intl Toronado Base) | **425** | 180 | 200 |
| (Custom Cruiser, Ciera SL Sdn, Cutlass Supreme, Ninety-Eight Elite) | **515** | 230 | 250 |

NOTE: Power brakes standard on all models. Anti-lock brakes standard on Custom Cruiser, Calais International and Ninety-Eight. Air bag standard on Custom Cruiser, Ninety-Eight and Toronado. Power window standard on Cutlass Supreme Convertible, Ninety-Eight and Toronado. Power door locks standard on Cutlass Supreme International, Ninety-Eight and Toronado. Power seat standard on Custom Cruiser, Ciera SL, Cutlass Supreme International, Ninety-Eight and Toronado.

## 1990

| Year/Model/Body/Type | Original List | Current Whlse | Average Retail |
|---|---|---|---|
| **CUSTOM CRUISER 8** | | | |
| 4 Dr Wgn | **17595** | 8175 | 9450 |
| **CUTLASS CALAIS 4*** | | | |
| 2 Dr Cpe | **11255** | 4825 | 5750 |
| 4 Dr Sdn | **11255** | 4825 | 5750 |
| 2 Dr S Cpe | **12155** | 5225 | 6150 |
| 4 Dr S Sdn | **12255** | 5225 | 6150 |
| 2 Dr SL Cpe | **13915** | 5950 | 6875 |
| 4 Dr SL Sdn | **14015** | 5950 | 6875 |
| 2 Dr International Cpe | **14895** | 7125 | 8275 |
| 4 Dr International Sdn | **14995** | 7125 | 8275 |

*For 6 cyl models add $300 whsle/$300 retail.

| Year/Model/Body/Type | Original List | Current Whlse | Average Retail |
|---|---|---|---|
| **CUTLASS CIERA 4*** | | | |
| 4 Dr Sdn | **12800** | 5025 | 5950 |
| 2 Dr S Cpe | **13000** | 5250 | 6175 |
| 4 Dr S Sdn | **13300** | 5350 | 6275 |
| 4 Dr Cruiser Wgn | **14200** | 5725 | 6650 |

| Year/Model/Body/Type | Original List | Current Whlse | Average Retail |
|---|---|---|---|
| 4 Dr SL Sdn (6 cyl) | **14695** | 6325 | 7350 |
| 4 Dr SL Cruiser Wgn (6 cyl) | **15295** | 6825 | 7950 |
| 2 Dr Intl Cpe (6 cyl) | **15995** | 7550 | 8775 |
| 4 Dr Intl Sdn (6 cyl) | **16795** | 7650 | 8875 |

*For 6 cyl models add $400 whsle/$400 retail.

| Year/Model/Body/Type | Original List | Current Whlse | Average Retail |
|---|---|---|---|
| **CUTLASS SUPREME 4*** | | | |
| 2 Dr Cpe | **14495** | 6600 | 7675 |
| 4 Dr Sdn | **14595** | 6600 | 7675 |
| 2 Dr International Cpe | **17995** | 8450 | 9750 |
| 4 Dr International Sdn | **17995** | 8450 | 9750 |
| 2 Dr SL Cpe (6 cyl) | **16095** | 7450 | 8650 |
| 4 Dr SL Sdn (6 cyl) | **16195** | 7450 | 8650 |

*For 6 cyl models add $200 whsle/$200 retail.

| Year/Model/Body/Type | Original List | Current Whlse | Average Retail |
|---|---|---|---|
| **EIGHTY-EIGHT ROYALE 6** | | | |
| 2 Dr Cpe | **15895** | 7325 | 8500 |
| 4 Dr Sdn | **15995** | 7475 | 8675 |
| 2 Dr Brougham Cpe | **17295** | 8275 | 9550 |
| 4 Dr Brougham Sdn | **17395** | 8425 | 9725 |
| **NINETY-EIGHT REGENCY 6** | | | |
| 4 Dr Sdn | **19995** | 8925 | 10300 |
| 4 Dr Brougham Sdn | **21595** | 9825 | 11325 |
| **TORONADO 6** | | | |
| 2 Dr Cpe | **21995** | 9925 | 11425 |
| 2 Dr Trofeo Cpe | **24995** | 11450 | 13225 |
| **TOURING SEDAN** | | | |
| 4 Dr Sdn | **26795** | 11625 | 13425 |
| *ADD FOR:* | | | |
| Air Bag Supplemental Restraint System (Eighty-Eight, Ninety-Eight) | **850** | 320 | 350 |
| Anti-Lock Brakes (Cutlass Supreme, Eighty-Eight, Toronado Base) | **925** | 350 | 380 |
| Visual Information Center (Toronado) | **1295** | 450 | 500 |
| 2.3 Liter Quad 4 Eng (Cutlass Calais S) | **660** | 250 | 270 |
| (Cutlass Calais Intl) | **400** | 150 | 160 |
| (Cutlass Supreme Base) | **325** | 120 | 130 |

NOTE: Power brakes standard on all models. Power door locks and power seat standard on Cutlass Supreme International.

## 1989

| Year/Model/Body/Type | Original List | Current Whlse | Average Retail |
|---|---|---|---|
| **CUSTOM CRUISER 8** | | | |
| 4 Dr Wgn | **16795** | 6550 | 7625 |

©1993 by Edmund Publications Corporation

*Refer to optional equipment schedules*

| Year/Model/Body/Type | Original List | Current Whlse | Average Retail |
|---|---|---|---|
| **CUTLASS CALAIS 4\*** | | | |
| 2 Dr Cpe | **11505** | 3875 | 4775 |
| 4 Dr Sdn | **11505** | 3875 | 4775 |
| 2 Dr S Cpe | **12585** | 4300 | 5225 |
| 4 Dr S Sdn | **12685** | 4300 | 5225 |
| 2 Dr SL Cpe | **13585** | 4650 | 5575 |
| 4 Dr SL Sdn | **13685** | 4650 | 5575 |
| 2 Dr International Cpe | **14910** | 5750 | 6675 |
| 4 Dr International Sdn | **15010** | 5750 | 6675 |

*For models with quad 4 or 6 cyl engs add $350 whlse/$350 retail.*

| Year/Model/Body/Type | Original List | Current Whlse | Average Retail |
|---|---|---|---|
| **CUTLASS CIERA 4\*** | | | |
| 2 Dr Cpe | **12721** | 3875 | 4775 |
| 4 Dr Sdn | **13221** | 3975 | 4875 |
| 4 Dr Cruiser Wgn | **14563** | 4275 | 5200 |
| 2 Dr SL Cpe | **13985** | 4400 | 5325 |
| 4 Dr SL Sdn | **14795** | 4500 | 5425 |
| 4 Dr SL Cruiser Wgn | **16014** | 4875 | 5800 |
| 2 Dr Intl Cpe (6 cyl) | **15995** | 5925 | 6850 |
| 4 Dr Intl Sdn (6 cyl) | **16795** | 6025 | 6950 |

*For 6 cyl models add $375 whlse/$375 retail.*

| Year/Model/Body/Type | Original List | Current Whlse | Average Retail |
|---|---|---|---|
| **CUTLASS SUPREME 6** | | | |
| 2 Dr Cpe | **14370** | 5300 | 6225 |
| 2 Dr SL Cpe | **15270** | 5925 | 6850 |
| 2 Dr International Cpe | **16995** | 6875 | 8000 |
| **EIGHTY-EIGHT ROYALE 6** | | | |
| 2 Dr Cpe | **15195** | 5825 | 6750 |
| 4 Dr Sdn | **15295** | 5975 | 6900 |
| 2 Dr Brougham Cpe | **16295** | 6625 | 7700 |
| 4 Dr Brougham Sdn | **16395** | 6750 | 7850 |
| **NINETY-EIGHT REGENCY 6** | | | |
| 4 Dr Sdn | **19295** | 6775 | 7875 |
| 4 Dr Brougham Sdn | **20495** | 7525 | 8725 |
| **TORONADO 6** | | | |
| 2 Dr Cpe | **21995** | 7800 | 9050 |
| 2 Dr Trofeo Cpe | **24995** | 8925 | 10300 |
| **TOURING SEDAN 6** | | | |
| 4 Dr Sdn | **25995** | 9150 | 10550 |
| *ADD FOR:* | | | |
| 2.3 Liter Quad 4 Eng (Cutlass Calais) | **660** | 200 | 220 |
| Quad 4 App Pkg (Cutlass Calais S) | **1180** | 360 | 400 |
| Anti-Lock Brakes (Cutlass Supreme, 88, 98, Toronado) | **925** | 270 | 300 |
| Visual Info Sys (Toronado) | **1295** | 360 | 400 |

NOTE: Power brakes standard on all models. Power windows, power locks and power seat standard on 98, Touring Sedan and Toronado.

| Year/Model/Body/Type | Original List | Current Whlse | Average Retail |
|---|---|---|---|
| **1988** | | | |
| **CUSTOM CRUISER 8** | | | |
| 4 Dr Wgn | **15655** | 5125 | 6050 |
| **CUTLASS CALAIS 4\*** | | | |
| 2 Dr Cpe | **11485** | 3250 | 4150 |
| 4 Dr Sdn | **11485** | 3250 | 4150 |
| 2 Dr SL Cpe | **12360** | 3550 | 4450 |
| 4 Dr SL Sdn | **12360** | 3550 | 4450 |
| 2 Dr Intl Cpe (quad 4 eng) | **14185** | 4375 | 5300 |
| 4 Dr Intl Sdn (quad 4 eng) | **14185** | 4375 | 5300 |

*For models with quad 4 or 6 cyl engs add $300 whlse/$300 retail.*

| Year/Model/Body/Type | Original List | Current Whlse | Average Retail |
|---|---|---|---|
| **CUTLASS CIERA 4\*** | | | |
| 2 Dr Cpe | **11770** | 2950 | 3850 |
| 4 Dr Sdn | **12431** | 3050 | 3950 |
| 4 Dr Cruiser Wgn | **13095** | 3250 | 4150 |
| 2 Dr SL Cpe | **12620** | 3375 | 4275 |
| 4 Dr Brougham Sdn | **13400** | 3475 | 4375 |
| 4 Dr Brougham Cruiser Wgn | **13770** | 3725 | 4625 |
| 2 Dr Intl Cpe (6 cyl) | **14995** | 4675 | 5600 |
| 4 Dr Intl Sdn (6 cyl) | **15825** | 4750 | 5675 |

*For 6 cyl models add $325 whlse/$325 retail.*

| Year/Model/Body/Type | Original List | Current Whlse | Average Retail |
|---|---|---|---|
| **CUTLASS SUPREME 6** | | | |
| 2 Dr Cpe | **13621** | 4325 | 5250 |
| 2 Dr SL Cpe | **14270** | 4800 | 5725 |
| 2 Dr International Cpe | **16259** | 5425 | 6350 |
| **CUTLASS SUPREME CLASSIC 8** | | | |
| 2 Dr Cpe | **13938** | 4825 | 5750 |
| 2 Dr Brougham Cpe | **14770** | 5325 | 6250 |
| **DELTA 88 ROYALE 6** | | | |
| 2 Dr Cpe | **14498** | 4050 | 4950 |
| 4 Dr Sdn | **14498** | 4200 | 5125 |
| 2 Dr Brougham Cpe | **15451** | 4725 | 5650 |
| 4 Dr Brougham Sdn | **15451** | 4850 | 5775 |
| **FIRENZA 4** | | | |
| 2 Dr Cpe | **10675** | 3000 | 3900 |
| 4 Dr Sdn | **10675** | 3100 | 4000 |
| 4 Dr Cruiser Wgn | **11375** | 3250 | 4150 |
| **NINETY-EIGHT REGENCY 6** | | | |
| 4 Dr Sdn | **17995** | 5075 | 6000 |
| 4 Dr Brougham Sdn | **19371** | 5750 | 6675 |
| **TORONADO 6** | | | |
| 2 Dr Cpe | **20598** | 5650 | 6575 |
| 2 Dr Trofeo Cpe | **22695** | 6325 | 7350 |
| **TOURING SEDAN 6** | | | |
| 4 Dr Sdn | **24470** | 7100 | 8250 |

| Year/Model/ Body/Type | Original List | Current Whlse | Average Retail |
|---|---|---|---|
| **ADD FOR:** | | | |
| Spt Option Pkg (Firenza) | **617** | 150 | 160 |
| Anti-Lock Braking (Ninety-Eight) | **925** | 220 | 240 |
| Deluxe Mobile Phone (Toronado) | **1795** | 150 | 160 |

NOTE: Power brakes standard on all models. Power seat standard on Touring Sedan and Toronado Series. Power windows and power door locks standard on Ninety-Eight Series, Touring Sedan and Toronado Series.

## 1987

### CALAIS 4*

| | Original List | Current Whlse | Average Retail |
|---|---|---|---|
| 2 Dr Cpe | **10906** | 2400 | 3275 |
| 4 Dr Sdn | **10906** | 2400 | 3275 |
| 2 Dr Supreme Cpe | **11562** | 2650 | 3550 |
| 4 Dr Supreme Sdn | **11562** | 2650 | 3550 |

*For 6 cyl models add $300 whsle/$300 retail.

### CUSTOM CRUISER 8

| | | | |
|---|---|---|---|
| 4 Dr Wgn | **14420** | 3700 | 4600 |

### CUTLASS CIERA 4*

| | | | |
|---|---|---|---|
| 2 Dr 'S' Cpe | **11715** | 2225 | 3075 |
| 4 Dr Sdn | **11715** | 2300 | 3175 |
| 4 Dr Cruiser | **12208** | 2525 | 3400 |
| 2 Dr 'SL' Cpe | **12522** | 2625 | 3525 |
| 4 Dr Brougham Sdn | **12522** | 2725 | 3625 |
| 4 Dr Brougham Cruiser | **12870** | 2950 | 3850 |

*For 6 cyl models add $300 whsle/$300 retail.

### CUTLASS SUPREME 6*

| | | | |
|---|---|---|---|
| 2 Dr Cpe | **12314** | 2975 | 3875 |
| 4 Dr Sdn | **12314** | 2775 | 3675 |
| 2 Dr Brougham Cpe | **13153** | 3275 | 4175 |
| 4 Dr Brougham Sdn | **13153** | 3125 | 4025 |
| 2 Dr Salon Cpe | **13472** | 3650 | 4550 |

*For 8 cyl models add $350 whsle/$350 retail.

### DELTA 88 ROYALE 6

| | | | |
|---|---|---|---|
| 2 Dr Cpe | **13639** | 3150 | 4050 |
| 4 Dr Sdn | **13639** | 3275 | 4175 |
| 2 Dr Brougham Cpe | **14536** | 3700 | 4600 |
| 4 Dr Brougham Sdn | **14536** | 3850 | 4750 |

### FIRENZA 4

| | | | |
|---|---|---|---|
| 2 Dr Cpe | **9931** | 1950 | 2800 |
| 2 Dr 'S' Hbk | **10366** | 2050 | 2900 |
| 4 Dr Sdn | **9889** | 2050 | 2900 |
| 4 Dr Cruiser Wgn | **10536** | 2175 | 3025 |
| 2 Dr 'LC' Cpe | **10804** | 2275 | 3150 |
| 2 Dr 'GT' Hbk (6 cyl) | **12199** | 2750 | 3650 |
| 4 Dr 'LX' Sdn | **10572** | 2375 | 3250 |

### NINETY-EIGHT 6

| | | | |
|---|---|---|---|
| 4 Dr Sdn | **17371** | 3700 | 4600 |

| Year/Model/ Body/Type | Original List | Current Whlse | Average Retail |
|---|---|---|---|
| 2 Dr Brougham Cpe | **18388** | 4100 | 5025 |
| 4 Dr Brougham Sdn | **18388** | 4250 | 5175 |
| 4 Dr Touring Sdn | **24107** | 5925 | 6850 |

### TORONADO 6

| | | | |
|---|---|---|---|
| 2 Dr Brougham Cpe | **19938** | 3975 | 4875 |

| **ADD FOR:** | | | |
|---|---|---|---|
| Calais GT Pkg (Base Calais) | **1350** | 330 | 360 |
| Ciera GT Pkg (S Cpe) (Base Ciera Sdn)' | **3060** | 730 | 810 |
| | **3060** | 730 | 810 |
| Ninety-Eight Grande Premium Interior Pkg (Ninety-Eight Regency) | **975** | 240 | 260 |
| Removable Glass Panels (Cutlass Supreme) | **895** | 220 | 240 |
| 3.8 Liter V6 SFI Eng (Cutlass Ciera) | **745** | 180 | 200 |

NOTE: Power brakes standard on all models. Power seat and power windows standard on Ninety-Eight Regency and Toronado.

## 1986

### CALAIS 4*

| | Original List | Current Whlse | Average Retail |
|---|---|---|---|
| 2 Dr Cpe | **10656** | 1600 | 2450 |
| 4 Dr Sdn | **10856** | 1600 | 2450 |
| 2 Dr Supreme Cpe | **11050** | 1775 | 2625 |
| 4 Dr Supreme Sdn | **11249** | 1775 | 2625 |

*For 6 cyl models add $250 whsle/$250 retail.

### CUSTOM CRUISER 8

| | | | |
|---|---|---|---|
| 4 Dr Wgn | **13838** | 3700 | 4600 |

### CUTLASS CIERA 4*

| | | | |
|---|---|---|---|
| 2 Dr LS Cpe | **11921** | 1425 | 2175 |
| 4 Dr LS Sdn | **11394** | 1525 | 2375 |
| 4 Dr LS Cruiser | **11774** | 1700 | 2550 |
| 2 Dr Brougham Cpe | **11420** | 1750 | 2600 |
| 4 Dr Brougham Sdn | **11921** | 1825 | 2675 |

*For 6 cyl models add $300 whsle/$300 retail.

### CUTLASS SUPREME 6*

| | | | |
|---|---|---|---|
| 2 Dr Cpe | **11821** | 2175 | 3025 |
| 4 Dr Sdn | **12001** | 2000 | 2850 |
| 2 Dr Brougham Cpe | **12554** | 2475 | 3350 |
| 4 Dr Brougham Sdn | **12703** | 2275 | 3150 |
| 2 Dr Salon Cpe | **12874** | 2825 | 3725 |

*For 8 cyl models add $325 whsle/$325 retail.

### DELTA 88 ROYALE 6

| | | | |
|---|---|---|---|
| 2 Dr Cpe | **12955** | 2350 | 3225 |
| 4 Dr Sdn | **12955** | 2500 | 3375 |
| 2 Dr Brougham Cpe | **13667** | 2825 | 3725 |

| Year/Model/ Body/Type | Original List | Current Whlse | Average Retail |
|---|---|---|---|
| 4 Dr Brougham Sdn | **13667** | 2975 | 3875 |
| **FIRENZA 4** | | | |
| 2 Dr Cpe | **9389** | 1475 | 2300 |
| 2 Dr S Hbk | **9566** | 1575 | 2425 |
| 4 Dr Sdn | **9663** | 1575 | 2425 |
| 4 Dr Cruiser Wgn | **9889** | 1675 | 2525 |
| 2 Dr LC Cpe | **10035** | 1750 | 2600 |
| 2 Dr GT Hbk (6 cyl) | **11232** | 2225 | 3075 |
| 4 Dr LX Sdn | **10051** | 1825 | 2675 |

*For 6 cyl models add $200 whsle/$200 retail.

| | Original List | Current Whlse | Average Retail |
|---|---|---|---|
| **NINETY-EIGHT 6** | | | |
| 2 Dr Regency Cpe | **16062** | 2725 | 3625 |
| 4 Dr Regency Sdn | **16509** | 2875 | 3775 |
| 2 Dr Regency Brougham Cpe | **17591** | 3200 | 4100 |
| 4 Dr Regency Brougham Sdn | **17509** | 3325 | 4225 |
| **TORONADO 6** | | | |
| 2 Dr Brougham Cpe | **19850** | 3175 | 4075 |

*ADD FOR:*

| | | | |
|---|---|---|---|
| Calais GT Pkg (Base Calais Cpe) | **1350** | 240 | 260 |
| Ciera ES Pkg (Base Ciera Sdn) | **1992** | 350 | 380 |
| Ciera GT Pkg (Base Ciera Cpe) | **3330** | 570 | 640 |
| (Base Ciera Sdn) | **2980** | 510 | 570 |
| Ciera Holiday Cpe Pkg (Ciera Brougham Cpe) | **680** | 120 | 130 |
| Cutlass 442 Pkg (Cutlass Supreme Salon) | **2075** | 360 | 400 |
| ES Sdn Pkg (Base Calais Sdn) | **995** | 170 | 190 |
| Ninety-Eight Grande Premium Interior Pkg (Ninety-Eight Regency Brougham) | **975** | 160 | 180 |
| Removable Glass Panels (Cutlass Supreme) | **895** | 160 | 170 |
| 2.8 Liter V6 MPFI Eng (Cutlass Ciera) | **485** | 80 | 90 |
| 3.8 Liter V6 SFI Eng (Delta 88 Royale) | **370** | 60 | 70 |

NOTE: Power windows standard on Ninety-Eight Regency and Toronado. Power seat standard on Toronado. Power brakes standard on all models.

## 1985

| **CALAIS 4*** | Original List | Current Whlse | Average Retail |
|---|---|---|---|
| 2 Dr Cpe | **9739** | 1250 | 1975 |
| 2 Dr Supreme Cpe | **10091** | 1550 | 2400 |

| Year/Model/ Body/Type | Original List | Current Whlse | Average Retail |
|---|---|---|---|
| **CUTLASS CIERA 4*** | | | |
| 2 Dr LS Cpe | **10243** | 1250 | 1975 |
| 4 Dr LS Sdn | **10437** | 1325 | 2050 |
| 4 Dr Cruiser | **10805** | 1475 | 2300 |
| 2 Dr Brougham Cpe | **10733** | 1475 | 2300 |
| 4 Dr Brougham Sdn | **10948** | 1575 | 2425 |

*For 6 cyl models add $250 whsle/$250 retail.

| **CUTLASS SUPREME 6*** | | | |
|---|---|---|---|
| 2 Dr Cpe | **10743** | 1600 | 2450 |
| 4 Dr Sdn | **10910** | 1400 | 2150 |
| 2 Dr Brougham Cpe | **11427** | 1825 | 2675 |
| 4 Dr Brougham Sdn | **11564** | 1675 | 2525 |
| 2 Dr Salon Cpe | **11735** | 2050 | 2900 |

*For 8 cyl models add $300 whsle/$300 retail.

| **DELTA 88 6*** | | | |
|---|---|---|---|
| 2 Dr Royale Cpe | **11448** | 1675 | 2525 |
| 4 Dr Royale Sdn | **11548** | 1775 | 2625 |
| 2 Dr Royale Brougham Cpe | **11938** | 2000 | 2850 |
| 4 Dr Royale Brougham Sdn | **12043** | 2150 | 3000 |
| 4 Dr Brougham LS Sdn (8 cyl) | **14618** | 2550 | 3425 |
| 4 Dr Custom Cruiser (8 cyl) | **12610** | 1800 | 2650 |

*For 8 cyl models add $375 whsle/$375 retail.

| **FIRENZA 4** | | | |
|---|---|---|---|
| 2 Dr S Cpe | **8873** | 1075 | 1800 |
| 4 Dr Sdn | **8964** | 1175 | 1900 |
| 2 Dr SX Cpe | **9465** | 1300 | 2025 |
| 4 Dr LX Sdn | **9325** | 1375 | 2125 |
| 4 Dr 2 Seat Wgn | **9183** | 1250 | 1975 |
| 4 Dr LX 3 Seat Wgn | **9562** | 1450 | 2225 |

| **NINETY-EIGHT 6** | | | |
|---|---|---|---|
| 2 Dr Regency Cpe | **15295** | 2000 | 2850 |
| 4 Dr Regency Sdn | **15224** | 2150 | 3000 |
| 2 Dr Regency Brougham Cpe | **16251** | 2375 | 3250 |
| 4 Dr Regency Brougham Sdn | **16181** | 2525 | 3400 |

| **TORONADO 8** | | | |
|---|---|---|---|
| 2 Dr Brougham Cpe | **17134** | 2450 | 3325 |

*ADD FOR:*

| | | | |
|---|---|---|---|
| Calais 500 Pkg (Base Calais) | **1595** | 170 | 190 |
| Caliente Pkg (Toronado) | **1970** | 210 | 230 |
| Ciera GT Pkg (Ciera LS Cpe) | **3295** | 350 | 380 |
| Cutlass 442 Pkg (Cutlass Supreme | | | |

| Year/Model/Body/Type | Original List | Current Whlse | Average Retail |
|---|---|---|---|
| Salon) | **1275** | 330 | 360 |
| ES Pkg (Cutlass Ciera LS Sdn) | **895** | 90 | 100 |
| GT Pkg (Firenza S Cpe) | **1360** | 150 | 160 |
| Holiday Cpe Pkg (Cutlass Ciera Brougham Cpe) | **565** | 70 | 70 |

NOTE: Power brakes standard on all models. Power windows standard on Delta 88 Brougham LS and Ninety-Eight. Power seat standard on Delta 88 and Ninety-Eight. Power locks standard on Delta 88 Brougham LS and Ninety-Eight.

## 1984

### CUTLASS CIERA 4*

| Year/Model/Body/Type | Original List | Current Whlse | Average Retail |
|---|---|---|---|
| 2 Dr LS Cpe | **9735** | 950 | 1675 |
| 4 Dr LS Sdn | **9924** | 1050 | 1775 |
| 4 Dr Cruiser Wgn | **10272** | 1175 | 1900 |
| 2 Dr Brougham Cpe | **10240** | 1150 | 1875 |
| 4 Dr Brougham Sdn | **10442** | 1225 | 1950 |

*For 6 cyl models add $150 whlse/$150 retail.

### CUTLASS SUPREME 6ᴬ

| | | | |
|---|---|---|---|
| 2 Dr Cpe | **10208** | 1250 | 1975 |
| 4 Dr Sdn | **10361** | 1075 | 1800 |
| 2 Dr Brougham Cpe | **10847** | 1450 | 2225 |
| 4 Dr Brougham Sdn | **10977** | 1300 | 2025 |
| 2 Dr Calais Cpe | **11106** | 1500 | 2350 |

*For 8 cyl models add $200 whlse/$200 retail.

### DELTA 88 ROYALE 6*

| | | | |
|---|---|---|---|
| 2 Dr Cpe | **10770** | 1175 | 1900 |
| 4 Dr Sdn | **10882** | 1300 | 2025 |
| 2 Dr Brougham Cpe | **11239** | 1450 | 2300 |
| 4 Dr Brougham Sdn | **11330** | 1500 | 2350 |
| 4 Dr Custom Cruiser (8 cyl) | **11669** | 1325 | 2050 |
| 4 Dr LS Sdn (8 cyl) | **13854** | 1850 | 2700 |

*For 8 cyl models add $300 whlse/$300 retail.

### FIRENZA 4

| | | | |
|---|---|---|---|
| 2 Dr S Cpe | **8435** | 675 | 1275 |
| 4 Dr Sdn | **8522** | 750 | 1475 |
| 4 Dr Cruiser | **8742** | 800 | 1500 |
| 2 Dr SX Cpe | **8974** | 825 | 1525 |
| 4 Dr LX Sdn | **8870** | 900 | 1625 |
| 4 Dr LX Cruiser | **9090** | 925 | 1650 |

### NINETY-EIGHT 8

| | | | |
|---|---|---|---|
| 2 Dr Regency Cpe | **13962** | 1700 | 2550 |
| 4 Dr Regency Sdn | **14139** | 1800 | 2650 |
| 4 Dr Regency Brougham Sdn | **15189** | 2100 | 2950 |

### OMEGA 4*

| | | | |
|---|---|---|---|
| 2 Dr Cpe | **8780** | 525 | 975 |

| | | | |
|---|---|---|---|
| 4 Dr Sdn | **8978** | 600 | 1125 |
| 2 Dr Brougham Cpe | **9069** | 700 | 1325 |
| 4 Dr Brougham Sdn | **9250** | 750 | 1475 |

*For 6 cyl models add $150 whlse/$150 retail.

### TORONADO 6*

| | | | |
|---|---|---|---|
| 2 Dr Brougham Cpe | **16096** | 2000 | 2850 |

*For 8 cyl models add $300 whlse/$300 retail.

NOTE: Power brakes standard on all models. Power windows standard on Ninety-Eight and Toronado. Vinyl roof standard on Ninety-Eight Brougham.

## 1983 — ALL BODY STYLES

| | | | |
|---|---|---|---|
| CUTLASS CIERA | — | 850 | 1550 |
| CUTLASS SUPREME | — | 1075 | 1800 |
| DELTA 88 | — | 1025 | 1750 |
| FIRENZA | — | 550 | 1025 |
| NINETY-EIGHT | — | 1350 | 2100 |
| OMEGA | — | 450 | 825 |
| TORONADO | — | 1425 | 2175 |

## PLYMOUTH

### 1992

#### ACCLAIM 4*

| | | | |
|---|---|---|---|
| 4 Dr Sdn | **12532** | 7900 | 9175 |

*For 6 cyl models add $475 whlse/$475 retail.

*ADD FOR:*

| | | | |
|---|---|---|---|
| Anti-Lock Brakes | **899** | 460 | 500 |
| Cast Aluminum Wheels | **328** | 220 | 240 |

#### LASER 4

| | | | |
|---|---|---|---|
| 2 Dr Hbk | **13375** | 9000 | 10400 |
| 2 Dr RS Hbk | **14915** | 9725 | 11200 |
| 2 Dr RS Turbo Hbk | **16965** | — | — |
| 2 Dr RS Turbo AWD Hbk (NA w/auto trans) | **17820** | — | — |

*ADD FOR:*

| | | | |
|---|---|---|---|
| Anti-Lock Brakes | **943** | 460 | 500 |
| Alloy Whls (RS, RS Turbo) | **321** | 210 | 230 |

#### SUNDANCE 4

| | | | |
|---|---|---|---|
| 2 Dr America Hbk | **9733** | 6425 | 7475 |
| 4 Dr America Sdn | **10131** | 6525 | 7600 |
| 2 Dr Highline Hbk | **10793** | 7275 | 8450 |
| 4 Dr Highline Sdn | **11193** | 7375 | 8550 |
| 2 Dr Duster Hbk (6 cyl) | **11439** | — | — |
| 4 Dr Duster Sdn (6 cyl) | **11839** | — | — |

*ADD FOR:*

| | | | |
|---|---|---|---|
| 2.5 Liter 4 Cyl Eng (Highline) | **286** | 190 | 210 |

| Year/Model/ Body/Type | Original List | Current Whlse | Average Retail |
|---|---|---|---|
| Aluminum Wheels | **328** | 220 | 240 |

## 1991

### ACCLAIM 4 *

| | | | |
|---|---|---|---|
| 4 Dr Sdn | **11423** | 6650 | 7750 |
| 4 Dr LE Sdn | **13752** | 7200 | 8350 |

*For 6 cyl models add $425 whsle/$425 retail.

### ACCLAIM LX 6

| | | | |
|---|---|---|---|
| 4 Dr Sdn | **15252** | 8350 | 9650 |

### LASER 4

| | | | |
|---|---|---|---|
| 3 Dr Lftbk Cpe | **13014** | 7850 | 9125 |
| 3 Dr RS Lftbk Cpe | **14269** | 8525 | 9850 |
| 3 Dr RS Turbo Lftbk Cpe | **15588** | 9900 | 11400 |

### SUNDANCE 4

| | | | |
|---|---|---|---|
| 3 Dr America Cpe | **9321** | 4850 | 5775 |
| 5 Dr America Sdn | **9621** | 4950 | 5875 |
| 3 Dr Highline Cpe | **10286** | 5625 | 6550 |
| 5 Dr Highline Sdn | **10586** | 5725 | 6650 |
| 3 Dr RS Cpe | **11486** | 6525 | 7600 |
| 5 Dr RS Sdn | **11812** | 6625 | 7700 |

*ADD FOR:*

| | | | |
|---|---|---|---|
| Anti-lock Brakes (Acclaim) | **899** | 440 | 480 |
| (Laser ex. Base) | **925** | 460 | 500 |

NOTE: Power brakes standard on all models. Air bag standard on Acclaim and Sundance.

## 1990

### ACCLAIM 4*

| | | | |
|---|---|---|---|
| 4 Dr Sdn | **10931** | 4750 | 5675 |
| 4 Dr LE Sdn | **13216** | 5225 | 6150 |

*For 6 cyl models add $400 whsle/$400 retail.

### ACCLAIM LX 6

| | | | |
|---|---|---|---|
| 4 Dr Sdn | **14670** | 6275 | 7300 |

### HORIZON 4

| | | | |
|---|---|---|---|
| 4 Dr Hbk | **8698** | 2975 | 3875 |

### LASER 4

| | | | |
|---|---|---|---|
| 3 Dr Lftbk Cpe | **12339** | 6025 | 6950 |
| 3 Dr RS Lftbk Cpe | **13384** | 6625 | 7700 |
| 3 Dr RS Turbo Lftbk Cpe (NA w/auto trans) | **14707** | 7975 | 9250 |

### SUNDANCE 4

| | | | |
|---|---|---|---|
| 3 Dr Lftbk Cpe | **10156** | 4325 | 5250 |
| 5 Dr Lftbk Sdn | **10356** | 4425 | 5350 |

*ADD FOR:*

| | | | |
|---|---|---|---|
| RS Pkg (Sundance) | **1071** | 470 | 520 |

| Year/Model/ Body/Type | Original List | Current Whlse | Average Retail |
|---|---|---|---|
| 2.0 Liter 4 Cyl Eng (Laser) | **873** | 380 | 420 |
| 2.5 Liter 4 Cyl Eng (Sundance) | **280** | 120 | 130 |
| 2.5 Liter 4 Cyl Turbo Eng (Acclaim) | **700** | 310 | 340 |
| (Sundance) | **552** | 250 | 270 |

NOTE: Power brakes standard on all models.

## 1989

### ACCLAIM 4

| | | | |
|---|---|---|---|
| 4 Dr Sdn | **11231** | 3850 | 4750 |
| 4 Dr LE Sdn | **12606** | 4325 | 5250 |

### ACCLAIM LX 6

| | | | |
|---|---|---|---|
| 4 Dr Sdn | **13970** | 5225 | 6150 |

### GRAN FURY SALON 8

| | | | |
|---|---|---|---|
| 4 Dr Sdn | **12850** | 3250 | 4150 |

### HORIZON AMERICA 4

| | | | |
|---|---|---|---|
| 5 Dr Hbk | **8298** | 2075 | 2925 |

### RELIANT AMERICA 4

| | | | |
|---|---|---|---|
| 2 Dr Sdn | **9299** | 2625 | 3525 |
| 4 Dr Sdn | **9299** | 2725 | 3625 |

### SUNDANCE 4

| | | | |
|---|---|---|---|
| 3 Dr Lftbk Cpe | **9706** | 3425 | 4325 |
| 5 Dr Lftbk Sdn | **9906** | 3525 | 4425 |

*ADD FOR:*

| | | | |
|---|---|---|---|
| 2.5 Liter 4 Cyl Turbo Eng (Acclaim Base & LE) | **678** | 260 | 280 |
| Turbo Eng Pkg (Sundance w/RS Pkg) | **610** | 230 | 250 |
| (Sundance w/Pop Equip Pkg) | **923** | 350 | 380 |

NOTE: Power brakes standard on all models.

## 1988

### CARAVELLE 4*

| | | | |
|---|---|---|---|
| 4 Dr Sdn | **11434** | 2425 | 3300 |

*For 153 CID 4 cyl eng models add $100 whsle/$100 rtl.

### CARAVELLE SE 4

| | | | |
|---|---|---|---|
| 4 Dr Sdn | **12403** | 2800 | 3700 |

### GRAN FURY 8

| | | | |
|---|---|---|---|
| 4 Dr Sdn | **12127** | 2750 | 3650 |

### GRAN FURY SALON 8

| | | | |
|---|---|---|---|
| 4 Dr Sdn | **12237** | 2300 | 3175 |

| Year/Model/ Body/Type | Original List | Current Whlse | Average Retail |
|---|---|---|---|
| **HORIZON AMERICA 4** | | | |
| 4 Dr Hbk | **7868** | 1550 | 2400 |
| **RELIANT AMERICA 4*** | | | |
| 2 Dr Sdn | **9064** | 2175 | 3025 |
| 4 Dr Sdn | **9064** | 2250 | 3100 |
| 4 Dr Wgn | **9664** | 2625 | 3525 |
| *For 153 CID 4 cyl eng models add $100 whlse/$100 rtl. | | | |
| **SUNDANCE 4*** | | | |
| 2 Dr Lftbk Cpe | **9225** | 2350 | 3225 |
| 4 Dr Lftbk Sdn | **9475** | 2450 | 3325 |
| *For 153 CID 4 cyl eng models add $100 whlse/$100 rtl. | | | |
| *ADD FOR:* | | | |
| RS Pkg (Sundance) | **1390** | 430 | 480 |
| Turbo Eng Pkg | | | |
| (Sundance w/RS Pkg) | **467** | 150 | 160 |
| (Sundance w/o RS Pkg) | **780** | 240 | 260 |
| 2.2 Liter 4 Cyl Turbo Eng (Base Caravelle w/o Convenience Pkg) | **399** | 120 | 130 |
| (Base Caravelle w/ Convenience Pkg, Caravelle SE) | **678** | 210 | 230 |

NOTE: Power brakes standard on Horizon America, Reliant America, Sundance, Caravelle Series and Gran Fury Series.

## 1987

| Year/Model/ Body/Type | Original List | Current Whlse | Average Retail |
|---|---|---|---|
| **CARAVELLE 4*** | | | |
| 4 Dr Sdn | **10595** | 1625 | 2475 |
| **CARAVELLE SE 4*** | | | |
| 4 Dr Sdn | **11309** | 1875 | 2725 |
| *For 158 CID 4 cyl eng models add $100 whlse/$100 rtl. | | | |
| **GRAN FURY SALON 8** | | | |
| 4 Dr HT | **11435** | 1650 | 2500 |
| **HORIZON AMERICA 4** | | | |
| 5 Dr Hbk | **7214** | 1075 | 1800 |
| **RELIANT 4** | | | |
| 2 Dr Sdn | **9430** | 1200 | 1925 |
| 4 Dr Sdn | **9430** | 1275 | 2000 |
| **RELIANT LE 4** | | | |
| 2 Dr Sdn | **9915** | 1400 | 2150 |
| 4 Dr Sdn | **9915** | 1500 | 2350 |
| 4 Dr Wgn | **10359** | 1800 | 2650 |
| **SUNDANCE 4** | | | |
| 2 Dr Lftbk Cpe | **8822** | 1700 | 2550 |
| 4 Dr Lftbk Sdn | **9022** | 1775 | 2625 |

| Year/Model/ Body/Type | Original List | Current Whlse | Average Retail |
|---|---|---|---|
| **TURISMO 4** | | | |
| 3 Dr Hbk | **8614** | 1425 | 2175 |
| *ADD FOR:* | | | |
| Salon Luxury Pkg (Gran Fury) | **545** | 130 | 140 |
| 2.2 Liter 4 Cyl Turbo Eng (Caravelle) | **678** | 160 | 180 |
| (Sundance) | **806** | 190 | 210 |

NOTE: Power brakes standard on all models.

## 1986

| Year/Model/ Body/Type | Original List | Current Whlse | Average Retail |
|---|---|---|---|
| **CARAVELLE 4*** | | | |
| 4 Dr Sdn | **10053** | 1200 | 1925 |
| **CARAVELLE SE 4*** | | | |
| 4 Dr Sdn | **10622** | 1425 | 2175 |
| *For 158 CID 4 cyl eng models add $50 whlse/$50 retail. | | | |
| **GRAN FURY SALON 8** | | | |
| 4 Dr HT | **10898** | 1200 | 1925 |
| **HORIZON 4** | | | |
| 4 Dr Hbk | **7719** | 800 | 1500 |
| **HORIZON SE 4** | | | |
| 4 Dr Hbk | **7955** | 1075 | 1800 |
| **RELIANT 4** | | | |
| 2 Dr Sdn | **8675** | 900 | 1625 |
| 4 Dr Sdn | **8792** | 1000 | 1725 |
| **RELIANT LE 4** | | | |
| 2 Dr Sdn | **9578** | 1200 | 1925 |
| 4 Dr Sdn | **9698** | 1275 | 2000 |
| 4 Dr Wgn | **10197** | 1575 | 2425 |
| **RELIANT SE 4** | | | |
| 2 Dr Sdn | **9130** | 1050 | 1775 |
| 4 Dr Sdn | **9250** | 1150 | 1875 |
| 4 Dr Wgn | **9677** | 1425 | 2175 |
| **TURISMO 4** | | | |
| 2 Dr Hbk | **8297** | 1125 | 1850 |
| **TURISMO 2.2 4** | | | |
| 2 Dr Hbk | **9129** | 1500 | 2350 |
| *ADD FOR:* | | | |
| Salon Luxury Pkg (Gran Fury) | **545** | 90 | 100 |
| Sun/Sound/Shade Pkg (Turismo 2.2) | **552** | 100 | 110 |
| 2.2 Liter 4 Cyl Turbo Eng (Caravelle) | **628** | 110 | 120 |

NOTE: Power brakes standard on all models.

*Refer to optional equipment schedules*

| Year/Model/Body/Type | Original List | Current Whlse | Average Retail |
|---|---|---|---|
| **1985** | | | |
| **CARAVELLE 4*** | | | |
| 4 Dr Sdn | **9764** | 975 | 1700 |
| **GRAN FURY SALON 8** | | | |
| 4 Dr HT | **10470** | 900 | 1625 |
| **HORIZON 4** | | | |
| 4 Dr Hbk | **7413** | 700 | 1325 |
| **HORIZON SE 4** | | | |
| 4 Dr Hbk | **7643** | 950 | 1675 |
| **RELIANT 4** | | | |
| 2 Dr Sdn | **8432** | 800 | 1500 |
| 4 Dr Sdn | **8547** | 875 | 1600 |
| **RELIANT LE 4** | | | |
| 2 Dr Sdn | **9054** | 1025 | 1750 |
| 4 Dr Sdn | **9187** | 1125 | 1850 |
| 4 Dr Wgn | **9554** | 1325 | 2050 |
| **RELIANT SE 4** | | | |
| 2 Dr Sdn | **8716** | 900 | 1625 |
| 4 Dr Sdn | **8834** | 975 | 1700 |
| 4 Dr Wgn | **9334** | 1225 | 1950 |
| **TURISMO 4** | | | |
| 2 Dr Hbk | **7998** | 975 | 1700 |
| **TURISMO 2.2 4** | | | |
| 2 Dr Hbk | **8816** | 1325 | 2050 |
| *ADD FOR:* | | | |
| Salon Luxury Pkg (Gran Fury) | **536** | ·60 | 60 |

NOTE: Power brakes standard on all models.

| **1984** | | | |
|---|---|---|---|
| **GRAN FURY 8** | | | |
| 4 Dr HT | **9961** | 625 | 1175 |
| **HORIZON 4** | | | |
| 4 Dr Hbk | **7236** | 250 | 500 |
| **HORIZON SE 4** | | | |
| 4 Dr Hbk | **7441** | 475 | 875 |
| **RELIANT 4** | | | |
| 2 Dr Cpe | **8337** | 400 | 725 |
| 4 Dr Sdn | **8449** | 475 | 875 |
| **RELIANT CUSTOM 4** | | | |
| 2 Seat Wgn | **9123** | 650 | 1225 |

| Year/Model/Body/Type | Original List | Current Whlse | Average Retail |
|---|---|---|---|
| **RELIANT SPECIAL EDITION 4** | | | |
| 2 Dr Cpe | **8858** | 575 | 1075 |
| 4 Dr Sdn | **8984** | 650 | 1225 |
| 2 Seat Wgn | **9371** | 850 | 1550 |
| **TURISMO 4** | | | |
| 2 Dr Hbk | **7900** | 525 | 975 |
| **TURISMO 2.2 4** | | | |
| 2 Dr Hbk | **8581** | 750 | 1475 |

NOTE: Power brakes standard on all models.

## 1983 — ALL BODY STYLES

| | Original List | Current Whlse | Average Retail |
|---|---|---|---|
| GRAN FURY | — | 325 | 600 |
| HORIZON | — | 110 | 300 |
| RELIANT | — | 250 | 500 |
| RELIANT CUSTOM | — | 425 | 775 |
| RELIANT SPECIAL EDITION | — | 450 | 825 |
| TURISMO | — | 200 | 400 |

## PONTIAC

| 1992 | Original List | Current Whlse | Average Retail |
|---|---|---|---|
| **BONNEVILLE 6** | | | |
| 4 Dr SE Sdn | **18599** | 13350 | 15675 |
| 4 Dr SSE Sdn | **23999** | 17400 | 20050 |
| 4 Dr SSEi | **28045** | — | — |
| *ADD FOR:* | | | |
| Anti-Lock Brakes (SE) | **450** | 460 | 500 |
| Leather Seat Trim (SSE) | **1419** | 260 | 290 |
| (SSEi) | **779** | 260 | 290 |
| Cast Alum Whls | **340** | 220 | 240 |
| **FIREBIRD 6*** | | | |
| 2 Dr Cpe | **13865** | 10100 | 11650 |
| 2 Dr Conv | **20205** | — | — |
| *For 8 cyl models add $500 whlse/$500 retail.* | | | |
| **FIREBIRD 8** | | | |
| 2 Dr Formula Cpe | **16735** | 11475 | 13250 |
| 2 Dr Trans Am Cpe | **18635** | 13800 | 16175 |
| 2 Dr Trans Am Conv | **24405** | — | — |
| 2 Dr Trans Am GTA Cpe | **25880** | — | — |
| *ADD FOR:* | | | |
| 5.0 Liter Tuned 8 Cyl Eng (Formula) | **745** | 490 | 540 |
| 5.7 Liter 8 Cyl Eng (Formula) | **1045** | 680 | 760 |
| (Trans Am) | **300** | 200 | 220 |
| T-Tops | **914** | 600 | 670 |
| Leather Seat Trim (Trans Am) | **780** | 260 | 290 |

*1988 Pontiac Grand Prix LE*

| Year/Model/Body/Type | Original List | Current Whlse | Average Retail |
|---|---|---|---|
| (GTA) | **475** | 260 | 290 |
| **GRAND AM 4** | | | |
| 2 Dr SE Cpe | **13284** | 9250 | 10650 |
| 4 Dr SE Sdn | **13384** | 9250 | 10650 |
| 2 Dr GT Cpe | **15084** | 10575 | 12200 |
| 4 Dr GT Sdn | **15184** | 10575 | 12200 |
| *ADD FOR:* | | | |
| 6 Cyl Eng (SE) | **460** | 300 | 330 |
| Quad 4 Eng (SE) | **410** | 270 | 300 |
| Aluminum Wheels | **300** | 200 | 220 |
| **GRAND PRIX 6** | | | |
| 4 Dr LE Sdn | **14890** | 10800 | 12475 |
| 2 Dr SE Cpe | **15390** | 11425 | 13200 |
| 4 Dr SE Sdn | **16190** | 11425 | 13200 |
| 2 Dr GT Cpe | **20340** | 13350 | 15675 |
| 4 Dr STE Sdn | **21635** | 13850 | 16225 |
| *ADD FOR:* | | | |
| 3.4 Liter 6 Cyl Eng | **995** | 680 | 680 |
| Anti-Lock Brakes (LE, SE) | **450** | 460 | 500 |
| Leather Seats | **475** | 330 | 360 |
| Aluminum Wheels | **275** | 180 | 200 |
| **LE MANS 4** | | | |
| 2 Dr Value Leader Aerocoupe (NA w/auto trans, power steering or air cond) | **8357** | 4600 | 5525 |
| 2 Dr SE Aerocoupe | **9455** | 5800 | 6725 |
| 4 Dr SE Sdn | **10870** | 6000 | 6925 |
| **SUNBIRD LE 4** | | | |
| 2 Dr Cpe | **10860** | 7075 | 8225 |

| Year/Model/Body/Type | Original List | Current Whlse | Average Retail |
|---|---|---|---|
| 4 Dr Sdn | **10960** | 7150 | 8300 |
| **SUNBIRD SE 4*** | | | |
| 2 Dr Cpe | **11620** | 7775 | 9025 |
| 4 Dr Sdn | **11720** | 7875 | 9150 |
| 2 Dr Conv | **16585** | 11350 | 13100 |
| *For 6 cyl models add $— whsle/$— retail. | | | |
| **SUNBIRD GT 6** | | | |
| 2 Dr Cpe | **14060** | 9700 | 11175 |
| *ADD FOR:* | | | |
| Aluminum Wheels | **275** | — | — |

NOTE: Power windows standard on Bonneville, Firebird GTA, Grand Prix GT & STE, Sunbird SE Convertible & GT. Power door locks standard on Bonneville, Firebird GTA, Grand Am, Grand Prix GT & STE and Sunbird. Power seat standard on Bonneville SSE & SSEi, Grand Prix GT & STE. Tilt steering wheel standard on Bonneville and Firebird. Cruise control standard on Bonneville SSEi and Firebird GTA.

## 1991

| | Original List | Current Whlse | Average Retail |
|---|---|---|---|
| **6000 LE 4*** | | | |
| 4 Dr Sdn | **13829** | 7450 | 8650 |
| *For 6 cyl models add $425 whsle/$425 retail. | | | |
| **6000 LE 6** | | | |
| 4 Dr Wgn | **16699** | 8300 | 9575 |
| **6000 SE 6** | | | |
| 4 Dr Sdn | **18399** | 8850 | 10225 |
| **BONNEVILLE 6** | | | |
| 4 Dr LE Sdn | **16834** | 9925 | 11425 |

| Year/Model/Body/Type | Original List | Current Whlse | Average Retail |
|---|---|---|---|
| 4 Dr SE Sdn | **20464** | 11300 | 13050 |
| 4 Dr SSE Sdn | **25264** | 14575 | 17100 |

**FIREBIRD 6***

| | | | |
|---|---|---|---|
| 2 Dr Cpe | **13520** | 7875 | 9150 |
| 2 Dr Conv | **19989** | 12375 | 14450 |

*For 8 cyl models add $450 whsle/$450 retail.

**FIREBIRD 8**

| | | | |
|---|---|---|---|
| 2 Dr Formula Cpe | **16060** | 9125 | 10500 |
| 2 Dr Trans Am Cpe | **18060** | 11200 | 12925 |
| 2 Dr Trans Am Conv | **23510** | 15725 | 18375 |
| 2 Dr Trans Am GTA Cpe | **24530** | — | — |

**GRAND AM 4***

| | | | |
|---|---|---|---|
| 2 Dr Cpe | **11474** | 6375 | 7425 |
| 4 Dr Sdn | **11674** | 6375 | 7425 |
| 2 Dr LE Cpe | **12424** | 6775 | 7875 |
| 4 Dr LE Sdn | **12626** | 6775 | 7875 |
| 2 Dr SE Cpe | **16899** | 8000 | 9300 |
| 4 Dr SE Sdn | **17099** | 8000 | 9300 |

*For quad 4 4 cyl LE models add $200 whsle/$200 retail.

**GRAND PRIX 4***

| | | | |
|---|---|---|---|
| 4 Dr LE Sdn | **14294** | 8500 | 9825 |
| 2 Dr SE Cpe | **14894** | 9000 | 10400 |
| 4 Dr SE Sdn | **15284** | 9000 | 10400 |

*For 3.4 liter 6 cyl models add $600 whsle/$600 retail.

**GRAND PRIX 6**

| | | | |
|---|---|---|---|
| 2 Dr GT Cpe | **19154** | 10775 | 12425 |
| 4 Dr STE Sdn | **19994** | 11225 | 12975 |

**LE MANS 4**

| | | | |
|---|---|---|---|
| 2 Dr Value Leader Aerocoupe (NA w/auto trans or power steering) | **7574** | 3725 | 4625 |
| 2 Dr LE Aerocoupe | **9709** | 4850 | 5775 |
| 4 Dr LE Sdn | **10159** | 5025 | 5950 |

**SUNBIRD 4**

| | | | |
|---|---|---|---|
| 2 Dr Cpe | **9924** | 5350 | 6275 |
| 4 Dr Sdn | **10024** | 5475 | 6400 |

**SUNBIRD LE 4**

| | | | |
|---|---|---|---|
| 2 Dr Cpe | **10684** | 6100 | 7000 |
| 4 Dr Sdn | **10784** | 6175 | 7200 |
| 2 Dr Conv | **15654** | 9225 | 10625 |

**SUNBIRD SE 4**

| | | | |
|---|---|---|---|
| 2 Dr Cpe | **11934** | 6700 | 7800 |

**SUNBIRD GT 6**

| | | | |
|---|---|---|---|
| 2 Dr Cpe | **13684** | 8350 | 9650 |

ADD FOR:
Aero Perf. Pkg

| Year/Model/Body/Type | Original List | Current Whlse | Average Retail |
|---|---|---|---|
| (Grand Prix SE & GT Cpes) | **2795** | 1370 | 1520 |
| Anti-lock Brakes (Bonneville LE & SE) | **925** | 460 | 500 |
| Leather Seats (Bonneville SSE) | **779** | 310 | 340 |
| (Firebird Trans Am GTA, Grand Prix GT) | **475** | 250 | 280 |
| Sport Perf. Pkg (Grand Am LE) | **1650** | 810 | 900 |
| T-Tops (Firebird) | **920** | 460 | 500 |

NOTE: Power brakes standard on all models. Anti-lock brakes standard on Bonneville SSE and Grand Am SE. Power seat standard on Bonneville SE & SSE, Grand Prix GT & STE. Power windows and power door locks standard on 6000 SE Sdn, Bonneville SE & SSE, Firebird Trans Am GTA, Grand Am SE, Grand Prix GT & STE.

# 1990

**6000 LE 4***

| | | | |
|---|---|---|---|
| 4 Dr Sdn | **12954** | 4825 | 5750 |

*For 6 cyl models add $400 whsle/$400 retail.

**6000 LE 6**

| | | | |
|---|---|---|---|
| 4 Dr Wgn | **15309** | 5575 | 6500 |

**6000 SE 6**

| | | | |
|---|---|---|---|
| 4 Dr Sdn | **16909** | 6125 | 7125 |
| 4 Dr Wgn | **18509** | 6500 | 7575 |

**BONNEVILLE 6**

| | | | |
|---|---|---|---|
| 4 Dr LE Sdn | **15774** | 7150 | 8300 |
| 4 Dr SE Sdn | **19144** | 8350 | 9650 |
| 4 Dr SSE Sdn | **23994** | 11350 | 13100 |

**FIREBIRD 6***

| | | | |
|---|---|---|---|
| 2 Dr Cpe | **12640** | 6450 | 7500 |

*For 8 cyl Base models add $400 whsle/$400 retail.

**FIREBIRD 8**

| | | | |
|---|---|---|---|
| 2 Dr Formula Cpe | **15125** | 7525 | 8725 |
| 2 Dr Trans Am Cpe | **17025** | 9500 | 10950 |
| 2 Dr Trans Am GTA Cpe | **23320** | 12300 | 14300 |

**GRAND AM 4***

| | | | |
|---|---|---|---|
| 2 Dr LE Cpe | **11804** | 5325 | 6250 |
| 4 Dr LE Sdn | **12004** | 5325 | 6250 |
| 2 Dr SE Cpe | **15434** | 6450 | 7500 |
| 4 Dr SE Sdn | **15734** | 6450 | 7500 |

*For quad 4 4 cyl LE models add $300 whsle/$300 retail.

**GRAND PRIX 4***

| | | | |
|---|---|---|---|
| 2 Dr LE Cpe | **14564** | 6450 | 7500 |
| 4 Dr LE Sdn | **14564** | 6450 | 7500 |

*For 6 cyl models add $200 whsle/$200 retail.

| Year/Model/ Body/Type | Original List | Current Whlse | Average Retail |
|---|---|---|---|
| **GRAND PRIX 6** | | | |
| 2 Dr SE Cpe | **18324** | 8025 | 9275 |
| 4 Dr STE Sdn | **19179** | 8675 | 10025 |
| 2 Dr Turbo SE Cpe | **25560** | — | — |
| 4 Dr Turbo STE Sdn | **23775** | — | — |
| **LE MANS 4** | | | |
| 2 Dr Value Leader Aerocoupe (NA w/auto trans or pwr strng) | **7683** | 2375 | 3250 |
| 2 Dr LE Aerocoupe | **9893** | 3350 | 4250 |
| 4 Dr LE Sdn | **10243** | 3550 | 4450 |
| 2 Dr GSE Aerocoupe | **11209** | 4075 | 5000 |
| **SUNBIRD LE 4** | | | |
| 2 Dr Cpe | **9984** | 4750 | 5675 |
| 4 Dr Sdn | **10084** | 4850 | 5775 |
| 2 Dr Conv | **15109** | 7650 | 8875 |
| **SUNBIRD SE 4** | | | |
| 2 Dr Cpe | **10389** | 4950 | 5875 |
| **SUNBIRD GT 4** | | | |
| 2 Dr Cpe | **12909** | 6775 | 7875 |
| *ADD FOR:* | | | |
| All-Whl Drv Pkg (6000 SE) | **3635** | 1590 | 1770 |
| Anti-Lock Brakes (Bonneville LE) | **925** | 400 | 440 |
| (Grand Prix) | **925** | 400 | 440 |
| 45/45 Leather Seats (Bonneville SSE) | **779** | 340 | 370 |
| T-Top Roof (Firebird) | **920** | 400 | 440 |
| Turbo Pkg (Sunbird LE Conv) | **1402** | 620 | 690 |
| 5.7 Liter V8 EFI Eng (Firebird Formula) | **1045** | 460 | 500 |
| (Firebird Trans Am) | **300** | 130 | 140 |

NOTE: Power brakes standard on Bonneville SSE. Anti-locking brakes standard on Grand Prix Turbo SE & STE. Power windows standard on 6000 SE, Bonneville SE & SSE, Firebird GTA, Grand Am SE, Grand Prix SE, STE, Turbo SE & Turbo STE. Power door locks standard on 6000 SE, Bonneville SE & SSE, Grand Am SE, Grand Prix SE, STE, Turbo SE and Turbo STE.

## 1989

| | Original List | Current Whlse | Average Retail |
|---|---|---|---|
| **6000 LE 4\*** | | | |
| 4 Dr Sdn | **12764** | 4075 | 5000 |

*For 6 cyl models add $375 whsle/$375 retail.

| | Original List | Current Whlse | Average Retail |
|---|---|---|---|
| **6000 LE 6** | | | |
| 4 Dr Wgn | **14564** | 4725 | 5650 |
| **6000 SE 6** | | | |
| 4 Dr Sdn | **16194** | 5100 | 6025 |

| Year/Model/ Body/Type | Original List | Current Whlse | Average Retail |
|---|---|---|---|
| 4 Dr Wgn | **17494** | 5400 | 6325 |
| **6000 STE 6** | | | |
| 4 Dr Sdn | **22599** | 7850 | 9125 |
| **BONNEVILLE 6** | | | |
| 4 Dr LE Sdn | **14829** | 5575 | 6500 |
| 4 Dr SE Sdn | **17199** | 6575 | 7650 |
| 4 Dr SSE Sdn | **22899** | 8950 | 10325 |
| **FIREBIRD 6\*** | | | |
| 2 Dr Cpe | **13309** | 4925 | 5850 |

*For 8 cyl models add $375 whsle/$375 retail.

| | Original List | Current Whlse | Average Retail |
|---|---|---|---|
| **FIREBIRD 8** | | | |
| 2 Dr Formula Cpe | **14464** | 5925 | 6850 |
| 2 Dr Trans Am Cpe | **16514** | 7700 | 8950 |
| 2 Dr Trans Am GTA Cpe | **20854** | 10200 | 11775 |
| **GRAND AM 4** | | | |
| 2 Dr LE Cpe | **11679** | 4450 | 5375 |
| 4 Dr LE Sdn | **11879** | 4450 | 5375 |
| 2 Dr SE Cpe | **14865** | 5400 | 6325 |
| 4 Dr SE Sdn | **15065** | 5400 | 6325 |

*For quad 4 4 cyl models add $300 whsle/$300 retail.

| | Original List | Current Whlse | Average Retail |
|---|---|---|---|
| **GRAND PRIX 6** | | | |
| 2 Dr Cpe | **13975** | 5475 | 6400 |
| 2 Dr LE Cpe | **14925** | 6100 | 7000 |
| 2 Dr SE Cpe | **16639** | 6925 | 8050 |
| **LE MANS 4** | | | |
| 2 Dr Value Leader Aerocoupe (NA w/auto trans or power steering) | **6906** | 1475 | 2300 |
| 2 Dr LE Aerocoupe | **9338** | 2300 | 3175 |
| 4 Dr LE Sdn | **9688** | 2500 | 3375 |
| 4 Dr SE Sdn | **11088** | 2975 | 3850 |
| 2 Dr GSE Aerocoupe | **10624** | 2800 | 3700 |
| **SAFARI 8** | | | |
| 4 Dr Wgn | **15659** | 5650 | 6575 |
| **SUNBIRD LE 4** | | | |
| 2 Dr Cpe | **10367** | 4000 | 4900 |
| 4 Dr Sdn | **10467** | 4100 | 5025 |
| **SUNBIRD SE 4** | | | |
| 2 Dr Cpe | **10617** | 4200 | 5125 |
| **SUNBIRD GT 4** | | | |
| 2 Dr Cpe | **12534** | 5775 | 6700 |
| 2 Dr Conv | **18034** | 8375 | 9675 |
| *ADD FOR:* | | | |
| 2.0 Liter 4 Cyl Turbo | | | |

| Year/Model/Body/Type | Original List | Current Whlse | Average Retail |
|---|---|---|---|
| Eng (Sunbird SE) | **1434** | 540 | 600 |
| 5.0 Liter V8 MFI Eng (Firebird Formula & Trans Am) | **745** | 270 | 300 |
| 5.7 Liter V8 MFI Eng (Firebird Formula & Trans Am) | **1045** | 390 | 430 |
| Anti-Lock Brakes (Grand Prix, Bonneville) | **925** | 350 | 380 |

NOTE: Power brakes standard on all models. Power windows standard on Sunbird Convertible, Firebird GTA, Bonneville SE, 6000 SE and 6000 STE. Power door locks standard on Sunbird Convertible, Firebird GTA, Bonneville SSE, 6000 SE and 6000 STE.

## 1988

### 6000 4*

| | Original List | Current Whlse | Average Retail |
|---|---|---|---|
| 4 Dr Sdn | **11974** | 3175 | 4075 |
| 4 Dr Wgn | **12414** | 3400 | 4300 |

### 6000 LE 4*

| | | | |
|---|---|---|---|
| 4 Dr Sdn | **12614** | 3200 | 4100 |
| 4 Dr Wgn | **13074** | 3425 | 4325 |

*For 6 cyl models add $350 whsle/$350 retail.

### 6000 SE 6

| | | | |
|---|---|---|---|
| 4 Dr Sdn | **13179** | 3800 | 4700 |
| 4 Dr Wgn | **14079** | 4050 | 4950 |

### 6000 STE 6

| | | | |
|---|---|---|---|
| 4 Dr Sdn | **18699** | 5800 | 6725 |

### BONNEVILLE 6

| | | | |
|---|---|---|---|
| 4 Dr LE Sdn | **14099** | 4300 | 5225 |
| 4 Dr SE Sdn | **16299** | 5050 | 5975 |
| 4 Dr SSE Sdn | **21879** | 7400 | 8600 |

### FIERO 4

| | | | |
|---|---|---|---|
| 2 Dr Cpe (NA w/power steering) | **10264** | 2425 | 3300 |
| 2 Dr Formula Cpe (6 cyl) (NA w/power steering) | **12264** | 3575 | 4475 |
| 2 Dr GT Cpe (6 cyl) | **15264** | 4700 | 5625 |

### FIREBIRD 6*

| | | | |
|---|---|---|---|
| 2 Dr Hbk Cpe | **12384** | 4000 | 4900 |

*For 8 cyl models add $350 whsle/$350 retail.

### FIREBIRD 8

| | | | |
|---|---|---|---|
| 2 Dr Formula | **13384** | 4750 | 5675 |
| 2 Dr Trans Am | **15384** | 6500 | 7575 |
| 2 Dr Trans Am GTA | **19299** | 8675 | 10025 |

### GRAND AM 4*

| | | | |
|---|---|---|---|
| 2 Dr Cpe | **11034** | 3100 | 4000 |

| Year/Model/Body/Type | Original List | Current Whlse | Average Retail |
|---|---|---|---|
| 4 Dr Sdn | **11234** | 3100 | 4000 |
| 2 Dr LE Cpe | **11734** | 3350 | 4250 |
| 4 Dr LE Sdn | **11934** | 3350 | 4250 |
| 2 Dr SE Cpe (quad 4) | **14034** | 4025 | 4925 |
| 4 Dr SE Sdn (quad 4) | **14264** | 4025 | 4925 |

*For quad 4 4 cyl models add $275 whsle/$275 retail.

### GRAND PRIX 6

| | | | |
|---|---|---|---|
| 2 Dr Cpe | **13314** | 4375 | 5300 |
| 2 Dr LE Cpe | **14014** | 4850 | 5775 |
| 2 Dr SE Cpe | **15864** | 5600 | 6525 |

### LE MANS 4

| | | | |
|---|---|---|---|
| 2 Dr Value Leader Aerocoupe (NA w/auto trans or power steering) | **6700** | 900 | 1625 |
| 2 Dr Aerocoupe | **8993** | 1700 | 2550 |
| 4 Dr Sdn | **9443** | 1850 | 2700 |
| 4 Dr SE Sdn | **10293** | 2150 | 3000 |

### SAFARI 8

| | | | |
|---|---|---|---|
| 4 Dr Wgn | **14519** | 4700 | 5625 |

### SUNBIRD 4

| | | | |
|---|---|---|---|
| 4 Dr Sdn | **9972** | 2650 | 3550 |

### SUNBIRD GT 4

| | | | |
|---|---|---|---|
| 2 Dr Cpe | **11989** | 4150 | 5075 |
| 2 Dr Conv | **17289** | 6500 | 7575 |

### SUNBIRD SE 4

| | | | |
|---|---|---|---|
| 2 Dr Cpe | **10072** | 2750 | 3650 |
| 4 Dr Sdn | **10272** | 2850 | 3750 |
| 4 Dr Wgn | **10872** | 3025 | 3925 |

ADD FOR:

| | | | |
|---|---|---|---|
| Hatchroof (Firebird) | **920** | 280 | 310 |
| 2.0 Liter 4 Cyl Turbo Eng (Grand Am LE) | **1173** | 360 | 400 |
| 5.0 Liter V8 MFI Eng (Firebird Formula & Trans Am) | **745** | 230 | 250 |
| 5.7 Liter V8 EFI Eng (Firebird Formula & Trans Am) | **1045** | 320 | 350 |

NOTE: Power brakes standard on all models. Power seat standard on Bonneville SSE. Power windows standard on Sunbird GT, Firebird GTA, Grand Prix LE, Bonneville SE and SSE and 6000 STE. Power door locks standard on Grand Am SE, Firebird GTA, Bonneville SSE and 6000 STE.

## 1987

### 1000 4

| | | | |
|---|---|---|---|
| 3 Dr Hbk | **7309** | 1000 | 1725 |
| 5 Dr Hbk | **7449** | 1100 | 1825 |

| Year/Model/Body/Type | Original List | Current Whlse | Average Retail |
|---|---|---|---|
| **6000 4\*** | | | |
| 2 Dr Cpe | **11274** | 1800 | 2650 |
| 4 Dr Sdn | **11274** | 1900 | 2750 |
| 4 Dr Wgn | **11674** | 2125 | 2975 |
| **6000 LE 4\*** | | | |
| 4 Dr Sdn | **11874** | 2200 | 3050 |
| 4 Dr Wgn | **12274** | 2400 | 3275 |
| *For 6 cyl models add $300 whsle/$300 retail.* | | | |
| **6000 SE 6** | | | |
| 4 Dr Sdn | **13164** | 2800 | 3700 |
| 4 Dr Wgn | **13824** | 3025 | 3925 |
| **6000 STE 6** | | | |
| 4 Dr Sdn | **18099** | 4425 | 5350 |
| **BONNEVILLE 6** | | | |
| 4 Dr Sdn | **13399** | 3350 | 4250 |
| 4 Dr LE Sdn | **14866** | 4000 | 4900 |
| **FIERO 4\*** | | | |
| 2 Dr Cpe | **9564** | 1700 | 2550 |
| 2 Dr Sport Cpe | **11254** | 2000 | 2850 |
| 2 Dr SE Cpe | **12504** | 2575 | 3450 |
| 2 Dr GT Cpe (6 cyl) | **14754** | 3875 | 4775 |
| *For 6 cyl models add $325 whsle/$325 retail.* | | | |
| **FIREBIRD 6\*** | | | |
| 2 Dr Cpe | **11624** | 2825 | 3725 |
| *For 8 cyl models add $300 whsle/$300 retail.* | | | |
| **FIREBIRD 8** | | | |
| 2 Dr Trans Am | **14524** | 4600 | 5525 |
| **GRAND AM 4\*** | | | |
| 2 Dr Cpe | **10464** | 2550 | 3450 |
| 4 Dr Sdn | **10664** | 2550 | 3450 |
| 2 Dr LE Cpe | **11164** | 2625 | 3525 |
| 4 Dr LE Sdn | **11364** | 2625 | 3525 |
| 2 Dr SE Cpe (6 cyl) | **13334** | 3475 | 4375 |
| 4 Dr SE Sdn (6 cyl) | **13574** | 3475 | 4375 |
| *For 6 cyl models add $300 whsle/$300 retail.* | | | |
| **GRAND PRIX 6\*** | | | |
| 2 Dr Cpe | **11844** | 2950 | 3850 |
| 2 Dr LE Cpe | **12574** | 3225 | 4125 |
| 2 Dr Brougham Cpe | **13294** | 3550 | 4450 |
| *For 8 cyl models add $350 whsle/$350 retail.* | | | |
| **SAFARI 8** | | | |
| 4 Dr Wgn | **13959** | 3500 | 4400 |
| **SUNBIRD 4** | | | |
| 4 Dr Sdn | **9211** | 2000 | 2850 |

| Year/Model/Body/Type | Original List | Current Whlse | Average Retail |
|---|---|---|---|
| 4 Dr Wgn | **9741** | 2125 | 2975 |
| **SUNBIRD GT 4** | | | |
| 2 Dr Cpe | **11389** | 3125 | 4025 |
| 4 Dr Sdn | **11439** | 3200 | 4100 |
| 3 Dr Hbk | **11789** | 3200 | 4100 |
| 2 Dr Conv | **16659** | 5225 | 6150 |
| **SUNBIRD SE 4** | | | |
| 2 Dr Cpe | **9191** | 2125 | 2975 |
| 3 Dr Hbk | **9711** | 2200 | 3050 |
| 2 Dr Conv | **14889** | 4350 | 5275 |
| *ADD FOR:* | | | |
| Formula Opt (Base Firebird) | **1070** | 260 | 280 |
| GTA Opt (Firebird Trans Am) | **2700** | 650 | 720 |
| SE Opt (Bonneville LE) | **940** | 220 | 240 |
| Hatchroof (Grand Prix) | **906** | 220 | 240 |
| (Firebird) | **920** | 220 | 240 |
| 5.7 Liter V8 Eng (Base Firebird, Firebird, Trans Am) | **1045** | 260 | 280 |

NOTE: Power brakes standard on all models except 1000. Power locks standard on 6000 STE. Power windows standard on Bonneville, 6000 STE, Bonneville LE and Grand Prix Brougham.

## 1986

| Year/Model/Body/Type | Original List | Current Whlse | Average Retail |
|---|---|---|---|
| **1000 4** | | | |
| 3 Dr Hbk | **7209** | 800 | 1500 |
| 5 Dr Hbk | **7349** | 875 | 1600 |
| **6000 4\*** | | | |
| 2 Dr Cpe | **10560** | 1225 | 1950 |
| 4 Dr Sdn | **10740** | 1300 | 2025 |
| 4 Dr Wgn | **11120** | 1475 | 2300 |
| **6000 LE 4\*** | | | |
| 2 Dr Cpe | **11070** | 1450 | 2225 |
| 4 Dr Sdn | **11220** | 1550 | 2400 |
| 4 Dr Wgn | **11610** | 1725 | 2575 |
| *For 6 cyl models add $300 whsle/$300 retail.* | | | |
| **6000 STE 6** | | | |
| 4 Dr Sdn | **16345** | 3225 | 4125 |
| **BONNEVILLE 6\*** | | | |
| 4 Dr Sdn | **10354** | 1650 | 2500 |
| 4 Dr LE Sdn | **11644** | 1850 | 2700 |
| 4 Dr Brougham Sdn | **12224** | 2125 | 2975 |
| *For 8 cyl models add $375 whsle/$375 retail.* | | | |

| Year/Model/Body/Type | Original List | Current Whlse | Average Retail |
|---|---|---|---|
| **FIERO 4** | | | |
| 2 Dr Cpe (NA w/auto trans) | **8421** | 1250 | 1975 |
| 2 Dr Sport Cpe | **10764** | 1500 | 2350 |
| 2 Dr SE Cpe | **11954** | 1975 | 2825 |
| 2 Dr GT Cpe (6 cyl) | **14314** | 3125 | 4025 |
| *For 6 cyl models add $300 whsle/$300 retail. | | | |
| **FIREBIRD 4\*** | | | |
| 2 Dr Cpe | **10760** | 2175 | 3025 |
| *For 6 cyl models add $300 whsle/$300 retail. | | | |
| **FIREBIRD 6\*** | | | |
| 2 Dr SE Cpe | **13210** | 2800 | 3700 |
| *For 8 cyl models add $300 whsle/$300 retail. | | | |
| **FIREBIRD 8** | | | |
| 2 Dr Trans Am | **13940** | 3700 | 4600 |
| **GRAND AM 4\*** | | | |
| 2 Dr Cpe | **9924** | 1725 | 2575 |
| 4 Dr Sdn | **10124** | 1725 | 2575 |
| 2 Dr LE Cpe | **10470** | 1925 | 2775 |
| 4 Dr LE Sdn | **10670** | 1925 | 2775 |
| 2 Dr SE Cpe (6 cyl) | **12474** | 2650 | 3550 |
| 4 Dr SE Sdn (6 cyl) | **12724** | 2650 | 3550 |
| *For 6 cyl models add $250 whsle/$250 retail. | | | |
| **GRAND PRIX 6\*** | | | |
| 2 Dr Cpe | **11354** | 1925 | 2775 |
| 2 Dr LE Cpe | **11914** | 2175 | 3025 |
| 2 Dr Brougham Cpe | **12724** | 2450 | 3325 |
| *For 8 cyl models add $325 whsle/$325 retail. | | | |
| **PARISIENNE 6\*** | | | |
| 4 Dr Sdn | **12294** | 1900 | 2750 |
| 4 Dr Wgn (8 cyl) | **12914** | 2425 | 3300 |
| 4 Dr Brougham Sdn | **13094** | 2375 | 3250 |
| *For 8 cyl models add $400 whsle/$400 retail. | | | |
| **SUNBIRD 4** | | | |
| 4 Dr Sdn | **9112** | 1475 | 2300 |
| 4 Dr Wgn | **9502** | 1575 | 2425 |
| **SUNBIRD GT 4** | | | |
| 2 Dr Cpe | **11069** | 2300 | 3175 |
| 4 Dr Sdn | **11119** | 2400 | 3275 |
| 3 Dr Hbk | **11445** | 2400 | 3275 |
| 2 Dr Conv | **15904** | 4075 | 5000 |
| **SUNBIRD SE 4** | | | |
| 2 Dr Cpe | **9076** | 1575 | 2425 |
| 3 Dr Hbk | **9462** | 1675 | 2525 |
| 2 Dr Conv | **14169** | 3350 | 4250 |
| *ADD FOR:* | | | |
| Brougham Landau | | | |

| Year/Model/Body/Type | Original List | Current Whlse | Average Retail |
|---|---|---|---|
| (Grand Prix Brougham) | **469** | 80 | 90 |
| Driver Enthusiast Pkg (Grand Am) | **699** | 120 | 130 |
| Turbo Eng Pkg (Sunbird except SE Conv) | **1511** | 260 | 280 |
| (Sunbird SE Conv) | **1296** | 220 | 240 |
| Hatchroof (Grand Prix) | **931** | 160 | 180 |
| (Firebird) | **895** | 160 | 170 |
| Spt Landau Roof (6000) | **712** | 120 | 130 |
| 2.8 Liter V6 EFI Eng (Base 6000, 6000 LE) | **610** | 110 | 120 |
| 5.0 Liter V8 Eng (Base Firebird) | **800** | 140 | 150 |
| 5.0 Liter HO V8 Eng (Trans Am) | **745** | 130 | 140 |

NOTE: Power windows standard on 6000 STE, Grand Prix Brougham and Sunbird Convertible. Power brakes standard on 6000 STE, Bonneville, Fiero, Firebird, Grand Am, Grand Prix, Parisienne and Sunbird.

## 1985

| Year/Model/Body/Type | Original List | Current Whlse | Average Retail |
|---|---|---|---|
| **1000 4** | | | |
| 3 Dr Hbk | **6860** | 675 | 1275 |
| 5 Dr Hbk | **7080** | 775 | 1500 |
| **6000 4\*** | | | |
| 2 Dr Cpe | **9839** | 1075 | 1800 |
| 4 Dr Sdn | **9999** | 1125 | 1850 |
| 4 Dr Wgn | **10349** | 1275 | 2000 |
| **6000 LE 4\*** | | | |
| 2 Dr Cpe | **10339** | 1250 | 1975 |
| 4 Dr Sdn | **10489** | 1325 | 2050 |
| 4 Dr Wgn | **10849** | 1475 | 2300 |
| *For 6 cyl models add $300 whsle/$300 retail. | | | |
| **6000 STE 6** | | | |
| 4 Dr Sdn | **15125** | 2475 | 3350 |
| **BONNEVILLE 6\*** | | | |
| 4 Dr Sdn | **10647** | 1275 | 2000 |
| 4 Dr LE Sdn | **10893** | 1425 | 2175 |
| 4 Dr Brougham Sdn | **11393** | 1650 | 2500 |
| *For 8 cyl models add $300 whsle/$300 retail. | | | |
| **FIERO 4** | | | |
| 2 Dr Cpe (NA w/auto trans) | **8607** | 950 | 1675 |
| 2 Dr Sport Cpe | **10170** | 1275 | 2000 |
| 2 Dr SE Cpe | **11170** | 1700 | 2550 |
| **FIERO 6** | | | |
| 2 Dr GT Cpe | **13020** | 2450 | 3325 |

| Year/Model/Body/Type | Original List | Current Whlse | Average Retail |
|---|---|---|---|
| **FIREBIRD 4*** | | | |
| 2 Dr Cpe | **10024** | 1450 | 2225 |
| *For 6 cyl models add $300 whsle/$300 retail. | | | |
| **FIREBIRD 6*** | | | |
| 2 Dr SE Cpe | **12470** | 2100 | 2950 |
| *For 8 cyl models add $300 whsle/$300 retail. | | | |
| **FIREBIRD 8** | | | |
| 2 Dr Trans Am Cpe | **12744** | 2775 | 3675 |
| **GRAND AM 4*** | | | |
| 2 Dr Cpe | **9319** | 1325 | 2050 |
| 2 Dr LE Cpe | **9829** | 1525 | 2375 |
| *For 6 cyl models add $200 whsle/$200 retail. | | | |
| **GRAND PRIX 6** | | | |
| 2 Dr Cpe | **10509** | 1500 | 2350 |
| 2 Dr LE Cpe | **11009** | 1700 | 2550 |
| 2 Dr Brougham Cpe | **11745** | 1950 | 2800 |
| *For 8 cyl models add $300 whsle/$300 retail. | | | |
| **PARISIENNE 6*** | | | |
| 4 Dr Sdn | **11497** | 1575 | 2425 |
| 4 Dr Wgn (8 cyl) | **12073** | 1850 | 2700 |
| 4 Dr Brougham Sdn | **12247** | 1950 | 2800 |
| *For 8 cyl models add $375 whsle/$375 retail. | | | |
| **SUNBIRD 4** | | | |
| 2 Dr Cpe | **8317** | 1075 | 1800 |
| 4 Dr Sdn | **8457** | 1175 | 1900 |
| 3 Dr Hbk | **8687** | 1175 | 1900 |
| 4 Dr Wgn | **8807** | 1250 | 1975 |
| **SUNBIRD LE 4** | | | |
| 2 Dr Cpe | **8905** | 1300 | 2025 |
| 4 Dr Sdn | **9105** | 1375 | 2125 |
| 4 Dr Wgn | **9435** | 1450 | 2225 |
| 2 Dr Conv | **13290** | 2725 | 3625 |
| **SUNBIRD SE 4** | | | |
| 2 Dr Cpe | **10549** | 1675 | 2525 |
| 4 Dr Sdn | **10719** | 1750 | 2600 |
| 3 Dr Hbk | **11049** | 1750 | 2600 |
| *ADD FOR:* | | | |
| Brougham Landau (Grand Prix) | **469** | 50 | 50 |
| Driver Enthusiast Pkg (Grand Am) | **670** | 70 | 80 |
| Hatch Roof (Grand Prix) | **850** | 120 | 130 |
| (Firebird) | **875** | 120 | 130 |
| 2.8 Liter V6 Eng (6000, 6000 LE) | **435** | 50 | 50 |

| Year/Model/Body/Type | Original List | Current Whlse | Average Retail |
|---|---|---|---|
| (Fiero SE) | **595** | 120 | 130 |
| 5.0 Liter EFI V8 Eng (Trans Am) | **695** | 80 | 90 |
| 5.0 Liter V8 Eng (Base Firebird) | **650** | 100 | 110 |
| (Bonneville, Grand Prix) | **490** | 100 | 110 |
| (Parisienne Sdn) | **340** | 120 | 130 |
| *DEDUCT FOR:* | | | |
| 4.3 Liter V6 Diesel Eng (6000, 6000 LE) | **335** | 330 | 360 |

NOTE: Power brakes standard on all models. Power windows standard on 6000 STE and Fiero GT. Power locks standard on 6000 STE.

## 1984

| Year/Model/Body/Type | Original List | Current Whlse | Average Retail |
|---|---|---|---|
| **1000 4** | | | |
| 3 Dr Hbk Cpe | **6843** | 225 | 475 |
| 5 Dr Hbk Sdn | **7046** | 300 | 575 |
| **2000 4** | | | |
| 2 Dr Cpe | **7933** | 700 | 1325 |
| 4 Dr Sdn | **8057** | 775 | 1500 |
| 3 Dr Hbk | **8253** | 775 | 1500 |
| 4 Dr Wgn | **8373** | 825 | 1525 |
| **2000 LE 4** | | | |
| 2 Dr Cpe | **8479** | 875 | 1600 |
| 4 Dr Sdn | **8645** | 900 | 1625 |
| 4 Dr Wgn | **8965** | 950 | 1675 |
| 2 Dr Conv | **12691** | 1825 | 2675 |
| **2000 SE 4** | | | |
| 2 Dr Cpe | **10034** | 1200 | 1925 |
| 4 Dr Sdn | **10200** | 1275 | 2000 |
| 3 Dr Hbk | **10504** | 1275 | 2000 |
| **6000 4*** | | | |
| 2 Dr Cpe | **9420** | 900 | 1625 |
| 4 Dr Sdn | **9594** | 1000 | 1725 |
| 4 Dr Wgn | **9942** | 1125 | 1850 |
| **6000 LE 4*** | | | |
| 2 Dr Cpe | **9863** | 1050 | 1775 |
| 4 Dr Sdn | **10013** | 1150 | 1875 |
| 4 Dr Wgn | **10333** | 1275 | 2000 |
| *For 6 cyl models add $200 whsle/$200 retail. | | | |
| **6000 STE 6** | | | |
| Sdn | **14428** | 1675 | 2525 |
| **BONNEVILLE 6*** | | | |
| 4 Dr Sdn | **9963** | 900 | 1625 |
| 4 Dr LE Sdn | **10190** | 1025 | 1750 |

*Refer to optional equipment schedules*

| Year/Model/Body/Type | Original List | Current Whlse | Average Retail |
|---|---|---|---|
| **BONNEVILLE BROUGHAM 6*** | | | |
| 4 Dr Sdn | **10667** | 1150 | 1875 |
| *For 8 cyl models add $200 whsle/$200 retail. | | | |
| **FIERO 4** | | | |
| 2 Dr Cpe | **8102** | 575 | 1075 |
| 2 Dr Sport Cpe | **9645** | 875 | 1600 |
| 2 Dr SE Cpe | **10742** | 1150 | 1875 |
| **FIREBIRD 4*** | | | |
| 2 Dr Cpe | **9706** | 1325 | 2050 |
| *For 6 cyl models add $200 whsle/$200 retail. | | | |
| **FIREBIRD 6*** | | | |
| 2 Dr S/E Cpe | **11776** | 1775 | 2625 |
| *For 8 cyl models add $200 whsle/$200 retail. | | | |
| **FIREBIRD 8** | | | |
| Trans Am | **11826** | 2350 | 3225 |
| **GRAND PRIX 6*** | | | |
| 2 Dr | **9977** | 1075 | 1800 |
| 2 Dr LE | **10456** | 1250 | 1975 |
| 2 Dr Brougham | **11131** | 1400 | 2150 |
| *For 8 cyl models add $200 whsle/$200 retail. | | | |
| **PARISIENNE 6** | | | |
| 4 Dr Sdn | **10712** | 1175 | 1900 |
| 4 Dr Wgn (8 cyl) | **11224** | 1300 | 2025 |
| **PARISIENNE BROUGHAM 6** | | | |
| 4 Dr Sdn | **11112** | 1425 | 2175 |
| *For 8 cyl models add $300 whsle/$300 retail. | | | |
| **PHOENIX 4*** | | | |
| 2 Dr Cpe | **8451** | 450 | 825 |
| 5 Dr Hbk | **8526** | 500 | 925 |
| **PHOENIX LE 4*** | | | |
| 2 Dr Cpe | **9044** | 600 | 1125 |
| 5 Dr Hbk | **9177** | 675 | 1275 |
| *For 6 cyl models add $175 whsle/$175 retail. | | | |
| **PHOENIX SE 6** | | | |
| 2 Dr Cpe | **10217** | 1000 | 1725 |

NOTE: Power brakes standard on Bonneville, Grand Prix, Firebird, Fiero, 2000 Series, 6000 Series and Phoenix SJ. Power windows standard on Grand Prix Brougham and 6000 STE.

### 1983 — ALL BODY STYLES

| | | | |
|---|---|---|---|
| 1000 | — | 150 | 350 |
| 2000 | — | 475 | 875 |
| 2000 LE | — | 600 | 1125 |
| 2000 SE | — | 800 | 1500 |

| Year/Model/Body/Type | Original List | Current Whlse | Average Retail |
|---|---|---|---|
| 2000 SUNBIRD CONV | — | 1250 | 1975 |
| 6000 | — | 800 | 1500 |
| 6000 LE | — | 875 | 1600 |
| 6000 STE | — | 1350 | 2100 |
| BONNEVILLE | — | 900 | 1625 |
| BONNEVILLE BROUGHAM | — | 1000 | 1725 |
| FIREBIRD | — | 1150 | 1875 |
| FIREBIRD SE | — | 1500 | 2350 |
| FIREBIRD TRANS AM | — | 2075 | 2925 |
| GRAND PRIX | — | 900 | 1625 |
| GRAND PRIX LJ | — | 1025 | 1750 |
| GRAND PRIX BROUGHAM | — | 1150 | 1875 |
| PARISIENNE | — | 975 | 1700 |
| PARISIENNE BROUGHAM | — | 1150 | 1875 |
| PHOENIX | — | 275 | 550 |
| PHOENIX LJ | — | 375 | 675 |
| PHOENIX SJ | — | 625 | 1175 |

## SATURN

### 1992

**SATURN 4**

| | Original List | Current Whlse | Average Retail |
|---|---|---|---|
| 4 Dr SL Sdn (NA w/power steering or auto trans) | **9220** | 7500 | 8700 |
| 4 Dr SL1 Sdn | **10745** | 7925 | 9200 |
| 4 Dr SL2 Sdn | **12145** | 10125 | 11675 |
| 2 Dr SC Cpe | **13525** | 11525 | 13300 |

*ADD FOR:*

| | | | |
|---|---|---|---|
| Anti-Lock Brakes | **595** | 400 | 450 |
| Leather Trim (SL2, SC) | **610** | 325 | 375 |

NOTE: Tilt steering wheel standard on all models.

### 1991

**SATURN 4**

| | Original List | Current Whlse | Average Retail |
|---|---|---|---|
| 4 Dr SL Sdn (NA w/pwr strng) | **9385** | 7075 | 8225 |
| 4 Dr SL1 Sdn | **9985** | 7425 | 8625 |
| 4 Dr SL2 Sdn | **11685** | 9475 | 10925 |
| 2 Dr SC Cpe | **13165** | 10650 | 12300 |

*ADD FOR:*

| | | | |
|---|---|---|---|
| Anti-lock Brakes | **895** | 410 | 460 |

NOTE: Power brakes standard on all models.

*1984 Chevrolet S-10 Extended Cab 2WD*

| Year/Model/ Body/Type | Original List | Current Whlse | Average Retail |
|---|---|---|---|
| **CHEVROLET** | | | |
| **1992** | | | |
| **S-10 BLAZER 2WD 6** | | | |
| 2 Dr Sport Utility | **15603** | 12850 | 15175 |
| 4 Dr Sport Utility | **16563** | 13600 | 15975 |
| *ADD FOR:* | | | |
| CAA2 Tahoe/Sport Equip Pkg | **1024** | 715 | 795 |
| CAA3 Tahoe/Sport Equip Pkg | **2870** | 1705 | 1895 |
| DAA2 Tahoe/Sport Equip Pkg | | | |
| (2WD 4 Dr) | **554** | 395 | 445 |
| (NA w/pwr strng) | **5607** | 550 | 975 |
| 3 Dr GVL Hbk | | | |
| (NA w/pwr strng) | **5837** | 650 | 1300 |

NOTE: Power brakes standard on all models.

| **K-1500 BLAZER 4WD 111.5" WB 8** | | | |
|---|---|---|---|
| Wgn | **20125** | 15600 | 17875 |
| *ADD FOR:* | | | |
| K5A2 Silverado Pkg | **2276** | 900 | 1000 |
| K5A3 Silverado Pkg | **2933** | 900 | 1000 |
| Sport Silverado Pkg | **2926** | 1100 | 1250 |

| **C-1500 PICKUPS 117.5" WB 6*** | | | |
|---|---|---|---|
| Fleetside | **13900** | 10850 | 12525 |
| Sportside | **14300** | 10700 | 12350 |

*For 8 cyl models add $475 whlse/$475 retail.

| **C-1500 PICKUPS 117.5" WB 8** | | | |
|---|---|---|---|
| 454 SS Fleetside | **20585** | — | — |

| Year/Model/ Body/Type | Original List | Current Whlse | Average Retail |
|---|---|---|---|
| **C-1500 PICKUPS 131.5" WB 6*** | | | |
| Fleetside | **14200** | 10975 | 12700 |
| Work Truck Fleetside | **11405** | 10400 | 12025 |

*For 8 cyl models add $475 whlse/$475 retail.

| **C-1500 EXTENDED PICKUPS 141.5" WB 6*** | | | |
|---|---|---|---|
| Fleetside | **14850** | 11525 | 13325 |
| Sportside | **15250** | 11400 | 13175 |

*For 8 cyl models add $475 whlse/$475 retail.

| **C-1500 EXTENDED PICKUPS 155.5" WB 6*** | | | |
|---|---|---|---|
| Fleetside | **15140** | 12350 | 14500 |

*For 8 cyl models add $475 whlse/$475 retail.

| *ADD FOR:* | | | |
|---|---|---|---|
| 5.7 Liter 8 Cyl Eng | **845** | 600 | 600 |
| 6.2 Liter 8 Cyl Diesel Eng. | **2400** | 1195 | 1335 |
| Work Truck Group 2 | **790** | 545 | 605 |
| Scottsdale Pkg | **738** | 505 | 565 |
| P1A3 Silverado Pkg | **1948** | 1375 | 1535 |
| P1A4 Silverado Pkg | **2820** | 1775 | 1975 |
| Sport Scottsdale Pkg | **1378** | 945 | 1055 |
| Sport Silverado Pkg | | | |
| (2WD) | **2881** | 1775 | 1975 |
| (4WD) | **3129** | 1915 | 2135 |

| **C-2500 PICKUP 131.5" WB 6*** | | | |
|---|---|---|---|
| Fleetside | **14840** | 12425 | 14650 |

*For 8 cyl models add $500 whlse/$500 retail.

| **C-2500 HD PICKUP 131.5" WB 6*** | | | |
|---|---|---|---|
| Fleetside | **15673** | 12675 | 14900 |

*For 8 cyl models add $500 whlse/$500 retail.

| Year/Model/ Body/Type | Original List | Current Whlse | Average Retail |
|---|---|---|---|
| **C-2500 EXTENDED PICKUP 141.5" WB 6*** | | | |
| Fleetside | **15960** | 13400 | 15600 |
| *For 8 cyl models add $500 whsle/$500 retail. | | | |
| **C-2500 EXTENDED PICKUP 155.5" WB 6*** | | | |
| Fleetside | **16240** | 13675 | 14950 |
| *For 8 cyl models add $500 whsle/$500 retail. | | | |
| **C-2500 HD EXTENDED PICKUP 155" WB 6*** | | | |
| Fleetside | **16733** | 13900 | 15275 |
| *For 8 cyl models add $500 whsle/$500 retail. | | | |
| ADD FOR: | | | |
| 5.7 Liter 8 Cyl Eng | **845** | 450 | 450 |
| 7.4 Liter 8 Cyl Eng | **1315** | 750 | 7500 |
| 6.2 Liter 8 Cyl Diesel Eng. | **2400** | 1100 | 1100 |
| 6.5 Liter 8 Cyl Turbo Diesel Eng | **3100** | 1500 | 1500 |
| Scottsdale Pkg | **853** | 585 | 655 |
| Silverado Pkg | **2453** | 1555 | 1735 |
| **S-10 PICKUPS4*** | | | |
| Fleetside EL (108" WB) | **9883** | 6825 | 7950 |
| Fleetside (108" WB) | **10888** | 7875 | 9200 |
| Fleetside (118" WB) | **11188** | 8000 | 9350 |
| Fleetside Maxi Cab (123" WB) | **12113** | 8550 | 9875 |
| *For 6 cyl models add $475 whsle/$475 retail. | | | |
| ADD FOR: | | | |
| 4.3 Liter 6 Cyl Eng | **620** | 525 | 525 |
| **C-1500 SUBURBAN 129.5" WB 8** | | | |
| Panel Doors | **19000** | 16100 | 18650 |
| ADD FOR: | | | |
| NA2 Silverado Pkg | **3507** | 1100 | 1250 |
| NA3 Silverado Pkg | **4796** | 1350 | 1500 |
| **C-2500 SUBURBAN 129.5" WB 8** | | | |
| Panel Doors | **20204** | 16700 | 19150 |
| ADD FOR: | | | |
| 7.4 Liter 8 Cyl Eng | **470** | 400 | 400 |
| Silverado Pkg | **4528** | 1350 | 1500 |
| **ASTRO 111" WB 2WD 6** | | | |
| Cargo Van | **14840** | 11100 | 12825 |
| Extended Cargo Van | **15510** | 11900 | 13750 |
| Pass Van | **16030** | 12650 | 14975 |
| Extended Pass Van | **16720** | 13425 | 15800 |
| ADD FOR: | | | |
| 4.3 Liter 6 Cyl Eng (2WD models) | **500** | 335 | 375 |
| CL Decor Pkg | **633** | 625 | 695 |
| LT Decor Pkg | **2848** | 1415 | 1575 |

| Year/Model/ Body/Type | Original List | Current Whlse | Average Retail |
|---|---|---|---|
| **LUMINA APV 6** | | | |
| Cargo Van | **15205** | — | — |
| Wgn | **16400** | 12700 | 15025 |
| CL Wgn | **17355** | 13425 | 15800 |
| ADD FOR: | | | |
| 3.8 Liter 6 Cyl Eng | **619** | 445 | 495 |
| **G-10 VANS 110" WB 6*** | | | |
| Chevyvan | **15290** | 11250 | 13000 |
| Sportvan | **17030** | 12725 | 15050 |
| *For 8 Cyl models add $475 whsle/$475 retail. | | | |
| **G-10 VANS 125" WB 6*** | | | |
| Chevyvan | **15570** | 11400 | 13175 |
| Sportvan | **17970** | 13150 | 15475 |
| *For 8 Cyl models add $475 whsle/$475 retail. | | | |
| ADD FOR: | | | |
| Beauville Group (Sportvan) | **3652** | 2135 | 2375 |
| Beauville Trim Pkg (Sportvan) | **818** | 625 | 695 |
| **G-20 VANS 125" WB 6*** | | | |
| Chevyvan | **15810** | 11650 | 13475 |
| Sportvan | **18160** | 13025 | 15350 |
| *For 8 Cyl models add $475 whsle/$475 retail. | | | |
| ADD FOR: | | | |
| 5.7 Liter 8 Cyl Eng | **845** | 585 | 655 |
| 6.2 Liter LD 8 Cyl Eng | **2400** | 1195 | 1335 |

## 1991

| Year/Model/ Body/Type | Original List | Current Whlse | Average Retail |
|---|---|---|---|
| **S-10 BLAZER 2WD 6** | | | |
| 2 Dr Sport Utility | **14625** | 10975 | 12575 |
| 4 Dr Sport Utility | **15865** | 11675 | 13375 |
| **V-1500 BLAZER 4WD 106.5" WB 8** | | | |
| Wgn | **18435** | 13025 | 15225 |
| Wgn, HD Diesel | **21363** | 13375 | 15625 |
| **C-1500 GAS PICKUPS 117.5" WB 6*** | | | |
| Fleetside | **12920** | 8750 | 10000 |
| Sportside | **13260** | 8875 | 10125 |
| 454 SS Fleetside (8 Cyl) | **19610** | 12650 | 14850 |
| Fleetside (131" WB) | **13220** | 9100 | 10375 |
| Fleetside Ext Cab (141" WB) | **13870** | 9650 | 11000 |
| Sportside Ext Cab (141" WB) | **14210** | 9725 | 11075 |
| Fleetside Ext Cab (155" WB) | **14160** | 9750 | 11125 |
| *For 8 cyl models add $425 whsle/$425 retail. | | | |
| **C-1500 DIESEL PICKUPS 131.5" WB 8** | | | |
| Fleetside | **16250** | 10050 | 11475 |
| Fleetside Extended Cab | | | |

| Year/Model/<br>Body/Type | Original<br>List | Current<br>Whlse | Average<br>Retail |
|---|---|---|---|
| (141" WB) | **16690** | 10450 | 11950 |
| Sportside Extended Cab | | | |
| (141" WB) | **17030** | 10525 | 12050 |
| Fleetside Extended Cab | | | |
| (155" WB) | **16980** | 10550 | 12075 |

### C-2500 GAS PICKUPS 131.5" WB 6*

| | | | |
|---|---|---|---|
| Fleetside | **13860** | 9525 | 10850 |
| Heavy Duty Fleetside | **14514** | 9775 | 11150 |
| Fleetside Extended Cab | | | |
| (141" WB) | **14980** | 10250 | 11725 |
| Fleetside Extended Cab | | | |
| (155" WB) | **15260** | 10375 | 11875 |
| Heavy Duty Fleetside | | | |
| Extended Cab | | | |
| (155" WB) | **15564** | 10675 | 12225 |

*For 8 Cyl models add $425 whsle/$425 retail.

### C-2500 DIESEL PICKUPS 131.5" WB 8

| | | | |
|---|---|---|---|
| Fleetside | **16320** | 10275 | 11750 |
| Heavy Duty Fleetside | **16793** | 10575 | 12100 |
| Fleetside Extended Cab | | | |
| (141" WB) | **17430** | 11125 | 12750 |
| Fleetside Extended Cab | | | |
| (155" WB) | **17720** | 11250 | 12900 |
| Heavy Duty Fleetside | | | |
| Extended Cab | | | |
| (155" WB) | **17904** | 11550 | 13225 |

### S-10 REG CAB PICKUPS 4*

| | | | |
|---|---|---|---|
| Fleetside EL (108" WB) | | | |
| (NA w/pwr strng) | **9350** | 5675 | 6475 |
| Fleetside (108" WB) | **10645** | 6250 | 7150 |
| Fleetside (118" WB) | **10945** | 6350 | 7275 |
| Fleetside Extended Cab | | | |
| (123" WB) | **12226** | 6850 | 7850 |

*For 6 Cyl models add $450 whsle/$450 retail.

### R-1500 SUBURBAN 129.5" WB 8

| | | | |
|---|---|---|---|
| Panel Doors | **17405** | 13200 | 15450 |
| Tailgate | **17565** | 13300 | 15550 |
| Panel Doors, Diesel | **19843** | 13650 | 15900 |
| Tailgate, Diesel | **19998** | 13750 | 16075 |

### R-2500 SUBURBAN 129.5" WB 8

| | | | |
|---|---|---|---|
| Panel Doors | **18963** | 13700 | 16025 |
| Tailgate | **19113** | 13800 | 16125 |
| Panel Doors, Diesel | **20701** | 14125 | 16525 |
| Tailgate, Diesel | **20861** | 14200 | 16600 |

### ASTRO 111" WB 6

| | | | |
|---|---|---|---|
| Cargo Van | **14305** | 9200 | 10475 |
| CS Pass Van | **15425** | 11050 | 12650 |
| CL Pass Van | **16505** | 11750 | 13475 |
| LT Pass Van | **18055** | 12250 | 14275 |

### ASTRO EXTENDED 111" WB 6

| | | | |
|---|---|---|---|
| Cargo Van | **14975** | 9950 | 11350 |
| CS Pass Van | **16115** | 11875 | 13600 |
| CL Pass Van | **17195** | 12500 | 14700 |
| LT Pass Van | **18745** | 13075 | 15275 |

### LUMINA APV 6

| | | | |
|---|---|---|---|
| Cargo Van | **14422** | 8900 | 10300 |
| Wgn | **15560** | 10900 | 12450 |
| CL Wgn | **16450** | 11600 | 13250 |

### G-10 VANS 110" WB 6*

| | | | |
|---|---|---|---|
| Chevyvan | **14585** | 9100 | 10375 |
| Sportvan | **16315** | 10500 | 12000 |
| Beauville (125" WB) | **18155** | 11750 | 13475 |
| w/125" WB add | | | |
| (Chevyvan) | **280** | 100 | 130 |
| (Sportvan) | **950** | 460 | 570 |

*For 8 Cyl models add $425 whsle/$425 retail.

### G-20 VANS 110" WB 6*

| | | | |
|---|---|---|---|
| Chevyvan | **14765** | 9275 | 10575 |
| Chevyvan Diese (8 Cyl) | **17438** | 10075 | 11500 |
| Chevyvan Diesel | | | |
| (125" WB) (8 Cyl) | **17728** | 10200 | 11675 |
| Sportvan (125" WB) | **17415** | 10825 | 12375 |
| Beauville Sportvan | | | |
| (125" WB) | **18295** | 11900 | 13650 |
| Sportvan Diesel | | | |
| (125" WB) (8 Cyl) | **20085** | 11675 | 13375 |
| Beauville Sportvan | | | |
| Diesel (125" WB) (8 Cyl) | **20838** | 12700 | 14900 |
| w/125" WB add | | | |
| (Chevyvan) | **290** | 100 | 130 |

*For 8 Cyl models add $425 whsle/$425 retail.

*ADD FOR:*

| | | | |
|---|---|---|---|
| Baja Equip | | | |
| (S-10 4WD Pickups) | **1260** | 640 | 800 |
| Scottsdale Pkg | | | |
| (C-K Pickups) | **573** | 240 | 300 |
| Silverado Pkg | | | |
| (V-1500 Blazer) | **1298** | 660 | 820 |
| (C-K Pickups) | **1012** | 1260 | 1540 |
| (Suburban) | **1600** | 1580 | 1920 |
| Tahoe Equip Pkg | | | |
| (S-10 Blazer) | **841** | 400 | 500 |
| (S-10 Pickup) | **587** | 240 | 310 |

## 1990

### S-10 BLAZER 2WD 100.5" WB 6

| | | | |
|---|---|---|---|
| Sport Utility | **13695** | 7475 | 8550 |

### V-10 BLAZER 4WD 106.5" WB 8

| | | | |
|---|---|---|---|
| Wgn | **17305** | 9875 | 11250 |

| Year/Model/Body/Type | Original List | Current Whlse | Average Retail |
|---|---|---|---|
| Wgn, Diesel | **19998** | 10250 | 11725 |

### C-1500 GAS PICKUPS 117.5" WB 6*

| | | | |
|---|---|---|---|
| Fleetside | **12080** | 6825 | 7825 |
| Sportside | **12405** | 6925 | 7925 |
| 454 SS Fleetside (8 cyl) | **18295** | 10075 | 11525 |
| Fleetside (131" WB) | **12380** | 7075 | 8100 |
| Fleetside Ext Cab (141" WB) | **12990** | 7650 | 8750 |
| Fleetside Ext Cab (155" WB) | **13270** | 7775 | 8900 |
| Fleetside Work Truck (131" WB) | **11347** | 6625 | 7575 |

*For 8 Cyl models add $400 whlse/$400 retail.

### C-1500 DIESEL PICKUPS 131.5" WB 8

| | | | |
|---|---|---|---|
| Fleetside | **15170** | 7750 | 8875 |
| Fleetside Ext Cab (141" WB) | **15600** | 8475 | 9675 |
| Fleetside Ext Cab (155" WB) | **15875** | 8600 | 9825 |

### C-2500 GAS PICKUPS 131.5" WB 6*

| | | | |
|---|---|---|---|
| Fleetside | **12985** | 7550 | 8650 |
| Heavy Duty Fleetside | **13609** | 7800 | 8925 |
| Fleetside Ext Cab (141" WB) | **14055** | 8300 | 9450 |
| Fleetside Ext Cab (155" WB) | **14335** | 8425 | 9600 |
| Heavy Duty Fleetside Ext Cab (155" WB) | **14624** | 8550 | 9750 |

*For 8 Cyl models add $400 whlse/$400 retail.

### C-2500 DIESEL PICKUPS 131.5" WB 8

| | | | |
|---|---|---|---|
| Fleetside | **15235** | 8400 | 9575 |
| Heavy Duty Fleetside | **15694** | 8600 | 9825 |
| Fleetside Extended Cab (141" WB) | **16305** | 9100 | 10375 |
| Fleetside Ext Cab (155" WB) | **16585** | 10325 | 11775 |
| Heavy Duty Fleetside Ext Cab (155" WB) | **16759** | 10325 | 11800 |

### S-10 REG CAB PICKUPS 4*

| | | | |
|---|---|---|---|
| Fleetside EL (108" WB) (NA w/pwr strng) | **8951** | 5000 | 5800 |
| Fleetside (108" WB) | **10265** | 5150 | 5950 |
| Fleetside (118" WB) | **10430** | 5275 | 6075 |
| Fleetside Ext Cab (123" WB) | **11215** | 6700 | 7675 |

*For 6 Cyl models add $425 whlse/$425 retail.

### R-1500 SUBURBAN 129.5" WB 8

| | | | |
|---|---|---|---|
| Panel Doors | **16435** | 10950 | 12550 |
| Tailgate | **16586** | 11050 | 12650 |
| Panel Doors, Diesel | **18703** | 11400 | 13050 |
| Tailgate, Diesel | **18848** | 11500 | 13175 |

### R-2500 SUBURBAN 129.5" WB 8

| | | | |
|---|---|---|---|
| Panel Doors | **17058** | 11350 | 13000 |
| Tailgate | **17203** | 11450 | 13125 |
| Panel Doors, HD Diesel | **19286** | 11800 | 13525 |
| Tailgate, HD Diesel | **19436** | 11900 | 13650 |

### ASTRO 111" WB 6

| | | | |
|---|---|---|---|
| Cargo Van (4 Cyl) | **12915** | 6550 | 7500 |
| CS Pass Van | **14610** | 8750 | 10000 |
| CL Pass Van | **15650** | 9350 | 10650 |
| LT Pass Van | **17145** | 9875 | 11250 |

### ASTRO EXTENDED 111" WB 6

| | | | |
|---|---|---|---|
| Cargo Van (4 Cyl) | **14217** | 7225 | 8275 |
| CS Pass Van | **15312** | 9425 | 10750 |
| CL Pass Van | **16352** | 9975 | 11400 |
| LT Pass Van | **17847** | 10500 | 12000 |

### LUMINA APV 6

| | | | |
|---|---|---|---|
| Cargo Van | **13700** | 7700 | 8950 |
| Wgn | **14800** | 9400 | 11150 |
| CL Wgn | **15745** | 10000 | 11775 |

### G-10 VANS 110" WB 6*

| | | | |
|---|---|---|---|
| Chevyvan | **13600** | 7025 | 8025 |
| Sportvan | **15515** | 8475 | 9675 |
| Beauville (125" WB) | **17270** | 9550 | 10875 |
| w/125" WB add | | | |
| (Chevyvan) | **270** | 120 | 150 |
| (Sportvan) | **905** | 360 | 460 |

*For 8 cyl models add $400 whlse/$400 retail.

### G-20 VANS 110" WB 6*

| | | | |
|---|---|---|---|
| Chevyvan | **13770** | 7150 | 8175 |
| Chevyvan Diesel (8 cyl) | **16408** | 8000 | 9175 |
| Chevyvan Diesel (125" WB) (8 cyl) | **16678** | 8150 | 9300 |
| Sportvan (125" WB) | **16565** | 8850 | 10100 |
| Beauville Sportvan (125" WB) | **17410** | 9700 | 11050 |
| Sportvan Diesel (125" WB) (8 cyl) | **18888** | 9650 | 11000 |
| Beauville Sportvan Diesel (125" WB) (8 Cyl) | **19678** | 10400 | 11900 |
| w/125" WB add | | | |
| (Chevyvan) | **280** | 120 | 150 |

*For 8 cyl models add $400 whlse/$400 retail.

### ADD FOR:

| | | | |
|---|---|---|---|
| Baja Equip (S-10 4WD Pickups) | **1260** | 550 | 680 |
| Scottsdale Pkg (C-K Pickups) | **557** | 180 | 240 |
| Silverado Pkg (V-10 Blazer) | **1281** | 560 | 690 |
| (Suburban) | **1583** | 710 | 880 |
| (C-K Pickups) | **1025** | 420 | 530 |
| Sport Pkg (S-10 Blazer) | **1038** | 430 | 540 |
| Tahoe Pkg (S-10 Blazer) | **841** | 330 | 420 |
| (S Pickups) | **574** | 200 | 260 |

| Year/Model/Body/Type | Original List | Current Whlse | Average Retail |
|---|---|---|---|
| **1989** | | | |
| **S-10 BLAZER 2WD 100.5" WB 6** | | | |
| Sport Utility | **11680** | 6300 | 7200 |
| **V-10 BLAZER 4WD 106.5" WB 8** | | | |
| Wgn | **15355** | 8525 | 9725 |
| Wgn, Diesel | **18085** | 8925 | 10200 |
| **C-10 GAS PICKUPS 117.5" WB 6*** | | | |
| Fleetside | **10335** | 5675 | 6475 |
| Sportside | **10553** | 5750 | 6550 |
| Fleetside Extended Cab (141" WB) | **11267** | 6525 | 7475 |
| Fleetside Extended Cab (155" WB) | **11467** | 6700 | 7675 |
| w/131" WB add | **200** | 105 | 130 |
| *For 8 cyl models add $375 whsle/$375 retail. | | | |
| **C-10 DIESEL PICKUPS 131.5" WB 8** | | | |
| Fleetside | **13318** | 6475 | 7400 |
| Fleetside Extended Cab (141" WB) | **13853** | 7300 | 8350 |
| Fleetside Extended Cab (155" WB) | **14053** | 7500 | 8575 |
| **C-20 GAS PICKUPS 131.5" WB 6*** | | | |
| Fleetside | **11143** | 6375 | 7300 |
| Heavy Duty Fleetside | **12378** | 6625 | 7575 |
| Fleetside Extended Cab (141" WB) | **12298** | 6925 | 7925 |
| Fleetside Extended Cab (155" WB) | **12498** | 7125 | 8150 |
| Heavy Duty Fleetside Extended Cab (155" WB) (8 cyl) | **13413** | 7700 | 8825 |
| *For 8 cyl models add $375 whsle/$375 retail. | | | |
| **C-20 DIESEL PICKUPS 131.5" WB 8** | | | |
| Fleetside | **13383** | 7150 | 8175 |
| Heavy Duty Fleetside | **13828** | 7400 | 8475 |
| Fleetside Extended Cab (141" WB) | **14538** | 7700 | 8825 |
| Fleetside Extended Cab (155" WB) | **14738** | 7900 | 9050 |
| Heavy Duty Fleetside Ext Cab (155" WB) | **14911** | 8100 | 9225 |
| **R-20 GAS PICKUPS 164.5" WB 8** | | | |
| Fleetside Bonus Cab | **14164** | 7650 | 8750 |
| Fleetside Crew Cab | **14664** | 7850 | 9000 |
| **R-20 HD DIESEL PICKUPS 164.5" WB 8** | | | |
| Fleetside Bonus Cab | **15164** | 8050 | 9175 |
| Fleetside Crew Cab | **15664** | 8250 | 9400 |

| Year/Model/Body/Type | Original List | Current Whlse | Average Retail |
|---|---|---|---|
| **S-10 REG CAB PICKUPS 4** | | | |
| Fleetside EL (108" WB) | **7474** | 4275 | 5075 |
| Fleetside (108" WB) | **8585** | 4450 | 5250 |
| Fleetside (118" WB) | **8750** | 4550 | 5350 |
| Fleetside Extended Cab (123" WB) | **9435** | 4900 | 5700 |
| *For 6 cyl models add $400 whsle/$400 retail. | | | |
| **R-10 SUBURBAN 129.5" WB 8** | | | |
| Panel Doors | **14545** | 9150 | 10425 |
| Tailgate | **14585** | 9250 | 10550 |
| Panel Doors, Diesel | **16895** | 9525 | 10850 |
| Tailgate, Diesel | **16935** | 9600 | 10950 |
| **R-20 SUBURBAN 129.5" WB 8** | | | |
| Panel Doors | **15184** | 9450 | 10775 |
| Tailgate | **15224** | 9525 | 10850 |
| Panel Doors, HD Diesel | **17464** | 9800 | 11175 |
| Tailgate, HD Diesel | **17504** | 9900 | 11275 |
| **ASTRO 111" WB 6*** | | | |
| Cargo Van (4 cyl) | **10400** | 4825 | 5625 |
| CS Pass Van | **11900** | 7025 | 8025 |
| CL Pass Van | **12633** | 7550 | 8650 |
| LT Pass Van | **14144** | 8100 | 9225 |
| *For 6 cyl models add $325 whsle/$325 retail. | | | |
| **G-10 VANS 110" WB 6*** | | | |
| Chevyvan | **11145** | 5050 | 5850 |
| Sportvan | **12638** | 6550 | 7500 |
| Beauville (125" WB) | **14221** | 7600 | 8700 |
| w/125" WB add | | | |
| (Chevyvan) | **260** | 90 | 120 |
| (Sportvan) | **280** | 100 | 130 |
| *For 8 cyl models add $375 whsle/$375 retail. | | | |
| **G-20 VANS 110" WB 6*** | | | |
| Chevyvan | **11455** | 5150 | 5950 |
| Chevyvan Diesel (8 cyl) | **13853** | 5975 | 6775 |
| Chevyvan (125" WB) | **11725** | 5275 | 6075 |
| Chevyvan Diesel (125" WB) (8 cyl) | **14114** | 6125 | 7000 |
| Sportvan (125" WB) | **13121** | 6775 | 7750 |
| Beauville Sportvan | **14440** | 7700 | 8825 |
| Sportvan Diesel (125" WB) (8 cyl) | **15498** | 7550 | 8650 |
| Beauville Sportvan Diesel (125" WB) (8 cyl) | **16759** | 8475 | 9675 |
| *For 8 cyl models add $375 whsle/$375 retail. | | | |
| *ADD FOR:* | | | |
| High Country Pkg (T Blazer) | **1063** | 360 | 460 |
| Sport Pkg (S/T Blazer) | **1089** | 370 | 470 |

| Year/Model/Body/Type | Original List | Current Whlse | Average Retail |
|---|---|---|---|
| (Astro) | **1070** | 370 | 460 |
| Tahoe Pkg | | | |
| (S/T Blazer) | **715** | 210 | 270 |
| (S/T Pickups) | **563** | 180 | 230 |
| Silverado Pkg | | | |
| (Blazer) | **1340** | 480 | 600 |
| (Suburban) | **1570** | 590 | 730 |
| (C-K10,20 Pickups) | **708** | 210 | 270 |

## 1988

### S-10 BLAZER 100.5" WB 4*

| | | | |
|---|---|---|---|
| Sport Utility | **10505** | 4225 | 5025 |

*For 6 cyl models add $300 whsle/$300 retail.

### V-10 BLAZER 106" WB 8

| | | | |
|---|---|---|---|
| Wgn | **14691** | 6850 | 7850 |
| Wgn, Diesel | **17422** | 7175 | 8200 |

### C-10 GAS PICKUPS 117.5" WB 6*

| | | | |
|---|---|---|---|
| Fleetside | **9894** | 3925 | 4700 |
| Sportside | **10102** | 4025 | 4800 |
| Fleetside Extended Cab (155" WB) | **10983** | 4800 | 5600 |
| w/131" WB add | **190** | 60 | 70 |

*For 8 cyl models add $325 whsle/$325 retail.

### C-10 DIESEL PICKUPS 131.5" WB 8

| | | | |
|---|---|---|---|
| Fleetside | **12868** | 4600 | 5400 |
| Fleetside Extended Cab (155" WB) | **13569** | 5475 | 6275 |

### C-20 GAS PICKUPS 131.5" WB 6*

| | | | |
|---|---|---|---|
| Fleetside | **10671** | 4475 | 5400 |
| Fleetside Extended Cab (155" WB) | **11976** | 5275 | 6075 |

*For 8 cyl models add $325 whsle/$325 retail.

### C-20 DIESEL PICKUPS 131.5" WB 8

| | | | |
|---|---|---|---|
| Fleetside | **12911** | 4950 | 5750 |
| Fleetside Extended Cab (155" WB) | **14216** | 5675 | 6475 |

### R-20 GAS PICKUPS 164.5" WB 8

| | | | |
|---|---|---|---|
| Fleetside Bonus Cab | **12922** | 5775 | 6575 |
| Fleetside Crew Cab | **13358** | 5975 | 6775 |

### R-20 HD DIESEL PICKUPS 164.5" WB 8

| | | | |
|---|---|---|---|
| Fleetside Bonus Cab | **14578** | 6125 | 7000 |
| Fleetside Crew Cab | **15015** | 6325 | 7225 |

### S-10 REG CAB PICKUPS 4*

| | | | |
|---|---|---|---|
| Fleetside EL (108" WB) | **6795** | 2525 | 3350 |
| Fleetside (108" WB) | **7890** | 2675 | 3525 |

*For 6 cyl models add $300 whsle/$300 retail.

### S-10 EXTENDED CAB 4*

| | | | |
|---|---|---|---|
| Fleetside | **8815** | 4100 | 4900 |

*For 6 cyl models add $300 whsle/$300 retail.

### R-10 SUBURBAN 129.5" WB 8

| | | | |
|---|---|---|---|
| Panel Doors | **13945** | 7175 | 8200 |
| Tailgate | **13968** | 7275 | 8325 |
| Panel Doors, Diesel | **16260** | 7525 | 8600 |
| Tailgate, Diesel | **16304** | 7625 | 8725 |

### R-20 SUBURBAN 129.5" WB 8

| | | | |
|---|---|---|---|
| Panel Doors | **14559** | 7475 | 8550 |
| Tailgate | **14602** | 7575 | 8675 |
| Panel Doors, Diesel | **16839** | 7825 | 8950 |
| Tailgate, Diesel | **16883** | 7925 | 9075 |

### ASTRO 111" WB 6*

| | | | |
|---|---|---|---|
| Cargo Van (4 cyl) | **9190** | 3025 | 3875 |
| CS Pass Van | **10696** | 5150 | 5950 |
| CL Pass Van | **11489** | 5650 | 6450 |
| LT Pass Van | **12828** | 6175 | 7075 |

### G-10 VANS 110" WB 6

| | | | |
|---|---|---|---|
| Chevyvan | **10240** | 3150 | 4000 |
| Sportvan | **11922** | 4650 | 5450 |
| Bonaventure (125" WB) | **13081** | 5475 | 6275 |
| Beauville (125" WB) | **13489** | 5650 | 6450 |
| w/125" WB add | | | |
| (Chevyvan) | **248** | 70 | 80 |
| (Sportvan) | **251** | 70 | 90 |

*For 8 cyl models add $325 whsle/$325 retail.

### G-20 VANS 110" WB 6*

| | | | |
|---|---|---|---|
| Chevyvan | **10865** | 3275 | 4125 |
| Chevyvan Diesel (8 cyl) | **13262** | 3975 | 4750 |
| Sportvan (125" WB) | **12423** | 4825 | 5625 |
| Bonaventure Sportvan (125" WB) | **13330** | 5525 | 6325 |
| Beauville Sportvan (125" WB) | **13736** | 5725 | 6525 |
| Sportvan Diesel (125" WB) (8 cyl) | **14800** | 5525 | 6325 |
| Bonaventure Sportvan Diesel (125" WB) (8 cyl) | **15735** | 6200 | 7100 |
| Beauville Sportvan Diesel (125" WB) (8 cyl) | **16055** | 6375 | 7300 |

*For 8 cyl models add $250 whsle/$250 retail.

### ADD FOR:

| | | | |
|---|---|---|---|
| High Country Pkg (T Blazer) | **1025** | 270 | 350 |
| Scottsdale Pkg | | | |
| (R-20 Pickups) | **243** | 70 | 80 |
| (C-K10,20 Pickups) | **326** | 100 | 120 |

*1985 Chevrolet Astro*

| Year/Model/Body/Type | Original List | Current Whlse | Average Retail |
|---|---|---|---|
| Silverado Pkg (Blazer) | **1249** | 350 | 440 |
| (Suburban) | **1300** | 370 | 470 |
| Sport Pkg | | | |
| (S/T Blazer) | **1068** | 280 | 360 |
| (S/T Pickups) | **925** | 230 | 300 |
| Tahoe Pkg | | | |
| (S/T Blazer) | **683** | 180 | 230 |
| (S/T Pickups) | **650** | 160 | 210 |

## 1987

### S-10 BLAZER 100.5" WB 4*

| | Original List | Current Whlse | Average Retail |
|---|---|---|---|
| Sport Utility | — | 3425 | 4325 |

*For 6 cyl models add $250 whsle/$250 retail.

### V-10 BLAZER 106" WB 8

| | Original List | Current Whlse | Average Retail |
|---|---|---|---|
| Wgn | **13066** | 5775 | 6575 |
| Wgn, Diesel | **16027** | 6075 | 6850 |

### EL CAMINO 117" WB 6*

| | Original List | Current Whlse | Average Retail |
|---|---|---|---|
| El Camino | **10453** | 3975 | 4750 |
| El Camino Super Sport | **10784** | 4350 | 5150 |

*For 8 cyl models add $275 whsle/$275 retail.

### R-10 PICKUPS 117.5" WB 6*

| | Original List | Current Whlse | Average Retail |
|---|---|---|---|
| Stepside | **8651** | 3050 | 3900 |
| Fleetside | **8503** | 3050 | 3900 |
| Stepside, Diesel (8 cyl) | **11842** | 4225 | 5025 |
| Fleetside, Diesel (8 cyl) | **11695** | 4225 | 5025 |
| w/131.5" WB add | **184** | 30 | 40 |

*For 8 cyl models add $275 whsle/$275 retail.

### R-20 PICKUPS 131.5" WB 6*

| | Original List | Current Whlse | Average Retail |
|---|---|---|---|
| Stepside | **10077** | 3650 | 4425 |
| Fleetside | **9929** | 3650 | 4425 |

*For 8 cyl models add $275 whsle/$275 retail.

### R-20 DIESEL PICKUPS 131.5" WB 8

| | Original List | Current Whlse | Average Retail |
|---|---|---|---|
| Stepside | **12722** | 4225 | 5025 |
| Fleetside | **12574** | 4225 | 5025 |

### R-20 HEAVY DUTY PICKUPS 131.5" WB 8

| | Original List | Current Whlse | Average Retail |
|---|---|---|---|
| Stepside | **11498** | 4125 | 4925 |
| Fleetside | **11351** | 4125 | 4925 |

### R-20 PICKUPS 164.5" WB 8

| | Original List | Current Whlse | Average Retail |
|---|---|---|---|
| Fleetside Bonus Cab | **12475** | 4700 | 5500 |
| Fleetside Crew Cab | **12842** | 4875 | 5675 |

### R-20 DIESEL PICKUPS 164.5" WB 8

| | Original List | Current Whlse | Average Retail |
|---|---|---|---|
| Fleetside Bonus Cab | **13693** | 4975 | 5775 |
| Fleetside Crew Cab | **14060** | 5175 | 5975 |

### S-10 EXTENDED CAB 4*

| | Original List | Current Whlse | Average Retail |
|---|---|---|---|
| Fleetside (122.9" WB) | **8167** | 2650 | 3500 |

*For 6 cyl models add $250 whsle/$250 retail.

### S-10 REG CAB PICKUPS 4*

| | Original List | Current Whlse | Average Retail |
|---|---|---|---|
| Fleetside EL (108" WB) | **6295** | 2100 | 2900 |
| Fleetside (108" WB) | **7435** | 2150 | 2950 |
| Fleetside (118" WB) | **7702** | 2200 | 3025 |

*For 6 cyl models add $250 whsle/$250 retail.

### R-10 SUBURBAN 129.5" WB 8

| | Original List | Current Whlse | Average Retail |
|---|---|---|---|
| Panel Doors | **12435** | 5325 | 6125 |
| Tailgate | **12477** | 5450 | 6250 |
| Panel Doors, Diesel | **15193** | 5675 | 6475 |
| Tailgate, Diesel | **15235** | 5750 | 6550 |

| Year/Model/Body/Type | Original List | Current Whlse | Average Retail |
|---|---|---|---|
| **R-20 SUBURBAN 129.5" WB 8** | | | |
| Panel Doors | 13036 | 5550 | 6350 |
| Tailgate | 13077 | 5675 | 6475 |
| Panel Doors, HD Diesel | 15669 | 5850 | 6650 |
| Tailgate, HD Diesel | 15712 | 5950 | 6750 |
| **ASTRO M10 111" WB 6*** | | | |
| Cargo Van (4 cyl) | 8797 | 2300 | 3125 |
| Pass Van | 9833 | 4000 | 4775 |
| CS Pass Van | 10314 | 4200 | 5000 |
| CL Pass Van | 11079 | 4400 | 5200 |
| LT Pass Van | 12370 | 4875 | 5675 |
| **G-10 VANS 110" WB 6*** | | | |
| Chevyvan | 9464 | 2300 | 3125 |
| Sportvan | 11162 | 3675 | 4450 |
| Bonaventure (125" WB) | 12279 | 4275 | 5075 |
| Beauville (125" WB) | 12631 | 4450 | 5250 |
| w/125" WB add | | | |
| (Chevyvan) | 242 | 50 | 60 |
| (Sportvan) | 242 | 50 | 60 |
| *For 8 cyl models add $275 whsle/$275 retail. | | | |
| **G-20 VANS 110" WB 6*** | | | |
| Chevyvan | 10131 | 2350 | 3175 |
| Chevyvan Diesel (8 cyl) | 12753 | 2850 | 3700 |
| Sportvan (125" WB) | 11609 | 3825 | 4600 |
| Bonaventure Sportvan (125" WB) | 12483 | 4350 | 5150 |
| Beauville Sportvan (125" WB) | 12833 | 4500 | 5300 |
| Sportvan Diesel (125" WB) (8 cyl) | 14211 | 4375 | 5175 |
| Bonaventure Sportvan Diesel (125" WB) (8 cyl) | 15113 | 4825 | 5625 |
| Beauville Sportvan Diesel (125" WB) (8 cyl) | 15379 | 5025 | 5825 |
| Chevyvan Diesel (125" WB) (8 cyl) | 12995 | 3025 | 3875 |
| *For 8 cyl models add $275 whsle/$275 retail. | | | |
| *ADD FOR:* | | | |
| Durango Pkg (S/T Pickup) | 313 | 70 | 90 |
| High Country Pkg (S/T Blazer) | 1025 | 200 | 260 |
| Scottsdale Pkg | | | |
| (Suburban Diesel) | 329 | 70 | 90 |
| (Suburban Gasoline) | 485 | 120 | 140 |
| (C-K Pickups) | 353 | 80 | 100 |
| (R-V Pickups) | 274 | 60 | 80 |
| Silverado Pkg (Blazer) | 1073 | 210 | 270 |
| (Suburban) | 1330 | 280 | 360 |
| (C-K Pickups) | 681 | 130 | 170 |
| Sport Pkg (S/T Blazer) | 1042 | 200 | 260 |

| Year/Model/Body/Type | Original List | Current Whlse | Average Retail |
|---|---|---|---|
| (S/T Pickups) | 965 | 180 | 230 |
| Tahoe Pkg (S/T Blazer) | 657 | 110 | 150 |
| (S/T Pickups) | 637 | 110 | 150 |
| **1986** | | | |
| **K-10 BLAZER 8** | | | |
| Utility w/HT | 12383 | 4700 | 5500 |
| Utility Diesel w/HT | 15330 | 4950 | 5750 |
| **S-10 BLAZER 100.5" WB 4*** | | | |
| Tailgate | 9582 | 2400 | 3225 |
| *For 6 cyl models add $225 whsle/$225 retail. | | | |
| **EL CAMINO 117" WB 6*** | | | |
| El Camino | 9850 | 3075 | 3925 |
| El Camino Super Sport | 10172 | 4450 | 5250 |
| *For 8 cyl models add $250 whsle/$250 retail. | | | |
| **C-10 PICKUPS 117.5" WB 6*** | | | |
| Stepside | 8133 | 2550 | 3400 |
| Fleetside | 7989 | 2550 | 3405 |
| Stepside, Diesel (8 cyl) | 11223 | 3025 | 3875 |
| Fleetside, Diesel (8 cyl) | 11080 | 3025 | 3875 |
| w/131.5" WB add | 179 | 20 | 30 |
| *For 8 cyl models add $250 whsle/$250 retail. | | | |
| **C-20 PICKUPS 131.5" WB 6*** | | | |
| Stepside | 9521 | 3000 | 3850 |
| Fleetside | 9377 | 3000 | 3850 |
| *For 8 cyl models add $250 whsle/$250 retail. | | | |
| **C-20 DIESEL PICKUPS 131.5" WB 8** | | | |
| Stepside | 12161 | 3575 | 4350 |
| Fleetside | 12017 | 3575 | 4350 |
| **C-20 HEAVY DUTY PICKUPS 131.5" WB 6*** | | | |
| Stepside | 10542 | 3175 | 4025 |
| Fleetside | 10399 | 3175 | 4025 |
| *For 8 cyl models add $250 whsle/$250 retail. | | | |
| **C-20 PICKUPS 164.5" WB 6*** | | | |
| Fleetside Bonus Cab | 11425 | 3800 | 4575 |
| Fleetside Crew Cab | 11783 | 4025 | 4800 |
| *For 8 cyl models add $250 whsle/$250 retail. | | | |
| **S-10 EXTENDED CAB 4*** | | | |
| Fleetside (122.9" WB) | 7909 | 1725 | 2525 |
| *For 6 cyl models add $225 whsle/$225 retail. | | | |
| **S-10 REG CAB PICKUPS 4*** | | | |
| Fleetside EL (108" WB) | 6161 | 1450 | 2250 |
| Fleetside (108" WB) | 7202 | 1500 | 2300 |
| Fleetside (118" WB) | 7444 | 1575 | 2375 |
| *For 6 cyl models add $225 whsle/$225 retail. | | | |

| Year/Model/Body/Type | Original List | Current Whlse | Average Retail |
|---|---|---|---|
| **C-10 SUBURBAN 129.5" WB 8** | | | |
| Panel Doors | **11769** | 4350 | 5150 |
| Tailgate | **11809** | 4425 | 5225 |
| Panel Doors, Diesel | **14518** | 4575 | 5375 |
| Tailgate, Diesel | **14559** | 4650 | 5450 |
| **C-20 SUBURBAN 129.5" WB 8** | | | |
| Panel Doors | **12613** | 4550 | 5350 |
| Tailgate | **12653** | 4650 | 5450 |
| Panel Doors, HD Diesel | **15241** | 4875 | 5675 |
| Tailgate, HD Diesel | **15282** | 4975 | 5775 |
| **ASTRO M10 111" WB 6*** | | | |
| Cargo Van (4 cyl) | **8290** | 1525 | 2325 |
| Pass Van | **9299** | 2875 | 3725 |
| CS Pass Van | **9767** | 3000 | 3850 |
| CL Pass Van | **10512** | 3300 | 4150 |
| **G-10 VANS 110" WB 6*** | | | |
| Chevyvan | **8876** | 1650 | 2450 |
| Sportvan | **10529** | 2750 | 3600 |
| Bonaventure (125" WB) | **11617** | 3225 | 4075 |
| Beauville (125" WB) | **11959** | 3475 | 4250 |
| w/125" WB add | | | |
| (Chevyvan) | **232** | 30 | 40 |
| (Sportvan) | **236** | 30 | 40 |
| **G-20 VANS 110" WB 6*** | | | |
| Chevyvan | **9525** | 1725 | 2525 |
| Chevyvan Diesel (8 cyl) | **12143** | 2200 | 3025 |
| Sportvan (125" WB) | **10964** | 2875 | 3725 |
| Bonaventure Sportvan (125" WB) | **11815** | 4350 | 5150 |
| Beauville Sportvan (125" WB) | **12156** | 4500 | 5300 |
| Sportvan Diesel (125" WB) (8 cyl) | **13562** | 3425 | 4200 |
| Bonaventure Sportvan Diesel (125" WB) (8 cyl) | **14440** | 3900 | 4675 |
| Beauville Sportvan Diesel (125" WB) (8 cyl) | **14699** | 4075 | 4875 |
| w/125" WB add (Chevyvan) | **235** | 45 | 55 |
| (Chevyvan Diesel 8 cyl) | **236** | 45 | 55 |
| *For 8 cyl models add $250 whlse/$250 retail. | | | |
| *ADD FOR:* | | | |
| Conquista (El Camino) | **232** | 30 | 40 |
| Durango Pkg (S/T Pickup) | **305** | 40 | 60 |
| Scottsdale Pkg (Suburban) | **—** | 80 | 100 |
| Silverado Pkg (Blazer) | **1045** | 150 | 190 |
| (Suburban) | **1145** | 170 | 220 |
| (C-K Pickups) | **—** | 80 | 110 |
| Sport Pkg (S/T Blazer) | **1015** | 150 | 190 |
| (S/T Pickups) | **940** | 130 | 170 |
| Tahoe Pkg (S/T Blazer) | **640** | 120 | 140 |
| (S/T Pickups) | **620** | 110 | 140 |

| Year/Model/Body/Type | Original List | Current Whlse | Average Retail |
|---|---|---|---|
| **1985** | | | |
| **K-10 BLAZER 8** | | | |
| Utility w/HT | **11380** | 3950 | 4725 |
| Utility Diesel w/HT | **14411** | 4225 | 5025 |
| **S-10 BLAZER 100.5" WB 4*** | | | |
| Tailgate | **8881** | 1950 | 2750 |
| *For 6 cyl models add $200 whlse/$200 retail. | | | |
| **EL CAMINO 117" WB 6*** | | | |
| El Camino | **9058** | 2350 | 3175 |
| El Camino Super Sport | **9327** | 2525 | 3350 |
| *For 8 cyl models add $225 whlse/$225 retail. | | | |
| **C-10 PICKUPS 117.5" WB 6*** | | | |
| Stepside | **7532** | 1975 | 2775 |
| Fleetside | **7397** | 1975 | 2775 |
| Stepside, Diesel | **10445** | 2375 | 3200 |
| Fleetside, Diesel | **10310** | 2375 | 3200 |
| w/131.5" WB add | **169** | 10 | 20 |
| *For 8 cyl models add $225 whlse/$225 retail. | | | |
| **C-20 PICKUPS 131.5" WB 6*** | | | |
| Stepside | **8798** | 2325 | 3150 |
| Fleetside | **8663** | 2325 | 3150 |
| *For 8 cyl models add $225 whlse/$225 retail. | | | |
| **C-20 DIESEL PICKUPS 131.5" WB 8** | | | |
| Stepside | **11274** | 2750 | 3600 |
| Fleetside | **11139** | 2750 | 3600 |
| **C-20 HEAVY DUTY PICKUPS 131.5" WB 6*** | | | |
| Stepside | **9756** | 2500 | 3325 |
| Fleetside | **9622** | 2500 | 3325 |
| *For 8 cyl models add $225 whlse/$225 retail. | | | |
| **C-20 HD DIESEL PICKUPS 131.5" WB 8** | | | |
| Stepside | **11575** | 2925 | 3775 |
| Fleetside | **11441** | 2925 | 3775 |
| **C-20 PICKUPS 164.5" WB 6*** | | | |
| Fleetside Bonus Cab | **10584** | 2900 | 3750 |
| Fleetside Crew Cab | **10920** | 3075 | 3925 |
| *For 8 cyl models add $225 whlse/$225 retail. | | | |
| **C-20 DIESEL PICKUPS 164.5" WB 8** | | | |
| Fleetside Bonus Cab | **12403** | 3425 | 4200 |
| Fleetside Crew Cab | **12379** | 3625 | 4400 |
| **S-10 EXTENDED CAB 4*** | | | |
| Fleetside (122.9" WB) | **7167** | 1375 | 2075 |
| Fleetside, Diesel (122.9" WB) | **7875** | 1075 | 1750 |
| *For 6 cyl models add $200 whlse/$200 retail. | | | |

| Year/Model/Body/Type | Original List | Current Whlse | Average Retail |
|---|---|---|---|
| **S-10 REG CAB PICKUPS 4\*** | | | |
| Fleetside (108" WB) | **5990** | 1150 | 1825 |
| Fleetside (118" WB) | **6702** | 1225 | 1900 |
| Fleetside, Diesel (108" WB) | **7349** | 850 | 1550 |
| Fleetside, Diesel (118" WB) | **7502** | 975 | 1650 |
| *For 6 cyl models add $200 whsle/$200 retail.* | | | |
| **C-10 SUBURBAN 129.5" WB 8** | | | |
| Panel Doors | **10812** | 3525 | 4300 |
| Tailgate | **10850** | 3625 | 4400 |
| Panel Doors, Diesel | **13369** | 3800 | 4575 |
| Tailgate, Diesel | **13407** | 3900 | 4675 |
| **C-20 SUBURBAN 129.5" WB 8** | | | |
| Panel Doors | **11598** | 3725 | 4500 |
| Tailgate | **11635** | 3825 | 4600 |
| Panel Doors, Diesel | **14042** | 4000 | 4775 |
| Tailgate, Diesel | **14079** | 4100 | 4900 |
| **ASTRO 111" WB 4** | | | |
| Cargo Van | **7821** | 1075 | 1750 |
| Pass Van | **8195** | 2100 | 2900 |
| CS Pass Van | **8623** | 2175 | 2975 |
| CL Pass Van | **9359** | 2375 | 3200 |
| **G-10 VANS 110" WB 6\*** | | | |
| Chevyvan | **8099** | 1175 | 1850 |
| Sportvan | **9650** | 2200 | 3025 |
| Bonaventure (125" WB) | **10661** | 2500 | 3325 |
| Beauville (125" WB) | **10979** | 2625 | 3475 |
| w/125" WB add | | | |
| (Chevyvan) | **215** | 10 | 20 |
| (Sportvan)0 | **220** | 10 | 20 |
| **G-20 VANS 110" WB 6\*** | | | |
| Chevyvan | **8701** | 1225 | 1900 |
| Chevyvan Diesel | **11128** | 1650 | 2450 |
| Sportvan (125" WB) | **10054** | 2250 | 3075 |
| Bonaventure (125" WB) | **10845** | 2525 | 3350 |
| Beauville (125" WB) | **11161** | 2675 | 3525 |
| Sportvan Diesel (125" WB) | **12468** | 2675 | 3525 |
| Bonaventure Diesel 125" WB) | **13284** | 2975 | 3825 |
| Beauville Diesel (125" WB) (8 cyl) | **13525** | 3100 | 3950 |
| Chevyvan (125" WB) | **8921** | 1275 | 1950 |
| Chevyvan Diesel (125" WB) (8 cyl) | **11346** | 1675 | 2475 |
| *For 8 cyl models add $225 whsle/$225 retail.* | | | |
| *ADD FOR:* | | | |
| Conquista (El Camino) Durango Pkg | **195** | 10 | 10 |

| Year/Model/Body/Type | Original List | Current Whlse | Average Retail |
|---|---|---|---|
| (S/T Pickups) | **289** | 20 | 30 |
| Scottsdale Pkg | | | |
| (Suburban Diesel) | **311** | 20 | 30 |
| (Suburban Gasoline) | **459** | 40 | 50 |
| Silverado Pkg (Blazer) | **1015** | 120 | 150 |
| (Suburban) | **—** | 100 | 130 |
| (C-K Pickups) | **695** | 80 | 90 |
| Sport Pkg (S/T Blazer) | **972** | 110 | 140 |
| (S/T Pickups) | **—** | 100 | 120 |
| Tahoe Pkg (S/T Blazer) | **585** | 60 | 80 |
| (S/T Pickups) | **—** | 60 | 80 |

## 1984

| | Original List | Current Whlse | Average Retail |
|---|---|---|---|
| **K-10 BLAZER 8** | | | |
| Utility w/HT | **10931** | 2950 | 3800 |
| Utility Diesel w/HT | **13664** | 3150 | 4000 |
| **S-10 BLAZER 100.5" WB 4\*** | | | |
| Tailgate | **8580** | 1650 | 2450 |
| *For 6 cyl models add $175 whsle/$175 retail.* | | | |
| **EL CAMINO 117" WB 6\*** | | | |
| El Camino | **8622** | 1800 | 2600 |
| El Camino Super Sport | **8881** | 1975 | 2775 |
| *For 8 cyl models add $200 whsle/$200 retail.* | | | |
| **C-10 PICKUPS 117.5" WB 6\*** | | | |
| Stepside | **7213** | 1650 | 2450 |
| Fleetside | **7082** | 1650 | 2450 |
| Stepside, Diesel | **10257** | 1975 | 2775 |
| Fleetside, Diesel | **10126** | 1975 | 2775 |
| w/131.5" WB add | **157** | — | — |
| *For 8 cyl models add $200 whsle/$200 retail.* | | | |
| **C-20 PICKUPS 131.5" WB 6\*** | | | |
| Stepside | **8431** | 1975 | 2775 |
| Fleetside | **8300** | 1975 | 2775 |
| *For 8 cyl models add $200 whsle/$200 retail.* | | | |
| **C-20 HEAVY DUTY PICKUPS 131.5" WB 6\*** | | | |
| Stepside | **8945** | 2125 | 2925 |
| Fleetside | **8814** | 2125 | 2925 |
| *For 8 cyl models add $200 whsle/$200 retail.* | | | |
| **C-20 DIESEL PICKUPS 131.5" WB 8** | | | |
| Stepside | **11038** | 2300 | 3125 |
| Fleetside | **10907** | 2300 | 3125 |
| **C-20 HD DIESEL PICKUPS 131.5" WB 8** | | | |
| Stepside | **11552** | 2425 | 3250 |
| Fleetside | **11421** | 2425 | 3250 |
| **C-20 PICKUPS 164.5" WB 6\*** | | | |
| Fleetside Bonus Cab | **9757** | 2525 | 3350 |

| Year/Model/ Body/Type | Original List | Current Whlse | Average Retail |
|---|---|---|---|
| Fleetside Crew Cab | **10087** | 2625 | 3475 |

*For 8 cyl models add $200 whsle/$200 retail.

### C-20 DIESEL PICKUPS 164.5" WB 8

| | | | |
|---|---|---|---|
| Fleetside Bonus Cab | **12364** | 2875 | 3725 |
| Fleetside Crew Cab | **12694** | 2975 | 3825 |

### S-10 EXTENDED CAB 4*

| | | | |
|---|---|---|---|
| Fleetside (122.9" WB) | **7036** | 1275 | 1950 |
| Fleetside, Diesel (122.9" WB) | **7939** | 1025 | 1700 |

### S-10 REG CAB PICKUPS 4*

| | | | |
|---|---|---|---|
| Fleetside (108" WB) | **6102** | 1075 | 1750 |
| Fleetside (118" WB) | **6663** | 1150 | 1825 |
| Fleetside, Diesel (108" WB) | **7413** | 800 | 1500 |
| Fleetside, Diesel (118" WB) | **7566** | 900 | 1575 |

*For 6 cyl models add $175 whsle/$175 retail.

### C-10 SUBURBAN 129.5" WB 8

| | | | |
|---|---|---|---|
| Panel Doors | **10444** | 2675 | 3525 |
| Tailgate | **10480** | 2750 | 3600 |
| Panel Doors, Diesel | **13004** | 2850 | 3700 |
| Tailgate, Diesel | **13040** | 2925 | 3775 |

### C-20 SUBURBAN 129.5" WB 8

| | | | |
|---|---|---|---|
| Panel Doors | **10691** | 2850 | 3700 |
| Tailgate | **10727** | 2925 | 3775 |
| Panel Doors, Diesel | **13820** | 3000 | 3850 |
| Tailgate, Diesel | **13856** | 3100 | 3950 |

### G-10 VANS 110" WB 6*

| | | | |
|---|---|---|---|
| Chevyvan | **7653** | 750 | 1425 |
| Sportvan | **9201** | 1650 | 2450 |
| Bonaventure (125" WB) | **10174** | 1900 | 2700 |
| Beauville (125" WB) | **10439** | 2000 | 2800 |
| w/125" WB add | | | |
| (Chevyvan) | **212** | 30 | 40 |
| (Sportvan) | **212** | 30 | 40 |

### G-20 VANS 110" WB 6*

| | | | |
|---|---|---|---|
| Chevyvan | **8288** | 800 | 1500 |
| Chevyvan Diesel | **10846** | 1125 | 1800 |
| Sportvan (125" WB) | **9589** | 1700 | 2500 |
| Bonaventure (125" WB) | **10350** | 1950 | 2750 |
| Beauville (125" WB) | **10615** | 2050 | 2850 |
| Sportvan Diesel (125" WB) | **12134** | 2050 | 2850 |
| Bonaventure Diesel (125" WB) | **12920** | 2250 | 3075 |
| Beauville Diesel (125" WB) | **13110** | 2325 | 3150 |
| Chevyvan (125" WB) | **8500** | 850 | 1550 |
| Chevyvan Diesel | | | |

| Year/Model/ Body/Type | Original List | Current Whlse | Average Retail |
|---|---|---|---|
| (125" WB) | **11056** | 1225 | 1900 |

*For 8 cyl models add $200 whsle/$200 retail.

## DODGE

### 1992

### AD-150S 2WD 106" WB 8

| | | | |
|---|---|---|---|
| Ramcharger S | **17575** | 12500 | 14675 |

### AD-150 2WD 106" WB 8

| | | | |
|---|---|---|---|
| Ramcharger | **19600** | 13450 | 15650 |
| *ADD FOR:* | | | |
| 5.9 Liter 8 Cyl Eng | **399** | 200 | 200 |
| LE Pkg | **1460** | 800 | 900 |
| Canyon Sport Pkg | **2365** | 1100 | 1250 |

### CARAVAN 4*

| | | | |
|---|---|---|---|
| Caravan, Base | **14358** | 11550 | 13350 |
| Caravan, SE | **16481** | 12725 | 15050 |
| Caravan, LE | **20340** | 14075 | 16550 |

*For 3.0 liter 6 cyl models add $500 whsle/$500 retail.

### CARAVAN 6

| | | | |
|---|---|---|---|
| Caravan, SE AWD | **19539** | 14725 | 17300 |
| Caravan, LE AWD | **22442** | 16125 | 18775 |
| Caravan, ES | **20883** | 14100 | 16475 |

### GRAND CARAVAN 6

| | | | |
|---|---|---|---|
| Caravan, Base | **18233** | 13075 | 15200 |
| Caravan SE | **18463** | 14200 | 16700 |
| Caravan LE | **21060** | 15575 | 18225 |
| Caravan ES | **21571** | 15725 | 18375 |

### CARAVAN CARGO VAN 112" WB 4*

| | | | |
|---|---|---|---|
| Van | **13772** | 10450 | 12100 |

*For 3.0 liter 6 cyl models add $500 whsle/$500 retail.

### CARAVAN CARGO VAN 119" WB 6

| | | | |
|---|---|---|---|
| Van | **16161** | 11200 | 12975 |
| *ADD FOR:* | | | |
| 3.3 Liter 6 Cyl Eng | **796** | 475 | 535 |
| ES Decor Group | **543** | 375 | 415 |

### DAKOTA 2WD 4*

| | | | |
|---|---|---|---|
| S Sweptline (112" WB) | **10117** | 8025 | 9375 |
| Sweptline (112" WB) | **11773** | 8575 | 9900 |
| Sweptline (124" WB) | **12056** | 8750 | 10100 |
| Club Cab (131" WB) | **13040** | 9425 | 10850 |
| Sport Sweptline (112" WB) | **10542** | 8200 | 9525 |

*For 6 cyl models add $500 whsle/$500 retail.

| Year/Model/ Body/Type | Original List | Current Whlse | Average Retail |
|---|---|---|---|
| **DAKOTA 4WD 6** | | | |
| Sweptline (112" WB) | **15081** | 10575 | 12225 |
| Sweptline (124" WB) | **15295** | 10775 | 12450 |
| Club Cab (131" WB) | **16235** | 11400 | 13175 |
| Sport Sweptline (112" WB) | **14269** | — | — |
| *ADD FOR:* | | | |
| 5.2 Liter 8 Cyl Eng | | | |
| (2WD) | **1118** | 675 | 675 |
| (4WD) | **587** | 475 | 475 |
| **RAM 50 2WD 4** | | | |
| Standard Cab (105" WB) | **9571** | 7425 | 8450 |
| Standard Cab (116" WB) | **10126** | — | — |
| SE Standard Cab (105" WB) | **10431** | — | — |
| **POWER RAM 50 4WD 4** | | | |
| Standard Cab (105" WB) | **12301** | — | — |
| **D150 PICKUPS 115" WB 6*** | | | |
| Sweptline | **13980** | 9825 | 11325 |
| *For 8 cyl models add $475 whsle/$475 retail. | | | |
| **D150 PICKUPS 131" WB 6*** | | | |
| Sweptline | **14197** | 10000 | 11550 |
| *For 8 cyl models add $475 whsle/$475 retail. | | | |
| **D150 PICKUPS 133" WB 8** | | | |
| Club Cab | **16062** | 10875 | 12550 |
| **D150 PICKUPS 149" WB 8** | | | |
| Club Cab | **16281** | 12025 | 13825 |
| **D250 PICKUP 131" WB 6*** | | | |
| Sweptline | **15138** | 11300 | 13075 |
| *For 8 cyl models add $475 whsle/$475 retail. | | | |
| **D250 PICKUPS 149" WB 8** | | | |
| Club Cab | **17022** | 12850 | 15175 |
| *ADD FOR:* | | | |
| 5.9 Liter 8 Cyl Eng | | | |
| (D250 Sweptline) | **857** | 555 | 615 |
| (D250 Club Cab, 4WD models) | **270** | — | — |
| 5.9 Liter 6 Cyl Cummins Turbo Diesel Eng | | | |
| (D250 Sweptline) | **4728** | 2000 | 2275 |
| (D250 Club Cab) | **4022** | 2000 | 2275 |
| (4WD Sweptline) | **3821** | 2000 | 2275 |
| (4WD Club Cab) | **3702** | 2000 | 2275 |
| **B150 VANS 6*** | | | |
| 109" WB Van | **14749** | 12000 | 14400 |

| Year/Model/ Body/Type | Original List | Current Whlse | Average Retail |
|---|---|---|---|
| 127" WB Van | **15578** | 12650 | 14700 |
| *For 8 cyl models add $400 whsle/$400 retail. | | | |
| **B250 VANS 6*** | | | |
| 109" WB Van | **15297** | 12500 | 14700 |
| 127" WB Van | **15991** | 12950 | 15000 |
| 127" WB Maxivan | **16978** | 13300 | 15350 |
| *For 8 cyl models add $450 whsle/$450 retail. | | | |
| *ADD FOR:* | | | |
| 5.9 Liter 8 Cyl Eng | **857** | 575 | 575 |
| **B150 WAGONS 6*** | | | |
| 109" WB Wgn | **16137** | 13400 | 15600 |
| 127" WB Wgn | **16995** | 13800 | 15975 |
| *For 8 cyl models add $450 whsle/$450 retail. | | | |
| **B250 WAGONS 6*** | | | |
| 127" WB Wgn | **17639** | 14150 | 16250 |
| *For 8 cyl models add $450 whsle/$450 retail. | | | |
| **B250 WAGONS 8** | | | |
| 127" WB Maxiwagon | **18925** | 14550 | 16650 |
| *ADD FOR:* | | | |
| 5.9 Liter 8 Cyl Eng | | | |
| (B250 ex. Maxiwagon) | **857** | 575 | 575 |
| (B250 Maxiwagon) | **270** | 150 | 150 |
| LE Pkg (B150 Wgn) | **2996** | 1100 | 1250 |
| (B250 ex. Maxiwagon) | **3140** | 1100 | 1250 |
| **1991** | | | |
| **AD-150S 106" WB 8*** | | | |
| Ramcharger S | **16494** | 9925 | 11325 |
| **AD-150 106" WB 8*** | | | |
| Ramcharger | **18656** | 10875 | 12450 |
| *For 360 CID 8 cyl Eng. add $300 whsle/$300 retail. | | | |
| **CARAVAN 4*** | | | |
| Caravan, Base | **14305** | 10025 | 11450 |
| Caravan, SE | **15551** | 10800 | 12350 |
| Caravan, LE | **17994** | 11550 | 13225 |
| *For 6 cyl models add $400 whsle/$400 retail. | | | |
| **CARAVAN 6** | | | |
| Caravan ES | **19489** | 11875 | 13600 |
| **GRAND CARAVAN 6** | | | |
| Caravan SE | **17301** | 12075 | 13900 |
| Caravan LE | **19604** | 12775 | 14975 |
| **CARAVAN CARGO VAN 112" WB 4*** | | | |
| Van | **13671** | 8300 | 9450 |
| *For 6 cyl models add $400 whsle/$400 retail. | | | |

| Year/Model/Body/Type | Original List | Current Whlse | Average Retail |
|---|---|---|---|
| **CARAVAN CARGO VAN 119" WB 6** | | | |
| Van | **15411** | 9525 | 10850 |
| **DAKOTA 2WD 4** | | | |
| S Sweptline (112" WB) | **9926** | 6175 | 7075 |
| Sweptline (112" WB) | **11377** | 6850 | 7850 |
| Sweptline (124" WB) | **11528** | 6975 | 8000 |
| Club Cab (131" WB) | **12657** | 7450 | 8525 |
| Sport Sweptline (112" WB) | **13798** | 8075 | 9200 |
| Sport Club Cab (131" WB) | **15128** | 8625 | 9850 |
| *6 cyl models add $500 whsle/$500 retail. | | | |
| **RAM 50 2WD 4** | | | |
| Standard Cab (105" WB) | **9213** | 6325 | 7225 |
| Standard Cab (116" WB) | **9746** | 6425 | 7350 |
| SE Sports Cab (116" WB) | **10471** | 7650 | 8750 |
| SE Standard Cab (105" WB) | **10175** | 6700 | 7675 |
| LE Sports Cab (116"WB) | **11900** | 8075 | 9200 |
| **D150 PICKUPS 115" WB 6*** | | | |
| S Sweptline | **11679** | 7575 | 8675 |
| Sweptline | **13144** | 8075 | 9200 |
| Club Cab (133" WB) (8 cyl) | **15185** | 9350 | 10650 |
| Club Cab (149" WB) (8 cyl) | **15394** | 9525 | 10850 |
| w/131" WB add | **209** | 120 | 140 |
| *For 8 cyl models add $425 whsle/$425 retail. | | | |
| **D250 PICKUPS 131" WB 6*** | | | |
| Sweptline | **14216** | 8825 | 10075 |
| Club Cab (149" WB) (8 cyl) | **16833** | 10075 | 11500 |
| *For 8 cyl models add $425 whsle/$425 retail. | | | |
| **B150 VANS 6*** | | | |
| 109" WB Van | **14456** | 9600 | 10950 |
| 127" WB Van | **15165** | 9775 | 11150 |
| *For 8 cyl models add $425 whsle/$425 retail. | | | |
| **B250 VANS 6*** | | | |
| 109" WB Van | **14697** | 9375 | 10675 |
| 127" WB Van | **15373** | 9950 | 11350 |
| 127" WB Maxivan | **16334** | 10075 | 11525 |
| *For 8 cyl models add $425 whsle/$425 retail. | | | |
| **B150 WAGONS 06*** | | | |
| 109" WB Wgn | **15719** | 10625 | 12150 |
| 127" WB Wgn | **16555** | 11200 | 12825 |
| *For 8 cyl models add $425 whsle/$425 retail. | | | |
| **B250 WAGONS 6*** | | | |
| 127" WB Wgn | **17183** | 10975 | 12575 |
| 127" WB Maxiwgn (8 cyl) | **18436** | 11875 | 13600 |
| *For 8 cyl models add $425 whsle/$425 retail. | | | |

| Year/Model/Body/Type | Original List | Current Whlse | Average Retail |
|---|---|---|---|
| *ADD FOR:* | | | |
| LE Decor Pkg (Dakota) | **1110** | 550 | 690 |
| (Ram Wagons) | **1152** | 580 | 720 |
| (Pickups) | **1160** | 580 | 720 |
| Premium Van Decor Pkg (Caravan Cargo Van) | **1451** | 750 | 930 |
| SE Decor Pkg (Dakota) | **682** | 300 | 380 |
| (Pickups) | **700** | 310 | 400 |
| **1990** | | | |
| **AD-150S 106" WB 8*** | | | |
| Ramcharger S | **15334** | 6550 | 7500 |
| **AD-150 106" WB 8*** | | | |
| Ramcharger | **17195** | 7425 | 8500 |
| *For 360 CID V8 Eng. add $250 whsle/$250 retail. | | | |
| **CARAVAN 4*** | | | |
| Caravan, Base | **12835** | 7800 | 8925 |
| Caravan, SE | **13515** | 8500 | 9700 |
| Caravan, LE | **16125** | 9175 | 10450 |
| Caravan, ES | **17350** | 9350 | 10650 |
| *For 6 cyl models add $375 whsle/$375 retail. | | | |
| **GRAND CARAVAN 6** | | | |
| Caravan, SE | **16235** | 9600 | 10950 |
| Caravan, LE | **18325** | 10175 | 11625 |
| **CARAVAN CARGO VAN 112" WB 4*** | | | |
| Van | **11965** | 5975 | 6775 |
| *For 6 cyl models add $375 whsle/$375 retail. | | | |
| **CARAVAN CARGO VAN 119" WB 6** | | | |
| Van | **14290** | 7125 | 8150 |
| **DAKOTA 2WD 4*** | | | |
| S Sweptline (112" WB) | **9290** | 4700 | 5500 |
| Sweptline (112" WB) | **10481** | 5250 | 6050 |
| Conv (112" WB) | **14126** | 6475 | 7400 |
| Sweptline (124" WB) | **10626** | 5375 | 6175 |
| Club Cab (131" WB) | **11781** | 5825 | 6625 |
| Sport Sweptline (112" WB) | **13006** | 6425 | 7350 |
| Sport Conv (112" WB) | **16281** | 7625 | 8725 |
| Sport Club Cab (131" WB) | **14081** | 7000 | 8025 |
| *For 6 cyl models add $375 whsle/$375 retail. | | | |
| **RAM 50 2WD 4** | | | |
| Standard Cab (105" WB) | **8780** | 4750 | 5550 |
| Standard Cab (116" WB) | **9313** | 4825 | 5625 |
| Sport Cab (116" WB) | **9819** | 5250 | 6050 |
| SE Standard Cab | | | |

| Year/Model/Body/Type | Original List | Current Whlse | Average Retail |
|---|---|---|---|
| (105" WB) | **9853** | 5125 | 5925 |
| LE Sport Cab (116" WB) | **12030** | 5900 | 6700 |
| **D150 PICKUPS 115" WB 6*** | | | |
| S Sweptline | **11470** | 5900 | 6700 |
| Sweptline | **12206** | 6300 | 7200 |
| Club Cab (133" WB) (8 cyl) | **14156** | 7525 | 8600 |
| Club Cab (149" WB) (8 cyl) | **14356** | 7675 | 8775 |
| w/131" WB add | **200** | 80 | 100 |
| *For 8 cyl models add $400 whsle/$400 retail. | | | |
| **D250 PICKUPS 131" WB 6*** | | | |
| Sweptline | **13181** | 7050 | 8050 |
| Club Cab (149" WB) (8 cyl) | **15681** | 8275 | 9425 |
| *For 8 cyl models add $400 whsle/$400 retail. | | | |
| **B150 VANS 6*** | | | |
| 109" WB Van | **13296** | 7100 | 8125 |
| 127" WB Van | **13976** | 7600 | 8700 |
| *For 8 cyl models add $400 whsle/$400 retail. | | | |
| **B250 VANS 6*** | | | |
| 109" WB Van | **13526** | 7275 | 8325 |
| 127" WB Van | **14176** | 7775 | 8900 |
| 127" WB Maxivan | **15096** | 8000 | 9175 |
| *For 8 cyl models add $400 whsle/$400 retail. | | | |
| **B150 WAGONS 6*** | | | |
| 109" WB Wgn | **15096** | 8525 | 9725 |
| 127" WB Wgn | **15896** | 9025 | 10275 |
| *For 8 cyl models add $400 whsle/$400 retail. | | | |
| **B250 WAGONS 6*** | | | |
| 127" WB Wgn | **16496** | 8825 | 10075 |
| 127" WB Maxiwagon (8 cyl) | **17696** | 9350 | 10650 |
| *For 8 cyl models add $400 whsle/$400 retail. | | | |
| *ADD FOR:* | | | |
| LE Decor Pkg (Ram Wagons) | **1130** | 480 | 600 |
| (Dakota Conv) | **—** | 250 | 320 |
| (Dakota) | **1102** | 470 | 590 |
| (D & W Series Pickups) | | 350 | 450 |
| Royal Decor Pkg (Caravan Cargo Van) | **1125** | 470 | 590 |
| SE Decor Pkg (Dakota Pickups) | **—** | 185 | 235 |
| (D150 Reg Cab Pickups) | **686** | 250 | 320 |
| (D250 Reg Cab Pickups) | **459** | 160 | 210 |

| Year/Model/Body/Type | Original List | Current Whlse | Average Retail |
|---|---|---|---|
| **1989** | | | |
| **AD-100 106" WB 8** | | | |
| Ramcharger | **12785** | 5200 | 6000 |
| **AD-150 106" WB 8** | | | |
| Ramcharger | **14927** | 6075 | 6850 |
| **CARAVAN 4*** | | | |
| Caravan, Base | **11312** | 6550 | 7500 |
| Caravan, Special Ed | **12039** | 7225 | 8275 |
| Caravan, Limited Ed | **13987** | 7825 | 8950 |
| *For 6 cyl models add $325 whsle/$325 retail. | | | |
| **GRAND CARAVAN 6** | | | |
| Caravan, Special Ed | **14526** | 8300 | 9450 |
| Caravan, Limited Ed | **16462** | 8900 | 10150 |
| **DAKOTA 2WD 4*** | | | |
| S Sweptline (112" WB) | **7497** | 3675 | 4450 |
| Sweptline (112" WB) | **9172** | 4275 | 5075 |
| Sweptline (124" WB) | **9228** | 4350 | 5150 |
| Sport Sweptline (112" WB) (6 cyl) | **11293** | 5200 | 6000 |
| Sport Conv (112" WB) (6 cyl) | **14425** | 6225 | 7125 |
| *For 6 cyl models add $325 whsle/$325 retail. | | | |
| **RAIDER 4*** | | | |
| Sport Utility | **12550** | 5675 | 6475 |
| *For 6 cyl models add $325 whsle/$325 retail. | | | |
| **RAM 50 2WD 4** | | | |
| Pickup (105" WB) | **7664** | 3750 | 4525 |
| Sport Pickup (105" WB) | **9496** | 4350 | 5150 |
| Pickup (116" WB) | **8320** | 3875 | 4650 |
| Extended Cab Pickup (116" WB) | **8680** | 4200 | 5000 |
| Custom Pickup (116" WB) | **8769** | 4300 | 5100 |
| Sport Extended Cab Pickup (116" WB) | **10407** | 4725 | 5525 |
| **D100 PICKUPS 115" WB 6*** | | | |
| Sweptline | **9865** | 4950 | 5750 |
| w/131" WB add | **187** | 70 | 90 |
| *For 8 cyl models add $375 whsle/$375 retail. | | | |
| **D150 PICKUPS 115" WB 6*** | | | |
| Sweptline | **10693** | 5325 | 6125 |
| w/131" WB add | **200** | 80 | 100 |
| *For 8 cyl models add $375 whsle/$375 retail. | | | |
| **D250 PICKUPS 131" WB 6*** | | | |
| Sweptline | **11722** | 6075 | 6850 |
| *For 8 cyl models add $375 whsle/$375 retail. | | | |

| Year/Model/Body/Type | Original List | Current Whlse | Average Retail |
|---|---|---|---|
| **B150 VANS 6*** | | | |
| 109" WB Van | **11430** | 5575 | 6375 |
| 109" WB Long Range Ram Van | **10729** | 5650 | 6450 |
| 127" WB Van | **12000** | 6025 | 6825 |
| 127" WB Long Range Ram Van | **11973** | 6100 | 6875 |
| *For 8 cyl models add $375 whsle/$375 retail. | | | |
| **B250 VANS 6*** | | | |
| 109" WB Van | **11741** | 5700 | 6500 |
| 127" WB Van | **12379** | 6150 | 7025 |
| 127" WB Maxivan | **13250** | 6625 | 7575 |
| *For 8 cyl models add $375 whsle/$375 retail. | | | |
| **B150 WAGONS 6*** | | | |
| 109" WB Ram Value Wgn | **13273** | 7075 | 8100 |
| 109" WB Ram Wgn | **13339** | 7150 | 8175 |
| 127" WB Ram Wgn | **13862** | 7650 | 8750 |
| *For 8 cyl models add $375 whsle/$375 retail. | | | |
| **B250 WAGONS 6*** | | | |
| 127" WB Ram Wgn | **14431** | 7275 | 8325 |
| 127" WB Maxiwagon | **15573** | 7775 | 8900 |
| *For 8 cyl Non-Maxiwagons add $375 whsle/$375 retail. For 8 cyl Maxiwagons add $375 whsle/$375 retail. | | | |
| *ADD FOR:* | | | |
| LE Decor Pkg (Ramcharger) | **718** | 210 | 270 |
| (Ram Wagons) | **1179** | 410 | 520 |
| Snow Commander Pkg (Ramcharger) | **1573** | 590 | 730 |
| Prospector Pkg 1 (Ramcharger) | **—** | 130 | 170 |
| (Ram Wagons) | **1179** | 410 | 520 |
| (Vans) | **320** | 120 | 150 |
| (Dakota) | **287** | 100 | 130 |
| (D & W 100 Pickups) | **655** | 130 | 180 |
| (D & W 250 Pickups) | **382** | 100 | 130 |
| Prospector Pkg 2 (Ramcharger) | **2171** | 850 | 1050 |
| (Ram Wagons) | **521** | 160 | 200 |
| (Vans) | **571** | 180 | 230 |
| (Dakota 2WD) | **691** | 200 | 260 |
| (Dakota 4WD) | **1186** | 420 | 520 |
| (D & W 150 Pickups) | **536** | 160 | 210 |
| (D & W 250 Pickups) | **595** | 175 | 225 |
| Prospector Pkg 3 (Ram Wagons) | **915** | 300 | 380 |
| (Vans) | **939** | 310 | 390 |
| (Dakota) | **1801** | 690 | 850 |
| (D & W 150 Pickups) | **621** | 185 | 245 |
| (D & W 250 Pickups) | **690** | 200 | 260 |
| Prospector Pkg 4 | | | |

| Year/Model/Body/Type | Original List | Current Whlse | Average Retail |
|---|---|---|---|
| (Ram Wagons) | **2888** | 1160 | 1420 |
| (Vans) | **1811** | 690 | 860 |
| SE Decor Pkg (Dakota) | **374** | 90 | 130 |
| **1988** | | | |
| **AD-100 106" WB 8** | | | |
| Ramcharger | **11776** | 3650 | 4425 |
| **AD-150 106"** | | | |
| Ramcharger | **13640** | 4375 | 5175 |
| **CARAVAN 4*** | | | |
| Caravan, Base | **10887** | 4825 | 5625 |
| Caravan, Special Ed | **11587** | 5450 | 6250 |
| Caravan, Limited Ed | **13462** | 5975 | 6775 |
| **GRAND CARAVAN 4*** | | | |
| Caravan, Special Ed | **12502** | 6150 | 7025 |
| Caravan, Ltd Ed (6 cyl) | **15509** | 6625 | 7575 |
| **MINI RAM VAN 4*** | | | |
| Mini Ram Van, Base | **9717** | 3150 | 4000 |
| Mini Ram Van, Ext | **10399** | 3625 | 4400 |
| *For 6 cyl models add $300 whsle/$300 retail. | | | |
| **DAKOTA 2WD 4*** | | | |
| S Sweptline (112" WB) | **6875** | 2675 | 3525 |
| Sweptline (112" WB) | **8244** | 2775 | 3625 |
| Sweptline (124" WB) | **8407** | 2875 | 3725 |
| Sport Sweptline (112" WB) (6 cyl) | **9995** | 3650 | 4425 |
| *For 6 cyl models add $300 whsle/$300 retail. | | | |
| **RAIDER 4** | | | |
| Sport Utility | **12053** | 4150 | 4950 |
| **RAM 50 2WD 4** | | | |
| Pickup (105" WB) | **7404** | 2300 | 3125 |
| Sport Pickup (105" WB) | **8976** | 2750 | 3600 |
| Pickup (116" WB) | **8060** | 2375 | 3200 |
| Extended Cab (116" WB) | **8416** | 2625 | 3475 |
| Custom Pickup (116" WB) | **8463** | 2625 | 3475 |
| Sport Extended Cab (116" WB) | **9886** | 3075 | 3925 |
| **D100 PICKUPS 115" WB 6*** | | | |
| Sweptline | **8853** | 2975 | 3825 |
| w/131.5" WB add | **177** | 70 | 80 |
| **D150 PICKUPS 115" WB 6*** | | | |
| Sweptline | **9988** | 3225 | 4075 |
| w/131" WB add | **191** | 60 | 80 |
| *For 8 cyl models add $325 whsle/$325 retail. | | | |

*Refer to optional equipment schedules*

| Year/Model/Body/Type | Original List | Current Whlse | Average Retail |
|---|---|---|---|
| **D250 PICKUPS 131" WB 6*** | | | |
| Sweptline | **11031** | 3900 | 4675 |
| *For 8 cyl models add $325 whsle/$325 retail. | | | |
| **B150 WAGONS 6*** | | | |
| 109" WB Ram Value Wgn | **12705** | 5175 | 5975 |
| 109" WB Ram Wgn | **12781** | 5100 | 5900 |
| **B250 WAGONS 6*** | | | |
| 127" WB Ram Wgn | **13714** | 5300 | 6100 |
| 127" WB Ram Maxiwagon (8 cyl) | **14812** | 6025 | 6825 |
| *For 8 cyl models add $325 whsle/$325 retail. | | | |
| *ADD FOR:* | | | |
| LE Decor Pkg (AD & AW 150 Ramcharger) | **625** | 110 | 140 |
| (Ram Wagons) | **1095** | 210 | 280 |
| (Caravan) | **603** | 100 | 140 |
| (Dakota) | **1073** | 210 | 270 |
| (D & W Pickups) | **469** | 110 | 140 |
| Prospector Pkg I (Ramcharger) | **—** | 240 | 310 |
| (Ram Value Wagon) | **725** | 140 | 180 |
| (Dakota) | **439** | 100 | 130 |
| Prospector Pkg II (Ramcharger) | **2006** | 470 | 590 |
| (Ram Wagons) | **465** | 110 | 140 |
| (Vans) | **450** | 110 | 140 |
| (Dakota) | **671** | 120 | 160 |
| Prospector Pkg III (Ram Wagons) | **803** | 190 | 250 |
| (Vans) | **800** | 190 | 250 |
| (Dakota 2WD) | **1031** | 270 | 350 |
| (D & W Pickups) | **1685** | 510 | 630 |
| Prospector Pkg IV (Ram Wagons) | **2869** | 940 | 1150 |
| (Vans) | **1875** | 580 | 720 |
| Royal Decor Pkg (Mini Ram Van) | **1043** | 280 | 360 |
| SE Decor Pkg (Dakota) | **499** | 110 | 140 |

## 1987

| Year/Model/Body/Type | Original List | Current Whlse | Average Retail |
|---|---|---|---|
| **AD-150 106" WB 8** | | | |
| Ramcharger | **12820** | 3525 | 4300 |
| **CARAVAN 4*** | | | |
| Caravan, Base | **10411** | 3475 | 4250 |
| Caravan, Special Ed | **10875** | 4025 | 4800 |
| Caravan, Limited Ed | **11741** | 4450 | 5250 |
| **GRAND CARAVAN 4*** | | | |
| Caravan, Special Ed | **11751** | 4500 | 5300 |

| Year/Model/Body/Type | Original List | Current Whlse | Average Retail |
|---|---|---|---|
| Caravan, Limited Ed | **12561** | 4875 | 5675 |
| *For 6 cyl models add $250 whsle/$250 retail. | | | |
| **MINI RAM VAN 4*** | | | |
| Mini Ram Van, Base | **9222** | 2250 | 3075 |
| Mini Ram Van, Royal | **10052** | 2525 | 3350 |
| *For 6 cyl models add $250 whsle/$250 retail. | | | |
| **DAKOTA 4 2WD*** | | | |
| S Sweptline (112" WB) | **6590** | 2325 | 3150 |
| Sweptline (112" WB) | **7529** | 2400 | 3225 |
| Sweptline (124" WB) | **7764** | 2475 | 3300 |
| *For 6 cyl S Sweptline add $250 whsle/$250 retail. | | | |
| **RAIDER 4** | | | |
| Sport Utility | **10501** | 3725 | 4500 |
| **RAM 50 4 2WD** | | | |
| Pickup (105" WB) | **6527** | 1650 | 2450 |
| Pickup (116" WB) | **6887** | 1725 | 2525 |
| Custom Pickup (116" WB) | **7289** | 1900 | 2700 |
| Sport Pickup (105" WB) | **7945** | 1975 | 2775 |
| **D100 PICKUPS 115" WB 6*** | | | |
| Sweptline | **7653** | 2375 | 3200 |
| w/131" WB add | **172** | 70 | 80 |
| **D150 PICKUPS 115" WB 6*** | | | |
| Sweptline | **8823** | 2575 | 3425 |
| w/131" WB add | **184** | 70 | 90 |
| *For 8 cyl models add $275 whsle/$275 retail. | | | |
| **D250 PICKUPS 131" WB 6*** | | | |
| Sweptline | **10493** | 3050 | 3900 |
| **B150 VANS 6*** | | | |
| 109" WB Van | **9939** | 2650 | 3500 |
| 109" WB Long Range Ram Van | **9295** | 2700 | 3550 |
| 127" WB Van | **10178** | 2950 | 3800 |
| 127" WB Long Range Ram Van | **10238** | 3000 | 3850 |
| *For 8 cyl models add $275 whsle/$275 retail. | | | |
| **B250 VANS 6*** | | | |
| 109" WB Van | **10401** | 2700 | 3550 |
| 127" WB Van | **10645** | 3000 | 3850 |
| 127" WB Maxivan | **11333** | 3075 | 3925 |
| *For 8 cyl models add $275 whsle/$275 retail. | | | |
| **B150 WAGONS 6*** | | | |
| 109" WB Ram Value Wgn | **11933** | 4150 | 4950 |

| Year/Model/Body/Type | Original List | Current Whlse | Average Retail |
|---|---|---|---|
| 109" WB Ram Wgn | **11980** | 4100 | 4900 |
| 127" WB Ram Wgn | **12220** | 4425 | 5225 |

*For 8 cyl models add $275 whsle/$275 retail.

### B250 WAGONS 6*

| | | | |
|---|---|---|---|
| 127" WB Ram Wgn | **12559** | 4525 | 5325 |
| 127" WB Ram Maxiwagon (8 cyl) | **14174** | 4775 | 5575 |

*For 8 cyl models add $275 whsle/$275 retail.

*ADD FOR:*

| | | | |
|---|---|---|---|
| LE Decor Pkg (Ramcharger) | **696** | 130 | 170 |
| (Ram Wgns) | **1203** | 240 | 310 |
| (D & W Pickups) | **630** | 110 | 150 |
| Prospector I Pkg (Dakota) | **607** | 100 | 140 |
| Prospector II Pkg (Dakota) | **1208** | 240 | 310 |
| Prospector III Pkg (Dakota) | **2599** | 640 | 800 |
| Prospector Van Conv Pkg (B150 & B250 Vans) | **2514** | 640 | 800 |

## 1986

### AD-150 106" WB 8

| | | | |
|---|---|---|---|
| Ramcharger | **11534** | 2750 | 3600 |

### CARAVAN 4

| | | | |
|---|---|---|---|
| Caravan, Base | **9659** | 2675 | 3525 |
| Caravan, Special Ed | **9938** | 3000 | 3850 |
| Caravan, Limited Ed | **10681** | 3425 | 4200 |

### MINI RAM VAN 4

| | | | |
|---|---|---|---|
| Mini Ram Van, Base | **8308** | 1525 | 2325 |
| Mini Ram Van, Royal | **9128** | 1750 | 2550 |

### D100 PICKUPS 115" WB 6*

| | | | |
|---|---|---|---|
| Sweptline | **7291** | 1725 | 2525 |
| w/131" WB add | **224** | 90 | 120 |

### D150 PICKUPS 115" WB 6*

| | | | |
|---|---|---|---|
| Sweptline | **8010** | 1875 | 2675 |
| w/131" WB add | **174** | 70 | 80 |

*For 8 cyl models add $250 whsle/$250 retail.

### D250 PICKUPS 131" WB 6*

| | | | |
|---|---|---|---|
| Sweptline | **9333** | 2275 | 3100 |

### B150 VANS 6*

| | | | |
|---|---|---|---|
| 109" WB Van | **9040** | 1925 | 2725 |
| 109" WB Long Range Ram Van | **9109** | 1975 | 2775 |
| 127" WB Van | **9266** | 2200 | 3025 |

| Year/Model/Body/Type | Original List | Current Whlse | Average Retail |
|---|---|---|---|
| 127" WB Long Range Ram Van | **9328** | 2225 | 3050 |

*For 8 cyl models add $250 whsle/$250 retail.

### B250 VANS 6*

| | | | |
|---|---|---|---|
| 109" WB Van | **9489** | 1975 | 2775 |
| 127" WB Van | **9718** | 2200 | 3025 |
| 127" WB Maxivan | **10349** | 2300 | 3125 |

*For 8 cyl models add $250 whsle/$250 retail.

### B150 WAGONS 6*

| | | | |
|---|---|---|---|
| 109" WB Ram Value Wgn | **10947** | 3050 | 3900 |
| 109" WB Ram Wgn | **10987** | 3000 | 3850 |
| 127" WB Ram Wgn | **11215** | 3200 | 4050 |

*For 8 cyl models add $250 whsle/$250 retail.

### B250 WAGONS 6*

| | | | |
|---|---|---|---|
| 127" WB Ram Wgn | **11535** | 3225 | 4075 |
| 127" WB Ram Maxiwagon (8 cyl) | **13024** | 3550 | 4325 |

*For 8 cyl models add $250 whsle/$250 retail.

*ADD FOR:*

| | | | |
|---|---|---|---|
| LE Pkg (Dakota) | **1074** | 160 | 200 |
| Popular Equip Pkg (Caravan SE) | **1155** | 170 | 220 |
| (Caravan LE) | **851** | 110 | 150 |
| Royal SE Pkg (Ramcharger) | **680** | 120 | 150 |
| (Ram Wgns) | **1087** | 160 | 200 |
| (D & W Pickups) | **591** | 100 | 130 |
| SE Pkg (Dakota) | **501** | 80 | 110 |

## 1985

### AD-150 106" WB 8

| | | | |
|---|---|---|---|
| Ramcharger | **10471** | 1925 | 2725 |

### CARAVAN 4

| | | | |
|---|---|---|---|
| Caravan, Base | **9238** | 2050 | 2850 |
| Caravan, Special Ed | **9487** | 2275 | 3100 |
| Caravan, Limited Ed | **10105** | 2525 | 3350 |

### MINI RAM VAN 4

| | | | |
|---|---|---|---|
| Mini Ram Van, Base | **8052** | 1025 | 1700 |
| Mini Ram Van, Royal | **8848** | 1225 | 1900 |

### D100 PICKUPS 115" WB 6*

| | | | |
|---|---|---|---|
| Sweptline | **6871** | 1225 | 1900 |
| w/131" WB add | **271** | 100 | 120 |

### D150 PICKUPS 115" WB 6*

| | | | |
|---|---|---|---|
| Utiline | **7693** | 1275 | 1950 |
| Sweptline | **7558** | 1300 | 2000 |

©1993 by Edmund Publications Corporation

*Refer to optional equipment schedules*

| Year/Model/Body/Type | Original List | Current Whlse | Average Retail |
|---|---|---|---|
| w/131" WB add | **168** | 50 | 70 |

*For 8 cyl models add $225 whsle/$225 retail.

**D250 PICKUPS 131" WB 6\***

| | | | |
|---|---|---|---|
| Utiline | **8645** | 1650 | 2450 |
| Sweptline | **8510** | 1700 | 2500 |

*For 8 cyl models add $225 whsle/$225 retail.

**B150 VANS 6\***

| | | | |
|---|---|---|---|
| 109" WB Van | **8574** | 1075 | 1750 |
| 109" WB Long Range Ram Van | **8660** | 1125 | 1800 |
| 127" WB Van | **8789** | 1225 | 1900 |
| 127" WB Long Range Ram Van | **8868** | 1275 | 1950 |

*For 8 cyl models add $225 whsle/$225 retail.

**B250 VANS 6\***

| | | | |
|---|---|---|---|
| 109" WB Van | **8994** | 1125 | 1800 |
| 127" WB Van | **9213** | 1250 | 1925 |
| 127" WB Maxivan | **9807** | 1425 | 2200 |

*For 8 cyl models add $225 whsle/$225 retail.

**B150 WAGONS 6\***

| | | | |
|---|---|---|---|
| 109" WB Ram Value Wgn | **10386** | 2125 | 2925 |
| 109" WB Ram Wgn | **10343** | 2100 | 2900 |
| 127" WB Ram Wgn | **10560** | 2225 | 3050 |

*For 8 cyl models add $225 whsle/$225 retail.

**B250 WAGONS 6\***

| | | | |
|---|---|---|---|
| 127" WB Ram Wgn | **10872** | 2175 | 2975 |
| 127" WB Ram Maxiwagon (8 cyl) | **12283** | 2525 | 3350 |

*For 8 cyl models add $225 whsle/$225 retail.

*ADD FOR:*

| | | | |
|---|---|---|---|
| Prospector Pkg I (Pickups) | **1087** | 80 | 110 |
| Prospector Pkg II (Pickups) | **1510** | 130 | 180 |
| Prospector Pkg III (Pickups) | **2427** | 230 | 300 |
| Royal SE Pkg (Ramcharger) | **1161** | 90 | 120 |
| (Ram Wgns) | **1123** | 80 | 110 |
| (Pickups) | **452** | 40 | 50 |
| Travel Equip Pkg (Caravan SE & LE) | **1003** | 120 | 140 |

## 1984

**AD-150 106" WB 8**

| | | | |
|---|---|---|---|
| Ramcharger | **9829** | 1575 | 2375 |

| Year/Model/Body/Type | Original List | Current Whlse | Average Retail |
|---|---|---|---|
| **AW-150 106" WB 8** | | | |
| Ramcharger | **10945** | 2175 | 2975 |

**CARAVAN 4**

| | | | |
|---|---|---|---|
| Caravan, Base | **8669** | 1750 | 2550 |
| Caravan Special Ed | **8906** | 1950 | 2750 |
| Caravan Limited Ed | **9494** | 2175 | 2975 |

**MINI RAM VAN 4**

| | | | |
|---|---|---|---|
| Mini Ram Van, Base | **7698** | 775 | 1450 |
| Mini Ram Van, Royal | **8457** | 950 | 1625 |

**D100 PICKUPS 115" WB 6\***

| | | | |
|---|---|---|---|
| Sweptline | **6535** | 925 | 1600 |
| w/131" WB add | **208** | 70 | 80 |

**D150 PICKUPS 115" WB 6\***

| | | | |
|---|---|---|---|
| Utiline | **7368** | 975 | 1650 |
| Sweptline | **7236** | 1050 | 1725 |
| w/131" WB add | **157** | 40 | 60 |

*For 8 cyl models add $200 whsle/$200 retail.

**D250 PICKUPS 131" WB 6\***

| | | | |
|---|---|---|---|
| Utiline | **8274** | 1275 | 1950 |
| Sweptline | **8143** | 1350 | 2050 |

*For 8 cyl models add $200 whsle/$200 retail.

**RAMPAGE 104" WB 4**

| | | | |
|---|---|---|---|
| Rampage | **6899** | 575 | 1125 |
| Rampage 2.2 | **7315** | 700 | 1400 |

**B150 VANS 6\***

| | | | |
|---|---|---|---|
| 109" WB Van | **7854** | 750 | 1425 |
| 109" WB Long Range Ram Van | **7954** | 775 | 1450 |
| 127" WB Van | **8064** | 825 | 1525 |
| 127" WB Long Range Ram Van | **8157** | 900 | 1575 |

*For 8 cyl models add $200 whsle/$200 retail.

**B250 VANS 6\***

| | | | |
|---|---|---|---|
| 109" WB Van | **8493** | 775 | 1450 |
| 127" WB Van | **8703** | 825 | 1525 |
| 127" WB Maxivan | **9322** | 1000 | 1675 |

*For 8 cyl models add $200 whsle/$200 retail.

**B150 WAGONS 6\***

| | | | |
|---|---|---|---|
| 109" WB Ram Value Wgn | **9659** | 1675 | 2475 |
| 109" WB Ram Wgn | **9559** | 1650 | 2450 |
| 127" WB Ram Wgn | **9768** | 1725 | 2525 |

*For 8 cyl models add $200 whsle/$200 retail.

**B250 WAGONS 6\***

| | | | |
|---|---|---|---|
| 127" WB Ram Wgn | **9987** | 1700 | 2500 |

# AMERICAN TRUCKS

*1991 Ford Explorer*

| Year/Model/ Body/Type | Original List | Current Whlse | Average Retail |
|---|---|---|---|
| 127" WB Ram | | | |
| Maxiwagon (8 cyl) | **11309** | 1850 | 2650 |
| *For 8 cyl models add $200 whsle/$200 retail. | | | |

## FORD

### 1992

#### EXPLORER 2WD 6

| | | | |
|---|---|---|---|
| 2 Dr XL | **15854** | 14225 | 16725 |
| 2 Dr Sport | **17780** | 15075 | 17725 |
| 2 Dr Eddie Bauer | **21208** | 16525 | 19175 |
| 4 Dr XL | **16692** | 15125 | 17775 |
| 4 Dr XLT | **19427** | 16175 | 18825 |
| 4 Dr Eddie Bauer | **22578** | 17275 | 19925 |
| *ADD FOR:* | | | |
| Leather Seats (Sport) | **1434** | 405 | 455 |
| (XLT) | **1368** | 405 | 455 |
| Cloth Sport Bucket | | | |
| Seats (Sport) | **1022** | 265 | 295 |
| (XLT) | **956** | 265 | 295 |

#### BRONCO 4WD 6

| | | | |
|---|---|---|---|
| Custom Wgn | **19697** | 15850 | 18525 |
| XLT Wgn | **21841** | 16850 | 19550 |
| XLT Nite Wgn | **23202** | 17050 | '19775 |
| Eddie Bauer Wgn | **23201** | 17600 | 20375 |
| *ADD FOR:* | | | |
| 5.0 Liter 8 Cyl Eng | | | |
| (Custom, XLT) | **637** | 350 | 350 |
| 5.8 Liter 8 Cyl Eng | | | |
| (Custom, XLT) | **857** | 450 | 450 |

| Year/Model/ Body/Type | Original List | Current Whlse | Average Retail |
|---|---|---|---|
| (XLT Nite, Eddie Bauer) | **221** | 125 | 125 |

#### ECONOLINE CLUB WAGON 138" WB 6

| | | | |
|---|---|---|---|
| Custom Wgn | **17713** | 14850 | 17250 |
| Custom HD Wgn | **18701** | 15050 | 17475 |
| Custom Super Wgn | **20751** | — | — |
| XLT Wgn | **20457** | 15850 | 18275 |
| XLT HD Wgn | **21667** | 16050 | 18500 |
| XLT Super Wgn | **22326** | — | — |
| Chateau Wgn | **23963** | 16350 | 18825 |
| Chateau HD Wgn | **24720** | 16600 | 19050 |
| *ADD FOR:* | | | |
| 5.0 Liter 8 Cyl Eng | **716** | 350 | 350 |
| 5.8 Liter 8 Cyl Eng | **937** | 450 | 450 |
| 7.5 Liter 8 Cyl Eng | **1421** | 600 | 600 |
| 7.3 Liter 8 Cyl | | | |
| Diesel Eng | **3733** | 1250 | 1250 |

#### E-150 ECONOLINE VAN 138" WB 6*

| | | | |
|---|---|---|---|
| Cargo | **15933** | 11950 | 13800 |
| *For 8 cyl models add $450 whsle/$450 retail. | | | |

#### E-250 ECONOLINE VANS 138" WB 6*

| | | | |
|---|---|---|---|
| Cargo | **16347** | 12250 | 14100 |
| Cargo, Heavy Duty | **16666** | 12475 | 14300 |
| Cargo, Super | **16997** | — | — |
| Cargo, Super HD | **17406** | — | — |
| *For 8 cyl models add $450 whsle/$450 retail. | | | |
| *ADD FOR:* | | | |
| 5.8 Liter 8 Cyl Eng | | | |
| (E-150) | **937** | 575 | 575 |

#### AEROSTAR VANS 119" WB 2WD 6

| | | | |
|---|---|---|---|
| Cargo | **14590** | 9975 | 11600 |

*Refer to optional equipment schedules*

| Year/Model/Body/Type | Original List | Current Whlse | Average Retail |
|---|---|---|---|
| Cargo, Extended | **15387** | 10725 | 12475 |
| Window | **14967** | 10175 | 11750 |
| Window, Extended | **15714** | 10300 | 11900 |
| *ADD FOR:* | | | |
| 4.0 Liter 6 Cyl Eng | | | |
| (2WD models) | **316** | 225 | 225 |

### AEROSTAR WAGONS 119" WB 2WD 6

| | | | |
|---|---|---|---|
| Wgn, XL | **14596** | 11850 | 13700 |
| Wgn, XL Extended | **16388** | 12700 | 15025 |
| Wgn, XL Plus | **16092** | 13200 | 14400 |
| Wgn, XL Plus Extended | **17277** | 13200 | 15525 |
| Wgn, XLT | **17944** | 12900 | 15225 |
| Wgn, XLT Extended | **18621** | 13725 | 16100 |
| Wgn, Eddie Bauer | **21636** | 13850 | 16225 |
| Wgn, Eddie Bauer Extended | **22604** | 15000 | 17650 |
| *ADD FOR:* | | | |
| 4.0 Liter 6 Cyl Eng | | | |
| (2WD models) | **300** | 225 | 225 |

### F-150 PICKUPS 117" WB 6*

| | | | |
|---|---|---|---|
| S Styleside | **11264** | 10125 | 11700 |
| Styleside | **13613** | 10700 | 12350 |
| Flareside | **14926** | 10825 | 12500 |

*For 8 cyl models add $450 whsle/$450 retail.

### F-150 PICKUPS 133" WB 6*

| | | | |
|---|---|---|---|
| S Styleside | **11500** | 10300 | 11900 |
| Styleside | **13957** | 10925 | 12625 |

*For 8 cyl models add $450 whsle/$450 retail.

### F-150 SUPER CAB PICKUPS 139" WB 6

| | | | |
|---|---|---|---|
| S Styleside | **13667** | 11150 | 12725 |
| Styleside | **14979** | 11750 | 13350 |
| Flareside | **15990** | 11750 | 13350 |

*For 8 cyl models add $450 whsle/$450 retail.

### F-150 SUPER CAB PICKUP 155" WB 6

| | | | |
|---|---|---|---|
| S Styleside | **13771** | 11300 | 13025 |

*For 8 cyl models add $450 whsle/$450 retail.

| *ADD FOR:* | | | |
|---|---|---|---|
| XL Pkg (2WD Styleside) | **621** | 425 | 475 |
| (4WD Styleside) | **465** | 425 | 475 |
| (Super Cab) | **416** | 425 | 475 |
| XLT Lariat Pkg | | | |
| (2WD Styleside) | **1263** | 835 | 935 |
| (4WD Styleside) | **1107** | 835 | 935 |
| (Flareside) | **1056** | 835 | 935 |
| (Super Cab) | **1257** | 835 | 935 |
| XLT Lariat Nite Pkg | | | |
| (2WD Styleside) | **2439** | 1275 | 1415 |
| (4WD Styleside) | **2283** | 1275 | 1415 |
| (Flareside) | **999** | 835 | 935 |
| (Styleside Super Cab) | **3227** | 1275 | 1415 |

| Year/Model/Body/Type | Original List | Current Whlse | Average Retail |
|---|---|---|---|
| (Flareside Super Cab) | **999** | 835 | 935 |
| 5.8 Liter 8 Cyl Eng | **857** | 555 | 615 |

### F-250 PICKUPS 133" WB 6

| | | | |
|---|---|---|---|
| Styleside (under 8500 lb. GVW) | **14697** | 12300 | 14000 |
| Styleside (over 8500 lb. GVW) | **15413** | 12600 | 14350 |

### F-250 SUPER CAB PICKUP 155" WB 8

| | | | |
|---|---|---|---|
| Styleside (over 8500 lb. GVW) | **17808** | 13700 | 15500 |
| *ADD FOR:* | | | |
| XLT Lariat Pkg | | | |
| (Styleside) | **2029** | 850 | 950 |
| (Super Cab) | **2179** | 850 | 950 |
| 5.0 Liter 8 Cyl Eng (Styleside under 8500 lb. GVW) | **637** | 400 | 400 |
| 5.8 Liter 8 Cyl Eng (2WD Styleside) | **857** | 550 | 550 |
| 7.3 Liter 8 Cyl Diesel Eng (2WD Styleside over 8500 lb. GVW) | **3072** | 1350 | 1350 |
| (4WD Styleside, Super Cab) | **2215** | 1150 | 1150 |
| 7.5 Liter 8 Cyl Eng (2WD Styleside over 8500 lb. GVW) | **1341** | 700 | 700 |
| (4WD Styleside, Super Cab) | **484** | 500 | 500 |

### RANGER S 2WD 4

| | | | |
|---|---|---|---|
| 108" WB | **9820** | 6975 | 8125 |

### RANGER 2WD 4*

| | | | |
|---|---|---|---|
| Sport 108" WB | **9759** | 7425 | 8625 |
| Sport 114" WB | **9916** | 7575 | 8800 |
| Custom 108" WB | **10905** | 8200 | 9400 |
| Custom 114" WB | **11225** | 8350 | 9575 |

### RANGER SUPER CAB 2WD 4

| | | | |
|---|---|---|---|
| 125" WB | **12216** | 8550 | 9875 |
| *ADD FOR:* | | | |
| 2.9 Liter 6 Cyl Eng (4WD Sport & Custom) | **556** | 375 | 375 |
| 4.0 Liter 6 Cyl Eng (2WD Sport & Custom) | **620** | 475 | 475 |
| (4WD Sport & Custom) | **735** | 475 | 475 |
| (4WD Super Cab) | **179** | 475 | 475 |
| Sport Pkg | — | 775 | 850 |
| STX Pkg | — | 725 | 800 |
| XLT Pkg | — | 575 | 650 |

| Year/Model/Body/Type | Original List | Current Whlse | Average Retail |
|---|---|---|---|
| **1991** | | | |
| **EXPLORER 2WD 6** | | | |
| 2 Dr XL | **14586** | 12000 | 13750 |
| 2 Dr Sport | **15961** | 12675 | 14875 |
| 2 Dr Eddie Bauer | **18882** | 13600 | 15850 |
| 4 Dr XL | **15541** | 12975 | 15175 |
| 4 Dr XLT | **17642** | 13800 | 16125 |
| 4 Dr Eddie Bauer | **20164** | 14525 | 17000 |
| **BRONCO 105" WB 6*** | | | |
| Wgn | **18463** | 13175 | 15425 |
| Silver Anniversary Wgn | **25690** | — | — |
| *For 8 cyl models add $425 whsle/$425 retail. | | | |
| **E-150 CLUB WAGON 138" WB 6*** | | | |
| 8 Pass Wgn | **17530** | 11350 | 13000 |
| *For 8 cyl models add $425 whsle/$425 retail. | | | |
| **E-250 CLUB WAGON 138" WB 6*** | | | |
| 12 Pass Wgn | **18614** | 11725 | 13425 |
| *For 8 cyl models add $425 whsle/$425 retail. | | | |
| **E-150 ECONOLINE VANS 138" WB 6*** | | | |
| Cargo | **14766** | 9175 | 10450 |
| Cargo, Super | **15712** | 9875 | 11250 |
| *For 8 cyl models add $425 whsle/$425 retail. | | | |
| **E-250 ECONOLINE VANS 138" WB 6*** | | | |
| Cargo | **15116** | 9300 | 10600 |
| Cargo, Heavy Duty | **15519** | 9475 | 10800 |
| Cargo, Super | **15851** | 10125 | 11575 |
| *For 8 cyl models add $425 whsle/$425 retail. | | | |
| **AEROSTAR VANS 119" WB 2WD 6*** | | | |
| Cargo | **13519** | 8400 | 9575 |
| Cargo, Extended | **14266** | 9150 | 10425 |
| Window | **13903** | 8475 | 9675 |
| Window, Extended | **14650** | 9250 | 10550 |
| *For 4.0 liter 6 cyl models add $200 whsle/$200 retail. | | | |
| **AEROSTAR WAGONS 119" WB 2WD 6*** | | | |
| Wgn, XL | **13986** | 10200 | 11675 |
| Wgn, XL Extended | **15121** | 11035 | 12650 |
| Wgn, XLT | **15909** | 11200 | 12825 |
| Wgn, XLT Extended | **16807** | 12000 | 13750 |
| Wgn, Eddie Bauer | **19025** | 12050 | 13825 |
| Wgn, Eddie Bauer Ext | **19922** | 12725 | 14925 |
| **F-150 PICKUPS 117" WB 6*** | | | |
| S Styleside | **11026** | 8375 | 9550 |
| Custom Styleside | **12745** | 8675 | 9900 |
| w/133" WB add (S) | **225** | 120 | 140 |
| (Custom) | **244** | 120 | 140 |
| *For 8 cyl models add $425 whsle/$425 retail. | | | |

| Year/Model/Body/Type | Original List | Current Whlse | Average Retail |
|---|---|---|---|
| **F-150 SUPER CAB PICKUPS 139" WB 6*** | | | |
| S Styleside | **12318** | 9325 | 10625 |
| Custom Styleside | **14129** | 9675 | 11025 |
| *For 8 cyl models add $425 whsle/$425 retail. | | | |
| **F-150 SUPER CAB PICKUPS 155" WB 6*** | | | |
| S Styleside | **12544** | 9475 | 10800 |
| Custom Styleside | **14363** | 9800 | 11175 |
| *For 8 cyl models add $425 whsle/$425 retail. | | | |
| **F-250 PICKUPS 133" WB 6*** | | | |
| Styleside (under 8500 lb. GVW) | **13854** | 9450 | 10775 |
| *For 8 cyl models add $425 whsle/$425 retail. | | | |
| **F-250 HD PICKUPS 133" WB 6*** | | | |
| Styleside (over 8500 lb. GVW) | **14271** | 9750 | 11125 |
| **F-250 HD SUPER CAB PICKUP 155" WB 8** | | | |
| Styleside (over 8500 lb. GVW) | **16680** | 10675 | 12225 |
| **RANGER S 2WD 4*** | | | |
| 108" WB | **9134** | 5500 | 6300 |
| *For 6 cyl models add $400 whsle/$400 retail. | | | |
| **RANGER 2WD 4*** | | | |
| Sport 108" WB | **9347** | 6525 | 7475 |
| Sport 114" WB | **9503** | 6625 | 7575 |
| Custom 108" WB | **10508** | 6700 | 7675 |
| Custom 114" WB | **10833** | 6825 | 7825 |
| *For 6 cyl models add $400 whsle/$400 retail. | | | |
| **RANGER SUPER CAB 2WD 4*** | | | |
| 125" WB | **12020** | 7100 | 8125 |
| *For 6 cyl models add $400 whsle/$400 retail. | | | |
| *ADD FOR:* | | | |
| XL Pkg | | | |
| (Econoline) | — | 210 | 280 |
| (F-150 Reg Cab) | **445** | 175 | 225 |
| (F-250 Reg Cab) | **340** | 130 | 170 |
| (F-250 Super Cab) | **244** | 120 | 150 |
| XLT Pkg | | | |
| (Bronco) | **2378** | 1305 | 1580 |
| (Econoline E-150 Club Wgn) | **2278** | 1240 | 1510 |
| (Econoline E-250 Club Wgn) | **4672** | 2625 | 3195 |
| XLT Nite Pkg (Bronco) | **3589** | 1985 | 2415 |
| XLT Lariat Trim | | | |
| (F-150) | — | 570 | 710 |
| (F-250) | — | 1140 | 1400 |
| XLT Lariat Nite Trim | | | |
| (F-150) | — | 1260 | 1530 |

| Year/Model/<br>Body/Type | Original<br>List | Current<br>Whlse | Average<br>Retail |
|---|---|---|---|
| Eddie Bauer Pkg<br>(Bronco) | **4044** | 2255 | 2745 |

## 1990

### BRONCO 105" WB 6*

| Wgn | **17619** | 9800 | 11175 |
|---|---|---|---|

*For 8 cyl models add $400 whsle/$400 retail.

### BRONCO II 94" WB 6

| Bronco II 2WD | **13769** | 7050 | 8050 |
|---|---|---|---|

### E-150 CLUB WAGON 138" WB 6*

| 8 Pass Wgn | **17569** | 9525 | 10850 |
|---|---|---|---|

*For 8 cyl models add $400 whsle/$400 retail.

### E-250 CLUB WAGON 138" WB 6*

| 12 Pass Wgn | **18094** | 9900 | 11275 |
|---|---|---|---|

*For 8 cyl models add $400 whsle/$400 retail.

### E-150 ECONOLINE VANS 124" WB 6*

| Cargo | **13713** | 7000 | 8025 |
|---|---|---|---|

*For 8 cyl models add $400 whsle/$400 retail.

### E-150 ECONOLINE VANS 138" WB 6*

| Cargo | **13983** | 7125 | 8150 |
|---|---|---|---|
| Cargo, Super | **14893** | 7825 | 8950 |

*For 8 cyl models add $400 whsle/$400 retail.

### E-250 ECONOLINE VANS 138" WB 6*

| Cargo | **14272** | 7275 | 8325 |
|---|---|---|---|
| Cargo, Super | **15031** | 7975 | 9125 |

*For 8 cyl models add $400 whsle/$400 retail.

### AEROSTAR VANS 119" WB 2WD 6*

| Cargo | **12726** | 6150 | 7025 |
|---|---|---|---|
| Cargo, Extended | **13473** | 6850 | 7850 |
| Window | **13110** | 6250 | 7150 |
| Window, Extended | **13857** | 7000 | 8025 |
| Wagon | **13152** | 8025 | 9150 |
| Wagon, Extended | **14050** | 8725 | 9950 |

*For 4.0 liter 6 cyl models add $200 whsle/$200 retail.

### F-150 PICKUPS 117" WB 6*

| S Styleside | **11151** | 6150 | 7025 |
|---|---|---|---|
| Styleside | **12017** | 6825 | 7825 |
| w/133" WB add | | | |
| (2WD) | **216** | 100 | 120 |
| (4WD) | **335** | 150 | 180 |

*For 8 cyl models add $400 whsle/$400 retail.

### F-150 SUPER CAB PICKUP 139" WB 6*

| Styleside | **13367** | 7675 | 8775 |
|---|---|---|---|

*For 8 cyl models add $400 whsle/$400 retail.

### F-150 SUPER CAB PICKUP 155" WB 6*

| Styleside | **13591** | 7800 | 8925 |
|---|---|---|---|

*For 8 cyl models add $400 whsle/$400 retail.

### F-250 PICKUPS 133" WB 6*

| Styleside<br>(under 8500 lb. GVW) | **12962** | 7550 | 8650 |
|---|---|---|---|
| Styleside<br>(over 8500 lb. GVW) | **13411** | 7850 | 9000 |

*For 8 cyl models (under 8500 lb. GVW) add $400 whsle/$400 retail. For 8 cyl models (over 8500 lb. GVW) add $400 whsle/$400 retail.

### F-250 SUPER CAB 2WD 155" WB 6

| Styleside<br>(over 8500 lb. GVW) | **15765** | 8425 | 9600 |
|---|---|---|---|

### F-250 SUPER CAB 4WD 155" WB 8

| Styleside<br>(over 8500 lb. GVW) | **18070** | 10000 | 11425 |
|---|---|---|---|

### RANGER 2WD 4*

| 108" WB | **10188** | 5100 | 5900 |
|---|---|---|---|
| 114" WB | **10351** | 5200 | 6000 |

*For 6 cyl models add $400 whsle/$400 retail.

### RANGER "S" 2WD 4

| 108" WB | **8607** | 4000 | 4775 |
|---|---|---|---|
| 114" WB | **8763** | 4100 | 4900 |

### RANGER SUPER CAB 2WD 4*

| 125" WB | **11461** | 5675 | 6475 |
|---|---|---|---|

*For 6 cyl models add $375 whsle/$375 retail.

*ADD FOR:*

| | Original<br>List | Current<br>Whlse | Average<br>Retail |
|---|---|---|---|
| Sport Appearance Pkg<br>(Bronco II) | **695** | 260 | 330 |
| Sport Trim Pkg<br>(Bronco II) | **824** | 320 | 410 |
| Eddie Bauer Pkg<br>(Bronco) | **3578** | 1740 | 2120 |
| (Aerostar) | **6668** | 3295 | 4005 |
| XL Pkg<br>(Econoline Van) | **794** | 300 | 390 |
| (F-150 Pickups) | **—** | 270 | 350 |
| (F-250 Pickups) | **767** | 290 | 370 |
| XL Plus Pkg<br>(Aerostar) | **2072** | 960 | 1180 |
| XL Sport Pkg<br>(Bronco II) | **799** | 300 | 390 |
| XLT Pkg<br>(Bronco II) | **640** | 230 | 300 |
| (Bronco) | **1197** | 520 | 640 |
| (Econoline Club Wgn) | **2416** | 1140 | 1400 |
| (Aerostar) | **3037** | 1460 | 1780 |
| (Ranger) | **—** | 130 | 180 |

| Year/Model/Body/Type | Original List | Current Whlse | Average Retail |
|---|---|---|---|
| XLT Plus Pkg (Aerostar) | **4360** | 2115 | 2575 |
| XLT Lariat Pkg (F-Pickups) | — | 750 | 920 |
| Plus Pkg (Ranger S) | — | 300 | 390 |

## 1989

### BRONCO 105" WB 6*
| | | | |
|---|---|---|---|
| Wgn | **15983** | 8500 | 9700 |

*For 8 cyl models add $375 whlse/$375 retail.

### BRONCO II 94" WB 6
| | | | |
|---|---|---|---|
| Bronco II 2WD | **12520** | 6000 | 6800 |

### E-150 CLUB WAGON 138" WB 6*
| | | | |
|---|---|---|---|
| 5 Pass Wgn | **15289** | 7550 | 8650 |

### E-250 CLUB WAGON 138" WB 6*
| | | | |
|---|---|---|---|
| 5 Pass Wgn | **16060** | 7825 | 8950 |

*For 8 cyl models add $375 whlse/$375 retail.

### E-150 ECONOLINE VANS 124" WB 6*
| | | | |
|---|---|---|---|
| Cargo | **11443** | 5375 | 6175 |

*For 8 cyl models add $375 whlse/$375 retail.

### E-150 ECONOLINE VANS 138" WB 6*
| | | | |
|---|---|---|---|
| Cargo | **11702** | 5550 | 6350 |
| Cargo, Super | **13291** | 6250 | 7150 |

*For 8 cyl models add $375 whlse/$375 retail.

### E-250 ECONOLINE VANS 138" WB 6*
| | | | |
|---|---|---|---|
| Cargo | **12684** | 5675 | 6475 |
| Cargo, Super | **13400** | 6375 | 7300 |

*For 8 cyl models add $375 whlse/$375 retail.

### AEROSTAR VANS 119" WB 6
| | | | |
|---|---|---|---|
| Cargo | **11126** | 4850 | 5650 |
| Cargo, Extended | **11666** | 5550 | 6350 |
| Window | **11509** | 4950 | 5750 |
| Window, Extended | **12049** | 5675 | 6475 |
| Wagon | **11645** | 6775 | 7750 |
| Wagon, Extended | **12292** | 7450 | 8525 |

### F-150 PICKUPS 117" WB 6*
| | | | |
|---|---|---|---|
| S Styleside | **10067** | 5550 | 6350 |
| Styleside | **10516** | 6175 | 7075 |
| w/133" WB add | **200** | 70 | 80 |

*For 8 cyl models add $375 whlse/$375 retail.

### F-150 SUPER CAB PICKUP 138" WB 6*
| | | | |
|---|---|---|---|
| Styleside | **12027** | 6575 | 7525 |

*For 8 cyl models add $375 whlse/$375 retail.

### F-150 SUPER CAB PICKUP 155" WB 6*
| | | | |
|---|---|---|---|
| Styleside | **12227** | 6700 | 7675 |

*For 8 cyl models add $375 whlse/$375 retail.

### F-250 PICKUPS 133" WB 6*
| | | | |
|---|---|---|---|
| Styleside (under 8500 lb. GVW) | **11419** | 6500 | 7450 |
| Styleside (over 8500 lb. GVW) | **11843** | 6825 | 7825 |

*For 8 cyl models (under 8500 lb. GVW) add $375 whlse/$375 retail. For 8 cyl models (over 8500 lb. GVW) add $375 whlse/$375 retail.

### F-250 SUPER CAB 2WD 155" WB 6
| | | | |
|---|---|---|---|
| Styleside (over 8500 lb. GVW) | **14250** | 7225 | 8275 |

### F-250 SUPER CAB 4WD 155" WB 8
| | | | |
|---|---|---|---|
| Styleside (over 8500 lb. GVW) | **16395** | 7550 | 8650 |

### RANGER 2WD 4*
| | | | |
|---|---|---|---|
| 108" WB | **9045** | 4575 | 5375 |
| 114" WB | **9208** | 4650 | 5450 |

### RANGER 'S' 2WD 4
| | | | |
|---|---|---|---|
| 108" WB | **7693** | 4000 | 4775 |

### RANGER SUPER CAB 2WD 4*
| | | | |
|---|---|---|---|
| 125" WB | **10458** | 5025 | 5825 |

*For 6 cyl 2WD models add $325 whlse/$325 retail. For 6 cyl 4WD models add $325 whlse/$325 retail.

### RANGER SUPER CAB 4WD 6
| | | | |
|---|---|---|---|
| 125" WB | **13451** | 6375 | 7300 |
| *ADD FOR:* | | | |
| XL Sport Pkg (Bronco II) | **1693** | 640 | 790 |
| XL Pkg (Econoline) | **590** | 175 | 225 |
| (F-Pickups) | **470** | 140 | 180 |
| XLT Pkg (Bronco II) | **1455** | 530 | 660 |
| (Bronco) | **1599** | 600 | 740 |
| (Aerostar) | **3770** | 1550 | 1890 |
| (Ranger) | **1400** | 510 | 640 |
| XLT Lariat Pkg (F-Pickups) | **2380** | 940 | 1160 |
| Eddie Bauer Pkg (Bronco II) | **3537** | 1440 | 1760 |
| (Bronco) | **5000** | 2065 | 2515 |
| (Aerostar) | **7350** | 220 | 290 |
| STX Pkg (Ranger) | **2500** | 90 | 110 |
| GT Pkg (Ranger) | **4655** | 1940 | 2350 |

99

*Refer to optional equipment schedules*

| Year/Model/Body/Type | Original List | Current Whlse | Average Retail |
|---|---|---|---|
| **1988** | | | |
| **BRONCO 105" WB 6*** | | | |
| Wgn | **15279** | 7175 | 8200 |
| *For 8 cyl models add $325 whsle/$325 retail. | | | |
| **BRONCO II 94" WB 6** | | | |
| Bronco II 2WD | **11707** | 4700 | 5500 |
| **E-150 CLUB WAGON 138" WB 6*** | | | |
| 5 Pass Wgn | **14621** | 6150 | 7025 |
| **E-250 CLUB WAGON 138" WB 6*** | | | |
| 5 Pass Wgn | **15462** | 6275 | 7175 |
| **E-150 ECONOLINE VANS 124" WB 6*** | | | |
| Cargo | **10949** | 3900 | 4675 |
| *For 8 cyl models add $325 whsle/$325 retail. | | | |
| **E-150 ECONOLINE VANS 138" WB 6*** | | | |
| Cargo | **11196** | 4025 | 4800 |
| Cargo, Super | **12724** | 4650 | 5450 |
| *For 8 cyl models add $325 whsle/$325 retail. | | | |
| **E-250 ECONOLINE VANS 138" WB 6*** | | | |
| Cargo | **12102** | 4075 | 4875 |
| Cargo, Super | **12818** | 4700 | 5500 |
| *For 8 cyl models add $325 whsle/$325 retail. | | | |
| **AEROSTAR VANS 119" WB 6** | | | |
| Cargo (4 cyl) | **10540** | 3550 | 4325 |
| Window | **10924** | 4725 | 5525 |
| Wagon | **11165** | 5450 | 6250 |
| **F-150 PICKUPS 117" WB 6*** | | | |
| S Styleside | **9676** | 3650 | 4425 |
| Styleside | **10038** | 3775 | 4550 |
| w/133" WB add | **189** | 60 | 80 |
| *For 8 cyl models add $325 whsle/$325 retail. | | | |
| **F-150 SUPERCAB PICKUP 138" WB 6*** | | | |
| Styleside | **11550** | 5200 | 6000 |
| *For 8 cyl models add $325 whsle/$325 retail. | | | |
| **F-150 SUPER CAB PICKUP 155" WB 6*** | | | |
| Styleside | **11739** | 5325 | 6125 |
| *For 8 cyl models add $325 whsle/$325 retail. | | | |
| **F-250 PICKUPS 133" WB 6*** | | | |
| Styleside (under 8500 lb. GVW) | **10849** | 5050 | 5850 |
| Styleside (over 8500 lb. GVW) | **11288** | 5425 | 6225 |
| *For 8 cyl models add $325 whsle/$325 retail. | | | |

| Year/Model/Body/Type | Original List | Current Whlse | Average Retail |
|---|---|---|---|
| **F-250 SUPER CAB 155" WB 6** | | | |
| Styleside (over 8500 lb. GVW) | **12898** | 6150 | 7025 |
| **F-250 SUPER CAB 4WD 155" WB 8** | | | |
| Styleside (over 8500 lb. GVW) | **15734** | 7700 | 8825 |
| **RANGER 4*** | | | |
| 108" WB | **8396** | 3450 | 4225 |
| 114" WB | **8558** | 3550 | 4325 |
| **RANGER 'S' 4** | | | |
| 108" WB | **7093** | 2600 | 3450 |
| *For 6 cyl models add $300 whsle/$300 retail. | | | |
| **RANGER SUPER CAB 2WD 4** | | | |
| 125" WB | **9691** | 3900 | 4675 |
| **RANGER SUPER CAB 4WD 6** | | | |
| 125" WB | **11956** | 5200 | 6000 |
| *ADD FOR:* | | | |
| XL Sport Pkg (Bronco II) | **1215** | 340 | 430 |
| XL Pkg (F-Pickups) | **430** | 90 | 120 |
| XLT Pkg (Bronco II) | **890** | 220 | 290 |
| (Bronco) | **1400** | 410 | 510 |
| XLT Lariat Pkg (F-Series) | **1440** | 420 | 530 |
| GT Pkg (Ranger) | **3460** | 1150 | 1410 |
| STX Pkg (Ranger) | **1460** | 430 | 540 |
| Eddie Bauer Pkg (Bronco II) | **3450** | 1150 | 1410 |
| (Bronco) | **3970** | 1340 | 1630 |
| **1987** | | | |
| **BRONCO 105" WB 6*** | | | |
| Wgn | **14166** | 5425 | 6225 |
| *For 8 cyl models add $275 whsle/$275 retail. | | | |
| **BRONCO II 94" WB 6** | | | |
| Bronco II 2WD | **11398** | 3000 | 3850 |
| **E-150 CLUB WAGON 138" WB 6*** | | | |
| 5 Pass Wgn | **13171** | 4725 | 5525 |
| **E-250 CLUB WAGON 138" WB 6*** | | | |
| 5 Pass Wgn | **14881** | 4825 | 5625 |
| **E-150 ECONOLINE VANS 124" WB 6*** | | | |
| Cargo | **10449** | 2375 | 3200 |
| Window | **10740** | 2450 | 3275 |
| *For 8 cyl models add $275 whsle/$275 retail. | | | |

| Year/Model/Body/Type | Original List | Current Whlse | Average Retail |
|---|---|---|---|
| **E-150 ECONOLINE VANS 138" WB 6*** | | | |
| Cargo | **10688** | 2475 | 3300 |
| Window | **10979** | 2550 | 3400 |
| Cargo, Super | **11599** | 2825 | 3675 |
| Window, Super | **11890** | 2900 | 3750 |
| *For 8 cyl models add $275 whsle/$275 retail. | | | |
| **E-250 ECONOLINE VANS 138" WB 6*** | | | |
| Cargo | **11589** | 2500 | 3325 |
| Window | **11880** | 2600 | 3450 |
| Cargo, Super | **12302** | 2775 | 3625 |
| *For 8 cyl models add $275 whsle/$275 retail. | | | |
| **AEROSTAR VANS 119" WB 6** | | | |
| Cargo (4 cyl) | **10045** | 1925 | 2725 |
| Window | **10428** | 2200 | 3025 |
| Wagon | **10682** | 3525 | 4300 |
| **F-150 PICKUPS 117" WB 6*** | | | |
| Styleside | **9509** | 3025 | 3875 |
| Flareside | **9772** | 3075 | 3925 |
| w/133" WB add | **184** | 70 | 90 |
| *For 8 cyl models add $275 whsle/$275 retail. | | | |
| **F-150 SUPER CAB PICKUP 155" WB 6*** | | | |
| Styleside (139" WB) | **11405** | 3650 | 4425 |
| *For 8 cyl models add $275 whsle/$275 retail. | | | |
| **F-250 PICKUPS 133" WB 6*** | | | |
| Styleside (under 8500 lb. GVW) | **10566** | 3650 | 4425 |
| Styleside (over 8500 lb. GVW) | **10874** | 3850 | 4625 |
| *For 8 cyl models add $275 whsle/$275 retail. | | | |
| **F-250 SUPER CAB 155" WB 6** | | | |
| Styleside (over 8500 lb. GVW) | **12686** | 4500 | 5300 |
| **F-250 SUPER CAB 4WD 155" WB 8** | | | |
| Styleside (over 8500 lb. GVW) | **15834** | 5425 | 6225 |
| **RANGER 4*** | | | |
| 108" WB | **7684** | 1950 | 2750 |
| 114" WB | **7845** | 2050 | 2850 |
| *For 6 cyl models add $250 whsle/$250 retail. | | | |
| **RANGER 'S' 4** | | | |
| 108" WB | **6393** | 1900 | 2700 |
| **RANGER SUPER CAB 2WD 4** | | | |
| 125" WB | **8846** | 2275 | 3100 |
| *ADD FOR:* | | | |
| XL Pkg (F-Pickups) | **395** | 90 | 120 |

| Year/Model/Body/Type | Original List | Current Whlse | Average Retail |
|---|---|---|---|
| XLT Pkg | | | |
| (Bronco II) | **830** | 170 | 220 |
| (Bronco) | **980** | 180 | 240 |
| (Ranger) | **780** | 150 | 200 |
| XLT Lariat Pkg | | | |
| (F-Pickups) | **—** | 185 | 245 |
| STX Pkg | | | |
| (Ranger) | **—** | 200 | 260 |
| Eddie Bauer Pkg | | | |
| (Bronco II) | **2260** | 550 | 680 |

## 1986

| Year/Model/Body/Type | Original List | Current Whlse | Average Retail |
|---|---|---|---|
| **BRONCO 104" WB 6*** | | | |
| Wgn | **12782** | 4375 | 5175 |
| *For 8 cyl models add $250 whsle/$250 retail. | | | |
| **BRONCO II 94" WB 6*** | | | |
| Bronco II 2WD | **10420** | 2400 | 3225 |
| **E-150 CLUB WAGON 138" WB 6*** | | | |
| 5 Pass Wgn | **12274** | 3425 | 4200 |
| **E-250 CLUB WAGON 138" WB 6*** | | | |
| 5 Pass Wgn | **13839** | 3525 | 4300 |
| **E-150 ECONOLINE VANS 124" WB 6*** | | | |
| Cargo | **9439** | 1650 | 2450 |
| Window | **9710** | 1725 | 2525 |
| *For 8 cyl models add $250 whsle/$250 retail. | | | |
| **E-150 ECONOLINE VANS 138" WB 6*** | | | |
| Cargo | **9663** | 1750 | 2550 |
| Window | **9934** | 1875 | 2675 |
| Cargo, Super | **10593** | 2325 | 3150 |
| Window, Super | **10863** | 2425 | 3250 |
| *For 8 cyl models add $250 whsle/$250 retail. | | | |
| **E-250 ECONOLINE VANS 138" WB 6*** | | | |
| Cargo | **10561** | 1800 | 2600 |
| Window | **10831** | 1950 | 2750 |
| Cargo, Super | **11221** | 2375 | 3200 |
| *For 8 cyl models add $250 whsle/$250 retail. | | | |
| **AEROSTAR VANS 119" WB 4** | | | |
| Cargo | **8774** | 1250 | 1925 |
| Window | **9822** | 1325 | 2025 |
| Wagon | **9553** | 2400 | 3225 |
| **F-150 PICKUPS 117" WB 6*** | | | |
| Styleside | **8373** | 2375 | 3225 |
| Flareside | **8626** | 2475 | 3300 |
| w/133" WB add | **174** | 70 | 80 |
| *For 8 cyl models add $250 whsle/$250 retail. | | | |

| Year/Model/Body/Type | Original List | Current Whsle | Average Retail |
|---|---|---|---|
| **F-150 SUPER CAB PICKUP 138" WB 6*** | | | |
| Styleside | **10272** | 2925 | 3775 |
| *For 8 cyl models add $250 whsle/$250 retail. | | | |
| **F-150 SUPER CAB PICKUP 155" WB 6*** | | | |
| Styleside | **10446** | 3025 | 3875 |
| *For 8 cyl models add $250 whsle/$250 retail. | | | |
| **F-250 PICKUPS 133" WB 6*** | | | |
| Styleside (under 8500 lb. GVW) | **9646** | 2925 | 3775 |
| Styleside (over 8500 lb. GVW) | **9978** | 3275 | 4125 |
| *For 8 cyl models under 8500 lb. GVW add $250 whsle/$250 retail. For 8 cyl models over 8500 lb. GVW add $250 whsle/$250 retail. | | | |
| **F-250 SUPER CAB 155" WB 6** | | | |
| Styleside (over 8500 lb. GVW) | **11645** | 3475 | 4250 |
| **F-250 SUPER CAB 4WD 155" WB 8** | | | |
| Styleside (over 8500 lb. GVW) | **14015** | 4350 | 5150 |
| **RANGER 4*** | | | |
| 108" WB Pickup | **7065** | 1400 | 2125 |
| 114" WB Pickup | **7221** | 1500 | 2300 |
| *For 6 cyl models add $225 whsle/$225 retail. | | | |
| **RANGER 'S' 4** | | | |
| 108" WB Pickup | **5993** | 1125 | 1800 |
| **RANGER SUPER CAB 2WD 4** | | | |
| 125" WB | **8053** | 1625 | 2425 |
| *For 6 cyl models add $225 whsle/$225 retail. | | | |
| *ADD FOR:* | | | |
| XL Pkg (F-Pickups) | **395** | 60 | 80 |
| XLT Pkg (Bronco II) | **830** | 100 | 140 |
| (Bronco) | **980** | 140 | 180 |
| (Ranger) | **780** | 100 | 130 |
| XLT Lariat Pkg (F-Pickups) | **625** | 110 | 140 |
| STX Pkg (Ranger) | **—** | 120 | 160 |

## 1985

| Year/Model/Body/Type | Original List | Current Whsle | Average Retail |
|---|---|---|---|
| **BRONCO 104" WB 6* E** | | | |
| Wgn | **12050** | 3425 | 4200 |
| Eddie Bauer Wgn | **16029** | 3975 | 4750 |
| *For 8 cyl models add $225 whsle/$225 retail. | | | |

| Year/Model/Body/Type | Original List | Current Whsle | Average Retail |
|---|---|---|---|
| **BRONCO II 94" WB 6*** | | | |
| Bronco II | **11102** | 2575 | 3425 |
| Bronco II Eddie Bauer | **13365** | 3000 | 3850 |
| **E-150 CLUB WAGON 124" WB 6*** | | | |
| 5 Pass Wgn | **11641** | 2300 | 3125 |
| **E-150 CLUB WAGON 138" WB 6*** | | | |
| 5 Pass Wgn | **13140** | 2400 | 3225 |
| **E-150 ECONOLINE VANS 124" WB 6*** | | | |
| Cargo | **8676** | 1075 | 1750 |
| Display | **8802** | 1150 | 1825 |
| Window | **8870** | 1175 | 1850 |
| *For 8 cyl models add $225 whsle/$225 retail. | | | |
| **E-150 ECONOLINE VANS 138" WB 6*** | | | |
| Cargo | **8888** | 1150 | 1825 |
| Display | **9015** | 1225 | 1900 |
| Window | **9082** | 1250 | 1925 |
| Cargo, Super | **9765** | 1375 | 2075 |
| Window, Super | **9959** | 1500 | 2300 |
| *For 8 cyl models add $225 whsle/$225 retail. | | | |
| **E-250 ECONOLINE VANS 138" WB 6*** | | | |
| Cargo | **9940** | 1225 | 1900 |
| Display | **10067** | 1275 | 1950 |
| Window | **10134** | 1325 | 2025 |
| Cargo, Super | **10570** | 1500 | 2300 |
| Window, Super | **10764** | 1575 | 2375 |
| *For 8 cyl models add $225 whsle/$225 retail. | | | |
| **F-150 PICKUPS 117" WB 6*** | | | |
| Styleside | **7902** | 1900 | 2700 |
| Flareside | **8066** | 1875 | 2675 |
| w/133" WB add | **166** | 50 | 70 |
| *For 8 cyl models add $225 whsle/$225 retail. | | | |
| **F-150 SUPERCAB PICKUP 139" WB 6*** | | | |
| Styleside | **9238** | 2200 | 3025 |
| *For 8 cyl models add $225 whsle/$225 retail. | | | |
| **F-150 SUPER CAB PICKUP 155" WB 6*** | | | |
| Styleside | **9404** | 2300 | 3125 |
| *For 8 cyl models add $225 whsle/$225 retail. | | | |
| **F-250 PICKUPS 133" WB 6*** | | | |
| Styleside (over 8500 lb. GVW) | **9563** | 2325 | 3150 |
| *For 8 cyl models under 8500 lb. GVW add $225 whsle/$225 retail. For 8 cyl models over 8500 lb. GVW add $225 whsle/$225 retail. | | | |
| **F-250 SUPER CAB 4WD 155" WB 8** | | | |
| Styleside (over 8500 lb. GVW) | **13177** | 4000 | 4775 |

*1984 Ford E-150 Econoline Van 124" WB 6*

| Year/Model/Body/Type | Original List | Current Whlse | Average Retail |
|---|---|---|---|
| **RANGER 4** | | | |
| 108" WB Pickup | **6675** | 1050 | 1725 |
| 114" WB Pickup | **6829** | 1125 | 1800 |
| **RANGER 'S' 4** | | | |
| 108" WB Pickup | **5995** | 1200 | 1875 |
| *ADD FOR:* | | | |
| California Pkg (E250 Club Wgn) | **492** | 50 | 60 |
| Camper Pkg (Econoline Vans) | **641** | 70 | 80 |
| Explorer Pkg A (F Series Pickups) | **525** | 50 | 70 |
| Explorer Pkg B (F Series Pickups) | **800** | 90 | 110 |
| Explorer Pkg C (F Series Pickups) | **1328** | 110 | 150 |
| Explorer Pkg D (F Series Pickups) | **1763** | 170 | 220 |
| XL Trim (Ranger) | **355** | 30 | 40 |
| (F Series Pickups) | **—** | 30 | 40 |
| XLT Trim (Ranger) | **737** | 80 | 100 |
| (F Series Pickups) | **655** | 70 | 80 |

## 1984

| Year/Model/Body/Type | Original List | Current Whlse | Average Retail |
|---|---|---|---|
| **BRONCO 104" WB 6★** | | | |
| Wgn | **11468** | 2850 | 3700 |

*For 8 cyl models add $200 whsle/$200 retail.

| Year/Model/Body/Type | Original List | Current Whlse | Average Retail |
|---|---|---|---|
| **BRONCO II 94" WB 6★** | | | |
| Bronco II | **10446** | 2100 | 2900 |

| Year/Model/Body/Type | Original List | Current Whlse | Average Retail |
|---|---|---|---|
| Bronco II Eddie Bauer | **12638** | 2325 | 3150 |
| **E-150 CLUB WAGON 124" WB 6★** | | | |
| 5 Pass Wgn | **9621** | 1775 | 2575 |
| **E-150 CLUB WAGON 138" WB 6★** | | | |
| 5 Pass Wgn | **9830** | 1875 | 2675 |
| **E-250 CLUB WAGONS 138" WB 6★** | | | |
| 11 Pass Wgn | **11474** | 1950 | 2750 |
| 5 Pass HD Extended Super Wgn | **11911** | 2500 | 3325 |
| 5 Pass Extended Super Wgn | **11584** | 2425 | 3250 |
| **E-150 ECONOLINE VANS 124" WB 6★** | | | |
| Cargo | **7835** | 1175 | 1850 |
| Display | **7957** | 1225 | 1900 |
| Window | **8023** | 1275 | 1950 |

*For 8 cyl models add $200 whsle/$200 retail.

| Year/Model/Body/Type | Original List | Current Whlse | Average Retail |
|---|---|---|---|
| **E-150 ECONOLINE VANS 138" WB 6★** | | | |
| Cargo | **8045** | 1250 | 1925 |
| Display | **8167** | 1300 | 2000 |
| Window | **8233** | 1350 | 2050 |
| Cargo, Super | **8984** | 1500 | 2300 |
| Display, Super | **9106** | 1575 | 2375 |
| Window, Super | **9172** | 1600 | 2400 |

*For 8 cyl models add $200 whsle/$200 retail.

| Year/Model/Body/Type | Original List | Current Whlse | Average Retail |
|---|---|---|---|
| **E-250 ECONOLINE VANS 138" WB 6★** | | | |
| Cargo | **8889** | 1000 | 1675 |
| Display | **9011** | 1075 | 1750 |
| Window | **9077** | 1150 | 1825 |
| Cargo, Super | **9496** | 1175 | 1850 |

| Year/Model/Body/Type | Original List | Current Whlse | Average Retail |
|---|---|---|---|
| Display, Super | **9618** | 1225 | 1900 |
| Window, Super | **9684** | 1300 | 2000 |
| *For 8 cyl models add $200 whsle/$200 retail. | | | |

### F-150 PICKUPS 117" WB 6*

| | | | |
|---|---|---|---|
| Styleside | **7209** | 1500 | 2300 |
| Flareside | **7371** | 1500 | 2300 |
| w/133" WB add | **157** | 30 | 40 |
| *For 8 cyl models add $200 whsle/$200 retail. | | | |

### F-150 SUPER CAB PICKUP 139" WB 6*

| | | | |
|---|---|---|---|
| Styleside | **8674** | 1825 | 2625 |
| *For 8 cyl models add $200 whsle/$200 retail. | | | |

### F-150 SUPER CAB PICKUP 155" WB 6*

| | | | |
|---|---|---|---|
| Styleside | **8832** | 1925 | 2725 |
| *For 8 cyl models add $200 whsle/$200 retail. | | | |

### F-250 PICKUPS 133" WB 6*

| | | | |
|---|---|---|---|
| Styleside (under 8500 lb. GVW) | **8130** | 1875 | 2675 |
| Styleside (over 8500 lb. GVW) | **9034** | 2125 | 2925 |
| *For 8 cyl models under 8500 lb. GVW add $200 whsle/$200 retail. For 8 cyl models over 8500 lb. GVW add $200 whsle/$200 retail. | | | |

### F-250 SUPER CAB 155" WB 6*

| | | | |
|---|---|---|---|
| Styleside (over 8500 lb. GVW) | **9811** | 2400 | 3225 |
| *For 8 cyl models add $200 whsle/$200 retail. | | | |

### RANGER 4

| | | | |
|---|---|---|---|
| 108" WB Pickup | **6453** | 900 | 1575 |
| 114" WB Pickup | **6612** | 1000 | 1675 |

### GMC
### 1992

### YUKON 4WD 112" WB

| | | | |
|---|---|---|---|
| 2 Dr Wgn | **20493** | 15700 | 17925 |
| ADD FOR: | | | |
| SLE Pkg (models w/o sport pkg) | **1135** | 600 | 700 |
| (models w/sport pkg) | **705** | 300 | 375 |
| Sport Pkg | **1197** | 650 | 750 |

### JIMMY 2WD 100.5" WB 6

| | | | |
|---|---|---|---|
| 2 Dr Sport Utility | **15802** | 13025 | 15350 |

### JIMMY 2WD 107" WB 6

| | | | |
|---|---|---|---|
| 4 Dr Sport Utility | **16762** | 14050 | 16525 |

| Year/Model/Body/Type | Original List | Current Whlse | Average Retail |
|---|---|---|---|
| ADD FOR: | | | |
| SLE Pkg | **815** | 555 | 615 |
| SLS Pkg (2WD models) | **991** | 625 | 695 |
| (4WD models) | **744** | 625 | 695 |

### TYPHOON 4WD 100.5" WB 6

| | | | |
|---|---|---|---|
| 2 Dr Sport Utility | **28995** | — | — |

### SONOMA REG CAB PICKUPS 2WD 4*

| | | | |
|---|---|---|---|
| Special Wideside (108" WB) | **10021** | 6725 | 7825 |
| Wideside (108" WB) | **11087** | 7925 | 9200 |
| Wideside (118" WB) | **11387** | 8075 | 9325 |
| *For 2.8 liter 6 cyl Eng. add $450 whsle/$450 retail. | | | |

### SONOMA GT 2WD 6

| | | | |
|---|---|---|---|
| Wideside | **16300** | — | — |

### SONOMA CLUB COUPE 2WD 4

| | | | |
|---|---|---|---|
| Wideside | **12312** | 8500 | 9825 |

### SONOMA SYCLONE TURBO 4WD 6

| | | | |
|---|---|---|---|
| Wideside | **26995** | — | — |
| ADD FOR: | | | |
| SLE Pkg | **522** | 405 | 455 |
| 4.3 Liter EFI 6 Cyl Eng (2WD models) | **620** | 475 | 475 |
| 4.3 Liter PFI 6 Cyl Eng (2WD models) | **1120** | 575 | 575 |
| (4WD models) | **500** | 375 | 375 |

### C-1500 PICKUPS 117.5" WB 6*

| | | | |
|---|---|---|---|
| Wideside | **14138** | 10850 | 12525 |
| Sportside | **14538** | 10925 | 12625 |
| *For 8 cyl models add $475 whsle/$475 retail. | | | |

### C-1500 PICKUPS 131.5" WB 6*

| | | | |
|---|---|---|---|
| Wideside | **14438** | 11000 | 12725 |
| Special Wideside | **11569** | 10575 | 12225 |
| *For 8 cyl models add $475 whsle/$475 retail. | | | |

### C-1500 CLUB COUPE PICKUPS 141.5" WB 6*

| | | | |
|---|---|---|---|
| Wideside | **15088** | 11825 | 13675 |
| Sportside | **15488** | 11825 | 13675 |
| *For 8 cyl models add $475 whsle/$475 retail. | | | |

### C-1500 CLUB COUPE PICKUP 155.5" WB 6*

| | | | |
|---|---|---|---|
| Wideside | **15378** | 11950 | 13825 |
| *For 8 cyl models add $475 whsle/$475 retail. | | | |
| ADD FOR: | | | |
| 5.7 Liter 8 Cyl Eng | **845** | 425 | 425 |
| 6.2 Liter 8 Cyl Diesel Eng | **2400** | 1475 | 1475 |
| SLE Pkg | **810** | 550 | 600 |
| SLX Pkg | **589** | 425 | 500 |

# AMERICAN TRUCKS

| Year/Model/ Body/Type | Original List | Current Whlse | Average Retail |
|---|---|---|---|
| Sport Pkg (2WD models) | **723** | 525 | 600 |
| (4WD models) | **1030** | 725 | 800 |
| Sport Handling Pkg | **805** | 265 | 295 |
| **C-2500 PICKUPS 131.5" WB 6\*** | | | |
| Wideside | **15078** | 12450 | 14150 |
| Heavy Duty Wideside | **15911** | 12700 | 14425 |
| *For 8 cyl models add $450 whlse/$450 retail.* | | | |
| **C-2500 CLUB COUPE PICKUP 141.5" WB 6\*** | | | |
| Wideside | **16198** | 13275 | 14950 |
| *For 8 cyl models add $450 whlse/$450 retail.* | | | |
| **C-2500 CLUB COUPE PICKUPS 155.5" WB 6\*** | | | |
| Wideside | **16478** | 13475 | 15200 |
| Heavy Duty Wideside | **16971** | 13700 | 15500 |
| *For 8 cyl models add $450 whlse/$450 retail.* | | | |
| *ADD FOR:* | | | |
| SLE Pkg | **794** | 550 | 600 |
| SLX Pkg | **589** | 400 | 450 |
| 5.7 Liter 8 Cyl Eng | **845** | 425 | 425 |
| 7.4 Liter 8 Cyl Eng | **1315** | 700 | 700 |
| 6.2 Liter 8 Cyl Diesel Eng | **2400** | 1400 | 1400 |
| 6.5 Liter 8 Cyl Turbo Diesel Eng | **3100** | — | — |
| **C-1500 SUBURBAN 2WD 131.5" WB 8** | | | |
| Panel Doors | **19238** | 16250 | 18000 |
| *ADD FOR:* | | | |
| SLE Pkg | **2109** | 1150 | 1250 |
| **C-2500 SUBURBAN 2WD 131.5" WB 8** | | | |
| Panel Doors | **20442** | 16800 | 18600 |
| *ADD FOR:* | | | |
| SLE Pkg | **2109** | 1150 | 1250 |
| 7.4 Liter 8 Cyl Eng | **470** | 350 | 350 |
| **SAFARI 2WD 111" WB 6** | | | |
| Cargo Van | **14908** | 11200 | 12900 |
| Extended Cargo Van | **15578** | 12000 | 13525 |
| Pass Van | **16249** | 12950 | 15275 |
| Extended Pass Van | **16939** | 13800 | 16175 |
| *ADD FOR:* | | | |
| SLE Pkg | **1092** | 875 | 1000 |
| SLT Pkg | **2952** | 1375 | 1550 |
| GT Sport Pkg (models w/SLE pkg) | **737** | 575 | 650 |
| (models w/o SLE pkg) | **1196** | 695 | 775 |
| 4.3 Liter CPI 6 Cyl Eng (2WD models) | **500** | 335 | 375 |
| **G-1500 VANS 110" WB 6\*** | | | |
| 1/2 Ton Vandura | **15358** | 11400 | 13150 |

| Year/Model/ Body/Type | Original List | Current Whlse | Average Retail |
|---|---|---|---|
| Rally Wgn | **17174** | 12850 | 15225 |
| *For 8 cyl models add $450 whlse/$450 retail.* | | | |
| **G-1500 VANS 125" WB 6\*** | | | |
| 1/2 Ton Vandura | **15638** | 11550 | 13325 |
| Rally Wgn | **18124** | 13025 | 15400 |
| *For 8 cyl models add $450 whlse/$450 retail.* | | | |
| *ADD FOR:* | | | |
| STX Pkg (Rally Wgn) | **838** | 575 | 650 |
| 5.7 Liter 8 Cyl Eng | **845** | 575 | 575 |
| **G-2500 VANS 110" WB 6** | | | |
| 3/4 Ton Vandura | **15578** | 11900 | 13625 |
| **G-2500 VANS 125" WB 6** | | | |
| 3/4 Ton Vandura | **15878** | 12050 | 13800 |
| Rally Wgn | **18314** | 13550 | 15900 |
| *ADD FOR:* | | | |
| STX Pkg (Rally Wgn) | **838** | 575 | 650 |
| 5.7 Liter 8 Cyl Eng | **845** | 575 | 575 |
| 6.2 Liter 8 Cyl Diesel Eng | **2400** | 1300 | 1300 |

## 1991

| **S-15 JIMMY 2WD 100.5" WB 6** | | | |
|---|---|---|---|
| 2 Dr Sport Utility | **14840** | 11050 | 12650 |
| **S-15 JIMMY 2WD 107" WB 6** | | | |
| 4 Dr Sport Utility | **16080** | 12000 | 13750 |
| **V-1500 JIMMY 106" WB 8** | | | |
| Wgn | **18519** | 13150 | 15350 |
| Wgn, Diesel | **21447** | 13475 | 15725 |
| **SONOMA REG CAB PICKUPS 4\*** | | | |
| Special Wideside (108" WB) | **9709** | 5275 | 6075 |
| Wideside (108" WB) | **10659** | 6375 | 7300 |
| Wideside (118" WB) | **10959** | 6525 | 7475 |
| *For 6 cyl models add $400 whlse/$400 retail.* | | | |
| **SONOMA CLUB COUPE 2WD 4** | | | |
| Wideside | **12240** | 6925 | 7925 |
| *For 6 cyl models add $400 whlse/$400 retail.* | | | |
| **SONOMA SYCLONE TURBO 4WD 6** | | | |
| Wideside | **25500** | — | — |
| **C-1500 GAS PICKUPS 117.5" WB 6\*** | | | |
| Wideside | **13214** | 8850 | 10100 |
| Sportside | **13554** | 8950 | 10225 |
| Special Wideside (131" WB) | **11572** | 8225 | 9375 |
| w/131" WB add | **300** | 110 | 140 |
| *For 8 cyl models add $425 whlse/$425 retail.* | | | |

| Year/Model/Body/Type | Original List | Current Whlse | Average Retail |
|---|---|---|---|

### C-1500 GAS CLUB CPE PICKUPS 141.5" WB 6*

| | | | |
|---|---|---|---|
| Wideside | **14164** | 9700 | 11050 |
| Sportside | **14504** | — | — |
| w/155" WB add | **290** | 100 | 130 |

*For 8 cyl models add $425 whsle/$425 retail.

### C-1500 DIESEL PICKUPS 131.5" WB 8

| | | | |
|---|---|---|---|
| Wideside | **16544** | 9775 | 11150 |

### C-1500 DIESEL CLUB CPE PICKUPS 141.5" WB 8

| | | | |
|---|---|---|---|
| Wideside | **16984** | 10125 | 11575 |
| Sportside | **17324** | — | — |
| w/155" WB add | **290** | 100 | 130 |

### C-2500 GAS PICKUPS 131.5" WB 6*

| | | | |
|---|---|---|---|
| Wideside | **14154** | 9600 | 10950 |
| Heavy Duty Wideside | **14807** | 9925 | 11325 |

*For 8 cyl models add $425 whsle/$425 retail.

### C-2500 GAS CLUB CPE PICKUPS 141.5" WB 6*

| | | | |
|---|---|---|---|
| Wideside | **15274** | 10750 | 12300 |
| Heavy Duty Wideside (155" WB) | **15858** | 11200 | 12825 |
| w/155" WB add | **280** | 100 | 130 |

*For 8 cyl models add $425 whsle/$425 retail.

### C-2500 DIESEL PICKUPS 131.5" WB 8

| | | | |
|---|---|---|---|
| Wideside | **16614** | 10400 | 11900 |
| Heavy Duty Wideside | **17088** | 10750 | 12300 |

### C-2500 DIESEL CLUB CPE PICKUPS 141.5" WB 8

| | | | |
|---|---|---|---|
| Wideside | **17724** | 11250 | 12900 |
| Heavy Duty Wideside (155" WB) | **18198** | 11575 | 13275 |
| w/155" WB add | **290** | 100 | 130 |

### R-1500 SUBURBAN 129.5" WB 8

| | | | |
|---|---|---|---|
| Panel Doors | **17620** | 13275 | 15525 |
| Tailgate | **17780** | 13375 | 15625 |
| Panel Doors, Diesel | **20098** | 13725 | 16050 |
| Tailgate, Diesel | **20253** | 13800 | 16125 |

### R-2500 SUBURBAN 129.5" WB 8

| | | | |
|---|---|---|---|
| Panel Doors | **19178** | 13800 | 16125 |
| Tailgate | **19328** | 13875 | 16225 |
| Panel Doors, HD Diesel | **20956** | 14200 | 16600 |
| Tailgate, HD Diesel | **21116** | 14300 | 16725 |

### SAFARI 111" WB 6*

| | | | |
|---|---|---|---|
| Cargo Van | **14389** | 9300 | 10600 |
| Extended Cargo Van | **15059** | 10050 | 11475 |
| SLX Pass Van | **15660** | 11150 | 12775 |
| SLX Extended Pass Van | **16350** | 11300 | 12950 |
| SLE Pass Van | **16740** | 11850 | 13575 |
| SLE Extended Pass Van | **17430** | 11975 | 13725 |
| SLT Pass Van | **18290** | 12350 | 14475 |
| SLT Extended Pass Van | **18980** | 12500 | 14700 |

*For 2WD models w/6 cyl high output Eng. add $200 whsle/$200 retail.

### G-1500 VANS 110" WB 6*

| | | | |
|---|---|---|---|
| ½ Ton Vandura | **14669** | 9125 | 10400 |
| Rally Wgn | **16485** | 10525 | 12050 |
| Rally STX Wgn (125" WB) | **18345** | 11775 | 13500 |
| w/125" WB add | | | |
| (Vandura) | **280** | 100 | 130 |
| (Rally) | **950** | 100 | 130 |

*For 8 cyl models add $425 whsle/$425 retail.

### G-2500 VANS 110" WB 6*

| | | | |
|---|---|---|---|
| ¾ Ton Vandura | **14849** | 9300 | 10600 |
| ¾ Ton Vandura Diesel (8 cyl) | **17522** | 10075 | 11525 |
| Rally Wgn (125" WB) | **17585** | 10875 | 12450 |
| Rally STX (125" WB) | **18485** | 11925 | 13675 |
| Rally Wgn Diesel (125" WB) | **20188** | 11750 | 13475 |
| Rally STX Diesel (125" WB) | **21028** | 12850 | 15050 |

*For 8 cyl models add $425 whsle/$425 retail.

### ADD FOR:

| | | | |
|---|---|---|---|
| SLE Comfort Pkg (Sonoma Reg Cab Pickup) | **548** | 220 | 280 |
| (Sonoma Club Cab Pickup) | **683** | 300 | 380 |
| SLE Decor Pkg (V-1500 Jimmy) | **1286** | 660 | 810 |
| (R Pickups) | **947** | 460 | 570 |
| (V Pickups) | **905** | 430 | 540 |
| (C-K Pickups) | **771** | 350 | 450 |
| (Suburban) | **1600** | 840 | 1040 |
| SLX Decor Pkg (C-K Reg Pickups) | **573** | 240 | 300 |
| (C-K Club Cab Pickups) | **458** | 175 | 235 |

## 1990

### S-15 JIMMY 100.5" WB 6

| | | | |
|---|---|---|---|
| Sport Utility | **13888** | 7575 | 8675 |

### V-1500 JIMMY 106" WB 8

| | | | |
|---|---|---|---|
| Wgn | **17367** | 9825 | 11200 |
| Wgn, Diesel | **20060** | 10200 | 11675 |

### C-1500 GAS PICKUPS 117.5" WB 6*

| | | | |
|---|---|---|---|
| Wideside | **12352** | 6875 | 7875 |
| Sportside | **12677** | 7000 | 8025 |
| Wideside Extended Cab (141" WB) | **13262** | 7700 | 8825 |

| Year/Model/Body/Type | Original List | Current Whlse | Average Retail |
|---|---|---|---|
| w/131" WB add | **280** | 120 | 150 |

*For 8 cyl models add $400 whsle/$400 retail.

### C-1500 DIESEL PICKUPS 131.5" WB 8

| Year/Model/Body/Type | Original List | Current Whlse | Average Retail |
|---|---|---|---|
| Wideside | **15442** | 7800 | 8925 |
| Wideside Extended Cab (141" WB) | **15872** | 8500 | 9700 |
| Wideside Extended Cab (155" WB) | **16147** | 8650 | 9875 |

### C-2500 GAS PICKUPS 131.5" WB 6*

| | | | |
|---|---|---|---|
| Wideside | **13257** | 7600 | 8700 |
| Heavy Duty Wideside | **13881** | 7925 | 9075 |
| Wideside Extended Cab (141" WB) | **14327** | 8350 | 9525 |
| Wideside Extended Cab (155" WB) | **14607** | 8475 | 9675 |
| Heavy Duty Wideside Extended Cab (155" WB) | **14896** | 8750 | 10000 |

*For 8 cyl models add $400 whsle/$400 retail.

### C-2500 DIESEL PICKUPS 131.5" WB 8

| | | | |
|---|---|---|---|
| Wideside | **15507** | 8425 | 9600 |
| Heavy Duty Wideside | **15966** | 8700 | 9925 |
| Wideside Extended Cab (141" WB) | **16577** | 9250 | 10550 |
| Wideside Extended Cab (155" WB) | **16857** | 9350 | 10650 |
| Heavy Duty Wideside Extended Cab (155" WB) | **17031** | 9625 | 10975 |

### S-15 REG CAB PICKUPS 4

| | | | |
|---|---|---|---|
| Wideside EL (108" WB) (NA w/pwr strng) | **8812** | 4525 | 5325 |
| Wideside (108" WB) | **10458** | 5200 | 6000 |
| Wideside (118" WB) | **10623** | 5325 | 6125 |
| Wideside Extended Cab (123" WB) | **11408** | 5775 | 6575 |

### R-1500 SUBURBAN 129.5" WB 8

| | | | |
|---|---|---|---|
| Panel Doors | **16628** | 10975 | 12575 |
| Tailgate | **16778** | 11075 | 12675 |
| Panel Doors, Diesel | **18896** | 11425 | 13100 |
| Tailgate, Diesel | **19041** | 11525 | 13200 |

### R-2500 SUBURBAN 129.5" WB 8

| | | | |
|---|---|---|---|
| Panel Doors | **17251** | 11375 | 13025 |
| Tailgate | **17396** | 11475 | 13150 |
| Panel Doors, HD Diesel | **19479** | 11775 | 13500 |
| Tailgate, HD Diesel | **19629** | 11875 | 13600 |

### SAFARI 111" WB 6

| | | | |
|---|---|---|---|
| Cargo Van (4 cyl) | **12977** | 6600 | 7550 |
| SLX Pass Van | **14823** | 8800 | 10050 |

| Year/Model/Body/Type | Original List | Current Whlse | Average Retail |
|---|---|---|---|
| SLE Pass Van | **15863** | 9375 | 10675 |
| SLT Pass Van | **17358** | 9925 | 11325 |

*For 6 cyl models add $375 whsle/$375 retail.

### G-1500 VANS 110" WB 6*

| | | | |
|---|---|---|---|
| ½ Ton Vandura | **13662** | 7050 | 8050 |
| Rally Wgn | **15663** | 8750 | 10000 |
| Rally STX (125" WB) | **17438** | 9575 | 10925 |
| w/125" WB add | | | |
| (Vandura) | **270** | 120 | 150 |
| (Rally) | **905** | 120 | 150 |

*For 8 cyl models add $400 whsle/$400 retail.

### G-2500 VANS 110" WB 6*

| | | | |
|---|---|---|---|
| ¾ Ton Vandura | **13832** | 7175 | 8200 |
| ¾ Ton Vandura Diesel (8 cyl) | **16470** | 8025 | 9150 |
| Rally Wgn (125" WB) | **16713** | 8875 | 10125 |
| Rally STX (125" WB) | **17578** | 9700 | 11050 |
| Rally Wgn Diesel (125" WB) (8 cyl) | **19036** | 9700 | 11050 |
| Rally STX Diesel (125" WB) (8 cyl) | **19846** | 10450 | 11950 |
| ¾ Ton Vandura (125" WB) (6 cyl) | **14112** | 7425 | 8500 |
| 3/4 Ton Vandura Diesel (125" WB) (8 cyl) | **16740** | 8275 | 9425 |

*For 8 cyl models add $400 whsle/$400 retail.

*ADD FOR:*

| | | | |
|---|---|---|---|
| Baja Equip (S15 4WD Pickups) | **1260** | 550 | 680 |
| Gypsy Pkg (S15 Jimmy) | **1239** | 530 | 660 |
| Safari GT Pkg (Safari 2WD SLE) | **905** | 360 | 460 |
| (Safari 2WD SLX) | **1309** | 570 | 700 |
| Sierra Classic Pkg (S-15 2WD Jimmy) | **841** | 330 | 420 |
| (S-15 4WD Jimmy) | **809** | 310 | 400 |
| (V1500 Jimmy) | **1281** | 560 | 690 |
| (Suburban) | **1583** | 710 | 880 |
| Sierra SLE Pkg (C & K Pickups) | **1040** | 430 | 540 |
| Sierra SLX Pkg (C & K Reg Cab Pickups) | **632** | 220 | 290 |
| (C & K Ext Cab Pickups) | **517** | 175 | 225 |

## 1989

### S-15 JIMMY 100.5" WB 6

| | | | |
|---|---|---|---|
| Sport Utility | **11680** | 6325 | 7225 |

### V-1500 JIMMY 106" WB 8

| | | | |
|---|---|---|---|
| Wgn | **15355** | 8575 | 9775 |
| Wgn, Diesel | **18085** | 8975 | 10225 |

| Year/Model/Body/Type | Original List | Current Whlse | Average Retail |
|---|---|---|---|
| **C-1500 GAS PICKUPS 117.5" WB 6*** | | | |
| Wideside | **10335** | 5750 | 6550 |
| Sportside | **10553** | 5825 | 6625 |
| Fleetside Extended Cab (141" WB) | **11267** | 6375 | 7300 |
| Wideside Extended Cab (155" WB) | **11467** | 6600 | 7550 |
| w/131" WB add | **200** | 70 | 80 |
| *For 8 cyl models add $375 whsle/$375 retail.* | | | |
| **C-1500 DIESEL PICKUPS 131.5" WB 8** | | | |
| Fleetside | **13318** | 6625 | 7575 |
| Fleetside Extended Cab (141" WB) | **13853** | 7125 | 8125 |
| Fleetside Extended Cab (155" WB) | **14053** | 7350 | 8400 |
| **C-2500 GAS PICKUPS 131.5" WB 6*** | | | |
| Wideside | **11143** | 6425 | 7350 |
| HD Fleetside | **12378** | 6725 | 7700 |
| Fleetside Extended Cab (141" WB) | **12298** | 7050 | 8050 |
| Wideside Extended Cab (155" WB) | **12498** | 7200 | 8225 |
| HD Fleetside Extended Cab (155" WB) (8 cyl) | **13413** | 7800 | 8925 |
| *For 8 cyl models add $375 whsle/$375 retail.* | | | |
| **C-2500 DIESEL PICKUPS 131.5" WB 8** | | | |
| Wideside | **13383** | 7200 | 8225 |
| HD Fleetside | **13828** | 7500 | 8575 |
| Fleetside Extended Cab (141" WB) | **14538** | 7800 | 8925 |
| Wideside Extended Cab (155" WB) | **14738** | 7975 | 9125 |
| HD Fleetside Extended Cab (155" WB) | **14911** | 8525 | 9725 |
| **R-2500 GAS PICKUPS 164.5" WB 8** | | | |
| Wideside Bonus Cab | **14164** | 7700 | 8825 |
| Wideside Crew Cab | **14664** | 7925 | 9075 |
| **R-2500 DIESEL PICKUPS 164.5" WB 8** | | | |
| HD Wideside Bonus Cab | **15164** | 8350 | 9525 |
| HD Wideside Crew Cab | **15664** | 8550 | 9750 |
| **S-15 REG CAB PICKUPS 4*** | | | |
| Wideside EL (108" WB) | **7474** | 3500 | 4275 |
| Wideside (108" WB) | **8585** | 4450 | 5250 |
| Wideside (118" WB) | **8750** | 4525 | 5325 |
| Wideside Extended Cab (123" WB) | **9435** | 4875 | 5675 |
| *For 6 cyl models add $375 whsle/$375 retail.* | | | |
| **R-1500 SUBURBAN 129.5" WB 8** | | | |
| Panel Doors | **14545** | 9200 | 10475 |

| Year/Model/Body/Type | Original List | Current Whlse | Average Retail |
|---|---|---|---|
| Tailgate | **14585** | 9300 | 10600 |
| Panel Doors, Diesel | **16895** | 9550 | 10875 |
| Tailgate, Diesel | **16935** | 9650 | 11000 |
| **R-2500 SUBURBAN 129.5" WB 8** | | | |
| Panel Doors | **15184** | 9550 | 10875 |
| Tailgate | **15224** | 9650 | 11000 |
| Panel Doors, HD Diesel | **17464** | 10075 | 11525 |
| Tailgate, HD Diesel | **17504** | 10150 | 11600 |
| **SAFARI 111" WB 6*** | | | |
| Cargo Van (4 cyl) | **10400** | 4850 | 5650 |
| SLX Pass Van | **11900** | 7100 | 8125 |
| SLE Pass Van | **12633** | 7625 | 8725 |
| SLT Pass Van | **14144** | 8200 | 9350 |
| *For 6 cyl models add $325 whsle/$325 retail.* | | | |
| **G-1500 VANS 110" WB 6*** | | | |
| 1/2 Ton Vandura | **11145** | 5100 | 5900 |
| Rally Wgn | **12638** | 6625 | 7575 |
| Rally STX (125" WB) | **14221** | 9650 | 11050 |
| w/125" WB add | | | |
| (Vandura) | **260** | 90 | 120 |
| (Rally) | **260** | 90 | 120 |
| *For 8 cyl models add $375 whsle/$375 retail.* | | | |
| **G-2500 VANS 110" WB 6*** | | | |
| 3/4 Ton Vandura | **11455** | 5225 | 6025 |
| 3/4 Ton Vandura Diesel (8 cyl) | **13853** | 6025 | 6825 |
| Rally Wgn (125" WB) | **13121** | 6850 | 7850 |
| Rally STX (125" WB) | **14440** | 7775 | 8900 |
| Rally Wgn Diesel (125" WB) (8 cyl) | **15498** | 7600 | 8700 |
| Rally STX Diesel (125" WB) (8 cyl) | **16759** | 8500 | 9700 |
| 3/4 Ton Vandura (125" WB) (6 cyl) | **11725** | 5350 | 6150 |
| 3/4 Ton Vandura Diesel (125" WB) (8 cyl) | **14114** | 6425 | 7350 |
| *For 8 cyl models add $375 whsle/$375 retail.* | | | |
| *ADD FOR:* | | | |
| Timberline Pkg (S/T Jimmy) | **1063** | 360 | 460 |
| Gypsy Pkg (S/T Jimmy) | **1089** | 370 | 470 |
| Sierra SLE Pkg (Suburban) | **1560** | 580 | 720 |
| (C-K Pickups) | **601** | 175 | 235 |
| Sierra Classic Pkg (S/T Jimmy) | **715** | 210 | 270 |
| (Jimmy) | **1340** | 480 | 600 |
| (S/T Pickups) | **535** | 160 | 210 |
| (R-V Pickups) | **956** | 320 | 400 |
| Safari GT Pkg (Safari) | **1070** | 370 | 460 |

| Year/Model/<br>Body/Type | Original<br>List | Current<br>Whlse | Average<br>Retail |
|---|---|---|---|
| **1988** | | | |
| **S-15 JIMMY 100.5" WB 4*** | | | |
| Sport Utility | **10505** | 4300 | 5100 |
| *For 6 cyl models add $300 whsle/$300 retail. | | | |
| **V-1500 JIMMY 106" WB 8** | | | |
| Wgn | **14691** | 6925 | 7925 |
| Wgn, Diesel | **17422** | 7250 | 8300 |
| **C-1500 GAS PICKUPS 117.5" WB 6*** | | | |
| Wideside | **9894** | 4125 | 4925 |
| Sportside | **10102** | 4225 | 5025 |
| Wideside Ext Cab<br>(155" WB) | **10983** | 4825 | 5625 |
| w/131" WB add | **190** | 50 | 60 |
| *For 8 cyl models add $325 whsle/$325 retail. | | | |
| **C-1500 DIESEL PICKUPS 131.5" WB 8** | | | |
| Fleetside | **12868** | 4825 | 5625 |
| Fleetside Extended Cab<br>(155" WB) | **13569** | 5550 | 6350 |
| **C-2500 GAS PICKUPS 131.5" WB 6*** | | | |
| Wideside | **10671** | 4650 | 5450 |
| Wideside Extended Cab<br>(155" WB) | **11976** | 5325 | 6125 |
| **C-2500 DIESEL PICKUPS 131.5" WB 8** | | | |
| Wideside | **12911** | 5300 | 6100 |
| Wideside Extended Cab<br>(155" WB) | **14216** | 6025 | 6825 |
| **R-2500 GAS PICKUPS 164.5" WB 6** | | | |
| Wideside Bonus Cab | **12922** | 5500 | 6300 |
| Wideside Crew Cab | **13358** | 5725 | 6525 |
| **R-2500 DIESEL PICKUPS 164.5" WB 8** | | | |
| Wideside Bonus Cab | **14578** | 6175 | 7075 |
| Wideside Crew Cab | **15015** | 6400 | 7325 |
| **S-15 REG CAB PICKUPS 4*** | | | |
| Wideside EL (108" WB) | **6795** | 2450 | 3275 |
| Wideside (108" WB) | **7890** | 2675 | 3525 |
| *For 6 cyl models add $300 whsle/$300 retail. | | | |
| **S-15 EXTENDED CAB 4** | | | |
| Wideside | **8815** | 3050 | 3900 |
| **R-1500 SUBURBAN 129.5" WB 8** | | | |
| Panel Doors | **13945** | 7225 | 8275 |
| Tailgate | **13988** | 7325 | 8375 |
| Panel Doors, Diesel | **16260** | 7575 | 8675 |
| Tailgate, Diesel | **16304** | 7675 | 8775 |
| **R-2500 SUBURBAN 129.5" WB 8** | | | |
| Panel Doors | **14559** | 7550 | 8650 |

| Year/Model/<br>Body/Type | Original<br>List | Current<br>Whlse | Average<br>Retail |
|---|---|---|---|
| Tailgate | **14602** | 7650 | 8750 |
| Panel Doors, HD Diesel | **16839** | 8000 | 9175 |
| Tailgate, HD Diesel | **16883** | 8100 | 9225 |
| **SAFARI 111" WB 6*** | | | |
| Cargo Van (4 cyl) | **9190** | 3100 | 3950 |
| SLX Pass Van | **10696** | 5225 | 6025 |
| SLE Pass Van | **11489** | 5750 | 6550 |
| SLT Pass Van | **12828** | 6300 | 7200 |
| **G-1500 VANS 110" WB 6*** | | | |
| 1/2 Ton Vandura | **10240** | 3175 | 4025 |
| Rally Wgn | **11922** | 4600 | 5400 |
| Rally Cust Wgn<br>(125" WB) | **13081** | 5375 | 6175 |
| Rally STX (125" WB) | **13489** | 5650 | 6450 |
| w/125" WB add (Vandura) | **248** | 80 | 110 |
| (Rally) | **251** | 90 | 110 |
| *For 8 cyl models add $325 whsle/$325 retail. | | | |
| **G-2500 VANS 110" WB 6*** | | | |
| 3/4 Ton Vandura | **10865** | 3275 | 4125 |
| 3/4 Ton Vandura<br>Diesel (8 cyl) | **13262** | 4025 | 4800 |
| Rally Wgn (125" WB) | **12423** | 4825 | 5625 |
| Rally Cust Wgn<br>(125" WB) | **13330** | 5500 | 6300 |
| Rally STX (125" WB) | **13736** | 5775 | 6575 |
| Rally Wgn Diesel<br>(125" WB) (8 cyl) | **14800** | 5550 | 6350 |
| Rally Cust Wgn Diesel<br>(125" WB) (8 cyl) | **15735** | 6200 | 7100 |
| Rally STX Diesel<br>(125" WB) (8 cyl) | **16055** | 6400 | 7325 |
| 3/4 Ton Vandura<br>(125" WB) (6 cyl) | **11117** | 3475 | 4250 |
| 3/4 Ton Vandura Diesel<br>(125" WB) (8 cyl) | **13513** | 4150 | 4950 |
| *ADD FOR:* | | | |
| Gypsy Pkg (S/T Jimmy) | **1068** | 280 | 360 |
| (S/T Pickups) | **925** | 230 | 300 |
| Sierra Classic Pkg | | | |
| (S/T Jimmy) | **683** | 180 | 230 |
| (Jimmy) | **1249** | 350 | 440 |
| (S/T Reg Cab Pickups) | **637** | 160 | 200 |
| (S/T Ext Cab Pickups) | **729** | 175 | 225 |
| (R1500 Suburban) | **1369** | 400 | 500 |
| (R2500 Suburban) | **1248** | 350 | 450 |
| | | | |
| **1987** | | | |
| **S-15 JIMMY 100.5" WB 4*** | | | |
| Sport Utility | **10124** | 3150 | 4000 |
| *For 6 cyl models add $250 whsle/$250 retail. | | | |

| Year/Model/Body/Type | Original List | Current Whlse | Average Retail |
|---|---|---|---|
| **V-1500 JIMMY 106" WB 8** | | | |
| Wgn | **13066** | 5850 | 6650 |
| Wgn, Diesel | **16027** | 6150 | 7025 |
| **CABALLERO 117" WB 6*** | | | |
| Caballero | **10453** | 3925 | 4700 |
| Caballero SS Diablo | **10784** | 4300 | 5100 |
| *For 8 cyl models add $275 whsle/$275 retail. | | | |
| **R-1500 PICKUPS 117.5" WB 6*** | | | |
| Fenderside | **8651** | 3075 | 3925 |
| Wideside | **8503** | 3150 | 4000 |
| Fenderside, Diesel (8 cyl) | **11842** | 3650 | 4425 |
| Wideside, Diesel (8 cyl) | **11695** | 3750 | 4525 |
| w/131.5" WB add | **183** | 40 | 60 |
| *For 8 cyl models add $275 whsle/$275 retail. | | | |
| **R-2500 PICKUPS 131.5" WB 6*** | | | |
| Fenderside | **10077** | 3675 | 4450 |
| Wideside | **9929** | 3725 | 4500 |
| *For 8 cyl models add $275 whsle/$275 retail. | | | |
| **R-2500 DIESEL PICKUPS 131.5" WB 8** | | | |
| Fenderside | **12722** | 4250 | 5050 |
| Wideside | **12574** | 4300 | 5100 |
| **R-2500 HEAVY DUTY PICKUPS 131.5" WB 8** | | | |
| Fenderside | **10077** | 3975 | 4875 |
| Wideside | **9929** | 4025 | 4800 |
| **R-2500 HD DIESEL PICKUPS 131.5" WB 8** | | | |
| Fenderside | **11498** | 4275 | 5075 |
| Wideside | **11351** | 4325 | 5125 |
| **R-2500 PICKUPS 164.5" WB 8** | | | |
| Wideside Bonus Cab | **12475** | 4725 | 5525 |
| Wideside Crew Cab | **12842** | 4925 | 5725 |
| **R-2500 DIESEL PICKUPS 164.5" WB 8** | | | |
| Wideside Bonus Cab | **13693** | 5000 | 5800 |
| Wideside Crew Cab | **14060** | 5225 | 6025 |
| **S-15 EXTENDED CAB 4*** | | | |
| Wideside (122.9" WB) | **8167** | 2400 | 3225 |
| **S-15 REG CAB PICKUPS 4*** | | | |
| Wideside EL (108" WB) | **6595** | 1975 | 2775 |
| Wideside (108" WB) | **7435** | 2125 | 2925 |
| Wideside (118" WB) | **7702** | 2200 | 3025 |
| *For 6 cyl models add $250 whsle/$250 retail. | | | |
| **R-1500 SUBURBAN 129.5" WB 8** | | | |
| Panel Doors | **12435** | 5375 | 6175 |
| Tailgate | **12477** | 5500 | 6300 |
| Panel Doors, Diesel | **15193** | 5700 | 6500 |
| Tailgate, Diesel | **15235** | 5800 | 6600 |
| **R-2500 SUBURBAN 129.5" WB 8** | | | |
| Panel Doors | **13036** | 5675 | 6475 |
| Tailgate | **13077** | 5750 | 6550 |
| Panel Doors, HD Diesel | **15669** | 5950 | 6750 |
| Tailgate, HD Diesel | **15712** | 6075 | 6850 |
| **SAFARI M15 111" WB 6*** | | | |
| Cargo Van (4 cyl) | **8797** | 2300 | 3125 |
| SL Pass Van | **9833** | 4025 | 4800 |
| SLX Pass Van | **10314** | 4225 | 5025 |
| SLE Pass Van | **11079** | 4500 | 5300 |
| SLT Pass Van | **12370** | 4925 | 5725 |
| **G-1500 VANS 110" WB 6*** | | | |
| 1/2 Ton Vandura | **9464** | 2300 | 3125 |
| Rally Wgn | **11404** | 3675 | 4450 |
| Rally Cust Wgn (125" WB) | **12279** | 4275 | 5075 |
| Rally STX (125" WB) | **12631** | 4450 | 5250 |
| w/125" WB add (Vandura) | **242** | 50 | 60 |
| (Rally) | **242** | 50 | 60 |
| *For 8 cyl models add $275 whsle/$275 retail. | | | |
| **G-2500 VANS 110" WB 6*** | | | |
| 3/4 Ton Vandura | **10131** | 2350 | 3175 |
| 3/4 Ton Vandura Diesel (8 cyl) | **12753** | 2850 | 3700 |
| Rally Wgn (125" WB) | **11609** | 3825 | 4600 |
| Rally Cust Wgn (125" WB) | **12483** | 4350 | 5150 |
| Rally STX (125" WB) | **12833** | 4500 | 5300 |
| Rally Wgn Diesel (125" WB) (8 cyl) | **14211** | 4350 | 5150 |
| Rally Cust Wgn Diesel (125" WB) (8 cyl) | **15113** | 4825 | 5625 |
| Rally STX Diesel (125" WB) (8 cyl) | **15379** | 5025 | 5825 |
| 3/4 Ton Vandura (125" WB) (8 cyl) | **10374** | 2700 | 3550 |
| 3/4 Ton Vandura Diesel (125" WB) (8 cyl) | **12995** | 2950 | 3800 |
| *For 8 cyl models add $275 whsle/$275 retail. | | | |
| *ADD FOR:* | | | |
| Gypsy Pkg (S/T Jimmy) | **1042** | 200 | 260 |
| (S/T Pickups) | **965** | 180 | 230 |
| High Sierra Pkg (Suburban Diesel) | **329** | 70 | 90 |
| (Suburban Gasoline) | **485** | 120 | 140 |
| (R-V Pickups) | **274** | 60 | 80 |
| Sierra Classic Pkg (S/T Jimmy) | **657** | 110 | 150 |
| (Jimmy) | **1073** | 210 | 270 |

*1990 GMC S-15 Jimmy*

| Year/Model/ Body/Type | Original List | Current Whlse | Average Retail |
|---|---|---|---|
| (Suburban) | **1330** | 280 | 360 |
| (S/T Pickups) | **637** | 110 | 150 |
| (R-V Pickups) | **—** | 120 | 160 |
| Sierra SLE Pkg (C-K Pickups) | **681** | 130 | 170 |
| Timberline Pkg (S/T Jimmy) | **1025** | 200 | 260 |

## 1986

### K-1500 JIMMY 8

| | | | |
|---|---|---|---|
| Utility w/HT | **12383** | 4750 | 5550 |
| Utility Diesel w/HT | **15330** | 5000 | 5800 |

### S-15 JIMMY 100.5" WB 4*

| | | | |
|---|---|---|---|
| Tailgate | **9582** | 2400 | 3225 |

### CABALLERO 117" WB 6*

| | | | |
|---|---|---|---|
| Caballero | **9850** | 3100 | 3950 |
| Caballero Diablo | **10172** | 3425 | 4200 |

*For 8 cyl models add $250 whsle/$250 retail.

### C-1500 PICKUPS 117.5" WB 6*

| | | | |
|---|---|---|---|
| Fenderside | **8133** | 2600 | 3450 |
| Wideside | **7989** | 2600 | 3450 |
| Fenderside, Diesel (8 cyl) | **11223** | 3025 | 3875 |
| Wideside, Diesel (8 cyl) | **11080** | 3025 | 3875 |
| w/131.5" WB add | **179** | 30 | 40 |

*For 8 cyl models add $250 whsle/$250 retail.

### C-2500 PICKUPS 131.5" WB 6*

| | | | |
|---|---|---|---|
| Fenderside | **9521** | 3025 | 3875 |
| Wideside | **9377** | 3025 | 3875 |

*For 8 cyl models add $250 whsle/$250 retail.

### C-2500 DIESEL PICKUPS 131.5" WB 8

| | | | |
|---|---|---|---|
| Fenderside | **12161** | 3275 | 4125 |
| Wideside | **12017** | 3275 | 4125 |

### C-2500 HEAVY DUTY PICKUPS 131.5" WB 6*

| | | | |
|---|---|---|---|
| Fenderside | **10542** | 3300 | 4150 |
| Wideside | **10399** | 3300 | 4150 |

*For 8 cyl models add $250 whsle/$250 retail.

### C-2500 PICKUPS 164.5" WB 6*

| | | | |
|---|---|---|---|
| Wideside Bonus Cab | **11425** | 4675 | 5475 |
| Wideside Crew Cab | **11783** | 4875 | 5675 |

*For 8 cyl models add $250 whsle/$250 retail.

### C-2500 HD DIESEL PICKUPS 131.5" WB 8

| | | | |
|---|---|---|---|
| Fenderside | **12482** | 3650 | 4425 |
| Wideside | **12339** | 3650 | 4425 |

### C-2500 HD DIESEL PICKUPS 164.5" WB 8

| | | | |
|---|---|---|---|
| Wideside Bonus Cab | **13365** | 4925 | 5725 |
| Wideside Crew Cab | **13723** | 5150 | 5950 |

### S-15 EXTENDED CAB 4*

| | | | |
|---|---|---|---|
| Wideside (122.9" WB) | **7909** | 1800 | 2600 |

### S-15 REG CAB PICKUPS 4*

| | | | |
|---|---|---|---|
| Wideside EL (108" WB) | **6161** | 1475 | 2275 |
| Wideside (108" WB) | **7202** | 1500 | 2300 |
| Wideside (118" WB) | **7444** | 1575 | 2375 |

*For 6 cyl models add $225 whsle/$225 retail.

### C-1500 SUBURBAN 129.5" WB 8

| | | | |
|---|---|---|---|
| Panel Doors | **11769** | 4350 | 5150 |
| Tailgate | **11809** | 4450 | 5250 |

111

*Refer to optional equipment schedules*

| Year/Model/Body/Type | Original List | Current Whlse | Average Retail |
|---|---|---|---|
| Panel Doors, Diesel | **14518** | 4600 | 5400 |
| Tailgate, Diesel | **14559** | 4675 | 5475 |
| **C-2500 SUBURBAN 129.5" WB 8** | | | |
| Panel Doors | **12613** | 4550 | 5350 |
| Tailgate | **12653** | 4650 | 5450 |
| Panel Doors, HD Diesel | **15241** | 4800 | 5600 |
| Tailgate, HD Diesel | **15282** | 4875 | 5675 |
| **SAFARI M15 111" WB 6** | | | |
| Cargo Van (4 cyl) | **8290** | 1550 | 2350 |
| SL Pass Van | **9299** | 2900 | 3750 |
| SLX Pass Van | **9767** | 3025 | 3875 |
| SLE Pass Van | **10512** | 3425 | 4200 |
| **G-1500 VANS 110" WB 6*** | | | |
| 1/2 Ton Vandura | **8876** | 1675 | 2475 |
| Rally Wgn | **10529** | 2750 | 3600 |
| Rally Cust Wgn (125" WB) | **11617** | 3200 | 4050 |
| Rally Wgn STX (125" WB) | **11959** | 3450 | 4225 |
| w/125" WB add | | | |
| (Vandura) | **232** | 30 | 40 |
| (Rally) | **236** | 30 | 40 |
| **G-2500 VANS 110" WB 6*** | | | |
| 3/4 Ton Vandura | **9525** | 1725 | 2525 |
| 3/4 Ton Vandura Diesel (8 cyl) | **12142** | 2175 | 2975 |
| Rally Wgn (125" WB) | **10964** | 2875 | 3725 |
| Rally Cust Wgn (125" WB) | **11815** | 3275 | 4125 |
| Rally STX (125" WB) | **12156** | 3525 | 4300 |
| Rally Wgn Diesel (125" WB) (8 cyl) | **13562** | 3400 | 4175 |
| Rally Cust Wgn Diesel (125" WB) (8 cyl) | **14440** | 3875 | 4650 |
| Rally STX Diesel (125" WB) (8 cyl) | **14699** | 4075 | 4875 |
| w/125" WB add (Vandura) | **237** | 30 | 40 |

*For 8 cyl models add $250 whsle/$250 retail.

| *ADD FOR:* | | | |
|---|---|---|---|
| Amarillo Pkg (Caballero) | **232** | 30 | 40 |
| Gypsy Pkg (S/T Jimmy) | **1015** | 150 | 190 |
| (S/T Pickups) | **940** | 130 | 170 |
| High Sierra Pkg (Suburban Diesel) | **320** | 50 | 60 |
| (Suburban Gasoline) | **472** | 80 | 100 |
| (S/T Pickup) | **305** | 40 | 60 |
| Sierra Classic Pkg (Jimmy) | **1045** | 150 | 190 |
| (S/T Jimmy) | **640** | 120 | 140 |
| (Suburban Diesel) | **1145** | 170 | 220 |

| Year/Model/Body/Type | Original List | Current Whlse | Average Retail |
|---|---|---|---|
| (Suburban Gasoline) | **1295** | 180 | 230 |
| (S/T Pickups) | **620** | 110 | 140 |
| (C-K Reg Pickups) | **720** | 80 | 110 |
| (C-K Bonus Pickups) | **800** | 100 | 130 |
| (C-K Crew Cab Pickups) | **885** | 110 | 150 |

## 1985

| **CABALLERO 117" WB 6*** | | | |
|---|---|---|---|
| Caballero | **9109** | 2375 | 3200 |
| Caballero Diablo | **9378** | 2550 | 3400 |

*For 8 cyl models add $225 whsle/$225 retail.

| **K-1500 JIMMY 8** | | | |
|---|---|---|---|
| Utility w/HT | **11431** | 4000 | 4775 |
| Utility Diesel HT | **14165** | 4275 | 5075 |

| **S-15 JIMMY 100.5" WB 4*** | | | |
|---|---|---|---|
| Tailgate | **8928** | 1950 | 2750 |

| **C-1500 PICKUPS 117.5" WB 6*** | | | |
|---|---|---|---|
| Fenderside | **7532** | 1975 | 2775 |
| Wideside | **7397** | 1975 | 2775 |
| Fenderside, Diesel | **10445** | 2200 | 3025 |
| Wideside, Diesel | **10310** | 2200 | 3025 |
| w/131.5" WB add | **169** | 30 | 40 |

*For 8 cyl models add $225 whsle/$225 retail.

| **C-2500 PICKUPS 131.5" WB 6*** | | | |
|---|---|---|---|
| Fenderside | **8798** | 2325 | 3150 |
| Wideside | **8663** | 2325 | 3150 |

*For 8 cyl models add $225 whsle/$225 retail.

| **C-2500 HD PICKUPS 131.5" WB 6*** | | | |
|---|---|---|---|
| Fenderside | **9756** | 2550 | 3400 |
| Wideside | **9622** | 2550 | 3400 |

*For 8 cyl models add $225 whsle/$225 retail.

| **C-2500 DIESEL PICKUPS 131.5" WB 8** | | | |
|---|---|---|---|
| Fenderside | **11274** | 2750 | 3600 |
| Wideside | **11139** | 2750 | 3600 |

| **C-2500 HD DIESEL PICKUPS 131.5" WB 8** | | | |
|---|---|---|---|
| Fenderside | **11575** | 3000 | 3850 |
| Wideside | **11441** | 3000 | 3850 |

| **C-2500 PICKUPS 164.5" WB 6*** | | | |
|---|---|---|---|
| Wideside Bonus Cab | **10584** | 2900 | 3850 |
| Wideside Crew Cab | **10920** | 3075 | 3925 |

*For 8 cyl models add $225 whsle/$225 retail.

| **C-2500 DIESEL PICKUPS 164.5" WB 8** | | | |
|---|---|---|---|
| Fenderside | **12403** | 3425 | 4200 |
| Wideside | **12379** | 3425 | 4200 |

| Year/Model/Body/Type | Original List | Current Whlse | Average Retail |
|---|---|---|---|
| **S-15 REG CAB PICKUPS 4\*** | | | |
| Wideside (108" WB) | **5990** | 1175 | 1850 |
| Wideside (118" WB) | **6702** | 1250 | 1925 |
| Wideside Diesel (108" WB) | **7349** | 850 | 1550 |
| Wideside Diesel (118" WB) | **7502** | 975 | 1650 |
| **S-15 EXTENDED CAB 4\*** | | | |
| Wideside (122.9" WB) | **7167** | 1425 | 2200 |
| Wideside, Diesel (122.9" WB) | **7875** | 1225 | 1900 |
| *For 6 cyl models add $200 whsle/$200 retail.* | | | |
| **C-1500 SUBURBAN 129.5" WB 8** | | | |
| Panel Doors | **10812** | 3525 | 4300 |
| Tailgate | **10850** | 3625 | 4400 |
| Panel Doors, Diesel | **13369** | 3800 | 4575 |
| Tailgate, Diesel | **13407** | 3900 | 4675 |
| **C-2500 SUBURBAN 129.5" WB 8** | | | |
| Panel Doors | **11598** | 3725 | 4500 |
| Tailgate | **11635** | 3825 | 4600 |
| Panel Doors, Diesel | **14042** | 4000 | 4775 |
| Tailgate, Diesel | **14079** | 4100 | 4900 |
| **G-1500 VANS 110" WB 6\*** | | | |
| 1/2 Ton Vandura | **8150** | 1150 | 1825 |
| Rally Wgn | **9701** | 2175 | 2975 |
| Rally Cust Wgn (125" WB) | **17012** | 2475 | 3300 |
| Rally Wgn STX (125" WB) | **11030** | 2600 | 3450 |
| w/125" WB add (Vandura) | **215** | 30 | 40 |
| (Rally Wgn) | **220** | 30 | 40 |
| *For 8 cyl models add $225 whsle/$225 retail.* | | | |
| **G-2500 VANS 110" WB 6\*** | | | |
| 3/4 Ton Vandura | **8752** | 1175 | 1850 |
| 3/4 Ton Vandura Diesel | **11183** | 1575 | 2375 |
| Rally Wgn (125" WB) | **10105** | 2225 | 3050 |
| Rally Cust Wgn (125" WB) | **10896** | 2525 | 3350 |
| Rally STX (125" WB) | **11212** | 2700 | 3550 |
| Rally Wgn Diesel (125" WB) | **12523** | 2650 | 3500 |
| Rally Cust Wgn Diesel (125" WB) (8 cyl) | **13339** | 2950 | 3800 |
| Rally STX Diesel (125" WB) (8 cyl) | **13580** | 3100 | 3950 |
| Vandura (125" WB) | **8972** | 1225 | 1900 |
| *For 8 cyl models add $225 whsle/$225 retail.* | | | |
| *ADD FOR:* | | | |
| Amarillo Pkg (Caballero) | **195** | 10 | 10 |

| Year/Model/Body/Type | Original List | Current Whlse | Average Retail |
|---|---|---|---|
| Gypsy Pkg (S/T Jimmy) | **972** | 110 | 140 |
| (S/T Pickups) | **868** | 100 | 120 |
| High Sierra Pkg (Suburban Diesel) | **311** | 20 | 30 |
| (Suburban Gasoline) | **459** | 40 | 50 |
| (S/T Pickups) | **295** | 20 | 30 |
| Sierra Classic Pkg (S/T Jimmy) | **595** | 60 | 80 |
| (Jimmy) | **1015** | 120 | 150 |
| (Suburban) | **—** | 100 | 130 |
| (S/T Reg Cab Pickups) | **605** | 60 | 80 |
| (S/T Ext Pickups) | **995** | 120 | 140 |
| (C-K Pickups) | **—** | 70 | 90 |
| Woody Dress Up Pkg (S/T Jimmy) | **1520** | 140 | 180 |

## 1984

| | | | |
|---|---|---|---|
| **CABALLERO 117" WB 6\*** | | | |
| Caballero | **8622** | 1800 | 2600 |
| Caballero SS Sport | **8881** | 2000 | 2800 |
| *For 8 cyl models add $200 whsle/$200 retail.* | | | |
| **K-1500 JIMMY 8** | | | |
| Utility w/HT | **10931** | 2950 | 3800 |
| Utility Diesel w/HT | **13664** | 3125 | 3975 |
| **S-15 JIMMY 100.5" WB 4\*** | | | |
| Tailgate | **8580** | 1650 | 2450 |
| **C-1500 PICKUPS 117.5" WB 6\*** | | | |
| Fenderside | **7213** | 1650 | 2450 |
| Wideside | **7082** | 1650 | 2450 |
| Fenderside, Diesel | **10257** | 2000 | 2800 |
| Wideside, Diesel | **10126** | 2225 | 3000 |
| w/131.5" WB add | **157** | 20 | 30 |
| *For 8 cyl models add $200 whsle/$200 retail.* | | | |
| **C-2500 PICKUPS 131.5" WB 6\*** | | | |
| Fenderside | **8431** | 1975 | 2775 |
| Wideside | **8300** | 1975 | 2775 |
| *For 8 cyl models add $200 whsle/$200 retail.* | | | |
| **C-2500 HEAVY DUTY PICKUPS 131.5" WB 6\*** | | | |
| Fenderside | **8945** | 2150 | 2950 |
| Wideside | **8814** | 2150 | 2950 |
| *For 8 cyl models add $200 whsle/$200 retail.* | | | |
| **C-2500 DIESEL PICKUPS 131.5" WB 8** | | | |
| Fenderside | **11038** | 2300 | 3125 |
| Wideside | **10907** | 2300 | 3125 |
| **C-2500 HD DIESEL PICKUPS 131.5" WB 8** | | | |
| Fenderside | **11552** | 2450 | 3275 |
| Wideside | **11421** | 2450 | 3275 |

| Year/Model/Body/Type | Original List | Current Whlse | Average Retail |
|---|---|---|---|
| **C-2500 PICKUPS 164.5" WB 6*** | | | |
| Wideside Bonus Cab | **9757** | 2450 | 3275 |
| Wideside Crew Cab | **10087** | 2650 | 3500 |
| *For 8 cyl models add $200 whsle/$200 retail. | | | |
| **C-2500 DIESEL PICKUPS 164.5" WB 8** | | | |
| Fenderside Bonus Cab | **12364** | 2800 | 3650 |
| Wideside Crew Cab | **12694** | 3000 | 3850 |
| **S-15 EXTENDED CAB 4*** | | | |
| Wideside (122.9" WB) | **7036** | 1275 | 1950 |
| Wideside, Diesel (122.9" WB) | **7939** | 1050 | 1725 |
| *For 6 cyl models add $175 whsle/$175 retail. | | | |
| **S-15 REG CAB PICKUPS 4*** | | | |
| Wideside (108" WB) | **6102** | 1100 | 1775 |
| Wideside (118" WB) | **6663** | 1150 | 1825 |
| Wideside, Diesel (108" WB) | **7413** | 800 | 1500 |
| Wideside, Diesel (118" WB) | **7566** | 900 | 1575 |
| *For 6 cyl models add $175 whsle/$175 retail. | | | |
| **C-1500 SUBURBAN 129.5" WB 8** | | | |
| Panel Doors | **10444** | 2675 | 3525 |
| Tailgate | **10480** | 2750 | 3600 |
| Panel Doors, Diesel | **13004** | 2850 | 3700 |
| Tailgate, Diesel | **13040** | 2925 | 3775 |
| **C-2500 SUBURBAN 129.5" WB 8** | | | |
| Panel Doors | **10691** | 2850 | 3700 |
| Tailgate | **10727** | 2925 | 3775 |
| Panel Doors, Diesel | **13820** | 3000 | 3850 |
| Tailgate, Diesel | **13856** | 3100 | 3950 |
| **G-1500 VANS 110" WB 6*** | | | |
| 1/2 Ton Vandura | **7653** | 750 | 1425 |
| Rally Wgn | **9201** | 1650 | 2450 |
| Rally Cust Wgn (125" WB) | **10174** | 1900 | 2700 |
| Rally Wgn STX (125" WB) | **10439** | 1975 | 2775 |
| w/125" WB add (Vandura) | **212** | 40 | 50 |
| (Rally Wgn) | **212** | 40 | 50 |
| *For 8 cyl models add $200 whsle/$200 retail. | | | |
| **G-2500 VANS 110" WB 6*** | | | |
| 3/4 Ton Vandura | **8288** | 775 | 1450 |
| 3/4 Ton Vandura Diesel | **10846** | 1125 | 1800 |
| Rally Wgn (125" WB) | **9589** | 1725 | 2525 |
| Rally Cust Wgn (125" WB) | **10350** | 1950 | 2750 |
| Rally STX (125" WB) | **10615** | 2050 | 2850 |

| Year/Model/Body/Type | Original List | Current Whlse | Average Retail |
|---|---|---|---|
| Rally Wgn Diesel (125" WB) | **12134** | 2075 | 2875 |
| Rally Cust Wgn Diesel (125" WB) | **13110** | 2250 | 3075 |
| Rally STX Diesel (125" WB) | **11056** | 2350 | 3175 |
| Vandura (125" WB) | **8500** | 825 | 1525 |
| *For 8 cyl models add $200 whsle/$200 retail. | | | |

## JEEP

### 1992

| | Original List | Current Whlse | Average Retail |
|---|---|---|---|
| **CHEROKEE 2WD 101" WB 4*** | | | |
| 2 Dr Cherokee | **14346** | 12025 | 13900 |
| 4 Dr Cherokee | **15357** | 12650 | 14975 |
| *For 6 cyl models add $475 whsle/$475 retail. | | | |
| **CHEROKEE BRIARWOOD 4WD 101" WB 6** | | | |
| 4 Dr Cherokee | **24949** | — | — |
| **CHEROKEE LIMITED 4WD 101" WB 6** | | | |
| 4 Dr Cherokee | **25484** | — | — |
| **COMANCHE 2WD 4*** | | | |
| Short Bed Pickup | **10673** | — | — |
| Long Bed Pickup | **11370** | — | — |
| *For 6 cyl models add $475 whsle/$475 retail. | | | |
| *ADD FOR:* | | | |
| Eliminator Pkg | **2217** | — | — |
| Pioneer Pkg | **1649** | — | — |
| Sport Pkg | **412** | — | — |
| **WRANGLER 4WD 4*** | | | |
| 2 Dr "S" | **11993** | 9800 | 11200 |
| 2 Dr Soft Top | **14067** | 11200 | 12700 |
| *For 6 cyl models add $450 whsle/$450 retail. | | | |
| *ADD FOR:* | | | |
| Islander Pkg | **1350** | 475 | 525 |
| Sahara Pkg | **2499** | 900 | 1050 |
| Renegade Pkg | **4864** | 1600 | 1800 |

### 1991

| | Original List | Current Whlse | Average Retail |
|---|---|---|---|
| **CHEROKEE 101" WB 4* 2WD** | | | |
| 2 Dr Cherokee | **14229** | 9825 | 11200 |
| 4 Dr Cherokee | **15212** | 10450 | 11950 |
| **CHEROKEE BRIARWOOD 101" WB 6 4WD** | | | |
| 4 Dr Cherokee | **24562** | 17800 | 20425 |
| **CHEROKEE LIMITED 101" WB 6 4WD** | | | |
| 4 Dr Cherokee | **25082** | 18100 | 21025 |

# AMERICAN TRUCKS

| Year/Model/Body/Type | Original List | Current Whlse | Average Retail |
|---|---|---|---|
| **COMANCHE 4* 2WD** | | | |
| Short Bed Pickup | **10331** | 6275 | 7175 |
| Long Bed Pickup | **10716** | 6575 | 7525 |
| *For 6 cyl models add $400 whsle/$400 retail. | | | |
| **GRAND WAGONEER 109" WB 8** | | | |
| 4 Dr Wgn | **29421** | — | — |
| **WRANGLER 4* 4WD** | | | |
| 2 Dr "S" | **10480** | 8200 | 9350 |
| 2 Dr Soft Top | **13534** | 9200 | 10475 |
| *For 6 cyl models add $400 whsle/$400 retail. | | | |
| *ADD FOR:* | | | |
| Hardtop Roof (Wrangler) | **755** | 320 | 400 |
| Eliminator Pkg (Comanche) | **3452** | 130 | 180 |
| Islander Pkg (Wrangler Base) | **738** | 330 | 420 |
| Pioneer Pkg (Comanche Short Bed) | **1635** | 860 | 1060 |
| (Comanche 2WD Long Bed) | **1434** | 740 | 920 |
| (Comanche 4WD Long Bed) | **1138** | 560 | 700 |
| Renegade Pkg (Wrangler Base) | **4266** | 2385 | 2905 |
| Sahara Pkg (Wrangler Base) | **1886** | 1020 | 1250 |
| **1990** | | | |
| **CHEROKEE 101" WB 4* 2WD** | | | |
| 2 Dr Cherokee | **14115** | 8050 | 9175 |
| 4 Dr Cherokee | **14965** | 8400 | 9575 |
| *For 6 cyl models add $375 whsle/$375 retail. | | | |
| **CHEROKEE LIMITED 101" WB 6 4WD** | | | |
| 2 Dr Cherokee | **24650** | 15000 | 17525 |
| 4 Dr Cherokee | **25775** | 15550 | 18075 |
| **COMANCHE 4* 2WD** | | | |
| Short Bed Pickup | **9511** | 4825 | 5625 |
| Long Bed Pickup | **11797** | 5100 | 5900 |
| *For 6 cyl models add $375 whsle/$375 retail. | | | |
| **GRAND WAGONEER 109" WB 8** | | | |
| 4 Dr Wgn | **27795** | 13000 | 15200 |
| **WAGONEER 101" WB 6** | | | |
| 4 Dr Limited | **24795** | 12900 | 15100 |
| **WRANGLER 4* 4WD** | | | |
| 2 Dr "S" | **9952** | 6175 | 7075 |
| 2 Dr Soft Top | **12754** | 7175 | 8200 |
| *For 6 cyl models add $375 whsle/$375 retail. | | | |

| Year/Model/Body/Type | Original List | Current Whlse | Average Retail |
|---|---|---|---|
| *ADD FOR:* | | | |
| Eliminator Pkg (Comanche) | **3384** | 1640 | 1990 |
| Islander Pkg (Wrangler) | **724** | 270 | 350 |
| Laredo Pkg (Wrangler) | **4023** | 1945 | 2365 |
| (Cherokee) | **3390** | 1640 | 2000 |
| Pioneer Pkg (Cherokee) | **1689** | 760 | 940 |
| (Comanche Short Bed) | **1603** | 720 | 890 |
| (Comanche 2WD Long Bed) | **1406** | 620 | 760 |
| (Comanche 4WD Long Bed) | **1116** | 470 | 590 |
| Sahara Pkg (Wrangler) | **1823** | 840 | 1030 |
| Sport Pkg (Cherokee) | **945** | 390 | 490 |
| **1989** | | | |
| **CHEROKEE 101" WB 4* 2WD** | | | |
| 2 Dr Cherokee | **12374** | 6550 | 7500 |
| 4 Dr Cherokee | **13186** | 7025 | 8025 |
| *For 6 cyl models add $325 whsle/$325 retail. | | | |
| **CHEROKEE LIMITED 101" WB 6 4WD** | | | |
| 2 Dr Cherokee | **23282** | 12650 | 14850 |
| 4 Dr Cherokee | **24386** | 13175 | 15375 |
| **COMANCHE 4* 2WD** | | | |
| Short Bed Pickup | **7757** | 3925 | 4700 |
| Long Bed Pickup | **8585** | 4125 | 4925 |
| *For 6 cyl models add $325 whsle/$325 retail. | | | |
| **GRAND WAGONEER 109" WB** | | | |
| 4 Dr Wgn | **26639** | 11850 | 13575 |
| **WAGONEER 101" WB 6** | | | |
| 4 Dr Limited | **23455** | 11150 | 12775 |
| **WRANGLER 4* 4WD** | | | |
| 2 Dr "S" | **8995** | 5250 | 6050 |
| 2 Dr | **11022** | 6125 | 7000 |
| 2 Dr Islander | **11721** | 6425 | 7350 |
| 2 Dr Sahara | **12853** | 6825 | 7825 |
| 2 Dr Laredo (6 cyl) | **14867** | 7600 | 8700 |
| *For 6 cyl models add $325 whsle/$325 retail. | | | |
| *ADD FOR:* | | | |
| Laredo Pkg (Cherokee) | **2937** | 1180 | 1440 |
| Pioneer Pkg (Cherokee) | **1217** | 440 | 550 |
| (Comanche Short Bed) | **1291** | 470 | 590 |
| (Comanche 2WD Long Bed) | **1100** | 380 | 480 |
| (Comanche 4WD Long Bed) | **810** | 260 | 330 |

| Year/Model/Body/Type | Original List | Current Whlse | Average Retail |
|---|---|---|---|
| Eliminator Pkg (Comanche) | **2961** | 1200 | 1460 |
| Sport Pkg (Cherokee) | **945** | 310 | 400 |
| Off Road Pkg (Comanche) | **951** | 320 | 400 |
| Big Ton Pkg (Comanche) | **739** | 220 | 290 |
| Sport Pkg Opt Grp (Cherokee) | **1450** | 530 | 660 |
| Eliminator Pkg Grp 1 (Comanche) | **2783** | 1120 | 1360 |
| Eliminator Pkg Grp 2 (Comanche) | **3268** | 1330 | 1620 |
| Pioneer Pkg Opt Grp 1 (Cherokee) | **2420** | 960 | 1180 |
| Pioneer Pkg Opt Grp 2 (Cherokee) | **3067** | 1240 | 1520 |
| Laredo Pkg Opt Grp (Cherokee) | **3612** | 1480 | 1810 |

## 1988

### CHEROKEE 101" WB 4* 2WD

| | Original List | Current Whlse | Average Retail |
|---|---|---|---|
| 2 Dr Cherokee | **11186** | 4450 | 5250 |
| 4 Dr Cherokee | **11798** | 4825 | 5625 |

*For 6 cyl models add $300 whsle/$300 retail.

### CHEROKEE LIMITED 101" WB 6 4WD

| | | | |
|---|---|---|---|
| 2 Dr Cherokee | **22260** | 10075 | 11500 |
| 4 Dr Cherokee | **23153** | 10475 | 11975 |

### COMANCHE 4* 2WD — Schedule E

| | | | |
|---|---|---|---|
| Short Bed Pickup | **7114** | 3025 | 3875 |
| Long Bed Pickup | **7906** | 3100 | 3950 |

*For 6 cyl models add $300 whsle/$300 retail.

### GRAND WAGONEER 109" WB 8

| | | | |
|---|---|---|---|
| 4 Dr Wgn | **24623** | 9475 | 10800 |

### JEEP TRUCK 8 4WD

| | | | |
|---|---|---|---|
| J-10 Pickup | **13128** | 5750 | 6550 |
| J-20 Pickup | **13525** | 6250 | 7150 |

### WAGONEER 101" WB 6

| | | | |
|---|---|---|---|
| 4 Dr Limited | **21926** | 9475 | 10800 |

### WRANGLER 4* 4WD

| | | | |
|---|---|---|---|
| 2 Dr "S" | **8995** | 3650 | 4425 |
| 2 Dr | **10595** | 4750 | 5550 |
| 2 Dr Sahara | **11995** | 5450 | 6250 |
| 2 Dr Laredo | **13395** | 6125 | 7000 |

*ADD FOR:*

| | | | |
|---|---|---|---|
| Chief Pkg (Cherokee) | **1881** | 580 | 720 |
| (Comanche) | **1322** | 380 | 480 |
| Eliminator Pkg | | | |

| Year/Model/Body/Type | Original List | Current Whlse | Average Retail |
|---|---|---|---|
| (Comanche) | **2929** | 960 | 1170 |
| Laredo Pkg (Cherokee) | **3204** | 1060 | 1300 |
| (Comanche) | **1428** | 410 | 520 |
| Pioneer Pkg (Base Cherokee) | **1158** | 320 | 400 |
| (Comanche) | **648** | 160 | 210 |
| (Jeep Trucks) | **304** | 90 | 110 |
| Olympic Pkg (Wrangler) | **1491** | 440 | 550 |
| (Cherokee) | **3037** | 1000 | 1220 |
| (Comanche) | **—** | 550 | 690 |

## 1987

### CHEROKEE 101" WB 4* 2WD

| | | | |
|---|---|---|---|
| 2 Dr Cherokee | **10741** | 3675 | 4450 |
| 4 Dr Cherokee | **11335** | 4125 | 4925 |

*For 6 cyl models add $250 whsle/$250 retail.

### CHEROKEE LIMITED 101" WB 6 4WD

| | | | |
|---|---|---|---|
| 4 Dr Cherokee | **22104** | 8425 | 9600 |

### COMANCHE 4* 2WD

| | | | |
|---|---|---|---|
| Short Bed Pickup | **6495** | 2200 | 3025 |
| Long Bed Pickup | **7860** | 2300 | 3125 |

*For 6 cyl models add $250 whsle/$250 retail.

### GRAND WAGONEER 109" WB 8

| | | | |
|---|---|---|---|
| 4 Dr Wgn | **23906** | 8175 | 9325 |

### JEEP TRUCK 6* 4WD

| | | | |
|---|---|---|---|
| J-10 Pickup | **11714** | 4425 | 5225 |

*For 8 cyl models add $250 whsle/$250 retail.

### JEEP TRUCK 8 4WD

| | | | |
|---|---|---|---|
| J-20 Pickup | **13131** | 4825 | 5625 |

### WAGONEER 101" WB 4*

| | | | |
|---|---|---|---|
| 4 Dr Wgn | **15531** | 6550 | 7500 |
| 4 Dr Limited | **20400** | 7575 | 8675 |

*For 6 cyl models add $250 whsle/$250 retail.

### WRANGLER 4* 4WD

| | | | |
|---|---|---|---|
| 2 Dr "S" | **8795** | 3650 | 4425 |
| 2 Dr | **10295** | 4250 | 5050 |

### WRANGLER LAREDO 4* 4WD

| | | | |
|---|---|---|---|
| 2 Dr | **12693** | 5000 | 5800 |

*For 6 cyl models add $250 whsle/$250 retail.

*ADD FOR:*

| | | | |
|---|---|---|---|
| Chief Pkg (Cherokee) | **1788** | 410 | 510 |
| (Comanche) | **1399** | 300 | 380 |
| Laredo Pkg (Cherokee) | **3249** | 830 | 1020 |

| Year/Model/ Body/Type | Original List | Current Whlse | Average Retail |
|---|---|---|---|
| (Comanche) Pioneer Pkg | **1299** | 270 | 350 |
| (Cherokee) | **1080** | 210 | 270 |
| (Comanche) | **699** | 130 | 170 |
| (Jeep Trucks) Sport Decor Grp | **586** | 100 | 130 |
| (Wrangler) | **750** | 150 | 190 |

## 1986

### CHEROKEE 101" WB 4* 2WD

| | | | |
|---|---|---|---|
| 2 Dr Cherokee | **9945** | 2825 | 3675 |
| 4 Dr Cherokee | **10464** | 3025 | 3875 |

*For 6 cyl models add $225 whsle/$225 retail.

### GRAND WAGONEER 109" WB 6*

| | | | |
|---|---|---|---|
| 4 Dr Wgn | **21599** | 5650 | 6450 |

*For 8 cyl models add $250 whsle/$250 retail.

### JEEP CJ 4* 4WD

| | | | |
|---|---|---|---|
| CJ-7 Open Body | **7725** | 3100 | 3950 |

*For 6 cyl models add $225 whsle/$225 retail.

### COMANCHE 4* 2WD

| | | | |
|---|---|---|---|
| Custom Pickup | **7199** | 1900 | 2700 |

*For 6 cyl models add $225 whsle/$225 retail.

### JEEP TRUCK 6* 4WD

| | | | |
|---|---|---|---|
| J-10 Townside | **10999** | 3500 | 4275 |

*For 8 cyl models add $250 whsle/$250 retail.

### JEEP TRUCK 8 4WD

| | | | |
|---|---|---|---|
| J-20 Townside | **12329** | 4050 | 4825 |

### WAGONEER 101" WB 4*

| | | | |
|---|---|---|---|
| 4 Dr Wgn | **14024** | 4750 | 5550 |
| 4 Dr Limited | **18994** | 5575 | 6375 |

*For 6 cyl models add $225 whsle/$225 retail.

### WRANGLER 4* 4WD

| | | | |
|---|---|---|---|
| 2 Dr Open Body | **9899** | — | — |

### WRANGLER LAREDO 4* 4WD

| | | | |
|---|---|---|---|
| 2 Dr Open Body | **12205** | — | — |

*For 6 cyl models add $225 whsle/$225 retail.

*ADD FOR:*

| | | | |
|---|---|---|---|
| Chief Pkg (Cherokee) | **1548** | 220 | 290 |
| Laredo Pkg (Cherokee) | **2969** | 530 | 660 |
| (CJ-7 Soft Top) | **2787** | 490 | 610 |
| (CJ-7 Hardtop) | **3304** | 2315 | 2815 |
| Pioneer Pkg (Cherokee) | **1039** | 150 | 190 |
| (Jeep Trucks) | **570** | 100 | 130 |

| | | | |
|---|---|---|---|
| Renegade Pkg (CJ-7) Sport Decor Pkg | **1253** | 175 | 235 |
| (Wrangler) | **721** | 80 | 110 |
| X Pkg (Comanche) | **605** | 110 | 140 |
| XLS Pkg (Comanche) | **931** | 130 | 170 |

## 1985

### CHEROKEE 101" WB 4 2WD

| | | | |
|---|---|---|---|
| 2 Dr Cherokee | **9195** | 1975 | 2775 |
| 4 Dr Cherokee | **9766** | 2200 | 3025 |

*For 6 cyl models add $200 whsle/$200 retail.

### GRAND WAGONEER 109" WB 6*

| | | | |
|---|---|---|---|
| 4 Dr Wgn | **20830** | 4525 | 5325 |

*For 8 cyl models add $225 whsle/$225 retail.

### JEEP CJ 4* 4WD

| | | | |
|---|---|---|---|
| CJ-7 Open Body | **7282** | 2625 | 3475 |

*For 6 cyl models add $200 whsle/$200 retail.

### JEEP TRUCK 6* 4WD

| | | | |
|---|---|---|---|
| J-10 Townside (131" WB) | **10497** | 2750 | 3600 |

*For 8 cyl models add $225 whsle/$225 retail.

### JEEP TRUCK 8 4WD

| | | | |
|---|---|---|---|
| J-20 Townside (131" WB) | **11578** | 3000 | 3850 |

### SCRAMBLER 4* 4WD

| | | | |
|---|---|---|---|
| Scrambler | **7282** | 2000 | 2800 |

*For 6 cyl models add $200 whsle/$200 retail.

### WAGONEER 101" WB 4*

| | | | |
|---|---|---|---|
| 4 Dr Wgn | **13427** | 4425 | 5225 |
| 4 Dr Limited | **18186** | 5325 | 6125 |

*For 6 cyl models add $200 whsle/$200 retail.

*ADD FOR:*

| | | | |
|---|---|---|---|
| Chief Pkg (Cherokee) Laredo Pkg | **1650** | 250 | 320 |
| (CJ-7 Soft Top) | **2678** | 470 | 580 |
| (CJ-7 Hardtop) | **3180** | 580 | 710 |
| (Scrambler Soft Top) | **2494** | 430 | 540 |
| (Scrambler Hardtop) | **2939** | 520 | 650 |
| (Cherokee) | **2907** | 510 | 640 |
| Pioneer Pkg (Cherokee) | **1171** | 180 | 230 |
| Renegade Pkg (CJ-7) | **1188** | 180 | 230 |
| (Scrambler) | **970** | 130 | 180 |

## 1984

### CHEROKEE 101" WB 4* 4WD

| | | | |
|---|---|---|---|
| 2 Dr Cherokee | **10097** | 2375 | 3200 |

| Year/Model/Body/Type | Original List | Current Whlse | Average Retail |
|---|---|---|---|
| 4 Dr Cherokee | **10547** | 2500 | 3325 |
| 2 Dr Cherokee Celebration Ed | **11810** | — | — |
| 4 Dr Cherokee Celebration Ed | **12260** | — | — |

*For 6 cyl models add $175 whsle/$175 retail.

### GRAND WAGONEER 109" WB 6*

| | | | |
|---|---|---|---|
| 4 Dr Wgn | **19556** | 4250 | 5050 |

*For 8 cyl models add $200 whsle/$200 retail.

### JEEP CJ 4* 4WD

| | | | |
|---|---|---|---|
| CJ-7 Basic | **7109** | 2250 | 3075 |

*For 6 cyl models add $175 whsle/$175 retail.

### JEEP TRUCK 6* 4WD

| | | | |
|---|---|---|---|
| J-10 Townside (119" WB) | **9813** | 2100 | 2900 |
| J-10 Townside (131" WB) | **9963** | 2200 | 3025 |

*For 8 cyl models add $200 whsle/$150 retail.

### JEEP TRUCK 8 4WD

| | | | |
|---|---|---|---|
| J-20 Townside (131" WB) | **10889** | 2400 | 3225 |

### SCRAMBLER 4* 4WD

| | | | |
|---|---|---|---|
| Scrambler | **7109** | 2100 | 2900 |

*For 6 cyl models add $175 whsle/$175 retail.

### WAGONEER 101" WB 4*

| | | | |
|---|---|---|---|
| 4 Dr Wgn | **12594** | 3750 | 4525 |
| 4 Dr Limited | **17226** | 4350 | 5150 |

*For 6 cyl models add $175 whsle/$175 retail.

## OLDSMOBILE

### 1992

#### BRAVADA 6

| | | | |
|---|---|---|---|
| Sport Utility | **24855** | 17900 | 20900 |
| ADD FOR: | | | |
| Leather Seats | **650** | 425 | 475 |

#### SILHOUETTE 6

| | | | |
|---|---|---|---|
| Wagon | **19095** | 14600 | 17150 |
| ADD FOR: | | | |
| 3.8 Liter 6 Cyl Eng | **800** | 555 | 615 |
| Leather Seats | **650** | 375 | 415 |

### 1991

#### BRAVADA 6

| | | | |
|---|---|---|---|
| Sport Utility | **23795** | 16575 | 19100 |

#### SILHOUETTE 6

| | | | |
|---|---|---|---|
| Wagon | **18195** | — | — |
| ADD FOR: | | | |
| Leather Pkg | **650** | 280 | 360 |

## PLYMOUTH

### 1992

#### VOYAGER 4*

| | | | |
|---|---|---|---|
| Voyager, Base | **14358** | 12025 | 14450 |
| Voyager, SE | **16481** | 13250 | 15625 |

For 6 cyl models add $475 whsle/$475 retail.

#### VOYAGER 6

| | | | |
|---|---|---|---|
| Voyager, SE AWD | **19539** | 15200 | 17850 |
| Voyager, LE | **20202** | 14600 | 17150 |
| Voyager, LX | **20883** | 14925 | 17575 |

#### GRAND VOYAGER 6

| | | | |
|---|---|---|---|
| Voyager, Base | **18233** | 13675 | 16050 |
| Voyager, SE | **18463** | 14650 | 17225 |
| Voyager, LE | **21011** | 15475 | 18125 |
| ADD FOR: | | | |
| 3.3 Liter 6 Cyl Eng | **796** | 335 | 375 |
| LX Decor Pkg | **776** | 375 | 415 |

### 1991

#### VOYAGER 4*

| | | | |
|---|---|---|---|
| Voyager, Base | **14305** | 10050 | 11625 |
| Voyager, Special Ed | **15551** | 10825 | 12375 |
| Voyager, Limited Ed | **17994** | 11575 | 13275 |

*For 6 cyl models add $400 whsle/$400 retail.

#### VOYAGER 6

| | | | |
|---|---|---|---|
| Voyager, LX | **19489** | 11900 | 13650 |

#### GRAND VOYAGER 6

| | | | |
|---|---|---|---|
| Voyager, Special Ed | **17301** | 12050 | 13825 |
| Voyager, Limited Ed | **19604** | 12800 | 15000 |
| ADD FOR: | | | |
| Luxury Equip Pkg (Voyager SE, Grand Voyager SE) | **2376** | 1300 | 1580 |
| (Voyager LE, LX & Grand Voyager LE) | **1892** | 1010 | 1240 |

| Year/Model/Body/Type | Original List | Current Whlse | Average Retail |
|---|---|---|---|
| **1990** | | | |
| **VOYAGER 4\*** | | | |
| Voyager, Base | **12835** | 7750 | 8875 |
| Voyager, Special Ed | **13515** | 8475 | 9675 |
| Voyager, Limited Ed | **16125** | 9125 | 10400 |
| Voyager, LX | **17240** | 8025 | 9150 |
| *For 6 cyl models add $375 whsle/$375 retail.* | | | |
| **GRAND VOYAGER 6** | | | |
| Voyager, Special Ed | **16235** | 9550 | 10875 |
| Voyager, Limited Ed | **18325** | 10150 | 11600 |
| *ADD FOR:* | | | |
| Luxury Equip Pkg | | | |
| (Voyager SE) | **2070** | 960 | 1180 |
| (Voyager Grand SE) | **1903** | 870 | 1070 |
| **1989** | | | |
| **VOYAGER 4\*** | | | |
| Voyager, Base | **11312** | 6525 | 7475 |
| Voyager, Special Ed | **12039** | 7200 | 8225 |
| Voyager, Limited Ed | **13987** | 7825 | 8950 |
| *For 6 cyl models add $325 whsle/$325 retail.* | | | |
| **GRAND VOYAGER 6** | | | |
| Voyager, Special Ed | **14526** | 8250 | 9400 |
| Voyager, Limited Ed | **16462** | 8850 | 10100 |
| *ADD FOR:* | | | |
| LX Decor Pkg | | | |
| (Voyager LE) | **1469** | 540 | 670 |
| Lux Equip Pkg (Voyager) | **1828** | 700 | 860 |
| **1988** | | | |
| **VOYAGER 4\*** | | | |
| Voyager, Base | **10887** | 4825 | 5625 |
| Voyager, Special Ed | **11587** | 5450 | 6250 |
| Voyager, Limited Ed | **13462** | 5950 | 6750 |
| **GRAND VOYAGER 4\*** | | | |
| Voyager, Special Ed | **12505** | 6150 | 7025 |
| Voyager, Limited Ed | **15509** | 6675 | 7650 |
| *For 6 cyl models add $300 whsle/$300 retail.* | | | |
| *ADD FOR:* | | | |
| LE Decor Pkg | | | |
| (Voyager LE) | **603** | 150 | 190 |
| Lux Equip Pkg (Voyager) | **1281** | 360 | 460 |
| **1987** | | | |
| **VOYAGER 4\*** | | | |
| Voyager, Base | **10411** | 3525 | 4300 |

| Year/Model/Body/Type | Original List | Current Whlse | Average Retail |
|---|---|---|---|
| Voyager, Special Ed | **10875** | 4075 | 4875 |
| Voyager, Limited Ed | **11741** | 4525 | 5325 |
| **GRAND VOYAGER 4\*** | | | |
| Voyager, Special Ed | **11751** | 4500 | 5300 |
| Voyager, Limited Ed | **12561** | 4925 | 5725 |
| *For 6 cyl models add $275 whsle/$275 retail.* | | | |
| *ADD FOR:* | | | |
| Lux Equip Pkg (Voyager) | **1722** | 400 | 500 |
| Travel Equip Pkg (Voyager SE & LE) | **1927** | 450 | 560 |
| (Voyager Grand Models) | **1538** | 340 | 430 |
| **1986** | | | |
| **VOYAGER 4** | | | |
| Voyager, Base | **9659** | 2650 | 3500 |
| Voyager, Special Ed | **9938** | 3000 | 3850 |
| Voyager, Limited Ed | **10681** | 3450 | 4225 |
| *ADD FOR:* | | | |
| Luxury Equip Pkg (Voyager) | **1443** | 210 | 270 |
| Travel Equip Pkg (Voyager SE & LE) | **1633** | 240 | 310 |
| **1985** | | | |
| **VOYAGER 4** | | | |
| Voyager, Base | **9238** | 2050 | 2850 |
| Voyager, Special Ed | **9487** | 2275 | 3100 |
| Voyager, Limited Ed | **10105** | 2525 | 3350 |
| *ADD FOR:* | | | |
| Luxury Equip Pkg (Voyager LE) | **1270** | 100 | 140 |
| Travel Equip Pkg (Voyager SE & LE) | **1003** | 120 | 140 |
| **1984** | | | |
| **VOYAGER 4** | | | |
| Voyager, Base | **8669** | 1750 | 2550 |
| Voyager, Special Ed | **8906** | 1950 | 2750 |
| Voyager, Limited Ed | **9494** | 2175 | 2975 |
| **PONTIAC** | | | |
| **1992** | | | |
| **TRANS SPORT SE 6** | | | |
| Wagon | **17055** | 13725 | 16100 |

| Year/Model/ Body/Type | Original List | Current Whlse | Average Retail | Year/Model/ Body/Type | Original List | Current Whlse | Average Retail |
|---|---|---|---|---|---|---|---|
| **TRANS SPORT GT 6** | | | | **TRANS SPORT SE 6** | | | |
| Wagon | **20935** | 14625 | 17200 | Wagon | **18889** | 12350 | 14475 |
| *ADD FOR:* | | | | *ADD FOR:* | | | |
| 3.8 Liter 6 Cyl Eng | **819** | 555 | 615 | 6 Pass Seating (Trans Sport) | **525** | 210 | 270 |
| **1991** | | | | 7 Pass Seating (Trans Sport) | **675** | 300 | 380 |
| **TRANS SPORT 6** | | | | | | | |
| Wagon | **16449** | 11675 | 13375 | | | | |

# FREE

# RECALL INFORMATION

An important part of buying a used car is to know the model's recall history; it will tell you what problems the manufacturer recalled the auto for.  •  A lot of recalls could mean that the model had problems. You should try to get the auto's service records to see if all recalls were complied with by the owner.  • To get recall data, call the National Highway Traffic Safety Administration at the following toll-free number:

# 1-800-424-9393

They will send you the auto's up-to-date recall history. There is no charge for this service. *Also, you can report any safety problems you have had with an auto to the same number.*

*1990 Acura Legend Sedan LS*

| Year/Model/Body/Type | Original List | Current Whlse | Average Retail |
|---|---|---|---|
| **ACURA** | | | |
| **1992** | | | |
| **INTEGRA 4** | | | |
| 3 Dr RS Htchbk (5 spd) | **14080** | 10325 | 11925 |
| 3 Dr LS Htchbk (5 spd) | **15685** | 11200 | 12925 |
| 3 Dr GS Htchbk (5 spd) | **17855** | 12700 | 15025 |
| 4 Dr RS Sdn (5 spd) | **15005** | 10525 | 12150 |
| 4 Dr LS Sdn (5 spd) | **16435** | 11425 | 13200 |
| 4 Dr GS Sdn (5 spd) | **18395** | 12900 | 15225 |
| 3 Dr GS-R VTEC | **19110** | — | — |
| ADD FOR: | | | |
| Leather Interior (GS) | **500** | 260 | 290 |
| **LEGEND 6** | | | |
| 4 Dr Base Sdn (5 spd) | **28000** | 21325 | 24625 |
| 4 Dr L Sdn (5 spd) | **30400** | 22800 | 26100 |
| 2 Dr L Cpe (5 spd) | **31850** | 24250 | 27550 |
| 4 Dr LS Sdn (5 spd) | **34900** | — | — |
| 2 Dr LS Cpe (5 spd) | **36250** | — | — |
| ADD FOR: | | | |
| Leather Interior (L) | **1500** | 330 | 360 |
| **NSX 6** | | | |
| 2 Dr Cpe (5 spd) | **65000** | — | — |
| ADD FOR: | | | |
| Auto Trans | **4000** | 2620 | 2910 |
| **VIGOR 5** | | | |
| 4 Dr Sdn (5 spd) | **23665** | — | — |
| 4 Dr GS Sdn (5 spd) | **25650** | 19150 | 22200 |

NOTE: Power windows standard on Integra LS, GS & GS-R, Legend, NSX and Vigor. Power door locks standard on Integra LS 4 Dr, GS & GS-R, Legend, NSX and Vigor. Power seat standard on Legend and NSX. Power sunroof standard on Integra LS, GS & GS-R, Legend L & LS, Vigor GS. Tilt steering wheel standard on Integra, Legend, NSX and Vigor. Cruise control standard on Integra LS, GS & GSR, Legend, NSX and Vigor.

| Year/Model/Body/Type | Original List | Current Whlse | Average Retail |
|---|---|---|---|
| **1991** | | | |
| **INTEGRA 4** | | | |
| 3 Dr RS Hbk (5 spd) | **13400** | 9250 | 10650 |
| 3 Dr LS Hbk (5 spd) | **15275** | 9975 | 11500 |
| 3 Dr LS Special Hbk (5 spd) | **15975** | 10150 | 11725 |
| 3 Dr GS Hbk (5 spd) | **17405** | 11000 | 12700 |
| 3 Dr GS Hbk w/Leather Trim (5 spd) | **17905** | 11275 | 13025 |
| 4 Dr RS Sdn (5 spd) | **14325** | 9450 | 10875 |
| 4 Dr LS Sdn (5 spd) | **16025** | 10150 | 11725 |
| 4 Dr GS Sdn (5 spd) | **17945** | 11175 | 12900 |
| 4 Dr GS Sdn w/Leather Trim (5 spd) | **18445** | 11475 | 13250 |
| **LEGEND 6** | | | |
| 4 Dr Base Sdn (5 spd) | **26800** | 19375 | 22425 |
| 4 Dr L Sdn w/Cloth Interior (5 spd) | **28800** | 20650 | 23700 |
| 4 Dr L Sdn w/Leather Interior (5 spd) | **30300** | 21075 | 24250 |
| 4 Dr LS Sdn (5 spd) | **33400** | 22875 | 26175 |
| 2 Dr L Cpe w/Cloth Interior (5 spd) | **30900** | 21975 | 25275 |
| 2 Dr L Cpe w/Leather Interior (5 spd) | **32400** | 22375 | 25675 |

| Year/Model/Body/Type | Original List | Current Whlse | Average Retail |
|---|---|---|---|
| 2 Dr LS Cpe (5 spd) | **35500** | 24225 | 27525 |

### NSX 6

| Year/Model/Body/Type | Original List | Current Whlse | Average Retail |
|---|---|---|---|
| 2 Dr Cpe (5 spd) | **61000** | 44250 | 48975 |
| 2 Dr Cpe (auto) | **65000** | 44950 | 49750 |

NOTE: Power brakes standard on all models. Power windows standard on Integra RS, LS and GS, Legend, NSX. Power door locks standard on Integra LS Sedan, LS Special and GS, Legend, NSX. Sunroof standard on Integra LS Hatchback, LS Special and GS, Legend L and LS. Power seat standard on Legend L and LS, NSX.

## 1990

### INTEGRA 4

| Year/Model/Body/Type | Original List | Current Whlse | Average Retail |
|---|---|---|---|
| 3 Dr RS Sdn (5 spd) | **13450** | 7950 | 9225 |
| 4 Dr RS Sdn (5 spd) | **14430** | 8150 | 9425 |
| 3 Dr LS Sdn (5 spd) | **14925** | 8675 | 10025 |
| 4 Dr LS Sdn (5 spd) | **15745** | 8875 | 10250 |
| 3 Dr GS Sdn (5 spd) | **17025** | 9450 | 10875 |
| 4 Dr GS Sdn (5 spd) | **17150** | 96505 | 11125 |

### LEGEND 6

| Year/Model/Body/Type | Original List | Current Whlse | Average Retail |
|---|---|---|---|
| 2 Dr Cpe (5 spd) | **24760** | 15000 | 17600 |
| 4 Dr Sdn (5 spd) | **22600** | 13750 | 16125 |
| 2 Dr L Cpe w/Cloth Interior (5 spd) | **27325** | 16000 | 18650 |
| 2 Dr L Cpe w/Leather Interior (5 spd) | **28275** | 16250 | 18900 |
| 4 Dr L Sdn w/Cloth Interior (5 spd) | **25900** | 14725 | 17275 |
| 4 Dr L Sdn w/Leather Interior (5 spd) | **26850** | 14950 | 17550 |
| 2 Dr LS Cpe (5 spd) | **30690** | 17150 | 19800 |
| 4 Dr LS Sdn (5 spd) | **29610** | 15875 | 18525 |

NOTE: Power brakes standard on Integra and Legend. Power windows and power door locks standard on Integra LS 4 Door, Integra GS and Legend. Power seat standard on Legend L and LS. Sunroof standard on Integra LS 3 Door, Integra GS and Legend. Anti-lock brake system standard on Integra GS and Legend L and LS.

## 1989

### INTEGRA 4

| Year/Model/Body/Type | Original List | Current Whlse | Average Retail |
|---|---|---|---|
| 3 Dr RS Hbk (5 spd) | **12260** | 6025 | 6950 |
| 5 Dr RS Hbk (5 spd) | **13060** | 6225 | 7250 |
| 3 Dr LS Hbk (5 spd) | **14070** | 6675 | 7775 |
| 5 Dr LS Hbk (5 spd) | **14900** | 6900 | 8025 |

### LEGEND 6

| Year/Model/Body/Type | Original List | Current Whlse | Average Retail |
|---|---|---|---|
| 4 Dr Sdn (5 spd) | **24660** | 11550 | 13350 |
| 2 Dr Cpe (5 spd) | **24760** | 12775 | 15100 |
| 4 Dr L Sdn w/Cloth Interior (5 spd) | **25900** | 12475 | 14650 |
| 4 Dr L Sdn w/Leather Interior (5 spd) | **26850** | 12725 | 15050 |

| Year/Model/Body/Type | Original List | Current Whlse | Average Retail |
|---|---|---|---|
| 2 Dr L Cpe w/Cloth Interior (5 spd) | **27325** | 16000 | 18650 |
| 2 Dr L Cpe w/Leather Interior (5 spd) | **28275** | 16225 | 18875 |
| 4 Dr LS Sdn (5 spd) | **29160** | 13275 | 15600 |
| 2 Dr LS Cpe (5 spd) | **30040** | 14525 | 17050 |

NOTE: Power brakes standard on Integra and Legend. Power windows and power door locks standard on Ingegra LS 5 Door. Sunroof standard on Integra LS 3 Door.

## 1988

### INTEGRA 4

| Year/Model/Body/Type | Original List | Current Whlse | Average Retail |
|---|---|---|---|
| 3 Dr RS Hbk (5 spd) | **10915** | 4200 | 5125 |
| 5 Dr RS Hbk (5 spd) | **11695** | 4400 | 5325 |
| 3 Dr LS Hbk (5 spd) | **12670** | 4700 | 5625 |
| 5 Dr LS Hbk (5 spd) | **13485** | 4875 | 5800 |
| 3 Dr LS SE Hbk (5 spd) | **13670** | 5025 | 5950 |

### LEGEND 6

| Year/Model/Body/Type | Original List | Current Whlse | Average Retail |
|---|---|---|---|
| 4 Dr Sdn (5 spd) | **21535** | 8475 | 9800 |
| 2 Dr Cpe (5 spd) | **23675** | 9675 | 11150 |
| 4 Dr L Sdn (5 spd) | **25625** | 9350 | 10775 |
| 2 Dr L Cpe (5 spd) | **27255** | 10475 | 12100 |
| 4 Dr LS Sdn (5 spd) | **28230** | 10050 | 11600 |
| 2 Dr LS Cpe (5 spd) | **29085** | 11225 | 12975 |

NOTE: Pwr strng standard on all models. Power windows standard on Integra LS 5 Door and Legend. Air conditioning standard on Legend. Electric sunroof standard on Legend L and LS.

## 1987

### INTEGRA 4

| Year/Model/Body/Type | Original List | Current Whlse | Average Retail |
|---|---|---|---|
| 3 Dr RS Hbk (5 spd) | **10039** | 3175 | 4075 |
| 5 Dr RS Hbk (5 spd) | **10754** | 3350 | 4250 |
| 3 Dr LS Hbk (5 spd) | **11589** | 3600 | 4500 |
| 5 Dr LS Hbk (5 spd) | **12404** | 3800 | 4700 |
| 3 Dr Sp LS Hbk (5 spd) | **12589** | 3975 | 4875 |

### LEGEND 6

| Year/Model/Body/Type | Original List | Current Whlse | Average Retail |
|---|---|---|---|
| 4 Dr Sdn (5 spd) | **20258** | 6650 | 7750 |
| 4 Dr Luxury Sdn (5 spd) | **22858** | 7225 | 8400 |
| 2 Dr Cpe (5 spd) | **22458** | 7775 | 9025 |
| 2 Dr LS Cpe (5 spd) | **—** | 8650 | 10100 |

## 1986

### INTEGRA 4

| Year/Model/Body/Type | Original List | Current Whlse | Average Retail |
|---|---|---|---|
| 3 Dr RS Hbk (5 spd) | **9298** | 2750 | 3650 |
| 5 Dr RS Hbk (5 spd) | **9948** | 2950 | 3850 |
| 3 Dr LS Hbk (5 spd) | **10593** | 3125 | 4025 |
| 5 Dr LS Hbk (5 spd) | **11343** | 3300 | 4200 |

### LEGEND 6

| Year/Model/Body/Type | Original List | Current Whlse | Average Retail |
|---|---|---|---|
| 4 Dr Sdn (5 spd) | **19298** | 5300 | 6225 |

# FOREIGN CARS & TRUCKS

| Year/Model/Body/Type | Original List | Current Whlse | Average Retail |
|---|---|---|---|

## ALFA ROMEO

### 1992

**SPIDER 4**

| | | | |
|---|---|---|---|
| Base Conv | 22259 | — | — |
| Veloce Conv | 25304 | — | — |

*ADD FOR:*

| | | | |
|---|---|---|---|
| Removable Hardtop | 2500 | — | — |
| Alloy Wheels | 350 | — | — |

**164 6**

| | | | |
|---|---|---|---|
| L Sdn | 29490 | | |
| S Sdn | 34990 | | |

*ADD FOR:*

| | | | |
|---|---|---|---|
| Luxury Pkg | 1950 | — | — |

NOTE: Power windows standard on Spider and 164. Power door locks, power seat, power sunroof and cruise control standard on 164.

### 1991

**SPIDER 4**

| | | | |
|---|---|---|---|
| Base Conv | 21945 | 11525 | 13300 |
| Veloce Conv | 22950 | 13150 | 15475 |

**164 6**

| | | | |
|---|---|---|---|
| Base Sdn | 24500 | 12675 | 15000 |
| L Sdn | 27500 | 14650 | 17200 |
| S Sdn | 29500 | 15525 | 18175 |

*ADD FOR:*

| | | | |
|---|---|---|---|
| Power Leather Seats (164 Base) | 1200 | 440 | 480 |
| Power Recaro Leather Seats (164 S) | 2000 | 720 | 800 |

NOTE: Power brakes standard on all models. Power windows standard on 164 and Spider. Power door locks and power seat standard on 164.

### 1990

**SPIDER 4**

| | | | |
|---|---|---|---|
| Graduate Conv (NA w/pwr strng) | 18590 | 9975 | 11700 |
| Veloce Conv (NA w/pwr strng) | 21945 | 11625 | 13550 |
| Quadrifoglio Conv w/Hardtop (NA w/pwr strng) | 23950 | 12175 | 14375 |

*ADD FOR:*

| | | | |
|---|---|---|---|
| Metallic Paint (Veloce, Quadrifoglio) | 275 | 60 | 70 |

NOTE: Power brakes standard on Spider Series. Power windows std. on Spider Veloce and Spider Quadrifoglio.

### 1989

**MILANO 6**

| | | | |
|---|---|---|---|
| Gold Sdn | 18475 | 6350 | 7400 |
| Platinum Sdn (auto) | 22500 | 7225 | 8400 |
| 3.0 Liter Sdn | 22700 | 7725 | 8975 |

**SPIDER 4**

| | | | |
|---|---|---|---|
| Graduate Conv (NA w/pwr strng) | 18340 | 7375 | 8550 |
| Veloce Conv (NA w/pwr strng) | 21195 | 8775 | 10125 |
| Quadrifoglio Conv w/Hardtop (NA w/pwr strng) | 23400 | 9725 | 11200 |

*ADD FOR:*

| | | | |
|---|---|---|---|
| Metallic Paint (Quadrifoglio) | 275 | 60 | 60 |

NOTE: Power door locks standard on Milano Series. Power brakes standard on Milano Series and Spider Series. Automatic transmission standard on Milano Platinum. Power windows standard on Milano Series, Spider Veloce and Spider Quadrifoglio.

### 1988

**MILANO 6**

| | | | |
|---|---|---|---|
| Gold Sdn | 17550 | 4225 | 5150 |
| Platinum Sdn (auto) | 21450 | 4875 | 5800 |
| Verde Sdn | 21650 | 5400 | 6325 |

**SPIDER 4**

| | | | |
|---|---|---|---|
| Graduate Conv | 15950 | 5825 | 6750 |
| Veloce Conv | 19380 | 7100 | 8250 |
| Quadrifoglio Conv w/Hardtop | 22440 | 7775 | 9025 |

*ADD FOR:*

| | | | |
|---|---|---|---|
| Metallic Paint (Veloce, Quadrifoglio) | 275 | 60 | 60 |
| (Milano) | 350 | 60 | 60 |

NOTE: Air conditioning standard on Spider Quadrifoglio and Milano models. Power windows standard on Spider Veloce, Spider Quadrifoglio and Milano models. Pwr strng standard on Milano models.

### 1987

**SPIDER 4**

| | | | |
|---|---|---|---|
| Graduate Conv | 14500 | 3850 | 4750 |
| Veloce Conv | 17195 | 4925 | 5850 |
| Quadrifoglio Conv w/Hardtop | 21000 | 5600 | 6525 |

**MILANO 6**

| | | | |
|---|---|---|---|
| Silver Sdn | 15400 | 2700 | 3600 |

| Year/Model/ Body/Type | Original List | Current Whlse | Average Retail |
|---|---|---|---|
| Gold Sdn | **16000** | 2825 | 3725 |
| Platinum Sdn | **20350** | 3250 | 4150 |
| **VERDE 6** | | | |
| Sdn | **19800** | 3275 | 4175 |
| *ADD FOR:* | | | |
| Metallic Paint | | | |
| (Veloce, Quadrifoglio) | **275** | 60 | 60 |
| (Milano, Verde) | **350** | 60 | 60 |
| Leather Seats | | | |
| (Milano Gold) | — | — | — |

NOTE: Air conditioning standard on Quadrifoglio, Milano and Verde. Power windows standard on Veloce, Quadrifoglio and Milano. Pwr strng standard on Milano. Sun roof standard on Milano Platinum.

## 1986

**GRADUATE CONV 4**

| | | | |
|---|---|---|---|
| Conv | **14639** | 3075 | 3975 |
| SPIDER VELOCE 4 | | | |
| Conv | **17639** | 4050 | 4950 |

**QUADRIFOGLIO CONV 4**

| | | | |
|---|---|---|---|
| Conv | **19600** | 4650 | 5575 |

**GTV-6 6**

| | | | |
|---|---|---|---|
| Cpe | **17144** | 3175 | 4075 |
| *ADD FOR:* | | | |
| Leather Seats (GTV-6) | **750** | 100 | 110 |

NOTE: Power brakes standard on all models. Power windows standard on Spider Veloce and GTV-6. Pwr strng standard on GTV-6. Air conditioning standard on Quadrifoglio and GTV-6.

## 1985

**GRADUATE CONV 4**

| | | | |
|---|---|---|---|
| Conv | **13495** | 2375 | 3250 |

**GTV-6 6**

| | | | |
|---|---|---|---|
| Cpe | **16500** | 2500 | 3375 |

**SPIDER VELOCE 4**

| | | | |
|---|---|---|---|
| Conv | **16500** | 3325 | 4225 |
| *ADD FOR:* | | | |
| Leather Seats (GTV-6) | **750** | 80 | 90 |
| Fiberglass Hardtop | | | |
| (Spider Veloce) | **1100** | 180 | 200 |

## 1984

**GTV-6 6**

| | | | |
|---|---|---|---|
| Cpe | **19000** | 2000 | 2850 |

| Year/Model/ Body/Type | Original List | Current Whlse | Average Retail |
|---|---|---|---|
| **SPIDER VELOCE 4** | | | |
| Conv | **16000** | 2750 | 3650 |

## 1983

**GTV-6 6**

| | | | |
|---|---|---|---|
| Cpe | **17995** | 1675 | 2525 |

**SPIDER VELOCE 4**

| | | | |
|---|---|---|---|
| Conv | **15495** | 2325 | 3200 |

## AUDI

## 1992

**80 5**

| | | | |
|---|---|---|---|
| 4 Dr Sdn | **22650** | — | — |
| 4 Dr Quattro 4WD Sdn | **26250** | — | — |
| *ADD FOR:* | | | |
| CD Changer | **890** | — | — |

**100 6**

| | | | |
|---|---|---|---|
| 4 Dr Sdn | **27700** | 19150 | 22200 |
| 4 Dr S Sdn | **29900** | 20425 | 23475 |
| 4 Dr CS Sdn | **32900** | 21750 | 25050 |
| *ADD FOR:* | | | |
| CD Changer (CS) | **790** | 325 | 375 |
| Leather Seat Trim | **1300** | 400 | 475 |
| Cellular Telephone | **990** | 300 | 375 |

**V8 QUATTRO 8**

| | | | |
|---|---|---|---|
| 4 Dr Sdn (auto) | **53100** | — | — |

NOTE: Power windows, power door locks and cruise control standard on all models. Power seat and power sunroof standard on 100 S & CS and V8 Quattro. Tilt steering wheel standard on 100 Series and V8 Quattro.

## 1991

**80 5**

| | | | |
|---|---|---|---|
| 4 Dr Sdn | **20750** | 12650 | 14975 |
| 4 Dr Quattro 4WD Sdn | **25200** | 14850 | 17425 |

**90 5**

| | | | |
|---|---|---|---|
| 4 Dr Sdn (auto) | **26250** | 14900 | 17500 |
| 4 Dr Quattro 4WD Sdn | **29200** | 17125 | 19775 |

**100 5**

| | | | |
|---|---|---|---|
| 4 Dr Sdn (auto) | **28750** | 15975 | 18625 |
| 4 Dr Quattro 4WD Sdn | **31150** | 18075 | 20750 |

**200 5**

| | | | |
|---|---|---|---|
| 4 Dr Turbo Sdn (auto) | **35500** | 18975 | 22025 |

| Year/Model/Body/Type | Original List | Current Whlse | Average Retail |
|---|---|---|---|
| 4 Dr Quattro Turbo 4WD Sdn | **43500** | 21100 | 24300 |
| 4 Dr Quattro Turbo 4WD Wgn | **43500** | 21450 | 24750 |
| **COUPE QUATTRO 5** | | | |
| 2 Dr Cpe | **31650** | 17800 | 20350 |
| **V8 QUATTRO 8** | | | |
| 4 Dr 4WD Sdn | **51500** | 28800 | 32150 |
| *ADD FOR:* | | | |
| Anti-Lock Brakes (80) | **1145** | 390 | 430 |
| Audi-Bose Radio System (100) | **625** | 250 | 270 |
| Leather Seats (90) | **1040** | 310 | 340 |
| (100) | **1300** | 310 | 340 |

NOTE: Power brakes, power windows and power door locks standard on all models. Power seat standard on 200 and V8 Quattro. Sunroof standard on 90, 100, 200, Coupe Quattro and V8 Quattro.

## 1990

### 80 4

| | | | |
|---|---|---|---|
| 4 Dr Sdn | **18900** | 9225 | 10625 |
| 4 Dr Quattro 4WD Sdn (5 spd) | **22800** | 10750 | 12425 |

### 90 5

| | | | |
|---|---|---|---|
| 4 Dr Sdn | **23990** | 11425 | 13200 |
| 4 Dr Quattro 4WD Sdn (5 spd) | **27500** | 13075 | 15200 |

### 100 5

| | | | |
|---|---|---|---|
| 4 Dr Sdn (auto) | **26900** | 12425 | 14550 |
| 4 Dr Quattro 4WD Sdn | **29470** | 14325 | 16825 |

### 200 5

| | | | |
|---|---|---|---|
| 4 Dr Turbo Sdn | **33405** | 14750 | 17325 |
| 4 Dr Quattro Turbo 4WD Sdn | **35805** | 16625 | 19275 |
| 4 Dr Quattro Turbo 4WD Wgn | **36930** | 16950 | 19600 |

### COUPE QUATTRO 5

| | | | |
|---|---|---|---|
| 2 Dr Cpe | **29750** | 14550 | 17075 |

### V8 QUATTRO 8

| | | | |
|---|---|---|---|
| 4 Dr Sdn (auto) | **47450** | 23225 | 26525 |
| *ADD FOR:* | | | |
| Anti-Lock Brakes (80) | **1100** | 330 | 360 |
| Audi-Bose Radio System (100) | **600** | 160 | 180 |
| Leather Seats (90) | **1000** | 250 | 270 |
| (100) | **1250** | 250 | 270 |

| Year/Model/Body/Type | Original List | Current Whlse | Average Retail |
|---|---|---|---|
| Pearlescent Paint (90, Quattro Cpe) | **395** | 100 | 110 |
| (100) | **900** | 150 | 160 |
| (Quattro Sdn) | **450** | 150 | 160 |

NOTE: Power brakes, power windows, power door locks and anti-lock brake system standard on all models. Sunroof standard on 90, 100, 200, V8 Quattro and Coupe Quattro. Power seat standard on V8 Quattro and 200 Series.

## 1989

### 80 4

| | | | |
|---|---|---|---|
| 4 Dr Sdn | **19845** | 7575 | 8800 |
| 4 Dr Quattro Sdn (5 spd) | **23610** | 8925 | 10300 |

### 90 5

| | | | |
|---|---|---|---|
| 4 Dr Sdn | **25310** | 9575 | 11025 |
| 4 Dr Quattro Sdn | **28840** | 10850 | 12525 |

### 100 5

| | | | |
|---|---|---|---|
| 4 Dr E Sdn (auto) | **25230** | 7950 | 9225 |
| 4 Dr Sdn | **27750** | 8875 | 10250 |
| 4 Dr Wgn | **29250** | 9175 | 10575 |
| 4 Dr Quattro Sdn | **31110** | 10600 | 12225 |

### 200 5

| | | | |
|---|---|---|---|
| 4 Dr Turbo Sdn | **34005** | 10875 | 12550 |
| 4 Dr Quattro Turbo Sdn | **37905** | 12650 | 14975 |
| 4 Dr Quattro Turbo Wgn | **38805** | 12950 | 15275 |
| *ADD FOR:* | | | |
| Leather Seat Trim (100 ex. E, 200 Turbo Sdn) | **1250** | 250 | 270 |
| (200 Turbo Sdn) | **900** | 250 | 270 |

NOTE: Pwr strng, power brakes, power windows and power door locks standard on all models. Sunroof standard on 90, 100 and 200 models.

## 1988

### 80 4

| | | | |
|---|---|---|---|
| 4 Dr Sdn | **18600** | 5700 | 6625 |
| 4 Dr Quattro Sdn | **22700** | 7450 | 8650 |

### 90 4

| | | | |
|---|---|---|---|
| 4 Dr Sdn (auto) | **24330** | 7150 | 8300 |

### 90 5

| | | | |
|---|---|---|---|
| 4 Dr Sdn | **24330** | 7150 | 8300 |
| 4 Dr Quattro Sdn | **27720** | 8950 | 10325 |

### 5000S 5

| | | | |
|---|---|---|---|
| 4 Dr Sdn | **22180** | 5875 | 6800 |
| 4 Dr Wgn | **23620** | 6150 | 7150 |
| 4 Dr Quattro Sdn | **26490** | 7550 | 8775 |

*Refer to optional equipment schedules*

| Year/Model/ Body/Type | Original List | Current Whlse | Average Retail |
|---|---|---|---|
| **5000CS 5** | | | |
| 4 Dr Sdn | **30010** | 7350 | 8525 |
| 4 Dr Quattro Sdn | **33800** | 9050 | 10425 |
| 4 Dr Quattro Wgn | **35250** | 9325 | 10750 |
| *ADD FOR:* | | | |
| Leather Seat Trim | | | |
| (5000S ex. Quattro, | | | |
| 5000CS ex. Quattro) | **1250** | 210 | 230 |

NOTE: Air conditioning, pwr strng and power windows standard on all models. Power sunroof standard on 90 and 5000CS.

## 1987

| | | | |
|---|---|---|---|
| **4000S 4** | | | |
| 4 Dr Sdn | **15875** | 3400 | 4300 |
| **4000CS 5** | | | |
| 4 Dr Quattro Sdn | **19850** | 4300 | 5225 |
| **5000S 5** | | | |
| 4 Dr Sdn (110 HP) | **20060** | 3700 | 4600 |
| 4 Dr Sdn (130 HP) | **20460** | 3800 | 4700 |
| 4 Dr Wgn | **21390** | 3950 | 4850 |
| **5000CS 5** | | | |
| 4 Dr Turbo Sdn | **26640** | 4725 | 5650 |
| 4 Dr Turbo Sp Edit Sdn | **27975** | 4950 | 5875 |
| 4 Dr Quattro Turbo Sdn | **31215** | 6275 | 7300 |
| 4 Dr Quattro Turbo Wgn | **32555** | 6525 | 7600 |
| **GT COUPE 5** | | | |
| 2 Dr Cpe | **17580** | 4100 | 5025 |
| *ADD FOR:* | | | |
| Anti-Lock Braking | | | |
| System (5000S, | | | |
| 5000CS ex. Quattro) | **1075** | 230 | 250 |
| Leather Seat Trim | | | |
| (4000CS, GT Cpe) | **1025** | 160 | 180 |
| (5000S, Base 5000CS) | **1185** | 160 | 180 |

NOTE: Air conditioning standard on 4000S, 4000CS, GT Coupe, 5000S and 5000CS. Sun roof standard on 5000CS. Power door locks standard on 4000S, 4000CS, 5000S and 5000CS. Pwr strng and power windows standard on 4000S, 4000CS, and GT Coupe. Anti-lock braking system standard on 5000CS Quattro.

## 1986

| | | | |
|---|---|---|---|
| **4000S 4** | | | |
| 4 Dr Sdn | **15315** | 2325 | 3200 |
| **4000CS 5** | | | |
| 4 Dr Quattro Sdn Commemorative Edition | **18670** | 3075 | 3975 |

| Year/Model/ Body/Type | Original List | Current Whlse | Average Retail |
|---|---|---|---|
| Quattro 4 Dr Sdn | **20365** | 3500 | 4400 |
| **5000S 5** | | | |
| 4 Dr Sdn | **18950** | 2650 | 3550 |
| 4 Dr Wgn | **20220** | 2875 | 3775 |
| **5000CS 5** | | | |
| 4 Dr Turbo Sdn | **25275** | 3275 | 4175 |
| 4 Dr Quattro Turbo Sdn | **29345** | 4675 | 5600 |
| 4 Dr Quattro Turbo Wgn | **30615** | 4850 | 5775 |
| Comm Edit 4 Dr Sdn | **21660** | 2950 | 3850 |
| **GT COUPE 5** | | | |
| 2 Dr Cpe | **16535** | 2825 | 3725 |
| Commemorative Edition | | | |
| 2 Dr Cpe | **18525** | 3125 | 4025 |
| *ADD FOR:* | | | |
| Anti-Lock Braking | | | |
| System (5000S, 5000CS) | **995** | 150 | 160 |

NOTE: Power windows, power brakes, pwr strng and air conditioning standard on all models. Power seat and sunroof standard on 5000CS Turbo and 5000CS Turbo Quattro. Power locks standard on 4000S, 4000CS Quattro, 5000S, 5000CS Turbo and 5000CS Turbo Quattro.

## 1985

| | | | |
|---|---|---|---|
| **4000S 4** | | | |
| 4 Dr Base Sdn | **14330** | 1800 | 2650 |
| 4 Dr Quattro Sdn | **17450** | 2450 | 3325 |
| **5000S 5** | | | |
| 4 Dr Sdn | **18090** | 2100 | 2950 |
| 4 Dr Wgn | **19300** | 2275 | 3150 |
| 4 Dr Turbo Sdn (auto) | **23875** | 2300 | 3175 |
| **GT COUPE 5** | | | |
| 2 Dr Cpe | **15630** | 2125 | 2975 |
| **QUATTRO 5** | | | |
| 2 Dr Cpe | — | — | — |
| *ADD FOR:* | | | |
| Man Tilt Seat (GT Coupe) | **495** | 50 | 50 |
| Leather Interior (5000S) | **1085** | 100 | 110 |
| Full Leather Interior | | | |
| (4000S Quattro) | **950** | 80 | 90 |

NOTE: Pwr strng standard on 4000S, 5000S, GT Coupe and Quattro. Air conditioning standard on 4000S, GT Coupe and Quattro. Power windows standard on 4000S, 5000S, GT Coupe and Quattro. Power seat standard on 5000S Turbo. Sunroof standard on 5000S Turbo Quattro.

## 1984

| | | | |
|---|---|---|---|
| **4000S 4** | | | |
| 2 Dr Sdn | **12750** | 1175 | 1900 |

| Year/Model/Body/Type | Original List | Current Whlse | Average Retail |
|---|---|---|---|
| 4 Dr Sdn | **13340** | 1275 | 2000 |
| 4 Dr Quattro Sdn | **16860** | 1875 | 2725 |
| **5000S 5** | | | |
| 4 Dr Sdn | **16840** | 1625 | 2475 |
| 4 Dr Wgn | **17840** | 1750 | 2600 |
| 4 Dr Turbo Sdn (auto) | **22250** | 1775 | 2625 |
| **GT COUPE 5** | | | |
| 2 Dr Cpe | **14860** | 1500 | 2350 |
| **QUATTRO 5** | | | |
| 2 Dr Cpe | **35000** | — | — |

### 1983 — ALL BODY STYLES

| | | | |
|---|---|---|---|
| 4000 | — | 850 | 1550 |
| 4000S | — | 900 | 1625 |
| 5000S | — | 1075 | 1800 |
| 5000T | — | 1225 | 1950 |
| COUPE | — | 1125 | 1850 |

## BMW

### 1992

**BMW 4**

| | | | |
|---|---|---|---|
| 318iC 2 Dr Conv | **28870** | — | — |
| 318iS 2 Dr Cpe | **23600** | — | — |
| 318i 4 Dr Sdn | **22900** | — | — |

**BMW 6**

| | | | |
|---|---|---|---|
| 325i 4 Dr Sdn | **27990** | 21375 | 24675 |
| 325iC 2 Dr Conv | **36320** | — | — |
| 325iS 2 Dr Cpe | **29100** | — | — |
| 525i 4 Dr Sdn | **35600** | 27600 | 30950 |
| 535i 4 Dr Sdn (auto) | **44350** | — | — |
| M5 4 Dr Sdn | **58600** | — | — |
| 735i 4 Dr Sdn (auto) | **52990** | — | — |
| 735iL 4 Dr Sdn (auto) | **56950** | — | — |

**BMW 12**

| | | | |
|---|---|---|---|
| 750iL 4 Dr Sdn (auto) | **76500** | — | — |
| 850i 2 Dr Cpe (auto) | **78500** | — | — |

*ADD FOR:*

| | | | |
|---|---|---|---|
| Auto Traction Control | | | |
| (535i) | **1290** | — | — |
| (735i, 735iL) | **1290** | — | — |
| (850i) | **1500** | — | — |
| Cellular Telephone | | | |
| (525i, 535i, M5 | | | |
| 735i, 735iL) | **800** | — | — |
| CD Player (735i, 735iL) | **825** | — | — |
| Electronic Damping | | | |

| Year/Model/Body/Type | Original List | Current Whlse | Average Retail |
|---|---|---|---|
| Suspension (850i) | **1470** | — | — |
| Forged Alloy Whls (850i) | **1000** | — | — |
| Leather Seats | | | |
| (325i Sdn) | **1100** | 450 | 525 |
| (525i) | **1200** | — | — |
| Special App Pkg | | | |
| (325iC) | **1850** | — | — |
| Wood & Leather Pkg | | | |
| (525i Base) | **2040** | — | — |

NOTE: Power windows and power door locks standard on all models. Power seats standard on 525, 535, M5, 735, 750 and 850. Sunroof standard on all models except Convs. Tilt steering wheel and cruise control standard on all models except 318.

### 1991

**BMW 4**

| | | | |
|---|---|---|---|
| 318i 4 Dr Sdn | **19900** | 13100 | 15425 |
| 318iS 2 Dr Sdn | **21500** | 13200 | 15525 |
| 318iC 2 Dr Conv | **28500** | 18350 | 21300 |
| M3 2 Dr Sdn | **35900** | 22250 | 25550 |

**BMW 6**

| | | | |
|---|---|---|---|
| 325i 2 Dr Sdn | **25600** | 16650 | 19300 |
| 325i 4 Dr Sdn | **26400** | 16550 | 19200 |
| 325iC 2 Dr Conv | **35700** | 23225 | 26525 |
| 325iX 4WD 2 Dr Sdn | **31100** | 19475 | 22525 |
| 325iX 4WD 4 Dr Sdn | **31900** | 19400 | 22450 |
| 525i 4 Dr Sdn | **34500** | 24050 | 27350 |
| 535i 4 Dr Sdn (auto) | **42600** | 28575 | 31925 |
| M5 4 Dr Sdn | **56600** | 36600 | 40625 |
| 735i 4 Dr Sdn (auto) | **50900** | 32600 | 36250 |
| 735iL 4 Dr Sdn (auto) | **55000** | 34600 | 38475 |

**BMW 12**

| | | | |
|---|---|---|---|
| 750iL 4 Dr Sdn (auto) | **74000** | 46200 | 50900 |
| 850i 2 Dr Sdn (auto) | **73600** | 48475 | 53425 |

*ADD FOR:*

| | | | |
|---|---|---|---|
| Forged Alloy Wheels | | | |
| (850i) | **1000** | 420 | 460 |
| Leather Seats | | | |
| (325i, 325iX) | **950** | 390 | 430 |
| (525i) | **1200** | 460 | 500 |
| Sport Pkg (325i) | **1920** | 700 | 780 |
| Touring Pkg (325i) | **1665** | 600 | 670 |

NOTE: Power brakes standard on all models. Power windows and power door locks standard on 3-Series, 5-Series, M3, M5, 7-Series and 8-Series. Sunroof standard on 325iX, M3, M5, 7-Series and 8-Series. Power seat standard on M5, 7-Series and 8-Series.

### 1990

**BMW 4**

| | | | |
|---|---|---|---|
| M3 2 Dr Sdn | **34950** | 19475 | 22525 |

*Refer to optional equipment schedules*

| Year/Model/Body/Type | Original List | Current Whlse | Average Retail |
|---|---|---|---|
| **BMW 6** | | | |
| 325i 2 Dr Sdn | **24650** | 14575 | 17100 |
| 325i 4 Dr Sdn | **25450** | 14500 | 17025 |
| 325iC 2 Dr Conv | **33850** | 20375 | 23425 |
| 325iS 2 Dr Sdn | **28950** | 16150 | 18800 |
| 325iX 4WD 2 Dr Sdn | **29950** | 17125 | 19775 |
| 325iX 4WD 4 Dr Sdn | **30750** | 17025 | 19675 |
| 525i 4 Dr Sdn | **33200** | 19350 | 22400 |
| 535i 4 Dr Sdn (auto) | **41500** | 23250 | 26550 |
| 735i 4 Dr Sdn (auto) | **49000** | 27050 | 30375 |
| 735iL 4 Dr Sdn (auto) | **53000** | 28575 | 31925 |
| **BMW 12** | | | |
| 750iL 4 Dr Sdn (auto) | **70000** | 35750 | 39675 |
| *ADD FOR:* | | | |
| Cellular Phone (735) | **1205** | 200 | 230 |
| Leather Interior | | | |
| (325i, 325iX) | **895** | 290 | 320 |
| (525) | **1100** | 330 | 360 |

NOTE: Power brakes standard on all BMW models. Power windows and anti-lock brakes standard on 325 Series, M3, 525, 535, 735, 750. Power door locks standard on 325 Series, M3, 750. Power seat standard on 525, 535, 735, 750. Sunroof standard on 325 Series except 325iC, M3, 525, 535, 735, 750.

### 1989

| | Original List | Current Whlse | Average Retail |
|---|---|---|---|
| **BMW 4** | | | |
| M3 2 Dr Sdn | **34950** | 15000 | 17600 |
| **BMW 6** | | | |
| 325i 2 Dr Sdn | **24650** | 10675 | 12325 |
| 325i 4 Dr Sdn | **25450** | 10575 | 12200 |
| 325iC 2 Dr Conv | **33850** | 16300 | 18950 |
| 325is 2 Dr Sdn | **28950** | 12200 | 14100 |
| 325iX 4WD 2 Dr Sdn | **29950** | 12950 | 15275 |
| 325iX 4WD 4 Dr Sdn | **30750** | 12850 | 15175 |
| 525i 4 Dr Sdn (auto) | **37000** | 16500 | 19150 |
| 535i 4 Dr Sdn (auto) | **43600** | 19250 | 22300 |
| 635CSi 2 Dr Cpe (auto) | **47000** | 22250 | 25550 |
| 735i 4 Dr Sdn (auto) | **54000** | 21825 | 25125 |
| 735iL 4 Dr Sdn (auto) | **58000** | 23325 | 26625 |
| **BMW 12** | | | |
| 750iL 4 Dr Sdn (auto) | **70000** | 28175 | 31525 |
| *ADD FOR:* | | | |
| Hard Top (325iC) | **3500** | 1270 | 1410 |
| Compact Disc (525i, 535, 635CSi, 735i, 735iL, 750iL) | **775** | 160 | 180 |

NOTE: Pwr strng, air conditioning, power brakes and power windows standard on all models. Automatic transmission standard on 525i, 535i, 635CSi, 735 Series and 750iL. Sunroof standard on M3, 325 Series except 325iC, 525i, 535i, 635CSi, 735 Series and 750iL. Anti lock

brakes standard on 325 Series, 525i, 535i, 635CSi, 735 and 750iL.

### 1988

| | Original List | Current Whlse | Average Retail |
|---|---|---|---|
| **BMW 4** | | | |
| M3 2 Dr Sdn | **34800** | 12750 | 15075 |
| **BMW 6** | | | |
| 325 2 Dr Sdn | **24350** | 8500 | 9825 |
| 325 4 Dr Sdn | **25150** | 8400 | 9700 |
| 325i 4 Dr Sdn | **28950** | 9825 | 11325 |
| 325i 2 Dr Conv | **32995** | 14075 | 16525 |
| 325is 2 Dr Sdn | **28950** | 9925 | 11425 |
| 325ix 2 Dr Sdn | **33290** | 10625 | 12250 |
| 528e 4 Dr Sdn | **31950** | 8400 | 9700 |
| 535i 4 Dr Sdn | **36700** | 11000 | 12700 |
| 535is 4 Dr Sdn | **37800** | 11575 | 13375 |
| 635CSi 2 Dr Cpe (auto) | **46000** | 17000 | 19650 |
| 735i 4 Dr Sdn (auto) | **54000** | 15500 | 18150 |
| 750iL 4 Dr Sdn (auto) | **69000** | 22350 | 25650 |
| M5 4 Dr Sdn | **47500** | 16350 | 19000 |
| M6 2 Dr Cpe | **55950** | 22050 | 25350 |
| *ADD FOR:* | | | |
| Leather Upholstery (528e) | **1090** | 290 | 320 |
| Hard Top (325iC) | **3500** | 1240 | 1370 |

NOTE: Air conditioning, pwr strng, anti-lock brakes and sunroof standard on all models. Power windows standard on all models except 325 Base.

### 1987

| | Original List | Current Whlse | Average Retail |
|---|---|---|---|
| **BMW 6** | | | |
| 325 2 Dr Sdn | **23180** | 6675 | 7775 |
| 325 4 Dr Sdn | **23765** | 6600 | 7675 |
| 325es 2 Dr Sdn | **24370** | 7250 | 8425 |
| 325e 4 Dr Sdn | **25150** | 7150 | 8300 |
| 325is 2 Dr Sdn | **27300** | 7975 | 9250 |
| 325i 4 Dr Sdn | **27300** | 7875 | 9150 |
| 325i 2 Dr Conv | **31000** | 12175 | 14050 |
| 528e 4 Dr Sdn | **28330** | 6650 | 7750 |
| 535i 4 Dr Sdn | **33600** | 8850 | 10225 |
| 535is 4 Dr Sdn | **35200** | 9675 | 11150 |
| 635CSi 2 Dr Cpe | **46965** | 13450 | 15775 |
| 735i 4 Dr Sdn (auto) | **42475** | 12300 | 14300 |
| L6 2 Dr Cpe | **49500** | 14200 | 16675 |
| L7 4 Dr Sdn (auto) | **46675** | 12600 | 14925 |
| M6 2 Dr Cpe | **55950** | 18350 | 21300 |
| *ADD FOR:* | | | |
| Leather Upholstery (528e) | **980** | 210 | 230 |
| TRX Wheels & Tires (735i) | **650** | 150 | 160 |

NOTE: Air conditioning, pwr strng, power brakes, power windows and sunroof standard on 325 Series, 528e, 535, 635CSi, L6, M6 and 735i. Anti-lock braking system

| Year/Model/Body/Type | Original List | Current Whlse | Average Retail |
|---|---|---|---|

standard on 325 Series, 528e, 635CSi and 735i. Automatic transmission standard on L6.

## 1986

### BMW 6

| | | | |
|---|---|---|---|
| 325 2 Dr Sdn | **19955** | 5825 | 6750 |
| 325 4 Dr Sdn | **20455** | 5725 | 6650 |
| 325es 2 Dr Sdn | **22540** | 6325 | 7350 |
| 325e 4 Dr Sdn | **23255** | 6225 | 7250 |

### 524 4 Dr Turbo Diesel

| | | | |
|---|---|---|---|
| Sdn (auto) | **26225** | 4350 | 5275 |
| 528e 4 Dr Sdn | **26980** | 5475 | 6400 |
| 535i 4 Dr Sdn | **31980** | 7250 | 8425 |
| 635CSi 2 Dr Cpe | **43055** | 10875 | 12550 |
| 735i 4 Dr Sdn | **39275** | 7900 | 9175 |
| L7 4 Dr Sdn | **44030** | 8600 | 9925 |

*ADD FOR:*
Leather Upholstery

| | | | |
|---|---|---|---|
| (325es) | **790** | 130 | 140 |
| (528e) | **1090** | 160 | 180 |
| TRX Whls & Tires (735i) | **850** | 130 | 140 |

NOTE: Power brakes, power locks, power windows, pwr strng, air conditioning and sunroof standard on all models. Automatic transmission standard on 524td and L7. Power seat standard on 524td, 528e, 535i, 635CSi, 735i and L7.

## 1985

### BMW 4

| | | | |
|---|---|---|---|
| 318i 2 Dr Sdn | **16935** | 3900 | 4850 |
| 318i 4 Dr Sdn | **17430** | 3800 | 4700 |

### BMW 6

| | | | |
|---|---|---|---|
| 325e 2 Dr Sdn | **20970** | 5150 | 6075 |
| 325e 4 Dr Sdn | **21105** | 5050 | 5975 |
| 524td 4 Dr Sdn (auto) | **24145** | 3850 | 4750 |
| 528e 4 Dr Sdn | **24565** | 4725 | 5650 |
| 535i 4 Dr Sdn | **30760** | 6325 | 7350 |
| 633CSi 2 Dr Cpe | **41315** | 9250 | 10650 |
| 735i 4 Dr Sdn | **36880** | 6825 | 7950 |

*ADD FOR:*
Leather Upholstery

| | | | |
|---|---|---|---|
| (325e) | **790** | 80 | 90 |
| (528e) | **1090** | 100 | 110 |

Metallic Paint

| | | | |
|---|---|---|---|
| (318i, 325e) | **420** | 50 | 50 |
| TRX Whls & Tires (735i) | **850** | 60 | 70 |

NOTE: Pwr strng, air conditioning and power windows standard on all models. Sunroof standard on all models except 318i.

## 1984

### BMW 4

| | | | |
|---|---|---|---|
| 318i 2 Dr Sdn | **16935** | 3325 | 4225 |

### BMW 6

| | | | |
|---|---|---|---|
| 325e 2 Dr Sdn | **20970** | 4325 | 5250 |
| 528e 4 Dr Sdn | **24565** | 4250 | 5175 |
| 533i 4 Dr Sdn | **30305** | 4900 | 5825 |
| 633CSi 2 Dr Cpe | **40705** | 8575 | 9900 |
| 733i 4 Dr Sdn | **36335** | 6275 | 7300 |

## 1983 — ALL BODY STYLES

| | | | |
|---|---|---|---|
| 320i | — | 2500 | 3375 |
| 528e | — | 3600 | 4500 |
| 533i | — | 4250 | 5175 |
| 633CSi | — | 7825 | 9075 |
| 733i | — | 5600 | 6525 |

## CHALLENGER

## 1983

### CHALLENGER 4

| | | | |
|---|---|---|---|
| 2 Dr Luxury HT | **8223** | 525 | 975 |

## COLT

## 1992

### COLT 4

| | | | |
|---|---|---|---|
| 3 Dr Hbk (NA w/pwr strng) | **8344** | — | — |
| 3 Dr GL Hbk | **9016** | — | — |

## 1991

### COLT 4

| | | | |
|---|---|---|---|
| 3 Dr Hbk (NA w/pwr strng) | **7919** | 3950 | 4850 |
| 3 Dr GL Hbk | **8815** | 4700 | 5625 |

NOTE: Power brakes standard on all models.

## 1990

### COLT 4

| | | | |
|---|---|---|---|
| 3 Dr Hbk (NA w/pwr strng) | **7590** | 2775 | 3675 |
| 3 Dr GL Hbk | **9297** | 3400 | 4300 |
| 3 Dr GT Hbk | **10482** | 4000 | 4900 |

129

| Year/Model/Body/Type | Original List | Current Whlse | Average Retail |
|---|---|---|---|
| 5 Dr 2WD DL Wgn | **10823** | 4550 | 5475 |
| 5 Dr 4WD DL Wgn | **12393** | 4825 | 5750 |

NOTE: Power brakes standard on all models.

## 1989

### COLT 4

| | | | |
|---|---|---|---|
| 3 Dr Hbk (NA w/pwr strng) | **6951** | 1875 | 2725 |
| 3 Dr E Hbk | **8037** | 2425 | 3300 |
| 3 Dr GT Hbk | **9420** | 3100 | 4000 |
| 5 Dr 2WD DL Wgn | **9848** | 3425 | 4325 |
| 5 Dr 4WD DL Wgn | **11418** | 3725 | 4625 |

*ADD FOR:*

| | | | |
|---|---|---|---|
| Cast Aluminum Wheels | **299** | 80 | 90 |

NOTE: Power brakes standard on all models.

## 1988

### COLT 4

| | | | |
|---|---|---|---|
| 3 Dr Hbk | **6148** | 625 | 1175 |
| 3 Dr E Hbk | **6845** | 1150 | 1875 |
| 4 Dr E Sdn | **8014** | 1325 | 2050 |
| 3 Dr DL Hbk | **8098** | 1600 | 2450 |
| 4 Dr DL Sdn | **8466** | 1775 | 2625 |
| 5 Dr DL Wgn | **9018** | 1900 | 2750 |
| 4 Dr Premier Sdn | **9386** | 2200 | 3050 |

*ADD FOR:*

| | | | |
|---|---|---|---|
| DL Turbo Pkg | **1271** | 330 | 360 |
| Turbo Pkg (Premier) | **748** | 210 | 230 |

NOTE: Power brakes standard on all models.

## 1987

### COLT 4

| | | | |
|---|---|---|---|
| 3 Dr Hbk | **5949** | 750 | 1475 |
| 4 Dr Sdn | **7421** | 850 | 1550 |
| 3 Dr DL Hbk | **7255** | 1150 | 1875 |
| 4 Dr DL Sdn | **7733** | 1250 | 1975 |
| 4 Dr Premier Sdn | **8706** | 1700 | 2550 |

*ADD FOR:*

| | | | |
|---|---|---|---|
| DL Turbo Pkg | **1248** | 270 | 300 |
| Premier Turbo Pkg | **720** | 160 | 180 |

NOTE: Power brakes standard on all models.

## 1986

### COLT 4

| | | | |
|---|---|---|---|
| 3 Dr E Hbk | **5727** | 625 | 1175 |
| 4 Dr E Sdn | **6627** | 725 | 1375 |
| 3 Dr DL Hbk | **6604** | 975 | 1700 |
| 4 Dr DL Sdn | **6956** | 1075 | 1800 |

| Year/Model/Body/Type | Original List | Current Whlse | Average Retail |
|---|---|---|---|
| 4 Dr Premier Sdn | **7893** | 1425 | 2175 |

*ADD FOR:*

| | | | |
|---|---|---|---|
| GTS Turbo Pkg (DL) | **1375** | 210 | 230 |
| Premier Turbo Pkg (Premier Sdn) | **664** | 160 | 180 |

NOTE: Power brakes standard on all models.

## 1985

### COLT 4

| | | | |
|---|---|---|---|
| 3 Dr E Hbk | **5462** | 425 | 775 |
| 5 Dr E Hbk | **6119** | 525 | 975 |
| 3 Dr DL Hbk | **6267** | 775 | 1500 |
| 4 Dr DL Sdn | **6582** | 875 | 1600 |
| 4 Dr Premier Sdn | **7499** | 1175 | 1900 |

*ADD FOR:*

| | | | |
|---|---|---|---|
| GTS Pkg (DL) | **512** | 60 | 60 |
| GTS Turbo Pkg (DL) | **1580** | 150 | 160 |
| Turbo Pkg (Premier) | **949** | 100 | 110 |
| Technica Pkg (Premier) | **690** | 70 | 80 |

## 1984

### COLT 4

| | | | |
|---|---|---|---|
| 3 Dr E Hbk | **5085** | 150 | 350 |
| 5 Dr E Hbk | **5729** | 225 | 475 |
| 3 Dr DL Hbk | **5983** | 350 | 625 |
| 5 Dr DL Hbk | **6119** | 425 | 775 |

## 1983 — ALL BODY STYLES

| | | | |
|---|---|---|---|
| COLT 4 | — | 200 | 400 |

## CONQUEST

## 1989

### CONQUEST 4

| | | | |
|---|---|---|---|
| 2 Dr TSi Lftbk | **19929** | 5700 | 6625 |

*ADD FOR:*

| | | | |
|---|---|---|---|
| Leather Seat Trim | **372** | 210 | 230 |

NOTE: Power brakes, power door locks, tinted glass, pwr strng and power windows standard.

## 1988

### CONQUEST 4

| | | | |
|---|---|---|---|
| 2 Dr Lftbk | **18683** | 3800 | 4700 |

*ADD FOR:*

| | | | |
|---|---|---|---|
| Leather Seat Trim | **542** | 180 | 200 |

NOTE: Power brakes, power door locks, pwr strng and power windows standard.

# FOREIGN CARS & TRUCKS

| Year/Model/ Body/Type | Original List | Current Whlse | Average Retail |
|---|---|---|---|
| **1987** | | | |
| **CONQUEST 4** | | | |
| 2 Dr Lftbk | **14417** | 3125 | 4025 |
| *ADD FOR:* | | | |
| TSi Intercooler Pkg | **2757** | 580 | 650 |
| NOTE: Power brakes, power door locks, pwr strng and power windows standard. | | | |
| **1986** | | | |
| **CONQUEST 4** | | | |
| 2 Dr Lftbk | **13837** | 1775 | 2625 |
| *ADD FOR:* | | | |
| Technica Pkg | **346** | 60 | 70 |
| NOTE: Pwr strng, power windows/power brakes standard. | | | |
| **1985** | | | |
| **CONQUEST 4** | | | |
| 2 Dr Lftbk | **12564** | 1225 | 1950 |
| NOTE: Pwr strng, power windows/power brakes standard. | | | |
| **1984** | | | |
| **CONQUEST 4** | | | |
| 2 Dr Lftbk | **12149** | 950 | 1675 |

## DAIHATSU

| Year/Model/ Body/Type | Original List | Current Whlse | Average Retail |
|---|---|---|---|
| **1992** | | | |
| **CHARADE (1.0 LITER) 3** | | | |
| 3 Dr SE Hbk (5 spd) (NA w/pwr strng) | **7751** | 5100 | 6025 |
| **CHARADE (1.3 LITER) 4** | | | |
| 3 Dr SE Hbk (5 spd) | **8710** | 5925 | 6850 |
| 4 Dr SE Sdn (5 spd) | **10010** | 5725 | 6650 |
| 4 Dr SX Sdn (auto) | **10951** | — | — |
| **ROCKY 4** | | | |
| 4WD SE Sport Soft Top | **12972** | — | — |
| 4WD SE Spt Hard Top | **13772** | — | — |
| 4WD SX Spt Hard Top | **14772** | — | — |
| *ADD FOR:* | | | |
| Soft Top Conversion Kit (Hardtop) | **387** | — | — |
| Alloy Wheels | **550** | — | — |
| NOTE: Manual sunroof standard on Rocky. Tilt steering wheel standard on Rocky SX. | | | |

| Year/Model/ Body/Type | Original List | Current Whlse | Average Retail |
|---|---|---|---|
| **1991** | | | |
| **CHARADE (1.0 LITER) 3** | | | |
| 3 Dr SE Hbk (NA w/pwr strng) | **7705** | 3775 | 4675 |
| **CHARADE (1.3 LITER) 3** | | | |
| 3 Dr SE Hbk (auto) | **9005** | 4325 | 5250 |
| 4 Dr SE Sdn (5 spd) | **9875** | 4325 | 5250 |
| 4 Dr SX Sdn (auto) | **11075** | 5075 | 6000 |
| **ROCKY 4** | | | |
| 4WD SE Sport Soft Top | **12761** | 7500 | 8700 |
| 4WD SE Sport Hard Top | **13561** | 7650 | 8875 |
| 4WD Full-Time SE Sport Hard Top | **13981** | 7800 | 9050 |
| 4WD SX Sport Hard Top | **14461** | 8025 | 9275 |
| *ADD FOR:* | | | |
| SX Plus Pkg (Rocky) | **1385** | 470 | 520 |
| NOTE: Power brakes standard on all models. Sunroof standard on Rocky. | | | |
| **1990** | | | |
| **CHARADE (1.0 LITER) 3** | | | |
| 3 Dr SE Hbk (NA w/pwr strng) | **7757** | 2825 | 3725 |
| 3 Dr SX Hbk (NA w/pwr strng) | **8257** | 3100 | 4000 |
| **CHARADE (1.3 LITER) 3** | | | |
| 3 Dr SE Hbk (auto) | **8948** | 3475 | 4375 |
| 4 Dr SE Sdn (5 spd) | **9598** | 2925 | 3825 |
| 3 Dr SX Hbk (5 spd) | **8948** | 2700 | 3600 |
| 4 Dr SX Sdn (5 spd) | **10131** | 3175 | 4075 |
| **ROCKY 4** | | | |
| 4WD SE Sport Soft Top | **12172** | 6100 | 7100 |
| 4WD SE Sport Hard Top | **12972** | 6275 | 7300 |
| 4WD SX Sport Soft Top | **12872** | 6400 | 7450 |
| 4WD SX Sport Hard Top | **13772** | 6550 | 7625 |
| *ADD FOR:* | | | |
| SX Plus Pkg (Rocky SX) | **1220** | 330 | 360 |
| NOTE: Power brakes standard on all models. | | | |
| **1989** | | | |
| **1CHARADE (1.0 LITER) 3** | | | |
| 3 Dr CES Hbk (NA w/pwr strng) | **7157** | 2100 | 2950 |

| Year/Model/Body/Type | Original List | Current Whlse | Average Retail |
|---|---|---|---|
| 3 Dr CLS Hbk (NA w/pwr strng) | **7657** | 2300 | 3175 |
| 3 Dr CLX Hbk (NA w/pwr strng) | **8457** | 2525 | 3400 |
| CHARADE (1.3 LITER) 3 | | | |
| 3 Dr CLS Hbk | **8298** | 2425 | 3300 |
| 3 Dr CLX Hbk | **9617** | 2675 | 3575 |

NOTE: Power brakes standard on all models.

## 1988

### 1CHARADE 3

| | | | |
|---|---|---|---|
| 3 Dr CLS Hbk | **6397** | 1275 | 2000 |
| 3 Dr CLX Hbk w/o auto restraint | **7650** | 1425 | 2175 |
| 3 Dr CLX Hbk w/auto restraint | **7725** | 1450 | 2225 |
| 3 Dr CSX Hbk | **9232** | 1825 | 2675 |

NOTE: Power brakes standard on all models. Air conditioning standard on CSX.

## DODGE D-50

### 1984

#### 2WD D-50 4

| | | | |
|---|---|---|---|
| Custom Pickup | **5767** | 975 | 1700 |
| Royal Pickup | **6290** | 1050 | 1775 |
| Sport Pickup | **7018** | 1100 | 1825 |

### 1983

#### 2WD D-50 4

| | | | |
|---|---|---|---|
| Base Pickup | **5754** | 675 | 1275 |
| Custom Pickup | **6266** | 800 | 1500 |
| Royal Pickup | **7135** | 825 | 1525 |
| Sport Pickup | **7732** | 875 | 1600 |

## GEO

### 1992

#### METRO 3

| | | | |
|---|---|---|---|
| 2 Dr XFi Hbk Cpe (NA w/pwr strng or air cond) | **7300** | 4875 | 5800 |
| 2 Dr Hbk Cpe (NA w/pwr strng) | **8020** | 5100 | 6025 |
| 4 Dr Hbk Sdn (NA w/pwr strng) | **8420** | 5200 | 6125 |
| 2 Dr LSi Hbk Cpe (NA w/pwr strng) | **9220** | 5650 | 6575 |

| Year/Model/Body/Type | Original List | Current Whlse | Average Retail |
|---|---|---|---|
| 4 Dr LSi Hbk Sdn (NA w/pwr strng) | **9620** | 5725 | 6650 |
| 2 Dr LSi Conv (NA w/pwr strng) | **11020** | 7125 | 8275 |

#### RIZM 4

| | | | |
|---|---|---|---|
| 4 Dr Sdn | **11010** | 7550 | 8775 |
| 4 Dr GSi Sdn | **13770** | 8800 | 10175 |

#### TORM 4

| | | | |
|---|---|---|---|
| 3 Dr 2+2 Sport Cpe | **12075** | 7575 | 8800 |
| 3 Dr Hbk Cpe | **12845** | 7525 | 8725 |
| 3 Dr GSi Sport Cpe | **14045** | 8825 | 10200 |

#### TRACKER 4

| | | | |
|---|---|---|---|
| 4WD 2 Dr HT | **13222** | 9475 | 10925 |
| 4WD 2 Dr LSi HT | **14522** | — | — |
| 2WD 2 Dr Conv | **11017** | 8025 | 9275 |
| 4WD 2 Dr Conv | **12822** | 9325 | 10750 |
| 4WD 2 Dr LSi Conv | **13620** | — | — |

NOTE: Tilt steering wheel standard on Prizm.

### 1991

#### METRO 3

| | | | |
|---|---|---|---|
| 2 Dr XFi Hbk Cpe (NA w/pwr strng) | **7096** | 3850 | 4750 |
| 2 Dr Hbk Cpe (NA w/pwr strng) | **7816** | 4050 | 4950 |
| 4 Dr Hbk Sdn (NA w/pwr strng) | **8016** | 4150 | 5075 |
| 2 Dr LSi Hbk Cpe (NA w/pwr strng) | **8816** | 4450 | 5375 |
| 4 Dr LSi Hbk Sdn (NA w/pwr strng) | **9016** | 4550 | 5475 |
| 2 Dr LSi Conv (NA w/pwr strng) | **10901** | 5925 | 6850 |

#### PRIZM 4

| | | | |
|---|---|---|---|
| 4 Dr Ntchbk Sdn | **10565** | 6375 | 7425 |
| 5 Dr Hbk Sdn | **11180** | 6500 | 7575 |
| 4 Dr GSi Ntchbk Sdn | **12940** | 7375 | 8550 |
| 5 Dr GSi Hbk Sdn | **13440** | 7475 | 8675 |

#### STORM 4

| | | | |
|---|---|---|---|
| 3 Dr 2+2 Sport Cpe | **11415** | 6425 | 7475 |
| 2 Dr Hbk Cpe | **12195** | 6375 | 7425 |
| 3 Dr GSi Sport Cpe | **13140** | 7450 | 8650 |

#### TRACKER 4

| | | | |
|---|---|---|---|
| 4WD 2 Dr HT | **12607** | 8075 | 9325 |
| 4WD 2 Dr LSi HT | **13907** | 8825 | 10200 |
| 2WD 2 Dr Conv | **10321** | 6725 | 7825 |
| 4WD 2 Dr Conv | **12207** | 7925 | 9200 |
| 4WD 2 Dr LSi Conv | **13317** | 8625 | 9950 |

NOTE: Power brakes standard on all models.

*1990 Honda Accord EX Coupe*

| Year/Model/Body/Type | Original List | Current Whlse | Average Retail |
|---|---|---|---|
| **1990** | | | |
| **METRO 3** | | | |
| 2 Dr XFi Hbk Cpe (NA w/pwr strng) | **6966** | 2025 | 2875 |
| 2 Dr Hbk Cpe (NA w/pwr strng) | **7666** | 2225 | 3075 |
| 4 Dr Hbk Sdn (NA w/pwr strng) | **7966** | 2275 | 3150 |
| 2 Dr LSi Hbk Cpe (NA w/pwr strng) | **8466** | 2575 | 3450 |
| 4 Dr LSi Hbk Sdn (NA w/pwr strng) | **8766** | 2675 | 3575 |
| **PRIZM 4** | | | |
| 4 Dr Ntchbk Sdn | **11424** | 4775 | 5700 |
| 5 Dr Hbk Sdn | **11724** | 4850 | 5775 |
| 4 Dr GSi Ntchbk Sdn | **12590** | 5550 | 6475 |
| 5 Dr GSi Hbk Sdn | **12975** | 5675 | 6600 |
| **STORM 4** | | | |
| 3 Dr 2+2 Sport Cpe | **11080** | 4925 | 5850 |
| 3 Dr GSi Sport Cpe | **12340** | 5800 | 6725 |
| **TRACKER 4** | | | |
| 2 Dr | **12307** | 6700 | 7800 |
| 2 Dr LSi | **13215** | 7175 | 8325 |
| 2 Dr Conv | **11997** | 6575 | 7650 |
| 2 Dr LSi Conv | **12765** | 7025 | 8150 |

NOTE: Power brakes standard on all models.

## 1989

### METRO 3

2 Dr Hbk Cpe

| Year/Model/Body/Type | Original List | Current Whlse | Average Retail |
|---|---|---|---|
| (NA w/pwr strng) | **6296** | 1550 | 2400 |
| 2 Dr LSi Hbk Cpe | **7851** | 1900 | 2750 |
| 4 Dr LSi Hbk Sdn | **8151** | 2000 | 2850 |
| **SPECTRUM 4** | | | |
| 2 Dr Hbk Cpe | **8256** | 2475 | 3350 |
| 4 Dr Ntchbk Sdn | **8756** | 4000 | 4900 |
| **TRACKER 4** | | | |
| 2 Dr HT (NA w/power steering) | **10796** | 5025 | 5950 |
| 2 Dr Conv (NA w/power steering) | **10496** | 4875 | 5800 |
| 2 Dr LSi Hbk Cpe (NA w/pwr strng) | **12796** | 5650 | 6575 |

## HONDA

### 1992

#### ACCORD 4

| | | | |
|---|---|---|---|
| 2 Dr DX Cpe (5 spd) | **14800** | 11025 | 12725 |
| 4 Dr DX Sdn (5 spd) | **15000** | 11325 | 13075 |
| 2 Dr LX Cpe (5 spd) | **15900** | 12100 | 13975 |
| 4 Dr LX Sdn (5 spd) | **16100** | 12400 | 14500 |
| 5 Dr LX Wgn (5 spd) | **17725** | 13200 | 15525 |
| 2 Dr EX Cpe (5 spd) | **18320** | 13600 | 15975 |
| 4 Dr EX Sdn (5 spd) | **18520** | 13900 | 16275 |
| 5 Dr EX Wgn (5 spd) | **20175** | 14675 | 17225 |
| **CIVIC 4** | | | |
| 3 Dr CX Hbk (5 spd) | **9400** | — | — |
| 3 Dr DX Hbk (5 spd) | **11150** | 8050 | 9300 |

| Year/Model/ Body/Type | Original List | Current Whlse | Average Retail |
|---|---|---|---|
| 4 Dr DX Sdn (5 spd) | **12055** | 8825 | 10200 |
| 3 Dr VX Hbk (5 spd) | **11850** | — | — |
| 3 Dr Si Hbk (5 spd) | **13200** | — | — |
| 4 Dr LX Sdn (5 spd) | **12885** | 9375 | 10800 |
| 4 Dr EX Sdn (5 spd) | **15075** | 10250 | 11825 |

### PRELUDE 4

| | | | |
|---|---|---|---|
| 2 Dr S Cpe (5 spd) | **17950** | — | — |
| 2 Dr Si Cpe (5 spd) | **19550** | — | — |
| 2 Dr Si 4WS Cpe (5 spd) | **21870** | — | — |

NOTE: Power windows standard on Civic LX, EX & Si, Accord LX, EX & Prelude. Power door locks standard on Civic LX & EX, Accord LX & EX, Prelude Si. Power sunroof standard on Prelude. Power moonroof standard on Civic EX & Si, Accord EX. Tilt steering wheel standard on Civic DX, LX, EX & Si, Accord and Prelude. Cruise control standard on Civic LX, EX & Si, Accord LX & EX and Prelude.

## 1991

### ACCORD 4

| | | | |
|---|---|---|---|
| 2 Dr DX Cpe (5 spd) | **14025** | 9500 | 10950 |
| 4 Dr DX Sdn (5 spd) | **14225** | 9800 | 11300 |
| 2 Dr LX Cpe (5 spd) | **15175** | 10425 | 12025 |
| 4 Dr LX Sdn (5 spd) | **15375** | 10725 | 12375 |
| 5 Dr LX Wgn (5 spd) | **17400** | 11500 | 13275 |
| 2 Dr EX Cpe (5 spd) | **16895** | 11775 | 13600 |
| 4 Dr EX Sdn (5 spd) | **17095** | 12050 | 13925 |
| 5 Dr EX Wgn (5 spd) | **19150** | 12825 | 15150 |
| 4 Dr SE Sdn (auto) | **19895** | 13475 | 15800 |

### CIVIC 4

| | | | |
|---|---|---|---|
| 3 Dr Hbk (4 spd) | **8295** | 5300 | 6225 |
| 4 Dr Wgn (5 spd) | **11780** | 7425 | 8625 |
| 4 Dr 4WD Wgn (6 spd) | **13865** | 8175 | 9450 |
| 3 Dr DX Hbk (5 spd) | **10120** | 6900 | 8025 |
| 4 Dr DX Sdn (5 spd) | **10945** | 7600 | 8825 |
| 4 Dr LX Sdn (5 spd) | **11955** | 8100 | 9350 |
| 4 Dr EX Sdn (5 spd) | **12650** | 8500 | 9825 |
| 3 Dr Si Hbk (5 spd) | **11670** | 7550 | 8775 |

### CRX 4

| | | | |
|---|---|---|---|
| 2 Dr HF Hbk (5 spd) | **10600** | 7325 | 8500 |
| 2 Dr Hbk (5 spd) | **10865** | 7650 | 8875 |
| 2 Dr Si Hbk (5 spd) | **12605** | 8575 | 9900 |

### PRELUDE 4

| | | | |
|---|---|---|---|
| 2 Dr 2.0 Si Cpe (5 spd) | **16595** | 11625 | 13425 |
| 2 Dr Si High-Output Cpe (5 spd) | **17445** | 12275 | 14225 |
| 2 Dr Si High-Output Cpe w/4 Wheel Steering (5 spd) | **18750** | 12775 | 15100 |
| 2 Dr Si High-Output Cpe w/Anti-Lock Brakes (5 spd) | **19000** | 12825 | 15150 |

NOTE: Power brakes standard on all models. Power

windows and power door locks standard on Accord LX and EX, Civic LX Sedan and EX and Prelude Si High-Output. Sunroof standard on Accord EX, Civic Si Hatchback and CRX Si. Power moonroof standard on Prelude.

## 1990

### ACCORD 4

| | | | |
|---|---|---|---|
| 2 Dr DX Cpe (5 spd) | **13645** | 8150 | 9425 |
| 4 Dr DX Sdn (5 spd) | **13845** | 8450 | 9750 |
| 2 Dr LX Cpe (5 spd) | **14695** | 8850 | 10225 |
| 4 Dr LX Sdn (5 spd) | **14895** | 9150 | 10550 |
| 2 Dr EX Cpe (5 spd) | **16395** | 9925 | 11425 |
| 4 Dr EX Sdn (5 spd) | **16595** | 10175 | 11750 |

### CIVIC 4

| | | | |
|---|---|---|---|
| 3 Dr Hbk (4 spd) | **7935** | 4550 | 5475 |
| 4 Dr Wgn (5 spd) | **11625** | 5975 | 6900 |
| 3 Dr DX Hbk (5 spd) | **9995** | 5475 | 6400 |
| 4 Dr DX Sdn (5 spd) | **10740** | 6150 | 7150 |
| 4 Dr LX Sdn (5 spd) | **11750** | 6650 | 7750 |
| 4 Dr Si Sdn (5 spd) | **12445** | 7000 | 8150 |
| 3 Dr Si Hbk (5 spd) | **11545** | 6125 | 7125 |
| 4 Dr 4WD Wgn (6 spd) | **13710** | 6650 | 7750 |

### CRX 4

| | | | |
|---|---|---|---|
| 2 Dr HF Hbk (5 spd) | **10445** | 5875 | 6800 |
| 2 Dr Hbk (5 spd) | **10710** | 6200 | 7225 |
| 2 Dr Si Hbk (5 spd) | **12430** | 6875 | 8000 |

### PRELUDE

| | | | |
|---|---|---|---|
| 2 Dr 2.0 S Cpe (5 spd) | **15145** | 8900 | 10275 |
| 2 Dr 2.0 Si Cpe (5 spd) | **16145** | 9400 | 10825 |
| 2 Dr Si Cpe (5 spd) | **16965** | 9975 | 11500 |
| 2 Dr Si Cpe w/4 Wheel Steering (5 spd) | **18450** | 10400 | 12000 |
| 2 Dr Si Cpe w/Anti-Lock Brakes (5 spd) | **18550** | 10375 | 11975 |

NOTE: Power brakes standard on all models. Power windows standard on Civic LX and EX, Prelude Si High-Output and Prelude Si High-Output w/4 wheel steering. Power door locks standard on Civic LX & EX and Prelude Si High-Output w/4 wheel steering. Sunroof standard on CRX Si. Moonroof standard on Civic Si and Prelude. Anti-lock brakes standard on Prelude Si High-Output w/anti-lock brakes.

## 1989

### ACCORD 4

| | | | |
|---|---|---|---|
| 3 Dr DX Hbk (5 spd) | **12230** | 6375 | 7425 |
| 4 Dr DX Sdn (5 spd) | **12770** | 7100 | 8250 |
| 2 Dr DX Cpe (5 spd) | **12650** | 6500 | 7750 |
| 4 Dr LX Sdn (5 spd) | **14180** | 7475 | 8675 |
| 3 Dr LXi Hbk (5 spd) | **14530** | 7500 | 8700 |
| 4 Dr LXi Sdn (5 spd) | **15920** | 8525 | 9850 |

| Year/Model/ Body/Type | Original List | Current Whlse | Average Retail |
|---|---|---|---|
| 2 Dr LXi Cpe (5 spd) | **14690** | 8000 | 9300 |
| 2 Dr SEi Cpe (5 spd) | **16975** | 8725 | 10075 |
| 4 Dr SEi Sdn (5 spd) | **17985** | 9225 | 10625 |

### CIVIC 4

| | | | |
|---|---|---|---|
| 3 Dr 1.5 Hbk (4 spd) | **7185** | 3775 | 4675 |
| 4 Dr 1.5 Wgn (5 spd) | **10925** | 5000 | 5925 |
| 4 Dr 1.5 Wagovan (5 spd) | **10645** | 4700 | 5625 |
| 4 Dr 1.6 4WD Wgn (6 spd) | **13010** | 5700 | 6625 |
| 3 Dr 1.5 DX Hbk (5 spd) | **9245** | 4600 | 5525 |
| 4 Dr 1.5 DX Sdn (5 spd) | **9990** | 5175 | 6100 |
| 3 Dr 1.6 Si Hbk (5 spd) | **10780** | 5150 | 6075 |
| 4 Dr 1.5 LX Sdn (5 spd) | **10950** | 5725 | 6650 |

### CRX 4

| | | | |
|---|---|---|---|
| 2 Dr 1.5 HF Hbk (5 spd) | **9695** | 5050 | 5975 |
| 2 Dr 1.5 Hbk (5 spd) | **10110** | 5325 | 6250 |
| 2 Dr 1.6 Si Hbk (5 spd) | **11730** | 5975 | 6900 |

### PRELUDE 4

| | | | |
|---|---|---|---|
| 2 Dr 2.0 S Cpe (5 spd) | **14945** | 7550 | 8775 |
| 2 Dr 2.0 Si Cpe (5 spd) | **16965** | 8400 | 9700 |
| 2 Dr 2.0 4WS Si Cpe (5 spd) | **18450** | 8800 | 10175 |

NOTE: Power brakes standard on all models. Sunroof standard on CRX Si. Moonroof standard on Civic Si Hatchback, Accord LXi Sedan & SEi Sedan and Prelude. Power windows standard on Civic LX Sedan, Prelude Si, Accord LXi Hatchback, Accord LXi Coupe and Accord LX Sedan. Power locks standard on Civic LX Sedan, Accord LX Sedan and Prelude Si 4WS.

## 1988

### ACCORD 4

| | | | |
|---|---|---|---|
| 3 Dr DX Hbk (5 spd) | **11270** | 4150 | 5075 |
| 4 Dr DX Sdn (5 spd) | **11800** | 4825 | 5750 |
| 4 Dr LX Sdn (5 spd) | **14165** | 5300 | 6325 |
| 3 Dr LXi Hbk (5 spd) | **14510** | 5225 | 6150 |
| 4 Dr LXi Sdn (5 spd) | **15880** | 6275 | 7200 |

### CIVIC 4

| | | | |
|---|---|---|---|
| 3 Dr 1.5 Hbk (4 spd) | **6515** | 2350 | 3225 |
| 4 Dr 1.5 Wgn (5 spd) | **9948** | 3400 | 4300 |
| 4 Dr 1.5 Wagovan (5 spd) | **9698** | 3025 | 3925 |
| 4 Dr 1.6 4WD Wgn (6 spd) | **11998** | 4000 | 4900 |
| 3 Dr 1.5 DX Hbk (5 spd) | **8540** | 3050 | 3950 |

| Year/Model/ Body/Type | Original List | Current Whlse | Average Retail |
|---|---|---|---|
| 4 Dr 1.5 DX Sdn (5 spd) | **9325** | 3575 | 4475 |
| 4 Dr 1.5 LX Sdn (5 spd) | **10280** | 4000 | 4900 |

### CRX 4

| | | | |
|---|---|---|---|
| 3 Dr 1.5 HF Hbk (5 spd) | **8985** | 3500 | 4400 |
| 3 Dr 1.5 DX Hbk (5 spd) | **9315** | 3725 | 4625 |
| 3 Dr 1.5 Si Hbk (5 spd) | **10950** | 4300 | 5225 |

### PRELUDE 4

| | | | |
|---|---|---|---|
| 2 Dr 2.0 S Cpe (5 spd) | **13870** | 5600 | 6600 |
| 2 Dr 2.0 Si Cpe (5 spd) | **17025** | 6825 | 8550 |
| 2 Dr 2.0 4WS Cpe (5 spd) | **18355** | 7150 | 8875 |

NOTE: Power brakes standard on all models. Pwr strng on Accord and Prelude Series. Power windows standard on Civic LX, Accord LX and LXi and Prelude Si. Power sunroof standard on Civic CRX Si. Power moonroof standard on Accord LXi Sedan and Prelude S. Air conditioning standard on Accord LX and LXi and Prelude Si. Power door locks standard on Accord LXi Sedan and LX.

## 1987

### ACCORD 4

| | | | |
|---|---|---|---|
| 3 Dr DX Hbk (5 spd) | **10120** | 3175 | 4075 |
| 4 Dr DX Sdn (5 spd) | **10795** | 3750 | 4650 |
| 4 Dr LX Sdn (5 spd) | **12998** | 4475 | 5400 |
| 3 Dr LXi Hbk (5 spd) | **13160** | 3900 | 4800 |
| 4 Dr LXi Sdn (5 spd) | **14680** | 4650 | 5575 |

### CIVIC 4

| | | | |
|---|---|---|---|
| 3 Dr 1.3 Std Hbk (4 spd) | **5849** | 1600 | 2450 |
| 4 Dr 1.5 Sdn (5 spd) | **8580** | 2475 | 3350 |
| 4 Dr 1.5 Wgn (5 spd) | **8455** | 2300 | 3175 |
| 4 Dr 1.5 Wagovan (5 spd) | **8200** | 2200 | 3050 |
| 4 Dr 1.5 4WD Wgn (6 spd) | **9895** | 2850 | 3750 |
| 3 Dr 1.5 DX Hbk (5 spd) | **7599** | 2050 | 2900 |
| 3 Dr 1.5 Si Hbk (5 spd) | **9035** | 2500 | 3375 |

### CRX 4

| | | | |
|---|---|---|---|
| 2 Dr 1.5 HF Cpe (5 spd) | **7759** | 2425 | 3300 |
| 2 Dr 1.5 Cpe (5 spd) | **8095** | 2625 | 3525 |
| 2 Dr 1.5 Si Cpe (5 spd) | **9539** | 3125 | 4025 |

### PRELUDE 4

| | | | |
|---|---|---|---|
| 2 Dr 1.8 Cpe (5 spd) | **12230** | 4625 | 5550 |
| 2 Dr 2.0 Si Cpe (5 spd) | **15245** | 5650 | 6575 |

*Refer to optional equipment schedules*

| Year/Model/Body/Type | Original List | Current Whlse | Average Retail |
|---|---|---|---|

NOTE: Power brakes standard on all models. Power windows and air conditioning standard on Accord LX and Prelude Si. Power door locks standard on Accord LX and LXi Sedan. Pwr strng standard on Civic Automatic Sedan, Civic Wagon, Accord Series and Prelude Series. Sunroof standard on CRX Si. Moonroof standard on Civic Si, Prelude and Accord LXi Sedan.

## 1986

### ACCORD 4

| | Original List | Current Whlse | Average Retail |
|---|---|---|---|
| 3 Dr DX Hbk (5 spd) | 9195 | 2550 | 3425 |
| 3 Dr LXi Hbk (5 spd) | 12115 | 3225 | 4125 |
| 4 Dr DX Sdn (5 spd) | 9998 | 3100 | 4000 |
| 4 Dr LX Sdn (5 spd) | 11979 | 3600 | 4500 |
| 4 Dr LXi Sdn (5 spd) | 13727 | 4025 | 4925 |

### CIVIC 4

| | | | |
|---|---|---|---|
| 3 Dr 1.3 Std Hbk (4 spd) | 5698 | 1125 | 1850 |
| 3 Dr 1.5 DX Hbk (5 spd) | 7094 | 1525 | 2375 |
| 3 Dr 1.5 Si Hbk (5 spd) | 8529 | 1925 | 2775 |
| 4 Dr 1.5 Wgn (5 spd) | 7884 | 1750 | 2600 |
| 4 Dr 1.5 4WD Wgn (6 spd) | 9239 | 2200 | 3050 |
| 4 Dr 1.5 Sdn (5 spd) | 7993 | 1900 | 2750 |
| 4 Dr Wagovan (5 spd) | 7619 | 1775 | 2625 |

### CRX 4

| | | | |
|---|---|---|---|
| 2 Dr 1.3 HF Cpe (5 spd) | 7198 | 1875 | 2725 |
| 2 Dr 1.5 Cpe (5 spd) | 7523 | 2050 | 2900 |
| 2 Dr 1.5 Si Cpe (5 spd) | 8865 | 2450 | 3325 |

### PRELUDE 4

| | | | |
|---|---|---|---|
| 2 Dr 1.8 Cpe (5 spd) | 11365 | 3375 | 4275 |
| 2 Dr 2.0 Si Cpe (5 spd) | 14079 | 4225 | 5150 |

NOTE: Power locks standard on Accord LX & LXi Sedan. Pwr strng standard on Accord and Prelude. Power brakes standard on Accord, Civic, CRX and Prelude. Power windows standard on Accord LXi Hatchback, Accord LX Sedan, Accord LXi Sedan and Prelude Si. Air conditioning standard on Accord LX and LXi and Prelude Si. Moonroof standard on Accord LXi Sedan, Civic Si and Prelude Si. Sunroof standard on CRX Si.

## 1985

### ACCORD 4

| | | | |
|---|---|---|---|
| 3 Dr Hbk (5 spd) | 7895 | 1900 | 2750 |
| 3 Dr LX Hbk (5 spd) | 9095 | 2100 | 2950 |
| 4 Dr Base Sdn (5 spd) | 8845 | 2350 | 3225 |
| 4 Dr LX Sdn (5 spd) | 10295 | 2550 | 3425 |
| 4 Dr SE-i (5 spd) | 12945 | 2925 | 3825 |

### CIVIC 4

| | | | |
|---|---|---|---|
| 2 Dr CRX Si Cpe (5 spd) | 7999 | 2150 | 3000 |
| 2 Dr CRX HF Cpe (5 spd) | 6479 | 1725 | 2575 |
| 2 Dr CRX Cpe (5 spd) | 6855 | 1825 | 2675 |
| 3 Dr Base Hbk | 5399 | 1075 | 1800 |
| 3 Dr DX Hbk (5 spd) | 6529 | 1350 | 2100 |

| Year/Model/Body/Type | Original List | Current Whlse | Average Retail |
|---|---|---|---|
| 3 Dr S Hbk (5 spd) | 7129 | 1675 | 2525 |
| 5 Dr Wgn (5 spd) | 7195 | 1550 | 2400 |
| 5 Dr 4WD Wgn (6 spd) | 8649 | 1950 | 2800 |
| 4 Dr Sdn (5 spd) | 7295 | 1700 | 2550 |

### PRELUDE 4

| | Original List | Current Whlse | Average Retail |
|---|---|---|---|
| 2 Dr Cpe (5 spd) | 10345 | 2975 | 3875 |

NOTE: Pwr strng standard on Accord LX Hatchback, Accord Base Sedan and Prelude. Air conditioning standard on Accord LX Sedan and Accord SE-i. Power windows standard on Accord LX Sedan. Moonroof standard on Accord SE-i and Prelude.

## 1984

### ACCORD 4

| | | | |
|---|---|---|---|
| 3 Dr Hbk (5 spd) | 7699 | 1400 | 2150 |
| 4 Dr Sdn (5 spd) | 8549 | 1700 | 2550 |
| 3 Dr LX Hbk (5 spd) | 8849 | 1525 | 2375 |
| 4 Dr LX Sdn (5 spd) | 9949 | 1800 | 2650 |

### CIVIC 4

| | | | |
|---|---|---|---|
| 2 Dr 1.3 CRX Cpe | 6149 | 950 | 1625 |
| 2 Dr 1.5 CRX Cpe | 6599 | 1250 | 1975 |
| 3 Dr Base Hbk | 5249 | 650 | 1225 |
| 3 Dr 1.5 DX Hbk | 6299 | 900 | 1625 |
| 3 Dr 1.5 S Hbk | 6849 | 1050 | 1775 |
| 5 Dr 1.5 Wgn | 6999 | 1050 | 1775 |
| 4 Dr 1.5 Sdn | 7099 | 1200 | 1925 |

### PRELUDE 4

| | | | |
|---|---|---|---|
| 2 Dr Cpe (5 spd) | 9995 | 2525 | 3400 |

## 1983 — ALL BODY STYLES

| | | | |
|---|---|---|---|
| ACCORD | — | 1175 | 1900 |
| ACCORD SEDAN | — | 1325 | 2050 |
| CIVIC 1300 | — | 425 | 775 |
| CIVIC 1500 | — | 700 | 1325 |
| PRELUDE | — | 1975 | 2825 |

## HYUNDAI

## 1992

### ELANTRA 4

| | | | |
|---|---|---|---|
| 4 Dr Base Sdn (5 spd) | 10125 | 6775 | 7875 |
| 4 Dr GLS Sdn (5 spd) | 10919 | 7275 | 8450 |

### EXCEL 4

| | | | |
|---|---|---|---|
| 3 Dr Base Hbk (4 spd) | 8010 | 4725 | 5650 |
| 3 Dr GS Hbk (5 spd) | 8654 | 5025 | 5950 |
| 4 Dr Base Sdn (4 spd) | 9110 | 4950 | 5875 |
| 4 Dr GL Sdn (5 spd) | 9554 | 5425 | 6350 |

| Year/Model/Body/Type | Original List | Current Whlse | Average Retail |
|---|---|---|---|
| **SCOUPE 4** | | | |
| 2 Dr Base Cpe (5 spd) | 10189 | 6625 | 7700 |
| 2 Dr LS Cpe (5 spd) | 10794 | 7200 | 8350 |
| **SONATA 4** | | | |
| 4 Dr Base Sdn (5 spd) | 12000 | 8975 | 10375 |
| 4 Dr GLS Sdn (5 spd) | 13995 | — | — |
| **SONATA 6** | | | |
| 4 Dr Base Sdn (auto) | 13540 | — | — |
| 4 Dr GLS Sdn (auto) | 15535 | — | — |

NOTE: Power windows and tilt steering wheel standard on Scoupe LS, Elantra GLS and Sonata. Power door locks standard on Elantra GLS and Sonata. Power seat standard on Scoupe LS and Elantra GLS.

## 1991

| Year/Model/Body/Type | Original List | Current Whlse | Average Retail |
|---|---|---|---|
| **EXCEL 4** | | | |
| 3 Dr Base Hbk (4 spd) | 7770 | 3675 | 4575 |
| 3 Dr GS Hbk (5 spd) | 8740 | 4000 | 4900 |
| 4 Dr Base Sdn (4 spd) | 8905 | 3925 | 4825 |
| 4 Dr GL Sdn (5 spd) | 9610 | 4350 | 5275 |
| 4 Dr GLS Sdn (5 spd) | 9815 | 4675 | 5600 |
| **SCOUPE 4** | | | |
| 2 Dr Base Cpe (5 spd) | 9605 | 5500 | 6425 |
| 2 Dr LS Cpe (5 spd) | 10620 | 6000 | 6925 |
| **SONATA 4** | | | |
| 4 Dr Base Sdn (5 spd) | 11725 | 6600 | 7675 |
| 4 Dr GLS Sdn (5 spd) | 13450 | 7375 | 8550 |
| **SONATA 6** | | | |
| 4 Dr Sdn (auto) | 13195 | 7550 | 8775 |
| 4 Dr GLS Sdn (auto) | 14920 | 8350 | 9650 |

NOTE: Power brakes standard on all models. Power windows standard on Scoupe LS and Sonata GLS. Power door locks standard on Sonata GLS.

## 1990

| Year/Model/Body/Type | Original List | Current Whlse | Average Retail |
|---|---|---|---|
| **EXCEL 4** | | | |
| 3 Dr Base Hbk (4 spd) (NA w/pwr strng) | 6969 | 2625 | 3525 |
| 3 Dr GS Hbk (5 spd) | 8329 | 3025 | 3925 |
| 5 Dr GL Hbk (5 spd) (NA w/pwr strng) | 8669 | 3150 | 4050 |
| 4 Dr Base Sdn (4 spd) (NA w/pwr strng) | 8069 | 2875 | 3775 |
| 4 Dr GL Sdn (5 spd) (NA w/pwr strng) | 8949 | 3250 | 4150 |
| 4 Dr GLS Sdn (5 spd) | 9514 | 3500 | 4400 |
| **SONATA 4** | | | |
| 4 Dr Base Sdn (5 spd) | 11114 | 4975 | 5900 |

| Year/Model/Body/Type | Original List | Current Whlse | Average Retail |
|---|---|---|---|
| 4 Dr GLS Sdn (5 spd) | 13129 | 5725 | 6650 |
| **SONATA 6** | | | |
| 4 Dr Base Sdn (auto) | 12504 | 5600 | 6525 |
| 4 Dr GLS Sdn (auto) | 14519 | 6275 | 7300 |
| *ADD FOR:* | | | |
| Leather Pkg (Sonata GLS) | 575 | 160 | 180 |

NOTE: Power brakes standard on all models. Power windows and power door locks standard on Sonata GLS.

## 1989

| Year/Model/Body/Type | Original List | Current Whlse | Average Retail |
|---|---|---|---|
| **EXCEL 4** | | | |
| 3 Dr L Hbk (4 spd) | 7014 | 1550 | 2400 |
| 4 Dr L Sdn (4 spd) | 7739 | 1775 | 2625 |
| 3 Dr GL Hbk (5 spd) | 8239 | 1850 | 2700 |
| 5 Dr GL Hbk (5 spd) | 8439 | 2000 | 2850 |
| 4 Dr GL Sdn (5 spd) | 8689 | 2100 | 2950 |
| 5 Dr GLS Hbk (5 spd) | 8844 | 2175 | 3025 |
| 4 Dr GLS Sdn (5 spd) | 8994 | 2275 | 3150 |
| 3 Dr GS Hbk (5 spd) | 8944 | 2225 | 3075 |
| **SONATA 4** | | | |
| 4 Dr Sdn (5 spd) | 10770 | 3400 | 4300 |
| 4 Dr GLS Sdn (5 spd) | 12770 | 3950 | 4850 |

NOTE: Power brakes standard on all models. Power windows and power door locks standard on Sonata GLS.

## 1988

| Year/Model/Body/Type | Original List | Current Whlse | Average Retail |
|---|---|---|---|
| **EXCEL 4** | | | |
| 3 Dr L Hbk (4 spd) | 5395 | 700 | 1325 |
| 4 Dr L Sdn (4 spd) | 5995 | 900 | 1625 |
| 3 Dr GL Hbk (5 spd) | 6495 | 925 | 1650 |
| 5 Dr GL Hbk (5 spd) | 6745 | 1050 | 1775 |
| 4 Dr GL Sdn (5 spd) | 6895 | 1125 | 1850 |
| 5 Dr GLS Hbk (5 spd) | 7495 | 1200 | 1925 |
| 4 Dr GLS Sdn (5 spd) | 7645 | 1300 | 2000 |
| 3 Dr GS Hbk (5 spd) | 7595 | 1275 | 2000 |

NOTE: Power brakes standard on all models.

## 1987

| Year/Model/Body/Type | Original List | Current Whlse | Average Retail |
|---|---|---|---|
| **EXCEL 4** | | | |
| 3 Dr Hbk (4 spd) | 5195 | 600 | 1125 |
| 5 Dr Hbk (4 spd) | 5495 | 750 | 1275 |
| 3 Dr GL Hbk (5 spd) | 6095 | 725 | 1375 |
| 5 Dr GL Hbk (5 spd) | 6395 | 875 | 1600 |
| 4 Dr GL Sdn (5 spd) | 6545 | 925 | 1650 |
| 3 Dr GLS Hbk (5 spd) | 6795 | 850 | 1550 |
| 5 Dr GLS Hbk (5 spd) | 7095 | 950 | 1675 |
| 4 Dr GLS Sdn (5 spd) | 7245 | 1050 | 1775 |

NOTE: Power brakes standard on all models.

| Year/Model/ Body/Type | Original List | Current Whlse | Average Retail |
|---|---|---|---|
| **1986** | | | |
| **EXCEL 4** | | | |
| 3 Dr Hbk (4 spd) | **5270** | 475 | 875 |
| 5 Dr Hbk (4 spd) | **5470** | 625 | 1175 |
| 3 Dr GL Hbk (5 spd) | **6170** | 525 | 975 |
| 5 Dr GL Hbk (5 spd) | **6370** | 675 | 1275 |
| 4 Dr GL Sdn (5 spd) | **6520** | 775 | 1500 |
| 3 Dr GLS Hbk (5 spd) | **6395** | 625 | 1175 |
| 5 Dr GLS Hbk (5 spd) | **6595** | 775 | 1500 |
| 4 Dr GLS Sdn (5 spd) | **6745** | 875 | 1600 |

## INFINITI

| Year/Model/ Body/Type | Original List | Current Whlse | Average Retail |
|---|---|---|---|
| **1992** | | | |
| **G20 4** | | | |
| 4 Dr Sdn (5 spd) | **19100** | 13900 | 16525 |
| *ADD FOR:* | | | |
| Leather Seat Trim | **1000** | 300 | 330 |
| **M30 6** | | | |
| 2 Dr Cpe (auto) | **25500** | 17950 | 20600 |
| 2 Dr Conv (auto) | **33700** | — | — |
| **Q45 8** | | | |
| 4 Dr Sdn (auto) | **44000** | 30850 | 34300 |
| 4 Dr Full Active Suspension Sdn (auto) | **48500** | | |
| *ADD FOR:* | | | |
| Touring Pkg | **2800** | 1300 | 1550 |
| Traction Control Pkg | **1500** | — | — |

NOTE: Power windows, power door locks, tilt steering wheel, and cruise control standard on all models. Power seat and power sunroof standard on M30, J30 and Q45.

| Year/Model/ Body/Type | Original List | Current Whlse | Average Retail |
|---|---|---|---|
| **1991** | | | |
| **G20 4** | | | |
| 4 Dr Sdn (5 spd) | **17750** | 11725 | 13550 |
| **M30 6** | | | |
| 2 Dr Cpe | **24500** | 14675 | 17225 |
| 2 Dr Conv | **31000** | 20425 | 23475 |
| **Q45 8** | | | |
| 4 Dr Performance Luxury Sdn | **40000** | 26650 | 29975 |
| 4 Dr Full Active Suspension Sdn | **45000** | 28400 | 31750 |
| *ADD FOR:* | | | |
| Q45 Touring Pkg | **2800** | 990 | 1100 |

NOTE: Power brakes, power windows and power door

locks standard on all models. Power seat standard on Q45. Sunroof standard on M30 and Q45.

| Year/Model/ Body/Type | Original List | Current Whlse | Average Retail |
|---|---|---|---|
| **1991** | | | |
| **M30 6** | | | |
| 2 Dr Cpe | **23500** | 12775 | 15100 |
| 2 Dr Conv | — | — | — |
| **Q45 8** | | | |
| 4 Dr Sdn | **38000** | 21575 | 24875 |
| *ADD FOR:* | | | |
| Q45 Touring Pkg | **2500** | 560 | 630 |

NOTE: Power brakes, power windows, power door locks, sunroof, power seat and anti-lock brakes standard on all models.

## ISUZU

| Year/Model/ Body/Type | Original List | Current Whlse | Average Retail |
|---|---|---|---|
| **1992** | | | |
| **2WD S PICKUPS (2.3 LITER) 4** | | | |
| Std Bed (5 spd) | **9624** | 6550 | 7625 |
| Long Bed (5 spd) | **10674** | 6650 | 7750 |
| **2WD S PICKUPS (2.6 LITER) 4** | | | |
| Std Bed (5 spd) | **10394** | — | — |
| 1 Ton Long Bed (5 spd) | **11629** | 6950 | 8100 |
| Spacecab (5 spd) | **11714** | 7175 | 8325 |
| **2WD LS PICKUPS (2.6 LITER) 4** | | | |
| Spacecab (5 spd) | **13899** | | |
| **4WD S PICKUP (3.1 LITER) 6** | | | |
| Std Bed (5 spd) | **13289** | — | — |
| **2WD AMIGO S (2.3 LITER) 4** | | | |
| Sport Utility (5 spd) | **12414** | 9700 | 11175 |
| **2WD AMIGO S (2.6 LITER) 4** | | | |
| Sport Utility (5 spd) | **13104** | — | — |
| **2WD AMIGO XS (2.6 LITER) 4** | | | |
| Sport Utility (5 spd) | **13479** | 10325 | 11925 |
| **2WD RODEO (2.6 LITER) 4** | | | |
| S Sport Utility (5 spd) | **14191** | 11075 | 12800 |
| **2WD RODEO (3.1 LITER) 6** | | | |
| S Sport Utility (5 spd) | **14806** | — | — |
| XS Sport Utility (5 spd) | **15579** | 12200 | 14100 |
| LS Sport Utility ( 5 spd) | **16889** | 13000 | 15325 |
| **TROOPER 6** | | | |
| 4WD S 4 Dr (5 spd) | **19650** | 15525 | 18175 |

| Year/Model/ Body/Type | Original List | Current Whlse | Average Retail |
|---|---|---|---|
| 4WD LS 4 Dr (5 spd) | **24250** | — | — |
| *ADD FOR:* | | | |
| Anti-lock Brakes (LS) | **1100** | 475 | 550 |
| **STYLUS 4** | | | |
| S Sdn (5 spd) | **10479** | 6900 | 8025 |
| RS Sdn (5 spd) | **11499** | 7800 | 9050 |

NOTE: Tilt steering wheel standard on LS Pickup and Rodeo LS. Cruise control, power windows and power door locks standard on Trooper LS.

## 1991

### 2WD S PICKUPS (2.3 LITER) 4

| | | | |
|---|---|---|---|
| Std Bed (5 spd) | **9244** | 5575 | 6500 |
| Long Bed (5 spd) | **10274** | 5725 | 6650 |

### 2WD S PICKUPS (2.6 LITER) 4

| | | | |
|---|---|---|---|
| Std Bed (5 spd) | **9974** | 5775 | 6700 |
| Long Bed (auto) | **11454** | 6325 | 7350 |
| 1 Ton Long Bed (5 spd) | **11129** | 5925 | 6850 |
| Spacecab (5 spd) | **10949** | 6125 | 7125 |

### 2WD LS PICKUPS (2.6 LITER) 4

| | | | |
|---|---|---|---|
| Spacecab (5 spd) | **13299** | 7125 | 8275 |

### 4WD S PICKUP (3.1 LITER) 6

| | | | |
|---|---|---|---|
| Std Bed (5 spd) | **12479** | 7300 | 8475 |

### 4WD LS PICKUP (3.1 LITER) 6

| | | | |
|---|---|---|---|
| Std Bed (5 spd) | **15099** | 8300 | 9575 |

### TROOPER 4

| | | | |
|---|---|---|---|
| 4WD S 4 Dr (5 spd) | **14849** | 10575 | 12200 |

### TROOPER 6

| | | | |
|---|---|---|---|
| 4WD S 4 Dr (5 spd) | **15349** | 11000 | 12700 |
| 4WD SE 4 Dr (5 spd) | **16599** | 11675 | 13475 |
| 4WD XS 4 Dr (5 spd) | **16419** | 11625 | 13425 |
| 4WD LS 4 Dr (5 spd) | **18569** | 12400 | 14500 |

### 2WD AMIGO S (2.3 LITER) 4

| | | | |
|---|---|---|---|
| Sport Utility (5 spd) | **11084** | 7050 | 8175 |

### 2WD AMIGO S (2.6 LITER) 4

| | | | |
|---|---|---|---|
| Sport Utility (5 spd) | **11734** | 7225 | 8400 |

### 2WD AMIGO XS (2.6 LITER) 4

| | | | |
|---|---|---|---|
| Sport Utility (5 spd) | **12434** | 7625 | 8850 |

### IMPULSE 4

| | | | |
|---|---|---|---|
| XS Cpe (5 spd) | **12799** | 7800 | 9050 |
| RS Cpe (5 spd) | **15599** | 9450 | 10875 |
| XS Hbk (5 spd) | **13349** | — | — |

### 2WD RODEO 4

| | | | |
|---|---|---|---|
| S Sport Utility (5 spd) | **13834** | 10325 | 11925 |

### 2WD RODEO 6

| | | | |
|---|---|---|---|
| S Sport Utility (5 spd) | **14409** | 10725 | 12375 |
| XS Sport Utility (5 spd) | **15049** | 11375 | 13150 |
| LS Sport Utility (5 spd) | **16619** | 12150 | 14025 |

### STYLUS 4

| | | | |
|---|---|---|---|
| S Sdn (5 spd) | **10159** | 5600 | 6525 |
| XS Sdn (5 spd) | **12049** | 6525 | 7600 |

| *ADD FOR:* | | | |
|---|---|---|---|
| Sport Pkg | | | |
| (Impulse XS) | **1195** | 540 | 600 |
| (Impulse RS) | **1850** | 830 | 920 |
| (Stylus XS) | **1295** | 580 | 650 |

NOTE: Power brakes standard on all models.

## 1990

### 2WD S PICKUPS (2.3 LITER) 4

| | | | |
|---|---|---|---|
| Std Bed (5 spd) | **8989** | 4100 | 5025 |
| Long Bed (5 spd) | **9819** | 4225 | 5150 |

### 2WD S PICKUPS (2.6 LITER)

| | | | |
|---|---|---|---|
| Std Bed (5 spd) | **9619** | 4300 | 5225 |
| Spacecab (5 spd) | **10624** | 4600 | 5525 |
| Long Bed (auto) | **11039** | 4650 | 5575 |
| 1 Ton Long Bed (5 spd) | **10744** | 4425 | 5350 |

### 2WD XS PICKUP (2.3 LITER) 4

| | | | |
|---|---|---|---|
| Std Bed (5 spd) | **9529** | 4400 | 5325 |

### 2WD XS PICKUP (2.6 LITER) 4

| | | | |
|---|---|---|---|
| Spacecab (5 spd) | **11254** | 4575 | 5500 |

### 2WD LS PICKUPS (2.6 LITER) 4

| | | | |
|---|---|---|---|
| Std Bed (5 spd) | **11554** | 4950 | 5875 |
| Spacecab (5 spd) | **12784** | 5475 | 6400 |

### 4WD XS PICKUP (2.6 LITER) 4

| | | | |
|---|---|---|---|
| Std Bed (5 spd) | **12834** | 5725 | 6650 |

### TROOPER 4

| | | | |
|---|---|---|---|
| 4WD S 4 Dr (5 spd) | **14559** | 9225 | 10625 |
| 4WD RS 2 Dr (5 spd) | **16199** | 9500 | 10950 |

### TROOPER 6

| | | | |
|---|---|---|---|
| 4WD S 4 Dr (5 spd) | **14809** | 9575 | 11025 |
| 4WD XS 4 Dr (5 spd) | **15649** | 10025 | 11575 |
| 4WD LS 4 Dr (5 spd) | **17749** | 10400 | 12000 |

### 2WD AMIGO S (2.3 LITER)

| | | | |
|---|---|---|---|
| Sport Utility (5 spd) | **10744** | 5850 | 6775 |

| Year/Model/Body/Type | Original List | Current Whlse | Average Retail |
|---|---|---|---|
| **2WD AMIGO S (2.6 LITER)** | | | |
| Sport Utility (5 spd) | 11344 | 6025 | 6950 |
| **2WD AMIGO XS (2.6 LITER)** | | | |
| Sport Utility (5 spd) | 11739 | 6325 | 7350 |
| **IMPULSE 4** | | | |
| XS Cpe (5 spd) | 12749 | 5875 | 6800 |
| *ADD FOR:* | | | |
| Aluminum Wheel Pkg | | | |
| (Amigo, Trooper S) | 900 | 210 | 230 |
| (Trooper XS & LS) | 700 | 160 | 180 |
| (4WD S Pickup) | 700 | 150 | 160 |
| (4WD LS Pickup) | 400 | 150 | 160 |
| Rear Seat | | | |
| (Trooper S & XS) | 420 | 150 | 160 |
| (Trooper LS) | 520 | 150 | 160 |
| Sport Pkg (Impulse) | 1195 | 420 | 460 |

NOTE: Power brakes standard on all models.

## 1989

| Year/Model/Body/Type | Original List | Current Whlse | Average Retail |
|---|---|---|---|
| **2WD S PICKUPS (2.3 LITER) 4** | | | |
| Std Bed (5 spd) | 8749 | 3350 | 4250 |
| Long Bed (5 spd) | 9339 | 3475 | 4375 |
| **2WD S PICKUPS (2.6 LITER) 4** | | | |
| Std Bed (5 spd) | 9129 | 3500 | 4400 |
| Spacecab (5 spd) | 10379 | 4050 | 4950 |
| Long Bed (auto) | 10429 | 3925 | 4825 |
| 1-Ton Long Bed (5 spd) | 10579 | 3650 | 4550 |
| **2WD XS PICKUP (2.3 LITER) 4** | | | |
| Std Bed (5 spd) | 9259 | 3575 | 4475 |
| **2WD XS PICKUP (2.6 LITER) 4** | | | |
| Spacecab (5 spd) | 10949 | 4250 | 5175 |
| **2WD LS PICKUPS (2.6 LITER) 4** | | | |
| Std Bed (5 spd) | 11094 | 4150 | 5075 |
| Spacecab (5 spd) | 12294 | 4600 | 5525 |
| **4WD XS PICKUPS (2.6 LITER) 4** | | | |
| Std Bed (5 spd) | 11694 | 4975 | 5900 |
| **TROOPER II 4** | | | |
| 4WD S 4 Dr (5 spd) | 14184 | 7725 | 8975 |
| 4WD XS 4 Dr (5 spd) | 14999 | 8075 | 9325 |
| 4WD LS 4 Dr (5 spd) | 16689 | 8325 | 9625 |
| 4WD RS 2 Dr (5 spd) | 15749 | 7825 | 9075 |
| **TROOPER II 6** | | | |
| 4WD S 4 Dr (5 spd) | 14434 | 8025 | 9275 |
| 4WD LS 4 Dr (5 spd) | 17409 | 8625 | 9950 |

| Year/Model/Body/Type | Original List | Current Whlse | Average Retail |
|---|---|---|---|
| **2WD AMIGO S (2.3 LITER) 4** | | | |
| Sport Utility | 10259 | 4875 | 5800 |
| **2WD AMIGO S (2.6 LITER) 4** | | | |
| Sport Utility | 10829 | 5000 | 5925 |
| **2WD AMIGO XS (2.6 LITER) 4** | | | |
| Sport Utility | 11529 | 5225 | 6150 |
| **I-MARK 4** | | | |
| 3 Dr S Hbk (5 spd) | 8864 | 2275 | 3150 |
| 4 Dr S Sdn (5 spd) | 9264 | 2425 | 3300 |
| 3 Dr XS Hbk (5 spd) | 10044 | 2650 | 3550 |
| 4 Dr XS Sdn (5 spd) | 10244 | 2825 | 3725 |
| 4 Dr RS Turbo Sdn (5 spd) | 10239 | 3325 | 4225 |
| 3 Dr RS Turbo Hbk (5 spd) | 10039 | 3175 | 4075 |
| 4 Dr LS Turbo Sdn (5 spd) | 12049 | 3375 | 4275 |
| **IMPULSE 4** | | | |
| 2 Dr Hbk (5 spd) | 14329 | 5050 | 5975 |
| 2 Dr Turbo Hbk (5 spd) | 16329 | 5650 | 6575 |
| *ADD FOR:* | | | |
| Recaro Pkg (I-Mark RS) | 1200 | 370 | 410 |
| Sunsport Pkg (I-Mark S Hbk) | 1200 | 370 | 410 |
| Rear Seat (Trooper II) | 420 | 100 | 110 |

## 1988 1/2

| Year/Model/Body/Type | Original List | Current Whlse | Average Retail |
|---|---|---|---|
| **I-MARK 4** | | | |
| 3 Dr S Hbk (5 spd) | 7659 | 1250 | 1975 |
| 4 Dr S Sdn (5 spd) | 8009 | 1350 | 2100 |
| 3 Dr XS Hbk (5 spd) | 9029 | 1475 | 2300 |
| 4 Dr XS Sdn (5 spd) | 9219 | 1775 | 2625 |
| 3 Dr RS Turbo Hbk (5 spd) | 9829 | 1925 | 2775 |
| 4 Dr LS Turbo Sdn (5 spd) | 11189 | 2000 | 2850 |

## 1988 1/2

| Year/Model/Body/Type | Original List | Current Whlse | Average Retail |
|---|---|---|---|
| **2WD S PICKUP (2.3 LITER) 4** | | | |
| Std Bed (5 spd) | 7199 | 1975 | 2825 |
| Long Bed (5 spd) | 7729 | 2100 | 2950 |
| **2WD S PICKUP (2.6 LITER) 4** | | | |
| Std Bed (5 spd) | 7649 | 2025 | 2875 |
| 1 Ton Long Bed (5 spd) | 8999 | 2225 | 3075 |
| **2WD LS PICKUP (2.6 LITER) 4** | | | |
| Std Bed (5 spd) | 10249 | 2600 | 3475 |
| Spacecab (5 spd) | 11399 | 3000 | 3900 |

| Year/Model/Body/Type | Original List | Current Whlse | Average Retail |
|---|---|---|---|
| **TROOPER II 4** | | | |
| 4WD S 2 Dr (5 spd) | **11909** | 5650 | 6575 |
| 4WD S 4 Dr (5 spd) | **12639** | 5975 | 6900 |
| 4WD XS 2 Dr (5 spd) | **12909** | 5950 | 6875 |
| 4WD XS 4 Dr (5 spd) | **13439** | 6275 | 7325 |
| 4WD LS 4 Dr (5 spd) | **14799** | 6525 | 7600 |
| 4WD Limited (5 spd) | **14499** | 6575 | 7650 |
| 4WD LX Ltd (5 spd) | **15399** | 6375 | 7425 |
| **I-MARK 4** | | | |
| 3 Dr S Hbk (5 spd) | **7629** | 1450 | 2225 |
| 4 Dr S Sdn (5 spd) | **7979** | 1625 | 2475 |
| 3 Dr XS Hbk (5 spd) | **8999** | 1750 | 2600 |
| 4 Dr XS Sdn (5 spd) | **9189** | 1900 | 2750 |
| 3 Dr Turbo Hbk (5 spd) | **10669** | 2075 | 2925 |
| 4 Dr Turbo Sdn (5 spd) | **10859** | 2225 | 3075 |
| **IMPULSE 4** | | | |
| 2 Dr Hbk (5 spd) | **14109** | 3125 | 4025 |
| 2 Dr Turbo Hbk (5 spd) | **16079** | 3525 | 4425 |

NOTE: Power brakes standard on all models. Sunroof standard on I-Mark Turbo, Impulse and LS Pickup. Air conditioning standard on Impulse. Pwr strng standard on Impulse, Trooper II, 4WD S Pickup, 1 Ton S Pickup and LS Pickup. Power windows standard on Impulse and Trooper II LX Limited. Power door locks standard on Impulse and Trooper II LX Limited.

## 1987

**2WD PICKUP (GAS) 4**

| Year/Model/Body/Type | Original List | Current Whlse | Average Retail |
|---|---|---|---|
| Std Bed (4 spd) | **6399** | 1350 | 2100 |
| Std Bed (5 spd) | **6649** | 1375 | 2125 |
| Long Bed (5 spd) | **6899** | 1475 | 2300 |
| Spacecab (5 spd) | **7849** | 1700 | 2550 |
| LS Std Bed (5 spd) | **8699** | 1800 | 2650 |
| LS Spacecab (5 spd) | **10199** | 2150 | 3000 |
| **2WD PICKUP (DIESEL) 4** | | | |
| MPG Std Bed (4 spd) | **7469** | 900 | 1625 |
| MPG Std Bed (5 spd) | **7469** | 925 | 1650 |
| Long Bed (5 spd) | **7719** | 1025 | 1750 |
| LS Spacecab Turbo (5 spd) | **11519** | — | — |
| **4WD PICKUP (DIESEL) 4** | | | |
| Long Bed Turbo (5 spd) | **10739** | 2150 | 3000 |
| **TROOPER II 4** | | | |
| 4WD Dlx 2 Dr (5 spd) | **10979** | 3525 | 4425 |
| 4WD Dlx 4 Dr (5 spd) | **11399** | 3775 | 4675 |
| 4WD LS 4 Dr (5 spd) | **13199** | 4100 | 5025 |
| 4WD Dlx 2 Dr Turbo Diesel (5 spd) | **12899** | 3250 | 4150 |
| 4WD Dlx 4 Dr Turbo Diesel (5 spd) | **13319** | 3550 | 4450 |

| Year/Model/Body/Type | Original List | Current Whlse | Average Retail |
|---|---|---|---|
| 4WD LS 4 Dr Turbo Diesel (5 spd) | **15119** | 3900 | 4800 |
| **I-MARK 4** | | | |
| 2 Dr S Hbk (5 spd) | **7229** | 975 | 1700 |
| 4 Dr S Ntchbk (5 spd) | **7569** | 1075 | 1800 |
| 2 Dr Hbk (5 spd) | **8369** | 1225 | 1950 |
| 4 Dr Ntchbk (5 spd) | **8549** | 1325 | 2050 |
| 2 Dr RS Turbo Hbk (5 spd) | **10149** | 1425 | 2175 |
| 4 Dr RS Turbo Ntchbk (5 spd) | **10329** | 1600 | 2450 |
| **IMPULSE 4** | | | |
| 2 Dr Turbo Cpe (5 spd) | **14859** | 2800 | 3700 |

NOTE: Power brakes, power windows and power door locks standard on all models. Air conditioning standard on Impulse. Sun roof standard on I-Mark Turbo and Spacecab Pickup. Pwr strng standard on I-Mark Turbo, Impulse, Trooper II Series, Spacecab Pickup, Deluxe Pickup and LS Pickup.

## 1986

**2WD PICKUP (GAS) 4**

| Year/Model/Body/Type | Original List | Current Whlse | Average Retail |
|---|---|---|---|
| Std Bed (4 spd) | **6326** | 1100 | 1825 |
| Long Bed (5 spd) | **6816** | 1225 | 1950 |
| Dlx Std Bed (5 spd) | **7366** | 1325 | 2050 |
| Dlx Long Bed (5 spd) | **7616** | 1425 | 2175 |
| Dlx Spacecab (5 spd) | **8399** | 1600 | 2450 |
| LS Std Bed (5 spd) | **8149** | 1325 | 2050 |
| LS Spacecab (5 spd) | **9499** | 1775 | 2625 |
| **2WD PICKUP (DIESEL) 4** | | | |
| MPG Plus Std Bed (4 spd) | **7336** | 650 | 1225 |
| Long Bed (5 spd) | **7586** | 725 | 1375 |
| Dlx Long Bed Turbo (5 spd) | **8669** | 1150 | 1875 |
| Dlx Spacecab Turbo (5 spd) | **9619** | 1250 | 1975 |
| LS Spacecab Turbo (5 spd) | **10719** | 1275 | 2000 |
| **4WD PICKUP (DIESEL) 4** | | | |
| Dlx Std Bed Turbo (5 spd) | **10846** | 1700 | 2550 |
| **TROOPER II** | | | |
| 4WD Dlx 2 Dr (5 spd) | **10389** | 2750 | 3650 |
| 4WD Dlx 4 Dr (5 spd) | **10809** | 2925 | 3825 |
| 4WD LS (5 spd) | **11649** | 3100 | 4000 |
| 4WD Dlx 2 Dr Turbo Diesel (5 spd) | **12309** | 2800 | 3700 |
| 4WD Dlx 4 Dr Turbo Diesel | **12729** | 2925 | 3825 |

*Refer to optional equipment schedules*

| Year/Model/Body/Type | Original List | Current Whlse | Average Retail |
|---|---|---|---|
| 4WD LS Turbo Diesel (5 spd) | **13509** | 3050 | 3950 |
| **I-MARK 4** | | | |
| 2 Dr S Hbk (5 spd) | **7249** | 750 | 1475 |
| 2 Dr Hbk (5 spd) | **8059** | 650 | 1275 |
| 4 Dr Ntchbk (5 spd) | **8169** | 900 | 1625 |
| 4 Dr S Ntchbk (5 spd) | **7439** | 800 | 1500 |
| **IMPULSE 4** | | | |
| 2 Dr S Cpe (5 spd) | **10979** | 1875 | 2650 |
| 2 Dr Cpe (5 spd) | **12279** | 1900 | 2750 |
| 2 Dr Turbo Cpe (5 spd) | **14439** | 2075 | 2925 |
| *ADD FOR:* | | | |
| Leather Pkg (Turbo Impulse) | **780** | 130 | 140 |

NOTE: Power windows and air conditioning standard on Impulse series. Power locks standard on Impulse Turbo. Pwr strng standard on Impulse series, Trooper II and LS Pickup, Power brakes standard on I-Mark, Impulse, Trooper II Deluxe and Pickups. Sunroof standard on LS Spacecab Pickup.

## 1985

### 2WD PICKUP (GAS)

| Year/Model/Body/Type | Original List | Current Whlse | Average Retail |
|---|---|---|---|
| Std Bed (4 spd) | **5942** | 900 | 1625 |
| Dlx Std Bed (5 spd) | **6519** | 1125 | 1850 |
| Dlx Std Bed w/Bucket Seats (5 spd) | **6669** | 1125 | 1850 |
| LS Std Bed (5 spd) | **7295** | 1100 | 1825 |
| LS Std Bed w/Bucket Seats (5 spd) | **7345** | 1125 | 1850 |
| Base Long Bed (4 spd) | **6097** | 1025 | 1750 |
| Dlx Long Bed (5 spd) | **6674** | 1250 | 1975 |
| Dlx Long Bed w/Bucket Seats (5 spd) | **6824** | 1275 | 2000 |
| LS Long Bed (5 spd) | **7450** | 1275 | 2000 |
| LS Long Bed w/Bucket Seats (5 spd) | **7500** | 1275 | 2000 |

### 2WD PICKUP (DIESEL)

| Year/Model/Body/Type | Original List | Current Whlse | Average Retail |
|---|---|---|---|
| Base Std Bed (4 spd) | **6707** | 425 | 775 |
| Base Std Bed (5 spd) | **6707** | 425 | 775 |
| Dlx Std Bed (5 spd) | **7284** | 625 | 1175 |
| Dlx Std Bed w/Bucket Seats (5 spd) | **7434** | 650 | 1225 |
| Base Long Bed (5 spd) | **6862** | 450 | 825 |
| Dlx Long Bed (5 spd) | **7439** | 725 | 1375 |
| Dlx Long Bed w/Bucket Seats (5 spd) | **7589** | 750 | 1475 |
| LS Long Bed (5 spd) | **8215** | 875 | 1600 |
| LS Long Bed w/Bucket Seats (5 spd) | **8265** | 900 | 1625 |

### TROOPER II 4

| Year/Model/Body/Type | Original List | Current Whlse | Average Retail |
|---|---|---|---|
| 4WD Utility (4 spd) | **8933** | 2275 | 3150 |

### I-MARK (GAS) 4

| Year/Model/Body/Type | Original List | Current Whlse | Average Retail |
|---|---|---|---|
| 4 Dr Dlx Sdn (5 spd) | **7020** | 775 | 1450 |
| 2 Dr Hbk (5 spd) | **7384** | 650 | 1225 |

### IMPULSE 4

| Year/Model/Body/Type | Original List | Current Whlse | Average Retail |
|---|---|---|---|
| 2 Dr Cpe (5 spd) | **11048** | 1400 | 2150 |
| *ADD FOR:* | | | |
| Decor Pkg (Trooper II) | **815** | 60 | 70 |

NOTE: Pwr strng, power windows, air conditioning and power door locks standard on Impulse. Power brakes standard on all models.

## 1984

### 2WD PICKUP (GAS) 4

| Year/Model/Body/Type | Original List | Current Whlse | Average Retail |
|---|---|---|---|
| Std Bed (4 spd) | **5942** | 475 | 875 |
| Dlx Std Bed (5 spd) | **6519** | 600 | 1125 |
| Dlx Std Bed w/Bucket Seats (5 spd) | **6669** | 600 | 1125 |
| LS Std Bed (5 spd) | **7295** | 600 | 1125 |
| LS Std Bed w/Bucket Seats (5 spd) | **7345** | 600 | 1125 |
| Base Long Bed w/Bucket Seats (4 spd) | **6097** | 550 | 1025 |
| Dlx Long Bed (5 spd) | **6674** | 700 | 1325 |
| Dlx Long Bed w/Bucket Seats (5 spd) | **6824** | 700 | 1325 |
| LS Long Bed (5 spd) | **7450** | 700 | 1325 |
| LS Long Bed w/Bucket Seats (5 spd) | **7500** | 700 | 1325 |

### 2WD PICKUP (DIESEL) 4

| Year/Model/Body/Type | Original List | Current Whlse | Average Retail |
|---|---|---|---|
| Base Std Bed (4 spd) | **6707** | 275 | 550 |
| Base Std Bed (5 spd) | **6707** | 275 | 550 |
| Dlx Std Bed (5 spd) | **7284** | 300 | 575 |
| Dlx Std Bed w/Bucket Seats (5 spd) | **7434** | 300 | 575 |
| Base Long Bed w/Bucket Seats (5 spd) | **6862** | 350 | 625 |
| Dlx Long Bed (5 spd) | **7439** | 375 | 675 |
| Dlx Long Bed w/Bucket Seats (5 spd) | **7589** | 375 | 675 |
| LS Long Bed (5 spd) | **8215** | 400 | 725 |
| LS Long Bed w/Bucket Seats (5 spd) | **8265** | 400 | 725 |

### I-MARK (GAS) 4

| Year/Model/Body/Type | Original List | Current Whlse | Average Retail |
|---|---|---|---|
| 4 Dr Dlx Sdn (5 spd) | **6770** | 300 | 575 |

### I-MARK (DIESEL) 4

| Year/Model/Body/Type | Original List | Current Whlse | Average Retail |
|---|---|---|---|
| 4 Dr Dlx Sdn (5 spd) | **7620** | 200 | 400 |
| 2 Dr Cpe (4 spd) | **6955** | 110 | 300 |

### IMPULSE 4

| Year/Model/Body/Type | Original List | Current Whlse | Average Retail |
|---|---|---|---|
| 2 Dr Cpe (5 spd) | **10498** | 1025 | 1750 |

| Year/Model/ Body/Type | Original List | Current Whlse | Average Retail |
|---|---|---|---|
| **TROOPER 4** | | | |
| 4WD Utility (4 spd) | **8933** | 1725 | 2575 |
| **1983 — ALL BODY STYLES** | | | |
| 2WD PICKUP (GAS) | — | 150 | 350 |
| 2WD PICKUP (DIESEL) | — | 70 | 250 |
| 4WD PICKUP (GAS) | — | 850 | 1550 |
| 4WD PICKUP (DIESEL) | — | 275 | 550 |
| I-MARK (GAS) | — | 150 | 350 |
| I-MARK (DIESEL) | — | 70 | 250 |
| IMPULSE | — | 725 | 1375 |

## JAGUAR

### 1992

#### XJ 6

| | Original List | Current Whlse | Average Retail |
|---|---|---|---|
| Base Sdn (auto) | **44500** | 34950 | 38875 |
| Sovereign Sdn (auto) | **49500** | 36800 | 40850 |
| Vanden Plas Sdn (auto) | **54500** | 38975 | 43250 |
| Majestic Sdn (auto) | **59500** | — | — |

#### XJS 12

| | | | |
|---|---|---|---|
| Base Cpe (auto) | **60500** | — | — |
| Conv (auto) | **67500** | — | — |

NOTE: Tilt steering wheel, cruise control, power windows, power door locks and power seat standard on all models. Power sunroof standard on Sovereign, Vanden Plas and Majestic.

### 1991

#### XJ 6

| | | | |
|---|---|---|---|
| Base Sdn (auto) | **43000** | 24150 | 27450 |
| Sovereign Sdn (auto) | **47800** | 26300 | 29625 |
| Vanden Plas Sdn (auto) | **52800** | 28300 | 31650 |

#### XJS 12

| | | | |
|---|---|---|---|
| Base Cpe (auto) | **49900** | 30450 | 33850 |
| Conv (auto) | **59900** | 36850 | 40900 |

NOTE: Power windows, power door locks, power seat and power brakes standard on all models. Sunroof standard on XJ6 Sovereign and Vanden Plas models.

### 1990

#### XJ 6

| | | | |
|---|---|---|---|
| Base Sdn (auto) | **39700** | 18550 | 21600 |
| Sovereign Sdn (auto) | **43000** | 20425 | 23475 |
| Vanden Plas Sdn (auto) | **48000** | 22100 | 25400 |
| Vanden Plas Majestic Sdn (auto) | **53000** | 23800 | 27100 |

### XJS 12

| | Original List | Current Whlse | Average Retail |
|---|---|---|---|
| Base Cpe (auto) | **48000** | 22150 | 25450 |
| Conv (auto) | **57000** | 31650 | 35200 |
| Collection Rouge Cpe (auto) | **51000** | — | — |

NOTE: Power windows, power door locks, and anti-lock power brakes standard on all models. Power sunroof standard on XJ6 Sovereign and Vanden Plas models.

### 1989

#### XJ 6

| | | | |
|---|---|---|---|
| Sdn (auto) | **44000** | 15500 | 18150 |
| Vanden Plas Sdn (auto) | **48000** | 16750 | 19400 |

#### XJS 12

| | | | |
|---|---|---|---|
| Cpe (auto) | **48000** | 16250 | 18900 |
| Conv (auto) | **57000** | 25025 | 28350 |

NOTE: Power brakes, power door locks and power windows standard on all models. Power sunroof standard on XJ6.

### 1988

#### XJ 6

| | | | |
|---|---|---|---|
| Sdn (auto) | **43500** | 10775 | 12425 |
| Vanden Plas Sdn (auto) | **47500** | 11725 | 13550 |

#### XJS 12

| | | | |
|---|---|---|---|
| Cpe (auto) | **44500** | 11875 | 13725 |

#### XJ-SC 12

| | | | |
|---|---|---|---|
| Cabriolet (auto) | **50450** | 16600 | 19250 |

NOTE: Air conditioning, power brakes, power door locks, pwr strng, power sunroof, automatic transmission, power windows, and anti-lock brake system standard.

### 1987

#### XJ 6

| | | | |
|---|---|---|---|
| Sdn (auto) | **37500** | 9650 | 11125 |
| Vanden Plas Sdn (auto) | **41500** | 10400 | 12000 |

#### XJS 12

| | | | |
|---|---|---|---|
| Cpe (auto) | **39700** | 10375 | 11975 |

#### XJ-SC 12

| | | | |
|---|---|---|---|
| Cabriolet (auto) | **44850** | 14800 | 17375 |

NOTE: Air conditioning, power brakes, power door locks, pwr strng, power sunroof, automatic transmission and power windows standard.

| Year/Model/Body/Type | Original List | Current Whlse | Average Retail |
|---|---|---|---|
| **1986** | | | |
| **XJ 6** | | | |
| Sdn (auto) | **33900** | 7600 | 8825 |
| Vanden Plas Sdn (auto) | **37400** | 8375 | 9675 |
| **XJS 12** | | | |
| Cpe (auto) | **37800** | 8600 | 9925 |

NOTE: Power locks, power windows, power brakes, automatic transmission, pwr strng and air conditioning standard on all models. Sunroof standard on XJ6 series.

| **1985** | | | |
|---|---|---|---|
| **XJ 6** | | | |
| Sdn (auto) | **32250** | 6950 | 8100 |
| Vanden Plas Sdn (auto) | **35550** | 7650 | 8875 |
| **XJS 12** | | | |
| Cpe (auto) | **36000** | 8150 | 9425 |

NOTE: Air conditioning, pwr strng, power brakes, power windows, and automatic transmission standard on all models. Sunroof standard on XJ.

| **1984** | | | |
|---|---|---|---|
| **XJ 6** | | | |
| Sdn (auto) | **31100** | 6325 | 7350 |
| Vanden Plas Sdn (auto) | **34200** | 6775 | 7875 |
| **XJS 12** | | | |
| Cpe (auto) | **34700** | 7600 | 8825 |

NOTE: Air conditioning, pwr strng, power brakes, power windows, and automatic transmission standard on all models. Sunroof standard on XJ.

| **1983** | | | |
|---|---|---|---|
| **XJ 6** | | | |
| Sdn (auto) | **31111** | 5375 | 6300 |
| Vanden Plas Sdn (auto) | **34226** | 5750 | 6675 |
| **XJS 12** | | | |
| Cpe (auto) | **34606** | 7375 | 8550 |

## LEXUS

| **1992** | | | |
|---|---|---|---|
| **ES 300 6** | | | |
| 4 Dr Sdn (5 spd) | **26550** | 21200 | 24500 |
| *ADD FOR:* | | | |
| Leather Pkg | **1200** | 450 | 550 |

| | Original List | Current Whlse | Average Retail |
|---|---|---|---|
| CD Player | **900** | 300 | 375 |
| **LS 400 8** | | | |
| 4 Dr Sdn (auto) | **44300** | 34400 | 38250 |
| *ADD FOR:* | | | |
| Memory System | **800** | — | — |
| Air Susp System | **1500** | — | — |
| Traction Control Pkg | **1700** | — | — |
| CD Player | **900** | 350 | 375 |
| **SC 300 6** | | | |
| 2 Dr Sport Cpe (5 spd) | **32700** | — | — |
| *ADD FOR:* | | | |
| Leather Pkg | **1700** | — | — |
| Traction Control System | **1600** | — | — |
| Premium Sound System | **1000** | — | — |
| CD Player | **900** | — | — |
| **SC 400 8** | | | |
| 2 Dr Sport Cpe (auto) | **39400** | 31800 | 35350 |
| *ADD FOR:* | | | |
| Traction Control System | **1600** | 900 | 1100 |
| Premium Sound System | **1000** | 375 | 425 |
| CD Player | **900** | 350 | 375 |

NOTE: Tilt steering wheel, cruise control, power windows, power door locks and power seats standard on all models.

| **1991** | | | |
|---|---|---|---|
| **ES 250 6** | | | |
| 4 Dr Sdn (5 spd) | **21500** | 14400 | 16900 |
| **LS 400 8** | | | |
| 4 Dr Sdn (auto) | **39000** | 29950 | 33300 |
| *ADD FOR:* | | | |
| Leather Pkg (ES 250) | **950** | 280 | 310 |
| (LS 400) | **1400** | 420 | 460 |
| Lexus/Nakamachi Radio Equip (LS 400) | **1000** | 290 | 320 |
| Traction Control System (LS 400) | **1600** | 750 | 830 |

NOTE: Power brakes, power windows/power door locks standard on all models. Power seat standard on LS 400.

| **1990** | | | |
|---|---|---|---|
| **ES 250 6** | | | |
| 4 Dr Sdn (5 spd) | **21050** | 12100 | 13975 |
| **LS 400 8** | | | |
| 4 Dr Sdn (auto) | **35000** | 24750 | 28050 |
| 4 Dr Sdn w/Luxury Group (auto) | **39400** | 26025 | 29350 |

# FOREIGN CARS & TRUCKS

| Year/Model/Body/Type | Original List | Current Whlse | Average Retail |
|---|---|---|---|
| ADD FOR: | | | |
| Air Suspension System | | | |
| (LS 400) | **1500** | 580 | 650 |
| Leather Pkg (ES 250) | **950** | 320 | 350 |
| (LS 400) | **1400** | 370 | 410 |
| Lexus/Nakamachi Radio | | | |
| Equip (LS 400) | **1000** | 210 | 230 |
| Traction Control | | | |
| System (LS 400) | **1600** | 620 | 690 |

NOTE: Anti-lock power brakes, power windows/power door locks standard on all models. Power seat standard on LS 400. Moonroof standard on LS 400 w/luxury group.

## MAZDA

### 1992

#### 323 4

| Year/Model/Body/Type | Original List | Current Whlse | Average Retail |
|---|---|---|---|
| 3 Dr Base Hbk (5 spd) | **8289** | 6650 | 7750 |
| 3 Dr SE Hbk (5 spd) | **10239** | 7225 | 8400 |

#### 626 4

| | Original List | Current Whlse | Average Retail |
|---|---|---|---|
| 4 Dr DX Sdn (5 spd) | **14525** | 10775 | 12425 |
| 4 Dr LX Sdn (5 spd) | **15645** | 11650 | 13450 |
| ADD FOR: | | | |
| Leather Pkg | **1000** | 330 | 360 |
| Anti-lock Brakes (DX, LX) | **950** | 460 | 500 |
| (ES) | **800** | 530 | 590 |
| CD Player (ES) | **700** | 460 | 500 |
| Aluminum Wheels (LX) | **425** | 280 | 310 |

#### MX-3 4

| | Original List | Current Whlse | Average Retail |
|---|---|---|---|
| 3 Dr Hbk (5 spd) | **12280** | 9200 | 10600 |

#### MX-3 6

| | Original List | Current Whlse | Average Retail |
|---|---|---|---|
| 3 Dr GS Hbk (5 spd) | **15080** | 11250 | 13000 |
| ADD FOR: | | | |
| Anti-lock Brakes | **900** | 460 | 500 |
| Aluminum Wheels (Base) | **425** | 280 | 310 |

#### MX-5 MIATA 4

| | Original List | Current Whlse | Average Retail |
|---|---|---|---|
| 2 Dr Conv (5 spd) | **16170** | 12675 | 15000 |
| 2 Dr Black/Tan Conv | | | |
| (5 spd) | **17880** | — | — |
| ADD FOR: | | | |
| Anti-lock Brakes | **900** | 460 | 500 |
| Detachable Hardtop | **1500** | 980 | 1090 |
| CD Player | **600** | 390 | 430 |

#### MX-6 4

| | Original List | Current Whlse | Average Retail |
|---|---|---|---|
| 2 Dr DX Cpe (5 spd) | **14315** | 11025 | 12725 |
| 2 Dr LX Cpe (5 spd) | **15635** | 11900 | 13750 |
| 2 Dr GT Cpe (5 spd) | **17955** | 13000 | 15325 |

| Year/Model/Body/Type | Original List | Current Whlse | Average Retail |
|---|---|---|---|
| ADD FOR: | | | |
| Anti-lock Brakes | **1000** | 460 | 500 |
| CD Player | **700** | 460 | 500 |
| Aluminum Wheels (LX) | **425** | 280 | 310 |

#### 929 6

| | Original List | Current Whlse | Average Retail |
|---|---|---|---|
| 4 Dr Sdn (auto) | **28500** | 21775 | 25075 |
| ADD FOR: | | | |
| Leather Seat Trim | **1300** | 330 | 360 |
| Premium Pkg | **3200** | 2090 | 2320 |
| CD Player | **700** | 460 | 500 |

#### PROTEGE 4

| | Original List | Current Whlse | Average Retail |
|---|---|---|---|
| 4 Dr DX Sdn (5 spd) | **11669** | 8225 | 9500 |
| 4 Dr LX Sdn (5 spd) | **12839** | 8900 | 10275 |
| ADD FOR: | | | |
| Aluminum Wheels | **425** | — | — |

#### MPV 4

| | Original List | Current Whlse | Average Retail |
|---|---|---|---|
| 2WD Van (auto) | **14979** | — | — |
| 2 WD Wgn/Van (auto) | **17149** | — | — |
| 2WD Wgn (auto) | **18569** | 13950 | 16325 |

#### MPV 6

| | Original List | Current Whlse | Average Retail |
|---|---|---|---|
| 2WD Wgn (auto) | **19349** | — | — |
| 4WD Wgn (auto) | **22219** | 16450 | 19100 |
| ADD FOR: | | | |
| Touring Pkg | **570** | — | — |
| CD Player | **699** | — | — |

#### NAVAJO 6

| | Original List | Current Whlse | Average Retail |
|---|---|---|---|
| 2WD DX Sport Utility (5 spd) | **16590** | 13175 | 15500 |
| 4WD DX Sport Utility (5 spd) | **18390** | 14700 | 17250 |
| 2WD LX Sport Utility (5 spd) | **18645** | 14125 | 16575 |
| 4WD LX Sport Utility (5 spd) | **20445** | 15625 | 18275 |
| ADD FOR: | | | |
| Leather Pkg | **3770** | 400 | 500 |

#### B2200 2WD PICKUPS 4

| | Original List | Current Whlse | Average Retail |
|---|---|---|---|
| Short Bed (5 spd) | **10130** | 6975 | 7925 |
| Long Bed (5 spd) | **10845** | 7150 | 8150 |
| Cab Plus (5 spd) | **10590** | 7650 | 8700 |
| ADD FOR: | | | |
| LE-5 Luxury Pkg | **850** | 560 | 620 |
| SE-5 Sport Pkg | **650** | 430 | 480 |

#### B2600i 2WD PICKUPS 4

| | Original List | Current Whlse | Average Retail |
|---|---|---|---|
| Short Bed (5 spd) | **10185** | — | — |
| Cab Plus (5 spd) | **11570** | — | — |

| Year/Model/Body/Type | Original List | Current Whlse | Average Retail |
|---|---|---|---|
| **B2600i 4WD PICKUPS 4** | | | |
| Short Bed (5 spd) | **12620** | 8775 | 10125 |
| Cab Plus (5 spd) | **14120** | 9425 | 10850 |
| *ADD FOR:* | | | |
| LE-5 Luxury Pkg | **850** | 560 | 620 |
| SE-5 Sport Pkg | **750** | 490 | 540 |

NOTE: Tilt steering wheel standard on MX-3 GS, 626, MX-6, 929 and MPV. Cruise control standard on Protege LX, 626 LX, MX-6 LX & GT and 929. Power windows standard on Protege LX, 626 LX, MX-6 LX & GT, MX-5 Miata Black/Tan, 929 and Navajo LX. Power door locks standard on Protege LX, 626 LX, MX-6 LX & GT, 929 and Navajo LX.

## 1991

| Year/Model/Body/Type | Original List | Current Whlse | Average Retail |
|---|---|---|---|
| **323 4** | | | |
| 3 Dr Base Hbk (5 spd) | **8444** | 5575 | 6500 |
| 3 Dr SE Hbk (5 spd) | **9494** | 6125 | 7125 |
| **626 4** | | | |
| 4 Dr DX Sdn (5 spd) | **14095** | 8500 | 9825 |
| 4 Dr LX Sdn (5 spd) | **15215** | 9325 | 10750 |
| 5 Dr LX Hbk (5 spd) | **15615** | 9525 | 10975 |
| 4 Dr LE Sdn (5 spd) | **16545** | 9850 | 11350 |
| 5 Dr GT Hbk (5 spd) | **17215** | 10250 | 11825 |
| **MX-5 MIATA 4** | | | |
| 2 Dr Conv (5 spd) | **16475** | 11675 | 13475 |
| 2 Dr Special Edit. Conv (5 spd) | **19249** | 12750 | 15075 |
| **MX-6 4** | | | |
| 2 Dr DX Cpe (5 spd) | **13895** | 8700 | 10050 |
| 2 Dr LX Cpe (5 spd) | **15215** | 9525 | 10975 |
| 2 Dr LE Cpe (5 spd) | **16545** | 9825 | 11325 |
| 2 Dr GT Cpe (5 spd) | **17535** | 10250 | 11825 |
| **929 6** | | | |
| 4 Dr Sdn (auto) | **23850** | 14550 | 17075 |
| 4 Dr S Sdn (auto) | **25350** | 15200 | 17850 |
| **PROTEGE 4** | | | |
| 4 Dr DX Sdn (5 spd) | **11044** | 7075 | 8225 |
| 4 Dr LX Sdn (5 spd) | **12194** | 7650 | 8875 |
| 4 Dr 4WD Sdn (5 spd) | **12484** | 7800 | 9050 |
| **RX-7 ROTARY** | | | |
| 2 Dr Base Cpe (5 spd) | **20000** | 12775 | 15100 |
| 2 Dr Conv (5 spd) | **28150** | 17100 | 19750 |
| 2 Dr Turbo Cpe (5 spd) | **27100** | 16175 | 18825 |
| **MPV 4** | | | |
| Van (auto) | **13674** | 10175 | 11750 |
| Wgn/Van (5 spd) | **14994** | 10825 | 12500 |
| Wgn (5 spd) | **16394** | 11775 | 13600 |

| Year/Model/Body/Type | Original List | Current Whlse | Average Retail |
|---|---|---|---|
| **MPV 6** | | | |
| 2WD Wgn (auto) | **17874** | 12725 | 15050 |
| **NAVAJO 6** | | | |
| 2 Dr 4WD Spt Utility (5 spd) | **18810** | 13000 | 15325 |
| **B2200 2WD PICKUPS 4** | | | |
| Short Bed (5 spd) | **9794** | 5875 | 6800 |
| Long Bed (5 spd) | **10454** | 6025 | 6950 |
| Cab Plus (5 spd) | **11314** | 6450 | 7500 |
| **B2600i 2WD PICKUPS 4** | | | |
| Short Bed (5 spd) | **10029** | 6200 | 7225 |
| Cab Plus (5 spd) | **11279** | 6725 | 7825 |
| *ADD FOR:* | | | |
| Detachable Hardtop (MX-5 Miata) | **1400** | 500 | 560 |
| Leather Pkg (929 Base) | **900** | 270 | 300 |
| (929 S) | **1150** | 270 | 300 |
| Luxury Pkg (929 Base) | **1400** | 420 | 460 |
| (929 S) | **1600** | 480 | 540 |

NOTE: Power brakes standard on all models. Power door locks standard on 626 LX, 626 GT, 626 LE, 929, MX-6 LX, MX-6 LE, MX-6 GT, Protege LX and RX-7. Power windows standard on 626 LX, 626 GT, 626 LE, 929, MX-5 Miata, MX-6 LX, MX-6 LE, MX-6 GT, Navajo, Protege LX and RX-7. Power seat standard on 929. Moonroof standard on 626 LE, 929 and MX-6 LE.

## 1990

| Year/Model/Body/Type | Original List | Current Whlse | Average Retail |
|---|---|---|---|
| **323 4** | | | |
| 3 Dr Base Hbk (5 spd) | **7634** | 4425 | 5350 |
| 3 Dr SE Hbk (5 spd) | **9364** | 4800 | 5725 |
| **626 4** | | | |
| 4 Dr DX Sdn (5 spd) | **13269** | 7375 | 8550 |
| 4 Dr LX Sdn (5 spd) | **14139** | 8125 | 9375 |
| 5 Dr LX Touring Sdn (5 spd) | **14939** | 8325 | 9625 |
| 5 Dr GT Turbo Touring Sdn (5 spd) | **16509** | 8900 | 10275 |
| **MX-5 MIATA 4** | | | |
| 2 Dr Conv (5 spd) | **15740** | 9875 | 11375 |
| **MX-6 4** | | | |
| 2 Dr DX Cpe (5 spd) | **13089** | 7550 | 8775 |
| 2 Dr LX Cpe (5 spd) | **14579** | 8300 | 9575 |
| 2 Dr GT Turbo Cpe (5 spd) | **16839** | 8875 | 10250 |
| 2 Dr 4WS Turbo Cpe (5 spd) | **18039** | 9325 | 10750 |
| **929 6** | | | |
| 4 Dr Sdn (auto) | **23300** | 11800 | 13625 |

| Year/Model/Body/Type | Original List | Current Whlse | Average Retail |
|---|---|---|---|
| 4 Dr S Sdn (auto) | **24800** | 12325 | 14350 |
| **RX-7 ROTARY** | | | |
| 2 Dr GTU Cpe (5 spd) | **18739** | 10275 | 11850 |
| 2 Dr GTUs Cpe (5 spd) | **20180** | 10375 | 11975 |
| 2 Dr GXL Cpe (5 spd) | **22330** | 11300 | 13050 |
| 2 Dr GXL 2+2 Cpe (5 spd) | **22830** | 11500 | 13275 |
| 2 Dr Turbo Cpe (5 spd) | **26530** | 12325 | 14350 |
| 2 Dr Conv (5 spd) | **26530** | 14500 | 17025 |
| **PROTEGE 4** | | | |
| 4 Dr SE Sdn (5 spd) | **10574** | 5525 | 6450 |
| 4 Dr LX Sdn (5 spd) | **11334** | 6100 | 7000 |
| 4 Dr 4WD Sdn (5 spd) | **12474** | 6225 | 7250 |
| **MPV 4** | | | |
| Van (5 spd) | **12548** | 8550 | 9875 |
| Wgn/Van (5 spd) | **14548** | 9000 | 10400 |
| Wgn (5 spd) | **15793** | 10475 | 12100 |
| **MPV 6** | | | |
| 2WD Wgn (auto) | **17243** | 11300 | 13050 |
| 4WD Wgn (5 spd) | **19743** | 12300 | 14300 |
| **B2200 2WD PICKUPS 4** | | | |
| Short Bed (5 spd) | **9009** | 4900 | 5825 |
| Long Bed (5 spd) | **9659** | 5025 | 5950 |
| Cab Plus (5 spd) | **10409** | 5400 | 6325 |
| **B2600i 2WD PICKUPS 4** | | | |
| SE-5 Short Bed (5 spd) | **10238** | 5300 | 6225 |
| LE-5 Short Bed (5 spd) | **10538** | 5575 | 6500 |
| SE-5 Cab Plus (5 spd) | **11638** | 5875 | 6800 |
| LE-5 Cab Plus (5 spd) | **11938** | 6100 | 7000 |
| **B2600i 4WD PICKUPS 4** | | | |
| Short Bed (5 spd) | **11879** | 6575 | 7650 |
| *ADD FOR:* | | | |
| Anti-Lock Braking System (626 LX) | **1150** | 260 | 290 |
| (626 GT) | **1000** | 230 | 250 |
| (MX-6 GT & 4WS) | **1000** | 230 | 250 |
| (MX-6 LX) | **1150** | 260 | 290 |
| (929 Base) | **1000** | 230 | 250 |
| Detachable Hardtop (MX-5 Miata) | **1100** | 260 | 280 |
| Leather Seat Trim (RX-7 GXL) | **850** | 190 | 210 |
| (RX-7 Turbo) | **1000** | 230 | 250 |
| (929) | **880** | 200 | 220 |
| LE-5 Luxury Pkg (2WD Short Bed & Cab Plus Pickups) | **779** | 170 | 190 |
| (4WD Pickups) | **879** | 200 | 220 |
| SE-5 Sport Pkg | | | |
| (2WD Short Bed & Cab Plus Pickups) | **479** | 110 | 120 |
| (4WD Pickups) | **579** | 130 | 150 |

NOTE: Power brakes standard on all models. Anti-lock brakes standard on RX-7 Turbo, 929 S and MPV. Sunroof standard on RX-7 GXL and Turbo. Moonroof standard on MX-6 4WS and 929 Series. Power windows standard on 626 LX, MX-6 LX, MX-6 GT, MX-6 4WS, RX-7 Conv, RX-7 GXL, RX-7 Turbo and 929 Series. Power door locks standard on Protege LX, 626 LX, MX-6 LX, MX-6 GT, MX-6 4WS, RX-7 Conv, RX-7 GXL, RX-7 Turbo and 929 Series.

## 1989½

| Year/Model/Body/Type | Original List | Current Whlse | Average Retail |
|---|---|---|---|
| **B2600i 4WD PICKUPS 4** | | | |
| Short Bed (5 spd) | **11653** | 5600 | 6525 |
| SE-5 Short Bed (5 spd) | **12153** | 5850 | 6775 |
| SE-5 Cab Plus (5 spd) | **13893** | 6375 | 7300 |
| LX Cab Plus (5 spd) | **14528** | 6575 | 7500 |
| *ADD FOR:* | | | |
| 4x4 Pkg (B2600i LX) | **430** | 180 | 200 |

NOTE: Power brakes standard on all models.

## 1989

| Year/Model/Body/Type | Original List | Current Whlse | Average Retail |
|---|---|---|---|
| **323 4** | | | |
| 3 Dr Base Hbk (4 spd) (NA w/radio) | **7459** | 3300 | 4200 |
| 4 Dr Base Sdn (5 spd) | **8909** | 3525 | 4425 |
| 3 Dr SE Hbk (5 spd) | **8659** | 3675 | 4575 |
| 4 Dr SE Sdn (5 spd) | **10059** | 4100 | 5025 |
| 4 Dr LX Sdn (5 spd) | **11259** | 4500 | 5425 |
| 3 Dr GTX Turbo Hbk (5 spd) | **14459** | 6700 | 7800 |
| **626 4** | | | |
| 4 Dr DX Sdn (5 spd) | **12699** | 5575 | 6500 |
| 4 Dr LX Sdn (5 spd) | **14199** | 6225 | 7250 |
| 5 Dr LX Touring Sdn (5 spd) | **14399** | 6425 | 7475 |
| 5 Dr Turbo Touring Sdn (5 spd) | **16049** | 7000 | 8150 |
| **929 6** | | | |
| 4 Dr Sdn (auto) | **22900** | 9050 | 10425 |
| **MX-6 4** | | | |
| 2 Dr DX Cpe (5 spd) | **12649** | 5725 | 6650 |
| 2 Dr LX Cpe (5 spd) | **14099** | 6375 | 7425 |
| 2 Dr GT Turbo Cpe (5 spd) | **16299** | 6950 | 8100 |
| 2 Dr 4WS Turbo Cpe (5 spd) | **17499** | 7325 | 8500 |
| **MPV 4** | | | |
| Van (5 spd) | **12048** | 7025 | 8125 |

| Year/Model/Body/Type | Original List | Current Whlse | Average Retail |
|---|---|---|---|
| Wgn/Van (5 spd) | **14048** | 7275 | 8450 |
| Wgn (5 spd) | **14898** | 8825 | 10200 |
| **MPV 6** | | | |
| 2WD Wgn (5 spd) | **15598** | 9225 | 10625 |
| 2WD Wgn (auto) | **16348** | 10625 | 12250 |
| **RX-7 ROTARY** | | | |
| 2 Dr GTU 2-Seater (5 spd) | **18159** | 8550 | 9875 |
| 2 Dr GTUS 2-Seater (5 spd) | **20459** | 8750 | 10100 |
| 2 Dr Conv (5 spd) | **26459** | 12750 | 14850 |
| 2 Dr GXL 2-Seater (5 spd) | **21600** | 9400 | 10825 |
| 2 Dr GXL 2+2 (5 spd) | **22100** | 9625 | 11100 |
| 2 Dr Turbo 2-Seater (5 spd) | **25950** | 10375 | 11975 |
| **B2200 2WD PICKUPS 4** | | | |
| Short Bed (5 spd) | **9049** | 3525 | 4425 |
| Long Bed (5 spd) | **9549** | 3650 | 4550 |
| Cab Plus (5 spd) | **10549** | 3975 | 4875 |
| SE-5 Short Bed (5 spd) | **9449** | 3775 | 4675 |
| SE-5 Long Bed (5 spd) | **9949** | 3900 | 4800 |
| SE-5 Cab Plus (5 spd) | **10849** | 4200 | 5125 |
| LX Short Bed (5 spd) | **10824** | 4325 | 5250 |
| LX Cab Plus (5 spd) | **11824** | 4725 | 5650 |
| *ADD FOR:* | | | |
| Anti-Lock Braking System (MX-6 GT, 626 Turbo, 929) | **1000** | 250 | 270 |
| Leather Power Seat (929, RX-7 GXL ex. Conv) | **880** | 250 | 270 |
| (RX-7 Turbo ex. Conv) | **1000** | 250 | 270 |

NOTE: Power brakes standard on all models. Power windows and power door locks standard on 929, MX-6 LX, MX-6 GT, MX-4 4WS, RX-7 Conv, RX-7 GXL and RX-7 Turbo. Sunroof standard on RX-7 GXL and RX-7 Turbo.

## 1988

### 323 4

| | Original List | Current Whlse | Average Retail |
|---|---|---|---|
| 3 Dr Hbk (4 spd) | **6149** | 1900 | 2750 |
| 4 Dr Sdn (5 spd) | **7299** | 2275 | 3150 |
| 5 Dr Wgn (5 spd) | **7999** | 2350 | 3225 |
| 3 Dr SE Hbk (5 spd) | **7149** | 2075 | 2925 |
| 4 Dr SE Sdn (5 spd) | **7999** | 2425 | 3300 |
| 4 Dr LX Sdn (5 spd) | **9299** | 2775 | 3675 |
| 4 Dr GT Turbo Sdn (5 spd) | **11799** | 3775 | 4675 |
| 3 Dr GTX Hbk (5 spd) | **12999** | 5000 | 5925 |

### 626 4

| | Original List | Current Whlse | Average Retail |
|---|---|---|---|
| 4 Dr DX Sdn (5 spd) | **10999** | 4075 | 5000 |
| 4 Dr LX Sdn (5 spd) | **12899** | 4450 | 5375 |
| 5 Dr LX Touring Sdn (5 spd) | **13099** | 4650 | 5575 |
| 4 Dr Turbo Sdn (5 spd) | **14549** | 4875 | 5800 |
| 5 Dr Turbo Touring Sdn (5 spd) | **14749** | 5075 | 6000 |
| 4 Dr Turbo 4WS Sdn (auto) | **17799** | 6050 | 6950 |

### MX-6 4

| | Original List | Current Whlse | Average Retail |
|---|---|---|---|
| 2 Dr DX Cpe (5 spd) | **11099** | 4175 | 5100 |
| 2 Dr LX Cpe (5 spd) | **12999** | 4550 | 5475 |
| 2 Dr GT Turbo Cpe (5 spd) | **15099** | 4975 | 5900 |

### RX-7 ROTARY

| | Original List | Current Whlse | Average Retail |
|---|---|---|---|
| 2 Dr Conv (5 spd) | **21550** | 9300 | 10725 |
| 2 Dr Conv w/Opt Pkg (5 spd) | **24050** | — | |
| 2 Dr SE Cpe (5 spd) | **16150** | 5525 | 6450 |
| 2 Dr SE 2+2 Cpe (5 spd) | **16650** | 5725 | 6650 |
| 2 Dr GTU Cpe (5 spd) | **18150** | 5775 | 6700 |
| 2 Dr GXL Cpe (5 spd) | **20050** | 6875 | 8000 |
| 2 Dr GXL 2+2 Cpe (5 spd) | **20550** | 7075 | 8225 |
| 2 Dr Turbo Cpe (5 spd) | **22750** | 7550 | 8775 |

### 929 6

| | Original List | Current Whlse | Average Retail |
|---|---|---|---|
| 4 Dr Sdn (5 spd) | **19850** | 6650 | 7750 |
| 4 Dr Sdn (auto) | **19850** | 7050 | 8175 |

### B2200 2WD PICKUPS 4

| | Original List | Current Whlse | Average Retail |
|---|---|---|---|
| Short Bed (5 spd) | **7549** | 2550 | 3425 |
| Long Bed (5 spd) | **8049** | 2675 | 3575 |
| Cab Plus (5 spd) | **8849** | 2950 | 3850 |
| SE-5 Short Bed (5 spd) | **7849** | 2650 | 3550 |
| SE-5 Long Bed (5 spd) | **8349** | 2700 | 3600 |
| SE-5 Cab Plus (5 spd) | **9149** | 3125 | 4025 |
| LX Short Bed (5 spd) | **9449** | 3125 | 4025 |
| LX Cab Plus (5 spd) | **10499** | 3525 | 4550 |

### B2600 4WD PICKUPS 4

| | Original List | Current Whlse | Average Retail |
|---|---|---|---|
| Short Bed (5 spd) | **10199** | 3900 | 4800 |
| Long Bed (5 spd) | **10699** | 4025 | 4925 |
| Cab Plus (5 spd) | **11599** | 4300 | 5225 |
| SE-5 Short Bed (5 spd) | **10699** | 4075 | 5000 |
| SE-5 Long Bed (5 spd) | **11199** | 4200 | 5125 |
| SE-5 Cab Plus (5 spd) | **12099** | 4500 | 5425 |
| LX Short Bed (5 spd) | **12399** | 4500 | 5425 |
| LX Long Bed (5 spd) | **12899** | 4625 | 5550 |
| LX Cab Plus (5 spd) | **13449** | 4900 | 5950 |

*ADD FOR:*
Anti-Lock Braking

| Year/Model/ Body/Type | Original List | Current Whlse | Average Retail |
|---|---|---|---|
| System (929) (MX-6 GT, RX-7 | **1650** | 180 | 200 |
| Turbo) | **1395** | 180 | 200 |
| Leather Power Seat (929) | **1275** | 210 | 230 |

NOTE: Power brakes standard on all models. Air conditioning standard on RX-7 GXL and Turbo, 929. Power windows standard on 626 LX, 626 Turbo and 626 4WS, MX-6 LX, MX-6 GT, RX-7 Conv and 929. Power door locks standard on 626 LX, 626 Turbo, 626 4WS, MX-6 LX, MX-6 GT and 929. Pwr strng standard on 323 GTX, 626, MX-6, RX-7 Series except Turbo, 929, 4WD Standard Pickup, SE-5 Pickup and LX Pickup.

## 1987

### 323 4

| | | | |
|---|---|---|---|
| 3 Dr Hbk (4 spd) | **6099** | 1325 | 2050 |
| 4 Dr Wgn (5 spd) | **8399** | 1950 | 2800 |
| 3 Dr SE Hbk (5 spd) | **6699** | 1450 | 2225 |
| 3 Dr Dlx Hbk (5 spd) | **7799** | 1650 | 2500 |
| 4 Dr Dlx Sdn (5 spd) | **8299** | 1875 | 2725 |
| 4 Dr Dlx Wgn (5 spd) | **8999** | 2000 | 2850 |
| 4 Dr Lux Sdn (5 spd) | **8999** | 2100 | 2950 |

### 626 4

| | | | |
|---|---|---|---|
| 4 Dr Dlx Sdn (5 spd) | **10149** | 2575 | 3450 |
| 2 Dr Dlx Cpe (5 spd) | **10199** | 2675 | 3575 |
| 4 Dr Lux Sdn (5 spd) | **11949** | 2925 | 3825 |
| 2 Dr Lux Cpe (5 spd) | **12149** | 2475 | 3350 |
| 5 Dr Lux Touring Sdn (5 spd) | **12649** | 3125 | 4025 |
| 4 Dr GT Turbo Sdn (5 spd) | **13399** | 3300 | 4200 |
| 2 Dr GT Turbo Cpe (5 spd) | **13699** | 3400 | 4300 |
| 5 Dr GT Turbo Touring Sdn (5 spd) | **14299** | 3500 | 4400 |

### RX-7 ROTARY

| | | | |
|---|---|---|---|
| 2 Dr Cpe (5 spd) | **14399** | 3550 | 4450 |
| 2 Dr 2+2 Cpe (5 spd) | **14899** | 3725 | 4625 |
| 2 Dr Sport Cpe (5 spd) | **16649** | 3850 | 4750 |
| 2 Dr SE Cpe (5 spd) | **15199** | 3750 | 4650 |
| 2 Dr 2+2 SE Cpe (5 spd) | **15699** | 3950 | 4850 |
| 2 Dr GXL Cpe (5 spd) | **18669** | 4725 | 5650 |
| 2 Dr 2+2 GXL Cpe (5 spd) | **19199** | 5300 | 6225 |
| 2 Dr Turbo Cpe (5 spd) | **20799** | 5175 | 6100 |

### B2200 2WD PICKUPS 4

| | | | |
|---|---|---|---|
| Std Short Bed | **6799** | 1825 | 2675 |
| Std Long Bed | **7299** | 2000 | 2850 |
| Std Cab Plus | **8299** | 2200 | 3050 |
| SE-5 Short Bed | **7299** | 2025 | 2875 |
| SE-5 Long Bed | **7799** | 2125 | 2975 |
| SE-5 Cab Plus | **8799** | 2375 | 3250 |

| Year/Model/ Body/Type | Original List | Current Whlse | Average Retail |
|---|---|---|---|
| LX Short Bed | **8699** | 2375 | 3250 |
| LX Long Bed | **9199** | 2525 | 3375 |
| LX Cab Plus | **9749** | 2775 | 3675 |

### B2600 2WD PICKUPS 4

| | | | |
|---|---|---|---|
| LX Short Bed | **9049** | 2400 | 3275 |
| LX Long Bed | **9549** | 2525 | 3400 |
| LX Cab Plus | **10099** | 2825 | 3725 |

### B2600 4WD PICKUPS 4

| | | | |
|---|---|---|---|
| Std Short Bed | **9499** | 3125 | 4025 |
| Std Long Bed | **9999** | 3300 | 4200 |
| Std Cab Plus | **10999** | 3525 | 4425 |
| SE-5 Short Bed | **9999** | 3225 | 4125 |
| SE-5 Long Bed | **10499** | 3450 | 4350 |
| SE-5 Cab Plus | **11499** | 3675 | 4575 |

*ADD FOR:*

| | | | |
|---|---|---|---|
| Leather Pkg (RX-7 GXL except 2+2) | **730** | 130 | 140 |
| (RX-7 GXL 2+2) | **930** | 130 | 140 |

NOTE: Power brakes standard on all models. Air conditioning and sunroof standard on RX-7 GXL and RX-7 Turbo. Power windows standard on 626 Luxury, RX-7 GXL and RX-7 Turbo. Power door locks standard on 626 Luxury. Pwr strng standard on 626 Luxury, RX-7 Sport, RX-7 GXL and 4WD Pickups. AM/FM stereo radio standard on Base RX-7, 2WD LX Pickups and 4WD LX Pickups.

## 1986

### 323 4

| | | | |
|---|---|---|---|
| 3 Dr Hbk (4 spd) | **6160** | 1050 | 1775 |
| 3 Dr Dlx Hbk (5 spd) | **7760** | 1275 | 2000 |
| 4 Dr Dlx Sdn (5 spd) | **8260** | 1475 | 2300 |
| 3 Dr Lux Hbk (5 spd) | **8460** | 1400 | 2150 |
| 4 Dr Luxury Sdn (5 spd) | **8860** | 1625 | 2475 |

### 626 4

| | | | |
|---|---|---|---|
| 4 Dr Dlx Sdn (5 spd) | **9660** | 1825 | 2675 |
| 2 Dr Dlx Cpe (5 spd) | **9910** | 1925 | 2775 |
| 4 Dr Luxury Sdn (5 spd) | **11045** | 2125 | 2975 |
| 2 Dr Lux Cpe (5 spd) | **11345** | 2200 | 3050 |
| 5 Dr Lux Touring Sdn (5 spd) | **11945** | 2275 | 3150 |
| 4 Dr GT Turbo Sdn (5 spd) | **12695** | 2475 | 3350 |
| 2 Dr GT Turbo Cpe (5 spd) | **12995** | 2575 | 3450 |
| 5 Dr GT Turbo Touring Sdn (5 spd) | **13595** | 2675 | 3575 |

### RX-7 ROTARY

| | | | |
|---|---|---|---|
| 2 Dr Cpe (5 spd) | **13595** | 2850 | 3750 |
| 2 Dr 2+2 Cpe (5 spd) | **14095** | 2925 | 3825 |
| 2 Dr GXL Cpe (5 spd) | **18445** | 3375 | 4275 |

*Refer to optional equipment schedules*

| Year/Model/Body/Type | Original List | Current Whlse | Average Retail |
|---|---|---|---|
| 2 Dr GXL 2+2 Cpe (5 spd) | **18945** | 3475 | 4375 |
| **B2000 PICKUPS 4** | | | |
| Std Short Bed | **6295** | 1550 | 2400 |
| Std Long Bed | **6495** | 1675 | 2525 |
| SE-5 Short Bed | **6990** | 1675 | 2525 |
| SE-5 Long Bed | **7190** | 1725 | 2575 |
| LX Short Bed | **7895** | 1950 | 2800 |
| LX Long Bed | **8095** | 2075 | 2925 |
| Std Cab Plus | **7695** | 1800 | 2650 |
| SE-5 Cab Plus | **8095** | 2100 | 2950 |
| LX Cab Plus | **8995** | 2225 | 3075 |
| *ADD FOR:* | | | |
| Leather Pkg (RX-7 GXL except 2+2) | **720** | 100 | 110 |
| Luxury Pkg (RX-7 GXL 2+2) | **900** | 100 | 110 |
| Sport Pkg (RX-7 Base 2-Seater) | **1550** | 160 | 180 |

NOTE: Power locks standard on 626 Luxury. Power windows and pwr strng standard on 626 Luxury and RX-7 Series. Sunroof standard on RX-7 Series. Power brakes standard on 323 Series, 626 Series and B2000 Pickups.

## 1985

### 626 4

| | Original List | Current Whlse | Average Retail |
|---|---|---|---|
| 2 Dr Dlx Cpe (5 spd) | **9170** | 1700 | 2550 |
| 2 Dr Lux Cpe (5 spd) | **10595** | 1925 | 2775 |
| 4 Dr Dlx Sdn (5 spd) | **8820** | 1625 | 2475 |
| 4 Dr Luxury Sdn (5 spd) | **10245** | 1825 | 2675 |
| 4 Dr Lux Touring Sdn (5 spd) | **11245** | 2025 | 2875 |
| 4 Dr Diesel Lux Sdn (5 spd) | **10795** | 1275 | 2000 |

### GLC 4

| | Original List | Current Whlse | Average Retail |
|---|---|---|---|
| 3 Dr Base Hbk (4 spd) | **5195** | 800 | 1500 |
| 3 Dr Dlx Hbk (5 spd) | **6420** | 950 | 1675 |
| 3 Dr Lux Hbk (5 spd) | **7120** | 1125 | 1850 |
| 4 Dr Dlx Sdn (5 spd) | **7020** | 1150 | 1875 |
| 4 Dr Luxury Sdn (5 spd) | **7720** | 1300 | 2025 |

### RX-7 ROTARY

| | Original List | Current Whlse | Average Retail |
|---|---|---|---|
| 2 Dr S Cpe (5 spd) | **10945** | 2325 | 3200 |
| 2 Dr GS Cpe (5 spd) | **11845** | 2425 | 3300 |
| 2 Dr GSL Cpe (5 spd) | **13645** | 2775 | 3675 |
| 2 Dr GSL-SE Cpe (5 spd) | **15645** | 2975 | 3875 |
| *ADD FOR:* | | | |
| Leather Pkg (RX-7) | **720** | 80 | 90 |

NOTE: Pwr strng, power windows and power locks standard on 626 Luxury. Air conditioning standard on RX-7 GSL-SE. Sunroof standard on RX-7 GSL and GSL-SE.

## 1984

### 626 4

| | Original List | Current Whlse | Average Retail |
|---|---|---|---|
| 2 Dr Dlx Cpe (5 spd) | **8615** | 1250 | 1975 |
| 2 Dr Lux Cpe (5 spd) | **9845** | 1475 | 2300 |
| 4 Dr Dlx Sdn (5 spd) | **8215** | 1200 | 1925 |
| 4 Dr Lux Sdn (5 spd) | **9445** | 1425 | 2175 |
| 4 Dr Lux Touring Sdn (5 spd) | **10395** | 1575 | 2425 |

### B2000 PICKUPS 4

| | Original List | Current Whlse | Average Retail |
|---|---|---|---|
| Base Short Bed | **5945** | 725 | 1375 |
| Long Bed | **6145** | 800 | 1500 |
| Sport SE-5 Short Bed | **6145** | 875 | 1575 |
| Sport SE-5 Long Bed | **6345** | 925 | 1650 |
| Sport Short Bed | **6745** | 950 | 1675 |
| Sport Long Bed | **6945** | 1050 | 1775 |
| SE-5 Short Bed | **6145** | 800 | 1500 |
| SE-5 Long Bed | **6445** | 875 | 1600 |

### B2200 PICKUPS 4

| | Original List | Current Whlse | Average Retail |
|---|---|---|---|
| Diesel Short Bed | **6695** | 375 | 675 |
| Diesel Long Bed | **6895** | 425 | 775 |

### GLC 4

| | Original List | Current Whlse | Average Retail |
|---|---|---|---|
| 3 Dr Base Hbk (4 spd) | **4995** | 425 | 755 |
| 3 Dr Dlx Hbk (5 spd) | **6175** | 600 | 1125 |
| 3 Dr Lux Hbk (5 spd) | **6775** | 725 | 1375 |
| 4 Dr Dlx Sdn (5 spd) | **6725** | 700 | 1325 |
| 4 Dr Lux Sdn (5 spd) | **7375** | 825 | 1525 |

### RX-7 ROTARY

| | Original List | Current Whlse | Average Retail |
|---|---|---|---|
| 2 Dr S Cpe (5 spd) | **10195** | 1875 | 2725 |
| 2 Dr GS Cpe (5 spd) | **11295** | 2000 | 2850 |
| 2 Dr GSL Cpe (5 spd) | **13095** | 2200 | 3050 |
| 2 Dr GSL-SE Cpe (5 spd) | **15095** | 2325 | 3200 |

### 1983 — ALL BODY STYLES

| | Original List | Current Whlse | Average Retail |
|---|---|---|---|
| 626 | — | 775 | 1475 |
| B2000 PICKUPS | — | 575 | 1075 |
| B2200 PICKUPS | — | 95 | 300 |
| GLC | — | 475 | 875 |
| RX-7 ROTARY | — | 1725 | 2575 |

## MERCEDES-BENZ

### 1992

#### 190 E 4

| | Original List | Current Whlse | Average Retail |
|---|---|---|---|
| 2.3 4 Dr Sdn (5 spd) | **28950** | 22025 | 25325 |
| 2.6 4 Dr Sdn (5 spd) | **34000** | 24650 | 27975 |

*1990 Mercedes Benz 500SL*

| Year/Model/<br>Body/Type | Original<br>List | Current<br>Whlse | Average<br>Retail |
|---|---|---|---|
| *ADD FOR:* | | | |
| Leather Seat Trim | **1550** | 500 | 600 |
| **300 D 5** | | | |
| 4 Dr Turbo Sdn (auto) | **42950** | 33900 | 37700 |
| **300 E 6** | | | |
| 2.6 4 Dr Sdn (auto) | **42950** | 32900 | 36575 |
| 3.0 4 Dr Sdn (auto) | **49500** | 36450 | 40450 |
| 3.0 4Matic 4 Dr<br>Sdn (auto) | **57100** | — | — |
| **300 CE 6** | | | |
| 2 Dr Cpe (auto) | **60400** | — | — |
| **300 TE 6** | | | |
| 4Matic 5 Dr Wgn (auto) | **61100** | — | — |
| 5 Dr Wgn (auto) | **53900** | — | — |
| **300 SD 6** | | | |
| 4 Dr Turbo Sdn (auto) | **69400** | — | — |
| **300 SE 6** | | | |
| 4 Dr Sdn (auto) | **69400** | — | — |
| **300 SL 6** | | | |
| 2 Dr Cpe/Rdstr (5 spd) | **82500** | — | — |
| *ADD FOR:* | | | |
| Leather Seat Trim<br>(300 D, 300 E w/2.6<br>liter eng, 300 TE) | **1550** | 550 | 650 |
| Four Place Seating Pkg | **5120** | — | — |
| **400 E 8** | | | |
| 4 Dr Sdn (auto) | **55800** | — | — |

| Year/Model/<br>Body/Type | Original<br>List | Current<br>Whlse | Average<br>Retail |
|---|---|---|---|
| **400 SE 8** | | | |
| 4 Dr Sdn (auto) | **77900** | 56700 | 62150 |
| *ADD FOR:* | | | |
| Four Place Seating Pkg | **5120** | — | — |
| **500 E 8** | | | |
| 4 Dr Sdn (auto) | **79200** | — | — |
| **500 SL 8** | | | |
| 2 Dr Cpe/Rdstr (auto) | **97500** | — | — |
| **500 SEL 8** | | | |
| 4 Dr Sdn (auto) | **93500** | 64700 | 70275 |
| *ADD FOR:* | | | |
| Four Place Seating Pkg | **5120** | — | — |
| **600 SEL 12** | | | |
| 4 Dr Sdn (auto) | **127800** | — | — |
| *ADD FOR:* | | | |
| Four Place Seating Pkg | **3900** | — | — |

NOTE: Cruise control, power windows, power door locks and power seat standard on all models. Tilt steering wheel standard on 300 Series models with 3.0 liter eng, 400 Series, 500 Series and 600 SEL.

## 1991

| Year/Model/<br>Body/Type | Original<br>List | Current<br>Whlse | Average<br>Retail |
|---|---|---|---|
| **190 E 4** | | | |
| 2.3 4 Dr Sdn (5 spd) | **28050** | 18575 | 21625 |
| 2.3 4 Dr Sdn (auto) | **28950** | 19275 | 22325 |
| **190 E 6** | | | |
| 2.6 4 Dr Sdn (5 spd) | **32800** | 20825 | 23875 |

| Year/Model/Body/Type | Original List | Current Whlse | Average Retail |
|---|---|---|---|
| 2.6 4 Dr Sdn (auto) | **33700** | 21525 | 24825 |
| **300 D 5** | | | |
| 2.5 4 Dr Turbo Sdn (auto) | **41000** | 27500 | 30850 |
| **300 E 6** | | | |
| 2.6 4 Dr Sdn (auto) | **41000** | 26750 | 30075 |
| 4 Dr Std Sdn (auto) | **47200** | 30450 | 33850 |
| 4Matic 4 Dr Sdn (auto) | **54150** | 34150 | 37975 |
| **300 SE 6** | | | |
| 4 Dr Sdn (auto) | **53900** | 38050 | 41775 |
| **300 SEL 6** | | | |
| 4 Dr Sdn (auto) | **57800** | 39025 | 43325 |
| **300 CE 6** | | | |
| 2 Dr Cpe (auto) | **57350** | 36800 | 40850 |
| **300 SL 6** | | | |
| 2 Dr Cpe/Rdstr (5 spd) | **77500** | 55850 | 61200 |
| 2 Dr Cpe/Rdstr (auto) | **78500** | 56550 | 61975 |
| **300 TE 6** | | | |
| 5 Dr Std Wgn (auto) | **51150** | 34250 | 38075 |
| 4Matic 5 Dr Wgn (auto) | **57900** | 37450 | 41575 |
| **350 SD 6** | | | |
| 4 Dr Turbo Sdn (auto) | **53900** | 36450 | 40450 |
| **350 SDL 6** | | | |
| 4 Dr Turbo Sdn (auto) | **57800** | 38425 | 42650 |
| **420 SEL 8** | | | |
| 4 Dr Sdn (auto) | **63600** | 41200 | 45600 |
| **500 SL 8** | | | |
| 2 Dr Cpe/Rdstr (auto) | **89300** | 65300 | 70925 |
| **560 SEL 8** | | | |
| 4 Dr Sdn (auto) | **75100** | 46800 | 51575 |
| **560 SEC 8** | | | |
| 2 Dr Cpe (auto) | **82900** | 51750 | 56725 |
| *ADD FOR:* | | | |
| Leather Seats (190 E) (300 D 2.5, | **1495** | 480 | 540 |
| 300 E 2.6, 300 TE) | **1495** | 480 | 540 |
| Velour Seats (190 E) (300 D 2.5, | **1495** | 480 | 540 |
| 300 E 2.6, 300 TE) | **1475** | 480 | 540 |
| Four Place Seating (350 SDL, 300 SEL, | | | |
| 420 SEL) | **3080** | 1060 | 1170 |
| (560 SEL) | **2390** | 1000 | 1110 |

| Year/Model/Body/Type | Original List | Current Whlse | Average Retail |
|---|---|---|---|
| Rear Facing Third Seat (300 TE) | **1120** | 360 | 400 |

NOTE: Power brakes, power door locks and power windows standard on all models. Power seat standard on 190 E 2.6, 300 Series, 420 Series and 500 Series. Power sunroof standard on 560 Series.

## 1990

| | Original List | Current Whlse | Average Retail |
|---|---|---|---|
| **190 E 6** | | | |
| 2.6 4 Dr Sdn (5 spd) | **31600** | 17175 | 19825 |
| 2.6 4 Dr Sdn (auto) | **32500** | 17750 | 20400 |
| **300 D 6** | | | |
| 2.5 4 Dr Turbo Sdn (auto) | **39700** | 22350 | 25650 |
| **300 E 6** | | | |
| 2.6 4 Dr Sdn (auto) | **39950** | 21900 | 25200 |
| 4 Dr Sdn (auto) | **45950** | 24950 | 28275 |
| 4Matic 4 Dr Sdn (auto) | **52550** | 28425 | 31775 |
| **300 CE 6** | | | |
| 2 Dr Cpe (auto) | **55700** | 31600 | 35150 |
| **300 TE 6** | | | |
| 5 Dr Wgn (auto) | **49650** | 28425 | 31775 |
| 4Matic 5 Dr Wgn (auto) | **56250** | 31850 | 35425 |
| **300 SE 6** | | | |
| 4 Dr Sdn (auto) | **52950** | 29500 | 32725 |
| **300 SEL 6** | | | |
| 4 Dr Sdn (auto) | **56800** | 30900 | 34350 |
| **300 SL 6** | | | |
| 2 Dr Cpe/Rdstr (5 spd) | **72500** | 54200 | 59300 |
| 2 Dr Cpe/Rdstr (auto) | **73500** | 53200 | 58300 |
| **350 SD 6** | | | |
| 4 Dr Turbo Sdn (auto) | **52950** | — | — |
| **350 SDL 6** | | | |
| 4 Dr Turbo Sdn (auto) | **56800** | 30700 | 34150 |
| **420 SEL 8** | | | |
| 4 Dr Sdn (auto) | **62500** | 33200 | 36925 |
| **560 SEL 8** | | | |
| 4 Dr Sdn (auto) | **73800** | 37700 | 41850 |
| **560 SEC 8** | | | |
| 2 Dr Cpe (auto) | — | 43150 | 47775 |
| **500 SL 8** | | | |
| 2 Dr Cpe/Rdstr (auto) | **83500** | 59750 | 65475 |

# FOREIGN CARS & TRUCKS

| Year/Model/Body/Type | Original List | Current Whlse | Average Retail |
|---|---|---|---|
| *ADD FOR:* | | | |
| Electric Front Seats (190 E, 500 SL) | **505** | 130 | 140 |
| Leather Seats (190 E) | **1460** | 360 | 390 |
| Velour Seats (190 E) | **1440** | 360 | 390 |
| Third Facing Rear Seat (300 TE, 300 TE 4Matic) | **1095** | 260 | 280 |
| Four Place Seating (420 SEL) | **3005** | 660 | 730 |
| (560 SEL) | **2330** | 560 | 630 |

NOTE: Anti-lock power brakes, power windows, power door locks and power seat standard on all models. Sunroof standard on 560 SEL and 560 SEC.

## 1989

### 190 D 5

| | | | |
|---|---|---|---|
| 2.5 4 Dr Sdn (auto) | **30980** | 12750 | 15075 |

### 190 E 6

| | | | |
|---|---|---|---|
| 2.6 4 Dr Sdn (5 spd) | **31590** | 15250 | 17900 |
| 2.6 4 Dr Sdn (auto) | **32500** | 15250 | 17900 |

### 260 E 6

| | | | |
|---|---|---|---|
| 2.6 4 Dr Sdn (auto) | **39200** | 17650 | 20300 |

### 300 E 6

| | | | |
|---|---|---|---|
| 4 Dr Sdn (auto) | **44850** | 20425 | 23475 |

### 300 CE 6

| | | | |
|---|---|---|---|
| 2 Dr Cpe (auto) | **53880** | 25950 | 29275 |

### 300 TE 6

| | | | |
|---|---|---|---|
| 4 Dr Wgn (auto) | **48210** | 23400 | 26700 |

### 300 SE 6

| | | | |
|---|---|---|---|
| 4 Dr Sdn (auto) | **51400** | 23050 | 26350 |

### 300 SEL 6

| | | | |
|---|---|---|---|
| 4 Dr Sdn (auto) | **55100** | 25150 | 28475 |

### 420 SEL 8

| | | | |
|---|---|---|---|
| 4 Dr Sdn (auto) | **61210** | 27150 | 30475 |

### 560 SEL 8

| | | | |
|---|---|---|---|
| 4 Dr Sdn (auto) | **64230** | 30650 | 34075 |

### 560 SEC 8

| | | | |
|---|---|---|---|
| 2 Dr Cpe (auto) | **79840** | 35950 | 39900 |

### 560 SL 8

| | | | |
|---|---|---|---|
| 2 Dr Cpe/Rdstr (auto) | **72280** | 36050 | 40025 |

*ADD FOR:*
Electric Front Bucket

| Year/Model/Body/Type | Original List | Current Whlse | Average Retail |
|---|---|---|---|
| Seats (190 Series, 260 E) | **950** | 160 | 180 |
| Electric 4 Place Seating (300 SEL, 420 SEL) | **2835** | 500 | 560 |
| (560 SEL) | **2175** | 380 | 420 |
| Leather Seats (190 Series, 260 E, 300 E, 300 TE) | **1425** | 250 | 270 |
| Velour Seats (190 Series, 260 E, 300 E, 300 TE) | **1405** | 250 | 270 |
| Third Facing Rear Seat (300 TE) | **1070** | 190 | 210 |

NOTE: Power brakes, power windows and power door locks standard on all models. Power sunroof standard on 560 SEL Sedan and 560 SEC Coupe.

## 1988

### 190 D 5

| | | | |
|---|---|---|---|
| 2.5 4 Dr Sdn (auto) | **29960** | 10725 | 12375 |

### 190 E 4

| | | | |
|---|---|---|---|
| 2.3 4 Dr Sdn | **29190** | 11750 | 13600 |
| 2.3 4 Dr Sdn (auto) | **29960** | 12200 | 14100 |

### 190 E 6

| | | | |
|---|---|---|---|
| 2.6 4 Dr Sdn | **33500** | 12850 | 15075 |
| 2.6 4 Dr Sdn (auto) | **34260** | 13250 | 15575 |

### 260 E 6

| | | | |
|---|---|---|---|
| 2.6 4 Dr Sdn | **37845** | 14675 | 17225 |
| 2.6 4 Dr Sdn (auto) | **38760** | 15150 | 17800 |

### 300 E 6

| | | | |
|---|---|---|---|
| 4 Dr Sdn | **43365** | 16850 | 19500 |
| 4 Dr Sdn (auto) | **44400** | 17300 | 19950 |

### 300 CE 6

| | | | |
|---|---|---|---|
| 2 Dr Cpe (auto) | **53340** | 22825 | 26125 |

### 300 TE 6

| | | | |
|---|---|---|---|
| 4 Dr Wgn (auto) | **47730** | 20125 | 23175 |

### 300 SE 6

| | | | |
|---|---|---|---|
| 4 Dr Sdn (auto) | **49900** | 18300 | 21200 |

### 300 SEL 6

| | | | |
|---|---|---|---|
| 4 Dr Sdn (auto) | **53490** | 20125 | 23175 |

### 420 SEL 8

| | | | |
|---|---|---|---|
| 4 Dr Sdn (auto) | **59080** | 21900 | 25200 |

### 560 SEL 8

| | | | |
|---|---|---|---|
| 4 Dr Sdn (auto) | **69760** | 26000 | 29325 |

| Year/Model/Body/Type | Original List | Current Whlse | Average Retail |
|---|---|---|---|
| **560 SEC 8** | | | |
| 2 Dr Cpe (auto) | **77065** | 31450 | 34975 |
| **560 SL 8** | | | |
| 2 Dr Cpe/Rdstr (auto) | **62110** | 29800 | 33150 |
| *ADD FOR:* | | | |
| Anti-Lock Brake System (190 D, 190 E) | **1685** | 350 | 380 |
| Electric Front Bucket Seats (190 Series, 260 E) | **920** | 150 | 160 |
| Electric 4 Place Seating (300 SEL, 420 SEL) | **2750** | 620 | 690 |
| (560 SEL) | **2110** | 550 | 610 |
| Leather Seats (190 Series, 260 E, 300 E, 300 TE) | **1425** | 260 | 280 |
| Velour Seats (190 Series, 260 E, 300 E, 300 TE) | **1405** | 260 | 280 |

NOTE: Pwr strng, power door locks, power brakes, air conditioning and power windows standard on all models. Power sun roof standard on 560 SEC and 560 SEL.

## 1987

| | | | |
|---|---|---|---|
| **190 D 5** | | | |
| 2.5 4 Dr Sdn | **28450** | 8750 | 10100 |
| 2.5 4 Dr Sdn (auto) | **29200** | 9200 | 10600 |
| 2.5 4 Dr Turbo-diesel Sdn (auto) | **32110** | 9800 | 11300 |
| **190 E 4** | | | |
| 2.3 4 Dr Sdn | **28450** | 9925 | 11425 |
| 2.3 4 Dr Sdn (auto) | **29200** | 10325 | 11925 |
| 2.3-16 4 Dr Sdn | **42670** | 14900 | 17500 |
| 2.3-16 4 Dr Sdn (auto) | **43420** | 15350 | 18000 |
| **190 E 6** | | | |
| 2.6 4 Dr Sdn (auto) | **33390** | 11025 | 12725 |
| **260 E 6** | | | |
| 2.6 4 Dr Sdn (auto) | **37180** | 13300 | 15625 |
| **300 D 6** | | | |
| 4 Dr Turbo-diesel Sdn (auto) | **42570** | 13900 | 16275 |
| **300 TD 6** | | | |
| 4 Dr Turbo-diesel Wgn (auto) | **45790** | 15850 | 18500 |
| **300 E 6** | | | |
| 4 Dr Sdn (auto) | **42570** | 14850 | 17425 |

| Year/Model/Body/Type | Original List | Current Whlse | Average Retail |
|---|---|---|---|
| **300 SDL 6** | | | |
| 4 Dr Turbo-diesel Sdn (auto) | **50650** | 17800 | 20450 |
| **420 SEL 8** | | | |
| 4 Dr Sdn (auto) | **56050** | 18300 | 21200 |
| **560 SEL 8** | | | |
| 4 Dr Sdn (auto) | **66260** | 21725 | 25025 |
| **560 SEC 8** | | | |
| 2 Dr Cpe (auto) | **73260** | 26850 | 30175 |
| **560 SL 8** | | | |
| 2 Dr Cpe/Rdstr (auto) | **59580** | 25350 | 28675 |
| *ADD FOR:* | | | |
| Anti-Lock Brake System (190 D except Turbo, 190 E) | **1635** | 310 | 340 |
| Electric Left Front Seat (190 D, 190 E, 260) | **465** | 110 | 120 |
| Electric 4 Place Seating (560 SEL) | **2050** | 440 | 480 |
| (420) | **2670** | 510 | 570 |
| Leather Seats (190 D, 190 E, 260, 300 D, 300 E, 300 TD) | **1385** | 220 | 240 |
| Velour Seats (190 D, 190 E, 260, 300 D, 300 E, 300 TD) | **1365** | 220 | 240 |

NOTE: Pwr strng, power locks, power brakes, air conditioning and power windows standard on all models. Power sun roof standard on 560 SEC and 560 SEL.

## 1986

| | | | |
|---|---|---|---|
| **190 D 5** | | | |
| 2.5 4 Dr Sdn | **25080** | 7200 | 8350 |
| 2.5 4 Dr Sdn (auto) | **25710** | 7500 | 8700 |
| **190 E 4** | | | |
| 2.3 4 Dr Sdn | **25080** | 8150 | 9425 |
| 2.3 4 Dr Sdn (auto) | **25710** | 8500 | 9825 |
| 2.3-16 4 Dr Sdn | **36820** | 12700 | 15025 |
| 2.3-16 4 Dr Sdn (auto) | **37450** | 13000 | 15325 |
| **300 E 6** | | | |
| 4 Dr Sdn | **25870** | 12450 | 14600 |
| 4 Dr Sdn (auto) | **36710** | 12750 | 15075 |
| **300 SDL 6** | | | |
| 4 Dr Turbo-diesel (auto) | **43800** | 15350 | 18000 |
| **420 SEL 8** | | | |
| 4 Dr Sdn (auto) | **47720** | 15800 | 18450 |

# FOREIGN CARS & TRUCKS

| Year/Model/Body/Type | Original List | Current Whlse | Average Retail |
|---|---|---|---|
| **560 SEL 8** | | | |
| 4 Dr Sdn (auto) | **56390** | 18650 | 21700 |
| **560 SEC 8** | | | |
| 2 Dr Cpe (auto) | **62110** | 23350 | 26650 |
| **560 SL 8** | | | |
| 2 Dr Cpe/Rdstr (auto) | **51000** | 23000 | 26300 |
| *ADD FOR:* | | | |
| Anti-Lock Brake System (190 D, 190 E) | **1405** | 180 | 200 |
| Electric Left Front Seat (190 D, 190 E) | **1265** | 130 | 140 |
| Electric 4 Place Seating (420 SEL) | **2300** | 360 | 400 |
| (560 SEL) | **1760** | 330 | 360 |
| Leather Seats (190 D, 190 E, 300 E) | **1190** | 180 | 200 |
| Velour Seats (190 D, 190 E, 300 E) | **1170** | 180 | 200 |

NOTE: Pwr strng, power locks, power brakes, air conditioning and power windows standard on all models.

## 1985

| Year/Model/Body/Type | Original List | Current Whlse | Average Retail |
|---|---|---|---|
| **190 D 4** | | | |
| 4 Dr Sdn | **22930** | 5975 | 6900 |
| 4 Dr Sdn (auto) | **23510** | 6375 | 7425 |
| **190 E 4** | | | |
| 4 Dr Sdn | **22850** | 6925 | 8050 |
| 4 Dr Sdn (auto) | **23430** | 7300 | 8475 |
| **300 D 5** | | | |
| 2 Dr Turbo-diesel Cpe (auto) | **35220** | 9975 | 11500 |
| 4 Dr Turbo-diesel Sdn (auto) | **31940** | 8450 | 9750 |
| **300 SD 5** | | | |
| 4 Dr Turbo-diesel Sdn (auto) | **39500** | 11725 | 13550 |
| **300 TD 5** | | | |
| 4 Dr Turbo-diesel Wgn (auto) | **35310** | 9750 | 11225 |
| **380 SE 8** | | | |
| 4 Dr Sdn (auto) | **42730** | 12950 | 15275 |
| **380 SL 8** | | | |
| 2 Dr Cpe/Rdstr (auto) | **43820** | 10525 | 12150 |
| **500 SEC 8** | | | |
| 2 Dr Cpe (auto) | **56800** | 18550 | 21600 |

| Year/Model/Body/Type | Original List | Current Whlse | Average Retail |
|---|---|---|---|
| **500 SEL 8** | | | |
| 4 Dr Sdn (auto) | **51200** | 14800 | 17375 |
| *ADD FOR:* | | | |
| Rear Facing Third Seat (300 TD) | **834** | 90 | 100 |
| Leather Seats (190 E, 190 D, 300 D, 300 TD, 300 CD) | **1083** | 130 | 140 |
| (300 SD, 380 SE) | **1124** | 130 | 140 |
| (380 SL) | **853** | 130 | 140 |
| Velour Seats (190 E, 190 D, 300 D, 300 TD, 300 CD) | **1073** | 130 | 140 |
| (300 SD, 380 SE) | **1117** | 130 | 140 |

## 1984

| Year/Model/Body/Type | Original List | Current Whlse | Average Retail |
|---|---|---|---|
| **190 D 4** | | | |
| 4 Dr Sdn | **22930** | 5200 | 6125 |
| 4 Dr Sdn (auto) | **23510** | 5600 | 6525 |
| **190 E 4** | | | |
| 4 Dr Sdn | **22850** | 6125 | 7125 |
| 4 Dr Sdn (auto) | **23430** | 6500 | 7575 |
| **300 D 5** | | | |
| 2 Dr Turbo-diesel Cpe (auto) | **35220** | 8875 | 10250 |
| 4 Dr Turbo-diesel Sdn (auto) | **31940** | 7350 | 8525 |
| **300 SD 5** | | | |
| 4 Dr Turbo-diesel Sdn (auto) | **39500** | 11075 | 12800 |
| **300 TD 5** | | | |
| 4 Dr Turbo-diesel Wgn (auto) | **35310** | 8625 | 9950 |
| **380 SE 8** | | | |
| 4 Dr Sdn (auto) | **42730** | 12575 | 14850 |
| **380 SL 8** | | | |
| 2 Dr Cpe/Rdstr (auto) | **43830** | 19900 | 22950 |
| **500 SEC 8** | | | |
| 2 Dr Cpe (auto) | **56800** | 18250 | 21100 |
| **500 SEL 8** | | | |
| 4 Dr Sdn (auto) | **51200** | 14350 | 16850 |

## 1983

| Year/Model/Body/Type | Original List | Current Whlse | Average Retail |
|---|---|---|---|
| **240 D 4** | | | |
| 4 Dr Sdn | **22470** | 4775 | 5700 |

| Year/Model/Body/Type | Original List | Current Whlse | Average Retail |
|---|---|---|---|
| 4 Dr Sdn (auto) | **23800** | 4950 | 5875 |
| **300 D 5** | | | |
| 2 Dr Turbo-diesel Cpe (auto) | **33750** | 8225 | 9500 |
| 4 Dr Turbo-diesel Sdn (auto) | **30530** | 6750 | 7850 |
| **300 SD 5** | | | |
| 4 Dr Sdn (auto) | **37970** | 9500 | 10900 |
| **300 TD 5** | | | |
| 4 Dr Turbo-diesel Wgn (auto) | **33850** | 7700 | 8950 |
| **380 SEC 8** | | | |
| Cpe (auto) | **53570** | 16400 | 19050 |
| **380 SEL 8** | | | |
| 4 Dr Sdn (auto) | **47870** | 12200 | 14100 |
| **380 SL 8** | | | |
| 2 Dr Cpe/Rdstr (auto) | **43030** | 17675 | 20325 |

## MITSUBISHI

### 1992

#### 2WD TRUCKS 4

| | | | |
|---|---|---|---|
| Mighty Max (5 spd) | **9509** | 6500 | 7575 |
| Mighty Max Macrocab (5 spd) | **10839** | 7125 | 8275 |
| Mighty Max 1-Ton (5 spd) | **10609** | 6825 | 7950 |

#### 4WD TRUCKS 6

| | | | |
|---|---|---|---|
| Mighty Max (5 spd) | **13519** | 8900 | 10275 |
| ADD FOR: | | | |
| Special Edit Pkg | **454** | 200 | 250 |

#### 3000 GT 6

| | | | |
|---|---|---|---|
| 2 Dr Base Hbk (5 spd) | **21739** | 17225 | 19875 |
| 2 Dr SL Hbk (5 spd) | **27289** | 20375 | 23425 |
| 2 Dr VR-4 Hbk (5 spd) | **34150** | 23800 | 27100 |
| ADD FOR: | | | |
| Anti-Lock Brakes (Base) | **1130** | 500 | 600 |
| Leather & Vinyl Seat Trim | **1120** | 500 | 600 |

#### DIAMANTE 6

| | | | |
|---|---|---|---|
| 4 Dr Base Sdn | | | |

| Year/Model/Body/Type | Original List | Current Whlse | Average Retail |
|---|---|---|---|
| (auto) | **21489** | 15650 | 18300 |
| 4 Dr LS Sdn (auto) | **26450** | 19000 | 22050 |
| ADD FOR: | | | |
| Euro Handling Pkg | **1670** | 450 | 550 |
| Leather Seat Pkg | **1741** | 450 | 550 |
| Alloy Wheels (Base) | **388** | 175 | 200 |

#### ECLIPSE 4

| | | | |
|---|---|---|---|
| 3 Dr 1.8 Liter Base Cpe (5 spd) | **12463** | 9775 | 11250 |
| 3 Dr 1.8 Liter GS Cpe (5 spd) | **13476** | 10300 | 11875 |
| 3 Dr 2.0 Liter GS Cpe (5 spd) | **14436** | 10950 | 12625 |
| 3 Dr GS Turbo Cpe (5 spd) | **17269** | 12075 | 13950 |
| 3 Dr GSX 4WD Turbo Cpe (5 spd) | **19029** | 12875 | 15200 |
| ADD FOR: | | | |
| Leather Pkg | **435** | 260 | 290 |
| Anti-Lock Brakes | **943** | 460 | 500 |
| Alloy Wheels | **321** | 210 | 230 |

#### EXPO 4

| | | | |
|---|---|---|---|
| 3 Dr LRV Lftbk (5 spd) | **12271** | 10100 | 11650 |
| 3 Dr LRV Sport Lftbk (5 spd) | **13290** | 10375 | 11975 |
| 3 Dr LRV Sport AWD Lftbk (5 spd) | **15190** | 11175 | 12900 |
| 4 Dr Base Lftbk (5 spd) | **14324** | 11675 | 13475 |
| 4 Dr SP Lftbk (5 spd) | **15284** | 12075 | 13950 |
| 4 Dr SP AWD Lftbk (5 spd) | **16614** | 12875 | 15200 |
| ADD FOR: | | | |
| Anti-Lock Brakes | **924** | 475 | 550 |
| Alloy Wheels | **291** | 175 | 200 |

#### GALANT 4

| | | | |
|---|---|---|---|
| 4 Dr Base Sdn (5 spd) | **13368** | 9650 | 11125 |
| 4 Dr LS Sdn (auto) | **16041** | 10875 | 12550 |
| 4 Dr GS Sport Sdn (5 spd) | **16441** | 11175 | 12900 |
| 4 Dr GSX 4WD Sport Sdn (auto) | **19041** | — | — |
| 4 Dr GSR Sport Sdn (5 spd) | **17991** | | |
| 4 Dr VR-4 4WD Turbo Sport Sdn (5 spd) | **23100** | — | — |
| ADD FOR: | | | |
| Anti-Lock Brakes (GSR, GSX) | **924** | 460 | 500 |
| Alloy Wheels (LS, GS, GSX) | **294** | 190 | 210 |

| Year/Model/Body/Type | Original List | Current Whlse | Average Retail |
|---|---|---|---|
| **MIRAGE 4** | | | |
| 3 Dr VL Hbk (4 spd) | **8735** | — | — |
| 3 Dr Base Hbk (5 spd) | **9550** | 7025 | 8150 |
| 3 Dr Special Edit Hbk (5 spd) | **9094** | — | — |
| 4 Dr Base Sdn (5 spd) | **10580** | 7200 | 8350 |
| 4 Dr LS Sdn (5 spd) | **11304** | 7475 | 8675 |
| 4 Dr GS Sdn (5 spd) | **12472** | — | — |
| *ADD FOR:* | | | |
| Alloy Wheels | **285** | 180 | 200 |
| **MONTERO 6** | | | |
| 4WD 4 Dr Base (5 spd) | **19924** | 14950 | 17550 |
| 4WD 4 Dr RS (5 spd) | **21089** | — | — |
| 4WD 4 Dr LS (auto) | **24560** | — | — |
| 4WD 4 Dr SR (auto) | **23985** | — | — |
| *ADD FOR:* | | | |
| Leather Pkg | **1213** | 400 | 475 |
| Anti-Lock Brakes (SR) | **1188** | 475 | 550 |
| **PRECIS 4** | | | |
| 3 Dr Base Hbk (4 spd) | **8068** | — | — |

NOTE: Tilt steering wheel standard on Mirage GS, Expo, Eclipse, Galant, Diamante, 3000 GT, Pickups and Montero. Cruise control standard on Eclipse GS Turbo & GSX, Galant LS, GS, GSX, GSR & VR-4, Diamante LS, 3000 GT SL & VR-4, Montero LS & SR. Power windows and power door locks standard on Galant LS, GS, GSX, GSR & VR-4, Diamante, 3000 GT and Montero LS & SR. Power seat standard on Galant LS, GS, GSX, GSR & VR-4, Diamante and 3000 GT SL & VR-4.

# 1991

### 2WD TRUCKS 4

| | Original List | Current Whlse | Average Retail |
|---|---|---|---|
| Mighty Max (5 spd) | **8969** | 5350 | 6275 |
| Mighty Max Macrocab (5 spd) | **10199** | 5875 | 6800 |
| Mighty Max 1-Ton (5 spd) | **9969** | 5700 | 6625 |

### 4WD TRUCKS 6

| | | | |
|---|---|---|---|
| Mighty Max (5 spd) | **12689** | 7650 | 8875 |

### 3000 GT 4

| | | | |
|---|---|---|---|
| 2 Dr Base Hbk (5 spd) | **19059** | 14675 | 17225 |
| 2 Dr Base Hbk (auto) | **19859** | 15200 | 17850 |
| 2 Dr SL Hbk (5 spd) | **24749** | 17650 | 20300 |
| 2 Dr VR-4 4WD Twin-Turbo Hbk (5 spd) | **30800** | 20825 | 23875 |

| Year/Model/Body/Type | Original List | Current Whlse | Average Retail |
|---|---|---|---|
| **ECLIPSE 4** | | | |
| 3 Dr Base Hbk (5 spd) | **11932** | 7725 | 8975 |
| 3 Dr GS Hbk (5 spd) | **12700** | 8275 | 9550 |
| 3 Dr GS DOHC Hbk (5 spd) | **13600** | 8775 | 10125 |
| 3 Dr GS DOHC Turbo Hbk (5 spd) | **15910** | 9675 | 11150 |
| 3 Dr GSX DOHC Turbo Hbk (5 spd) | **17570** | 11300 | 13050 |
| **GALANT 4** | | | |
| 4 Dr Base Sdn (5 spd) | **12355** | 8550 | 9875 |
| 4 Dr LS Sdn (auto) | **14781** | 9750 | 11225 |
| 4 Dr GS Sport Sdn (5 spd) | **15061** | 9975 | 11500 |
| 4 Dr GSR Sport Sdn (5 spd) | **17371** | 10525 | 12150 |
| 4 Dr 4WD GSX Sport Sdn (auto) | **17761** | 11275 | 13025 |
| 4 Dr 4WD VR-4 Turbo Sport Sdn (5 spd) | **21000** | 13900 | 16275 |
| **MIRAGE 4** | | | |
| 3 Dr VL Hbk (4 spd) (NA w/pwr strng) | **8165** | 5150 | 6075 |
| 3 Dr Standard Hbk (5 spd) | **8907** | 5825 | 6750 |
| 4 Dr Base Sdn (5 spd) | **9837** | 6025 | 6950 |
| 4 Dr LS Sdn (5 spd) | **10407** | 6225 | 7250 |
| 4 Dr GS Sdn (5 spd) | **11772** | 6875 | 8000 |
| **MONTERO 6** | | | |
| 4WD 4 Dr Base (5 spd) | **16805** | 11800 | 13625 |
| 4WD 4 Dr RS (auto) | **17985** | 12225 | 14175 |
| 4WD 4 Dr LS (5 spd) | **19609** | 12925 | 15250 |
| **PRECIS 4** | | | |
| 3 Dr Base Hbk (4 spd) (NA w/pwr strng) | **7522** | 3825 | 4725 |
| 3 Dr RS Hbk (5 spd) | **8418** | 4050 | 4950 |
| *ADD FOR:* | | | |
| Anti-Lock Brakes (Eclipse GS DOHC Turbo, Galant GS & GSX) | **924** | 440 | 480 |
| Leather Pkg (3000GT) | **1120** | 530 | 590 |
| (Eclipse GSX) | **427** | 220 | 240 |

NOTE: Power brakes standard on all models. Power door locks standard on 3000GT SL & VR-4, Eclipse, Galant except Base, Montero LS and Pickups. Power windows standard on 3000GT SL and VR-4, Galant except Base and Montero LS. Power seat standard on Galant VR-4.

*Refer to optional equipment schedules*

| Year/Model/<br>Body/Type | Original<br>List | Current<br>Whlse | Average<br>Retail |
|---|---|---|---|
| **1990** | | | |
| **2WD TRUCKS 4** | | | |
| Mighty Max (5 spd) | **8969** | 4100 | 5025 |
| Mighty Max Macrocab<br>(5 spd) | **9909** | 4550 | 5475 |
| Mighty Max 1-Ton<br>(5 spd) | **9969** | 4375 | 5300 |
| **VAN/WAGON 4** | | | |
| Van (auto) | **11950** | 6450 | 7500 |
| Wagon (auto) | **17134** | 8750 | 10100 |
| Wagon w/LS Pkg (auto) | **18005** | 9475 | 10925 |
| **ECLIPSE 4** | | | |
| 3 Dr Hbk (5 spd) | **11871** | 6650 | 7750 |
| 3 Dr GS Hbk (5 spd) | **12560** | 7150 | 8300 |
| 3 Dr GS DOHC Hbk<br>(5 spd) | **13490** | 7500 | 8700 |
| 3 Dr GS DOHC Turbo<br>Hbk (5 spd) | **15450** | 8150 | 9425 |
| 3 Dr GSX DOHC Turbo<br>Hbk (5 spd) | **17260** | 9800 | 11300 |
| **GALANT 4** | | | |
| 4 Dr Sdn (5 spd) | **12343** | 6425 | 7475 |
| 4 Dr LS Sdn (auto) | **14777** | 7325 | 8500 |
| 4 Dr GS Sport Sdn<br>(5 spd) | **16477** | 8075 | 9325 |
| 4 Dr 4WD GSX Sport<br>Sdn (5 spd) | **17171** | 8775 | 10125 |
| **MIRAGE 4** | | | |
| 3 Dr VL Hbk (4 spd)<br>(NA w/pwr strng) | **8012** | 3575 | 4475 |
| 3 Dr Hbk (5 spd) | **8875** | 4200 | 5125 |
| 3 Dr RS Hbk (5 spd) | **9824** | 4450 | 5375 |
| 3 Dr EXE Spec Edit<br>(5 spd) | **8339** | 3850 | 4750 |
| 4 Dr Sdn (5 spd) | **9595** | 4400 | 5325 |
| 4 Dr EXE Spec Edit<br>(5 spd) | **9509** | 4475 | 5400 |
| **MONTERO 6** | | | |
| 4WD 2 Dr SP (5 spd) | **15086** | 9675 | 11150 |
| 4WD 2 Dr Sport (auto) | **16219** | 10175 | 11750 |
| 4WD 4 Dr (5 spd) | **16835** | 10375 | 11975 |
| 4WD 4 Dr RS (5 spd) | **18949** | 10875 | 12550 |
| 4WD 4 Dr LS (auto) | **20309** | 11900 | 13750 |
| **PRECIS 4** | | | |
| 3 Dr Hbk (4 spd) | **7212** | 2825 | 3725 |
| 3 Dr RS Hbk (5 spd) | **8312** | 3275 | 4175 |
| **SIGMA 6** | | | |
| 4 Dr Lux Sdn (auto) | **17879** | 8650 | 10000 |

| Year/Model/<br>Body/Type | Original<br>List | Current<br>Whlse | Average<br>Retail |
|---|---|---|---|
| *ADD FOR:* | | | |
| Anti-Lock Brakes<br>(Galant GS & GSX<br>Sport, Sigma) | **1495** | 420 | 460 |
| Eurotech Pkg (Sigma) | **2042** | 530 | 590 |
| Leather Pkg<br>(Eclipse GSX) | **427** | 160 | 180 |
| (Sigma) | **816** | 200 | 220 |

NOTE: Power windows standard on Galant LS, GS & GSX, Sigma, Van/Wagon LS, Montero LS & RS. Power door locks standard on Galant LS, GS & GSX, Sigma, Van/Wagon Series and Montero Series.

| Year/Model/<br>Body/Type | Original<br>List | Current<br>Whlse | Average<br>Retail |
|---|---|---|---|
| **1989** | | | |
| **2WD TRUCKS 4** | | | |
| Mighty Max (5 spd) | **8861** | 3125 | 4025 |
| Mighty Max Macrocab<br>Ext. Cab (5 spd) | **10071** | 3475 | 4375 |
| Mighty Max 1-Ton<br>(5 spd) | **9841** | 3325 | 4225 |
| Mighty Max Sport<br>Short Bed (5 spd) | **9751** | 3525 | 4425 |
| Mighty Max Sport<br>Long Bed (5 spd) | **10341** | 3650 | 4550 |
| SPX Macrocab Ext.<br>Cab (5 spd) | **11654** | 4175 | 5100 |
| **4WD TRUCKS 4** | | | |
| SPX Short Bed (5 spd) | **13289** | 5675 | 6600 |
| **VAN/WAGON 4** | | | |
| L Cargo Van (auto) | **11950** | 3925 | 4825 |
| Wgn (auto) | **17134** | 5875 | 6800 |
| Wgn w/LS Pkg (auto) | **18005** | 6275 | 7300 |
| **GALANT 4** | | | |
| 4 Dr Sdn (5 spd) | **11761** | 4625 | 5550 |
| 4 Dr LS Sdn (auto) | **14369** | 5475 | 6400 |
| 4 Dr GS Sdn (5 spd) | **16059** | 5775 | 6700 |
| **MIRAGE 4** | | | |
| 3 Dr VL Hbk (5 spd) | **9158** | 2700 | 3600 |
| 4 Dr VL Sdn (5 spd) | **9818** | 2875 | 3775 |
| 3 Dr Hbk (5 spd) | **10048** | 2875 | 3775 |
| 4 Dr Sdn (5 spd)<br>(NA w/pwr strng) | **9956** | 3175 | 4075 |
| 4 Dr LS Sdn (5 spd) | **11505** | 3475 | 4375 |
| 3 Dr Turbo Spt Hbk<br>(5 spd) | **13265** | 3850 | 4750 |
| **MONTERO 6** | | | |
| 4WD 2 Dr SP (5 spd)<br>(4 cyl) | **13109** | 7150 | 8300 |
| 4WD 2 Dr SP (5 spd) | **14759** | 7375 | 8550 |
| 4WD 2 Dr Sport (auto) | **16209** | 8050 | 9300 |
| 4 Dr Sport (5 spd) | | | |

| Year/Model/Body/Type | Original List | Current Whlse | Average Retail |
|---|---|---|---|
| (6 cyl) | **17909** | 8750 | 10100 |
| 4 Dr LS Sport (auto) | **19199** | 9725 | 11200 |
| **PRECIS 4** | | | |
| 3 Dr Hbk (4 spd) (NA w/pwr strng) | **6019** | 1775 | 2625 |
| 3 Dr RS Hbk (5 spd) (NA w/pwr strng) | **7244** | 2075 | 2925 |
| 3 Dr LS Hbk (5 spd) | **8594** | 2375 | 3250 |
| 5 Dr LS Hbk (5 spd) | **8109** | 2525 | 3400 |
| **SIGMA 6** | | | |
| 4 Dr Sdn (auto) | **17069** | 6725 | 7825 |
| **STARION 4** | | | |
| ESI Turbo 2+2 Cpe (5 spd) | **19859** | 6625 | 7700 |
| *ADD FOR:* | | | |
| Anti-Lock Brakes (Galant, Sigma) | **1495** | 380 | 420 |
| Eurotech Pkg (Sigma) | **2042** | 460 | 500 |
| Leather Seats (Starion) | **626** | 160 | 180 |
| (Sigma) | **816** | 180 | 200 |

NOTE: Power brakes standard on all models. Power door locks standard on Galant LS & GS, Sigma, Starion, Montero Series and Van/Wagon. Power windows standard on Galant LS & GS, Sigma, Starion and LS Van/Wagon.

## 1988

### 2WD TRUCKS 4

| Year/Model/Body/Type | Original List | Current Whlse | Average Retail |
|---|---|---|---|
| Mighty Max (5 spd) | **6999** | 1925 | 2775 |
| Mighty Max Macrocab (5 spd) | **8109** | 2250 | 3100 |
| Mighty Max 1-Ton (5 spd) | **8159** | 2150 | 3000 |
| Mighty Max Sport Short Bed (5 spd) | **7919** | 2275 | 3150 |
| Mighty Max Sport Long Bed (5 spd) | **8469** | 2375 | 3250 |
| Mighty Max SPX Macrocab (5 spd) | **9589** | 2875 | 3775 |

### 4WD TRUCKS

| | Original List | Current Whlse | Average Retail |
|---|---|---|---|
| SPX (5 spd) | **11469** | 3875 | 4775 |

### VAN/WAGON 4

| | Original List | Current Whlse | Average Retail |
|---|---|---|---|
| Cargo Van (auto) | **10789** | 2500 | 3375 |
| Cargo Van w/Converter Conv Pkg (auto) | **11549** | 2750 | 3650 |
| Wgn (auto) | **14269** | 4100 | 5025 |
| Wgn w/LS Pkg (auto) | **15789** | 4500 | 5425 |

### CORDIA 4

| | Original List | Current Whlse | Average Retail |
|---|---|---|---|
| 2 Dr L Sport Hbk | **10829** | 1825 | 2675 |

| Year/Model/Body/Type | Original List | Current Whlse | Average Retail |
|---|---|---|---|
| **GALANT SIGMA 6** | | | |
| 4 Dr Luxury Sdn | **16129** | 4775 | 5750 |
| **MIRAGE 4** | | | |
| 4 Dr Sdn | **8619** | 1700 | 2550 |
| 2 Dr Turbo Sport Hbk | **9239** | 1950 | 2800 |
| **MONTERO 4** | | | |
| 3 Dr SP (5 spd) | **11929** | 4600 | 5525 |
| 3 Dr Sport (5 spd) | **14259** | 5100 | 6025 |
| **PRECIS 4** | | | |
| 3 Dr Hbk | **5395** | 900 | 1625 |
| 3 Dr RS Hbk | **6499** | 1150 | 1875 |
| 3 Dr LS Hbk | **7249** | 1375 | 2125 |
| 5 Dr LS Hbk | **7499** | 1525 | 2375 |
| **STARION 4** | | | |
| ESI Turbo 2+2 Cpe (5 spd) | **17129** | 5175 | 6100 |
| ESI-R Turbo 2+2 Cpe (5 spd) | **19789** | 5700 | 6625 |
| **TREDIA 4** | | | |
| 4 Dr L Sdn | **10039** | 1850 | 2700 |
| 4 Dr LS Sdn (auto) | **11109** | 2150 | 3000 |
| 4 Dr Turbo Sdn (5 spd) | **10949** | 2350 | 3225 |
| *ADD FOR:* | | | |
| Eurotech Pkg (Galant Sigma) | **1920** | 360 | 400 |
| Leather Seats (Galant Sigma) | **753** | 180 | 200 |
| (Starion ESI-R) | **563** | 150 | 160 |

NOTE: Air conditioning standard on Galant Sigma and Starion ESI-R. Power windows standard on Tredia LS, Tredia Turbo, Galant Sigma, Starion Series, Converter Convenience Van and LS Wagon. Power door locks standard on Tredia LS, Tredia Turbo, Galant Sigma, Starion ESI-R and Van/Wagon Series. Pwr strng standard on Tredia Series, Cordia Series, Galant Sigma, Starion Series, LS Wagon, Mighty Max Pickups except 2WD Base and Montero Series. Power brakes standard on all models.

## 1987

### 2WD TRUCKS 4

| | Original List | Current Whlse | Average Retail |
|---|---|---|---|
| Mighty Max (5 spd) | **6499** | 825 | 1525 |
| Mighty Max 1-Ton (5 spd) | **7329** | 975 | 1700 |
| Mighty Max Sport Short Bed (5 spd) | **7299** | 1075 | 1800 |
| Mighty Max Sport Long Bed (5 spd) | **7589** | 1200 | 1925 |
| SPX (5 spd) | **7779** | 1325 | 2050 |

| Year/Model/Body/Type | Original List | Current Whlse | Average Retail |
|---|---|---|---|
| **4WD TRUCKS 4** | | | |
| Mighty Max Long Bed (5 spd) | **9569** | 2100 | 2950 |
| **VAN/WAGON 4** | | | |
| Cargo Van (auto) | **9839** | 2100 | 2950 |
| Cargo Van w/Converter Pkg (auto) | **10529** | 2200 | 3100 |
| Wgn (auto) | **13099** | 3300 | 4200 |
| Wgn w/LS Pkg (auto) | **14649** | 3600 | 4500 |
| **CORDIA 4** | | | |
| 2 Dr L Sport Hbk | **9999** | 1450 | 2225 |
| 2 Dr L Sport Hbk (auto) | **10439** | 1775 | 2625 |
| 2 Dr Turbo Sport Hbk | **11619** | 1700 | 2550 |
| **GALANT 4** | | | |
| 4 Dr Luxury Sdn | **14339** | 2925 | 3825 |
| **MIRAGE 4** | | | |
| 2 Dr Base Hbk | **5969** | 950 | 1675 |
| 4 Dr Base Sdn | **8069** | 1250 | 1975 |
| 2 Dr L Hbk | **7479** | 1150 | 1875 |
| 2 Dr Turbo Sport Hbk | **8479** | 1350 | 2100 |
| **MONTERO 4** | | | |
| 4WD 3 Dr (5 spd) | **10089** | 3200 | 4100 |
| 4WD 3 Dr Sport (5 spd) | **12399** | 3525 | 4425 |
| **PRECIS 4** | | | |
| 3 Dr Hbk | **5195** | 550 | 1025 |
| 3 Dr LS Hbk | **6499** | 900 | 1625 |
| 5 Dr LS Hbk | **6799** | 1025 | 1750 |
| **STARION 4** | | | |
| LE Turbo 2+2 Cpe (5 spd) | **15959** | 4000 | 4900 |
| ESI-R Turbo 2+2 Cpe (5 spd) | **18479** | 4400 | 5325 |
| **TREDIA 4** | | | |
| 4 Dr L Sdn | **9699** | 1325 | 2050 |
| 4 Dr LS Sdn (auto) | **10749** | 1575 | 2425 |
| 4 Dr Turbo Sdn (5 spd) | **10589** | 1575 | 2425 |
| *ADD FOR:* | | | |
| ECS Pkg (Galant) | **670** | 150 | 160 |
| Leather Seat Trim (Galant LS) | **669** | 150 | 160 |
| (Starion LE) | **389** | 110 | 120 |

NOTE: Power brakes standard on all models. Air conditioning standard on Galant and Starion. Power door locks standard on Galant, Starion Series, Van, LS Wagon. Power windows standard on Tredia LS, Galant, Starion

Series, Converter Convenience Van and LS Wagon. Pwr strng standard on Mirage Turbo w/automatic transmission, Tredia Series, Cordia Series, Galant, Starion Series, LS Wagon and Mighty Max Sport Pickup.

## 1986

| Year/Model/Body/Type | Original List | Current Whlse | Average Retail |
|---|---|---|---|
| **2WD TRUCKS 4** | | | |
| Mighty Max (5 spd) | **6208** | 650 | 1225 |
| Mighty Max Sport (5 spd) | **6668** | 850 | 1550 |
| SPX (5 spd) | **7458** | 1000 | 1725 |
| **CORDIA 4** | | | |
| 2 Dr L Sport Hbk | **9319** | 1050 | 1775 |
| 2 Dr Turbo Sport Hbk | **10799** | 1250 | 1975 |
| **GALANT 4** | | | |
| 4 Dr Luxury Sdn (auto) | **13899** | 2125 | 2975 |
| **MIRAGE 4** | | | |
| 2 Dr Base Hbk | **6152** | 650 | 1225 |
| 2 Dr L Hbk | **7352** | 800 | 1500 |
| 2 Dr L Hbk (auto) | **7752** | 900 | 1625 |
| 2 Dr Turbo Hbk | **8636** | 950 | 1675 |
| 2 Dr Turbo Hbk (auto) | **9226** | 1000 | 1725 |
| **MONTERO 4** | | | |
| 4WD 3 Dr (5 spd) | **9588** | 2775 | 3675 |
| 4WD 3 Dr w/Sport Group (5 spd) | **10599** | 2950 | 3850 |
| **STARION 4** | | | |
| LE Turbo 2+2 Cpe (5 spd) | **15209** | 2800 | 3700 |
| ESI-R Turbo Cpe (5 spd) | **17569** | 3125 | 4025 |
| **TREDIA 4** | | | |
| 4 Dr Base Sdn | **8150** | 825 | 1525 |
| 4 Dr L Sdn | **9079** | 925 | 1650 |
| 4 Dr LS Sdn (auto) | **10279** | 1250 | 1975 |
| 4 Dr Turbo Sdn | **10089** | 1125 | 1850 |
| *ADD FOR:* | | | |
| ECS Pkg (Galant) | **670** | 110 | 120 |
| Sport Group (Montero) | **865** | 150 | 160 |
| Leather/Digital Pkg (Starion LE) | **640** | 90 | 100 |
| Off-Road Pkg (4WD Pickup) | **474** | 90 | 100 |

NOTE: Power brakes standard on all models. Power locks, power windows, automatic transmission and air conditioning standard on Galant and Starion Series. Pwr strng standard on Mirage Turbo, Cordia Series, Galant, Starion Series, Montero and 4WD Mighty Max.

*1984 Mitsubishi Cordia LS*

| Year/Model/ Body/Type | Original List | Current Whlse | Average Retail |
|---|---|---|---|
| **1985** | | | |
| **2WD TRUCKS 4** | | | |
| Mighty Max (4 spd) | **5948** | 600 | 1125 |
| SP (5 spd) | **6868** | 875 | 1600 |
| SP Turbodiesel (5 spd) | **7798** | 500 | 925 |
| SPX (5 spd) | **7239** | 1000 | 1725 |
| SPX Turbodiesel (5 spd) | **8109** | 850 | 1550 |
| **CORDIA 4** | | | |
| 2 Dr L Hbk | **8449** | 925 | 1650 |
| 2 Dr Turbo Hbk | **9959** | 1125 | 1850 |
| **GALANT 4** | | | |
| 4 Dr Luxury Sdn (auto) | **11989** | 1725 | 2575 |
| **MIRAGE 4** | | | |
| 2 Dr Base Hbk | **5389** | 600 | 1125 |
| 2 Dr L Hbk | **6576** | 700 | 1325 |
| 2 Dr LS Hbk | **7056** | 800 | 1500 |
| 2 Dr Turbo Hbk | **8076** | 875 | 1600 |
| **MONTERO 4** | | | |
| 4WD 3 Dr (5 spd) | **9955** | 2500 | 3375 |
| **STARION 4** | | | |
| LS Turbo 2+2 Cpe (5 spd) | **12629** | 1600 | 2450 |
| LE Turbo 2+2 Cpe (5 spd) | **14869** | 1800 | 2650 |
| LE Turbo 2+2 Cpe (auto) | **15409** | 2250 | 3100 |
| ES Turbo 2+2 Cpe (5 spd) | **14489** | 2150 | 3000 |

| Year/Model/ Body/Type | Original List | Current Whlse | Average Retail |
|---|---|---|---|
| **TREDIA 4** | | | |
| 4 Dr Base Sdn | **7112** | 775 | 1500 |
| 4 Dr L Sdn | **8189** | 875 | 1600 |
| 4 Dr Turbo Sdn | **9279** | 1025 | 1750 |
| *ADD FOR:* | | | |
| Sport Group (Montero) | **770** | 70 | 80 |
| ECS Pkg (Galant) | **910** | 90 | 100 |
| LS Pkg (Tredia L) | **760** | 90 | 100 |
| (Cordia L) | **699** | 90 | 100 |

NOTE: Pwr strng standard on Cordia, Tredia L, Tredia Turbo, Starion, Galant, Montero, 2WD SPX Truck and 4WD Trucks. Air conditioning standard on Starion LE, Starion ES and Galant. Power windows standard on Starion and Galant. Power brakes standard on all models. Power door locks standard on Starion LE and Galant. Automatic transmission standard on Galant.

## 1984

| | Original List | Current Whlse | Average Retail |
|---|---|---|---|
| **2WD TRUCKS 4** | | | |
| Mighty Max (4 spd) | **5841** | 350 | 625 |
| SP (5 spd) | **6941** | 475 | 875 |
| SP Turbodiesel (5 spd) | **7861** | 250 | 500 |
| SPX (5 spd) | **7839** | 600 | 1125 |
| SPX Turbodiesel (5 spd) | **8819** | 375 | 675 |
| **CORDIA 4** | | | |
| 2 Dr Base Sport Hbk | **7482** | 475 | 875 |
| 2 Dr L Sport Hbk | **8179** | 550 | 1025 |
| 2 Dr LS Sport Hbk | **9419** | 650 | 1225 |
| 2 Dr Turbo Spt Hbk | **9809** | 725 | 1375 |
| **MONTERO 4** | | | |
| 4WD 3 Dr Base (5 spd) | **9778** | 1750 | 2600 |

| Year/Model/Body/Type | Original List | Current Whlse | Average Retail |
|---|---|---|---|
| 4WD 3 Dr Sport (5 spd) | **10309** | 1800 | 2650 |
| **STARION 4** | | | |
| LS Turbo 2+2 Cpe (5 spd) | **12509** | 1200 | 1925 |
| LE Turbo 2+2 Cpe (5 spd) | **14279** | 1350 | 2100 |
| ES Turbo 2+2 Cpe (5 spd) | **14559** | 1525 | 2375 |
| **TREDIA 4** | | | |
| 4 Dr Base Sdn | **7040** | 325 | 600 |
| 4 Dr L 4+4 Sdn | **7879** | 400 | 725 |
| 4 Dr LS 4+4 Sdn | **9019** | 500 | 925 |
| 4 Dr Turbo Sdn | **9349** | 600 | 1125 |
| **1983 — ALL BODY STYLES** | | | |
| MIGHTY MAX | — | 150 | 350 |
| 2WD S TRUCKS | — | 150 | 350 |
| 2WD SP TRUCKS | — | 225 | 475 |
| 2WD SPX TRUCKS | — | 325 | 600 |
| 4WD S TRUCKS | — | 725 | 1375 |
| 4WD SP TRUCKS | — | 475 | 875 |
| 4WD SPX TRUCKS | — | 900 | 1625 |
| CORDIA | — | 300 | 575 |
| MONTERO | — | 1200 | 1925 |
| STARION | — | 900 | 1625 |
| TREDIA | — | 150 | 350 |

## NISSAN

### 1992

| Year/Model/Body/Type | Original List | Current Whlse | Average Retail |
|---|---|---|---|
| **2WD PICKUPS 4** | | | |
| 2 Dr Reg Cab | **10260** | 7025 | 8150 |
| 2 Dr King Cab | **11605** | 7650 | 9500 |
| **2WD PICKUPS 6** | | | |
| 2 Dr Reg Cab Long Bed | **11710** | 7725 | 8975 |
| 2 Dr SE King Cab | **14585** | 9200 | 10600 |
| **4WD PICKUPS 4** | | | |
| 2 Dr Reg Cab | **13185** | 8850 | 10225 |
| 2 Dr King Cab | **14845** | 9500 | 10950 |
| **4WD PICKUPS 6** | | | |
| 2 Dr SE King Cab | **16700** | 11000 | 12700 |
| ADD FOR: | | | |
| Chrome Pkg | **825** | 350 | 425 |
| Power Plus Pkg | | | |
| (SE 2WD) | **1540** | — | — |
| (SE 4WD) | **2109** | — | — |

| Year/Model/Body/Type | Original List | Current Whlse | Average Retail |
|---|---|---|---|
| **240SX 4** | | | |
| 2 Dr Base Cpe | **15365** | 12250 | 14200 |
| 2 Dr SE Cpe | **17840** | 13450 | 15775 |
| 2 Dr Base Fstbk | **16115** | 12350 | 14400 |
| 2 Dr SE Fstbk | **18285** | 13550 | 15925 |
| 2 Dr LE Fstbk | **19320** | — | — |
| ADD FOR: | | | |
| Anti-Lock Brakes | **995** | 460 | 500 |
| Handling Pkg | **500** | 330 | 360 |
| **300ZX 6** | | | |
| 2-Seater Cpe w/o T-Bar Roof | **29705** | 22500 | 25800 |
| 2-Seater Cpe w/T-Bar Roof | **31815** | — | — |
| 2+2 Cpe w/T-Bar Roof | **33090** | 23900 | 27200 |
| Turbo Cpe w/T-Bar Roof | **36610** | — | — |
| ADD FOR: | | | |
| Leather Pkg | **1075** | — | — |
| Bose Radio System (models w/o T-bar roof) | **700** | — | — |
| **MAXIMA 6** | | | |
| 4 Dr GXE Sdn (auto) | **20425** | 14900 | 17500 |
| 4 Dr SE Sdn | **21490** | 16000 | 18650 |
| ADD FOR: | | | |
| Anti-Lock Brakes | **995** | 460 | 500 |
| Leather Seat Trim (GXE) | **1000** | 330 | 360 |
| (SE) | **1400** | 330 | 360 |
| **NX 4** | | | |
| 3 Dr 1600 Cpe | **12770** | 9800 | 11300 |
| 3 Dr 2000 Cpe | **14530** | 11150 | 12875 |
| ADD FOR: | | | |
| Anti-Lock Brakes | **700** | — | — |
| T-Bar Roof | **900** | — | — |
| **2WD PATHFINDER 6** | | | |
| XE Sport | **18805** | 16250 | 18900 |
| **4WD PATHFINDER 6** | | | |
| XE Sport | **20515** | 17750 | 20400 |
| SE Sport | **22735** | 19225 | 22275 |
| ADD FOR: | | | |
| Leather Seat Trim | **1000** | 450 | 525 |
| Power Pkg | **1050** | 275 | 350 |
| Sport/Power Pkg | **2000** | 650 | 800 |
| **SENTRA 4** | | | |
| 2 Dr E Sdn | **9795** | 8000 | 9300 |
| 4 Dr E Sdn | **11200** | 8100 | 9350 |
| 2 Dr XE Sdn | **11530** | 8725 | 10075 |
| 4 Dr XE Sdn | **12215** | 8825 | 10200 |

| Year/Model/Body/Type | Original List | Current Whlse | Average Retail |
|---|---|---|---|
| 2 Dr SE Sdn | **12210** | 8875 | 10250 |
| 2 Dr SE-R Sdn | **13465** | 9725 | 11200 |
| 4 Dr GXE Sdn | **13265** | 10025 | 11575 |
| *ADD FOR:* | | | |
| Anti-Lock Brakes | **700** | 460 | 500 |
| **STANZA 4** | | | |
| 4 Dr XE Sdn | **13225** | 10575 | 12200 |
| 4 Dr GXE Sdn (auto) | **17465** | 12450 | 14600 |
| 4 Dr SE Sdn | **17090** | 12050 | 13925 |
| *ADD FOR:* | | | |
| Anti-Lock Brakes | **995** | 460 | 500 |

NOTE: Tilt steering wheel standard on Sentra, Stanza, 240SX, NX, Maxima, Pathfinder and SE Pickup. Cruise control, power windows and power door locks standard on Sentra GXE, Stanza GXE & SE, 240SX SE & LE, Maxima, 300ZX and Pathfinder SE. Power seat standard on 300ZX.

## 1991

### 2WD PICKUPS 4

| | Original List | Current Whlse | Average Retail |
|---|---|---|---|
| 2 Dr Std Short Bed | **9710** | 6250 | 7275 |
| 2 Dr Std King Cab | **11015** | 6775 | 7875 |
| **2WD PICKUPS 6** | | | |
| 2 Dr Std Long Bed | **10780** | 6925 | 8050 |
| 2 Dr SE King Cab | **13955** | 8275 | 9550 |

### 240SX 4

| | | | |
|---|---|---|---|
| 2 Dr Base Cpe | **14945** | 10475 | 12100 |
| 2 Dr SE Cpe | **16200** | 11575 | 13375 |
| 3 Dr Base Fstbk | **15200** | 10575 | 12200 |
| 3 Dr SE Fstbk | **16390** | 11675 | 13475 |
| 3 Dr LE Fstbk | **18170** | 12550 | 14800 |

### 300ZX 6

| | | | |
|---|---|---|---|
| Base 2-Seater Cpe | **28175** | 19400 | 22450 |
| Turbo 2-Seater Cpe | **34570** | 22350 | 25650 |
| 2+2 Cpe | **31270** | 20650 | 23700 |

### MAXIMA 6

| | | | |
|---|---|---|---|
| 4 Dr GXE Sdn (auto) | **19375** | 12200 | 14100 |
| 4 Dr SE Sdn | **20495** | 13200 | 15525 |

### NX 4

| | | | |
|---|---|---|---|
| 3 Dr 1600 Cpe | **12390** | 8300 | 9575 |
| 3 Dr 2000 Cpe | **13820** | 9600 | 11050 |
| 2WD PATHFINDER 6 | | | |
| XE Sport | **17485** | 14275 | 16750 |

### 4WD PATHFINDER 6

| | | | |
|---|---|---|---|
| SE Sport | **21205** | 16775 | 19425 |

### SENTRA 4

| | | | |
|---|---|---|---|
| 2 Dr E Sdn (power steering available only w/auto trans) | **9140** | 6500 | 7575 |
| 4 Dr E Sdn (power steering available only w/auto trans) | **10075** | 6600 | 7675 |
| 2 Dr XE Sdn | **10380** | 7150 | 8300 |
| 4 Dr XE Sdn | **11065** | 7225 | 8400 |
| 2 Dr SE Sdn | **10960** | 7275 | 8450 |
| 2 Dr SE-R Sdn | **11370** | 7925 | 9200 |
| 4 Dr GXE Sdn | **12485** | 8425 | 9725 |

### STANZA 4

| | | | |
|---|---|---|---|
| 4 Dr XE Sdn | **13680** | 8350 | 9650 |
| 4 Dr GXE Sdn | **15825** | 9450 | 10875 |

| *ADD FOR:* | | | |
|---|---|---|---|
| Leather Pkg (300ZX Std & Turbo 2-Seater) | **1300** | 360 | 400 |
| (300ZX 2+2) | **1500** | 420 | 460 |
| (Maxima, Pathfinder SE) | **1000** | 280 | 310 |
| Luxury Pkg (Maxima GXE) | **1900** | 530 | 590 |
| T-Bar Roof (NX 2000) | **900** | — | — |
| Sport/Power Pkg (Pathfinder XE) | **1050** | 290 | 320 |
| (Pathfinder SE) | **2000** | 560 | 630 |

NOTE: Power brakes standard on all models. Power door locks and power windows standard on 240SX SE & LE, 300ZX, Maxima, Pathfinder SE, Sentra GXE and Stanza GXE. Power seat standard on 240SX SE & LE. Power sunroof standard on Maxima SE.

## 1990

### 2WD PICKUPS 4

| | Original List | Current Whlse | Average Retail |
|---|---|---|---|
| 2 Dr E Reg Cab | **9289** | 4700 | 5625 |
| 2 Dr E King Cab | **10574** | 5150 | 6075 |

### 2WD PICKUPS 6

| | | | |
|---|---|---|---|
| 2 Dr E Reg Cab | **10349** | 5100 | 6025 |
| 2 Dr SE King Cab | **13424** | 6625 | 7700 |

### VAN 4

| | | | |
|---|---|---|---|
| 7-Passenger XE | **14799** | 7600 | 8825 |
| 7-Passenger GXE (auto) | **17449** | 8725 | 10075 |

### 240SX 4

| | | | |
|---|---|---|---|
| 2 Dr XE Cpe | **14074** | 8025 | 9275 |
| 3 Dr SE Fstbk | **14324** | 8125 | 9375 |

### 300ZX 6

| | | | |
|---|---|---|---|
| GS Hbk Cpe | **27900** | 15150 | 17800 |
| GS 2+2 Hbk Cpe | **29100** | 15550 | 18200 |
| Turbo Hbk Cpe | **33000** | 17875 | 20525 |

### AXXESS 4

| | | | |
|---|---|---|---|
| XE Wgn | **14849** | 7875 | 9150 |

*Refer to optional equipment schedules*

| Year/Model/ Body/Type | Original List | Current Whlse | Average Retail |
|---|---|---|---|
| SE Wgn (auto) | **16749** | 8650 | 10000 |
| **MAXIMA 6** | | | |
| 4 Dr GXE Sdn (auto) | **17899** | 10150 | 11725 |
| 4 Dr SE Sdn | **18949** | 11025 | 12725 |
| **2WD PATHFINDER 6** | | | |
| XE Sport | **14855** | 12025 | 13900 |
| **4WD PATHFINDER 6** | | | |
| SE 2 Dr Sport | **21814** | 13875 | 16250 |
| SE 4 Dr Sport | **20149** | 14375 | 16875 |
| **PULSAR NX 4** | | | |
| 2 Dr XE Hbk Cpe | **13074** | 6925 | 8050 |
| **SENTRA 4** | | | |
| 2 Dr Sdn (NA w/pwr strng) | **8224** | 4225 | 5150 |
| 2 Dr XE Sdn | **9774** | 4925 | 5850 |
| 4 Dr XE Sdn | **10374** | 5025 | 5950 |
| 4 Dr XE Wgn | **11124** | 5300 | 6225 |
| 2 Dr XE Hbk Cpe | **11824** | 5725 | 6650 |
| 2 Dr SE Hbk Cpe | **13124** | 6175 | 7200 |
| **STANZA 4** | | | |
| 4 Dr XE Sdn | **12875** | 6925 | 8050 |
| 4 Dr GXE Sdn | **14975** | 7850 | 9125 |
| *ADD FOR:* | | | |
| Anti-Lock Braking System (240SX SE) | **995** | 240 | 260 |
| Convenience/Sport Pkg (240SX XE) | **2300** | 560 | 620 |
| (240SX SE) | **2100** | 510 | 570 |
| Sport Pkg (240SX) | **1150** | 280 | 310 |
| Electronic Equipment Pkg (300ZX ex. Turbo) | **1600** | 390 | 430 |
| (300ZX Turbo) | **900** | 220 | 240 |
| (Maxima GXE) | **1550** | 370 | 410 |
| Leather Trim Pkg (300ZX GS 2-Seater) | **1000** | 250 | 270 |
| (300ZX GS 2+2) | **1200** | 290 | 320 |
| (Maxima) | **950** | 230 | 250 |
| Luxury Pkg (Maxima GXE) | **1900** | 460 | 520 |
| SE Sport Pkg (Maxima SE) | **995** | 240 | 260 |
| Power Plus Pkg (2WD V6 SE King Cab Pickup) | **1540** | 370 | 410 |
| (4WD V6 SE King Cab Pickup) | **2109** | 510 | 570 |

NOTE: Power brakes standard on all models. Anti-lock brakes standard on 300ZX Series. Power windows standard on Stanza GXE, Axxess SE, Maxima Series, 300ZX Series, Van GXE and Pathfinder SE. Power door locks standard on Stanza GXE, Axxess Series, Maxima Series, 300ZX Series, Van GXE and Pathfinder SE. Sunroof standard on Sentra SE, Axxess SE and Maxima SE.

## 1989

| Year/Model/ Body/Type | Original List | Current Whlse | Average Retail |
|---|---|---|---|
| **2WD PICKUP 4** | | | |
| 2 Dr E Reg Bed | **8689** | 3500 | 4400 |
| 2 Dr E King Cab | **9974** | 3950 | 4850 |
| 2 Dr Special Reg Cab | **10089** | 3950 | 4850 |
| 2 Dr Special King Cab | **10974** | 4400 | 5325 |
| **2WD PICKUP 6** | | | |
| 2 Dr E Reg Bed | **10089** | 4075 | 5000 |
| 2 Dr Special Reg Cab | **11089** | 4525 | 5450 |
| 2 Dr SE King Cab | **13024** | 5325 | 6250 |
| **240SX 4** | | | |
| 2 Dr XE Cpe | **13249** | 7075 | 8225 |
| 3 Dr SE Fstbk | **13499** | 7150 | 8300 |
| **300ZX 6** | | | |
| GS Hbk Cpe | **23449** | 10175 | 11750 |
| GS 2+2 Hbk Cpe | **24649** | 10325 | 11925 |
| Turbo Hbk Cpe | **25949** | 11000 | 12700 |
| **MAXIMA 6** | | | |
| 4 Dr GXE Sdn (auto) | **17499** | 8650 | 10000 |
| 4 Dr SE Sdn | **18549** | 9250 | 10650 |
| **2WD PATHFINDER 6** | | | |
| XE Sport | **16224** | 9100 | 10475 |
| **4WD PATHFINDER 6** | | | |
| SE Sport | **20499** | 11100 | 12825 |
| **PULSAR NX 4** | | | |
| 2 Dr XE Hbk Cpe | **12824** | 5275 | 6200 |
| 2 Dr SE Hbk Cpe | **13824** | 5775 | 6700 |
| **SENTRA 4** | | | |
| 2 Dr Sdn | **7824** | 2600 | 3475 |
| 2 Dr E Sdn | **9074** | 3250 | 4150 |
| 4 Dr E Sdn | **9624** | 3350 | 4250 |
| 2WD E Wgn | **10324** | 3600 | 4500 |
| 2 Dr XE Sdn | **10774** | 3650 | 4550 |
| 4 Dr XE Sdn | **11424** | 3750 | 4650 |
| 2 Dr XE Cpe | **11824** | 4000 | 4900 |
| 2WD XE Wgn | **11874** | 4000 | 4900 |
| 4WD XE Wgn | **12424** | 4650 | 5575 |
| 2 Dr SE Cpe | **13124** | 4375 | 5300 |
| **STANZA 4** | | | |
| 4 Dr E Ntchbk Sdn | **13198** | 5275 | 6200 |
| 4 Dr GXE Ntchbk Sdn | **15074** | 5825 | 6750 |
| *ADD FOR:* | | | |
| Convenience/Sport Pkg | | | |

| Year/Model/Body/Type | Original List | Current Whlse | Average Retail |
|---|---|---|---|
| (240SX SE) | **2100** | 360 | 400 |
| Sport Pkg (240SX SE) | **1150** | 200 | 220 |
| (Pathfinder SE) | **2000** | 350 | 380 |
| Anti-Lock Braking System (240SX SE) | **1450** | 260 | 280 |
| (Maxima SE) | **1450** | 260 | 280 |
| Electronic Equipment Pkg (Maxima GXE) | **1550** | 270 | 300 |
| (300ZX) | **1375** | 240 | 260 |
| Luxury Pkg (Maxima GXE) | **1900** | 340 | 370 |
| Power Plus Pkg (2WD XE Pathfinder) | **1700** | 300 | 330 |
| (4WD XE Pathfinder) | **1900** | 340 | 370 |
| (2WD SE Pickup) | **1390** | 250 | 270 |
| (4WD SE Pickup) | **1959** | 350 | 380 |
| Leather Seat Trim (Maxima SE) | **1450** | 260 | 280 |
| (300ZX ex. 2+2, 300ZX Turbo) | **1055** | 180 | 200 |
| (300ZX GS 2+2) | **1215** | 210 | 230 |

NOTE: Power brakes standard on all models. Sunroof standard on Maxima SE and Sentra SE. Power windows and power door locks standard on 300ZX Series, Maxima Series, Pathfinder SE and Stanza GXE.

## 1988

### 2WD PICKUP 4

| | | | |
|---|---|---|---|
| 2 Dr Std Reg Bed | **7349** | 2525 | 3400 |
| 2 Dr E Reg Bed | **7724** | 2900 | 3800 |
| 2 Dr E Long Bed | **8424** | 3025 | 3925 |
| 2 Dr E King Cab | **8724** | 3250 | 4150 |
| 2 Dr XE King Cab | **10174** | 3675 | 4575 |

### 2WD PICKUP 6

| | | | |
|---|---|---|---|
| 2 Dr E HD Long Bed | **9249** | 3025 | 3925 |
| 2 Dr SE King Cab | **11324** | 4175 | 5100 |

### 4WD PICKUP 6

| | | | |
|---|---|---|---|
| 2 Dr E Reg Bed | **11224** | 4650 | 5575 |
| 2 Dr SE Reg Bed | **12874** | 5125 | 6050 |

### PATHFINDER 6

| | | | |
|---|---|---|---|
| XE Sport Utility | **15299** | 8475 | 9800 |
| SE Sport Utility | **17349** | 9100 | 10475 |

### VAN 4

| | | | |
|---|---|---|---|
| 7-Passenger XE | **14599** | 4825 | 5750 |
| 7-Passenger GXE (auto) | **16849** | 5200 | 6125 |

### 200SX 4

| | | | |
|---|---|---|---|
| 2 Dr XE Ntchbk | **12349** | 3725 | 4625 |
| 2 Dr XE Hbk | **12599** | 3825 | 4725 |

### 200SX 6

| | | | |
|---|---|---|---|
| 2 Dr SE Hbk | **15399** | 4400 | 5325 |

### 300ZX 6

| | | | |
|---|---|---|---|
| GS Hbk Cpe | **21199** | 7875 | 9150 |
| GS 2+2 Hbk Cpe | **22349** | 7975 | 9250 |
| Turbo Hbk Cpe | **23699** | 8475 | 9800 |
| Limited Turbo Hbk Cpe | **24699** | 8900 | 10275 |

### MAXIMA 6

| | | | |
|---|---|---|---|
| 4 Dr GXE Sdn (auto) | **17449** | 6625 | 7700 |
| 4 Dr GXE Wgn (auto) | **18699** | 6525 | 7600 |
| 4 Dr SE Sdn (5 spd) | **17699** | 6650 | 7750 |
| 4 Dr SE Special Edit. (5 spd) | **18699** | 6775 | 7875 |

### PULSAR NX 4

| | | | |
|---|---|---|---|
| 3 Dr XE Hbk | **11649** | 3550 | 4450 |
| 2 Dr XE Sportbak | **12199** | 3750 | 4650 |
| 3 Dr SE Hbk Cpe | **12999** | 4000 | 4900 |
| 2 Dr SE Sportbak | **13549** | 4175 | 5100 |

### SENTRA 4

| | | | |
|---|---|---|---|
| 2 Dr Std Sdn | **6499** | 1825 | 2675 |
| 2 Dr E Sdn | **7449** | 2275 | 3150 |
| 3 Dr E Hbk Sdn | **7349** | 2175 | 3025 |
| 4 Dr E Sdn | **8649** | 2350 | 3225 |
| 2WD E Wgn | **9099** | 2575 | 3450 |
| 2 Dr XE Sdn | **9149** | 2600 | 3475 |
| 4 Dr XE Sdn | **9749** | 2700 | 3600 |
| 2WD XE Wgn | **10049** | 2925 | 3825 |
| 2 Dr XE Cpe | **9999** | 2975 | 3875 |
| 4WD XE Wgn | **10849** | 3475 | 4375 |
| 4 Dr GXE Sdn | **10349** | 2900 | 3800 |
| 2 Dr SE Cpe | **11249** | 2575 | 3450 |

### STANZA 4

| | | | |
|---|---|---|---|
| 4 Dr E Ntchbk Sdn | **11249** | 3700 | 4600 |
| 2WD XE Wgn | **12349** | 3875 | 4775 |
| 4WD XE Wgn | **13899** | 4475 | 5400 |
| 4 Dr GXE Ntchbk Sdn | **13199** | 4125 | 5050 |

### ADD FOR:

| | | | |
|---|---|---|---|
| Electronic Pkg (300ZX) | **1300** | 110 | 120 |
| (Maxima GXE Sdn) | **845** | 100 | 110 |
| Desert Runner Pkg (4WD Pickup) | **3000** | 360 | 390 |
| Sport Pkg (2WD Pickup) | **750** | 90 | 100 |
| (4WD Pickup) | **1300** | 160 | 170 |
| (Pathfinder XE) | **900** | 110 | 120 |
| (Pathfinder SE) | **2000** | 240 | 260 |
| Leather Trim Pkg (Maxima GXE) | **785** | 90 | 100 |

*Refer to optional equipment schedules*

| Year/Model/Body/Type | Original List | Current Whlse | Average Retail |
|---|---|---|---|
| (300ZX) | **1100** | 130 | 140 |
| Suede Trim (Maxima SE) | **785** | 90 | 100 |

NOTE: Power brakes standard on all models. Power windows standard on Stanza GXE, 200SX SE, Maxima Series, 300ZX Series, Van GXE and Pathfinder SE. Air conditioning standard on Maxima Series, 300ZX Series and Vans. Power door locks standard on Stanza GXE, Maxima Series, Van GXE and Pathfinder SE. Sunroof standard on Sentra SE, Maxima GXE Wagon, Maxima SE and Maxima Special Edition. Pwr strng standard on Sentra E with automatic transmission, Sentra XE, Sentra GXE, Sentra SE, Stanza Series, Pulsar NX Series, 200SX Series, Maxima Series, 300ZX Series, Vans, Pathfinder Pickup E V6, Pickup XE and Pickup SE.

## 1987

### 2WD PICKUP 4

| Year/Model/Body/Type | Original List | Current Whlse | Average Retail |
|---|---|---|---|
| 2 Dr Std Reg Bed | **6999** | 1975 | 2825 |
| 2 Dr E Reg Bed | **7399** | 2250 | 3100 |
| 2 Dr E Long Bed | **8199** | 2350 | 3225 |
| 2 Dr E King Cab | **8899** | 2575 | 3450 |
| 2 Dr XE Long Bed | **9249** | 2725 | 3625 |
| 2 Dr XE King Cab | **9949** | 2950 | 3850 |

### 2WD PICKUP 6

| | | | |
|---|---|---|---|
| 2 Dr HD Long Bed | **9449** | 2850 | 3750 |
| 2 Dr SE Std Reg Bed | **10349** | 3100 | 4000 |
| 2 Dr SE Std King Cab | **11499** | 3400 | 4300 |

### PATHFINDER 4

| | | | |
|---|---|---|---|
| E Sport Utility | **12899** | 5850 | 6775 |

### PATHFINDER 6

| | | | |
|---|---|---|---|
| XE Sport Utility | **14899** | 6500 | 7575 |
| SE Sport Utility | **16299** | 6875 | 8000 |

### VAN 4

| | | | |
|---|---|---|---|
| 7-Passenger XE | **12849** | 3625 | 4525 |
| 7-Passenger GXE (auto) | **15099** | 4075 | 5000 |

### 200SX 4

| | | | |
|---|---|---|---|
| 2 Dr XE Ntchbk | **11649** | 2725 | 3625 |
| 3 Dr XE Hbk | **11899** | 2825 | 3725 |
| 200SX 6 3 Dr SE Hbk | **15199** | 3300 | 4200 |

### 300ZX 6

| | | | |
|---|---|---|---|
| GS Hbk Cpe w/o T-Bar Roof | **18999** | 6275 | 7300 |
| GS Hbk Cpe w/T-Bar Roof | **20449** | 6575 | 7650 |
| GS 2+2 Hbk Cpe w/T-Bar Roof | **21599** | 6350 | 7400 |
| Turbo Hbk Cpe w/T-Bar Roof | **22699** | 6700 | 7800 |
| Turbo Hbk Cpe w/Limited Slip | | | |

| Year/Model/Body/Type | Original List | Current Whlse | Average Retail |
|---|---|---|---|
| Differential | **22949** | 6725 | 7825 |

### MAXIMA 6

| | | | |
|---|---|---|---|
| 4 Dr GXE Sdn (auto) | **16799** | 4975 | 5900 |
| 4 Dr GXE Wgn (auto) | **17999** | 4875 | 5800 |
| 4 Dr SE Sdn (5 spd) | **16999** | 4950 | 5875 |
| 4 Dr SE Sdn (auto) | **17749** | 5350 | 6275 |

### PULSAR NX 4

| | | | |
|---|---|---|---|
| 3 Dr XE Hbk Cpe | **11399** | 2775 | 3675 |
| 3 Dr SE Hbk Cpe | **12599** | 3125 | 4025 |

### SENTRA 4

| | | | |
|---|---|---|---|
| 2 Dr Std Sdn | **6399** | 1325 | 2050 |
| 2 Dr E Sdn | **7599** | 1725 | 2575 |
| 3 Dr E Hbk Sdn | **7499** | 1650 | 2500 |
| 4 Dr E Sdn | **8349** | 1800 | 2650 |
| 2WD E Wgn | **8799** | 2000 | 2850 |
| 2 Dr XE Sdn | **8849** | 1900 | 2750 |
| 3 Dr XE Hbk Sdn | **8699** | 1800 | 2650 |
| 4 Dr XE Sdn | **9449** | 2000 | 2850 |
| 2WD XE Wgn | **9749** | 2175 | 3025 |
| 4WD XE Wgn | **10499** | 2700 | 3600 |
| 2 Dr XE Cpe | **9699** | 2225 | 3075 |
| 4 Dr GXE Sdn | **10049** | 2200 | 3050 |
| 2 Dr SE Cpe | **10899** | 2550 | 3425 |

### STANZA 4

| | | | |
|---|---|---|---|
| 4 Dr E Ntchbk Sdn | **10949** | 3025 | 3925 |
| 5 Dr XE Hbk Sdn | **12049** | 3125 | 4025 |
| 2WD XE Wgn | **11949** | 3125 | 4025 |
| 4WD XE Wgn | **13499** | 3650 | 4550 |
| 4 Dr GXE Ntchbk Sdn | **12899** | 3325 | 4225 |

### ADD FOR:

| | | | |
|---|---|---|---|
| Elec Pkg (300ZX) | **1300** | 90 | 100 |
| (Maxima GXE Sdn) | **825** | 90 | 100 |
| Leather Trim Pkg (Maxima GXE Sdn) | **750** | 90 | 100 |
| Sport/Power Pkg (2WD SE Pickup, Pathfinder SE) | **1950** | 150 | 160 |
| (4WD SE Pickup) | **2350** | 170 | 190 |
| Sportbak Rear Canopy (Pulsar NX) | **925** | 200 | 220 |

NOTE: Power brakes standard on all models. Air conditioning standard on Maxima Series and 300ZX Series. Power door locks standard on Stanza GXE, Maxima Series and 300ZX Series. Power windows standard on Stanza GXE, Maxima Series, 200SX SE, 300ZX Series and Van GXE. Sunroof standard on Sentra SE, 200SX SE, Maxima GXE Wagon and Maxima SE. Pwr strng standard on Sentra E with automatic transmission, Sentra XE, Sentra GXE, Sentra SE, Stanza Series, Pulsar NX Series, 200SX Series, Maxima Series, 300ZX Series, Van Series, Pathfinder Series, HD Pickups and XE Pickups.

# FOREIGN CARS & TRUCKS

| Year/Model/<br>Body/Type | Original<br>List | Current<br>Whlse | Average<br>Retail |
|---|---|---|---|
| **1986½** | | | |
| **2WD PICKUP 4** | | | |
| 2 Dr Std Reg Bed | **6299** | 1750 | 2600 |
| 2 Dr E Reg Bed | **6949** | 1950 | 2800 |
| 2 Dr E Long Bed | **7249** | 2075 | 2925 |
| 2 Dr E King Cab | **8049** | 2225 | 3075 |
| 2 Dr HD Long Bed | **8549** | 2150 | 3000 |
| 2 Dr XE Long Bed | **8199** | 2375 | 3250 |
| 2 Dr XE King Cab | **8999** | 2550 | 3425 |
| 2 Dr SE Reg Bed | **9399** | 2700 | 3600 |
| 2 Dr SE King Cab | **10499** | 3000 | 3900 |
| **1986** | | | |
| **2WD PICKUP 4** | | | |
| 2 Dr Std Reg Bed | **6199** | 1700 | 2550 |
| 2 Dr Std King Cab | **7699** | 1975 | 2825 |
| 2 Dr Dlx Reg Bed | **7599** | 1900 | 2750 |
| 2 Dr ST Reg Bed | **8639** | 2175 | 3025 |
| 2 Dr Std Long Bed | **6549** | 1800 | 2650 |
| 2 Dr ST Long Bed | **8799** | 2275 | 3150 |
| 2 Dr Dlx King Cab | **8219** | 2175 | 3025 |
| 2 Dr ST King Cab | **9259** | 2125 | 2975 |
| **4WD PICKUP 4** | | | |
| 2 Dr Dlx Long Bed | **9619** | 3050 | 3950 |
| **200SX 4** | | | |
| 2 Dr E Ntchbk | **9899** | 2275 | 3150 |
| 2 Dr E Hbk | **10199** | 2350 | 3225 |
| 2 Dr XE Ntchbk | **11299** | 2375 | 3250 |
| 2 Dr XE Hbk | **11899** | 2475 | 3350 |
| 2 Dr Turbo Hbk | **13549** | 2525 | 3400 |
| **300ZX 4** | | | |
| 2 Dr Cpe w/o<br>T-Bar Roof | **17999** | 4375 | 5300 |
| 2 Dr Cpe w/T-Bar Roof | **18999** | 4600 | 5525 |
| 2 Dr 2+2 Cpe<br>w/T-Bar Roof | **20149** | 4425 | 5350 |
| 2 Dr Turbo Cpe<br>w/T-Bar Roof | **20999** | 4750 | 5675 |
| **MAXIMA 6** | | | |
| 4 Dr SE Sdn | **14459** | 3475 | 4375 |
| 4 Dr GL Sdn (auto) | **14459** | 3425 | 4325 |
| 4 Dr GL Wgn (auto) | **15399** | 3350 | 4250 |
| **PULSAR 4** | | | |
| 2 Dr Cpe | **9099** | 1450 | 2225 |
| **SENTRA 4** | | | |
| 2 Dr Std Sdn | **5649** | 925 | 1650 |
| 2 Dr MPG Diesel Sdn | **7449** | 825 | 1525 |

| Year/Model/<br>Body/Type | Original<br>List | Current<br>Whlse | Average<br>Retail |
|---|---|---|---|
| 2 Dr Dlx Sdn | **6969** | 1275 | 2000 |
| 4 Dr Dlx Sdn | **7169** | 1325 | 2050 |
| 4 Dr Dlx Wgn | **7699** | 1500 | 2350 |
| 2 Dr XE Sdn | **7649** | 1400 | 2150 |
| 4 Dr XE Sdn | **7849** | 1500 | 2350 |
| 2 Dr XE Hbk | **8169** | 1550 | 2400 |
| 4 Dr XE Wgn | **8379** | 1675 | 2525 |
| 2 Dr SE Hbk | **9109** | 1775 | 2625 |
| **STANZA 4** | | | |
| 4 Dr GL Ntchbk | **10069** | 1725 | 2575 |
| 4 Dr XE Wgn | **10799** | 1775 | 2625 |
| 4 Dr 4WD E Wgn | **11429** | 2175 | 3025 |
| 4 Dr 4WD XE Wgn | **12099** | 2250 | 3100 |
| *ADD FOR:* | | | |
| Electronic Pkg<br>(Maxima) | **600** | 60 | 60 |
| Leather Pkg (Maxima) | **600** | 70 | 80 |

NOTE: Power brakes standard on all models. Power windows standard on Stanza GL, Maxima, 200SX SE and 300ZX. Sunroof standard on Sentra SE, Maxima Wagon, Maxima SE and 200SX Turbo. Power locks standard on Stanza GL, Maxima and 300ZX. Automatic transmission standard on Maxima and 300ZX. Pwr strng standard on Sentra XE, Sentra SE, Stanza, Maxima, 200SX E, 300ZX, Deluxe Pickups and ST Pickups.

| Year/Model/<br>Body/Type | Original<br>List | Current<br>Whlse | Average<br>Retail |
|---|---|---|---|
| **1985** | | | |
| **2WD PICKUP 4** | | | |
| 2 Dr Std Reg Bed | **5999** | 1650 | 2500 |
| 2 Dr Dlx Reg Bed | **7295** | 1800 | 2650 |
| 2 Dr ST Reg Bed | **8295** | 2100 | 2950 |
| 2 Dr Std Long Bed | **6299** | 1750 | 2600 |
| 2 Dr ST Long Bed | **8445** | 2175 | 3025 |
| 2 Dr Std King Cab | **7395** | 1875 | 2725 |
| 2 Dr Dlx King Cab | **7895** | 2075 | 2925 |
| 2 Dr ST King Cab | **8895** | 2175 | 3025 |
| **4WD PICKUP 4** | | | |
| 2 Dr Dlx Long Bed | **9245** | 2800 | 3700 |
| **200SX 4** | | | |
| 2 Dr Dlx Ntchbk | **8999** | 2050 | 2900 |
| 2 Dr XE Ntchbk | **10249** | 2125 | 2975 |
| 3 Dr Dlx Hbk | **9199** | 2150 | 3000 |
| 3 Dr XE Hbk | **10749** | 2200 | 3050 |
| 3 Dr Turbo Htchck | **12349** | 2225 | 3075 |
| **300ZX 6** | | | |
| 2 Seater Cpe | **17199** | 3600 | 4500 |
| 2+2 Cpe | **18399** | 3650 | 4550 |
| 2 Dr Turbo Cpe | **19699** | 3900 | 4800 |
| **MAXIMA 6** | | | |
| 4 Dr SE Sdn | **13499** | 3250 | 4150 |

| Year/Model/Body/Type | Original List | Current Whlse | Average Retail |
|---|---|---|---|
| 4 Dr GL Wgn (auto) | **14399** | 3150 | 4000 |
| 4 Dr GL Sdn (auto) | **13499** | 3175 | 4075 |
| **PULSAR 4** | | | |
| 2 Dr Cpe | **8249** | 1325 | 2050 |
| **SENTRA 4** | | | |
| 2 Dr Std Sdn | **5499** | 925 | 1650 |
| 2 Dr Dlx Sdn | **6649** | 1150 | 1875 |
| 2 Dr MPG Diesel Sdn | **7099** | 700 | 1325 |
| 2 Dr XE Sdn | **7299** | 1275 | 2000 |
| 4 Dr Dlx Sdn | **6849** | 1250 | 1975 |
| 4 Dr XE Sdn | **7499** | 1325 | 2050 |
| 4 Dr Dlx Wgn | **7349** | 1350 | 2100 |
| 4 Dr XE Wgn | **7999** | 1475 | 2300 |
| 3 Dr XE Hbk | **7799** | 1375 | 2125 |
| 3 Dr SE Hbk | **8699** | 1625 | 2475 |
| **STANZA 4** | | | |
| 4 Dr XE Hbk | **8949** | 1500 | 2350 |
| 4 Dr GL Sdn | **9549** | 1600 | 2450 |
| *ADD FOR:* | | | |
| ST Pkg (Dlx King Cab) | **1000** | 70 | 80 |
| Electronic Pkg (300ZX) | **1200** | 70 | 80 |
| Leather Pkg (300ZX) | **1200** | 70 | 80 |

NOTE: Pwr strng standard on Pulsar, Stanza, 200SX, Sentra XE, Maxima, 300ZX, 2WD Deluxe Pickups and 2WD ST Pickups. Air conditioning and power windows standard on Maxima and 300ZX. Power seat standard on Maxima and 300ZX. Sunroof standard on Pulsar and Maxima. Power brakes standard on all models. Power door locks standard on Maxima and 300ZX. Automatic transmission standard on Maxima.

## 1984

| 200SX 4 | | | |
|---|---|---|---|
| 2 Dr Dlx Ntchbk | **8699** | 1500 | 2350 |
| 2 Dr XE Ntchbk | **9949** | 1600 | 2450 |
| 3 Dr Dlx Hbk | **8899** | 1575 | 2425 |
| 3 Dr XE Hbk | **10249** | 1675 | 2525 |
| 3 Dr Turbo Htchck | **11949** | 1675 | 2525 |
| **300ZX 6** | | | |
| 2 Seater Cpe | **16199** | 2825 | 3725 |
| 2+2 Cpe | **17399** | 2850 | 3750 |
| 2 Seater Turbo Cpe | **18699** | 3100 | 4000 |
| 50th Anniversary Edit. Turbo | **25999** | 3500 | 4400 |
| **2WD PICKUP 4** | | | |
| 2 Dr Std Reg Bed MPG | **5999** | 1150 | 1875 |
| 2 Dr Std Reg Bed | **5999** | 1150 | 1875 |
| 2 Dr Dlx Reg Bed | **7195** | 1275 | 2000 |
| 2 Dr Spt Truck Reg Bed | **8145** | 1275 | 2000 |
| 2 Dr Dlx Long Bed | **7345** | 1325 | 2050 |
| 2 Dr HD Dlx Long Bed | **7445** | 1325 | 2050 |

| Year/Model/Body/Type | Original List | Current Whlse | Average Retail |
|---|---|---|---|
| 2 Dr Std King Cab MPG | **6895** | 1275 | 2000 |
| 2 Dr Dlx King Cab | **7795** | 1500 | 2350 |
| 2 Dr Dlx Diesel King Cab | **8635** | 1200 | 1925 |
| 2 Dr XE King Cab | **8895** | 1525 | 2375 |
| **MAXIMA 4** | | | |
| 4 Dr Sdn | **11899** | 1775 | 2625 |
| 4 Dr Wgn (auto) | **13299** | 1700 | 2550 |
| **PULSAR 4** | | | |
| 2 Dr NX Cpe | **8099** | 900 | 1625 |
| **SENTRA 4** | | | |
| 2 Dr Std Sdn | **5399** | 475 | 875 |
| 2 Dr Dlx Sdn | **6549** | 675 | 1275 |
| 4 Dr Dlx Sdn | **6749** | 750 | 1475 |
| 4 Dr Dlx Wgn | **7249** | 875 | 1600 |
| 2 Dr MPG Sdn | **6999** | 400 | 725 |
| 2 Dr XE Sdn | **7199** | 825 | 1525 |
| 4 Dr XE Sdn | **7399** | 900 | 1625 |
| 4 Dr XE Wgn | **7899** | 950 | 1675 |
| 2 Dr XE Hbk Cpe | **7699** | 900 | 1625 |
| **STANZA 4** | | | |
| 2 Dr XE Hbk | **8649** | 925 | 1650 |
| 4 Dr XE Hbk | **8849** | 1025 | 1750 |
| 4 Dr GL Sdn | **9449** | 1125 | 1850 |

## 1983 — ALL BODY STYLES

| | | | |
|---|---|---|---|
| 200SX | — | 950 | 1675 |
| 280-ZX | — | 2225 | 3075 |
| PICKUP | — | 1000 | 1725 |
| MAXIMA GL | — | 1400 | 2150 |
| PULSAR | — | 450 | 825 |
| SENTRA | — | 450 | 825 |
| STANZA | — | 650 | 1225 |

### PEUGEOT

## 1991

| 405 4 | | | |
|---|---|---|---|
| DL 4 Dr Sdn | **15490** | 7075 | 8225 |
| S 4 Dr Sdn | **17990** | 8050 | 9300 |
| Mi16 4 Dr Sdn | **21990** | 9150 | 10550 |
| DL 4 Dr Sportswagon | **16180** | 7550 | 8775 |
| S 4 Dr Sportswagon | **18785** | 8550 | 9875 |
| **505 4** | | | |
| DL 2.2i 5 Dr Wgn | **18950** | 7950 | 9225 |
| SW8 2.2i 5 Dr Wgn | **20800** | 9225 | 10625 |
| SW8 5 Dr Turbo Wgn (auto) | **26300** | 11625 | 13425 |

NOTE: Power brakes and power door locks standard on all models. Power windows standard on 405 S and Mi16,

505 SW8 2.2i and Turbo SW8. Power seat standard on 405 Mi16. Power sunroof standard on 405 Mi16.

## 1990

### 405 4

| Year/Model/Body/Type | Original List | Current Whlse | Average Retail |
|---|---|---|---|
| DL 4 Dr Sdn | **15390** | 5550 | 6475 |
| S 4 Dr Sdn | **17700** | 6275 | 7300 |
| Mi16 4 Dr Sdn | **21990** | 7775 | 9025 |
| DL 5 Dr Sportswagon | **15990** | 5950 | 6875 |
| S 5 Dr Sportswagon | **18495** | 6725 | 7825 |

### 505 4

| | | | |
|---|---|---|---|
| S 2.2i 4 Dr Sdn | **19945** | — | — |
| S V6 4 Dr Sdn | **22485** | — | — |
| DL 2.2i 5 Dr Wgn | **18590** | — | — |
| SW8 2.2i 5 Dr Wgn | **20400** | — | — |
| 5 Dr Turbo Wgn (auto) | **25940** | — | — |
| SW8 5 Dr Turbo Wgn (auto) | **26100** | — | — |

NOTE: Power brakes and power door locks standard on all models. Anti-lock power brakes standard on 405 Mi16. Sunroof standard on 505 S 2.2i and 505 S V6. Power seat standard on 405 Mi16. Moonroof standard on 405 S Sedan and 405 Mi16 Sedan. Power windows standard on 405 S, 405 MI16, 505 SW8 2.2i and 505 Turbo Wagon.

## 1989

### 405 4

| | | | |
|---|---|---|---|
| DL 4 Dr Sdn | **14500** | 3750 | 4600 |
| S 4 Dr Sdn | **17700** | 4250 | 5175 |
| Mi 16 4 Dr Sdn | **20700** | 5225 | 6150 |

### 505 4

| | | | |
|---|---|---|---|
| DL 4 Dr Wgn | **17590** | 4200 | 5125 |
| S 4 Dr Sdn | **19295** | 4950 | 5875 |
| S 4 Dr Sdn (6 cyl) | **21435** | 5400 | 6325 |
| SW8 5 Dr Wgn | **19995** | 5275 | 6200 |
| STX 4 Dr Sdn (6 cyl) | **25895** | 7300 | 8475 |
| 4 Dr Turbo Sdn | **26335** | 7550 | 8775 |
| 5 Dr Turbo Wgn (auto) | **25540** | 7850 | 9125 |
| SW8 5 Dr Turbo Wgn (auto) | **25695** | 8025 | 9275 |

*ADD FOR:*

| | | | |
|---|---|---|---|
| Leather Package | | | |
| (405 S) | **1300** | 160 | 180 |
| (505 Turbo Sdn) | **960** | 160 | 180 |

NOTE: Power brakes and power door locks standard on all models. Power moonroof standard on 405 S and 405 Mi16. Sunroof standard on 505 Series except DL. Power windows standard on 405 S, 405 Mi16, 505 S, 505 SW8, 505 STX, 505 Turbo and 505 SW8 Turbo.

## 1988

### 505 4

| | | | |
|---|---|---|---|
| DL 4 Dr Sdn | **15950** | 2075 | 2950 |
| DL 4 Dr Wgn | **16975** | 2350 | 3250 |
| GLS 4 Dr Sdn | **18290** | 2625 | 3525 |
| GLS 5 Dr Wgn | **18475** | 2825 | 3725 |
| SW8 5 Dr Wgn | **19200** | 3150 | 4050 |
| GLX 4 Dr Sdn | **20425** | 2950 | 3850 |
| STI 4 Dr Sdn (auto) | **20890** | 3800 | 4700 |
| STX 4 Dr Sdn | **24690** | 4625 | 5550 |
| S 4 Dr Turbo Sdn | **25330** | 4700 | 5625 |
| S 5 Dr Wgn (auto) | **24330** | 5200 | 6125 |

*ADD FOR:*

| | | | |
|---|---|---|---|
| Leather Upholstery | | | |
| (505 STI, STX & S) | **950** | 150 | 160 |

NOTE: Pwr strng and power brakes standard on all models. Power windows standard on 505 GLS, 505 SW8, 505 GLX and 505 STI. Sunroof standard on 505 GLS Sedan, 505 SW8 Sedan, 505 GLX and 505 STI.

## 1987

### 505 4

| | | | |
|---|---|---|---|
| GL 4 Dr Sdn | **14160** | 1675 | 2500 |
| Liberte 4 Dr Sdn (auto) | **16100** | 1875 | 2725 |
| Liberte 5 Dr Wgn (auto) | **17100** | 2150 | 3075 |
| GLS 4 Dr Sdn | **16170** | 2050 | 2900 |
| STI 4 Dr Sdn | **18870** | 2450 | 3325 |
| STI 4 Dr Sdn (6 cyl) | **21100** | 2825 | 3725 |
| STX 4 Dr Sdn | **23750** | 3350 | 4250 |
| 4 Dr Turbo Sdn | **18990** | 2550 | 3425 |
| 5 Dr Turbo Wgn | **20200** | 2800 | 3700 |
| S 4 Dr Turbo Sdn | **23100** | 3350 | 4250 |
| S 5 Dr Turbo Wgn | **22750** | 3600 | 4500 |
| GLS 4 Dr Turbodiesel Sdn (auto) | **18550** | — | — |
| GLS 5 Dr Turbodiesel Wgn (auto) | **19450** | — | — |

*ADD FOR:*

| | | | |
|---|---|---|---|
| Anti-Lok Braking System (505 STI w/6 Cyl) | **1300** | 230 | 250 |
| Leather Upholstery (505 STI w/4 Cyl, 505 S Turbo) | **380** | 100 | 110 |

NOTE: Pwr strng and power brakes standard on all models. Power windows standard on 505 Liberte, 505 GLS, 505 STI, 505 STX, 505 Turbo, 505 S Turbo and 505 GSL Turbo-diesel Wagon. Sunroof standard on 505 Liberte Sedan, 505 GLS, 505 STI, 505 Turbo, 505 S Turbo and 505 GLS Turbo-diesel. Air conditioning standard on 505 GL, 505 GLS, 505 STI w/6 cyl, 505 STX, 505 Turbo, 505 S Turbo and 505 GLS Turbo-diesel.

| Year/Model/ Body/Type | Original List | Current Whlse | Average Retail |
|---|---|---|---|
| **1986** | | | |
| **505 4** | | | |
| GL 4 Dr Sdn | **12895** | 1000 | 1725 |
| S 4 Dr Sdn | **16245** | 1450 | 2225 |
| STI 4 Dr Sdn | **17295** | 1725 | 2575 |
| GL 4 Dr Wgn | **13495** | 1300 | 2025 |
| S 4 Dr Wgn | **17445** | 1675 | 2525 |
| 4 Dr Turbo Sdn | **19345** | 2000 | 2850 |
| 4 Dr Turbo Wgn (auto) | **20495** | 2425 | 3300 |
| *ADD FOR:* | | | |
| Leather Upholstery (505 S Gasoline, Turbo Gasoline Sdn & Wgn) | **750** | 90 | 100 |

NOTE: Power brakes and pwr strng standard on all models. Power windows and air conditioning standard on all models except 505 GL. Sunroof standard on all models except wagons and 505 GL Sedan. Automatic transmission standard on 505 GL Turbodiesel Wagon and 505 S Turbodiesel Wagon.

| Year/Model/ Body/Type | Original List | Current Whlse | Average Retail |
|---|---|---|---|
| **1985** | | | |
| **505 4** | | | |
| GL 4 Dr Sdn | **11900** | 850 | 1550 |
| S 4 Dr Sdn | **15580** | 1150 | 1875 |
| STI 4 Dr Sdn | **16630** | 1325 | 2050 |
| GL 4 Dr Wgn | **12440** | 975 | 1700 |
| S 4 Dr Wgn | **16695** | 1300 | 2025 |
| 4 Dr Turbo Sdn | **18150** | 1450 | 2225 |
| GL 4 Dr Turbodiesel Sdn | **13220** | 700 | 1325 |
| S 4 Dr Turbodiesel Sdn | **16900** | 900 | 1625 |
| STI 4 Dr Turbodiesel Sdn | **17950** | 1075 | 1800 |
| GL 4 Dr Turbodiesel Wgn | **13860** | 825 | 1525 |
| S 4 Dr Turbodiesel Wgn | **17965** | 1025 | 1750 |
| *ADD FOR:* | | | |
| Metallic Paint (505 GL) | **350** | 40 | 40 |
| Leather Upholstery (505 S Wgn) | **675** | 80 | 90 |

NOTE: Power brakes and pwr strng standard on all models. Power windows and air conditioning standard on all models except 505 GL. Sunroof standard on all models except wagons and 505 GL Sedan. Automatic transmission standard on 505 GL Turbodiesel Wagon and 505 S Turbodiesel Wagon.

| Year/Model/ Body/Type | Original List | Current Whlse | Average Retail |
|---|---|---|---|
| **1984** | | | |
| **505 4** | | | |
| GL 4 Dr Sdn | **11300** | 500 | 925 |

| Year/Model/ Body/Type | Original List | Current Whlse | Average Retail |
|---|---|---|---|
| GL 4 Dr Wgn | **11990** | 600 | 1125 |
| GL 4 Dr Turbodiesel Sdn | **12800** | 150 | 350 |
| GL 4 Dr Turbodiesel Wgn (auto) | **13680** | 225 | 475 |
| S 4 Dr Sdn | **14845** | 800 | 1500 |
| S 4 Dr Wgn | **16095** | 875 | 1600 |
| S 4 Dr Turbodiesel Sdn | **16345** | 450 | 825 |
| S 4 Dr Turbodiesel Wgn (auto) | **17695** | 525 | 975 |
| STI 4 Dr Sdn | **15800** | 925 | 1650 |
| STI 4 Dr Turbodiese Sdn | **17300** | 600 | 1125 |
| **604 4** | | | |
| 4 Dr Turbodiesel Sdn | **20885** | 625 | 1175 |
| **1983** | | | |
| **504 4** | | | |
| Diesel 4 Dr Wgn | **12085** | 110 | 300 |
| **505 4** | | | |
| 4 Dr Sdn | **11865** | 350 | 625 |
| Diesel 4 Dr Sdn | **12575** | 110 | 300 |
| Turbodiesel 4 Dr Sdn | **14445** | 110 | 300 |
| **604 4** | | | |
| Turbodiesel 4 Dr Sdn | **19780** | 500 | 925 |

### PORSCHE

| Year/Model/ Body/Type | Original List | Current Whlse | Average Retail |
|---|---|---|---|
| **1992** | | | |
| **911 CARRERA 2 6** | | | |
| 2 Dr Cpe (5 spd) | **63900** | — | — |
| 2 Dr Cpe (Tiptronic) | **67050** | — | — |
| 2 Dr Targa (5 spd) | **65500** | — | — |
| 2 Dr Targa (Tiptronic) | **68650** | — | — |
| 2 Dr Cabriolet (5 spd) | **72900** | — | — |
| 2 Dr Cabriolet (Tiptronic) | **76050** | — | — |
| 2 Dr American Rdstr Cabriolet (5 spd) | **87900** | — | — |
| 2 Dr American Rdstr Cabriolet (Tiptronic) | **91050** | — | — |
| **911 CARRERA 4 6** | | | |
| 2 Dr Cpe (5 spd) | **75780** | — | — |
| 2 Dr Targa (5 spd) | **77380** | — | — |
| 2 Dr Cabriolet (5 spd) | **84780** | — | — |
| **911 TURBO COUPE 6** | | | |
| 2 Dr Cpe (5 spd) | **98875** | — | — |

*1991 Porsche 928 Manual*

| Year/Model/ Body/Type | Original List | Current Whlse | Average Retail |
|---|---|---|---|
| *ADD FOR:* | | | |
| 5-Spoke Wheels | **1352** | — | — |
| Hardtop Roof (Cabriolet) | **9670** | — | — |
| CD Player | **755** | — | — |
| **968 4** | | | |
| 2 Dr Cpe (6 spd) | **39850** | — | — |
| 2 Dr Cpe (Tiptronic) | **43000** | — | — |
| 2 Dr Cabriolet (6 spd) | **51000** | — | — |
| 2 Dr Cabriolet (Tiptronic) | **54150** | — | — |
| *ADD FOR:* | | | |
| 5-Spoke Turbo Wheels | **1352** | — | — |
| Special Chassis | **1976** | — | — |
| CD Player | **1250** | — | — |

NOTE: Power windows/power door locks standard on all models. Cruise control and power seat standard on 911 Carrera, 911 American Roadster, 911 Turbo Coupe and 968. Power sunroof standard on 911 Carrera 2 Coupe and 968 Coupe.

## 1991

### 911 CARRERA 2 6

| | Original List | Current Whlse | Average Retail |
|---|---|---|---|
| 2 Dr Cpe (5 spd) | **61915** | 43200 | 47825 |
| 2 Dr Cpe (Tiptronic) | **64925** | 42375 | 46900 |
| 2 Dr Targa (5 spd) | **63445** | 43975 | 48675 |
| 2 Dr Targa (Tiptronic) | **66455** | 44900 | 49700 |
| 2 Dr Cabriolet (5 spd) | **70690** | 48375 | 53300 |
| 2 Dr Cabriolet (Tiptronic) | **73695** | 48800 | 53775 |

### 911 CARRERA 4 6

| | Original List | Current Whlse | Average Retail |
|---|---|---|---|
| 2 Dr Cpe (5 spd) | **73440** | 48225 | 53150 |
| 2 Dr Targa (5 spd) | **74970** | 48525 | 53475 |
| 2 Dr Cabriolet (5 spd) | **82215** | 53550 | 58700 |

| Year/Model/ Body/Type | Original List | Current Whlse | Average Retail |
|---|---|---|---|
| **911 TURBO COUPE 6** | | | |
| 2 Dr Cpe (5 spd) | **95000** | — | — |
| **928 8** | | | |
| 2 Dr S4 Cpe (auto) | **77500** | 45950 | 50625 |
| 2 Dr GT (5 spd) | **77500** | 46750 | 51525 |
| **944 S2 4** | | | |
| 2 Dr Cpe (5 spd) | **43350** | 25250 | 28575 |
| 2 Dr Cabriolet (5 spd) | **50350** | 29025 | 32375 |
| *ADD FOR:* | | | |
| Hardtop Roof (911 Cabriolet) | **8582** | 4750 | 5270 |

NOTE: Power brakes, power door locks, power windows, power seat and sunroof standard on all models.

## 1990

### 911 CARRERA 2 6

| | Original List | Current Whlse | Average Retail |
|---|---|---|---|
| 2 Dr Cpe (5 spd) | **58500** | 37450 | 41575 |
| 2 Dr Cpe (Tiptronic) | **61280** | 38450 | 42675 |
| 2 Dr Targa (5 spd) | **59900** | 38150 | 42350 |
| 2 Dr Targa (Tiptronic) | **62680** | 39150 | 43450 |
| 2 Dr Cabriolet (5 spd) | **66800** | 42800 | 47375 |
| 2 Dr Cabriolet (Tiptronic) | **69580** | 43750 | 48425 |

### 911 CARRERA 4 6

| | Original List | Current Whlse | Average Retail |
|---|---|---|---|
| 2 Dr Cpe (5 spd) | **69500** | 42700 | 47275 |
| 2 Dr Targa (5 spd) | **70900** | 43250 | 47875 |
| 2 Dr Cabriolet (5 spd) | **77800** | 47525 | 52375 |

### 928S 8

| | Original List | Current Whlse | Average Retail |
|---|---|---|---|
| 2 Dr Cpe (5 spd) | **74545** | 40700 | 45050 |
| 2 Dr Cpe (auto) | **74545** | 41500 | 46000 |

| Year/Model/ Body/Type | Original List | Current Whlse | Average Retail |
|---|---|---|---|
| **944 S2 4** | | | |
| 2 Dr Cpe (5 spd) | **41900** | 21425 | 24725 |
| 2 Dr Cabriolet (5 spd) | **48600** | 24700 | 28000 |

NOTE: Power windows, power door locks and anti-lock power brakes standard on all models. Power seat standard on 911 and 944. Sunroof standard on 911 Coupe, 944 Coupe and 928.

## 1989

### 911 6

| | | | |
|---|---|---|---|
| Cpe (5 spd) | **51205** | 30350 | 33750 |
| Targa (5 spd) | **52435** | 31000 | 34475 |
| Cabriolet (5 spd) | **59200** | 34750 | 38650 |
| Speedster (5 spd) | **65480** | 43975 | 48675 |
| Turbo Cpe (5 spd) | **70975** | 38900 | 43175 |
| Turbo Targa (5 spd) | **77065** | 39950 | 44350 |
| Turbo Cabriolet (5 spd) | **85060** | 44250 | 48975 |

### 928S 4

| | | | |
|---|---|---|---|
| Cpe (auto) | **74545** | 31375 | 34900 |

### 944 4

| | | | |
|---|---|---|---|
| Cpe (5 spd) | **33245** | 13950 | 16325 |
| Cpe (auto) | **34215** | 14175 | 16650 |
| S Cpe (5 spd) | **41900** | 15650 | 18300 |
| Turbo Cpe (5 spd) | **44900** | 17750 | 20400 |

*ADD FOR:*

| | | | |
|---|---|---|---|
| 930 Slant Nose Pkg (911) | **29555** | — | — |
| 930 Turbo Look (911) | **14218** | — | — |

NOTE: Power brakes, sunroof and power windows standard on all models. Power door locks standard on 911 Series.

## 1988

### 911 6

| | | | |
|---|---|---|---|
| 5 Spd Cpe | **45895** | 24425 | 27725 |
| 5 Spd Targa | **48230** | 25000 | 28325 |
| 5 Spd Cabriolet | **52895** | 28775 | 32125 |
| 4 Spd Turbo Cpe | **68670** | 36350 | 40350 |
| 4 Spd Turbo Targa | **77065** | 37875 | 40350 |
| 4 Spd Turbo Cabriolet | **85060** | 40350 | 44675 |

### 924S 4

| | | | |
|---|---|---|---|
| 5 Spd Cpe | **26560** | 5875 | 5800 |
| Cpe (auto) | **27660** | 6000 | 6925 |

### 928S 8

| | | | |
|---|---|---|---|
| Cpe (auto) | **69680** | 24300 | 27600 |

### 944 4

| | | | |
|---|---|---|---|
| 5 Spd Cpe | **30995** | 10300 | 11875 |
| Cpe (auto) | **32115** | 10500 | 12125 |

| Year/Model/ Body/Type | Original List | Current Whlse | Average Retail |
|---|---|---|---|
| 5 Spd S Cpe | **36830** | 11625 | 13425 |
| 5 Spd Turbo Cpe | **39765** | 13325 | 15650 |

*ADD FOR:*

| | | | |
|---|---|---|---|
| Turbo Look (911 Non-Turbo) | **13970** | — | — |
| Turbo Pkg (944S) | **5510** | 1850 | 2050 |
| Anti-Lock Brake System (944) | **2368** | 790 | 880 |
| Special Edit. Pkg (924S) | **918** | 310 | 340 |
| (911 Non-Turbo Cpe) | **3819** | 1270 | 1410 |
| (911 Non-Turbo Targa, 911 Non-Turbo Cabriolet) | **2411** | 810 | 900 |
| (944) | **2486** | 840 | 930 |

NOTE: Air conditioning and power windows standard on 924S, 944 Series, 911 Series and 928S. Power locks standard on 944 Series. Sunroof standard on 911 Turbo Coupe and 928. Pwr strng standard on 924S, 944 Series and 928. Power brakes standard on 924S, 944 Series and 911 Series.

## 1987

### 911 6

| | | | |
|---|---|---|---|
| 5 Spd Cpe | **41440** | 21175 | 24450 |
| 5 Spd Targa | **43590** | 21725 | 25025 |
| 5 Spd Cabriolet | **47895** | 25200 | 28525 |
| 5 Spd Turbo Cpe | **63295** | 33250 | 36975 |
| 5 Spd Turbo Targa | **71035** | 33550 | 37300 |
| 5 Spd Turbo Cabriolet | **78415** | 38600 | 42850 |

### 924S 4

| | | | |
|---|---|---|---|
| 5 Spd Cpe | **24408** | 4225 | 5150 |
| Cpe (auto) | **25523** | 4350 | 5275 |

### 928S 8

| | | | |
|---|---|---|---|
| Cpe (auto) | **63520** | 20425 | 23475 |

### 944 4

| | | | |
|---|---|---|---|
| 5 Spd Cpe | **28338** | 7975 | 9250 |
| Cpe (auto) | **29453** | 8075 | 9325 |
| 5 Spd S Cpe | **31348** | 8625 | 9950 |
| 5 Spd Turbo Cpe | **36798** | 10700 | 12350 |

*ADD FOR:*

| | | | |
|---|---|---|---|
| Forged Alloy Wheels (944 ex. Turbo) | **3191** | 840 | 930 |
| (944 Turbo) | **2255** | 590 | 660 |
| Pressure Cast Magnesium Wheels (944 ex. Turbo) | **2655** | 690 | 770 |
| (944 Turbo) | **1744** | 460 | 500 |
| 16" Forged Alloy Wheels (944 ex. Turbo) | **2139** | 560 | 630 |

NOTE: Air conditioning and power windows standard on 911 Series, 928S, 924S and 944 Series. Pwr strng

| Year/Model/Body/Type | Original List | Current Whlse | Average Retail |
|---|---|---|---|

standard on 924S, 928S and 944 Series. Sunroof and power door locks standard on 911 Turbo and 928S.

## 1986

### 911 6

| | | | |
|---|---|---|---|
| 5 Spd Cpe | 34632 | 20125 | 23175 |
| 5 Spd Targa | 36157 | 20625 | 23675 |
| 5 Spd Cabriolet | 39407 | 23650 | 26950 |
| 5 Spd Turbo Cpe | 53475 | 31250 | 34750 |

### 928S 8

| | | | |
|---|---|---|---|
| 5 Spd Cpe | 51900 | 13400 | 15725 |
| Cpe (auto) | 51900 | 13550 | 15925 |

### 944 4

| | | | |
|---|---|---|---|
| 5 Spd Cpe | 25157 | 6900 | 8025 |
| Cpe (auto) | 25657 | 7000 | 8150 |
| 5 Spd Turbo Cpe | 30457 | 9125 | 10500 |

NOTE: Power windows, power brakes, pwr strng and air conditioning standard on all models. Automatic transmission standard on 928S and 944. Power locks, sunroof and power seat standard on 928S.

## 1985

### 911 CARRERA 6

| | | | |
|---|---|---|---|
| 5 Spd Cpe | 31950 | 18100 | 20800 |
| 5 Spd Targa | 33450 | 18550 | 21600 |
| 5 Spd Cabriolet | 36450 | 21350 | 24650 |

### 928S 8

| | | | |
|---|---|---|---|
| 5 Spd Cpe | 50000 | 13150 | 15475 |
| Cpe (auto) | 50000 | 13425 | 15750 |

### 944 4

| | | | |
|---|---|---|---|
| 5 Spd Hbk | 22950 | 5775 | 6700 |
| Hbk (auto) | 23450 | 5875 | 6800 |

NOTE: Pwr strng standard on 928 and 944. Air conditioning and power windows standard on all models. Power seat standard on 928. Sunroof standard on 944.

## 1984

### 911 CARRERA 6

| | | | |
|---|---|---|---|
| 5 Spd Cpe | 32550 | 16550 | 19200 |
| 5 Spd Targa | 34050 | 17100 | 19750 |
| 5 Spd Cabriolet | 37050 | 20000 | 23050 |

### 928S 8

| | | | |
|---|---|---|---|
| 5 Spd Cpe | 44600 | 12600 | 14925 |
| Cpe (auto) | 44600 | 12800 | 15125 |

### 944 4

| | | | |
|---|---|---|---|
| 5 Spd Hbk | 22040 | 5125 | 6050 |

| | | | |
|---|---|---|---|
| Hbk (auto) | 22540 | 5325 | 6250 |

## 1983

### 911 SC 6

| | | | |
|---|---|---|---|
| 5 Spd Cpe | 30745 | 15950 | 18600 |

### 911 SC TARGA 6

| | | | |
|---|---|---|---|
| 5 Spd Rdstr | 32245 | 16100 | 18750 |
| 5 Spd Cabriolet | 35245 | 18750 | 21800 |

### 928S 8

| | | | |
|---|---|---|---|
| 5 Spd Cpe | 43795 | 11425 | 13200 |

### 944 4

| | | | |
|---|---|---|---|
| 5 Spd Cpe | 19775 | 4700 | 5625 |
| Hbk (auto) | 19475 | 4775 | 5700 |

## RANGE ROVER

## 1992

### RANGE ROVER 8

| | | | |
|---|---|---|---|
| 4WD Standard Rover | 38900 | — | — |
| 4WD County Rover | 44500 | — | — |

*ADD FOR:*

| | | | |
|---|---|---|---|
| LSE Sport & Trim Pkg | 4000 | — | — |

NOTE: Tilt steering wheel, cruise control, power windows, power door locks, power seat and power sunroof standard on all models.

## 1991

### RANGE ROVER 8

| | | | |
|---|---|---|---|
| 4WD Hunter Rover | 36500 | — | — |
| 4WD Standard Rover | 43000 | 26400 | 29725 |
| 4WD County SE Rover | 47300 | 27650 | 31000 |

NOTE: Power brakes, power door locks and power windows standard on all models. Power seat standard on Standard and County SE. Sunroof standard on County SE.

## 1990

### RANGE ROVER 8

| | | | |
|---|---|---|---|
| 4WD Base Rover | 38025 | 22000 | 25300 |
| 4WD County Rover | 40125 | 22750 | 26050 |

*ADD FOR:*

| | | | |
|---|---|---|---|
| Premium Radio (Range Rover County) | 1600 | 420 | 460 |

NOTE: Power door locks, power windows, anti-lock power brakes and power seat standard.

# FOREIGN CARS & TRUCKS

| Year/Model/ Body/Type | Original List | Current Whlse | Average Retail |
|---|---|---|---|
| **1989** | | | |
| **RANGE ROVER 8** | | | |
| 4WD Base Rover | **36600** | 17675 | 20325 |
| 4WD County Rover | **43100** | 19600 | 22650 |
| *ADD FOR:* | | | |
| Leather Interior (Base Rover) | **1125** | 380 | 420 |

NOTE: Power brakes, power windows and power door locks standard on all models. Power sunroof standard on County Rover.

| **1988** | | | |
|---|---|---|---|
| **RANGE ROVER 8** | | | |
| 4WD Rover | **34400** | 13725 | 16100 |
| *ADD FOR:* | | | |
| Leather Interior | **1125** | 350 | 380 |

NOTE: Air conditioning, power brakes, pwr strng, automatic transmission and power windows standard.

| **1987** | | | |
|---|---|---|---|
| **RANGE ROVER 8** | | | |
| 4WD Rover | **30825** | 11075 | 12800 |
| *ADD FOR:* | | | |
| Leather Interior | **1025** | 240 | 260 |

NOTE: Air conditioning, power disc brakes, power door locks, pwr strng, automatic transmission, power windows and AM/FM stereo cassette radio standard.

## RENAULT

| **1986** | | | |
|---|---|---|---|
| **SPORTWAGON 4** | | | |
| Sportwagon | **10199** | 575 | 1075 |
| Sportwgn Touring Edit. | **12024** | 675 | 1275 |

NOTE: Power brakes, pwr strng and air conditioning standard on Sportwagon. Power locks and power windows standard on Sportwagon Touring Edition.

| **1985** | | | |
|---|---|---|---|
| **FUEGO 4** | | | |
| Fuego Cpe | **9295** | 425 | 775 |
| **SPORTWAGON 4** | | | |
| Sportwagon | **9895** | 350 | 625 |
| Sportwgn Touring Edit. | **11700** | 450 | 825 |

NOTE: Pwr strng standard on Fuego and Sportwagon. Air conditioning standard on Sportwagon. Power brakes stan. on Fuego and Sportwagon. Power windows and power door locks standard on Sportwagon Touring Edition.

| Year/Model/ Body/Type | Original List | Current Whlse | Average Retail |
|---|---|---|---|
| **1984** | | | |
| **FUEGO 4** | | | |
| Fuego Cpe Fuel Inj. | **8995** | 150 | 350 |
| Fuego Turbo Cpe | **11395** | 150 | 350 |
| **SPORTWAGON 4** | | | |
| Sportwagon | **9595** | 110 | 300 |
| Sportwgn Touring Edit. | **11350** | 200 | 400 |
| **1983** — ALL BODY STYLES | | | |
| 18i | — | 110 | 300 |
| FUEGO | — | 110 | 300 |
| LE CAR | — | 110 | 300 |

## SAAB

| **1992** | | | |
|---|---|---|---|
| **900 4** | | | |
| 3 Dr Hbk | **19880** | 14525 | 17050 |
| 4 Dr Sdn | **20495** | 14600 | 17150 |
| 3 Dr S Hbk | **23980** | 16575 | 19225 |
| 4 Dr S Sdn | **24595** | 16675 | 19325 |
| 2 Dr S Conv | **31360** | — | — |
| 3 Dr Turbo Hbk | **29360** | — | — |
| 2 Dr Turbo Conv | **36230** | — | — |
| **9000 4** | | | |
| 5 Dr Hbk | **25465** | — | — |
| 5 Dr S Hbk | **28795** | — | — |
| 4 Dr CD Sdn (auto) | **30950** | — | — |
| 5 Dr Turbo Hbk | **36945** | — | — |
| 4 Dr CD Turbo Sdn (5 spd or auto) | **37615** | — | — |
| CD Griffin Edition Sdn (auto) | **42195** | — | — |

NOTE: Power windows and power door locks standard on all models. Cruise control standard on 900 S & Turbo, 9000 S, 9000 CD, 9000 Turbo, Turbo CD & Turbo CD Griffin Edition. Power seat standard on 900 S Convertible & Turbo, 9000 CD, 9000 Turbo, Turbo CD & Turbo CD Griffin Edition.

| **1991** | | | |
|---|---|---|---|
| **900 4** | | | |
| 3 Dr Hbk | **18295** | 11150 | 12875 |
| 4 Dr Sdn | **18815** | 11250 | 13000 |
| S 3 Dr Hbk | **22445** | 13100 | 15425 |
| S 4 Dr Sdn | **22995** | 13200 | 15525 |
| Turbo 3 Dr Hbk | **26295** | 15400 | 17950 |
| Turbo 2 Dr Conv | **33295** | 21625 | 24925 |
| SPG Turbo 3 Dr Hbk | **29295** | 16650 | 19150 |
| S Conv | **29495** | — | — |

| Year/Model/Body/Type | Original List | Current Whlse | Average Retail |
|---|---|---|---|
| **9000 4** | | | |
| 5 Dr Hbk | **22895** | 13275 | 15600 |
| S 5 Dr Hbk | **26995** | 14800 | 17375 |
| CD 4 Dr Sdn | **28995** | 15775 | 18425 |
| Turbo 5 Dr Hbk | **32995** | 18250 | 21100 |
| CD Turbo 4 Dr Sdn | **33995** | 19225 | 22275 |

NOTE: Power brakes and power door locks standard on all models. Power windows standard on 900 S, 900 Turbo, 900 Turbo SPG and 9000. Power seat standard on 900 Turbo Convertible, 9000 CD, 9000 Turbo Hatchback and 9000 Turbo CD. Power sunroof standard on 900 S, 900 Turbo, 900 Turbo SPG, 9000 S, 9000 CD, 9000 Turbo Hatchback and 9000 Turbo CD.

## 1990

| **900 4** | | | |
|---|---|---|---|
| 3 Dr Hbk | **16995** | 9125 | 10500 |
| 4 Dr Sdn | **17515** | 9225 | 10625 |
| S 3 Dr Hbk | **20995** | 10850 | 12525 |
| S 4 Dr Sdn | **21545** | 10950 | 12625 |
| Turbo 3 Dr Hbk | **25495** | 12925 | 15250 |
| Turbo 4 Dr Sdn | **26045** | 13025 | 15350 |
| 2 Dr Conv | **32995** | 18650 | 21700 |
| SPG Turbo 3 Dr Hbk | **28995** | 13775 | 16150 |

| **9000 4** | | | |
|---|---|---|---|
| S 5 Dr Hbk | **25495** | 12325 | 14350 |
| S 4 Dr Sdn | **25995** | 12825 | 15150 |
| Turbo 5 Dr Hbk | **32495** | 15575 | 18225 |
| CD Turbo 4 Dr Sdn | **32995** | 16075 | 18725 |

*ADD FOR:*
| Leather Package (9000 S Hbk, 9000 S Sdn) | **1995** | 360 | 400 |
|---|---|---|---|

NOTE: Anti-lock power brakes standard on all models. Power windows and sunroof standard on 900 S, 900 Turbo and 900 SPG. Power door locks standard on 900 Series, 900 Turbo and 900 SPG.

## 1989

| **900 4** | | | |
|---|---|---|---|
| 3 Dr Hbk | **16995** | 7025 | 8150 |
| 4 Dr Sdn | **17515** | 7125 | 8275 |
| S 3 Dr Hbk | **19695** | 8275 | 9550 |
| S 4 Dr Sdn | **20245** | 8375 | 9675 |
| Turbo 3 Dr Hbk | **23795** | 9975 | 11500 |
| Turbo 4 Dr Sdn | **24345** | 10050 | 11600 |
| Turbo Convertible | **32095** | 15175 | 17825 |
| SPG 3 Dr Hbk | **26895** | — | — |

| **9000 4** | | | |
|---|---|---|---|
| S 5 Dr Hbk | **24445** | 9175 | 10575 |
| Turbo 5 Dr Sdn | **30795** | 11500 | 13275 |

| Year/Model/Body/Type | Original List | Current Whlse | Average Retail |
|---|---|---|---|
| Turbo CD 4 Dr Sdn w/Cloth Interior | **30895** | 12000 | 13850 |
| Turbo CD 4 Dr Sdn w/Leather Interior | **31995** | 12675 | 15000 |

*ADD FOR:*
| Leather Package (900 Turbo Hbk & Sdn) | **1295** | 310 | 340 |
|---|---|---|---|
| (9000S) | **1595** | 310 | 340 |
| Air Bag Restraint System (9000 Turbo) | **895** | 330 | 360 |

NOTE: Power brakes and power door locks standard on all models. Sunroof and power windows standard on all models except 900 Base.

## 1988

| **900 4** | | | |
|---|---|---|---|
| 3 Dr Sdn | **15432** | 5175 | 6100 |
| 4 Dr Sdn | **15935** | 5275 | 6200 |
| S 3 Dr Sdn | **19280** | 6125 | 7125 |
| S 4 Dr Sdn | **19783** | 6200 | 7225 |
| Turbo 3 Dr Sdn | **22655** | 7325 | 8500 |
| Turbo Convertible | **30632** | 12450 | 14600 |

| **9000 4** | | | |
|---|---|---|---|
| S 5 Dr Sdn | **24037** | 6100 | 7000 |
| Turbo 5 Dr Sdn | **28985** | 7250 | 8425 |

*ADD FOR:*
| Leather Package (900 Turbo, 9000 S) | **1151** | 270 | 300 |
|---|---|---|---|
| Special Performance Group (900 Turbo) | **2960** | 620 | 700 |

NOTE: Air conditioning, pwr strng, power brakes and power locks standard on all models. Sunroof and power windows standard on all models except 900 Base.

## 1987

| **900 4** | | | |
|---|---|---|---|
| 3 Dr Sdn | **14395** | 3675 | 4575 |
| 4 Dr Sdn | **14805** | 3775 | 4675 |
| S 3 Dr Sdn | **17935** | 4275 | 5200 |
| S 4 Dr Sdn | **18345** | 4375 | 5300 |
| Turbo 3 Dr Sdn | **20815** | 5125 | 6050 |
| Turbo Convertible | **27115** | 10375 | 11975 |

| **9000 4** | | | |
|---|---|---|---|
| 5 Dr Sdn | **22245** | 4825 | 5750 |
| Turbo 5 Dr Sdn | **26025** | 5650 | 6575 |

*ADD FOR:*
| Leather Package (900 Turbo) | **1030** | 220 | 240 |
|---|---|---|---|
| (9000 S) | **1030** | 220 | 240 |
| Special Performance | | | |

| Year/Model/Body/Type | Original List | Current Whlse | Average Retail |
|---|---|---|---|
| Group (900 Turbo) | **2680** | 560 | 630 |

NOTE: Air conditioning, pwr strng, power brakes and power door locks standard on 900, 900 S, 900 Turbo, 9000 S and 9000 Turbo. Power windows and sunroof standard on 900 S, 900 Turbo, 9000 S and 9000 Turbo).

## 1986

### 900 4

| | | | |
|---|---|---|---|
| 3 Dr Sdn | **12585** | 2325 | 3200 |
| 4 Dr Sdn | **12985** | 2425 | 3300 |
| S 2 Dr Sdn | **15795** | 2800 | 3700 |
| S 3 Dr Sdn | **16095** | 2900 | 3800 |
| S 4 Dr Sdn | **16495** | 3000 | 3900 |
| Turbo 3 Dr Sdn | **18895** | 3725 | 4625 |
| Turbo Convertible | **25390** | 9400 | 10825 |

### 9000 4

| | | | |
|---|---|---|---|
| Turbo 5 Dr Sdn | **22145** | 3925 | 4825 |

*ADD FOR:*
| | | | |
|---|---|---|---|
| Metallic Paint | **395** | 70 | 80 |
| Special Black Paint | **395** | 70 | 80 |
| Exclusive Appointment Pkg (900 Turbo) | **1360** | 220 | 240 |
| Leather Package (900 Turbo) | **1800** | 160 | 180 |
| Special Performance Group (900 Turbo) | **2820** | 490 | 540 |

NOTE: Power brakes standard on all models. Pwr strng and air conditioning standard on 900 Series and 900 Turbo. Sunroof standard on 900 S and 900 Turbo. Power locks standard on 900 Series. Power windows standard on 900 S, 900 Turbo and 9000 Turbo.

## 1985

### 900 4

| | | | |
|---|---|---|---|
| 3 Dr Sdn | **11850** | 1775 | 2625 |
| 4 Dr Sdn | **12170** | 1875 | 2725 |
| S 3 Dr Sdn | **15040** | 2275 | 3150 |
| S 4 Dr Sdn | **15510** | 2350 | 3225 |
| Turbo 3 Dr Sdn | **18150** | 2950 | 3850 |
| Turbo 4 Dr Sdn | **18620** | 3050 | 3950 |

*ADD FOR:*
| | | | |
|---|---|---|---|
| Exclusive Appointment Pkg (900 Turbo) | **1330** | 130 | 140 |
| Special Performance Group (900 Turbo) | **2860** | 340 | 370 |

NOTE: Pwr strng, power brakes and air conditioning standard on all models. Power windows and sunroof standard on 900 S and 900 Turbo.

## 1984

### 900 4

| | | | |
|---|---|---|---|
| 3 Dr Sdn | **11110** | 1450 | 2225 |

| Year/Model/Body/Type | Original List | Current Whlse | Average Retail |
|---|---|---|---|
| 4 Dr Sdn | **11420** | 1525 | 2375 |
| S 3 Dr Sdn | **13850** | 1750 | 2600 |
| S 4 Dr Sdn | **14310** | 1800 | 2650 |
| Turbo 3 Dr Sdn | **16940** | 2275 | 3150 |
| Turbo 4 Dr Sdn | **17400** | 2325 | 3200 |

## 1983 — ALL BODY STYLES

| | | | |
|---|---|---|---|
| 900 | — | 1125 | 1850 |
| 900 S | — | 1025 | 1750 |
| 900 TURBO | — | 1350 | 2100 |

## SAPPORO

## 1983

### SAPPORO 4

| | | | |
|---|---|---|---|
| 2 Dr Luxury Cpe | **8323** | 500 | 925 |

## STERLING

## 1991

### 827 6

| | | | |
|---|---|---|---|
| Si (5 spd) | **26500** | 10325 | 12025 |
| SLi (auto) | **28500** | 12000 | 13850 |
| SL (auto) | **28500** | 12000 | 13850 |

NOTE: Power brakes, power door locks, power windows, power seat and power moonroof standard on all models.

## 1990

### 827 6

| | | | |
|---|---|---|---|
| S (5 spd) | **23550** | 9100 | 10475 |
| Si (5 spd) | **26500** | 9650 | 11125 |
| SL (5 spd) | **28500** | 10275 | 11850 |
| SLi (auto) | **28500** | 10825 | 12500 |
| Oxford Edition (auto) | — | 10825 | 12500 |

*ADD FOR:*
| | | | |
|---|---|---|---|
| Anti-Lock Braking System (S) | **1250** | 530 | 590 |
| Leather Seat Trim (S) | **1150** | 350 | 380 |

NOTE: Power windows, power door locks and moonroof standard on all models. Anti-lock power brakes standard on 827Si, 827SL, 827SLi and Oxford Edition.

## 1989

### 827 6

| | | | |
|---|---|---|---|
| S (5 spd) | **23300** | 6650 | 7750 |
| SL (auto) | **29675** | 7925 | 9200 |
| SLi (auto) | **29675** | 7925 | 9200 |
| LE (auto) | **30150** | 8225 | 9500 |

| Year/Model/ Body/Type | Original List | Current Whlse | Average Retail |
|---|---|---|---|
| *ADD FOR:* | | | |
| Anti-Lock Brakes (S) | **1225** | 250 | 280 |
| Leather Seats (S) | **1100** | 270 | 300 |

NOTE: Power brakes, power windows, power door locks and power moonroof standard on all models.

## 1988

### 825 6

| Year/Model/ Body/Type | Original List | Current Whlse | Average Retail |
|---|---|---|---|
| S (5 spd) | **20804** | 4450 | 5375 |
| SL (auto) | **25995** | 5400 | 6325 |
| *ADD FOR:* | | | |
| Anti-Lock Braking System (S) | **1150** | 260 | 280 |
| Leather Seat Trim (S) | **1025** | 200 | 220 |

NOTE: Air conditioning, power brakes, power door locks, pwr strng, power windows and electric moonroof standard on all models.

## 1987

### 825 6

| Year/Model/ Body/Type | Original List | Current Whlse | Average Retail |
|---|---|---|---|
| S (5 spd) | **19000** | 3250 | 4150 |
| SL (auto) | **23900** | 4025 | 4925 |
| *ADD FOR:* | | | |
| Anti-Lock Braking System (S) | **940** | 240 | 260 |
| Leather Trim (S) | **950** | 160 | 180 |

NOTE: Air conditioning, power disc brakes, power door locks, electric moonroof, pwr strng and power windows standard on all models. Power seats and anti-lock braking system standard on 825SL.

# SUBARU

## 1992

### JUSTY 3

| Year/Model/ Body/Type | Original List | Current Whlse | Average Retail |
|---|---|---|---|
| 3 Dr Hbk (5 spd) (NA w/pwr strng or radio) | **6945** | — | — |
| 3 Dr GL Hbk (5 spd) | **8349** | 6725 | 7825 |
| 5 Dr GL 4WD Hbk (5 spd) (NA w/pwr strng) | **9249** | 6900 | 8025 |
| *ADD FOR:* | | | |
| On-Demand 4WD (GL 3 Dr) | **800** | 500 | 575 |

### LEGACY 4

| Year/Model/ Body/Type | Original List | Current Whlse | Average Retail |
|---|---|---|---|
| 4 Dr L Sdn (5 spd) | **14564** | 9975 | 11500 |
| 5 Dr L Wgn (5 spd) | **15064** | 10275 | 11850 |
| 4 Dr LS Sdn (auto) | **19649** | 12600 | 14925 |
| 5 Dr LS Wgn (auto) | **20149** | 12950 | 15275 |
| 4 Dr LSi (auto) | **21049** | — | — |
| 4 Dr Sport 4WD Turbo Sdn (5 spd) | **21645** | — | — |
| *ADD FOR:* | | | |
| Anti-Lock Brakes (L) | **1100** | 460 | 500 |
| Full-Time 4WD (L Sdn) | **1100** | 720 | 800 |
| (L Wgn) | **1600** | 1050 | 1160 |
| (LS, LSi) | **1500** | 980 | 1090 |

### LOYALE 4

| Year/Model/ Body/Type | Original List | Current Whlse | Average Retail |
|---|---|---|---|
| 4 Dr Sdn (5 spd) | **10049** | 7375 | 8550 |
| 5 Dr Wgn (5 spd) | **10899** | 7725 | 8975 |
| *ADD FOR:* | | | |
| On-Demand 4WD (Sdn) | **1350** | 880 | 980 |
| (Wgn) | **1500** | 980 | 1090 |

### SVX 6

| Year/Model/ Body/Type | Original List | Current Whlse | Average Retail |
|---|---|---|---|
| 2 Dr Cpe (auto) | **26250** | — | — |
| *ADD FOR:* | | | |
| Touring Pkg | **3000** | — | — |

NOTE: Tilt steering wheel standard on Loyale, Legacy and SVX. Cruise control standard on Legacy LS, LSi, LE 4WD & Sport 4WD and SVX. Power windows and power door locks standard on SVX. Moonroof standard on Legacy LS, LSi, LE 4WD & Sport 4WD.

## 1991

### JUSTY 3

| Year/Model/ Body/Type | Original List | Current Whlse | Average Retail |
|---|---|---|---|
| 2 Dr Hbk (5 spd) (NA w/pwr strng) | **6295** | 4400 | 5325 |
| 2 Dr GL Hbk (5 spd) (NA w/pwr strng) | **7699** | 5175 | 6100 |
| 5 Dr GL 4WD Hbk (5 spd) (NA w/power steering) | **8599** | 6000 | 6925 |

### LEGACY 4

| Year/Model/ Body/Type | Original List | Current Whlse | Average Retail |
|---|---|---|---|
| 4 Dr L Sdn (5 spd) | **12924** | 8550 | 9875 |
| 5 Dr L Wgn (5 spd) | **13524** | 8850 | 10225 |
| 4 Dr LS Sdn (5 spd) | **17324** | 10425 | 12025 |
| 5 Dr LS Wgn (5 spd) | **17924** | 10725 | 12375 |
| 4 Dr LSi Sdn (auto) | **19024** | — | — |
| 4 Dr Sport 4WD Turbo Sdn (5 spd) | **19224** | 11625 | 13425 |

### LOYALE 4

| Year/Model/ Body/Type | Original List | Current Whlse | Average Retail |
|---|---|---|---|
| 4 Dr Sdn (5 spd) | **9499** | 6925 | 8050 |
| 5 Dr Wgn (5 spd) | **10499** | 7200 | 8350 |

### XT GL 4

| Year/Model/ Body/Type | Original List | Current Whlse | Average Retail |
|---|---|---|---|
| 2 Dr Cpe (5 spd) | **13438** | 7550 | 8775 |



**Refer to optional equipment schedules**

| Year/Model/Body/Type | Original List | Current Whlse | Average Retail |
|---|---|---|---|
| **XT6 6** | | | |
| 2 Dr Cpe (auto) | **17478** | 9225 | 10625 |
| *ADD FOR:* | | | |
| Full Time 4WD | | | |
| (XT6 w/manual trans) | **840** | 400 | 440 |
| (XT6 w/auto trans) | **1610** | 470 | 520 |
| (Legacy L Sdn) | **1280** | 550 | 610 |
| (Legacy L Wgn, Legacy LSi) | **1300** | 550 | 610 |
| (Legacy LS Sdn) | **1500** | 550 | 610 |
| (Legacy LS Wgn) | **1400** | 550 | 610 |
| On-Demand 4WD | | | |
| (Justy GL) | **800** | 290 | 320 |
| (Loyale) | **1500** | 510 | 570 |
| Anti-Lock Braking System (Legacy L) | **895** | 400 | 440 |

NOTE: Power brakes standard on all models. Power door locks and power windows standard on Legacy L, Loyale, XT and XT6. Power moonroof standard on Legacy LS, LSi and Legacy Sport Sedan.

## 1990

| Year/Model/Body/Type | Original List | Current Whlse | Average Retail |
|---|---|---|---|
| **JUSTY 3** | | | |
| 2 Dr DL Hbk (5 spd) (NA w/pwr strng) | **5866** | 2900 | 3800 |
| 2 Dr GL Hbk (5 spd) (NA w/pwr strng) | **7251** | 3400 | 4300 |
| 5 Dr GL 4WD Hbk (5 spd) (NA w/power steering) | **8156** | 4150 | 5075 |
| **LEGACY 4** | | | |
| 4 Dr Sdn (5 spd) | **11299** | 5875 | 6800 |
| 5 Dr Wgn (5 spd) | **11849** | 6175 | 7200 |
| 4 Dr L Sdn (5 spd) | **13494** | 6650 | 7750 |
| 5 Dr L Wgn (5 spd) | **14044** | 6925 | 8050 |
| 4 Dr LS Sdn (5 spd) | **14699** | 6450 | 7500 |
| 5 Dr LS Wgn (5 spd) | **15249** | 6900 | 8025 |
| **LOYALE 4** | | | |
| 4 Dr Sdn (5 spd) | **9299** | 4900 | 5825 |
| 3 Dr Cpe (5 spd) | **9599** | 4850 | 5775 |
| 5 Dr Wgn (5 spd) | **9999** | 5175 | 6100 |
| 5 Dr Touring Wgn | **10699** | 5400 | 6325 |
| *ADD FOR:* | | | |
| Full Time 4WD | | | |
| (Loyale Sdn & Wgn) | **3750** | 530 | 590 |
| (Loyale Touring Wgn) | **3400** | 530 | 590 |
| (Loyale Cpe) | **4100** | 530 | 590 |
| (Legacy L) | **1200** | 510 | 570 |
| (Legacy LS) | **1800** | 510 | 570 |
| On Demand 4WD | | | |
| (Justy GL) | **700** | 270 | 300 |
| (Loyale Cpe) | **—** | 530 | 590 |

| Year/Model/Body/Type | Original List | Current Whlse | Average Retail |
|---|---|---|---|
| (Loyale Sdn) | **—** | 530 | 590 |
| (Loyale Wgn) | **—** | 530 | 590 |
| Anti-Lock Braking System (Legacy LS) | **1095** | 350 | 380 |

NOTE: Power brakes standard on all models. Power windows standard on Legacy L and Legacy LS. Power door locks standard on Loyale Coupe, Legacy L and Legacy LS. Sunroof standard on Legacy LS.

## 1989

| Year/Model/Body/Type | Original List | Current Whlse | Average Retail |
|---|---|---|---|
| **DL 4** | | | |
| 4 Dr Sdn (5 spd) | **9731** | 3500 | 4400 |
| 3 Dr Cpe (5 spd) | **10031** | 3450 | 4350 |
| 4 Dr Wgn (5 spd) | **10181** | 3750 | 4650 |
| **GL 4** | | | |
| 3 Dr Hbk (5 spd) | **8596** | 2725 | 3625 |
| 4 Dr Sdn (5 spd) | **11521** | 3925 | 4825 |
| 3 Dr Cpe (5 spd) | **11821** | 3875 | 4775 |
| 4 Dr Wgn (5 spd) | **11971** | 4175 | 5100 |
| 4 Dr Touring Wgn (5 spd) | **12171** | 4275 | 5200 |
| 4 Dr Turbo Sdn (auto) | **12521** | 4275 | 5200 |
| 4 Dr Turbo Wgn (auto) | **12971** | 4800 | 5725 |
| 2 Dr XT Cpe (5 spd) | **13071** | 4450 | 5375 |
| **GL-10 4** | | | |
| 4 Dr Sdn (auto) | **16401** | 4425 | 5350 |
| 4 Dr Wgn (auto) | **16851** | 4675 | 5600 |
| 4 Dr Touring Wgn (auto) | **16851** | 4850 | 5775 |
| **JUSTY 3** | | | |
| 2 Dr DL Hbk (5 spd) | **5866** | 1850 | 2700 |
| 2 Dr GL Hbk (5 spd) | **7251** | 2275 | 3150 |
| 2 Dr RS 4WD Hbk (5 spd) | **8351** | 3000 | 3900 |
| **RX 4** | | | |
| 3 Dr 4WD Cpe (5 spd) | **16361** | 4525 | 5450 |
| **XT 6** | | | |
| 2 Dr Cpe (auto) | **17111** | 5925 | 6850 |
| *ADD FOR:* | | | |
| 4WD (DL, GL) | **—** | 450 | 510 |
| (XT 6) | **—** | 330 | 390 |

NOTE: Power brakes standard on all models. Power windows standard on GL except Hatchback, GL-10, RX and XT-6. Power door locks standard on GL Turbo Sedan and Turbo Wagon, GL-10, RX and XT-6. Sunroof standard on GL-10.

## 1988

| Year/Model/Body/Type | Original List | Current Whlse | Average Retail |
|---|---|---|---|
| **DL 4** | | | |
| 4 Dr Sdn (5 spd) | **9748** | 2100 | 2950 |

| Year/Model/Body/Type | Original List | Current Whlse | Average Retail |
|---|---|---|---|
| 3 Dr Cpe (5 spd) | **10048** | 2050 | 2900 |
| 4 Dr Wgn (5 spd) | **10198** | 2275 | 3150 |
| 2 Dr XT Cpe (5 spd) | **10413** | 1700 | 2550 |
| **GL 4** | | | |
| 3 Dr Hbk (5 spd) | **8693** | 1450 | 2225 |
| 4 Dr Sdn (5 spd) | **11393** | 2350 | 3225 |
| 3 Dr Cpe (5 spd) | **11693** | 2300 | 3175 |
| 4 Dr Wgn (5 spd) | **11843** | 2575 | 3450 |
| 2 Dr XT Cpe (5 spd) | **12915** | 2250 | 3100 |
| **GL-10 4** | | | |
| 4 Dr Sdn (auto) | **14928** | 3025 | 3925 |
| 4 Dr Wgn (auto) | **15378** | 3425 | 4325 |
| **JUSTY 3** | | | |
| 2 Dr Hbk (5 spd) | **6088** | 650 | 1225 |
| 2 Dr GL Hbk (5 spd) | **7213** | 950 | 1675 |
| 2 Dr RS 4WD Hbk (5 spd) | **8213** | 1550 | 2400 |
| **RX 4** | | | |
| 4 Dr 4WD Turbo Sdn (5 spd) | **15913** | 4000 | 4900 |
| 3 Dr 4WD Turbo Cpe (5 spd) | **15913** | 3950 | 4850 |
| **XT-6 6** | | | |
| 2 Dr Cpe (auto) | **16663** | 3775 | 4675 |
| *ADD FOR:* | | | |
| Full Time 4WD (GL-10) | **2600** | 400 | 440 |
| (XT6) | **1600** | 220 | 240 |
| On-Demand 4WD (Justy GL, GL Hbk, DL Wgn) | **600** | 200 | 220 |
| (GL Wgn w/Turbo Eng) | **2450** | 400 | 440 |
| Turbo Eng (GL-10) | **1550** | 400 | 440 |

NOTE: Power brakes standard on all models. Pwr strng standard on DL Series, GL Series except Hatchback, GL-10 Series, RX Series and XT-6. Power door locks standard on GL Series except Hacthback, RX Series and XT-6. Sunroof standard on GL-10 Series. Air conditioning standard on GL-10 Series, RX Series and XT-6. Power windows standard on GL Series except Hatchback, GL-10 Series, RX Series and XT-6.

## 1987

| **DL 4** | | | |
|---|---|---|---|
| 2 Dr XT Cpe (5 spd) | **9531** | 1325 | 2050 |
| **GL 4** | | | |
| 2 Dr XT Cpe (5 spd) | **11653** | 1700 | 2550 |
| 2 Dr 4WD XT Cpe (5 spd) | **12728** | 2150 | 3000 |
| **GL-10 4** | | | |
| 2 Dr XT Cpe (auto) | **14264** | 2500 | 3375 |

| Year/Model/Body/Type | Original List | Current Whlse | Average Retail |
|---|---|---|---|
| 2 Dr 4WD Turbo XT Cpe (5 spd) | **16224** | 2725 | 3625 |
| **RX 4** | | | |
| 3 Dr 4WD Turbo Cpe (5 spd) | **14153** | 3000 | 3900 |
| *ADD FOR:* | | | |
| Turbo Eng (GL XT 2 Dr Cpe) | **1863** | 490 | 540 |
| (GL-10 XT 2 Dr w/man trans) | **735** | 190 | 210 |
| (GL-10 XT 2 Dr Cpe w/auto trans) | **1285** | 340 | 370 |

NOTE: Pwr strng standard on GL, GL-10 and RX. Power brakes standard on all models. Air conditioning standard on GL-10 and RX. Power windows standard on RX. Power door locks and sunroof standard on GL-10.

## 1987

| **DL 4** | | | |
|---|---|---|---|
| 4 Dr Sdn (5 spd) | **8908** | 1625 | 2475 |
| 3 Dr Cpe (5 spd) | **9208** | 1575 | 2425 |
| 4 Dr Wgn (5 spd) | **9308** | 1775 | 2625 |
| **GL 4** | | | |
| 3 Dr Hbk (5 spd) | **7688** | 1050 | 1775 |
| 4 Dr Sdn (5 spd) | **9938** | 1800 | 2650 |
| 3 Dr Cpe (5 spd) | **10238** | 1775 | 2625 |
| 4 Dr Wgn (5 spd) | **10338** | 2000 | 2850 |
| 3 Dr 4WD Hbk (4 spd) | **8393** | 1550 | 2400 |
| 4 Dr 4WD Sdn (5 spd) | **10408** | 2300 | 3175 |
| 3 Dr 4WD Cpe (5 spd) | **10708** | 2275 | 3150 |
| 4 Dr 4WD Wgn (5 spd) | **10808** | 2500 | 3375 |
| 4 Dr 4WD Brat (4 spd) | **8453** | 1200 | 1925 |
| **GL-10 4** | | | |
| 4 Dr Sdn (auto) | **12448** | 2425 | 3300 |
| 4 Dr Wgn (auto) | **12848** | 2600 | 3475 |
| 4 Dr 4WD Turbo Sdn (5 spd) | **15168** | 2800 | 3700 |
| 4 Dr 4WD Turbo Wgn (5 spd) | **14788** | 3000 | 3900 |
| **JUSTY 3** | | | |
| 2 Dr DL Hbk (5 spd) | **5366** | 325 | 600 |
| 2 Dr GL Hbk (5 spd) | **6166** | 525 | 975 |
| **RX 4** | | | |
| 4 Dr 4WD Turbo Sdn (5 spd) | **13933** | 3000 | 3900 |
| **STANDARD 4** | | | |
| 3 Dr 4WD Hbk (4 spd) | **7355** | 400 | 600 |
| *ADD FOR:* | | | |

*Refer to optional equipment schedules*

| Year/Model/Body/Type | Original List | Current Whlse | Average Retail |
|---|---|---|---|
| Turbo Eng | — | 300 | 370 |

NOTE: Power brakes standard on Standard Series, DL Series, GL Series, GL-10 Series, RX and Brat. Power windows, power door locks and air conditioning standard on GL-10 Series and RX. Sunroof standard on GL-10 4WD. Pwr strng standard on GL Coupe, Sedan and Wagon, RX and GL-10 Series.

## 1986

### BRAT 4

| | Original List | Current Whlse | Average Retail |
|---|---|---|---|
| 2 Dr 4WD (4 spd) | 8235 | 900 | 1625 |

### DL 4

| | Original List | Current Whlse | Average Retail |
|---|---|---|---|
| 2 Dr XT Cpe (5 spd) | 9192 | 1000 | 1725 |
| 4 Dr Sdn (5 spd) | 8168 | 1225 | 1950 |
| 4 Dr Wgn (5 spd) | 8490 | 1350 | 2100 |
| 4 Dr 4WD Wgn (5 spd) | 9080 | 1800 | 2650 |

### GL SERIES 4

| | Original List | Current Whlse | Average Retail |
|---|---|---|---|
| 2 Dr XT Cpe (5 spd) | 11030 | 1375 | 2125 |
| 3 Dr Hbk (5 spd) | 7509 | 650 | 1225 |
| 3 Dr 4WD Hbk (4 spd dual range) | 8174 | 1100 | 1825 |
| 4 Dr Sdn (5 spd) | 8803 | 1325 | 2050 |
| 4 Dr 4WD Sdn (5 spd dual range) | 10013 | 1775 | 2625 |
| 4 Dr Wgn (5 spd) | 9125 | 1500 | 2350 |
| 4 Dr Wgn (5 spd dual range) | 9715 | 1725 | 2575 |

### GL-10 SERIES

| | Original List | Current Whlse | Average Retail |
|---|---|---|---|
| 2 Dr XT Turbo Cpe (5 spd) | 13930 | 2450 | 3325 |
| 2 Dr 4WD Turbo Cpe (5 spd) | 14925 | 2750 | 3650 |
| 4 Dr Sdn (auto) | 12080 | 2200 | 3050 |
| 4 Dr Turbo Sdn (5 spd) | 12811 | 2300 | 3175 |
| 4 Dr 4WD Turbo Sdn (5 spd) | 13806 | 2575 | 3450 |
| 4 Dr Wgn (auto) | 12262 | 2275 | 3150 |
| 4 Dr Turbo Wgn (5 spd) | 12997 | 2300 | 3175 |
| 4 Dr 4WD Turbo Wgn (5 spd) | 13587 | 2550 | 3425 |
| 4 Dr 4WD Turbo Wgn (auto) | 14412 | 2700 | 3600 |

### RX 4

| | Original List | Current Whlse | Average Retail |
|---|---|---|---|
| 4 Dr 4WD Turbo Sdn (5 spd) | 12643 | 2275 | 3150 |

### STANDARD SERIES 4

| | Original List | Current Whlse | Average Retail |
|---|---|---|---|
| 3 Dr Hbk (4 spd) | 5379 | 350 | 550 |

NOTE: Power brakes standard on all models. Power windows, power door locks and air conditioning standard on GL-10 and RX Turbo Sedan. Sunroof standard on GL-10. Pwr strng standard on GL XT Coupe, GL-10 and RX Turbo Sedan..............................

## 1985

### BRAT 4

| | Original List | Current Whlse | Average Retail |
|---|---|---|---|
| 2 Dr GL 4WD (4 spd) | 7783 | 800 | 1500 |

### DL SERIES 4

| | Original List | Current Whlse | Average Retail |
|---|---|---|---|
| 4 Dr Sdn (4 spd) | 7109 | 1125 | 1850 |
| 4 Dr Sdn (5 spd) | 7208 | 1125 | 1850 |
| 4 Dr Wgn (5 spd) | 7509 | 1275 | 2000 |
| 4 Dr 4WD Wgn | 8059 | 1675 | 2525 |
| 2 Dr XT Cpe (5 spd) | 7889 | 900 | 1625 |

### GL SERIES 4

| | Original List | Current Whlse | Average Retail |
|---|---|---|---|
| 3 Dr Hbk | 6924 | 750 | 1475 |
| 3 Dr 4WD Hbk | 7474 | 1150 | 1875 |
| 4 Dr Sdn | 7758 | 1225 | 1950 |
| 4 Dr 4WD Sdn (auto) | 9281 | 1625 | 2475 |
| 4 Dr 4WD Turbo Sdn (5 spd) | 11453 | 2000 | 2850 |
| 5 Dr Wgn | 8059 | 1325 | 2050 |
| 5 Dr 4WD Wgn | 8609 | 1750 | 2600 |
| 5 Dr 4WD Turbo Wgn (auto) | 11917 | 2100 | 2950 |
| 2 Dr XT Cpe (5 spd) | 9899 | 1275 | 2000 |

### RX 4 —

| | Original List | Current Whlse | Average Retail |
|---|---|---|---|
| 4 Dr 4WD Turbo Sdn | 11031 | 1825 | 2675 |

### STANDARD SERIES 4 —

| | Original List | Current Whlse | Average Retail |
|---|---|---|---|
| 3 Dr Hbk | 4989 | 300 | 500 |

*ADD FOR:*

| | Original List | Current Whlse | Average Retail |
|---|---|---|---|
| GL-10 Pkg (GL Sdn) | 2419 | 260 | 290 |
| (GL Wgn) | 2290 | 260 | 290 |
| GL-10T Pkg (GT Sdn) | 2869 | 310 | 340 |
| (GL Wgn) | 2740 | 310 | 340 |

NOTE: Pwr strng, power door locks and power windows standard on GL Turbo. Air conditioning standard on GL Turbo and RX. Power brakes standard on all models.

## 1984

### BRAT 4

| | Original List | Current Whlse | Average Retail |
|---|---|---|---|
| 2 Dr GL 4WD | 8043 | 350 | 625 |
| 2 Dr Turbo 4WD (auto) | 10413 | 425 | 775 |

### DL SERIES 4

| | Original List | Current Whlse | Average Retail |
|---|---|---|---|
| 3 Dr Hbk | 6398 | 350 | 625 |
| 4 Dr Sdn | 6935 | 500 | 925 |
| 2 Dr HT | 7051 | 600 | 1125 |
| 4 Dr Wgn | 7174 | 625 | 1175 |
| 4 Dr 4WD Wgn | 7723 | 975 | 1700 |

### GL SERIES 4

| | Original List | Current Whlse | Average Retail |
|---|---|---|---|
| 3 Dr Hbk | 7129 | 475 | 875 |
| 3 Dr 4WD Hbk | 7678 | 850 | 1550 |
| 2 Dr HT | 7727 | 725 | 1375 |

| Year/Model/Body/Type | Original List | Current Whlse | Average Retail |
|---|---|---|---|
| 2 Dr 4WD Turbo HT (auto) | 11338 | 1200 | 1925 |
| 4 Dr Sdn | 7534 | 625 | 1175 |
| 4 Dr 4WD Sdn (auto) | 8955 | 975 | 1700 |
| 4 Dr Wgn | 7773 | 750 | 1475 |
| 4 Dr 4WD Wgn | 8322 | 1100 | 1825 |
| 4 Dr 4WD Turbo Wgn (auto) | 10578 | 1200 | 1925 |

**STANDARD SERIES 4**

| | | | |
|---|---|---|---|
| 3 Dr Hbk | 5393 | 150 | 350 |

**1983 — ALL BODY STYLES**

| | | | |
|---|---|---|---|
| BRAT | — | 225 | 475 |
| DL SERIES | — | 350 | 625 |
| GL SERIES | — | 450 | 825 |
| STANDARD SERIES | — | 150 | 325 |

## SUZUKI

### 1992

**SAMURAI 4**

| | | | |
|---|---|---|---|
| 2WD JA Soft Top (NA w/pwr strng) | 6399 | 4575 | 5500 |
| 4WD JL Soft Top (NA w/pwr strng) | 8299 | 6200 | 7225 |

**SIDEKICK 4**

| | | | |
|---|---|---|---|
| 2WD JS-Plus 2 Dr Soft Top (NA w/pwr strng) | 10799 | 7800 | 9050 |
| 4WD JX 2 Dr Soft Top | 12139 | 9100 | 10475 |
| 4WD JX LTD 2 Dr Soft Top | 13299 | — | — |
| 4WD JX 4 Dr Hard Top | 12649 | 9250 | 10650 |
| 4WD JLX 4 Dr Hard Top | 13849 | 9825 | 11325 |
| 4WD JLX LTD 4 Dr Hard Top | 15199 | — | — |

**SWIFT 4**

| | | | |
|---|---|---|---|
| 3 Dr GA Hbk | 6999 | 4625 | 5550 |
| 3 Dr GT Hbk | 9699 | 6025 | 6950 |
| 4 Dr GA Sdn | 7799 | 4750 | 5675 |
| 4 Dr GS Sdn | 9199 | 5500 | 6425 |

NOTE: Tilt steering wheel, power door locks and power windows standard on Sidekick JLX & JLX Limited Edition.

### 1991

**SAMURAI 4**

2WD JA Soft Top

| Year/Model/Body/Type | Original List | Current Whlse | Average Retail |
|---|---|---|---|
| (NA w/pwr strng) | 5999 | 3550 | 4450 |
| 2WD JS Soft Top (NA w/pwr strng) | 6999 | 3950 | 4850 |
| 4WD JL Soft Top (NA w/pwr strng) | 8299 | 5100 | 6025 |

**SIDEKICK 4**

| | | | |
|---|---|---|---|
| 2WD JS 2 Dr Soft Top (NA w/pwr strng) | 10299 | 7275 | 8450 |
| 4WD JX 2 Dr Soft Top | 11799 | 8475 | 9800 |
| 4WD JX 4 Dr Hard Top | 11999 | 8625 | 9950 |
| 4WD JLX 4 Dr Hard Top | 12999 | 9025 | 10400 |

**SWIFT 4**

| | | | |
|---|---|---|---|
| GA 3 Dr Hbk | 6699 | 3850 | 4750 |
| GT 3 Dr Hbk | 9399 | 5000 | 5925 |
| GA 4 Dr Sdn | 7499 | 4000 | 4900 |
| GS 4 Dr Sdn | 8599 | 4625 | 5550 |

NOTE: Power brakes standard on all models. Power windows standard on Sidekick JLX.

### 1990

**SAMURAI 4**

| | | | |
|---|---|---|---|
| Soft Top (NA w/pwr strng) | 7999 | 4200 | 5125 |

**SIDEKICK 4**

| | | | |
|---|---|---|---|
| 2WD JS Soft Top | 9999 | 5175 | 6100 |
| 4WD JX Soft Top | 10799 | 6025 | 6950 |
| 4WD JX Hard Top | 11099 | 6175 | 7200 |
| 4WD JLX Hard Top | 12499 | 6650 | 7750 |
| 4WD JLX Soft Top | 12299 | 6525 | 7600 |

**SWIFT 4**

| | | | |
|---|---|---|---|
| GA 3 Dr Hbk | 6399 | 2800 | 3700 |
| GA 4 Dr Sdn | 7399 | 2950 | 3850 |
| GL 3 Dr Hbk | 6799 | 2975 | 3875 |
| GL 4 Dr Sdn | 7899 | 3125 | 4025 |
| GS 4 Dr Sdn | 8599 | 3400 | 4300 |
| GT 3 Dr Hbk | 9399 | 3850 | 4750 |
| GLX 3 Dr Hbk | 7799 | 3000 | 3900 |

*ADD FOR:*

| | | | |
|---|---|---|---|
| Sport/Convenience Pkg B (Sidekick JX) | 528 | 260 | 280 |

NOTE: Power brakes standard on all models.

### 1989

**SAMURAI STANDARD PLUS 4**

| | | | |
|---|---|---|---|
| Soft Top (NA w/pwr strng) | 9774 | 3175 | 4075 |
| Hard Top | | | |

| Year/Model/Body/Type | Original List | Current Whlse | Average Retail |
|---|---|---|---|
| (NA w/pwr strng) | 9874 | 3300 | 4200 |
| **SIDEKICK 4** | | | |
| Std Convertible 2 Passenger (NA w/pwr strng) | 8995 | 4050 | 4950 |
| Deluxe Convertible 2 Passenger (NA w/pwr strng) | 11660 | 4775 | 5700 |
| Deluxe Convertible 4 Passenger (NA w/pwr strng) | 12215 | 5025 | 5950 |
| Deluxe Hardtop 2 Passenger (auto) (NA w/pwr strng) | 13160 | 5400 | 6325 |
| Deluxe Hardtop 4 Passenger (auto) (NA w/pwr strng) | 13679 | 5650 | 6575 |
| Custom Convertible 2 Passenger (auto) (NA w/pwr strng) | 13260 | 5600 | 6525 |
| Custom Convertible 4 Passenger (auto) (NA w/pwr strng) | 13959 | 5825 | 6750 |
| Custom Hardtop 2 Passenger (auto) | 14260 | 5825 | 6750 |
| Custom Hardtop 4 Passenger (auto) | 14939 | 6100 | 7000 |
| **SWIFT 4** | | | |
| GLX 5 Dr Hbk (auto) | 7495 | 2150 | 3000 |
| GTi 3 Dr Hbk | 8995 | 2375 | 3250 |

NOTE: Power brakes standard on all models. Power windows standard on Sidekick Custom Hardtop. Power door locks standard on Sidekick Custom Hardtop and Swift.

## 1988

| | Original List | Current Whlse | Average Retail |
|---|---|---|---|
| **SAMURAI 4** | | | |
| Std Convertible | 7995 | 2750 | 3650 |
| Std Hardtop | 8095 | 2900 | 3800 |
| Deluxe Convertible 2-Seater | 8695 | 3125 | 4025 |
| Deluxe Hardtop 2-Seater | 8725 | 3325 | 4225 |
| Deluxe Convertible 4-Seater | 8945 | 3275 | 4175 |
| Deluxe Hardtop 4-Seater | 8995 | 3525 | 4425 |
| *ADD FOR:* | | | |
| Fiberglass Hardtop | 1395 | 460 | 520 |

NOTE: Power brakes standard on all models.

## 1988

| Year/Model/Body/Type | Original List | Current Whlse | Average Retail |
|---|---|---|---|
| **SAMURAI 4** | | | |
| Std Convertible | 7995 | 2475 | 3350 |
| Std Hardtop | 8095 | 2200 | 3050 |
| Deluxe Convertible 2-Seater | 8695 | 2775 | 3675 |
| Deluxe Hardtop 2-Seater | 8725 | 2850 | 3750 |
| Deluxe Convertible 4-Seater | 8945 | 2800 | 3700 |
| Deluxe Hardtop 4-Seater | 8995 | 2875 | 3775 |
| *ADD FOR:* | | | |
| Fiberglass Hardtop | 1395 | 460 | 520 |

NOTE: Power brakes standard on all models.

## 1987

| | Original List | Current Whlse | Average Retail |
|---|---|---|---|
| **SAMURAI 4** | | | |
| Convertible Truck | 6695 | 1800 | 2650 |
| Hardtop Truck | 6900 | 1925 | 2775 |
| JA Std Convertible | 7495 | 2075 | 2925 |
| JA Std Hardtop | 7495 | 2200 | 3050 |
| JX Deluxe Convertible | 8545 | 2200 | 3050 |
| JX Deluxe Hardtop | 8665 | 2275 | 3150 |
| JX Deluxe II Convertible | 8635 | 2250 | 3100 |
| JX Deluxe II Hardtop | 8795 | 2325 | 3200 |
| *ADD FOR:* | | | |
| Automatic Hub Set | 250 | 60 | 70 |
| Fiberglass Hardtop | 1395 | 360 | 400 |

NOTE: Power front disc brakes standard on all models.

## 1986

| | Original List | Current Whlse | Average Retail |
|---|---|---|---|
| **SAMURAI 4** | | | |
| Convertible Truck | 6456 | 1425 | 2175 |
| Hardtop Truck | 6856 | 1500 | 2350 |
| Base Convertible | 6951 | 1500 | 2350 |
| Base Hardtop | 7121 | 1650 | 2500 |
| JX Deluxe Convertible | 7375 | 1550 | 2400 |
| JX Deluxe Hardtop | 7530 | 1725 | 2575 |
| JX Deluxe II Convertible | 8115 | 1675 | 2525 |
| JX Deluxe II Hardtop | 8275 | 1775 | 2625 |
| *ADD FOR:* | | | |
| Fiberglass Hardtop | 1399 | 270 | 300 |
| Automatic Hub Set | 210 | 40 | 50 |

NOTE: Power front disc brakes standard on all models. Air conditioning standard on JX Deluxe II models.

*1984 Toyota Camry*

| Year/Model/ Body/Type | Original List | Current Whlse | Average Retail |
|---|---|---|---|
| **TOYOTA** | | | |
| **1992** | | | |
| **2WD 4RUNNER SR5 6** | | | |
| 4 Dr (auto) | 20758 | — | — |
| **4WD 4RUNNER SR5 4** | | | |
| 4 Dr (5 spd) | 19918 | 17425 | 20075 |
| 4 Dr 4WDemand (5 spd) | 20118 | — | — |
| **4WD 4RUNNER SR5 6** | | | |
| 2 Dr (5 spd) | 22098 | 17525 | 20175 |
| 4 Dr 4WDemand (5 spd) | 21618 | — | — |
| *ADD FOR:* | | | |
| Leather Pkg | 1390 | 475 | 550 |
| Sports Pkg (4 Dr Models) | 440 | 200 | 250 |
| Aluminum Wheels | 490 | 175 | 200 |
| **2WD PICKUPS 4** | | | |
| Std Short Bed (5 spd) | 10338 | 7150 | 8300 |
| Dlx Short Bed (5 spd) | 11278 | 7625 | 8850 |
| Dlx Long Bed (5 spd) | 11808 | 7750 | 9000 |
| Dlx Xtracab (5 spd) | 12708 | 8275 | 9550 |
| **2WD PICKUPS 6** | | | |
| Dlx Xtracab (5 spd) | 13538 | — | — |
| SR5 Xtracab (5 spd) | 15188 | 9775 | 11250 |
| 1-Ton (5 spd) | 13148 | 8125 | 9375 |
| **4WD PICKUPS 4** | | | |
| Dlx Short Bed (5 spd) | 14488 | 9475 | 10925 |

| Year/Model/ Body/Type | Original List | Current Whlse | Average Retail |
|---|---|---|---|
| Dlx Short Bed 4WDemand (5 spd) | 14688 | — | — |
| Dlx Long Bed (5 spd) | 15098 | 9600 | 11050 |
| Dlx Long Bed 4WDemand (5 spd) | 15298 | — | — |
| Dlx Xtracab (5 spd) | 15928 | 10075 | 11625 |
| Dlx Xtracab 4WDemand (5 spd) | 16128 | — | — |
| **4WD PICKUPS 6** | | | |
| Dlx Short Bed (5 spd) | 15378 | 9975 | 11500 |
| Dlx Long Bed (5 spd) | 15958 | 10100 | 11650 |
| Dlx Xtracab (5 spd) | 16788 | 10600 | 12225 |
| SR5 Xtracab (5 spd) | 17548 | 11550 | 13350 |
| **CAMRY 4** | | | |
| 4 Dr Dlx Sdn | 15818 | 11950 | 13800 |
| 4 Dr LE Sdn (auto) | 17498 | 13450 | 15775 |
| 4 Dr XLE Sdn (auto) | 19428 | 14950 | 17550 |
| 5 Dr Dlx Wgn (auto) | 17768 | 12975 | 15300 |
| 5 Dr LE Wgn (auto) | 18798 | 13850 | 16225 |
| **CAMRY 6** | | | |
| 4 Dr Dlx Sdn (auto) | 17328 | 13175 | 15550 |
| 4 Dr LE Sdn (auto) | 19228 | 14000 | 16375 |
| 4 Dr SE Sdn (5 spd) | 18528 | — | — |
| 4 Dr XLE Sdn (auto) | 21178 | 15500 | 18150 |
| 5 Dr LE Wgn (auto) | 20528 | 14675 | 17225 |
| *ADD FOR:* | | | |
| Anti-Lock Brakes | 1245 | 460 | 500 |
| Leather Seat Trim | 950 | 330 | 360 |
| Aluminum Alloy Wheels | 420 | 270 | 300 |
| **CELICA 4** | | | |
| 2 Dr ST Spt Cpe | 14788 | 10875 | 12550 |

| Year/Model/Body/Type | Original List | Current Whlse | Average Retail |
|---|---|---|---|
| 2 Dr GT Spt Cpe | **17248** | 12025 | 13900 |
| 2 Dr GT Lftbk | **17388** | 12100 | 13975 |
| 2 Dr GT Conv | **22208** | — | — |
| 2 Dr GT-S Lftbk | **19118** | 13250 | 15575 |
| 2 Dr All-Trac Turbo Lftbk | **23998** | — | — |
| *ADD FOR:* | | | |
| Anti-Lock Brakes | | | |
| (GT, GT-S) | **1360** | 475 | 550 |
| (All-Trac) | **1130** | 475 | 550 |
| Leather Pkg (GT) | **1420** | 400 | 475 |
| Aluminum Alloy Wheels | **420** | 200 | 250 |
| **COROLLA 4** | | | |
| 4 Dr Std Sdn | **11128** | 7825 | 9075 |
| 4 Dr Dlx Sdn | **12148** | 8275 | 9550 |
| 4 Dr Dlx Wgn | **12838** | 8625 | 9950 |
| 5 Dr All-Trac Wgn | **14508** | 9425 | 10850 |
| 4 Dr LE Sdn (auto) | **13798** | 9575 | 11025 |
| *ADD FOR:* | | | |
| Aluminum Alloy Wheels | **410** | 200 | 250 |
| **CRESSIDA 6** | | | |
| 4 Dr Sdn (auto) | **24428** | 17075 | 19725 |
| *ADD FOR:* | | | |
| Anti-Lock Brakes | **1130** | — | — |
| **LAND CRUISER 6** | | | |
| 4 Dr Wgn (auto) | **27548** | 24100 | 27400 |
| *ADD FOR:* | | | |
| Third Rear Seat | **800** | — | — |
| **MR2 4** | | | |
| 2 Dr Cpe | **19128** | 13675 | 16050 |
| 2 Dr Cpe w/T-Bar Roof | **20128** | — | — |
| 2 Dr Turbo Cpe | **21748** | 15125 | 17775 |
| 2 Dr Turbo Cpe w/T-Bar Roof | **22688** | — | — |
| *ADD FOR:* | | | |
| Anti-Lock Brakes | **1130** | 400 | 475 |
| Leather Pkg (Base) | **1750** | 400 | 450 |
| (Turbo) | **1275** | 375 | 425 |
| Aluminum Alloy Wheels (Base) | **400** | 200 | 250 |
| **PASEO 4** | | | |
| 2 Dr Cpe | **11558** | 8500 | 9825 |
| *ADD FOR:* | | | |
| Aluminum Alloy Wheels | **455** | 175 | 225 |
| **PREVIA 4** | | | |
| 2WD Dlx | **19358** | 14800 | 17375 |
| 4WD Dlx | **22188** | 16275 | 18925 |
| 2WD LE (auto) | **22748** | 17375 | 20025 |
| 4WD LE (auto) | **25518** | 18850 | 21900 |

| Year/Model/Body/Type | Original List | Current Whlse | Average Retail |
|---|---|---|---|
| *ADD FOR:* | | | |
| Anti-Lock Brakes | **1405** | 450 | 525 |
| Third Seat (Dlx) | **600** | 250 | 300 |
| **SUPRA 6** | | | |
| 2 Dr Lftbk | **26290** | — | — |
| 2 Dr Turbo Lftbk | **29900** | — | — |
| 2 Dr Turbo Lftbk w/Sport Roof | **30960** | — | — |
| *ADD FOR:* | | | |
| Anti-Lock Brakes (Base) | **1130** | — | — |
| Leather Seat Pkg | **1100** | — | — |
| Sports Pkg (Base) | **795** | — | — |
| (Turbo) | **360** | — | — |
| **TERCEL 4** | | | |
| 2 Dr Std Sdn (NA w/pwr strng) | **8208** | 5725 | 6650 |
| 2 Dr DX Sdn | **10158** | 7000 | 8150 |
| 4 Dr DX Sdn | **10258** | 7100 | 8250 |
| 4 Dr LE Sdn (auto) | **11388** | 8200 | 9475 |

NOTE: Tilt steering wheel standard on Corolla LE, Camry, Celica GT, GT-S & All-Trac, Supra, MR2, Cressida, Previa, 4Runner V6 and Land Cruiser. Cruise control standard on Camry LE & XLE, Celica All-Trac, Supra, Cressida and Previa. Power windows and power door locks standard on Camry LE & XLE, Celica All-Trac, Supra, Cressida, Previa LE and Land Cruiser. Moonroof standard on Camry XLE.

## 1991

| | Original List | Current Whlse | Average Retail |
|---|---|---|---|
| **2WD 4RUNNER SR5 4** | | | |
| 4 Dr (auto) | **16488** | 13950 | 16325 |
| **2WD 4RUNNER SR5 6** | | | |
| 4 Dr (auto) | **19013** | 14450 | 16975 |
| **4WD 4RUNNER SR5 4** | | | |
| 2 Dr (5 spd) | **17308** | 14300 | 16800 |
| 4 Dr (5 spd) | **17298** | 14775 | 17350 |
| **4WD 4RUNNER SR5 6** | | | |
| 2 Dr (5 spd) | **20293** | 14775 | 17350 |
| 4 Dr 4WDemand (5 spd) | **19793** | 15300 | 17950 |
| **2WD PICKUPS 4** | | | |
| Std Short Bed (5 spd) | **9738** | 6125 | 7125 |
| Dlx Short Bed (5 spd) | **10558** | 6575 | 7650 |
| Dlx Long Bed (5 spd) | **11088** | 6675 | 7775 |
| Dlx Std Xtracab Short Bed (5 spd) | **11798** | 7125 | 8275 |
| **2WD PICKUPS 6** | | | |
| Dlx Xtracab Short Bed (5 spd) | **12578** | 7600 | 8825 |
| SR5 Xtracab Short Bed (5 spd) | **14308** | 8300 | 9575 |

| Year/Model/Body/Type | Original List | Current Whlse | Average Retail |
|---|---|---|---|
| 1-Ton (5 spd) | **12368** | 7025 | 8150 |
| **4WD PICKUPS 6** | | | |
| Dlx Short Bed (5 spd) | **14138** | 8300 | 9575 |
| Dlx Long Bed (5 spd) | **14698** | 8425 | 9725 |
| **CAMRY 4** | | | |
| 4 Dr Sdn | **13353** | 8850 | 10225 |
| 4 Dr Dlx Sdn | **14043** | 9550 | 11000 |
| 4 Dr LE Sdn (auto) | **16103** | 10875 | 12550 |
| 4 Dr Dlx All-Trac 4WD Sdn (auto) | **16713** | 10825 | 12500 |
| 4 Dr LE All-Trac 4WD Sdn (auto) | **18093** | 11625 | 13425 |
| 5 Dr Dlx Wgn (auto) | **15513** | 10425 | 12025 |
| **CAMRY 6** | | | |
| 4 Dr Dlx Sdn | **15323** | 10000 | 11525 |
| 4 Dr LE Sdn (auto) | **17668** | 11375 | 13150 |
| 5 Dr LE Wgn (auto) | **18458** | 11775 | 13600 |
| **CELICA 4** | | | |
| 2 Dr ST Spt Cpe | **13623** | 9450 | 10875 |
| 2 Dr GT Spt Cpe | **15293** | 10375 | 11975 |
| 2 Dr GT Conv | **20153** | 13700 | 16075 |
| 2 Dr GT Lftbk | **15543** | 10475 | 12100 |
| 2 Dr GT-S Lftbk | **17758** | 11575 | 13375 |
| 2 Dr All-Trac Turbo Lftbk | **22498** | 13450 | 15775 |
| **COROLLA 4** | | | |
| 4 Dr Std Sdn | **10383** | 6625 | 7700 |
| 4 Dr Dlx Sdn | **11383** | 7025 | 8150 |
| 4 Dr LE Sdn | **12403** | 7600 | 8825 |
| 4 Dr Dlx Wgn | **12053** | 7325 | 8500 |
| 5 Dr 4WD Dlx All-Trac Wgn | **13753** | 8075 | 9325 |
| 2 Dr SR5 Spt Cpe | **12923** | 7850 | 9125 |
| 2 Dr GT-S Spt Cpe | **14513** | 8950 | 10325 |
| **CRESSIDA 6** | | | |
| 4 Dr Lux Sdn (auto) | **22698** | 15550 | 18200 |
| **LAND CRUISER** | | | |
| 4 Dr Wgn (auto) | **24378** | 19625 | 22675 |
| **MR2 4** | | | |
| 2 Dr Cpe | **16873** | 11650 | 13450 |
| 2 Dr Cpe w/T-Bar Roof | **17823** | 12175 | 14050 |
| 2 Dr Turbo Cpe | **20203** | 12975 | 15300 |
| 2 Dr Turbo Cpe w/T-Bar Roof | **21103** | 13525 | 15900 |
| **PREVIA 4** | | | |
| 2WD Dlx | **16448** | 12650 | 14975 |
| 2WD LE (auto) | **19598** | 14625 | 17175 |

| Year/Model/Body/Type | Original List | Current Whlse | Average Retail |
|---|---|---|---|
| **SUPRA 6** | | | |
| 2 Dr Lftbk | **24320** | 14900 | 17500 |
| 2 Dr Turbo Lftbk | **27790** | 15950 | 18600 |
| 2 Dr Turbo Lftbk w/Sport Roof | **28810** | 16500 | 19150 |
| **TERCEL** | | | |
| 2 Dr Std Sdn (NA w/pwr strng) | **7553** | 4650 | 5575 |
| 2 Dr DX Sdn | **9213** | 5825 | 6750 |
| 4 Dr DX Sdn | **9313** | 5925 | 6850 |
| 4 Dr LE Sdn | **10483** | 6375 | 7425 |
| *ADD FOR:* | | | |
| Leather/Power Seat Pkg | | | |
| (Camry LE) | **1080** | 420 | 460 |
| (Celica GT-S) | **1530** | 490 | 540 |
| (Celica GT Cpe) | **1830** | 490 | 540 |
| (Celica All-Trac Turbo) | **950** | 490 | 540 |
| (Cressida) | **1585** | 490 | 540 |
| Leather Trim Pkg | | | |
| (MR2 Base) | **1710** | 330 | 360 |
| (MR2 Turbo) | **1235** | 330 | 360 |
| (Supra) | **1010** | 350 | 380 |
| Dual Sunroofs | | | |
| (Previa LE 2WD) | **1370** | 550 | 610 |

NOTE: Power brakes standard on all models. Power door locks standard on Camry LE 6 cyl, Celica All-Trac Turbo, Cressida, Previa LE and Supra. Power windows standard on Camry LE 6 cyl, Celica All-Trac Turbo, Cressida and Supra.

## 1990

| Year/Model/Body/Type | Original List | Current Whlse | Average Retail |
|---|---|---|---|
| **2WD 4RUNNER SR5 4** | | | |
| 4 Dr (auto) | **16783** | 11650 | 13450 |
| **2WD 4RUNNER SR5 6** | | | |
| 4 Dr (auto) | **18393** | 12025 | 13900 |
| **4WD 4RUNNER SR5 4** | | | |
| 2 Dr (5 spd) | **17208** | 11950 | 13800 |
| **4WD 4RUNNER SR5 6** | | | |
| 2 Dr (5 spd) | **18788** | 12300 | 14300 |
| **2WD PICKUPS 4** | | | |
| Std Short Bed (4 spd) | **9288** | 4825 | 5750 |
| Dlx Short Bed (5 spd) | **9878** | 5225 | 6150 |
| Dlx Long Bed (5 spd) | **10408** | 5350 | 6275 |
| Dlx Xtracab (5 spd) | **11048** | 5750 | 6675 |
| SR5 Long Bed (5 spd) | **10998** | 5950 | 6875 |
| SR5 Xtracab (5 spd) | **11998** | 6325 | 7350 |
| **2WD PICKUPS 6** | | | |
| Dlx Long Bed (5 spd) | **11408** | 5750 | 6675 |

| Year/Model/Body/Type | Original List | Current Whlse | Average Retail |
|---|---|---|---|
| Dlx Xtracab (5 spd) | **12048** | 6150 | 7150 |
| SR5 Xtracab (5 spd) | **13778** | 6675 | 7775 |
| 1-Ton Long Bed (5 spd) | **12048** | 6100 | 7000 |
| **4WD PICKUPS 4** | | | |
| SR5 Short Bed (5 spd) | **13228** | 7450 | 8650 |
| **4WD PICKUPS 6** | | | |
| Dlx Short Bed (5 spd) | **13468** | 7325 | 8500 |
| SR5 Short Bed (5 spd) | **15448** | 7900 | 9175 |
| **CAMRY 4** | | | |
| 4 Dr Sdn | **12743** | 7150 | 8300 |
| 4 Dr Dlx Sdn | **13543** | 7750 | 9000 |
| 4 Dr All Trac Sdn | **15323** | 8450 | 9750 |
| 5 Dr Wgn (auto) | **14923** | 8625 | 9950 |
| 4 Dr LE Sdn (auto) | **15483** | 9025 | 10400 |
| 4 Dr LE All Trac Sdn (auto) | **17473** | 9725 | 11200 |
| **CAMRY 6** | | | |
| 4 Dr Dlx Sdn | **14028** | 8200 | 9475 |
| 5 Dr Dlx Wgn (auto) | **15408** | 9075 | 10450 |
| 4 Dr LE Sdn (auto) | **17078** | 9450 | 10875 |
| 5 Dr LE Wgn (auto) | **17868** | 9825 | 11325 |
| **CELICA 4** | | | |
| 2 Dr ST Spt Cpe | **13093** | 7650 | 8875 |
| 2 Dr GT Spt Cpe | **14763** | 8450 | 9750 |
| 2 Dr GT Lftbk | **15013** | 8550 | 9875 |
| 2 Dr GT-S Lftbk | **17258** | 8600 | 11050 |
| 2 Dr 4WD All Trac Turbo Lftbk | **21998** | 11375 | 13150 |
| **COROLLA 4** | | | |
| 4 Dr Std Sdn | **10103** | 5425 | 6350 |
| 4 Dr Dlx Sdn | **10843** | 5800 | 6725 |
| 5 Dr Dlx Wgn | **11483** | 6125 | 7125 |
| 4 Dr Dlx All Trac Sdn | **12113** | 6500 | 7575 |
| 5 Dr 4WD Dlx All Trac Wgn | **13193** | 6775 | 7875 |
| 4 Dr LE Sdn | **11703** | 6350 | 7400 |
| 2 Dr SR5 Spt Cpe | **12423** | 6600 | 7675 |
| 5 Dr 4WD SR5 All Trac Wgn | **14013** | 7575 | 8800 |
| 2 Dr GT-S Spt Cpe | **14013** | 7425 | 8625 |
| **CRESSIDA** | | | |
| 4 Dr Lux Sdn (auto) | **21498** | 13025 | 15350 |
| **LAND CRUISER 6** | | | |
| 4 Dr Wgn (auto) | **20898** | 14550 | 17075 |
| **SUPRA 6** | | | |
| 2 Dr Lftbk | **22860** | 13175 | 15500 |
| 2 Dr Lftbk w/Sport Roof | **23930** | 13675 | 16050 |
| 2 Dr Turbo Lftbk | **25200** | 14125 | 16575 |

| Year/Model/Body/Type | Original List | Current Whlse | Average Retail |
|---|---|---|---|
| 2 Dr Turbo Lftbk w/Sport Roof | **26220** | 14550 | 17075 |
| **TERCEL 4** | | | |
| 3 Dr Base Lftbk (NA w/pwr strng) | **7433** | 4425 | 5350 |
| 3 Dr EZ Lftbk (NA w/pwr strng) | **6698** | 3675 | 4575 |
| 2 Dr Std Cpe | **8813** | 4525 | 5450 |
| 3 Dr Std Lftbk | **8753** | 4700 | 5625 |
| 2 Dr Dlx Cpe | **9973** | 5075 | 6000 |
| *ADD FOR:* | | | |
| Anti-Lock Braking System | — | 450 | 500 |
| Leather/Power Seat Pkg | — | 310 | 380 |

NOTE: Power brakes standard on all models. Anti-lock brakes standard on 4Runner 6 Cyl. Power windows standard on Camry LE 6 Cyl, Celica All-Trac, Supra Series, Cressida and 4Runner. Power door locks standard on Camry LE 6 Cyl, Celica All-Trac, Supra Series and Cressida.

## 1989

| **4RUNNER 4** | Original List | Current Whlse | Average Retail |
|---|---|---|---|
| Dlx 2 Pass (5 spd) | **14478** | 9475 | 10925 |
| Dlx 5 Pass (5 spd) | **16458** | 9850 | 11350 |
| SR5 2 Pass (5 spd) | **18413** | 10575 | 12200 |
| Dlx 2 Pass V6 (5 spd) | **16083** | 9650 | 11125 |
| SR5 5 Pass V6 (5 spd) | **19223** | 10225 | 11800 |
| **2WD PICKUPS 4** | | | |
| Std Short Bed (4 spd) | **8488** | 3600 | 4500 |
| Dlx Short Bed (5 spd) | **9198** | 3975 | 4875 |
| Dlx Long Bed (5 spd) | **9728** | 4100 | 5025 |
| Dlx Xtracab (5 spd) | **10438** | 4425 | 5350 |
| SR5 Long Bed (5 spd) | **10478** | 4650 | 5575 |
| SR5 Xtracab (5 spd) | **11478** | 4925 | 5850 |
| **2WD PICKUPS 6** | | | |
| Dlx Long Bed (5 spd) | **10858** | 4550 | 5475 |
| Dlx Xtracab (5 spd) | **11498** | 4925 | 5850 |
| SR5 Xtracab (5 spd) | **12788** | 5325 | 6250 |
| 1-Ton Long Bed (5 spd) | **11218** | 4700 | 5625 |
| **4WD PICKUPS 4** | | | |
| SR5 Short Bed (5 spd) | **12708** | 6000 | 6925 |
| SR5 Short Bed w/4WD Demand (5 spd) | **12908** | 6150 | 7150 |
| **4WD PICKUPS 6** | | | |
| Dlx Short Bed (5 spd) | **12918** | 5850 | 6775 |
| SR5 Short Bed (5 spd) | **14458** | 6400 | 7450 |
| **CAMRY 4** | | | |
| 4 Dr Sdn | **12613** | 6250 | 7275 |
| 4 Dr Dlx Sdn | **13453** | 6750 | 7850 |

| Year/Model/Body/Type | Original List | Current Whlse | Average Retail |
|---|---|---|---|
| 4 Dr Dlx All Trac Sdn | **15233** | 7400 | 8600 |
| 5 Dr Wgn | **14143** | 7075 | 8225 |
| 4 Dr LE Sdn (auto) | **15453** | 7825 | 9075 |
| 4 Dr LE All Trac Sdn (auto) | **17443** | 8475 | 9800 |
| 5 Dr LE Wgn (auto) | **16233** | 8125 | 9375 |

### CAMRY 6

| | | | |
|---|---|---|---|
| 4 Dr Dlx Sdn | **14763** | 7250 | 8450 |
| 5 Dr Dlx Wgn (auto) | **16203** | 7525 | 8725 |
| 4 Dr LE Sdn (auto) | **16428** | 8000 | 9300 |
| 5 Dr LE Wgn | **17218** | 8300 | 9575 |

### CELICA 4

| | | | |
|---|---|---|---|
| 2 Dr ST Spt Cpe | **12603** | 5725 | 6650 |
| 2 Dr GT Spt Cpe | **14203** | 6450 | 7500 |
| 2 Dr GT Lftbk | **14453** | 6550 | 7625 |
| 2 Dr GT Convertible | **19113** | 9500 | 10950 |
| 2 Dr GT-S Spt Cpe | **16348** | 7325 | 8500 |
| 2 Dr GT-S Lftbk | **16698** | 7425 | 8625 |
| 2 Dr 4WD All Trac Turbo Lftbk | **21838** | 9225 | 10625 |

### COROLLA 4

| | | | |
|---|---|---|---|
| 4 Dr Dlx Sdn | **10403** | 4625 | 5550 |
| 5 Dr Dlx Wgn | **10993** | 4850 | 5775 |
| 4 Dr Dlx All Trac Sdn (5 spd) | **11843** | 5225 | 6150 |
| 4 Dr Dlx All Trac 4WD Wgn | **12703** | 5525 | 6450 |
| 4 Dr LE Sdn | **11413** | 5100 | 6025 |
| 2 Dr SR5 Spt Cpe | **11953** | 5200 | 6125 |
| 4 Dr SR5 All Trac 4WD Wgn | **14163** | 6275 | 7300 |
| 2 Dr GT-S Spt Cpe | **13723** | 6000 | 6925 |

### CRESSIDA 6

| | | | |
|---|---|---|---|
| 4 Dr Luxury Sdn (auto) | **21498** | 10125 | 11675 |

### LAND CRUISER 6

| | | | |
|---|---|---|---|
| 4 Dr Wgn (auto) | **21788** | 11725 | 13550 |

### MR2 4

| | | | |
|---|---|---|---|
| 2 Dr Cpe | **14593** | 7275 | 8450 |
| 2 Dr Cpe w/T-Bar Roof | **16063** | 7850 | 9125 |
| 2 Dr Supercharged Cpe w/T-Bar Roof | **18423** | 8250 | 9525 |

### SUPRA 6

| | | | |
|---|---|---|---|
| 2 Dr Lftbk | **22360** | 10150 | 11725 |
| 2 Dr Lftbk w/Sport Roof | **23430** | 10650 | 12300 |
| 2 Dr Turbo Lftbk | **24700** | 10875 | 12550 |
| 2 Dr Turbo Lftbk w/Sport Roof | **25720** | 11425 | 13200 |

### TERCEL 4

| | | | |
|---|---|---|---|
| 3 Dr Base Lftbk | | | |

| Year/Model/Body/Type | Original List | Current Whlse | Average Retail |
|---|---|---|---|
| (NA w/pwr strng) | **7273** | 3200 | 4100 |
| 3 Dr EZ Lftbk | | | |
| (NA w/pwr strng) | **6538** | 2725 | 3625 |
| 2 Dr Std Cpe | **8533** | 3275 | 4175 |
| 3 Dr Std Lftbk | **8373** | 3525 | 4425 |
| 2 Dr Dlx Cpe | **9593** | 3800 | 4700 |
| 3 Dr Dlx Lftbk | **9493** | 3700 | 4600 |
| 5 Dr Dlx Lftbk | **9733** | 3800 | 4700 |

### VANS 4

| | | | |
|---|---|---|---|
| Dlx Van | **15663** | 6500 | 7575 |
| Window | **11418** | 4850 | 5775 |
| Panel | **11118** | 4625 | 5550 |
| LE Van | **16958** | 7150 | 8300 |
| 4WD Deluxe Van | **17848** | 7450 | 8650 |
| 4WD Panel (auto) | **14018** | 6125 | 7125 |
| 4WD LE Van (auto) | **18448** | 8700 | 10050 |

*ADD FOR:*

| | | | |
|---|---|---|---|
| Anti-Lock Braking System | — | 350 | 400 |
| Leather Seat Trim | | | |
| (Camry 2WD LE) | **1080** | 440 | 480 |
| (Celica GT-S) | **1550** | 640 | 710 |
| (Celica All-Trac) | **1160** | 470 | 520 |
| (Supra) | **1010** | 410 | 460 |
| (Cressida) | **905** | 360 | 400 |
| Leather/Power Seal Pkg | **1240** | 290 | 320 |

NOTE: Power brakes standard on all models. Pwr strng standard on Camry, Celica, Cressida, Land Cruiser, Supra, 4WD Van, LE Van, Corolla SR5 All-Trac, 4Runner Deluxe 6 Cyl, 4Runner SR5. Power windows standard on Cressida and Supra. Power door locks standard on Cressida, Supra and LE Van. Air conditioning standard on Camry LE V6, Cressida and Supra.

### 1988

### 4RUNNER 4

| | | | |
|---|---|---|---|
| Dlx 2 Pass (5 spd) | **13618** | 7825 | 9075 |
| Dlx 5 Pass (5 spd) | **14278** | 8225 | 9500 |
| SR5 2 Pass (5 spd) | **14718** | 8525 | 9850 |
| SR5 2 Pass V6 (5 spd) | **15528** | 8825 | 10200 |
| SR5 5 Pass V6 (5 spd) | **16698** | 9325 | 10750 |

### 2WD PICKUP 4

| | | | |
|---|---|---|---|
| Std Short Bed (4 spd) | **7698** | 2400 | 3275 |
| Std Short Bed (5 spd) | **8078** | 2425 | 3300 |
| Std Long Bed (5 spd) | **8608** | 2525 | 3400 |
| Std Xtracab Long Bed (5 spd) | **9068** | 2925 | 3825 |
| Dlx Long Bed (5 spd) | **8818** | 2875 | 3775 |
| Dlx Xtracab Long Bed (5 spd) | **9358** | 3250 | 4150 |
| SR5 Xtracab (5 spd) | **10758** | 3575 | 4475 |
| SR5 Xtracab Turbo (5 spd) | **11918** | 3925 | 4825 |
| 1-Ton Long Bed (5 spd) | **9478** | 2675 | 3575 |

| Year/Model/ Body/Type | Original List | Current Whlse | Average Retail |
|---|---|---|---|
| **4WD PICKUP 4** | | | |
| Std Short Bed V6 (5 spd) | **11808** | 4100 | 5025 |
| Dlx Long Bed V6 (5 spd) | **12628** | 4575 | 5500 |
| Dlx Xtracab V6 (5 spd) | **12858** | 4825 | 5750 |
| SR5 Short Bed (5 spd) | **12598** | 4575 | 5500 |
| SR5 Short Bed V6 (5 spd) | **13408** | 4875 | 5800 |
| SR5 Xtracab V6 (5 spd) | **13898** | 5275 | 6200 |
| **CAMRY 4** | | | |
| 4 Dr Sdn | **11248** | 4550 | 5475 |
| 4 Dr Dlx Sdn | **12098** | 5000 | 5925 |
| 4 Dr 4WD Dlx Sdn | **13828** | 5525 | 6450 |
| 5 Dr Wgn | **12788** | 5175 | 6100 |
| 4 Dr LE Sdn (auto) | **14438** | 5825 | 6750 |
| 4 Dr 4WD LE Sdn | **15488** | 5975 | 6900 |
| 5 Dr LE Wgn (auto) | **15208** | 6175 | 7200 |
| **CAMRY 6** | | | |
| 4 Dr Dlx Sdn | **13148** | 5300 | 6225 |
| 5 Dr Dlx Wgn | **14568** | 5600 | 6525 |
| 4 Dr LE Sdn (auto) | **15998** | 6100 | 7000 |
| 5 Dr LE Wgn (auto) | **16788** | 6500 | 7575 |
| **CELICA 4** | | | |
| 2 Dr ST Spt Cpe | **11548** | 4000 | 4900 |
| 2 Dr GT Spt Cpe | **13288** | 4550 | 5475 |
| 2 Dr GT Lftbk | **13538** | 4650 | 5575 |
| 2 Dr GT Convertible | **18248** | 7150 | 8300 |
| 2 Dr GT-S Spt Cpe | **15298** | 5325 | 6250 |
| 2 Dr GT-S Lftbk | **15648** | 5425 | 6350 |
| 2 Dr 4WD Turbo Lftbk | **20698** | 7025 | 8150 |
| **COROLLA 4** | | | |
| 4 Dr Dlx Sdn | **8998** | 3450 | 4350 |
| 5 Dr Dlx Wgn | **9548** | 3700 | 4600 |
| 4 Dr 4WD Wgn | **10948** | 4300 | 5225 |
| 4 Dr LE Sdn | **10248** | 3875 | 4775 |
| 2 Dr SR5 Spt Cpe | **10348** | 3950 | 4850 |
| 4 Dr 4WD SR5 Wgn | **12418** | 4775 | 5700 |
| 2 Dr GT-S Spt Cpe | **12478** | 4625 | 5550 |
| 3 Dr FX Lftbk | **7948** | 2200 | 3050 |
| 3 Dr FX-16 Lftbk | **9978** | 2850 | 3750 |
| 3 Dr FX-16 Gt-S Lftbk | **10968** | 3325 | 4225 |
| **CRESSIDA 6** | | | |
| 4 Dr Luxury Sdn (auto) | **20998** | 8075 | 9325 |
| **LAND CRUISER 6** | | | |
| 4 Dr Wgn (auto) | **20398** | 9475 | 10925 |
| **MR2 4** | | | |
| 2 Dr Cpe | **13458** | 4975 | 5900 |
| 2 Dr Cpe w/T-Bar Roof | **14808** | 5325 | 6250 |
| 2 Dr Supercharged | | | |

| Year/Model/ Body/Type | Original List | Current Whlse | Average Retail |
|---|---|---|---|
| Cpe w/T-Bar Roof | **17068** | 5925 | 6850 |
| **SUPRA 6** | | | |
| 2 Dr Lftbk | **21740** | 7550 | 8775 |
| 2 Dr Lftbk w/Sport Roof | **22780** | 7950 | 9225 |
| 2 Dr Turbo Lftbk | **24210** | 8200 | 9475 |
| 2 Dr Turbo Lftbk w/Sport Roof | **25200** | 8575 | 9900 |
| **TERCEL 4** | | | |
| 3 Dr EZ Lftbk | **6148** | 1775 | 2625 |
| 2 Dr Std Cpe | **7148** | 2300 | 3175 |
| 3 Dr Std Lftbk | **6988** | 2225 | 3075 |
| 3 Dr Std Cpe (auto) | **7458** | 2700 | 3600 |
| 2 Dr Dlx Cpe | **8238** | 2700 | 3600 |
| 3 Dr Dlx Lftbk | **8088** | 2600 | 3475 |
| 5 Dr Sdn | **8328** | 2750 | 3650 |
| 5 Dr Lftbk (auto) | **8798** | 2700 | 3600 |
| 4 Dr 4WD Dlx Wgn | **10698** | 3400 | 4300 |
| 4 Dr 4WD SR5 Wgn | **11718** | 3900 | 4800 |
| **VANS 4** | | | |
| Dlx Van | **13198** | 4375 | 5300 |
| Window | **10808** | 3300 | 4200 |
| Panel | **10508** | 3125 | 4025 |
| LE Van | **15258** | 4925 | 5850 |
| 4WD Panel | **12928** | 3975 | 4875 |
| 4WD LE Van | **17328** | 5850 | 6775 |

NOTE: Power brakes stanard on all models. Power windows standard on Celica 4WD, Supra Series and Cressida Series. Power door locks standard on Celica 4WD, Supra Series, Cressida Series and Van LE. Pwr strng standard on Corolla FX16, Corolla FX16 GT-S, Camry Series, Celica Series, Supra Series, Cressida Series, Van 4WD, Van Deluxe, Van LE, Pickup SR5, 4Runner SR5 and Land Cruiser. Air conditioning standard on Camry LE with V6 eng, Supra Series and Cressida Series.

## 1987

| **TERCEL 4** | | | |
|---|---|---|---|
| 2 Dr Std Cpe | **6738** | 1900 | 2750 |
| 2 Dr Dlx Cpe (auto) | **8298** | 2550 | 3425 |

NOTE: Power front disc brakes standard.

## 1987

| **4RUNNER 4** | | | |
|---|---|---|---|
| Dlx (5 spd) | **12998** | 6325 | 7350 |
| SR5 2 Pass (5 spd) | **14548** | 6925 | 8050 |
| SR5 Wgn (5 spd) | **15248** | 7300 | 8475 |
| SR5 Turbo (5 spd) | **18698** | 7900 | 9175 |
| **2WD PICKUP 4** | | | |
| Std Short Bed (4 spd) | **6998** | 2150 | 3000 |
| Std Short Bed (5 spd) | **7378** | 2175 | 3025 |
| Std Long Bed (5 spd) | **7898** | 2250 | 3100 |

| Year/Model/Body/Type | Original List | Current Whlse | Average Retail |
|---|---|---|---|
| Xtracab Long Bed (5 spd) | 8498 | 2575 | 3450 |
| Dlx Long Bed (5 spd) | 8245 | 2550 | 3425 |
| Dlx Xtracab Long Bed (5 spd) | 8778 | 2900 | 3800 |
| SR5 Xtracab (5 spd) | 10188 | 3150 | 4050 |
| SR5 Xtracab Turbo (5 spd) | 12488 | 3425 | 4325 |
| 1-Ton Long Bed (5 spd) | 8898 | 2350 | 3225 |

### 4WD PICKUP 4

| | | | |
|---|---|---|---|
| Std Short Bed Turbo (5 spd) | 11638 | 3650 | 4550 |
| SR5 Short Bed (5 spd) | 11988 | 4075 | 5000 |

### CAMRY 4

| | | | |
|---|---|---|---|
| 4 Dr Sdn | 10798 | 3425 | 4325 |
| 4 Dr Dlx Sdn | 11448 | 3750 | 4650 |
| 5 Dr Dlx Wgn | 12138 | 4000 | 4900 |
| 4 Dr LE Sdn (auto) | 13798 | 4625 | 5550 |
| 5 Dr LE Wgn (auto) | 14568 | 4850 | 5775 |

### CELICA 4

| | | | |
|---|---|---|---|
| 2 Dr ST Spt Cpe | 10948 | 3175 | 4075 |
| 2 Dr GT Spt Cpe | 12638 | 3650 | 4550 |
| 2 Dr GT Lftbk | 12888 | 3750 | 4650 |
| 2 Dr GT Convertible | 17598 | 6025 | 6950 |
| 2 Dr GT-S Spt Cpe | 14648 | 4350 | 5275 |
| 2 Dr GT-S Lftbk | 15368 | 4450 | 5375 |

### COROLLA 4

| | | | |
|---|---|---|---|
| 4 Dr Dlx Sdn | 8478 | 2475 | 3350 |
| 5 Dr Dlx Lftbk (auto) | 9408 | 2950 | 3850 |
| 4 Dr LE Sdn | 9628 | 2775 | 3675 |
| 2 Dr SR5 Spt Cpe | 9998 | 2925 | 3825 |
| 2 Dr GT-S Spt Cpe | 10998 | 3425 | 4325 |
| 3 Dr FX Lftbk | 7878 | 1575 | 2425 |
| 3 Dr FX-16 Lftbk | 9678 | 2150 | 3000 |
| 3 Dr FX-16 Gt-S Lftbk | 10668 | 2575 | 3450 |

### CRESSIDA 6

| | | | |
|---|---|---|---|
| 4 Dr Lux Sdn (5 spd or auto) | 20250 | 6025 | 6950 |
| 4 Dr Lux Wgn (auto) | 20310 | 6200 | 7225 |

### LAND CRUISER 6

| | | | |
|---|---|---|---|
| 4 Dr Wgn | 18148 | 7500 | 8700 |
| 4 Dr Wgn w/o Rear Seat | 17448 | 7300 | 8475 |

### MR2 4

| | | | |
|---|---|---|---|
| 2 Dr Cpe | 12848 | 3725 | 4625 |
| 2 Dr Cpe w/T-Bar Roof | 14038 | 4025 | 4925 |

### SUPRA 6

| | | | |
|---|---|---|---|
| 2 Dr Lftbk | 20890 | 6350 | 7400 |

| Year/Model/Body/Type | Original List | Current Whlse | Average Retail |
|---|---|---|---|
| 2 Dr Lftbk w/Sport Roof (auto) | 22660 | 6725 | 7825 |
| 2 Dr Turbo Lftbk | 23210 | 6950 | 8100 |
| 2 Dr Turbo Lftbk w/Sport Roof | 24210 | 7225 | 8400 |

### TERCEL 4

| | | | |
|---|---|---|---|
| 3 Dr EZ Lftbk | 5848 | 1050 | 1775 |
| 3 Dr Lftbk | 6328 | 1450 | 2225 |
| 3 Dr Dlx Lftbk | 7638 | 1775 | 2625 |
| 5 Dr Dlx Lftbk (auto) | 8338 | 2150 | 3000 |
| 5 Dr Dlx Wgn | 8898 | 1975 | 2825 |
| 4 Dr 4WD Dlx Wgn | 10138 | 2475 | 3350 |
| 4 Dr 4WD SR5 Wgn | 11208 | 2925 | 3825 |

### VANS 4

| | | | |
|---|---|---|---|
| Dlx Van | 12338 | 2850 | 3750 |
| Window | 9948 | 2000 | 2850 |
| Panel | 9648 | 1800 | 2650 |
| LE Van (auto) | 14998 | 3625 | 4525 |
| 4WD Panel | 12018 | 2550 | 3425 |
| 4WD LE Van | 16428 | 4050 | 4950 |

### ADD FOR:

| | | | |
|---|---|---|---|
| Sports Pkg (Supra) | 700 | 180 | 200 |
| (Celica GT-S) | 800 | 210 | 230 |
| Leather Pkg (MR2) | 760 | 200 | 220 |
| (Cressida Sdn) | 760 | 200 | 220 |

NOTE: Power brakes standard on all models. Air conditioning standard on Cressida and Supra. Power windows standard on Cressida, Supra and 4Runner. Power door locks standard on Cressida, Van LE, SR5 Turbo Pickup and Supra. Sunroof standard on Corolla FX-16 GT-S. Pwr strng standard on Corolla FX-16, Camry, Celica, Cressida, Van LE, SR5 Pickup, 4Runner, Supra and Land Cruiser.

## 1986

### 4RUNNER 4

| | | | |
|---|---|---|---|
| Std (5 spd) | 12398 | 4775 | 5700 |
| Dlx (auto) | 13778 | 5175 | 6100 |
| SR5 (5 spd) | 14578 | 5550 | 6475 |
| SR5 Turbo Diesel (auto) | 17678 | 5375 | 6300 |

### 2WD PICKUPS

| | | | |
|---|---|---|---|
| Std Short Bed (4 spd) | 6298 | 1825 | 2675 |
| Std Long Bed (5 spd) | 7128 | 1950 | 2800 |
| Dlx Long Bed (5 spd) | 7438 | 2200 | 3050 |
| Dlx Xtracab Long Bed (5 spd) | 8168 | 2350 | 3225 |
| SR5 Long Bed (5 spd) | 9188 | 2525 | 3400 |
| SR5 Xtracab (5 spd) | 9388 | 2700 | 3600 |
| SR5 Xtracab Turbo (5 spd) | 11868 | 2600 | 3475 |
| 1-Ton Long Bed (5 spd) | 8088 | 2075 | 2925 |

| Year/Model/ Body/Type | Original List | Current Whlse | Average Retail |
|---|---|---|---|
| **4WD PICKUPS** | | | |
| Std Short Bed Turbo (5 spd) | **10738** | 2975 | 3875 |
| SR5 Short Bed (5 spd) | **11438** | 3550 | 4450 |
| SR5 Xtracab Turbo (auto) | **14838** | 3850 | 4750 |
| **CAMRY 4** | | | |
| 4 Dr Dlx Sdn | **10198** | 2550 | 3425 |
| 4 Dr Turbo-diesel Dlx Sdn (auto) | **12208** | 2300 | 3175 |
| 4 Dr LE Sdn | **11738** | 3000 | 3900 |
| 5 Dr LE Lftbk (auto) | **12758** | 3275 | 4175 |
| **CELICA 4** | | | |
| 2 Dr ST Spt Cpe | **10098** | 2300 | 3175 |
| 2 Dr GT Spt Cpe | **11398** | 2750 | 3650 |
| 2 Dr GT Lftbk | **11648** | 2850 | 3750 |
| 2 Dr GT-S Spt Cpe | **13348** | 3250 | 4150 |
| 2 Dr GT-S Lftbk | **13698** | 3350 | 4250 |
| **COROLLA 4** | | | |
| 4 Dr Dlx Sdn | **7798** | 2175 | 3025 |
| 5 Dr Dlx Lftbk | **8158** | 2250 | 3100 |
| 4 Dr LE Sdn | **8818** | 2400 | 3275 |
| 4 Dr LE LTD Sdn (auto) | **10778** | 2700 | 3600 |
| 2 Dr GT-S Spt Cpe | **10198** | 3050 | 3950 |
| 2 Dr GT-S Lftbk | **10378** | 2975 | 3875 |
| 2 Dr SR5 Spt Cpe | **9108** | 2525 | 3400 |
| 2 Dr SR5 Lftbk | **9288** | 2500 | 3375 |
| **CRESSIDA 6** | | | |
| 4 Dr Lux Sdn | **18280** | 4625 | 5550 |
| 4 Dr Lux Wgn (auto) | **18340** | 4725 | 5650 |
| **LAND CRUISER 6** | | | |
| 4 Dr Wgn | **16548** | 5600 | 6525 |
| **MR2 4** | | | |
| 2 Dr Cpe | **12548** | 2675 | 3575 |
| **SUPRA 6** | | | |
| 2 Dr Lftbk | **16558** | 4875 | 5800 |
| 1986.5 SUPRA 6 | | | |
| 2 Dr Lftbk | **17990** | 5550 | 6475 |
| 2 Dr Sport Lftbk | **18790** | 5750 | 6675 |
| **TERCEL 4** | | | |
| 3 Dr Std Lftbk | **5798** | 1225 | 1950 |
| 3 Dr Dlx Lftbk | **7038** | 1475 | 2300 |
| 5 Dr Dlx Lftbk | **7188** | 1575 | 2425 |
| 5 Dr Dlx Wgn | **7888** | 1675 | 2525 |
| 5 Dr Dlx 4WD Wgn (auto) | **9018** | 2125 | 2975 |
| 5 Dr SR5 4WD Wgn | **9948** | 2425 | 3300 |
| **VANS 4** | | | |
| Dlx Van | **11148** | 2100 | 2950 |

| Year/Model/ Body/Type | Original List | Current Whlse | Average Retail |
|---|---|---|---|
| LE Van (auto) | **13538** | 2700 | 3600 |
| Cargo Van | **8998** | 1375 | 2125 |
| *ADD FOR:* | | | |
| Leather Pkg (MR2) | **730** | 140 | 150 |
| (Celica GT-S) | **770** | 150 | 160 |
| (Cressida Sdn) | **670** | 130 | 140 |
| Luxury Pkg (Cargo Van) | **800** | 160 | 170 |
| Sports Pkg (Cressida) | **670** | 130 | 140 |
| Converter Pkg (Cargo Van) | **295** | 150 | 160 |

NOTE: Power brakes standard on Camry Deluxe, Corolla Series, Tercel Series, Celica Series, MR2, Supra, Cressida, Vans, 4Runner and Pickups. Air conditioning and power windows standard on Cressida and Supra. Power locks standard on Corolla LE Sedan, Corolla SR5, Corolla GTS, Supra, Cressida and LE Van. Pwr strng standard on Camry Series, Corolla Deluxe diesel models, Corolla LE, Corolla SR5, Corolla GT-S, Celica GT, Celica GT-S, Supra, Cressida, LE Van, SR5 4Runner and SR5 4WD Pickups.

## 1985

| | Original List | Current Whlse | Average Retail |
|---|---|---|---|
| **4RUNNER 4** | | | |
| Std (5 spd) | **10668** | 4250 | 5175 |
| Dlx (auto) | **12068** | 4600 | 5525 |
| SR5 (5 spd) | **12568** | 4925 | 5850 |
| **PICKUP 4** | | | |
| Std (4 spd) | **5998** | 1725 | 2575 |
| Long Bed (5 spd) | **6498** | 1825 | 2675 |
| Dlx Long Bed (5 spd) | **6898** | 2075 | 2925 |
| Dlx Xtracab (5 spd) | **7288** | 2200 | 3050 |
| SR5 Std Bed (5 spd) | **8098** | 2200 | 3050 |
| SR5 Long Bed (5 spd) | **8268** | 2300 | 3175 |
| SR5 Xtracab (5 spd) | **8448** | 2450 | 3325 |
| SR5 Xtracab Turbo (auto) | **10378** | 2375 | 3250 |
| Dlx Long Bed Diesel (5 spd) | **7648** | 1700 | 2550 |
| Dlx Long Bed Turbo-diesel (5 spd) | **7888** | 1875 | 2725 |
| Dlx Xtracab Std Bed Turbodiesel (5 spd) | **8788** | 1800 | 2650 |
| 1-Ton Long Bed (5 spd) | **7338** | 1925 | 2775 |
| **CAMRY 4** | | | |
| 4 Dr Dlx Sdn | **9248** | 2225 | 3075 |
| 4 Dr LE Sdn (auto) | **10898** | 2625 | 3525 |
| 5 Dr Dlx Lftbk (auto) | **10288** | 2275 | 3150 |
| 5 Dr LE Lftbk (auto) | **11248** | 2700 | 3600 |
| 4 Dr Dlx Turbodiesel Sdn | **10998** | 1775 | 2625 |
| **CELICA 4** | | | |
| 2 Dr ST Spt Cpe | **8449** | 2150 | 3000 |
| 2 Dr GT-S Spt Cpe | **11199** | 3000 | 3900 |

*Refer to optional equipment schedules*

| Year/Model/Body/Type | Original List | Current Whlse | Average Retail |
|---|---|---|---|
| 2 Dr GT Spt Cpe | **10099** | 2500 | 3375 |
| 2 Dr GT-S Lftbk | **11549** | 3100 | 4000 |
| 2 Dr GT Lftbk | **9989** | 2600 | 3475 |
| 2 Dr GT-S Convertible | **17669** | 5700 | 6625 |

### COROLLA 4

| | | | |
|---|---|---|---|
| 4 Dr Dlx Sdn | **7163** | 1850 | 2700 |
| 4 Dr LE Sdn | **7738** | 2050 | 2900 |
| 4 Dr LE LTD Sdn (auto) | **9258** | 2175 | 3025 |
| 5 Dr Dlx Lftbk | **7423** | 1925 | 2775 |
| 5 Dr LE Lftbk (auto) | **8358** | 2125 | 2975 |
| 4 Dr Dlx Diesel Sdn (auto) | **7898** | 1575 | 2425 |
| 5 Dr Dlx Diesel Lftbk (5 spd) | **7788** | 1600 | 2450 |
| 2 Dr SR5 Spt Cpe | **8058** | 2100 | 2950 |
| 2 Dr SR5 Lftbk | **8238** | 2075 | 2925 |
| 2 Dr GT-S Spt Cpe | **9298** | 2350 | 3225 |
| 2 Dr GT-S Lftbk | **9538** | 2350 | 3225 |

### CRESSIDA 6

| | | | |
|---|---|---|---|
| 4 Dr Lux Sdn | **15690** | 3900 | 4800 |
| 4 Dr Lux Wgn (auto) | **15750** | 3800 | 4700 |

### LAND CRUISER 6

| | | | |
|---|---|---|---|
| 4 Dr Wgn | **14570** | 4900 | 5825 |

### MR2 4

| | | | |
|---|---|---|---|
| 2 Dr Cpe | **10999** | 2625 | 3525 |

### SUPRA 6

| | | | |
|---|---|---|---|
| 2 Dr Lftbk | **16558** | 3575 | 4475 |
| 2 Dr L Lftbk (auto) | **16558** | 3375 | 4275 |

### TERCEL 4

| | | | |
|---|---|---|---|
| 3 Dr Lftbk | **5573** | 1050 | 1775 |
| 3 Dr Dlx Lftbk | **6563** | 1275 | 2000 |
| 5 Dr Dlx Lftbk | **6713** | 1350 | 2100 |
| 5 Dr Dlx Wgn | **7143** | 1425 | 2175 |
| 5 Dr Dlx 4WD Wgn (auto) | **8433** | 1825 | 2675 |
| 5 Dr SR5 4WD Wgn | **8778** | 2200 | 3050 |

### VAN WAGON 4

| | | | |
|---|---|---|---|
| Dlx Wgn | **10013** | 1900 | 2750 |
| LE Wgn | **11348** | 2250 | 3100 |
| Cargo Wgn | **9198** | 1275 | 2000 |

*ADD FOR:*

| | | | |
|---|---|---|---|
| Leather Seat Pkg | — | 70 | 80 |
| Leather Sport Seats (Supra L) | **700** | 80 | 90 |
| Converter Pkg (Cargo Van) | **1300** | 150 | 160 |

NOTE: Power brakes standard on all models. Pwr strng standard on Corolla, Corolla SR5 Sport, Corolla GT-S, Camry except Sdn, Celica GT, Celica GT-S, Supra, Cressida, LE Van and 4Runner. Air conditioning standard on Celica GT-S, Supra and Cressida. Power windows standard on Supra and Cressida.

## 1984

### PICKUP 4

| Year/Model/Body/Type | Original List | Current Whlse | Average Retail |
|---|---|---|---|
| Std Short Bed (4 spd) | **5998** | 1225 | 1950 |
| Std Long Bed (5 spd) | **6298** | 1300 | 2025 |
| Std Long Bed (4 spd) | **6728** | 1300 | 2025 |
| Dlx Long Bed (5 spd) | **7268** | 1500 | 2350 |
| Dlx Extra Cab (5 spd) | **7508** | 1675 | 2525 |
| SR5 Short Bed (5 spd) | **8308** | 1550 | 2400 |
| SR5 Long Bed (5 spd) | **8478** | 1650 | 2500 |
| SR5 Extra Cab (5 spd) | **8548** | 1775 | 2625 |
| Dlx Long Bed Diesel (5 spd) | **7868** | 950 | 1675 |
| Ton Long Bed (5 spd) | **6998** | 1325 | 2050 |
| Dlx 4WD Long Bed Diesel (5 spd) | **7868** | 1550 | 2400 |

### CAMRY 4

| | | | |
|---|---|---|---|
| 4 Dr Dlx Sdn | **8498** | 1700 | 2550 |
| 5 Dr Dlx Lftbk (auto) | **9448** | 1775 | 2625 |
| 4 Dr Dlx Turbodiesel Sdn | **9598** | 1275 | 2000 |
| 4 Dr LE Sdn (auto) | **10498** | 2025 | 2875 |
| 5 Dr LE Lftbk (auto) | **10848** | 2125 | 2975 |

### CELICA 4

| | | | |
|---|---|---|---|
| 2 Dr ST Spt Cpe | **8334** | 1525 | 2375 |
| 2 Dr GT Spt Cpe | **9149** | 1725 | 2575 |
| 2 Dr GT Lftbk | **9499** | 1800 | 2650 |
| 2 Dr GT-S Spt Cpe | **10919** | 2100 | 2950 |
| 2 Dr GT-S Lftbk | **11269** | 2175 | 3025 |

### COROLLA 4

| | | | |
|---|---|---|---|
| 4 Dr Dlx Sdn | **7018** | 1325 | 2050 |
| 4 Dr Dlx Diesel Sdn (auto) | **7938** | 950 | 1675 |
| 5 Dr Dlx Sdn | **7268** | 1350 | 2100 |
| 5 Dr Dlx Diesel Lftbk | **7818** | 900 | 1625 |
| 4 Dr LE Sdn | **7498** | 1450 | 1625 |
| 2 Dr SR5 HT | **7898** | 1525 | 2375 |
| 2 Dr SR5 Lftbk | **8078** | 1500 | 2350 |

### CRESSIDA 6

| | | | |
|---|---|---|---|
| 4 Dr Lux Sdn | **14259** | 2650 | 3550 |
| 4 Dr Lux Wgn (auto) | **14819** | 2550 | 3425 |

### LAND CRUISER 6

| | | | |
|---|---|---|---|
| 4 Dr Wgn | **14218** | 3875 | 4775 |

### STARLET 4

| | | | |
|---|---|---|---|
| 3 Dr Lftbk | **6168** | 700 | 1325 |

### SUPRA 6

| | | | |
|---|---|---|---|
| 2 Dr L Lftbk (auto) | **15438** | 2300 | 3175 |
| 2 Dr Lftbk (5 spd) | **16088** | 2325 | 3200 |

### TERCEL 4

| | | | |
|---|---|---|---|
| 3 Dr Lftbk | **5248** | 675 | 1275 |
| 3 Dr Dlx Lftbk | **6418** | 875 | 1600 |

| Year/Model/Body/Type | Original List | Current Whlse | Average Retail |
|---|---|---|---|
| 5 Dr Dlx Lftbk | **6608** | 900 | 1625 |
| 5 Dr Dlx Wgn | **7008** | 950 | 1675 |
| 5 Dr Dlx 4WD Wgn | **8288** | 1325 | 2050 |
| 3 Dr SR5 Lftbk | **6968** | 1050 | 1775 |
| 5 Dr SR5 4WD Wgn | **8528** | 1550 | 2400 |

**VAN WAGON 4**

| | | | |
|---|---|---|---|
| Dlx Wgn | **9698** | 1100 | 1825 |
| Dlx LE Wgn | **10948** | 1325 | 2050 |

**1983 — ALL BODY STYLES**

| | | | |
|---|---|---|---|
| HALF TON PICKUPS | — | 1050 | 1775 |
| 4WD PICKUPS | — | 1700 | 2550 |
| TON PICKUPS | — | 1050 | 1775 |
| CAMRY | — | 1350 | 2100 |
| CELICA | — | 1725 | 2575 |
| COROLLA | — | 900 | 1625 |
| COROLLA TERCEL | — | 750 | 1475 |
| CRESSIDA | — | 1950 | 2800 |
| LAND CRUISER | — | 3225 | 4125 |
| STARLET | — | 525 | 975 |
| SUPRA | — | 2275 | 3150 |

## VISTA

### 1992

**VISTA 4**

| | | | |
|---|---|---|---|
| 5 Dr 2WD Wgn | **12331** | — | — |
| 5 Dr 4WD Wgn | **14403** | — | — |
| 5 Dr 2WD SE Wgn | **12894** | — | — |

*ADD FOR:*

| | | | |
|---|---|---|---|
| Anti-Lock Brakes | **913** | — | — |

NOTE: Tilt steering wheel standard on 4WD models.

### 1991

**VISTA 4**

| | | | |
|---|---|---|---|
| 5 Dr 2WD Wgn | **13367** | 7225 | 8400 |
| 5 Dr 4WD Wgn | **14334** | 7525 | 8725 |

NOTE: Power brakes standard on all models.

### 1990

**VISTA 4**

| | | | |
|---|---|---|---|
| 5 Dr 2WD Wgn | **12628** | 5800 | 6725 |
| 5 Dr 4WD Wgn | **13595** | 6125 | 7125 |

NOTE: Power brakes standard on all models.

### 1989

**VISTA 4**

| | | | |
|---|---|---|---|
| 5 Dr 2WD Wgn | **12789** | 4575 | 5500 |
| 5 Dr 4WD Wgn | **13840** | 4850 | 5775 |

NOTE: Power brakes and tinted glass standard on all models. Pwr strng standard on Vista 4WD.

### 1988

**VISTA 4**

| | | | |
|---|---|---|---|
| 5 Dr 2WD Wgn | **11461** | 3025 | 3925 |
| 5 Dr 4WD Wgn | **12775** | 3275 | 4175 |

*ADD FOR:*

| | | | |
|---|---|---|---|
| Custom Pkg (2WD) | **433** | 150 | 160 |
| (4WD) | **359** | 150 | 160 |

NOTE: Power brakes standard on all models. Pwr strng standard on Vista 4WD model.

### 1987

**VISTA 4**

| | | | |
|---|---|---|---|
| 5 Dr 2WD Wgn | **10644** | 2450 | 3325 |
| 5 Dr 4WD Wgn | **11888** | 2775 | 3675 |

NOTE: Power brakes and tinted glass standard on all models.

### 1986

**VISTA 4**

| | | | |
|---|---|---|---|
| 5 Dr 2WD Wgn | **9577** | 2075 | 2925 |
| 5 Dr 4WD Wgn | **10701** | 2450 | 3325 |

*ADD FOR:*

| | | | |
|---|---|---|---|
| Custom Pkg (2WD) | **298** | 60 | 60 |
| (4WD) | **257** | 50 | 50 |

NOTE: Power brakes standard on all models.

### 1985

**VISTA 4**

| | | | |
|---|---|---|---|
| 5 Dr Wgn | **8721** | 1675 | 2525 |

*ADD FOR:*

| | | | |
|---|---|---|---|
| Custom Pkg | **292** | 40 | 40 |

NOTE: Power brakes and tinted glass standard.

### 1984

**VISTA 4**

| | | | |
|---|---|---|---|
| 5 Dr Wgn | **8115** | 1100 | 1825 |

NOTE: Power brakes and tinted glass standard.

*1991 Volkswagen Corrado*

| Year/Model/Body/Type | Original List | Current Whlse | Average Retail |
|---|---|---|---|
| **VOLKSWAGEN** | | | |
| **1992** | | | |
| **CABRIOLET 4** | | | |
| 2 Dr Conv (5 spd) | 18215 | — | — |
| 2 Dr Carat Conv (5 spd) | 19845 | — | — |
| **CORRADO 4** | | | |
| 2 Dr Cpe (5 spd) | 19860 | — | — |
| 2 Dr SLC Cpe (5 spd) | 22170 | — | — |
| *ADD FOR:* | | | |
| Anti-Lock Brakes (Base) | 835 | — | — |
| Leather Seat Trim | 770 | — | — |
| **FOX 4** | | | |
| 2 Dr Sdn (4 spd) (NA w/pwr strng) | 8335 | 6275 | 7300 |
| 4 Dr GL Sdn (NA w/pwr strng) | 9335 | 7075 | 8225 |
| **GOLF 4** | | | |
| 2 Dr GL Hbk (5 spd) | 11255 | 8300 | 9575 |
| 4 Dr GL Hbk (5 spd) | 11565 | 8400 | 9700 |
| **GTI 4** | | | |
| 2 Dr Hbk (5 spd) | 12460 | 9225 | 10625 |
| 2 Dr 16V Hbk | 15455 | 10900 | 12575 |
| **JETTA 4** | | | |
| 4 Dr GL Sdn (5 spd) | 12720 | 9200 | 10600 |
| 4 Dr GL ECO Diesel Sdn (5 spd) | 13030 | 8700 | 10050 |
| 4 Dr Carat Sdn (5 spd) | 13915 | 9750 | 11225 |

| Year/Model/Body/Type | Original List | Current Whlse | Average Retail |
|---|---|---|---|
| 4 Dr GLI Sdn (5 spd) | 16550 | 11575 | 13375 |
| *ADD FOR:* | | | |
| Anti-Lock Brakes | 835 | 460 | 500 |
| Alloy Wheels (GL) | 395 | 260 | 280 |
| **PASSAT 4** | | | |
| 4 Dr CL Sdn (5 spd) | 16350 | — | — |
| 4 Dr GL Sdn (5 spd) | 17810 | 12875 | 15200 |
| 4 Dr GL Wgn (5 spd) | 18240 | 13125 | 15450 |
| *ADD FOR:* | | | |
| Anti-Lock Brakes | 835 | 450 | 500 |
| Leather Seat Trim | 770 | 375 | 425 |
| Cast Alloy Wheels | 395 | 200 | 250 |
| Forged Alloy Wheels | 625 | 225 | 275 |

NOTE: Tilt steering wheel standard on Corrado, GTi and Jetta. Cruise control standard on Cabriolet Carat and Corrado. Power windows standard on Cabriolet and Corrado. Power door locks standard on Jetta Carat & GLi.

| **1991** | | | |
|---|---|---|---|
| **CABRIOLET 4** | | | |
| 2 Dr Convertible (5 spd) | 17400 | 11425 | 13200 |
| 2 Dr Carat Convertible (5 spd) | 18960 | 11975 | 13700 |
| 2 Dr Etienne Aigner Convertible (5 spd) | 19260 | 11800 | 13625 |
| **CORRADO 4** | | | |
| 2 Dr Cpe (5 spd) | 19100 | 11500 | 13275 |
| **FOX 4** | | | |
| 2 Dr Sdn (4 spd) | | | |

*Refer to optional equipment schedules*

| Year/Model/Body/Type | Original List | Current Whlse | Average Retail |
|---|---|---|---|
| (NA w/pwr strng) | 8515 | 5175 | 6100 |
| 4 Dr GL Sdn (5 spd) (NA w/pwr strng) | 9705 | 5975 | 6900 |
| **GOLF 4** | | | |
| 2 Dr GL Hbk (5 spd) | 10720 | 7000 | 8150 |
| 4 Dr GL Hbk (5 spd) | 11020 | 7075 | 8225 |
| **GTI 4** | | | |
| 2 Dr Hbk (5 spd) | 11990 | 7675 | 8900 |
| 2 Dr 16V Hbk (5 spd) | 14680 | 9450 | 10875 |
| **JETTA 4** | | | |
| 2 Dr GL Sdn (5 spd) | 11795 | 7675 | 8900 |
| 4 Dr GL Sdn (5 spd) | 12095 | 7875 | 9150 |
| 4 Dr GL Diesel Sdn (5 spd) | 12095 | 7375 | 8550 |
| 4 Dr ECO Diesel Sdn (5 spd) | 12395 | 7625 | 8850 |
| 4 Dr Carat Sdn (5 spd) | 13220 | 8375 | 9675 |
| 4 Dr GLI Sdn (5 spd) | 15720 | 10150 | 11725 |
| **PASSAT 4** | | | |
| 4 Dr GL Sdn (5 spd) | 15590 | 10725 | 12375 |
| 4 Dr GL Wgn (5 spd) | 16010 | 11000 | 12700 |
| **VANAGON 4** | | | |
| Base 7-Seater (4 spd) | 16365 | 9575 | 11025 |
| GL 7-Seater (4 spd) | 17855 | 11600 | 13400 |
| Carat 7-Seater (4 spd) | 19555 | 12850 | 15175 |
| Multi-Van 7-Seater (4 spd) | 22035 | — | — |
| GL Camper (4 spd) | 22625 | 14625 | 17175 |
| *ADD FOR:* | | | |
| Leather Upholstery (Corrado, Passat) | 740 | 410 | 460 |

NOTE: Power brakes standard on all models. Power door locks standard on Corrado, Jetta Carat, Vanagon Carat and Multi-Van. Power windows standard on Cabriolet, Corrado, Jetta Carat, Vanagon Carat and Multi-Van.

## 1990

| | Original List | Current Whlse | Average Retail |
|---|---|---|---|
| **CABRIOLET 4** | | | |
| 2 Dr Convertible (5 spd) | 16310 | 9475 | 10925 |
| 2 Dr Best Seller Convertible (5 spd) | 17005 | 9675 | 11150 |
| 2 Dr Boutique Convertible (5 spd) | 17565 | 9825 | 11325 |
| **CORRADO 4** | | | |
| 2 Dr Cpe (5 spd) | 17900 | 9475 | 10925 |
| **FOX 4** | | | |
| 2 Dr Sdn (NA w/pwr strng) | 8370 | 3700 | 4600 |

| Year/Model/Body/Type | Original List | Current Whlse | Average Retail |
|---|---|---|---|
| 2 Dr GL Sport Sdn (NA w/pwr strng) | 9740 | 4600 | 5525 |
| 4 Dr GL Sdn (NA w/pwr strng) | 9455 | 4450 | 5375 |
| 2 Dr GL Wgn (NA w/pwr strng) | 9695 | 4475 | 5400 |
| **GOLF 4** | | | |
| 2 Dr GL Hbk (5 spd) | 10075 | 5075 | 6000 |
| 4 Dr GL Hbk (5 spd) | 10375 | 5175 | 6100 |
| **GTI 4** | | | |
| 2 Dr Hbk (5 spd) | 11100 | 5800 | 6725 |
| **JETTA 4** | | | |
| 2 Dr GL Sdn (5 spd) | 11100 | 6450 | 7500 |
| 4 Dr GL Sdn (5 spd) | 11400 | 6650 | 7750 |
| 4 Dr GL Diesel Sdn (5 spd) | 11600 | 6150 | 7150 |
| 4 Dr Carat Sdn (5 spd) | 12095 | 7050 | 8175 |
| 4 Dr GLI Sdn (5 spd) | 15005 | 8875 | 10250 |
| **PASSAT 4** | | | |
| 4 Dr GL Sdn (5 spd) | 15070 | 8700 | 10050 |
| 4 Dr GL Wgn (auto) | 16185 | 9325 | 10750 |
| **VANAGON 4** | | | |
| Base 7-Seater (4 spd) | 15460 | 7725 | 8975 |
| GL 7-Seater (4 spd) | 16840 | 9725 | 11200 |
| Carat 7-Seater (auto) | 19020 | 10950 | 12400 |
| Multi-Van 7-Seater (4 spd) | 20780 | 12200 | 14100 |
| GL Camper (4 spd) | 21340 | 12525 | 14750 |
| *ADD FOR:* | | | |
| Anti-Lock Braking System (Corrado, Jetta, Passat) | 835 | 400 | 440 |
| Leather Upholstery (Corrado, Passat) | 710 | 350 | 380 |

NOTE: Power brakes standard on all models. Power windows standard on Cabriolet, Corrado, Vanagon.Carat, Vanagon Multi-Van and GL Syncro Camper. Power door locks standard on Corrado, Jetta Carat, Vanagon Multi-Van and GL Syncro Camper.

## 1989

| | Original List | Current Whlse | Average Retail |
|---|---|---|---|
| **CABRIOLET 4** | | | |
| 2 Dr Convertible (5 spd) | 16310 | 8125 | 9375 |
| 2 Dr Best Seller Convertible (5 spd) | 17005 | 8300 | 9575 |
| 2 Dr Best Seller Wolfsburg LTD Edit Convertible (5 spd) | 17005 | 8450 | 9750 |
| 2 Dr Boutique Convertible (5 spd) | 17565 | 8625 | 9950 |

| Year/Model/Body/Type | Original List | Current Whlse | Average Retail |
|---|---|---|---|
| **FOX 4** | | | |
| 2 Dr Sdn (4 spd) (NA w/pwr strng) | **8035** | 2850 | 3750 |
| 2 Dr GL Sdn (4 spd) (NA w/pwr strng) | **8865** | 3250 | 4150 |
| 4 Dr GL Sdn (4 spd) (NA w/pwr strng) | **9065** | 3450 | 4350 |
| 2 Dr GL Wgn (4 spd) (NA w/pwr strng) | **9295** | 3475 | 4375 |
| 2 Dr GL Spt Sdn (5 spd) (NA w/pwr strng) | **9340** | 3475 | 4375 |
| 4 Dr GL Spt Sdn (5 spd) (NA w/pwr strng) | **9540** | 3675 | 4575 |
| 2 Dr GL Wolfsburg LTD Edit Sdn (5 spd) (NA w/pwr strng) | **9920** | 3825 | 4725 |
| **GOLF 4** | | | |
| 2 Dr Hbk (5 spd) | **10025** | 3725 | 4625 |
| 2 Dr GL Hbk (5 spd) | **10730** | 4125 | 5050 |
| 4 Dr GL Hbk (5 spd) | **10940** | 4225 | 5150 |
| 4 Dr GL Wolfsburg LTD Edit Hbk (5 spd) | **11515** | 4425 | 5350 |
| **GTI 4** | | | |
| 2 Dr Hbk (5 spd) | **15040** | 6150 | 7150 |
| **JETTA 4** | | | |
| 2 Dr Sdn (5 spd) | **11295** | 4750 | 5675 |
| 4 Dr Sdn (5 spd) | **11515** | 4925 | 5850 |
| 4 Dr Diesel Sdn (5 spd) | **11715** | 4325 | 5250 |
| 4 Dr GL Sdn (5 spd) | **12575** | 5325 | 6250 |
| 4 Dr GL Wolfsburg LTD Edit Sdn (5 spd) | **12975** | 5550 | 6475 |
| 4 Dr GLI Sdn (5 spd) | **14770** | 6950 | 8100 |
| 4 Dr GLI Wolfsburg LTD Edit Sdn (5 spd) | **17575** | 7125 | 8275 |
| 4 Dr Carat Sdn (5 spd) | **15140** | 5875 | 6800 |
| **VANAGON GL 4** | | | |
| 7-Seater (4 spd) | **18690** | 8175 | 9450 |
| Carat 7-Seater (4 spd) | **21010** | 9225 | 10625 |
| Carat Wolfsburg LTD Edit 7-Seater (4 spd) | **20545** | 9375 | 12475 |
| GL Camper (4 spd) | **23265** | 10800 | 12475 |
| *ADD FOR:* | | | |
| Anti-Lock Brakes (Jetta) | **995** | 310 | 340 |

NOTE: Power brakes standard on all models. Sunroof and power door locks standard on Jetta GLI Wolfsburg LTD Edition and Jetta Carat. Power windows standard on Jetta GLI Wolfsburg LTD Edition, Jetta Carat, Vanagon Carat and Vanagon LTD Edition.

## 1988

### CABRIOLET 4

| | | | |
|---|---|---|---|
| 2 Dr Convertible (5 spd) | **14750** | 6500 | 7575 |

| Year/Model/Body/Type | Original List | Current Whlse | Average Retail |
|---|---|---|---|
| 2 Dr Best Seller Convertible (5 spd) | **15425** | 6650 | 7750 |
| 2 Dr Boutique Convertible (5 spd) | **16390** | 6850 | 7975 |
| **FOX 4** | | | |
| 2 Dr Sdn (4 spd) | **6290** | 1425 | 2175 |
| 4 Dr GL Sdn (4 spd) | **7280** | 1825 | 2675 |
| 2 Dr GL Wgn (4 spd) | **7380** | 1825 | 2675 |
| **GOLF 4** | | | |
| 2 Dr Hbk (5 spd) | **7990** | 2375 | 3250 |
| 2 Dr GL Hbk (5 spd) | **8695** | 2650 | 3550 |
| 4 Dr GL Hbk (5 spd) | **8905** | 2750 | 3650 |
| 2 Dr GT Hbk (5 spd) | **10175** | 3250 | 4150 |
| 4 Dr GT Hbk (5 spd) | **10385** | 3325 | 4225 |
| **GTI 4** | | | |
| 2 Dr Hbk (5 spd) | **12995** | 4350 | 5275 |
| **JETTA 4** | | | |
| 2 Dr Sdn (5 spd) | **9195** | 3200 | 4100 |
| 4 Dr Sdn (5 spd) | **9415** | 3375 | 4275 |
| 4 Dr GL Sdn (5 spd) | **10590** | 3550 | 4450 |
| 4 Dr GLI Sdn (5 spd) | **14080** | 5025 | 5950 |
| 4 Dr Carat Sdn (5 spd) | **14570** | 4525 | 5425 |
| **QUANTUM 5** | | | |
| 4 Dr GL Sdn (5 spd) | **17975** | 4700 | 5625 |
| 4 Dr GL Wgn (5 spd) | **18375** | 4725 | 5650 |
| 4 Dr GL Syncro Wgn (5 spd) | **21205** | 5375 | 6300 |
| **SCIROCCO 4** | | | |
| 2 Dr Cpe (5 spd) | **14440** | 4650 | 5575 |
| **VANAGON 4** | | | |
| GL 7-Seater (4 spd) | **16590** | 5225 | 6150 |
| GL Wolfsburg 7-Seater (4 spd) | **18990** | 5875 | 6800 |
| GL Camper (4 spd) | **21690** | 7725 | 8975 |
| *ADD FOR:* | | | |
| Weekender Pkg (Vanagon GL) | **295** | 100 | 110 |
| Leather Interior (Scirocco) | **685** | 180 | 200 |

NOTE: Power brakes standard on all models. Pwr strng standard on GTI, Jetta GL, Jetta GLI 16-Valve, Jetta Carat, Cabriolet, Scirocco, Quantum and Vanagon. Power door locks and sunroof standard on Quantum. Air conditioning standard on Jetta Carat and Quantum.

## 1987

### CABRIOLET 4

| | | | |
|---|---|---|---|
| 2 Dr Convertible (5 spd) | **13750** | 4950 | 5875 |
| 2 Dr Wolfsburg | | | |

*Refer to optional equipment schedules*

| Year/Model/Body/Type | Original List | Current Whlse | Average Retail |
|---|---|---|---|
| Convertible (5 spd) | **15350** | 4700 | 5625 |
| **FOX 4** | | | |
| 2 Dr Sdn (4 spd) | **5690** | 1000 | 1725 |
| 4 Dr GL Sdn (4 spd) | **6490** | 1375 | 2125 |
| 2 Dr GL Wgn (4 spd) | — | 1500 | 2375 |
| **GOLF 4** | | | |
| 2 Dr GL Hbk (5 spd) | **8390** | 1800 | 2650 |
| 4 Dr GL Hbk (5 spd) | **8600** | 1900 | 2750 |
| 2 Dr GL Diesel Hbk (5 spd) | — | 1350 | 2100 |
| 4 Dr GL Diesel Hbk (5 spd) | — | 1425 | 2175 |
| 2 Dr GT Hbk (5 spd) | **9975** | 2175 | 3025 |
| 4 Dr GT Hbk (5 spd) | **10185** | 2275 | 3150 |
| **GTI 4** | | | |
| 2 Dr Hbk (5 spd) | **10325** | 2775 | 3675 |
| 2 Dr 16-Valve Hbk (5 spd) | **12240** | 3300 | 4200 |
| **JETTA 4** | | | |
| 2 Dr Sdn (5 spd) | **9590** | 2275 | 3150 |
| 4 Dr Sdn (5 spd) | **9810** | 2475 | 3350 |
| 2 Dr Wolfsburg Sdn (5 spd) | **11340** | 2675 | 3575 |
| 4 Dr GL Sdn (5 spd) | **10340** | 2625 | 3525 |
| 4 Dr GLI Sdn (5 spd) | **12100** | 3125 | 4025 |
| **QUANTUM 5** | | | |
| 4 Dr Wgn (5 spd) | **13920** | 2475 | 3350 |
| 4 Dr Syncro Wgn (5 spd) | **17230** | 2975 | 3875 |
| 4 Dr GL Sdn (5 spd) | **15510** | 2875 | 3775 |
| 4 Dr GL Wgn (5 spd) | **15910** | 3025 | 3925 |
| 4 Dr GL Syncro Wgn (5 spd) | **18870** | 3250 | 4150 |
| **SCIROCCO 4** | | | |
| 2 Dr Cpe (5 spd) | **11110** | 3150 | 4050 |
| 2 Dr 16-Valve Cpe (5 spd) | **13500** | 3700 | 4600 |
| **VANAGON 4** | | | |
| Conversion Bus (4 spd) | **12020** | 2500 | 3375 |
| GL 7-Seater (4 spd) | **15320** | 3800 | 4700 |
| GL Wolfsburg 7-Seater (4 spd) | **17315** | 4350 | 5275 |
| Camper (4 spd) | **17325** | 4950 | 5875 |
| Camper GL (4 spd) | **20100** | 6100 | 7000 |
| *ADD FOR:* | | | |
| Bestseller Pkg (Cabriolet) | **630** | 160 | 180 |
| Weekender Pkg (Vanagon GL) | **280** | 90 | 100 |

NOTE: Power brakes standard on all models. Air conditioning standard on Quantum. Power windows standard on Quantum GL. Power door locks standard on Vanagon GL Wolfsburg. Pwr strng standard on GTI 16-Valve, Jetta Wolfsburg, Jetta GL, Jetta GLI, Cabriolet Wolfsburg, Scirocco 16-Valve, Quantum and Camper GL.

## 1986

| Year/Model/Body/Type | Original List | Current Whlse | Average Retail |
|---|---|---|---|
| **CABRIOLET 4** | | | |
| 2 Dr Convertible (5 spd) | **11995** | 3900 | 4800 |
| **GOLF 4** | | | |
| 2 Dr Diesel Hbk (5 spd) | **7665** | 1000 | 1725 |
| 2 Dr Hbk (5 spd) | **7865** | 1325 | 2050 |
| 4 Dr Diesel Hbk (5 spd) | **7875** | 1050 | 1775 |
| 4 Dr Hbk (5 spd) | **8075** | 1400 | 2150 |
| 2 Dr Wolfsburg Hbk (5 spd) | **8170** | 1450 | 2225 |
| 4 Dr Wolfsburg Hbk (5 spd) | **8380** | 1500 | 2350 |
| **GTI 4** | | | |
| 2 Dr Hbk (5 spd) | **9925** | 2000 | 2850 |
| **JETTA 4** | | | |
| 2 Dr Diesel Cpe (5 spd) | **9035** | 1575 | 2425 |
| 2 Dr Cpe (5 spd) | **9235** | 1925 | 2775 |
| 4 Dr Diesel Sdn (5 spd) | **9255** | 1700 | 2550 |
| 4 Dr Sdn (5 spd) | **9455** | 2100 | 2950 |
| 4 Dr GL Sdn (5 spd) | **9800** | 2225 | 3075 |
| 4 Dr GLI Sdn (5 spd) | **11415** | 2575 | 3450 |
| 4 Dr GLI Wolfsburg (5 spd) | **11420** | 2650 | 3550 |
| 4 Dr GLI Wolfsburg (auto) | **10075** | 2875 | 3775 |
| **QUANTUM 5** | | | |
| 4 Dr (5 spd) | **13995** | 1500 | 2300 |
| 4 Dr Wgn (5 spd) | **12570** | 1525 | 2375 |
| 4 Dr Syncro (5 spd) | **15645** | 1850 | 2700 |
| **SCIROCCO 4** | | | |
| 2 Dr Cpe | **10370** | 1900 | 7500 |
| **VANAGON 4** | | | |
| Conversion Bus (4 spd) | **11320** | 2275 | 3150 |
| L 7-Seater (4 spd) | **13490** | 2650 | 3550 |
| L 9-Seater (4 spd) | **13545** | 2675 | 3575 |
| GL 7-Seater (4 spd) | **14340** | 3050 | 3950 |
| Camper (4 spd) | **16150** | 3925 | 4825 |
| Camper GL (4 spd) | **18640** | 4850 | 5775 |
| Camper Syncro 4WD (4 spd) | **18325** | 4975 | 5900 |
| *ADD FOR:* | | | |
| Bestseller Pkg (Cabriolet) | **595** | 110 | 120 |
| Weekender Pkg (Vanagon GL & L) | **265** | 60 | 60 |
| Leather Trim (GTI) | **495** | 90 | 100 |

| Year/Model/ Body/Type | Original List | Current Whlse | Average Retail |
|---|---|---|---|
| NOTE: Power brakes standard on all models. Power windows standard on Quantum Sedan. Power locks standard on Quantum Sedan. Pwr strng standard on Jetta GLI, Scirocco, Camper GL, Quantum and Vanagon GL. Air conditioning standard on Quantum. | | | |

## 1985

### CABRIOLET 4

| | | | |
|---|---|---|---|
| 2 Dr Convertible (auto) | **11595** | 3375 | 4275 |

### GOLF 4

| | | | |
|---|---|---|---|
| 2 Dr Diesel Hbk (5 spd) | **7085** | 875 | 1600 |
| 2 Dr Hbk (5 spd) | **7285** | 1275 | 2000 |
| 4 Dr Diesel Hbk (5 spd) | **7295** | 950 | 1675 |
| 4 Dr Hbk (5 spd) | **7495** | 1325 | 2050 |

### GTI 4

| | | | |
|---|---|---|---|
| 2 Dr Hbk (5 spd) | **9285** | 1875 | 2725 |

### JETTA 4

| | | | |
|---|---|---|---|
| 2 Dr Base Diesel Cpe (5 spd) | **8350** | 1275 | 2000 |
| 2 Dr Base Cpe (5 spd) | **8550** | 1675 | 2525 |
| 4 Dr Base Diesel Sdn (5 spd) | **8570** | 1400 | 2150 |
| 4 Dr Base Sdn (5 spd) | **8770** | 1825 | 2675 |
| 4 Dr GL Sdn (5 spd) | **9070** | 1925 | 2775 |
| 4 Dr GLI Sdn (5 spd) | **10570** | 2275 | 3150 |

### QUANTUM 5

| | | | |
|---|---|---|---|
| 4 Dr GL Sdn (5 spd) | **13295** | 1425 | 2175 |
| 4 Dr Wgn (5 spd) | **11570** | 1125 | 1850 |

### SCIROCCO 4

| | | | |
|---|---|---|---|
| 2 Dr Cpe (5 spd) | **9980** | 1600 | 2450 |

### VANAGON 4

| | | | |
|---|---|---|---|
| 7-Seater L (4 spd) | **12865** | 2400 | 3275 |
| 9-Seater L (4 spd) | **12920** | 2425 | 3300 |
| 7-Seater GL (4 spd) | **13715** | 2750 | 3650 |
| Campmobile (4 spd) | **17190** | 3850 | 4750 |
| 5-Seat Conversion Bus | **11790** | 2275 | 3150 |

*ADD FOR:*

| | | | |
|---|---|---|---|
| Triple White Bestseller Pkg (Cabriolet) | **500** | 70 | 80 |
| Leather Trim (Scirocco) | **735** | 90 | 100 |

NOTE: Power brakes standard on all models. Pwr strng standard on Jetta GLI, Quantum and Vanagon Camper. Air conditioning standard on Jetta GLI and Quantum. Power windows standard on Quantum.

## 1984

### JETTA 4

| | | | |
|---|---|---|---|
| 2 Dr Diesel Sdn (4 spd) | **7955** | 825 | 1525 |
| 2 Dr Sdn (5 spd) | **7955** | 1150 | 1875 |
| 4 Dr Diesel Sdn (4 spd) | **8175** | 875 | 1600 |
| 4 Dr Sdn (5 spd) | **8415** | 1225 | 1950 |
| 4 Dr GL Sdn (5 spd) | **8775** | 1400 | 2150 |
| 4 Dr Turbo Diesel Sdn (5 spd) | **9775** | 1050 | 1775 |
| 4 Dr GLI Sdn (5 spd) | **9255** | 1725 | 2575 |

### QUANTUM 4

| | | | |
|---|---|---|---|
| 4 Dr GL Turbo Diesel Sdn (5 spd) | **13530** | 875 | 1600 |
| 4 Dr GL Sdn (5 spd) | **12980** | 1025 | 1750 |
| 4 Dr Wolfsburg Ltd Ed Sdn (5 spd) | **13480** | 1125 | 1850 |
| 4 Dr GL Turbo Diesel Wgn (5 spd) | **14330** | 875 | 1600 |
| 4 Dr GL Wgn (5 spd) | **13780** | 900 | 1625 |
| 4 Dr Wolfsburg Ltd Ed Wgn (5 spd) | **14280** | 1050 | 1775 |

### RABBIT 4

| | | | |
|---|---|---|---|
| 2 Dr Conv (5 spd) | **10980** | 2425 | 3300 |
| 2 Dr Conv Wolfsburg Ltd Ed (5 spd) | **11380** | 2500 | 3375 |
| 2 Dr L Hbk (4 spd) | **6695** | 700 | 1325 |
| 2 Dr L Diesel Hbk (4 spd) | **6555** | 200 | 400 |
| 2 Dr Wolfsburg Ltd Ed Hbk (4 spd) | **7160** | 725 | 1375 |
| 2 Dr GTI Hbk (5 spd) | **8515** | 1125 | 1850 |
| 4 Dr L Hbk (4 spd) | **6905** | 750 | 1475 |
| 4 Dr L Diesel Hbk (4 spd) | **6765** | 350 | 625 |
| 4 Dr Wolfsburg Ltd Ed Hbk (4 spd) | **7370** | 800 | 1500 |
| 4 Dr GL Hbk (4 spd) | **7295** | 875 | 1600 |

### SCIROCCO 4

| | | | |
|---|---|---|---|
| 2 Dr Cpe (5 spd) | **10870** | 1250 | 1975 |
| 2 Dr Wolfsburg Ltd Ed (5 spd) | **9975** | 1275 | 2000 |

### VANAGON 4

| | | | |
|---|---|---|---|
| 7-Seater (4 spd) | **12240** | 1700 | 2550 |
| 9-Seater (4 spd) | **12295** | 1700 | 2550 |
| 7-Seater GL (4 spd) | **12740** | 1850 | 2700 |
| 7-Seater Wolfsburg Ltd Ed (4 spd) | **13140** | 1875 | 2725 |
| Campmobile (4 spd) | **16365** | 2925 | 3825 |
| Campmobile Wolfsburg Ltd Ed (4 spd) | **17365** | 3025 | 3925 |

## 1983 — ALL BODY STYLES

| | | | |
|---|---|---|---|
| JETTA 4 | — | 900 | 1625 |
| QUANTUM | — | 750 | 1475 |
| RABBIT CONVERTIBLE | — | 1700 | 2550 |

| Year/Model/ Body/Type | Original List | Current Whlse | Average Retail |
|---|---|---|---|
| RABBIT HATCHBACKS | — | 550 | 1025 |
| RABBIT PICKUPS | — | 110 | 300 |
| SCIROCCO | — | 1000 | 1725 |
| VANAGON | — | 1325 | 2050 |
| CAMPMOBILE | — | 2375 | 3250 |

## VOLVO

### 1992

**240 4**

| | Original List | Current Whlse | Average Retail |
|---|---|---|---|
| 4 Dr Sdn (5 spd) | 20820 | 15700 | 17550 |
| 5 Dr Wgn (5 spd) | 21320 | 16450 | 18400 |
| 4 Dr GL Sdn (5 spd) | 21495 | — | — |

*ADD FOR:*

| | | | |
|---|---|---|---|
| Anti-Lock Brakes | 995 | 500 | 550 |
| Leather Seat Trim | 595 | 400 | 450 |
| Alloy Wheels | 325 | 175 | 200 |

**740 4**

| | | | |
|---|---|---|---|
| 4 Dr Sdn (auto) | 24285 | 18700 | 21750 |
| 5 Dr Wgn (auto) | 24965 | 19525 | 22575 |
| 5 Dr GL Wgn (auto) | 25675 | — | — |
| 5 Dr Turbo Wgn (auto) | 27795 | — | — |

*ADD FOR:*

| | | | |
|---|---|---|---|
| Leather Seat Trim | 895 | 450 | 500 |
| Alloy Wheels (Turbo) | 225 | 175 | 200 |
| (Base, GL) | 325 | 175 | 200 |

**940 4**

| | | | |
|---|---|---|---|
| 4 Dr GL Sdn (auto) | 24995 | 19850 | 22900 |
| 4 Dr Turbo Sdn (auto) | 30795 | — | — |
| 5 Dr Turbo Wgn (auto) | 31475 | — | — |

*ADD FOR:*

| | | | |
|---|---|---|---|
| Leather Seat Trim (GL) | 895 | | |
| Alloy Wheels (GL) | 325 | | |

**960 6**

| | | | |
|---|---|---|---|
| 4 Dr Sdn (auto) | 33975 | — | — |
| 5 Dr Wgn (auto) | 34655 | — | — |

NOTE: Cruise control standard on 940. Power windows and power door locks standard on all models. Power sunroof standard on 240 GL, 740 Turbo and 940.

### 1991

**240 4**

| | | | |
|---|---|---|---|
| 4 Dr Sdn (5 spd) | 19620 | 12650 | 14825 |
| 5 Dr Wgn (5 spd) | 20115 | 13300 | 15625 |
| 5 Dr SE Wgn (5 spd) | 22855 | 14200 | 16675 |

**740 4**

| | | | |
|---|---|---|---|
| 4 Dr Sdn (auto) | 23175 | 14575 | 17100 |

| | Original List | Current Whlse | Average Retail |
|---|---|---|---|
| 5 Dr Wgn (auto) | 23855 | 15350 | 18000 |
| 4 Dr Turbo Sdn (5 spd) | 25310 | 16000 | 18650 |
| 5 Dr Turbo Wgn | 25990 | 16800 | 19450 |
| 4 Dr SE Sdn (auto) | 28455 | 17900 | 20550 |
| 5 Dr SE Wgn (auto) | 29135 | 17000 | 19650 |

**940 4**

| | | | |
|---|---|---|---|
| 4 Dr GLE Sdn (auto) | 27885 | 18575 | 21625 |
| 4 Dr Turbo Sdn (auto) | 29985 | 19875 | 22925 |
| 4 Dr SE Sdn (auto) | 33775 | 21725 | 25025 |
| 5 Dr GLE Wgn (auto) | 28565 | 19375 | 22425 |
| 5 Dr Turbo Wgn (auto) | 30665 | 20700 | 23750 |
| 5 Dr SE Wgn (auto) | 34455 | 22500 | 25800 |

**COUPE 4**

| | | | |
|---|---|---|---|
| 2 Dr Turbo Cpe (auto) | 41945 | — | — |

*ADD FOR:*

| | | | |
|---|---|---|---|
| Anti-Lock Brakes (240 Base, 740 Base) | 995 | 440 | 480 |
| Leather Upholstery (240 Base) | 595 | 260 | 290 |
| (740, 940 GLE) | 895 | 400 | 440 |

NOTE: Power brakes, power door locks and power windows standard on all models. Pwr strng standard on 940 Turbo & SE and Coupe. Power sunroof standard on 740 Turbo & SE, 940 and Coupe.

### 1990

**240 4**

| | | | |
|---|---|---|---|
| 4 Dr Sdn (5 spd) | 16725 | 8800 | 10175 |
| 5 Dr Wgn (5 spd) | 17215 | 9550 | 11000 |

**240 DL 4**

| | | | |
|---|---|---|---|
| 4 Dr Sdn (5 spd) | 18820 | 9600 | 11050 |
| 5 Dr Wgn (5 spd) | 19310 | 10275 | 11850 |

**740 BASE**

| | | | |
|---|---|---|---|
| 4 Dr Sdn (5 spd) | 21095 | 10400 | 12000 |
| 5 Dr Wgn (5 spd) | 21775 | 11150 | 12875 |

**740 GL 4**

| | | | |
|---|---|---|---|
| 4 Dr Sgn (5 spd) | 22135 | 10925 | 12600 |
| 5 Dr Wgn (5 spd) | 22815 | 11675 | 13475 |

**740 GLE 4**

| | | | |
|---|---|---|---|
| 4 Dr Sdn (5 spd) | 25950 | 12350 | 14400 |
| 5 Dr Wgn (5 spd) | 26630 | 13100 | 15425 |

**740 TURBO 4**

| | | | |
|---|---|---|---|
| 4 Dr Sdn (4 spd) | 26285 | 12800 | 15125 |
| 5 Dr Wgn (4 spd) | 26965 | 13550 | 15925 |

**760 GLE 6**

| | | | |
|---|---|---|---|
| 4 Dr Sdn (auto) | 33965 | 15150 | 17800 |

| Year/Model/Body/Type | Original List | Current Whlse | Average Retail |
|---|---|---|---|
| **760 TURBO 4** | | | |
| 4 Dr Sdn (auto) | **33965** | 15725 | 18375 |
| 5 Dr Wgn (auto) | **34645** | 16475 | 19125 |
| **780 GLE 6** | | | |
| 2 Dr Cpe (auto) | **38735** | 17800 | 20450 |
| **780 TURBO 4** | | | |
| 2 Dr Cpe (auto) | **39950** | 18375 | 21350 |
| *ADD FOR:* | | | |
| Anti-Lock Braking System (740 Base & GL) | **1175** | 380 | 420 |
| Leather Upholstery (740) | **895** | 330 | 360 |

NOTE: Power brakes and power door locks standard on all models. Anti-lock brakes standard on 740 GLE, 740 Turbo, 760 Series and 780 Series. Power windows standard on 240 DL, 740 Series, 760 Series and 780 Series. Sunroof standard on 240 DL Sedan, 740 GL, 740 GLE, 740 Turbo, 760 Series and 780 Series.

## 1989

| Year/Model/Body/Type | Original List | Current Whlse | Average Retail |
|---|---|---|---|
| **240 DL 4** | | | |
| 4 Dr Sdn (5 spd) | **17250** | 8175 | 9450 |
| 5 Dr Wgn (5 spd) | **17740** | 8875 | 10250 |
| **240 GL 4** | | | |
| 4 Dr Sdn (auto) | **20110** | 9800 | 11300 |
| 5 Dr Wgn (auto) | **20850** | 10650 | 12300 |
| **740 GL 4** | | | |
| 4 Dr Sdn (5 spd) | **20685** | 9100 | 10475 |
| 5 Dr Wgn (5 spd) | **21365** | 9800 | 11300 |
| **740 GLE 4** | | | |
| 4 Dr Sdn (5 spd) | **24565** | 10275 | 11850 |
| 5 Dr Wgn (5 spd) | **26140** | 11175 | 12900 |
| **740 TURBO 4** | | | |
| 4 Dr Sdn (5 spd) | **24925** | 10725 | 12375 |
| 5 Dr Wgn (5 spd) | **25605** | 11425 | 13200 |
| **760 GLE 6** | | | |
| 4 Dr Sdn (auto) | **32155** | 12700 | 15025 |
| **760 TURBO 4** | | | |
| 4 Dr Sdn (auto) | **32940** | 13225 | 15550 |
| 5 Dr Wgn (auto) | **32940** | 13925 | 16300 |
| **780 GLE 6** | | | |
| 2 Dr Cpe (auto) | **37790** | 15225 | 17875 |
| **780 TURBO 4** | | | |
| 2 Dr Cpe (auto) | **38975** | 15750 | 18400 |

NOTE: Power brakes and power door locks standard on all models. Power windows standard on 240 GL, 740 Series, 760 Series and 780 Series. Power sunroof standard on 240 GL, 740 Series (manual on 740 GL), 760 Series and 780 Series.

## 1988

| Year/Model/Body/Type | Original List | Current Whlse | Average Retail |
|---|---|---|---|
| **240 DL 4** | | | |
| 4 Dr Sdn (5 spd) | **17250** | 6400 | 7450 |
| 5 Dr Wgn (5 spd) | **17740** | 7000 | 8150 |
| **240 GL 4** | | | |
| 4 Dr Sdn (auto) | **20035** | 7675 | 8900 |
| 5 Dr Wgn (auto) | **20775** | 8450 | 9750 |
| **740 GLE 4** | | | |
| 4 Dr Sdn (4 spd) | **21850** | 7725 | 8975 |
| 5 Dr Wgn (5 spd) | **23425** | 8500 | 9825 |
| 4 Dr Turbo Sdn (5 spd) | **24925** | 8500 | 9825 |
| 5 Dr Turbo Wgn (4 spd) | **25605** | 9100 | 10475 |
| **760 GLE 6** | | | |
| 4 Dr Sdn (auto) | **32155** | 10350 | 11950 |
| 4 Dr Turbo Sdn (auto) | **32940** | 10825 | 12500 |
| 5 Dr Turbo Wgn (auto) | **32940** | 11425 | 13200 |
| **780 GLE 6** | | | |
| 2 Dr Cpe (auto) | **39880** | 12575 | 14850 |
| *ADD FOR:* | | | |
| Anti-Lock Braking System (740 GLE) | **1175** | 270 | 300 |
| Leather Upholstery (240 GL Sdn) | **785** | 220 | 240 |
| (740 GLE Sdn, 740 GLE Sdn, 740 GLE Turbo Sdn & Wgn) | **895** | 240 | 260 |
| Metallic Paint (240 DL) | **380** | 70 | 80 |
| Pearlescent Paint (780 GLE) | **320** | 70 | 80 |
| Restraint System (740 GLE Sdn & Wgn) | **850** | 180 | 200 |

NOTE: Pwr strng, power brakes, power door locks and air conditioning standard on all models. Power windows standard on 240 GL, 740 GLE, 760 GLE and 780 GLE. Sunroof standard on 240 GL, 740 GLE and 760 GLE. Power seat standard on 760 GLE and 780 GLE. Moonroof standard on 780 GLE.

## 1987

| Year/Model/Body/Type | Original List | Current Whlse | Average Retail |
|---|---|---|---|
| **240 DL 4** | | | |
| 4 Dr Sdn (5 spd) | **15690** | 4575 | 5500 |
| 5 Dr Wgn (5 spd) | **16180** | 5075 | 6000 |
| **240 GL 4** | | | |
| 4 Dr Sdn (auto & | | | |

| Year/Model/Body/Type | Original List | Current Whlse | Average Retail |
|---|---|---|---|
| sunroof) | 18385 | 5275 | 6200 |
| 5 Dr Wgn (auto & sunroof) | 19070 | 5975 | 6900 |
| **740 GLE 4** | | | |
| 4 Dr Sdn (4 spd & sunroof) | 20695 | 5800 | 6725 |
| 5 Dr Wgn (4 spd & sunroof) | 22150 | 6500 | 7575 |
| 4 Dr Turbo Sdn (4 spd & sunroof) | 22710 | 6400 | 7500 |
| 5 Dr Turbo Wgn (4 spd & sunroof) | 23310 | 6875 | 8000 |
| **760 GLE 4** | | | |
| 4 Dr Turbo Sdn (auto & sunroof) | 28340 | 6875 | 8000 |
| 5 Dr Turbo Wgn (auto & sunroof) | 27765 | 7400 | 8600 |
| 4 Dr Sdn (6 cyl) (auto & sunroof) | 28290 | 6500 | 7575 |
| **780 GLE 6** | | | |
| 2 Dr Cpe (auto & moonroof) | 34785 | 9100 | 10475 |
| *ADD FOR:* | | | |
| Leather Upholstery (240 GL Sdn) | 730 | 180 | 200 |
| (740 GLE Sdn ex. Turbo) | 855 | 200 | 220 |
| Metallic Paint (240 DL) | 380 | 70 | 80 |
| Restraint System (740 GLE, 760 Turbos) | 850 | 180 | 200 |

NOTE: Air conditioning, pwr strng, power brakes and power door locks standard on all models. Power windows and sunroof standard on 240 GL, 740 GLE, 760 GLE and 780 GLE.

## 1986

| Year/Model/Body/Type | Original List | Current Whlse | Average Retail |
|---|---|---|---|
| **DL 4** | | | |
| 4 Dr Sdn (4 spd) | 14615 | 3650 | 4550 |
| 5 Dr Wgn (4 spd) | 15105 | 4150 | 5075 |
| **GL 4** | | | |
| 4 Dr Sdn (4 spd & sunroof) | 16695 | 4250 | 5175 |
| 5 Dr Wgn (4 spd) | 17280 | 4725 | 5650 |
| **740 GLE 4** | | | |
| 4 Dr Sdn (4 spd & sunroof) | 18525 | 4450 | 5375 |
| 4 Dr Turbo Sdn (4 spd & sunroof) | 20505 | 4850 | 5775 |
| 5 Dr Wgn (4 spd & sunroof) | 19750 | 4900 | 5825 |

| Year/Model/Body/Type | Original List | Current Whlse | Average Retail |
|---|---|---|---|
| 5 Dr Turbo Wgn (4 spd & sunroof) | 20995 | 5325 | 6250 |
| 4 Dr Turbo Diesel Sdn (6 cyl) (auto) | 20095 | 4100 | 5025 |
| 4 Dr Turbo Diesel Wgn (auto & sunroof) | 21320 | 4225 | 5150 |
| **760 GLE 4** | | | |
| 4 Dr Turbo Sdn (4 spd & sunroof) | 24480 | 4850 | 5975 |
| 4 Dr Turbo Wgn (auto & sunroof) | 25425 | 5800 | 6725 |
| 4 Dr Sdn (6 cyl) (auto & sunroof) | 23625 | 4950 | 5875 |
| *ADD FOR:* | | | |
| Leather Upholstery (GL Sdn) | 630 | 120 | 130 |
| (740 GLE Sdn except Turbo) | 735 | 140 | 150 |
| Metallic Paint (DL) | 380 | 60 | 60 |

NOTE: Power brakes, power locks and pwr strng standard on all models. Power windows and sunroof standard on GL, 740 GLE and 760 GLE. Power seat and air conditioning standard on 760 GLE. Automatic transmission standard on 740 GLE Turbo Diesel and 760 GLE (gas & turbo).

## 1985

| Year/Model/Body/Type | Original List | Current Whlse | Average Retail |
|---|---|---|---|
| **DL 4** | | | |
| 4 Dr Sdn (4 spd) | 13920 | 2850 | 3750 |
| 5 Dr Wgn (4 spd) | 14395 | 3250 | 4150 |
| **GL 4** | | | |
| 4 Dr Sdn (4 spd & sunroof) | 16225 | 3300 | 4200 |
| 5 Dr Wgn (4 spd) | 16755 | 3750 | 4650 |
| 5 Dr Wgn (auto) | 17190 | 4000 | 4900 |
| **GLT 4** | | | |
| 4 Dr Turbo Sdn (4 spd & sunroof) | 18420 | 3650 | 4550 |
| 5 Dr Turbo Wgn (4 spd) | 18950 | 4100 | 5025 |
| 5 Dr Turbo Wgn (auto) | 19385 | 4350 | 5275 |
| **740 GLE 4** | | | |
| 4 Dr Sdn (4 spd &sunroof) | 18150 | 3650 | 4550 |
| 4 Dr Turbo Sdn (4 spd & sunroof) | 20130 | 4000 | 4900 |
| 4 Dr Turbo Diesel Sdn (4 spd w/overdrive) | 19015 | 3050 | 3950 |
| 5 Dr Wgn (4 spd w/overdrive & sunroof) | 19360 | 4100 | 5025 |
| 5 Dr Turbo Diesel Wgn (4 spd w/overdrive & sunroof) | 20760 | 3450 | 4350 |

| Year/Model/Body/Type | Original List | Current Whlse | Average Retail |
|---|---|---|---|
| 5 Dr Turbo Wgn (4 spd w/overdrive & sunroof) | 21340 | 4450 | 5375 |

**760 GLE 4**

| Year/Model/Body/Type | Original List | Current Whlse | Average Retail |
|---|---|---|---|
| 4 Dr Sdn (auto & sunroof) | 21985 | 3700 | 4600 |
| 4 Dr Turbo Sdn (4 spd & sunroof) | 22965 | 4050 | 4950 |
| 4 Dr Diesel Turbo Sdn (auto & sunroof) | 23185 | 3100 | 4000 |
| 5 Dr Turbo Wgn (4 spd w/overdrive & sunroof) | 23440 | 4500 | 5425 |
| *ADD FOR:* | | | |
| Metallic Paint (DL) | 380 | 50 | 50 |
| Audio Pkg (740 GLE) | 800 | 90 | 100 |
| Leather Upholstery (740 GLE) | 735 | 90 | 100 |
| (GL Turbo Sdn) | 590 | 70 | 80 |

NOTE: Pwr strng, power brakes and air conditioning standard on all models. Sunroof and power windows standard on GL, GLT and 740 GLE and 760 GLE. Power door locks standard on GLT, 740 GLE and 760 GLE.

## 1984

**760 6**

| Year/Model/Body/Type | Original List | Current Whlse | Average Retail |
|---|---|---|---|
| 4 Dr (auto & sunroof) | 21657 | 3000 | 3900 |
| 4 Dr Turbo (4 spd) | 22353 | 3350 | 4250 |
| 4 Dr Turbo Diesel (4 spd) | 22655 | 2850 | 3750 |

**DL 4**

| | | | |
|---|---|---|---|
| 2 Dr (4 spd) | 11953 | 2450 | 3325 |
| 4 Dr (4 spd) | 12583 | 2550 | 3425 |
| 5 Dr Wgn (4 spd) | 13008 | 2925 | 3825 |

**GL 4**

| | | | |
|---|---|---|---|
| 4 Dr (4 spd & sunroof) | 15673 | 2725 | 3625 |
| 4 Dr Diesel (4 spd & sunroof) | 15705 | 2275 | 3150 |
| 5 Dr Wgn (4 spd) | 16228 | 3075 | 3975 |
| 5 Dr Diesel Wgn (4 spd) | 16260 | 2550 | 3425 |

**GLT 4**

| | | | |
|---|---|---|---|
| 2 Dr Turbo (4 spd & sunroof) | 17142 | 2850 | 3750 |
| 4 Dr Turbo (4 spd & sunroof) | 17452 | 2950 | 3850 |
| 5 Dr Turbo Wgn (4 spd) | 18007 | 3275 | 4175 |

**1983 — ALL BODY STYLES**

| | | | |
|---|---|---|---|
| 760 GLE | — | 2475 | 3350 |
| DL 4 | — | 2100 | 2950 |
| GL 4 | — | 2275 | 3150 |
| GLT 4 | — | 2450 | 3325 |

## YUGO

### 1991
**YUGO 4**

| Year/Model/Body/Type | Original List | Current Whlse | Average Retail |
|---|---|---|---|
| 3 Dr GV Plus Hbk (NA w/pwr strng) | 5824 | — | — |
| 2 Dr Cabrio Conv (NA w/pwr strng) | 10168 | — | — |

NOTE: Power brakes standard on all models.

### 1990
**YUGO 4**

| | | | |
|---|---|---|---|
| 3 Dr GV Plus Hbk (NA w/pwr strng) | 4435 | — | — |
| 2 Dr Cabrio Conv (NA w/pwr strng) | 10168 | — | — |

NOTE: Power brakes standard on all models.

### 1989
**YUGO 4**

| | | | |
|---|---|---|---|
| 3 Dr GV Hbk (NA w/pwr strng) | 5607 | 500 | 925 |
| 3 Dr GVL Hbk (NA w/pwr strng) | 5837 | 600 | 1125 |

NOTE: Power brakes standard on all models.

### 1988
**YUGO 4**

| | | | |
|---|---|---|---|
| 3 25 | 600 | | |
| 3 Dr GVL Hbk (4 spd) | 4599 | 425 | 775 |
| 3 Dr GVX Hbk 5 spd) | 5699 | 525 | 975 |

NOTE: Power brakes standard on all models.

### 1987
**YUGO 4**

| | | | |
|---|---|---|---|
| 3 Dr GV Hbk (4 spd) | 3990 | 225 | 475 |
| 3 Dr GVX Hbk (5 spd) | — | 450 | 825 |

NOTE: Power brakes standard on all models.

### 1986
**YUGO 4**

| | | | |
|---|---|---|---|
| 3 Dr Hbk | 3990 | 110 | 300 |

NOTE: Power brakes standard.

# USED CAR BUYING WORK SHEET

| ITEM: | CAR A | CAR B | CAR C | CAR D |
|---|---|---|---|---|
| **BODY:** | $ | $ | $ | $ |
| RUST | | | | |
| DENT | | | | |
| CHROME | | | | |
| PAINT | | | | |
| GLASS | | | | |
| **MOTOR:** | | | | |
| VALVES | | | | |
| PISTONS | | | | |
| RINGS | | | | |
| **TRANSMISSION:** | | | | |
| ADJUST | | | | |
| OVERHAUL | | | | |
| **TIRES:** | | | | |
| RETREAD | | | | |
| WORN | | | | |
| **BRAKES:** | | | | |
| ADJUST | | | | |
| REPLACE | | | | |
| **ELECTRICAL:** | | | | |
| BATTERY | | | | |
| WIRING | | | | |
| GENERATOR | | | | |
| REGULATOR | | | | |
| PLUGS & POINTS | | | | |
| **TUNE UP:** | | | | |
| MISCELLANEOUS | | | | |
| **COOLING SYSTEM:** | | | | |
| HOSE | | | | |
| RADIATOR | | | | |
| WATER PUMP | | | | |
| **EXHAUST:** | | | | |
| MUFFLER | | | | |
| FRONT EXHAUST | | | | |
| TAIL PIPE | | | | |
| **LIGHTS:** | | | | |
| HEAD | | | | |
| TAIL | | | | |
| DIRECTIONAL | | | | |
| **WIPER:** | | | | |
| BLADES | | | | |
| MOTOR | | | | |
| **TOTAL REPAIR COST** | $ | $ | $ | $ |
| **ASKING PRICE OF CAR** | | | | |
| + OR - = **NET PRICE** | | | | |

# USED CAR BUYING WORK SHEET

| ITEM: | CAR A | CAR B | CAR C | CAR D |
|---|---|---|---|---|
| **BODY:** | $ | $ | $ | $ |
| RUST | | | | |
| DENT | | | | |
| CHROME | | | | |
| PAINT | | | | |
| GLASS | | | | |
| **MOTOR:** | | | | |
| VALVES | | | | |
| PISTONS | | | | |
| RINGS | | | | |
| **TRANSMISSION:** | | | | |
| ADJUST | | | | |
| OVERHAUL | | | | |
| **TIRES:** | | | | |
| RETREAD | | | | |
| WORN | | | | |
| **BRAKES:** | | | | |
| ADJUST | | | | |
| REPLACE | | | | |
| **ELECTRICAL:** | | | | |
| BATTERY | | | | |
| WIRING | | | | |
| GENERATOR | | | | |
| REGULATOR | | | | |
| PLUGS & POINTS | | | | |
| **TUNE UP:** | | | | |
| MISCELLANEOUS | | | | |
| **COOLING SYSTEM:** | | | | |
| HOSE | | | | |
| RADIATOR | | | | |
| WATER PUMP | | | | |
| **EXHAUST:** | | | | |
| MUFFLER | | | | |
| FRONT EXHAUST | | | | |
| TAIL PIPE | | | | |
| **LIGHTS:** | | | | |
| HEAD | | | | |
| TAIL | | | | |
| DIRECTIONAL | | | | |
| **WIPER:** | | | | |
| BLADES | | | | |
| MOTOR | | | | |
| **TOTAL REPAIR COST** | $ | $ | $ | $ |
| **ASKING PRICE OF CAR** | | | | |
| **+ OR - = NET PRICE** | | | | |

# NATIONWIDE
## Auto Brokers, Inc.

17517 West 10 Mile Road, Southfield, Michigan 48075

**(313) 559-6661**    Mon-Fri — 9-5 pm Eastern Standard Time

## Car Salesmen Give The Impression Of Not Telling Me Everything. Why Would NATIONWIDE Be Any Different?

We have no reason to keep things from you. Our 20 plus year approach has been to be straightforward in working with our clients. The printout you receive clearly reveals our "hand".

## I Don't Live In Michigan, How Will I Get My New Vechicle?

You have three options -
1) You may designate a local dealership as your pick up point. (Please provide us with a choice of three.)
2) We will deliver your vehicle to your home via a licensed ICC driveaway service.
3) Your vehicle may be picked up at our headquarters in Southfield, MI.

## When I Buy From NATIONWIDE, Is The Vehicle Under Warranty?

All cars and trucks sold by NATIONWIDE Auto Brokers, Inc are fully factory warranteed and all authorized dealerships throughout the United States and Canada will honor the warranty.

---

**MASTERCARD/VISA CUSTOMERS ONLY! 1-800-521-7257**

Monday - Friday — 9 am to 8 pm: Saturday — 9 am to 1 pm Eastern Time

Please have your credit card number and expiration date ready for our operators

FAX PRICE: $6.95 for first two quotes of $11.95 each. $2.50 each additional fax.

---

# Nationwide Auto Brokers, Inc.  ⒺⒹ

17517 West Ten Mile Road ● Southfield, Michigan 48075

Name_____

Address_____

City_____ State _____ Zip _____

❏ MC/Visa/Discover  ❏ Check  ❏ Money Order

MC/Visa/Discover Card No. _____

Exp. Date _____ Signature _____

| MAKE | MODEL/ DESCRIP. | BODY TYPE (Check all that apply) | PRICE EACH |
|---|---|---|---|
| | | ☐ 2 door ☐ 4 door ☐ station wagon<br>☐ diesel ☐ turbo ☐ automatic<br>☐ manual ☐ hatchback ☐ notchback<br>☐ front wheel drive ☐ all wheel drive | $11.95 |
| | | ☐ 2 door ☐ 4 door ☐ station wagon<br>☐ diesel ☐ turbo ☐ automatic<br>☐ manual ☐ hatchback ☐ notchback<br>☐ front wheel drive ☐ all wheel drive | $11.95 |
| | | ☐ 2 wheel drive ☐ 4 wheel drive<br>☐ diesel ☐ turbo<br>☐ ½ ton ☐ ¾ ton ☐ 1 ton | $11.95 |

---

*FAX PRICE: $6.95 for first two quotes of $11.95 each. $2.50 each additional fax.*

NOTE: Attach sheet with additional body type specs only if necessary (do NOT list options).

Each Quote $11.95                    TOTAL _____

---

**PLEASE NOTE: Some specialty imports and limited production models and vehicles may not be available for delivery to your area or through our pricing service. A message on your printout will advise you of this eventuality. You will still be able to use the printout in negotiating the best deal with the dealer of your choice. New car pricing and purchasing services void where prohibited by law. Some limited vehicles are slightly higher.**

# Edmund's   SINGLE COPIES / ORDER FORM

### Please send me:

❏ **USED CAR PRICES** *(includes S&H)* ..................................$ 7.99

❏ **NEW CAR PRICES** *(includes S&H)*....................................$ 6.99

❏ **VAN, PICKUP, SPORT UTILITY BUYER'S GUIDE** *(includes S&H)*....$ 6.99

❏ **IMPORT CAR PRICES** *((includes S&H)* ...........................$ 6.99

❏ **ECONOMY CAR BUYING GUIDE** *(includes S&H)* ...........................$ 7.99

Name

Address

City, State, Zip

Phone

SU2702

**PAYMENT:** ❏ MASTERCARD ❏ VISA ❏ CHECK or MONEY ORDER $_____
*Make check or money order payable to:*
**Edmund Publications Corporation,** *P.O. Box 338, Shrub Oak, NY 10588*

Credit Card #                                             Exp. Date:

CardHolder Name                                          Signature

*Prices above are for shipping within the U.S. and Canada only. Other countries please add $5.00 to the cover price per book (via air mail) and $2.00 to the cover price per book (surface mail). Please pay through an American Bank or with American currency. Rates subject to change without notice.*

## *Edmund's* SUBSCRIPTIONS / ORDER FORM

**Please send me 1 year subscription for:**

❑ **USED CAR PRICES** *(includes bulk rate shipping/handling)* ...............$ **34.25**
FOREIGN COUNTRIES *(includes air mail shipping/handling)* ...........................$ 44.25
— includes (6 updated books per year)

❑ **NEW VEHICLE PRICES** *(includes bulk rate shipping/handling)* .........$ **49.95**
FOREIGN COUNTRIES *(includes air mail shipping/handling)* .......................$ 74.95
— *includes the complete automotive market*
*of new vehicles (10 books):*

    3 NEW CAR PRICES (Domestic)
    3 IMPORT CAR PRICES
    3 VAN, PICKUP, SPORT UTILITY
    1 ECONOMY CAR BUYING GUIDE

❑ **NEW & USED CAR PRICES***(includes bulk rate shipping/handling)* .....$ **62.50**
FOREIGN COUNTRIES*(includes air mail shipping/handling)* ...........................$ 87.50
— *includes (11 books):*

    6 USED CAR PRICES
    3 NEW CAR PRICES (Domestic)
    3 IMPORT CAR PRICES

❑ **PREMIUM SUBSCRIPTION***(includes bulk rate shipping/handling)* .....$ **81.25**
FOREIGN COUNTRIES*(includes air mail shipping/handling)* ...........................$ 113.25
— *includes all of the above (16 books)*

Name _____

Address _____

City, State, Zip _____

Phone _____

SU2702

**PAYMENT:** ❑ MASTERCARD ❑ VISA ❑ CHECK or MONEY ORDER $_____
*Make check or money order payable to: **Edmund Publications Corporation,***
*P.O. Box 338, Shrub Oak, NY 10588* —*Rates subject to change without notice.*

Credit Card # _____ Exp. Date: _____

CardHolder Name _____ Signature _____

# Edmund's

## SCHEDULED RELEASE DATES FOR 1993*

| VOL. 27 | | RELEASE DATE | COVERDATE |
|---|---|---|---|
| U2701 | USED CAR PRICES | JAN 93 | APR 93 |
| N2701 | NEW CAR PRICES [Domestic] | FEB 93 | JUN 93 |
| S2701 | VAN, PICKUP, SPORT UTILITY BUYER'S GUIDE | FEB 93 | JUN 93 |
| I2701 | IMPORT CAR PRICES | MAR 93 | JUL 93 |
| E2701 | ECONOMY CAR BUYER'S GUIDE | FEB 93 | 1993 |
| U2702 | USED CAR PRICES | MAR 93 | JUN 93 |
| N2702 | NEW CAR PRICES [Domestic] | MAY 93 | NOV 93 |
| S2702 | VAN, PICKUP, SPORT UTILITY BUYER'S GUIDE | MAY 93 | NOV 93 |
| U2703 | USED CAR PRICES | MAY 93 | OCT 93 |
| I2702 | IMPORT CAR PRICES | JUN 93 | DEC 93 |
| U2704 | USED CAR PRICES | JUL 93 | SEP 93 |
| U2705 | USED CAR PRICES | SEP 93 | NOV 93 |
| N2703 | NEW CAR PRICES [Domestic] | NOV 93 | FEB 94 |
| S2703 | VAN, PICKUP, SPORT UTILITY BUYER'S GUIDE | NOV 93 | FEB 94 |
| U2706 | USED CAR PRICES | NOV 93 | JAN 94 |
| I2703 | IMPORT CAR PRICES | DEC 93 | APR 94 |

*Subject to Change